PERCEPTUAL EXPEF

Perceptual Experience

Edited by
TAMAR SZABÓ GENDLER
and
JOHN HAWTHORNE

CLARENDON PRESS · OXFORD

OXFORD

UNIVERSITY PRESS

Great Clarendon Street, Oxford OX2 6DP

Oxford University Press is a department of the University of Oxford.
It furthers the University's objective of excellence in research, scholarship,
and education by publishing worldwide in

Oxford New York

Auckland Cape Town Dar es Salaam Hong Kong Karachi
Kuala Lumpur Madrid Melbourne Mexico City Nairobi
New Delhi Shanghai Taipei Toronto

With offices in

Argentina Austria Brazil Chile Czech Republic France Greece
Guatemala Hungary Italy Japan Poland Portugal Singapore
South Korea Switzerland Thailand Turkey Ukraine Vietnam

Oxford is a registered trade mark of Oxford University Press
in the UK and in certain other countries

Published in the United States
by Oxford University Press Inc., New York

British Library Cataloguing in Publication Data

Data available

Library of Congress Cataloging in Publication Data

Perceptual experience / edited by Tamar Szabó Gendler and John Hawthorne.
p. cm.
Includes bibliographial references and index.
1. Perception (Philosophy) 2. Experience. I. Gendler, Tamar. II. Hawthorne, John (John P.)
B828.45.P478 2006 121'.34—dc22 2005025711

Typeset by Newgen Imaging Systems (P) Ltd., Chennai, India
Printed in Great Britain
on acid-free paper by
Biddles Ltd., King's Lynn, Norfolk

ISBN 978–0–19–928975–2
ISBN 978–0–19–928976–9 (Pbk.)

5 7 9 10 8 6 4

Acknowledgements

Two anonymous referees provided excellent counsel on the volume's overall structure, and incisive suggestions concerning a number of the chapters; their influence can be seen at many points throughout the book. Many others made important contributions to one or more of the individual papers; acknowledgements of these contributions can be found in the papers themselves.

Syracuse, Cornell and Rutgers Universities offered financial support for the preparation of this volume. Thanks are also due to Peter Momtchiloff and Rebecca Bryant of Oxford University Press for seeing the publication through from beginning to end, and to the other staff at OUP who played a role in its production along the way.

All of the authors were enormously cooperative in meeting deadlines and responding to suggestions and queries, which made our editorial task much lighter. Authors were also gracious enough to circulate early drafts of their essays to other contributors, resulting in fruitful discussion and cross-references.

Three graduate students played important roles in bringing the volume to fruition. Karson Kovakovich helped at the preliminary stages with both administrative and editorial work. John Wynne did an extraordinary job preparing an absolutely first-rate index. And Emily Esch saw the book through its final months, providing outstanding advice and support at every step of the way.

Contents

Contributors

JOHN CAMPBELL is Willis S. and Marion Slusser Professor of Philosophy at the University of California, Berkeley

DAVID J. CHALMERS is Professor of Philosophy, ARC Federation Fellow, and Director of the Centre for Consciousness, in the Research School of Social Sciences, Australian National University

TIM CRANE is Professor of Philosophy at UCL and Director of the Institute of Philosophy at the University of London

FRED DRETSKE is Senior Research Scholar at Duke University

TAMAR SZABÓ GENDLER is Associate Professor of Philosophy at Cornell University

ANIL GUPTA is Distinguished Professor of Philosophy at the University of Pittsburgh

JOHN HAWTHORNE is Professor of Philosophy at Rutgers University

SUSAN HURLEY is Professor of Philosophy at the University of Bristol and is a fellow of All Souls College, Oxford

MARK JOHNSTON is Walter Cerf Professor of Philosophy at Princeton University

GEOFFREY LEE is a Doctoral Student in Philosophy at New York University

ERIC LORMAND is Associate Professor of Philosophy at the University of Michigan, Ann Arbor

M. G. F. MARTIN is Professor of Philosophy at UCL

ALVA NOË is Associate Professor of Philosophy at the University of California, Berkeley

JESSE J. PRINZ is Associate Professor of Philosophy at the University of North Carolina, Chapel Hill

SYDNEY SHOEMAKER is Susan Linn Sage Professor Emeritus at Cornell University

SUSANNA SIEGEL is Associate Professor of Philosophy and John L. Loeb Associate Professor of the Humanities at Harvard University

MICHAEL TYE is Professor of Philosophy at the University of Texas, Austin

Introduction: Perceptual Experience

Tamar Szabó Gendler and John Hawthorne

Much contemporary discussion of perceptual experience can be traced to two observations. The first is that perception seems to put us in direct contact with the world around us: when perception is successful, we come to recognize— immediately—that certain objects have certain properties. The second is that perceptual experience may fail to provide such knowledge: when we fall prey to illusion or hallucination, the way things appear may differ radically from the way things actually are. For much of the twentieth century, many of the most important discussions of perceptual experience could be fruitfully understood as responses to this pair of observations.

In recent years, the debates surrounding the issue of perceptual experience have become more complex. Lines of influence are often difficult to trace—and a number of independently motivated avenues of investigation have opened up. The philosophers in this volume take up a cluster of questions that represent this new generation of issues. The conceptual terrain they are exploring is difficult to chart: there is no agreed-upon methodology, no clear common ideological ground, and no shared paradigm of philosophical progress in the area. Introducing such a volume is thus both difficult and exciting. Rather than providing a premature road map of territory whose very nature is contested, our aim is to articulate a series of questions that—together—can provide the reader with a sense of the sorts of issues that the essays in this volume concern.

In the first part of the introduction, we look at two important responses to the observations described above, and explain the role they play in motivating the volume's chapters; in the remainder, we identify a series of further questions whose answers provide a framework for thinking about the essays that follow.[1]

For comments, discussion, and suggestions, we are grateful to Wylie Breckenridge, Emily Esch, Benj Hellie, Karson Kovakovich, Sarah Moss, Richard Price, and Susanna Siegel.

[1] Recent collections of influential essays on these matters include Byrne and Hilbert (eds.) (1997b), Crane (ed.) (1992a), Dancy (ed.) (1988), Noë and Thompson (eds.) (2002), and Smith and Jokic (eds.) (2003). Representative book-length treatments concerned specifically with issues of perceptual experience include Alston (1993), Armstrong (1961, 1968), Austin (1962) Chisholm (1957), Dretske (1969), Hardin (1988), and Jackson (1977), Peacocke (1983), Pitcher (1971), Robinson (1994), Russell (1912), Smith (2002), Hintan (1973), Valberg (1992); there is also an extensive literature on consciousness in general. More detailed introductions to many of the issues

PART I: PERCEPTUAL DIRECTNESS AND PERCEPTUAL DISTORTION

Perceptual Directness: Transparency

What must perceptual experience be like in order for perception to put us in direct contact with reality? One answer that has been especially influential in recent years is that perceptual experience is *transparent* or *diaphanous*: when we set out to attend to perceptual experience itself, we find ourselves instead attending to the objects around us. G. E. Moore puts the observation this way:

In general, that which makes a sensation of blue a mental fact seems to escape us: it seems, if I may use a metaphor, to be transparent—we look through it and see nothing but the blue... When we try to introspect the sensation of blue, all we can see is the blue: the other element is as if it were diaphanous. (Moore 1903/1993)

And Gilbert Harman maintains, in a widely cited passage:[2]

When you see a tree, you do not experience any features as intrinsic features of your experience. Look at a tree and try to turn your attention to intrinsic features of your visual experience. I predict you will find that the only features there to turn your attention to will be features of the presented tree. (Harman 1990: 39)[3]

While it is far from clear that advocates of transparency hold that we are *never* in a position to attend to our experience,[4] the mainstream view has been to accept that when we reflect on our perceptual experience, we do so *most naturally* by attending to the objects that that experience (purportedly) presents.[5] And some have held the stronger view that when we reflect on our perceptual experience, we can do so *only* by attending to the objects (purportedly) presented.[6]

addressed in this volume can be found in BonJour (2001), Crane (2005), and Siegel (2005), each of which includes a comprehensive bibliography.

[2] For further discussion, see also Crane (2001), Dretske (1995), Kriegel (2002), Loar (2002), Lycan (1996), Shoemaker (1990, 1991), Sturgeon (2000), Tye (1991), (1995), (2000) and papers cited below.

[3] Here, as elsewhere in the literature on perceptual experience, the majority of discussion has focused on cases of *visual* experience. Though there are interesting questions to be raised about other sensory modalities—and, indeed, interesting questions to be raised about the individuation and classification of sensory modalities (see Eilan, McCarthy, and Brewer (eds) (1993), Grice (1962), Keeley (2002), Leon (1988), Lopes (2000), Nelkin (1990), Noë (2002))—we will generally restrict ourselves to visual examples in our discussion below.

[4] The Moore passage just cited continues with the concessionary observation that "the other element... *can* be distinguished if we look attentively enough, and if we know that there is something to look for" (Moore (1903), 25). One might, for example, concede that when we see colors, what we are really doing is attending to some inner element that is then projected outward—even though naive phenomenology may seem to suggest otherwise. (Such a model is suggested by certain of Lormand's remarks, chapter 9.) We can thus distinguish the thesis that experience is in fact transparent from the thesis that unreflective common sense takes it to be so.

[5] One of the few dissenters is Ned Block, who responds to Harman's observation by noting that: "As a point about introspection, this seems to me to be straightforwardly wrong" (Block (1996), 27).

[6] Amy Kind calls the first of these theses *weak transparency*, and the second *strong transparency*; for further discussion, see Kind (2003).

Assuming that some version of this phenomenological observation is correct, what constraints does it put on a proper account of perceptual experience? A number of authors—most notably Michael Tye (e.g. 2000) and Gilbert Harman (1990)—have argued that the transparency of experience (in this stronger sense) provides direct support for the view that the phenomenal character of experience supervenes on the representational content of experience. (For further discussion of this issue, see question three on page 17.) Transparency is also used to argue for a thesis about introspection (see Tye 1995, 2000, and Dretske 1995): that our access to the nature of our own experiences is derivative, available to us only by reflection on the features of our environment; we are aware *that* we have experiences only by being aware *of* those things we are (apparently) experiencing.[7]

A number of authors in this volume use transparency as a springboard for their discussions. Eric Lormand (chapter 9) contends that what distinguishes phenomenal experiences from other sorts of conscious states is that they engender impressions either of transparency or its converse.[8] Tim Crane (chapter 3), in the course of arguing that recent discussions of perceptual experience have mislocated the central point of dispute, maintains that the degree to which perceptual experience is transparent has been overstated.[9] David Chalmers (chapter 2) offers an account of what experience represents that aims to stay true to the phenomenology that we have direct access to objects and their properties. And Sydney Shoemaker (chapter 13) holds as one of the constraints on a successful account of perceptual experience that it do justice to a version of transparency according to which, when we attend to our perceptual experience, what we attend to is what that experience represents.

Perceptual Distortion: Illusion, Hallucination and Their Kin

At the same time, it is undeniable that there are cases where perceptual experience seems to present the world in a distorted way. As A. J. Ayer observes, following numerous predecessors:[10]

It is remarked that a coin which looks circular from one point of view may look elliptical from another; or that a stick which normally appears straight looks bent when it appears

---

[7] Cf. Tye (2000): "We attend to . . . the external surfaces and qualities—and . . . *thereby* we are aware of something else, the 'feel' of our experience" (51–2). Or Dretske (1995): "If one is asked to introspect one's current gustatory experience . . . one finds oneself attending, not to one's experience of the wine, but to the wine itself (or perhaps the tongue or palate). There seems to be no other relevant place to direct one's attention" (62).

[8] More precisely, he hypothesizes that all and only those states that engender impressions of *transparency* or *images* are associated with phenomenal experiences. On Lormand's account, the impression of transparency—which is typically manifest most strongly in normal perceptual experiences—is the impression that we introspect only environmental properties; the impression of images—which is typically manifest most strongly in imaginative experiences—is the impression that we introspect special phenomenal objects with normal environmental properties (color, shape, etc.).

[9] For related discussions, see Martin (2002), Kind (2003), Siewart (2004), Stoljar (forthcoming).

[10] Discussion of these issues appears prominently in the work of Descartes, Locke, Berkeley, Hume, and Reid. A typical passage from Hume brings out the well-wornedness of these

in water; or that to people who take drugs such as mescal, things appear to change their colours. The familiar cases of mirror images, and double images, and complete hallucinations, such as the mirage, provide further examples . . . [Likewise] it may be pointed out, for example, that the taste a thing appears to have may vary with the condition of the palate; or that a liquid will appear to have a different temperature according as the hand that is feeling it is itself hot or cold; or that a coin seems larger when it is placed on the tongue than when it is held in the palm of the hand. (Ayer 1940)

Many have thought that these observations have implications for what the immediate or direct objects of perceptual experience might be. Numerous early- and mid-twentieth-century philosophers—among them Ayer, Broad, Moore, Price, and Russell[11]—were moved by a family of arguments, commonly referred to as *arguments from illusion, arguments from hallucination,* and *arguments from perceptual relativity.*[12] In rough form, the reasoning runs as follows. In cases of illusion or hallucination, the qualities that seem to hold of the direct object of perceptual experience are qualities which are not held by any mind-independent physical object, so the direct object of perceptual experience cannot be any of them. In cases of perceptual relativity and sensory variability, since an object with quality-profile Q may produce R-like experiences in one subject and S-like experiences in another, the direct object of perceptual experience cannot in both cases be the object itself, and so, for parity reasons, must be something distinct from it. But— and this step is crucial—there must be some object that actually bears the properties that the subject is experiencing. Since no external object will do the trick, the direct object of perceptual experience must be some special mental entity that bears those properties: it must be some sort of *sense datum.*[13]

***

observations: "I need not insist on the more trite topics, employed by the skeptics in all ages, against the evidence of *sense*; such as those that are derived from the imperfection and fallaciousness of our organs, on numberless occasions; the crooked appearance of an oar in water; the various aspects of objects, according to their different distances; the double images which arise from the pressing of one eye" (Hume, *Enquiries,* 151). For discussion of the history of these issues, see Hamlyn (1961) and Yolton (1984, 1996).

[11] For discussion, see for example Ayer (1936, 1940, 1973), Broad (1923, 1952), Chisholm (1942, 1950), Moore (1903, 1910, 1925), Price (1932, 1940), Russell (1912). A fine sample of relevant papers appears in Swartz (ed.) (1965).

[12] In cases of *illusion,* one misrepresents the properties of an object that one perceives: a straight stick submerged in water may appear bent. In cases of *hallucination,* one seems to perceive something where there is nothing to be perceived: a dagger may appear before one's eyes where there is only empty space. In cases of *perceptual relativity,* one's perceptual experience of an object varies with one's physical relation to it: a tabletop may appear to have different shapes when viewed from different angles. And in cases of *sensory variability,* the range of one's experience varies with the character of one's sensory apparati: a bee may perceive ultraviolet light that is invisible to humans. (Note that certain of these labels are elsewhere deployed differently in the perceptual experience literature—for instance, arguments that purport to move from facts of intersubjective variation to the conclusion that there are no objective facts about color are often called arguments from perceptual relativity.)

[13] For discussion of some of the subtleties surrounding the use of this term, see BonJour (2001), Crane (2005), Huemer (2004). For an accessible overview and defense, see Robinson (1994). For recent discussion, see Hellie (forthcoming b), Siegel (forthcoming), Smith (2002).

Traditional sense-data theories have fallen on hard times. Grounds for dissent vary. Some, motivated by physicalist commitments, see no way to make room in their metaphysics for the non-physical entities that traditional sense-data are supposed to be. Others, following Chisholm, worry that since perceptual experience is often indeterminate, no actual object could serve as the corresponding sense datum.[14] Yet others are troubled that, on such a theory, all perception of the external world—even in successful cases—is indirect. And many, following Austin, deny the sense-data theorist's motivating assumption that when it appears to us that a certain property is instantiated, then there must be some (mental or non-mental) entity that actually has that property.[15]

Still, certain of the motivations for sense-data theories—that the nature of experience is grounded in one's inner life and that experience consists in the presentation of properties that need not be instantiated by one's external surroundings—find contemporary voice in *representationalism* (see question three on page 17), and in related discussions about the existence and nature of qualia.[16] And the facts that gave rise to the sense-data response—the possibility of hallucination, illusion, perceptual relativity, and their kin—are among the central facts to be accommodated by any account of perceptual experience. Accounting for these possibilities plays an important role in the chapters by David Chalmers (chapter 2), Tim Crane (chapter 3), Anil Gupta (chapter 5), Mark Johnston (chapter 7), Eric Lormand (chapter 9), Alva Noë (chapter 11), and Sydney Shoemaker (chapter 13).

PART II: QUESTIONS

In the remainder of the introduction, we turn to a set of questions about perceptual experience which lie at the heart of many recent discussions. We begin with (1) a cluster of questions about the representational nature of perceptual experience: what reasons do we have for thinking that perceptual experience represents the world as being a certain way, and (assuming that it does) what sorts of features do we have reason to think that it represents? We then turn to (2) a cluster of questions about the content of perceptual experience: assuming that it has representational content, what is that content like? Consideration of these issues leads naturally to (3) a highly contested question about the

[14] Cf. Chisholm (1942).

[15] Cf. Austin: "If . . . a church were cunningly camouflaged so that it looked like a barn, how could any serious question be raised about what we see when we look at it? We see, of course, a *church* that now *looks like a barn*. We do *not* see an immaterial barn, an immaterial church, or an immaterial anything else. And what in this case could seriously tempt us to say that we do?" (1962), 30.

[16] For an overview, see Tye (2003); see also Dennett (1988, 1991), and Lormand (1994). Related issues are addressed in Crane (chapter 3).

representational content of perceptual experience: what is the relation between the representational content of perceptual experience, and its phenomenal character? We then turn to (4) a question about the relation between perceptual experience and perceptual success: how are the two related, and can the one be analyzed in terms of the other? Finally, we turn briefly to (5) a question about the *subjects* of perceptual experience: what does the structure of perceptual experience tell us about our own physical and cognitive make-up?

Question One: What Features does Experience Represent?

It is common ground among the authors in this volume that our experiential life is not to be understood as a body of semantically inert events that serve as mere signs or symptoms of the goings on outside. Rather, perceptual experience is understood as making a distinctive contribution to our epistemic lives by representing the world as being one way rather than another:[17] it has *representational content*.

As is typical with such cases of first-order consensus, however, philosophical discord lurks just below the surface. One set of questions concerns the issue of what might count as decisive reasons for endorsing the view that perceptual experience has such content. Another set of questions—addressed in some way or another by nearly all of our authors—concerns a cluster of issues about the nature of this representational content: What properties does it represent as obtaining in the core cases? What range of properties does it represent directly? What kinds of objects figure as the objects of perceptual representation? Relatedly, we might wonder about the content of this experience: Is it truth-evaluable? What is its logical form? Is it conceptual or non-conceptual? In the next two sections, we explore each of these sub-questions in turn.

Why Think that Experience is Representational in the First Place?

Many will content themselves with one or another of the simple answers to this question. Some will think that introspection by itself is decisive: if we look inwards, we can just *tell* that our experience represents the world as being this way or that. Some will appeal to semantico-linguistic considerations such as the behavior of the constructions that we use to describe our experiential life— "it looks to be the case that P," "it tastes as if Q," "he sounds R," and so on. Some will appeal to specific empirical results: such-and-such promising class of psychological theories presuppose that experience is representational, and it is good epistemic practice to believe the best scientific theories available. And some may appeal to transparency—our experiences are not the objects of our attention; they are vehicles that enable us to attend to things in the world: perceptual experience could play this role only if it were fundamentally representational.

---

[17] See Armstrong (1968), Peacocke (1983); for additional discussion, see Siegel (2005), section 2.

Some will appeal to more complicated reasoning. Suppose one subscribes to the empiricist view that in order to have certain (perhaps any) concepts, we must have (at least the capacity for) certain sorts of (perceptual) experience. On reflection, one might think that (perceptual) experience could provide such grounding only by being representational in the relevant sense. For, if it were not, it is hard to see how it could play the role of "putting us in touch" with the relevant properties (redness, smoothness, quickness) which thereby become available as contents for our concepts.

Others may make appeal to specifically epistemic considerations, pointing out that perceptual experience seems to play a justificatory role with respect to our beliefs about the external world:[18] not only does thus and such perceptual experience causally occasion thus and such belief—it helps explain what makes that belief a reasonable one.[19] Assuming that the datum is accepted, one might now argue that experience could play such an epistemic role only if it had representational properties. For, if perceptual experiences were semantically inert, they might *cause* our external world beliefs, and might play a crucial role in a reliable belief-forming mechanism, but it is hard to see how they could play the requisite *epistemic* role. In related fashion, one might maintain, as Johnston does (chapter 7), that perceptual experience plays a distinctive epistemic role by directly acquainting us with the objects, stuff, states, and events of which the world is composed. Understanding perceptual experience in this way, Johnston contends, transforms the terms of the debate in ways that permit an effective rebuff of skeptical challenges. (Related issues are discussed in Gupta (chapter 5) and Martin (chapter 10), this volume).

What Properties does Experience Represent as Obtaining in the Core Cases?

There is some dispute as to the range of phenomena that are represented in perceptual experience (see next sub-question). But those who accept that experience is representational agree about certain core cases. In the case of visual experience, for example, nearly everyone agrees that there is a good sense in which we represent shape, color, and motion.[20] But what exactly does this "good sense" amount to? When we experience an object as red and circular and motionless, which properties are represented, such that the object needs to have them in order for the experience to be veridical? The question invites a

---

[18] On this picture, beliefs stand in need of justification, but can only be justified by something with representational content. If that justifier is another belief, then the justifier itself requires justification, and regress sets in. But since perceptual experiences have content without themselves standing in need of justification, regress is averted and justification provided.

[19] See McDowell (1994a), Brewer (1999).

[20] As already noted, we will follow the literature in largely restricting our discussion to cases involving visual experience. Analogous discussion of other modalities would presumably focus on properties such as pitch and direction (hearing), intensity and valence (touch), and so on.

platitudinous answer: the required properties are redness, circularity, and motionlessness.

The platitudinous answer appeals to what might be called the Harmony Thesis:

> *Harmony Thesis*: The properties semantically expressed by "red," "circular," and the like are the very properties that are represented by the kinds of perceptual experiences that we standardly give voice to by utterances such as "It looks red" and "It looks circular".[21]

The Harmony Thesis accords well with a number of our practices: we seem to use color words, for example, to pick out the properties that our color experiences putatively represent objects as having.[22]

But a number of puzzles lurk in the vicinity: exactly what properties is experience representing as obtaining? Does experience represent red things as homogeneously red, so that the experience would be non-veridical if the thing turned out to be made of various multicolored small dots? Does experience represent redness as categorical rather than relational, so that if certain accounts of color are correct, then color experience misrepresents reality? If an object that looks circular is slightly ovoid or slightly bumpy, does the property that experience represents as obtaining fail to be instantiated? Does experience represent space as Euclidean, so that there is a problem saying what condition is being placed on the spatial objects by this or that aspect of experience when space is not in fact Euclidean?

Certain answers to these questions put pressure on the Harmony Thesis. If experience does represent colors as categorical—and if color terms in fact designate relational properties—then the Harmony Thesis will be hard to maintain. If we allow that "is circular" applies to objects with some degree of ovoidness or bumpiness, but we say of a roughly circular object that it turned out (on close inspection) not to be the way it looked (on initial inspection)—then again, Harmony is in trouble.

An additional source of mismatch may arise from the context dependence of natural language. In the context of a geometrical discussion we might point to a plate that we earlier classified using the predicate "circular" and say: "That is not circular." Semanticists typically accommodate such data in a charitable way by alleging that the term "circular" is context dependent. But do we wish to say the

---

[21] Cf. Jackson's "prime intuition about color": " 'red' denotes the property of an object putatively presented in visual experience when that object looks red" (Jackson (1996), Jackson and Pargetter (1987)); see also Campbell (1993). We will set aside the somewhat tricky matter of exactly what property is being ascribed when we predicate "is square" or "is circular" to a three-dimensional object. (Thanks to Richard Price for raising this issue.)

[22] In a related vein, John Campbell (chapter 1) argues that what is key to our possession of color concepts are color experiences which involve conscious attention to the colors of objects as properties upon which direct intervention is selectively possible; it is this, he maintains, that explains our intuition that colors are categorical properties.

same about the representational content of the perceptual experience itself? There is strong intuitive pressure to say that some property is common to what is represented by the experiences that induce the report "it looks circular," even if the semantic value of "circular" itself fluctuates across contexts.[23]

Yet another prima facie difficulty for Harmony is raised by the case of spectrum inversion. Suppose we allow the possibility that:

[B]y the different Structure of our Organs, it were so ordered, That *the same Object should produce in several Men's Minds different* Ideas at the same time; *v.g.*, if the *Idea* that a *Violet* produced in one Man's Mind by his Eyes, were the same that a *Marigold* produced in another Man's, and *vice versa*. (Locke 1689/1975: II.xxxii.15)

In such a case it is natural to suppose that when the second man has the kind of experience that the first would express by "looks violet," then the property that looks to him to obtain thanks to that experience is the property that the first man perceptually represents as obtaining when he looks at marigolds. Call that property P. Thinking about such a case suggests a potential mismatch between the semantic value of our color words and the properties that we perceptually represent. Suppose, as many hold, that the first man's term "violet" picks out a certain physical property, say a reflectance property: call that V. It seems difficult to maintain that the second man is perceptually representing V as obtaining when he looks at marigolds. So, contra Harmony, V is not identical to P.[24]

The Harmony Thesis is intimately connected with a second thesis, which might be called the Veridicality Thesis:

Veridicality Thesis: In very many cases, ordinary objects have the properties that we represent in experience.

If we accept Harmony, there is a natural way to argue for Veridicality. For we can move from the claim that things are often red and circular when we report

---

[23] Likewise, if the representational mechanisms of perceptual content are informationally encapsulated (Fodor (1983))—that is, if their representational content is unaffected by central processing—then perceptual content will not be subject to the vicissitudes that produce semantic context dependence for language and the vehicles of belief: conversational accommodation, varying paradigms, changes in what is salient, shifting standards, and so on. (For a related discussion of encapsulation and perceptual content, see Siegel (chapter 14).

[24] Cf. Horgan and Tienson (2002). Similar considerations apply if the semantic value of "violet" in my mouth is a dispositional property relativized to my local community, i.e. something of the form: being disposed to produce response R in community C under relevant settings S. (An extra complication arises if response R is described by appeal to representational facts about experience. Crudely, if "violet" has the same meaning as "is disposed to look violet under normal conditions," and "violet" occurs with its normal meaning within the scope of "looks", then "looks violet" means "looks to be disposed to look violet under normal conditions," and so on.) If "violet" in my mouth picks out some property relativized to some community C to which I belong, it seems difficult to maintain that a tribe of spectrum-inverted martians would be perceptually representing that property when they looked at marigolds. Again, on the assumption that the property that I perceptually represent when I look at violets is what they represent when they look at marigolds, we get the conclusion that the representational contents of color perception do not match the semantic values of color words.

them as looking to be red and circular to the conclusion that, in such cases, there are ways that we represent things as being—namely red and circular—such that they are that way.

If we reject Harmony, we lose this natural argument for Veridicality. Moreover, as we have seen, the ways that people have motivated rejection of the Harmony Thesis often create very specific pressures to reject the Veridicality Thesis, since the relevant lines of thought often motivate the idea that experience puts representational constraints on the world that the world falls short of meeting.

Given some such line of thought, a number of responses are available. One might reject the attempt to show that experience is demanding in the relevant respect. Or one might concede that experience places some relevant metaphysical demands on the world, and embrace a correspondingly ample ontology. So, for example, one might take the view that color experience requires for its veridicality a non-microphysical "paint" (an emergent property not reducible to microphysics) and acquiesce to a certain kind of non-reductive physicalism—paint supplied—to accommodate Veridicality.[25] Finally, one might concede that experience is demanding, but adopt an error theory about experience rather than be metaphysically expansionist.

David Chalmers (chapter 2) takes up many of these issues in his chapter. He contends that our perceptual experience is regulated by the ideal of an "Edenic world"—a world of perfect colors and shapes, where objects and properties are revealed to us directly—and goes on to try to reconcile the fact that the world is not Edenic with a version of Veridicality.

What Range of Properties are Represented in Perceptual Experience?

Let us put the previous worries to one side and grant that we perceptually represent shape, motion, and color in some way or other. What other properties are represented in experience?[26] Our use of terms like "looks" and "tastes" might seem to suggest that the range is a broad one.[27] Not only do we say things like: that looks red, that sounds loud, that tastes sweet; we also say things like: that looks elegant, that sounds ominous, or that tastes French. Of course, there may be uses of such terms that have nothing to do with sensory perception. If, during the course of a proof I say "step three looks to follow from step two" and you reply "that sounds unlikely" or "that smells fishy," neither of us is making a direct claim about the content of our sensory experience. But something more is going on in claims like "the team looks to be in a losing situation" or "he sounds happy." In these cases, it is not that the sensory term is being used metaphorically; rather, it seems, sensory terminology has been recruited to describe belief contents

---

[25] Cf. Block (1996). One might even allow multiple paint jobs on a single object so that spectrally inverted subjects all have a suitable paint to notice.

[26] For additional discussion of these issues, see Siegel (2005).   [27] Cf. Austin (1962).

which we are prompted to entertain as the result of having had a certain sort of sensory experience, but which are not straightforwardly represented by the experience itself. If it turns out that the team is not losing, or that our friend is not happy, then—while we have made some sort of mistake—our perceptual experience may still have been veridical. It would be a different sort of mistake entirely if I said "the team looks to be wearing blue shirts" when, as a matter of fact, their shirts were red. Some contents, it seems, we perceive *directly* (say, that such and such is red); others we perceive *indirectly* (say, that such-and-such team is winning).

We have, then, a putative distinction, but one whose extension turns out to be extremely difficult to determine. When I see a table, and it looks to have a back, is that something that is represented by the experience itself, or is it instead something that I conclude on the basis of the experience, or which is prompted by the experience? When it looks like one billiard ball causes the other to move, should we say with Hume that my experience would be perfectly veridical so long as the patterns of motions occur—even with causality absent—or should we say that the experience itself requires the presence of causality in order to be veridical? When someone looks to be in pain, does my experience merely "say" that the person is jumping up and down and making noises, or does it also include the content that he is actually in pain? Upon reflection one might begin to wonder whether the distinction between the direct and indirect cases is a cogent one after all (cf. Noë, chapter 11).[28]

Though the question of which properties are directly represented by perceptual experience is murky, it seems premature to give up completely on the distinction between direct and indirect altogether. Suppose you poke your head around the corner: in some good sense you look to be a thing with two feet. Suppose instead you walk around the corner: here again you look to be a thing with two feet. But it seems hard to deny that there is a difference in kind between the two cases of looking to have two feet. How, if at all, can that difference be expressed in a principled way?

A number of authors in the volume address related issues. Jesse Prinz (chapter 12) argues that perception involves matching incoming percepts to percepts stored in memory, in such a way that the incoming percepts may inherit their semantic content from their stored counterparts. Since the range of contents available to the stored percepts is unlimited, so too is the in-principle range of contents of direct perception: we can directly perceive not only redness and tigerness and carburetorness, but also primeness and injustice and truth.

Susanna Siegel (chapter 14) also argues that a relatively rich range of properties are represented perceptually, and suggests a principled way of distinguishing what is directly perceived from what is not: by considering which differences make a phenomenological difference. If we want to know whether

---

[28] Thanks to Richard Price for discussion of these issues.

being a pine tree is a property represented in visual experience, we need to ask whether there is the right sort of phenomenological difference between the visual experiences one has before and after one develops a capacity to recognize pine trees as such.

Alva Noë (chapter 11) maintains that our perceptual systems in fact represent much less than we think they do, and that our mind "fills in" to complete a perceptual scene supplying detail where the perceptual system does not. Since ordinary phenomenological testing will not allow us to reliably distinguish what is filled in from what is not, it cannot decisively settle questions about what is part of perceptual experience. Careful attention to the nature of perceptual experience reveals that experiences are not like snapshots; even in paradigm cases of veridical perception, what we experience visually outstrips what we actually see at any given moment.

What Stands at the Other End of Perceptual Relations?

Assuming that perception is relational, one might correspondingly wonder what stands at the other end of perceptual relations.[29] Here, as above, the original concerns are not hard to motivate—but it is even more difficult to see how the issues can be regimented. If we play hide-and-seek and I catch a glimpse of your foot,[30] I might exclaim "I see you!" But are you—as opposed to merely your foot—an object of my (direct) perception in this case?

Traditional sense-data theories offer one sort of contractionist response to this conundrum: in all cases, the objects of perception are simply mental entities. A less extreme contractionist view—though one that has likewise fallen out of favor—holds that we perceive only the exposed surfaces of physical objects.[31]

Those who find such views unpalatable may make appeal to a "by" locution to distinguish the hide-and-seek case from the ordinary one. In the former case, I see you (indirectly) by seeing your shoe (directly); in the latter, I see you

[29] Note that when we ask what is at the other end of perceptual relations, we are interested in the relations expressed by perceptual success verbs that take noun phrases: he sees the bus, she hears the radio, I smell hot cocoa, etc. We are not presupposing that the relation expressed by *see* in "He saw that P" is the same as that expressed in "He saw S."

[30] Or, more likely, your shoe. When does a covering prevent you from seeing a thing, when not? Does ordinary usage track some deeper difference in these cases? (Remember Descartes' admonition in the *Second Meditation*: "We say that we see the wax itself, if it is there before us, not that we judge it to be there from its colour or shape; and this might lead me to conclude without more ado that knowledge of the wax comes from what the eye sees, and not from the scrutiny of the eye alone. But then if I look out of the window and see men crossing the square, as I just happen to have done, I normally say that I see the men themselves, just as I say that I see the wax. Yet do I see any more than hats and coats which could conceal automatons? I *judge* that they are men. And so something which I thought I was seeing with my eyes is in fact grasped solely by the faculty of judgment which is in my mind" (Descartes 1641/1986).

[31] As Austin (1962) stresses, the objects of perception include many things other than physical objects: we see and hear claps of thunder, whispers, explosions, and weddings. Indeed, events may be even more prevalent as the reported objects of perception than we may realize (cf. Higginbotham (1983)). (Related issues are discussed in Noë (chapter 11) and Prinz (chapter 12).)

(directly). But such a view faces problems from two directions. After all, even in the ordinary case, I am directly impinged upon by some of your parts and not others: so it seems that no ordinary three-dimensional objects can be perceived directly.[32] At the same time, the view seems to make it all too easy to perceive things indirectly: if I can perceive you by perceiving a part of you, why can't I perceive the whole universe in the same way—after all, I directly perceive at least one of its parts? Regimentation seems hard to come by.

Question Two: What kind of Content does Perceptual Experience Have?

Begin with an ordinary declarative sentence. Various kinds of semantic taxonomies can be brought to bear on the sentence. Most basically we can evaluate the sentence for truth or falsity. Less basically we can ask after the intension of a sentence—which determines, for each possible world, whether or not it is true or false at that world. We can ask after the semantic values of the semantically significant subsentential segments of the sentence—or segments of the deep "logical form" that underlies the overt production of the sentence—and seek to explain the truth value of the sentence in terms of such semantic values and the logical form of the sentence in question. We might distinguish sentences with singular content—where some individual object figures as semantic value, from non-singular sentences—such as certain kinds of quantificational claims—where no such object figures. We might—if we are from certain traditions—apply some sort of Fregean sense-reference distinction to this or that expression, where the sense of the expression plays a crucial role in accounting for the cognitive significance of that expression in the relevant individual's cognitive life. And we might develop the view in such a way that we cling to Frege's insistence that sense determines reference, or else to his insistence that sense is to be tied to cognitive significance. Finally, if we are from certain traditions we will regard the notion of "concept" as explanatorily basic and will explain the cognitive significance of a sentence in terms of which concepts it gives voice to, combined with some picture of what makes a concept the concept that it is. For each of these questions, analogous questions might be raised with regard to the content of perceptual experience.[33]

Can Perceptual Representations be Evaluated for Truth and Falsity?

Most basically we can ask whether perceptual representations can be evaluated for truth and falsity. Here again, if we take our clue from ordinary language, the

---

[32] And if matter is "gunky," so that every part has proper parts and every part has finite thickness, there being no part as thin as a geometrical line, should we then say that we perceive every material object indirectly?

[33] A number of these matters are taken up in detail in Chalmers (chapter 2).

answer seems to be clear. For perceptual representations described using "that-clauses"—"It looks to be the case that . . ."—the representation is true iff the that-clause is true. For representations described using predicates "He looked F," the representation is true just in case the subject of the complex predicate "looked F" has the property expressed by the modifier "F". And so on. Indeed, it is the rough consensus that perceptual representations—and not just the beliefs they trigger—are evaluable for truth and falsity.

But there are dissenters. There are those who think that perceptual experience, considered in itself, does not have content at all—it merely serves as the occasion for beliefs with content. It is also possible to have a view according to which the kind of content possessed by perceptual experience is not evaluable for truth and falsity. Anil Gupta defends such a view, arguing that the content of belief is not anything like a function from possible worlds to truth values, or a truth-evaluable proposition, but instead a function from belief inputs to belief outputs—roughly, it is a rule for updating beliefs which is silent on what views one brings as input and thus, in abstraction from doxastic input, silent on what one should have as output[34] (see Gupta, chapter 5).

If we do adopt the consensus view that perceptual representations are evaluable for truth and falsity, difficult semantic questions remain to be settled. One obvious decision point is whether one can speak of the logical form of a perceptual representation.[35] Another concerns whether something like the sense-reference distinction holds in the perceptual realm.[36] A related issue is whether perceptual contents are always, or at least sometimes, singular contents about the objects perceived.[37] One question that has received special attention is considered in the section below.

Is the Representational Content of Experience Non-Conceptual?

Those who hold that there is non-conceptual content maintain that there are mental states which represent the world, even though their subject lacks the concepts that would enable her to specify their content.

---

[34] Notice that for Gupta a number of the issues raised in the previous section are based on misconceptions. No experience represents any property *simpliciter*: rather it delivers outputs about a certain property F only relative to certain informational inputs that are brought to the experience.

[35] Some hold that the notion of logical form can only be applied to sentence-like representations and argue that since perceptual representations are more map-like than sentence-like, the notion of logical form fails to apply.

[36] It is natural, for example, to think that tactile and visual perception of circularity involve the same property—the same referent—presented by means of different senses. But to progress beyond such semantic free association requires careful articulation of what the sense-reference distinction comes to.

[37] Suppose a thing X looks red to me. Wouldn't it be a gross distortion to claim that the content of my experience is not the singular proposition that X is red, but rather the general proposition that there is something at such-and-such an orientation that is red? (Prima facie, it would seem that singular representation has a foundational role to play insofar as it is to epistemically ground singular beliefs.)

One might think that the project is a non-starter. One might think it impossible that there could be any contentful mental state that is not conceptual; as Kant famously held that "Intuitions without concepts are blind."[38] Or one might think that the role perceptual experience plays in our epistemic lives means that it has to be conceptual: since perceptual experiences provide us with reasons for belief, and since the only way they could do so would be if their content were conceptual, then the content of perceptual experience must be conceptual.[39]

Alternatively, one might think that we are not clear enough on what it is for something to be conceptual for the question to be well-enough defined to answer. Is the point of saying that experience is non-conceptual that it lacks a logical form? Or that it lacks an intension?[40] The issue of whether content could be non-conceptual cannot be evaluated except against the background of some theory about the nature and role of concepts. One popular heuristic is the idea that a perceptual representation of some property is conceptual only if that property is available as part of the content of a belief and desire. And one way of building a theory on this basis would be to claim that it is of the nature of concepts that their possessor is able to freely recombine them, syntax permitting,[41] and that this kind of productivity only happens at the level of the central propositional attitudes.

Setting aside these worries, let us see what sorts of reasons have been given in favor of an affirmative answer. Some have thought that perceptual experience is clearly non-conceptual as a result of thinking about the range of beings who (presumably) have perceptual experiences, or as the result of reflection on the phenomenology of human perceptual experience itself. Two main arguments have been offered for this view, both offered in embryonic form in Gareth

---

[38] Kant writes: "Our nature is so constituted that our *intuition* can never be other than sensible; that is, it contains only the mode in which we are affected by objects. The faculty, on the other hand, which enables us to *think* the object of sensible intuition is the understanding. To neither of these powers may a preference be given over the other. Without sensibility no object would be given to us, without understanding no object would be thought. Thoughts without content are empty, intuitions without concepts are blind. It is, therefore, just as necessary to make our concepts sensible, that is, to add the concept to them in intuition, as to make our intuitions intelligible, that is, to bring them under concepts. These two powers or capacities cannot exchange their functions. The understanding can intuit nothing, the senses can think nothing. Only through their union can knowledge arise." (Kant 1781/1787/1929, A51/B75). Of course, Kant is using *intuition* here as a term of art.

[39] Cf. Brewer (1999a and b), McDowell (1994 a and b). Objectors maintain that perceptual experience may logically support or provide evidence for beliefs, despite lacking conceptual content; for instance, certain experiences might be consistent with, or render more probable, certain contents. Cf. Peacocke (2001a), Heck (2000).

[40] Where the intension of a sentence is a function from possible worlds to truth values. Given a perception, can we, for any possible world ask whether the perception is true relative to that world (in the way that we can, for a given utterance, ask whether it is true relative to any given possible world)?

[41] Cf. Evans's (1982) Generality Constraint. For recent discussion of its relation to the question of non-conceptual content, see Camp (2004) and Heck (forthcoming).

Evans's *Varieties of Reference*. The first—the Argument from Overlap—finds voice in the writings of Christopher Peacocke:[42]

Nonconceptual content has been recruited for many purposes. In my view the most fundamental reason—the one on which other reasons must rely if the conceptualist presses hard—lies in the need to describe correctly the overlap between human perception and that of some of the nonlinguistic animals. While being reluctant to attribute concepts to the lower animals, many of us would also want to insist that the property of (say) representing a flat brown surface as being at a certain distance from one can be common to the perceptions of humans and of lower animals. (Peacocke 2001b: 613)

But it is unclear to many that the perceptual experiences of humans and animals are common in the ways that Peacocke suggests, and unclear to others why we cannot ascribe beliefs to the animals in question.

The second—the Argument from Richness (or Fineness of Grain)—has been widely endorsed.[43] Here is a recent formulation:[44]

My experience of [the things around me] represents them far more precisely . . . far more distinctively, it would seem, than any other characterization I could hope to formulate, for myself or others, in terms of the concepts I presently possess. The problem is not lack of time, but lack of descriptive resources, that is, lack of the appropriate concepts. (Heck 2000: 490)

One line of response—which appeals to the notion of demonstrative reference— has been explored by John McDowell. Even if we lack a non-demonstrative word to serve as the vehicle for indicating a shade perceptually represented on a particular occasion, we can symmetrically encode each property represented by a rich experience at the level of judgement by referring to the shade by "that shade" (1994).[45] If the test for whether perceptual representation of

---

[42] Cf. Evans: "Two of . . . the operations of the informational system are [operations that] we share with animals; and I do not think we can properly understand the mechanism whereby we gain information from others unless we realize that it is already operative at a stage of human intellectual development that pre-dates the applicability of the more sophisticated notion" (Evans (1982), 124).

[43] Two related arguments are (1) *The Argument from Analogue Information*: Whereas propositional attitudes represent the world in digital form (that is, when they carry the information that S is F, they carry no further information about S other than that it is F), perceptual experiences represent the world in analogue form (that is, when they carry the information that s is F, they also carry additional information about s) cf. Dretske (1981); and (2) *The Argument from Remembered Experience*: Remembered reassessments of perceptual experiences can bring to light features of the experience that were in some sense absent from one's original representation of it; so one can perceive things without noticing them, and without deploying concepts (cf. Martin (1992), Dretske (chapter 4)). Michael Tye (chapter 15) takes up this theme in his discussion of Sperling's memory experiments, which Dretske (chapter 4) and Noë (chapter 11) also discuss.

[44] Cf. Evans: "[T]he content of the simplest photograph . . . will be something that can be specified conceptually only with some loss" (Evans (1982), 125, n. 9). "Do we really understand the proposal that we have as many colour concepts as there are shades of colour that we can sensibly discriminate?" (Evans (1982), 229). For additional discussion, see Chuard (under review).

[45] Such an account faces difficulties when the actual and apparent shades differ. In such a case it will not do to say that "that shade" refers to the actual shade, since the actual shade is not how things look. And it will not do to say that "that shade" refers to the apparent shade, since the point

some property is conceptual in subject S is whether the property is available as an object of judgment by S, then (modulo other worries) McDowell's method passes the test. But ultimate evaluation of his proposal requires (as noted above) getting clear on what, if any, the further tests for conceptuality are going to be.[46]

Michael Tye (chapter 15) explores these issues in detail, spelling out what is meant by "richness" and "fineness of grain" in light of a number of recent results from empirical psychology in order to defend a subtle version of the view that experiences have non-conceptual content.[47]

Question Three: What is the Relationship between Representational Content and Phenomenal Character?

Our perceptual experience has a "what it's like" aspect: there is something that it's like to be undergoing this or that kind of perceptual experience.[48] Call that the phenomenological aspect of experience. Meanwhile, if the consensus view is correct, it also has a representational aspect: a particular perceptual experience (directly) represents the world as being a certain way. Call this the representational aspect. What is the relationship between the two? Here it is particularly pertinent to consider in turn a pair of supervenience theses which have, in effect, been topics of much discussion in recent years.

(i) The phenomenological character of our perceptual experience supervenes on its representational content[49] (duplicate the representational properties of experience and one will have duplicated the phenomenological properties of experience[50]).

(ii) The representational content of our perceptual experience supervenes on its phenomenological character (duplicate the phenomenological character and one will duplicate the representational character).

---

of McDowell's account is to explain the apparent shade in terms of the demonstrative representative. (For discussion, see Heck 2000.)

[46] For further discussion, see Brewer (1999, 2005), Bermudez (1994, 1995, 2003), Byrne (2005), Crane (1988a, 1988b, 1992a), Cussins (1990), Gunther, (ed.) (2003), Hurley (1998), Kelly (2001a, 2001b), Martin (1992), McDowell (1994a, 1994b), Peacocke (1994, 1998, 2001a, 2001b), Stalnaker (1998).

[47] See also Crane, Johnston, and Martin (this volume, chapter 3, 7 and 10).

[48] Note that to claim this is not to prejudge the question of whether all cases of *perception* involve perceptual experience (see Dretske, chapter 4). Nor is it to prejudge the question of what determines this phenomenal character, and in particular whether it is reducible to physical or functional states (sometimes called the question of *qualia*.) (See, e.g. Dennett (1988, 1991), Lormand (1994), Tye (2003).)

[49] Thesis (i) is typically referred to as "intentionalism," "representationalism," or "representationism." Contemporary formulation of the view can be traced to Armstrong (1968); for terminology, cf. Byrne (2001).

[50] Subtleties aside, the idea of a thesis that A facts supervene on B facts is that duplication of B facts ensures duplication of A facts.

One or the other have been defended, in some form, in an ever-burgeoning body of literature.[51] Yet both face a number of challenges.

Begin with thesis (i). One prima facie worry is that representational properties are not generally associated with unique phenomenological characters, so why would they be in the case of perceptual representation? Beliefs, after all, can have representational properties without associated phenomenology, and the representational aspects of perceptual experience seem to be something that they share with belief, while the phenomenological aspects seem to be something that divides them from belief. Why, then, would the phenomenological character of perceptual experience be explained in terms of its representational content? (Such prima facie reasons are not decisive, of course.)

A more specific challenge to (i) arises from contemplating (apparently) possible cases where two subjects seem to share representational contents, but where these are associated with very different phenomenological properties (arguably, cases of spectrum inversion) or with the absence of any phenomenology at all (zombies). Such cases challenge the straightforward endorsement of (i), since they seem to describe cases where representational content is held constant, while phenomenological character varies. Sydney Shoemaker and Michael Thau,[52] among others, have argued that spectrum inversion is in fact compatible with (i), since, on their view, the representational content of perceptual experience represents what Shoemaker calls "appearance properties"[53]—"nameless properties that are correlated with colors in the experience of a particular sort of subject but could in principle be associated with different colors in the experience of different sorts of subject." In his chapter for this volume Shoemaker (chapter 13) defends this view against a number of recent criticisms that have been leveled against it.

A related challenge to both theses comes from the possibility of unconscious perceptual contents. It is arguable that there is much that we perceptually represent that we are not perceptually aware of and which is thereby not manifest in our phenomenological life. (Fred Dretske (chapter 4) presents and critically assesses a number of experimental studies that purportedly demonstrate the prevalence of such unconscious perception.) Such contents are not fixed by our phenomenology, as (ii) requires. And unless there are such things as representational contents which can only be represented unconsciously, such cases provide a challenge to (i) as well.

---

[51] The bulk of discussion has been devoted to (i). Among advocates of (some version of) (i) are Byrne (2001), Byrne and Hilbert (1997a), Dretske (1995, 1996), Harman (1990, 1996), Lycan (1995, 1996), McDowell (1994a), Rey (1992, 1998), Shoemaker (1994b, 2000), and Tye (1995, 2000). Among its notable critics are Boghossian and Velleman (1989, 1991), Burge (1997, 2003), Block (1990, 1995, 1996, 1999, 2003, forthcoming), Chalmers (1996), Levine (1997, 2001); McGinn (1991), and Peacocke (1983, 1984). For discussion of (some version of) (ii), see Chalmers (2004), Hellie (forthcoming a), Horgan and Tienson (2002), Loar (2003), Searle (1990), Siewert (1998), Strawson (1994).   [52] Shoemaker (1994a, 1994b, 2000); Thau (2002).

[53] In earlier work (1994b), Shoemaker called these "phenomenal properties;" he has since (2000) changed his terminology to "appearance properties."

Another consideration in this family is raised by what Eric Lormand (chapter 9) calls, following Sartre, the "illusion of immanence."[54] Our inner phenomenology often appears to have some of the very properties that things in the world have: our afterimage actually appears to be circular; our mental image actually appears to be rotating. This illusion of immanence seems central to the phenomenology of our inner life. But do the facts about what our perceptual experience represents all by themselves secure the immanence phenomena, as (i) would require? Couldn't there be a being that represents the world the same way in perceptual experience but for which these phenomena were absent? It is interesting to consider, in this light, whether something analogous to Shoemaker's appearance properties could provide the requisite retort.

A set of related issues seems to cut directly against (i) and indirectly against (ii). So, for example, there seem to be phenomenological aspects of our perceptual experience that do not have a representational role, and that can consequently be varied without varying representational content, or fixed without fixing representational content. Consider the "mood" of our experience. When we are happy, it is arguable that our visual phenomenology is subtly different from when we are sad, ostensibly without this affecting what properties are represented by it. Or consider the phenomenon of color constancy. We represent a surface as being of the same color despite the illumination of the surface having a different "look" in different patches. Or consider the representation of shape, in which a particular object is represented as having a constant shape, while manifesting different "looks" as we encounter it from different angles (such cases are discussed by Lormand, chapter 9). Unless these differences in looks and feels can be cashed out in terms of differences in which properties are represented as obtaining in the world (again, see Shoemaker, chapter 13), then it is hard to see how representational facts can fix phenomenological facts as (i) requires. And if we allow the phenomenological facts to be free-floating in the way that introspection seems to suggest, then it becomes more dubious that they fix representational content in the way that (ii) requires. Similar considerations arise from consideration of cross-modal perception.[55] It might be argued that when we perceive something as circular by touch and perceive something as circular by vision, the phenomenology is radically different but the property represented is the same, contrary to (i). Those who wish to block this argument are likely to do so in two ways. One might deny that the property represented in touch when

---

[54] Sartre (1940).

[55] Discussion of these issues is sometimes framed in terms of Molyneux's Problem: "Suppose a man born blind, and now adult, and taught by his touch to distinguish between a cube and a sphere of the same metal, and nighly of the same bigness, so as to tell, when he felt one and the other, which is the cube, which the sphere. Suppose then the cube and sphere placed on a table, and the blind man to be made to see; *quaere*, Whether by his sight, before he touched them, he could now distinguish and tell which is the globe, and which the cube?" (Locke (1689/1975) *Essay* II, ix, 8). See, for example, Bach-y-Rita (1996), Campbell (1996), Eilan, McCarthy, and Brewer (eds) (1993), Evans (1985), Morgan (1977).

things seem circular is the same as that represented in vision (thus denying the Harmony Thesis). Or one might contend that the phenomenological difference between visual and tactile experience of circularity is to be accounted for by a difference in their additional modality-specific representational content: vision gives both circularity and color; touch gives both circularity and texture.

A further consideration which raises equally powerful problems for (i) and for (ii) comes from the manifest incompatibility of two popular ideas: that the representational facts about experience are fixed by the ways that the experience is nomically connected to features of the outside world, whereas phenomenological facts are intrinsic to us. If so, then they could not covary in the ways that either (i) or (ii) requires. The problem is particularly pressing if we allow that perceptual representation can have singular content, or if we allow that the phenomenology of hallucination and perception can be identical. For, if I represent of a particular thing X that *it* is red, then the singular proposition represented obviously does not supervene on my phenomenology.

This is not to deny that there is room for maneuver. Gupta (chapter 5), for example, maintains that the content of perceptual experience does not determine a truth condition at all but rather a belief-updating rule. Perhaps Gupta content, as it were, is intrinsic, even though the content of truth-conditional states is not. Or one might argue that representational content does not have a single dimension, but, like other sorts of content—that it has two dimensions—and that phenomenology determines a character, or "primary intension" even if it does not determine a "content" or "secondary intension." (This proposal is discussed by Chalmers, chapter 2.) Or one might maintain that it is a profound though natural illusion to suppose that there is some set of intrinsic properties that determine our conscious/phenomenological life.

Question Four: What is the Relation between Perceptual Experience and Perceptual Success?

Some ways of describing our perceptual lives record perceptual success. When we say "He saw that P," "He heard that P" (in the non-testimonial use), or "She perceived that P" (in the literal use), we use perceptual experience verbs in a *factive* way, where X Φs that P is factive iff it entails that P. Another kind of success is recorded by perceptual verbs that take transparent noun phrases as complements:[56] if you hear the shout and the shout is the yell made by Jim, then you heard the yell made by Jim.[57] A third way of recording perceptual success is by naked infinitival constructions like "He saw the Titanic sink".[58] But there are

---

[56] That is, cases where the truth value of the reports are unaffected by substitution of co-referential noun phrases.

[57] In this case the verb expresses not a factive propositional attitude but rather a relation that holds between the subject and an object (be it an event or a physical object) in the world.

[58] Cf. Higginbotham (1983).

also success-neutral descriptions which can be used to report cases subjectively indistinguishable from the success cases. Consider "It is as if I see that P," "I seem to see that P," "I seem to see an F," "I see an F," (on the use that is compatible with an illusion), or "It looks as if there is an F."[59] What is the relationship between success cases and neutral cases?[60]

Two analytical projects present themselves. *Factorizing accounts* seek to characterize the success state in terms of the neutral state: a subject is in the success state S iff she is in the neutral state s, *and* some additional conditions obtain. (Consider, by analogy, the view that knowledge (the success state) can be factorized into belief (the neutral state) plus some other ingredients.) *Disjunctive accounts* seek to characterize the neutral state in terms of the success state:[61] a subject is in the neutral state s iff she is either in the success state S, *or* in a state which she cannot distinguish from S.[62] (Consider, by analogy, the view that belief is to be analyzed as that which is indiscriminable from knowledge.[63])

The idea that there is some natural kind that is common to cases of perceiving that P and their hallucinatory counterparts might seem to favor factorizing approaches.[64] If you and I are in subjectively identical states, but you see whereas I hallucinate that there is a coffee cup on the desk before us, it seems prima facie obvious that there is some set of experiential properties—both phenomenological and representational—that serve as the common ground of our respective experiences. Shouldn't it be possible to build the success case from this with the addition of some kind of supplement? As it turns out, the task of articulating just what that supplement amounts to is daunting at best.[65] Consider the following

[59] Cf. Hinton (1967).

[60] There are also constructions that encode success on one dimension while remaining neutral on the other: "Something looks to be F" requires that there is some x that is actually seen, but does not require that one sees that x is F. These intermediate states may, of course, be recruited in the analytical projects described below.

[61] Disjunctivists differ in their choice of success state. Hinton (1967) proposes "see NP." But, as Snowdon (1980–1) observes, the transparency of this construction (in its success use) makes it a poor choice as a basis for analyzing such states as "it looks like there is a NP" due to the possibility of perceptual illusion. Martin (chapter 10) opts for "veridically perceives x as F" as his springboard success state. A selection of recent papers—including essays by Campbell, Dretske, Johnston, Martin, and Siegel—can be found in *Philosophical Studies* (2004) 120 (1–3).

[62] Some disjunctivist accounts invite a slightly more metaphysical spin. The relevant disjunction is intended to articulate the natural kinds that are at work in the various cases, and need not be treated as a conceptual or semantic analysis (of course the relevant equivalences must still hold). (Martin (chapter 10) is relevant here.)

[63] This view is considered though not endorsed by Williamson (2002); see also his critical discussion of factorizing accounts of knowledge.

[64] Of course, even if there were some natural kind in common, there could be some additional explanatory natural kind present in the success cases. Consider the analogy with action. When I play electric guitar there is some natural motion kind in common with the case where I play air guitar—but there may also be a natural kind of event that is present only in cases of actual guitar playing.

[65] As Williamson (2002) emphasizes in related discussion of knowledge and belief, even if being colored is a common factor to being red and being blue, this should not lead us to expect that being red can be analyzed as being colored plus some (non-circular) supplementary condition. And if seeing that P entails knowing that P, then the problems that arise in the case of knowledge will confront us even more directly.

first pass at an analysis: seeing that P is equivalent to its looking to be the case that P plus P. The proposal runs aground in cases of veridical hallucinations,[66] for although both conditions are met in such cases, one does not see that P[67] (see Johnston, chapter 7).

Disjunctive accounts also face something of an uphill battle. Prima facie, introspection seems to count against the view. And, again prima facie, the conception of perceptual input systems recommended by cognitive science—according to which false representations of an input system have a reality that does not turn on what discriminative use the central processor makes of them—sits ill with the disjunctivist picture.[68]

Moreover, it is not an easy matter to come up with an appropriately disjunctive analysis of "looks to be the case that" and "looks F" (on the uses that report how things are perceptually rather than what one is inclined to believe) that survives obvious counterexample. One can get a feeling for the dialectic by considering the following toy analysis. Suppose I say that it looks to be the case that P (neutral case) just in case I either successfully perceive that P (success case) or I cannot tell (by introspection alone) that I am not perceiving that P.[69] (i) If we allow that "perceives that P" entails "knows that P"[70] and that "knows that P" entails "believes that P," then in any case where I know that I am not believing that P, I am in a position to easily tell that I am not perceiving that P. But surely there are cases of this sort where it still looks to be the case that P—contra the proposed analysis. (ii) Suppose that Judy and Trudy are so similar that I cannot tell them apart by looking. You see that Judy is brushing her teeth. I am intrinsically just like you except I am hallucinating—no one anywhere near me is brushing her teeth. Clearly, I cannot know by looking that I am not perceiving that Judy is brushing her teeth—nor can I know by looking that I am not perceiving that Trudy is brushing her teeth. But it seems inappropriate to say—as the proposed analysis requires—that it looks to me that Judy is brushing her teeth and it looks to me that Trudy is brushing her teeth. (iii) The intransitivity of discriminability seems to suggest that two experiences may present different colors c_1 and c_2 without my knowing it: if something looks to be c_1, then I cannot know by introspection that it does not present c_2.[71] The proposed analysis leads to the unwelcome conclusion that in such a case, it looks to me that something is c_2. (iv) Suppose I am so dreadful at introspecting that reflection

---

[66] Some might think that, strictly speaking, the only propositions that ever look to obtain are ones of the form "perceiving that P." Then veridical hallucination could not obtain, but neither could "perceives" be analyzed in terms of "looks."

[67] Instead, Johnston suggests, what we learn from thinking about the relation between successful and unsuccessful cases of (apparent) perception is that the function of sensory awareness is to disclose the sensible truthmakers for our immediate judgments about the external world.

[68] These challenges are addressed explicitly in Martin (2004).

[69] And not because I am asleep or inattentive or lacking the requisite concepts. (These qualifications raise issues which are beyond the scope of this introduction.)

[70] Cf. Williamson (2002), chapter 1.   [71] Cf. Williamson (1990).

tells me little about what I am or am not perceiving. On the proposed analysis, it will be all too easy to credit me with being in a state where it looks to be the case that P (for discussion, see Martin, chapter 10).[72]

It is not our place here to judge whether any of these concerns are decisive. Crane (chapter 3) offers a response to several of these worries, and Martin (chapter 10) offers a refined account of disjunctivism which seeks to fend off certain of these objections.

Question Five: What is the Relation between Embodiment and Perceptual Experience?

It is natural to think that the character of our perceptual experience—in either its phenomenological or representational aspects—puts no interesting constraints on the physical features of the perceiver (and certainly no interesting a priori constraints). For example: it is natural to think that simple immaterial Cartesian mind could share all the experiences I have perceptually, even if I am an extended physical thing that is engaged with the world. Several of the chapters in the volume argue that this impression of neutrality is mistaken.

Geoffrey Lee (chapter 8) discusses the case of a subject who is left–right inverted—a being who is exactly like us in his classificatory, discriminatory, and behavioral dispositions, but whose experiences when presented with an object on his left are qualitatively identical to those that we have when an object is presented on our right. Accounting for the possibility of such a being turns out to put surprising constraints on what sorts of physical structure we might have.

Other of the chapters challenge the pre-reflective and rather compelling idea that our knowledge of perceptual experience is responsive to some intrinsic set of phenomenological states that bear no constitutive relationship to action.

Alva Noë (chapter 11) argues for an intimate connection between perceptual experience and action, suggesting that it may be an illusion to suppose that perceptual experience can be detached from action in the way that certain philosophical thought experiments would have us believe. On the theory he sketches—enactive externalism—the content of perceptual experience depends on the possession and exercise of sensorimotor skill.

Finally, Susan Hurley (chapter 6) advances a view that she calls "the shared circuits hypothesis," which describes a unified framework for the mechanisms that enable control, imitation, and simulation. Hurley maintains that perception

[72] It is also not clear how to extend the analysis to cover cases where something has an oval look but does not look to be oval, or where the look of different portions of the carpet is different but the carpet does not look to have non-uniform color. (Additional discussion of such cases can be found in Noë, chapter 11 and Lormand, chapter 9.) Note also that if Lormand is correct that in many cases what naively seems like the presentation of a worldly property is actually a projection outwards of a property of the experience itself, then the sort of disjunctivist project just adverted to is a non-starter.

and action are dynamically co-constituted and suggests that cognitively significant resources, such as distinctions between self and other and between the imagined and the real, and information for action understanding and planning, can be seen as emerging from the information space that action and perception share.

REFERENCES

Alston, William P. (1993), *The Reliability of Sense Perception* (Ithaca, NY: Cornell University Press).

Armstrong, David (1961), *Perception and the Physical World* (London: Routledge and Kegan Paul).

Armstrong, David (1968), *A Materialist Theory of the Mind* (London: Routledge and Kegan Paul).

Austin, John (1962), *Sense and Sensibilia* (Oxford: Oxford University Press).

Ayer, A. J. (1936), *Language, Truth, and Logic* (London: Gollancz. (2nd Edition, 1946)).

Ayer, A. J. (1940), *The Foundations of Empirical Knowledge* (London: Macmillan).

Ayer, A. J. (1973), *The Central Questions of Philosophy* (London: Weidenfeld).

Bach-y-Rita, Paul (1996), "Sensory Substitution and Qualia," in J. Proust (ed.), *Perception et Intermodalite* (Paris: Presses Universitaires de France); reprinted in Alva Noë and Evan Thompson (eds) (2002), *Vision and Mind: Selected Readings in the Philosophy of Perception* (Cambridge, Mass.: MIT Press).

Berkeley, George (1713/1979), *Three Dialogues between Hylas and Philonous* (Cambridge, Mass.: Hackett Publishers).

Bermúdez, José (1994), "Peacocke's Argument against the Autonomy of Nonconceptual Content," *Mind and Language* 9: 402–18.

Bermúdez, José (1995), "Nonconceptual Content: From Perceptual Experience to Subpersonal Computational States," *Mind and Language* 10: 333–69.

Bermúdez, José (2003), *Thinking without Words* (New York: Oxford University Press).

Block, Ned (1990), "Inverted Earth," in James Tomberlin (ed.), *Philosophical Perspectives, 4: Action Theory and Philosophy of Mind* (Atascadero, Calif.: Ridgeview Press).

Block, Ned (1995), "On a Confusion about a Function of Consciousness," *Behavioral and Brain Sciences* 18: 227–47.

Block, Ned (1996), "Mental Paint and Mental Latex," in Ernesto Villanueva (ed.), *Philosophical Issues, 7: Perception* (Atascadero, Calif.: Ridgeview Press), 19–49.

Block, Ned (1999), "Sexism, Racism, Ageism and the Nature of Consciousness," in *Philosophical Topics*, 26 (1&2).

Block, Ned (2003), "Mental Paint," in Martin Hahn and Bjorn Ramberg (eds), *Reflections and Replies: Perspectives on the Philosophy of Tyler Burge* (Cambridge, Mass.: MIT Press).

Block, Ned (forthcoming), "Bodily Sensations as an Obstacle for Representationism," in a special issue of *Consciousness and Emotion*, Murat Aydede (ed.).

Boghossian, Paul, and Velleman David (1989), "Colour as a secondary quality," *Mind* 98: 81–103.

Boghossian, Paul, and Velleman David (1991), "Physicalist Theories of Color," *Philosophical Review* 100: 67–106.

BonJour, Laurence (2001), "Epistemological Problems of Perception," *The Stanford Encyclopedia of Philosophy (Fall 2001 Edition)*, Edward N. Zalta (ed.), URL = <http://plato.stanford.edu/archives/fall2001/entries/perception-episprob/>.

Brewer, Bill (1999), *Perception and Reason* (Oxford: Oxford University Press).

Brewer, Bill (2005), "Do Sense Experiential States have Conceptual Content?," debate with Alex Byrne, in Ernest Sosa and Matthias Steup (eds), *Contemporary Debates in Epistemology* (Oxford: Blackwell).

Broad, C. D. (1923), "The Theory of Sensa," reprinted in R. J. Swartz (ed.), (1965), *Perceiving, Sensing, Knowing: A Book of Readings from Twentieth Century Sources in the Philosophy of Perception* (Garden City, NY: Doubleday).

Broad, C. D. (1952), "Some Elementary Reflexions on Sense-Perception," *Philosophy* 27: 3–17.

Burge, Tyler (1997), "Interlocution, Perception, and Memory," *Philosophical Studies* (April 86) 1: 21–47.

Burge, Tyler (2003), "Qualia and Intentional Content: Reply to Block," in Martin Hahn and Bjorn Ramberg, (eds), *Reflections and Replies: Perspectives on the Philosophy of Tyler Burge* (Cambridge, Mass.: MIT Press), 405–17.

Byrne, Alex (2001), "Intentionalism Defended," the *Philosophical Review* 110: 199–240.

Byrne, Alex (2005), "Perception and Conceptual Content," *Contemporary Debates in Epistemology*, Ernest Sosa and Matthias Steup, (eds) (Oxford: Blackwell, 231–50).

Byrne, Alex and Hilbert, David (1997a), "Colors and Reflectances," in Byrne and Hilbert (eds), *Readings on Color, vol. 1: The Philosophy of Color* (Cambridge, Mass.: MIT Press).

Byrne, Alex and Hilbert, David (eds), (1997b), *Readings on Color, vol. 1: The Philosophy of Color* (Cambridge, Mass.: MIT Press).

Camp, Elisabeth (2004), "The Generality Constraint, Nonsense, and Categorial Restrictions," *Philosophical Quarterly* 54: 215, 209–31.

Campbell, John (1993), "A Simple View of Colour," in John Haldane and Crispin Wright (eds), *Reality: Representation and Projection* (Oxford: Oxford University Press), 257–68.

Campbell, John (1996), "Molineux's Question," in Ernesto Villanueva (ed.), *Philosophical Issues, 7: Perception* (Atascadero, Calif.: Ridgeview Press), 301–18.

Campbell, John (2002), *Reference and Consciousness* (Oxford: Oxford University Press).

Campbell, John (2004), "Reference as Attention," *Philosophical Studies* 120: 265–76.

Chalmers, David (1996), *The Conscious Mind* (Oxford: Oxford University Press).

Chalmers, David (2004), "The Representational Character of Experience," in Brian Leiter (ed.), *The Future for Philosophy* (Oxford: Oxford University Press).

Chisholm, Roderick (1942), "The Problem of the Speckled Hen," *Mind* 51: 368–73.

Chisholm, Roderick (1950), "The Theory of Appearing," in Max Black (ed.), *Philosophical Analysis* (Ithaca, NY: Cornell University Press).

Chisholm, Roderick (1957), *Perceiving: A Philosophical Study* (Ithaca, NY: Cornell University Press).

Chuard, Philippe (under review), "The Riches of Experience."

Crane, Tim (1988a), "The Waterfall Illusion," *Analysis* 48: 142–7.

Crane, Tim (1988b), "Concepts in Perception," *Analysis* 48: 150–3.

Crane, Tim (ed.) (1992a), *The Contents of Experience* (Cambridge: Cambridge University Press).

Crane, Tim (1992b), "The Non-conceptual Content of Experience," in Tim Crane (ed.), *The Contents of Experience* (Cambridge: Cambridge University Press).

Crane, Tim (2001), *Elements of Mind* (Oxford: Oxford University Press).

Crane, Tim (2005), "The Problem of Perception," *The Stanford Encyclopedia of Philosophy (Spring 2005 Edition)* Edward N. Zalta (ed.), URL = <http://plato.stanford.edu/archives/spr2005/entries/perception-problem/>.

Cussins, Adrian (1990), "The Connectionist Construction of Concepts," in Margaret Boden (ed.), *The Philosophy of Artificial Intelligence* (Oxford: Oxford University Press).

Dancy, Jonathan, (ed.) (1988), *Perceptual Knowledge* (Oxford: Oxford University Press).

Dennett, Daniel (1988), "Quining Qualia," in A. Marcel and E. Bisiach (eds), *Consciousness in Modern Science* (Oxford: Oxford University Press), 42–77.

Dennett, Daniel (1991), *Consciousness Explained* (Boston: Little, Brown and Company).

Descartes, Rene (1641/1986), *Meditations on a First Philosophy*, trans. John Cottingham, (New York: Cambridge University Press).

Dretske, Fred (1969), *Seeing and Knowing* (Chicago: University of Chicago Press).

Dretske, Fred (1981), *Knowledge and the Flow of Information* (Cambridge, Mass.: MIT Press).

Dretske, Fred (1990), "Seeing, Believing and Knowing," in Daniel Osherson, Stephen Kosslyn, and John Hollerbach (eds), *Visual Cognition and Action*, (Cambridge, Mass,: MIT Press).

Dretske, Fred (1995), *Naturalizing the Mind* (Cambridge, Mass.: MIT Press).

Dretske, Fred (1996), "Phenomenal Externalism," in Ernesto Villanueva (ed.), *Philosophical Issues, 7: Perception*, (Atascadero, Calif.: Ridgeview Press).

Dretske, Fred (2004), "Change Blindness," *Philosophical Studies* 120: 1–18.

Eilan, Naomi, McCarthy, Rosaleen, and Brewer, Bill (eds) (1993), *Spatial Representation: Problems in Philosophy and Psychology* (Cambridge, Mass.: Blackwell).

Evans, Gareth (1982), *The Varieties of Reference* (Oxford: Oxford University Press).

Evans, Gareth (1985), "Molyneux's Question," in *Collected Papers* (Oxford: Clarendon Press).

Fodor, Jerry (1983), *The Modularity of Mind: An Essay on Faculty Psychology* (Cambridge, Mass.: MIT Press).

Foster, John (2000), *The Nature of Perception* (Oxford: Oxford University Press).

Grice, H. Paul (1962/1989), "Some Remarks about the Senses," in R. J. Butler (ed.), (1962), *Analytical Philosophy*, Series I. (Oxford: Oxford University Press); reprinted in Grice, Paul (1989), *Studies in the Ways of Words* (Cambridge, Mass.: Harvard University Press), 248–68.

Gunther, York (ed.) (2003), *Essays on Nonconceptual Content* (Cambridge, Mass.: MIT Press).

Hamlyn, D. W. (1961), *Sensation and Perception: A History of the Philosophy of Perception* (London: Routledge & Kegan Paul).

Hardin, C. L. (1988), *Colors for Philosophers* (Indianapolis: Hackett).

Harman, Gilbert (1990), "The Intrinsic Quality of Experience," in James Tomberlin (ed.), *Philosophical Perspectives* 4 (Atascadero, Calif.: Ridgeview Press).

Harman, Gilbert (1996), "Qualia and Color Concepts," *Philosophical Issues 7: Perception*, Villanueva, Enrique (ed.) (Atascadero, Calif.: Ridgeview Press).

Heck, Richard (2000), "Nonconceptual Content and the 'Space of Reasons,'" *Philosophical Review* 109: 483–523.

Heck, Richard (forthcoming), "Are There Different Kinds of Content?," in Brian McLaughlin and Jonathan Cohen (eds), *Contemporary Debates in Philosophy of Mind* (Oxford: Blackwell).

Hellie, Benj (forthcoming a), "The Trouble with Relation Intentionalism," *Philosophical Studies*.

Hellie, Benj (forthcoming b), "Seeing into Sense-Data" (manuscript).

Higginbotham, James (1983), "The Logic of Perceptual Reports: An Extensional Alternative to Situation Semantics," *Journal of Philosophy* 80 (2): 100–27.

Hinton, J. M. (1967), "Visual Experiences," *Mind* 76 (302): 217–27.

Hinton, J. M. (1973), *Experiences* (Oxford: Clarendon Press).

Horgan, Terence and Tienson, John (2002), "The Intentionality of Phenomenology and the Phenomenology of Intentionality," in David Chalmers (ed.), *Philosophy of Mind: Classical and Contemporary Readings* (Oxford: Oxford University Press).

Huemer, Michael (2004), "Sense-Data," *The Stanford Encyclopedia of Philosophy (Fall 2004 Edition)*, Edward N. Zalta (ed.), URL = <http://plato.stanford.edu/archives/fall2004/entries/sense-data/>.

Hume, David (1751/1999), *An Enquiry concerning Human Understanding* Tom L. Beauchamp (ed.), (New York: Oxford University Press).

Hurley, Susan (1998), *Consciousness in Action* (Cambridge, Mass.: MIT Press).

Jackson, Frank (1977), *Perception: A Representative Theory* (Cambridge: Cambridge University Press).

Jackson, Frank (1996), "The Primary Quality View of Color," in James Tomberlin (ed.), *Philosophical Perspectives*, vol. 10 (Atascadero, Calif.: Ridgeview Press).

Jackson, Frank and Pargetter, Robert (1987), "An Objectivist's Guide to Subjectivism about Colour," *Revue-Internationale-de-Philosophie* 41: 127–41.

Johnston, Mark (2004), "The Obscure Object of Hallucination," *Philosophical Studies* 120: 113–83.

Kant, Immanuel (1781/1787/1929), *Critique of Pure Reason*, trans. Norman Kemp Smith (New York: St Martin's Press).

Keeley, Brian (2002), "Making Sense of the Senses: Individuating Modalities in Humans and Other Animals," *Journal of Philosophy* 99: 5–28.

Kelly, Sean (2001a), "The Non-conceptual Content of Perceptual Experience: Situation Dependence and Fineness of Grain," *Philosophy and Phenomenological Research* 62: 601–8.

Kelly, Sean (2001b), "Demonstrative Concepts and Experience," *Philosophical Review* 110 (3): 397–420.

Kind, Amy (2003), "What's So Transparent about Transparency?", *Philosophical Studies* 115: 225–44.

Kriegel, Uriah (2002), "Phenomenal Content," *Erkenntnis* 57: 175–98.

Leon, Mark (1988), "Characterising the Senses," *Mind and Language* 3: 243–70.

Levine, Joseph (1997), "Are Qualia Just Representations? A Critical Notice of Michael Tye's Ten Problems of Consciousness," *Mind & Language* 12 (1): 101–13.

Levine, Joseph (2001), *Purple Haze* (Oxford: Oxford University Press).

Loar, Brian (1990/1997), "Phenomenal States," *Philosophical Perspectives* 4: 81–108; revised edition in Ned Block, Owen Flanagan, and Guven Güzeldere (eds), *The Nature of Consciousness* (Cambridge, Mass.: MIT Press).

Loar, Brian (2002), "Transparent Experience and the Availability of Qualia," in Quentin Smith and Aleksander Jokic (eds), *Consciousness: New Philosophical Perspectives* (Oxford: Oxford University Press), 77–96.

Loar, Brian (2003), "Phenomenal Intentionality as the Basis of Mental Content," in Martin Hahn and Bjorn Ramberg (eds), *Reflections and Replies: Essays on the Philosophy of Tyler Burge* (Cambridge, Mass.: MIT Press).

Locke, John (1689/1975), *An Essay concerning Human Understanding*, Peter Nidditch (ed.) (Oxford: Clarendon Press).

Lopes, Dominic McIver (2000), "What is it Like to See with your Ears? The Representational Theory of Mind," *Philosophy and Phenomenological Research*, LX: 439–53.

Lormand, Eric (1994), *"Qualia!* (Now Showing at a Theater near You)," *Philosophical Topics* 22: 127–56.

Lycan, William (1995), "A Limited Defense of Phenomenal Information," in Thomas Metzinger (ed.), *Conscious Experience* (Tucson: University of Arizona Press), 243–58.

Lycan, William (1996), *Consciousness and Experience* (Cambridge, Mass.: MIT Press).

Lycan, William (1998), "In Defense of the Representational Theory of Qualia (Replies to Neander, Rey and Tye)," in James Tomberlin (ed.), *Philosophical Perspectives, Vol. 12: Language, Mind and Ontology* (Atascadero, Calif.: Ridgeview Press), 479–87.

McDowell, John (1994a), *Mind and World* (Cambridge, Mass.: Harvard University Press).

McDowell, John (1994b), "The Content of Perceptual Experience," *Philosophical Quarterly* 44: 190–205.

McGinn, Colin (1988), "Consciousness and Content," *Proceedings of the British Academy* 74: 219–39.

McGinn, Colin (1991), *The Problem of Consciousness* (Oxford: Blackwell).

Martin, Michael (1992), "Perception, Concepts and Memory," *Philosophical Review* 101: 745–63.

Martin, Michael (2002), "The Transparency of Experience," *Mind and Language* 17: 376–425.

Martin, Michael (2004), "The Limits of Self-Awareness," *Philosophical Studies* 120: 37–89.

Moore, G. E. (1903), "The Refutation of Idealism," in *Philosophical Studies* (London: Routledge & Kegan Paul); reprinted in Moore (1993).

Moore, G. E. (1910), "Sense Data," reprinted in Moore (1993).

Moore, G. E. (1925), "In Defense of Common Sense," reprinted in Moore (1993).

Moore, G. E. (1993), *Selected Writings*, Thomas Baldwin (ed.) (London: Routledge).

Morgan, M.J. (1977), *Molyneux's Question* (Cambridge: Cambridge University Press).

Nelkin, Norton (1990), "Categorising the Senses," *Mind & Language* 5:149–65.

Noë, Alva (2002), "On What We See," *Pacific Philosophical Quarterly* 83, (1): 57–80.

Noë, Alva and Thompson Evan (eds), (2002), *Vision and Mind: Selected Readings in the Philosophy of Perception* (Cambridge, Mass.: MIT Press).

Peacocke, Christopher (1983), *Sense and Content* (Oxford: Oxford University Press).

Peacocke, Christopher (1984), "Colour Experiences and Colour Concepts," *Synthese* 58: 365–81.

Peacocke, Christopher (1994), "Nonconceptual Content: Kinds, Rationales, and Relations," *Mind and Language* 4: 419–29.

Peacocke, Christopher (1998), "Nonconceptual Content Defended," *Philosophy and Phenomenological Research* 58,(2): 381–8.

Peacocke, Christopher (2001a), "Does Perception Have a Nonconceptual Content?," *Journal of Philosophy* 98: 239–64.

Peacocke, Christopher (2001b), "Phenomenology and Nonconceptual Content," *Philosophy and Phenomenological Research* 62: 609–15.

Pitcher, G. (1971), *Perception* (Princeton: Princeton University Press).

Price, H. H. (1932), *Perception* (London: Methuen).

Price, H. H. (1940) *Hume's Theory of The External World* (Oxford: Clarendon Press).

Reid, Thomas (1764/1970), *An Inquiry into the Human Mind*, Timothy Duggan (ed.) (Chicago: University of Chicago Press).

Rey, Georges (1992), "Sensational Sentences Switched," *Philosophical Studies* 67: 73–103.

Rey, Georges (1998), "A Narrow Representationalist Account of Qualitative Experience," *Philosophical Perspectives* 12: 435–58.

Robinson, Howard (1994), *Perception* (London: Routledge).

Russell, Bertrand (1912), *The Problems of Philosophy* (New York: Henry Holt and Company).

Sartre, Jean-Paul (1940), *The Psychology of Imagination*, trans. anon. 1948 (New York: Philosophical Library).

Searle, John (1983), *Intentionality* (Cambridge: Cambridge University Press).

Searle, John (1990), "Consciousness, Explanatory Inversion and Cognitive Science," *Behavioral and Brain Sciences* 13: 585–642.

Shoemaker, Sydney (1990), "Qualities and Qualia: What's in the Mind?," *Philosophy and Phenomenological Research* 50, Supplement: 109–31.

Shoemaker, Sydney (1991), "Qualia and Consciousness," *Mind* 100: 507–24.

Shoemaker, Sydney (1994a), "Self-knowledge and 'inner sense': Lecture III: The Phenomenal Character of Experience," *Philosophy and Phenomenological Research* 54: 219–314.

Shoemaker, Sydney (1994b), "Phenomenal Character," *Noûs* 28: 21–38.

Shoemaker, Sydney (2000), "Phenomenal Character Revisited," *Philosophy and Phenomenological Research* 60, 2: 465–7.

Siegel, Susanna (2004), "Indiscriminability and the Phenomenal," *Philosophical Studies* 120: 90–112.

Siegel, Susanna (2005), "The Contents of Perception," *The Stanford Encyclopedia of Philosophy (Spring 2005 Edition)*, Edward N. Zalta (ed.), URL = <http://plato.stanford.edu/archives/spr2005/entries/perception-contents/>.

Siegel, Susanna (forthcoming), "Direct Realism and Perceptual Consciousness," *Philosophy and Phenomenological Research*.

Siewert, Charles (1998), *The Significance of Consciousness* (Princeton: Princeton University Press).

Siewert, Charles (2004), "Is Experience Transparent?" *Philosophical Studies* 117(1–2): 15–41.

Smith, A. D. (2002), *The Problem of Perception* (Cambridge, Mass.: Harvard University Press).

Smith, Quentin and Jokic, Aleksander (eds) (2003), *Consciousness: New Philosophical Perspectives* (New York: Oxford University Press).

Snowdon, Paul (1980–1), "Perception, Vision and Causation," *Proceedings of the Aristotelian Society* 81: 175–192.

Sperling, G. (1960), "The Information available in Brief Visual Presentations," *Psychological Monographs* 74: 1–29.

Stalnaker, Robert (1998), "What Might Nonconceptual Content Be?," *Philosophical Issues* 9, Ernesto Villanueva (ed.) (Atascadero, Calif.: Ridgeview Press).

Stoljar, Daniel (forthcoming), "The Argument from Diaphanousness," *New Essays in Philosophy of Language and Mind, Canadian Journal of Philosophy*, Suppl. Vol. Maite Escurdia, Robert. J. Stainton and Chris Viger (eds).

Strawson, Galen (1994), *Mental Reality* (Cambridge, Mass.: MIT Press).

Sturgeon, Scott (2000), *Matters of Mind: Consciousness, Reason and Nature* (New York: Routledge).

Swartz, R. J. (ed.) (1965), *Perceiving, Sensing, Knowing: A book of Readings from Twentieth Century Sources in the Philosophy of Perception* (Garden City, NY: Doubleday).

Thau, Michael (2002), *Consciousness and Cognition* (Oxford: Oxford University Press).

Travis, Charles (2004), "The Silence of the Senses," *Mind* 113: 449.

Tye, Michael (1991), *The Imagery Debate* (Cambridge, Mass.: MIT Press).

Tye, Michael (1995), *Ten Problems of Consciousness* (Cambridge, Mass.: MIT Press).

Tye, Michael (2000), *Consciousness, Color and Content* (Cambridge, Mass.: MIT Press).

Tye, Michael (2003), "Qualia," *The Stanford Encyclopedia of Philosophy (Summer 2003 Edition)* Edward N. Zalta (ed.), URL = <http://plato.stanford.edu/archives/sum2003/entries/qualia/>.

Valberg, J. J., (1992), *The Puzzle of Experience* (Oxford: Clarendon Press).

Williamson, Timothy (1990), *Identity and Discrimination* (Oxford: Blackwell).

Williamson, Timothy (2002), *Knowledge and its Limits* (Oxford: Oxford University Press) (paperback with corrections).

Yolton, John (1984), *Perceptual Acquaintance: From Descartes to Reid* (Minneapolis: University of Minnesota Press).

Yolton, John (1996), *Perception and Reality: A History from Descartes to Kant* (Ithaca, NY: Cornell University Press).

1

Manipulating Colour: Pounding an Almond

John Campbell

It seems a compelling idea that experience of colour plays some role in our having concepts of the various colours, but in trying to explain the role experience plays the first thing we have to describe is what sort of colour experience matters here. I will argue that the kind of experience that matters is conscious attention to the colours of objects as an aspect of them on which direct intervention is selectively possible. As I will explain this idea, it is a matter of being able to use experience to inform linguistic or conceptual thought about what would happen were there to be various interventions on an object.

Against this background, I will review Locke's fundamental argument that, since we can change the colour of an almond by pounding it, there must be an error embodied in our ordinary concepts of colour: there is no such thing as intervening directly on the colour of an object. The analysis I present brings out the force of Locke's argument. But I will propose a vindication of our common-sense conception of colour as an aspect of objects on which direct intervention is selectively possible.

1 ATTENTION TO COLOURS

Let us go over the idea that experience of the colours plays a role in our understanding of colour concepts. Someone who is blind or entirely colour-blind

I have benefited from discussion of early drafts at NYU, Oxford, the University of California at Santa Barbara, the University of Southern California and the Center for Advanced Study at Stanford. I am particularly grateful for comments by Kevin Falvey when I presented this material at UCSB, and to Jerry Fodor and Christopher Peacocke for comments at their NYU seminar. Victor Caston also gave me a helpful set of comments, as did the editors of this volume, Tamar Gendler and John Hawthorne, and an anonymous referee. Thanks also to Alison Gopnik, Thomas Richardson and Ken Kendler, and to Christopher Hitchcock and James Woodward. This article was completed while on leave at the Center for Advanced Study in the Behavioral Sciences at Stanford and I am grateful to the Center for its support.

from birth, or someone who is normally sighted but simply never encounters colours, cannot understand colour predicates as we ordinarily understand them. Experience of the colours does some work in our ordinary grasp of colour concepts. Still, the kind of colour experience demanded needs careful explanation. Recall the kind of test for colour vision that consists of a number of variously coloured dots of various sizes in a single display. The colouring of the dots may be so organized that someone with ordinary colour vision can quite plainly see a figure, say the numeral 5, picked out in some one colour, say gold. For anyone without colour vision, though, all that they can see is an array of variously shaded and variously sized dots. So an ability to identify that there is a number 5 in the array provides good evidence that the subject has ordinary colour vision. Someone who can see the figure 5 in this kind of display need not, however, be capable of visually attending to the colours of things; they may not realize that there is such a thing as colour at all. This subject is attending only to the object, the number 5, not to the characteristics which allowed him to discriminate the object. Such a person might, for all that I have said so far, be unable to report the colours of objects, or to match different objects which are the same colour.

An analogy might be helpful. Our ordinary visual world is full of shadows as well as highlights. And these shadows and highlights are very important to us in allowing us to see how objects are oriented with respect to us, providing some indications as to the character of the illuminant, and so on. But you could accept that is so while still pointing out that you might go through your whole life without ever paying attention explicitly to the shadows of the things around you. You could be such an inattentive person; inattentive just to the shadows, that is, though they do help you, did you but know it, in discriminating and perceiving the objects around you. Just so, someone could use the colours, did she but know it, to allow her to identify objects, but never have attended to those colours. We might find this hard to imagine. We might find it hard to imagine because we find it hard to imagine not attending to so salient an aspect of our environment. That idea is consistent with the main point I want to make, which is that it is one thing to have full colour vision and be experiencing a coloured environment, and it is a further matter whether you attend to the colours in your environment.

We can draw a distinction, then, between colour as an object-defining characteristic, in the sense in which it is only the colours of the blobs in the display that define the figure 5, and colour as a characteristic to which the subject attends. Colour can be functioning as an object-defining characteristic even though the subject is not yet able to attend to colour. Notice, though, that if colour is to be functioning as an object-defining characteristic for a perceiver, the colours of the things seen must be showing up in the visual experience of the subject. If the colours of the blobs were not showing up in the experience of the subject, there would be nothing in the experience of the array itself which would differentiate the figure 5 from its background. Suppose a subject can see the figure 5 in the display I described. The subject has, we can suppose, ordinary colour vision, but as yet no ability to attend specifically to the colours of things. It seems quite evident that this subject need not have realized that there is such a characteristic as colour, despite the fact that the content of her vision includes experience of the colours. The natural formulation, in the light of what I have said so far, is that for experience to provide knowledge of the colours, the subject must not only have colour experience, but must be capable of visually attending to the colours of the things she sees.

There are, though, many tasks that involve attention to colours which do not seem to involve an understanding of colour concepts. Suppose we have a subject who performs the following tasks. When given two rows of coloured paper, she can match each paper in one row to the same-coloured paper in the other row. Or, again, when she is given a pile of chips of two slightly different shades of green, she sorts them successfully. She can correctly arrange a series of reds in order from bright red at one end to pink at the other. Given coloured papers or crayons and a group of line drawings of familiar objects, she can correctly match the colours to the objects, for example, the yellow crayon to the banana. In performing these tasks she is plainly attending to the perceived colours of objects. Let us suppose that she also passes the tests I mentioned earlier: she can use colour as an object-defining property. She performs well on the American Optical Company and the Ishihara pseudo-isochromatic tests of colour vision—that is, discerning the figure 5 in a pattern of blobs, and so on. Yet this attention merely for the purposes of matching colour samples, together with the use of colour as an object-defining characteristic, does not seem to be enough for knowledge of what the colours are.

It is not, though, as if what is missing is a battery of purely verbal skills. Geschwind and Fusillo (1997) describe a patient, fifty-eight years old, whose performance in tasks of colour identification was as I have just described. However, when he was asked to name the colour of a figure shown, his replies were wildly inaccurate. For example, a card which showed a bright red 7 on a grey background was described as having a grey 7. When the patient was shown an array of variously coloured objects, such as several sheets of paper, and asked to 'show me the red one', for example, he usually failed; he also answered at chance when shown a sheet of paper and asked, 'Is this red?' When presented with coloured sheets of paper, and asked to name their colours, he gave incorrect answers in almost all cases, including cases in which he was presented with sheets of black, white or grey paper. When the patient was presented with colour pictures of objects such as neckties or curtains, which can be any of a variety of colours, and asked to name their colours, he made similar errors. When shown coloured pictures of objects such as bananas or milk, which have standard colours, and asked to name those colours, the patient again was almost invariably wrong.

There was not, however, a specifically verbal problem here. The patient could identify the objects verbally, as bananas or milk and so on. And, when asked the usual colours of objects such as bananas or milk, the patient performed without error. When asked to give examples of objects which standardly have a certain colour, he again performed without error. Geschwind and Fusillo comment:

The patient failed in all tasks in which he was required to match the seen colour with its spoken name. Thus, the patient failed to give the names of colours and failed to choose a colour in response to its name. By contrast, he succeeded in all tasks where the matching was either purely verbal or purely nonverbal. Thus, he could give verbally the names of colours corresponding to named objects and vice versa. He could match seen colours to each other and to pictures of objects and could sort colours without error. By no nonverbal criterion could our patient be shown to have any deficit in colour vision. (1997: 271)

Suppose we extrapolate somewhat from the Geschwind and Fusillo results. Suppose that this patient is successful in all purely verbal tests of knowledge of the colours. That is, he knows, for example, that nothing can be both green and red all over. He can verbally order the colours, can say that orange is between yellow and red, and so on. And he also passes all the purely non-verbal tests for colour vision. His problems come only with the liaisons between colour names and colour vision. How are we to characterize the kind of liaison between colour names and colour vision that is required for grasp of colour concepts?

So much for an initial statement of the problem I aim to address. I think that the best way to present the analysis I propose is to state immediately my response to the question. Then I will set out the general considerations about the notion of 'grasp of a concept' which seem to me to matter for evaluation of the response. Finally, I will look at a classical argument for error theories of colour.

2 INTERVENTIONISM

In this section I want to try to describe a particular kind of awareness of colour: awareness of colour as an aspect of an object on which intervention is selectively possible. I draw the notion of an 'intervention' I will be using from the literature on causal reasoning (for excellent philosophical discussions, see Woodward and Hitchcock 2003; Woodward 2003; and references therein). Suppose you have noticed that there is a correlation between smoking and cancer, or between the position of a speedometer needle and the speed of a car, and you wonder in each case whether the first is causing the second. What exactly is it that you are asking? The interventionist proposal is: you are asking whether, were there to be an intervention on the smoking, there would be a difference in the level of cancer, or, were there to be an intervention on the position of the speedometer, there would be a difference in the speed of the car. This is an intuitively appealing analysis, but evidently it depends on it being possible to explain just what is meant by an 'intervention'. Not just any way of affecting the target variable will do. If your only way of affecting the position of the speedometer pointer is by affecting the speed of the car, then you will, trivially, find that the position of the speedometer continues to be correlated with the speed of the car under such 'interventions'. What we want to be asking is whether, if some external force comes from outside the system and changes the position of the pointer on the speedometer—for example, if someone physically grasps and moves the pointer—there would be a corresponding change in the speed of the car. If there would be such a change, that constitutes the existence of a causal link between the position of the pointer and the speed of the car. Of course, there is no such link in this case, though there is in the case of smoking and cancer: external interventions on the level of smoking are correlated with changes in the level of cancer.

Just to spell out the notion a bit more fully. An 'intervention' on one variable X with respect to another, Y, should be a way of affecting the value of X, and ideally it should take full control of the value of X (when moving the speedometer needle you want to have total control over the position of the needle, and to have suspended the usual control of the position of the needle by the speed of the car). And the way in which you affect the value of X should affect only the value of X, and not have any impact on the value of Y otherwise than by affecting the value of X. Moreover, you do not want there to be any bias—you do not want to find that intervening on X is correlated with cases in which, as it happens, there was going to be a change in the value of Y anyway. Suppose we are armed with this notion of an intervention. And suppose it's true that, were there to be an intervention on X, there would be a change in the value of Y. On the interventionist analysis, that constitutes the existence of a causal relation between X and Y. (Here I follow Woodward and Hitchcock 2003; Woodward 2003; and the interventionist tradition within which they are working.) I want now to focus on how this notion of an intervention might illuminate our ordinary understanding of colour concepts, our knowledge of what the colours are.

It is often observed that the colours of objects have predictive value. The particular colours of various foods are predictive of their nutritional value. The exact colours of particular people and plants are good predictors of their health. And so on. Even though the correlations are typically specific to particular types of context, they have some generality. It is important, though, in considering such cases, to distinguish between colour as a symptom and colour as a cause.

I suggest that our ordinary understanding that colour is in these cases a symptom rather than a cause is provided by our grasp of what will happen under interventions. To say that colour is merely a symptom of nutritional value or of health is to say that nutritional value and health cannot be manipulated by manipulating the colours of objects. Consider the contrast between colour on the one hand, and shape or size on the other. Being able to attend specifically to such dimensions as the size and shape of a seen object means that one grasps the implications for other variables of interventions on the size and shape of the seen object. You know what would happen if there were an intervention from outside to affect the size and shape of the thing. So, for example, you might squash and compress an envelope to get it through a letter box. You know how specific sizes and shapes of envelope are correlated with the possibility of getting the thing through a letter box. But you do not just have knowledge of correlations here. You have something more: knowledge of what would happen were there to be interventions on the size and shape of the envelope. Contrast the case of knowing, say, the correlation between the redness of a tomato and how ripe it is. You may use that information when choosing which tomato to eat. But you have some grasp of causal role here too, although of a different kind. Even if you are able to intervene on the colour of the object—say, by painting it—it would simply not occur to most of us to think that you could affect the ripeness of the tomato by manipulating the colour of the thing. This contrast between the kinds of manipulations we would ordinarily try to perform on shape, size and colour displays something of our ordinary grasp of the causal roles of these properties.

To sum up, when we think about interventions on the colour of an object, we find some quite special characteristics of colour. In the case of shape, there are many purposes to which we can put manipulation of shape. You may want to manipulate the shapes of things to roll them, to stack them together for easy carrying, to wrap them around you, or to use them as tools. But colour does not have the same causal significance. Of course, colour is often symptomatic of the further characteristics of an object. This is particularly so for children living in present-day environments full of colour-coded toys. But, even in the wild, colour is important for pursuits like finding good food, or deep water. You can't, though, in general, change the further characteristics of an object by changing its colour. It would be very unusual for it even to occur to someone to try to affect whether or not the water was deep by manipulating its colour. There is no analogue, for colour, of trying to get the envelope through the letter box by manipulating its shape. The exception is, of course, that by manipulating the colours of objects you can make a difference to the experiences that people will have when they look at those objects.

We usually take it that perception of an object as having a property is due to the operation of two different sorts of factor: the object having the property, and the perceiver being appropriately positioned, looking in the right way, and so on, with respect to the object. Whether the object is red is one thing, and whether I am so positioned as to be able to see that it is, is another thing. What this distinction comes to, I think, is that we ordinarily take it that there is a difference between changing the colour of the object itself, and merely changing the way it looks to an observer by manipulating the conditions of perception. We ordinarily experience the colours of objects as dimensions of them on which intervention is selectively possible. There are indeed cases, such as the colour of a star in the night sky, where we have no idea what it would be to intervene to affect the colour of the thing itself, as opposed to merely affecting our perceptions of colour. And these, of course, are cases in which we have no idea what it would mean to talk about the colour the object itself has, as opposed to the appearance it presents. In contrast, we would usually have no trouble in distinguishing between making a door look white by shining a bright light on it, and making the door look white by painting it white; in the latter case, but not the former, there has been a change in the colour of the thing itself. We experience colour as an aspect of an object on which intervention is selectively possible. That is, there are external causes which can change that aspect of the object in particular. Most strikingly, there are the paints, pigments, inks and dyes that have reliable specific effects on the colours of things. There are also causes that affect many manifest aspects of an object simultaneously, as when fire scorches an object, affecting its colour but also perhaps melting it. The contrast here between merely changing perceptions of the object, as opposed to changing the colour of the object itself, shows up in how the change affects perceptions of the object in different types of context. If I just shine a light on the door, that will have no implications for how it would look in ordinary sunlight. If I paint the door, in contrast, that will have implications for how it would look in sunlight; and in other types of context too.

My question has been how to characterize the type of liaison between colour experience and verbal or conceptual thought that is demanded for grasp of colour concepts. We saw that it isn't enough merely that you have colour experience; you must be able to attend specifically to the colours of objects. But, then, what type of attention is needed? I want now to argue that the kind of visual attention that is needed is attention to colour as an aspect of objects on which selective intervention is possible.

3 CONCEPTS: TRUTH-CONDITIONS VS. REASONS

On a classical semantic theory, a name makes its contribution to the meaning of a sentence by standing for an object. And a predicate makes its contribution to the truth or falsity of a sentence containing it by standing for, in Michael Dummett's phrase, a mapping from objects to truth-values (Dummett 1973). Understanding a predicate such as 'is red' is a matter of knowing which mapping from objects to truth-values is associated with the predicate. That is what it is to know which property the predicate stands for.

The account I am proposing of the role of experience in an understanding of colour concepts appeals to this classical conception of what it is to understand a predicate. The proposal is that the role of colour experience is to provide knowledge of various mappings from objects to truth-values. Colour experience can be seen to play that role when we conceive of colour experience as a matter of attention to colour as an aspect of objects on which selective intervention is possible.

There are two different levels at which you might have the conception of colour as an aspect of objects on which selective intervention is possible. It might be an entirely practical matter, of the skills that you have in interacting with your surroundings. You might have a capacity to affect the colours of objects by whatever means—paints or inks, for example—and you might in practice be able to recognize the upshot of those interventions for your own experiences, and those of other people. There might in this be some implicit recognition that your own actions are of the same general types as those of other people: for instance, you might be able to imitate the interventions of other people, or to recognize when you are being imitated yourself. You could have this practical grasp of colour as an aspect of objects on which selective intervention is possible without having any explicit conception of experience at all; it may never have occurred to you explicitly that you and others have experiences of the world, you just are in practice able to affect what those experiences will be by manipulating the colours of objects. Someone who has this capacity has evidently gone far beyond a subject who is capable merely of matching colour samples, or using colour as an object-defining property.

When I speak of 'intervention being possible' I am not talking about the possibility of specifically human action; it is the general notion of something external making a change in the colour of the object, of which human action is one example. And it is this modal fact that we exploit when in practice we do manipulate colours. So we can contrast the purely practical understanding I just described, of colour as an aspect of objects on which selective intervention is possible, with a theoretical grasp of colour as an aspect of objects on which selective intervention is possible. You can have a theoretical understanding of those modal facts which does not simply consist of the capacity to exploit them in manipulating the colours of objects. Attending to colour as an aspect of the object on which selective intervention is possible can be a purely practical matter of the range of interactions with the object of which you are capable. But attention to colour can also have to do with your theoretical understanding of the modal facts that you exploit when interacting with the object. This kind of understanding has to do with the way you would use the names of colours in saying what would happen in various counterfactual situations, such as those in which there are interventions on the colour of the object. And it is conscious attention to the colours of things, informed by this general theoretical understanding, that, I suggest, constitutes grasp of the ordinary colour concepts. It is when you have reached this point that you have a grasp of what it is for it to be true that an object has a particular colour.

Our common-sense picture of colour is that the observed colour of an object is the very property on which we intervene, when we act to change the colour of the object. When we ink over or paint or dye an object, we take ourselves to be acting directly on the very property of the object that we observe; we do not assume that the ink or paint or dye operates directly on some quite hidden aspect of the object, and only consequently affects the observed colour of the thing. It is in this sense that we do not ordinarily suppose colour to be merely a power that objects have to produce experiences in us. Were colours mere powers, it would not be possible to affect them directly; you could affect them only by affecting their bases. But we do assume that we can affect the observed colours of objects directly. And even if we cannot in practice do this, because of the limitations of the technologies available to us, we take it that when we observe the colour of any object, we are observing an aspect of it on which direct intervention is in principle possible. That is, we take it that we are observing a categorical property of the object.

There is a quite different account you might give of the role of experience in understanding colour concepts. On this account, the role of experience in understanding colour concepts is to provide us with reasons for making judgements of colour. Learning a colour concept, on this view, is a matter of learning which experiences constitute reasons for making judgements in which the concept is applied to an object. There is nothing more fundamental, in grasp of a colour concept, than knowledge of which experiences constitute reasons for making which colour judgements. I will call this the 'pure reasons-based approach'. The classical approach I have just recommended did not discuss the notion of experience providing reasons for belief at all. The pure reasons-based approach did not discuss the notion of grasp of truth-condition at all. Obviously a variety of mixed views are possible; but let me pursue the pure reasons-based approach for a moment.

A reason is always a reason-for something. So, on the face of it, for colour experiences to provide reasons for colour judgements, there must be such a thing as grasp of the truth-conditions of those judgements. That grasp of truth-condition will provide an understanding of what one is aiming at in verifying a colour proposition. The problem then for the pure reasons-based approach is to explain how we can have this conception of the truth-condition of a colour judgement, and what the role, if any, might be of experience in providing one with such a conception. On the pure reasons-based approach, the role of the colour experience can't be directly to provide knowledge of what it is for an object to have a particular colour. That is just what is meant by saying that what is fundamental is the role of experiences in providing reasons, rather than knowledge of truth-conditions.

The pure reasons-based approach might acknowledge that colour experience has a further role to play, over and above providing a reason for making a judgement about the colour of a seen object. Colour experience also plays a role in providing the subject with the conceptions of particular types of colour experience. And once we know what it is for someone to have a particular type of colour experience, we can form the conception of an object's having a tendency to produce that type of experience. And if you have an experience of that type, that may of itself prompt the hypothesis that the object you perceive has a tendency to produce that type of experience. So the pure reasons-based approach may propose that the natural conjecture for us to form about the truth-conditions of colour judgements is the dispositionalist one. On the dispositionalist account, the truth of a colour judgement depends on whether the object has a tendency to produce the right type of colour experiences in us.

Many philosophers—the classical sources are Galileo and Locke—have said that science shows that there is a mistake embodied in our ordinary understanding of colour concepts. We commonsensically take colours to be categorical properties of objects, whose nature is apparent to us in vision, but in fact there are only complex microphysical structures and the consequent tendencies of objects to produce ideas in us. Those who have followed Locke in holding that there are only the microphysical structures and the tendencies to produce experiences in us have often also agreed that there is an error that we naively fall into here: that of supposing that colours are categorical properties of objects, displayed to us in vision. Even if, like Locke, you think that the naive conception is mistaken, it does seem to be the conception of colour that we have pre-scientifically. And we ought to be able to explain how it is that we have this conception of colour as categorical.

The pure reasons-based account, as I have developed it, makes error theories of colour impossible. The account is in effect arguing that we could not have the conception of colour as a categorical characteristic which, the error theorist says, science has shown to be mistaken. For, the pure reasons-based theorist is arguing, the only conception of colour we could have formed is the conception of colour as a disposition of objects to produce colour experiences in us.

It therefore seems worth pursuing the classical account further, even if we acknowledge that it has to be supplemented with an account of the role of experience in providing reasons for colour judgements. That is, we should try to articulate the notion that the role of colour experience in understanding colour concepts is not in the first instance to provide one with knowledge of what constitutes a reason for making a colour judgement. Nor is the role of experience to provide one with the concept of colour experience itself. Rather, the role of colour experience is to provide one with knowledge of which categorical properties the colours are. Such an account will explain how it is that we have the conception of colour that error theories attack. This is the conception of colour as a categorical property, which can be specifically manipulated.

4 POUNDING AN ALMOND

I think that the simplest way to interpret the error theorist is as accepting something like the account I have given of our ordinary concept of colour as categorical. On this account, knowledge of the colours is provided by conscious attention to colour as an aspect of the object on which direct intervention is selectively possible. Nonetheless, the error theorist says, it is a mistake to suppose that experience directly confronts you with the variable you are manipulating when you intervene to change the colour of an object, and thereby make a difference to the values of other variables. Here is Locke:

Pound an Almond, and the clear white *Colour* will be altered into a dirty one, and the sweet *Taste* into an oily one. What real Alteration can the beating of the Pestle make in any Body, but an Alteration in the *Texture* of it? (*Essay* (1975), II/viii/20)

The general question is how to characterize the variables on which you are intervening in a manipulation. The challenge is: what we take to be interventions on the colour of an object are more properly thought of as interventions on the microphysical properties of the object. The point is to look at what it is that a pestle does, in general, to the object it pounds. The pestle is not in general a device that changes the colours of things. It would be a kind of magic, if in the case of almonds specifically, the pestle had the capacity to change the colour of the thing directly, rather than by manipulating any other variable. Rather, the pestle does what it always does, and operates mechanically to affect shape, size and motion. It is when we regard it as affecting the shape, size and motion of atoms, Locke is saying, and only consequently affecting the colour of the almond, that we make sense of the situation.

When we pound the almond, we change the colour of the object. There is then a change in the colour experiences of observers. But we have changed the colour of the almond only by affecting the microphysical properties of the almond. The question then is how we are to determine whether the changed microphysical properties of the almond have not affected the colour experiences of the observers directly; that is, otherwise than by affecting the presumed categorical colour of the almond.

We could put the same point another way by saying that the threat is that the microphysical facts about the almond will screen off the colour experiences of observers from the categorical colour of the almond. Learning the facts about the colour of the almond will not provide any additional information about the experiences observers will have, once we know the microphysical facts about the almond. Or, again, the probability that observers will have particular colour experiences on looking at the almond, given that it has a particular microphysical constitution, is no different from the probability that observers will have a particular colour experience, on looking at the almond, given that it has a particular microphysical constitution and that it has a particular colour. The use of this kind of reasoning to determine that one factor rather than another is causally relevant to an outcome is ubiquitous. The error theorist is in effect using this kind of reasoning to establish that when we take ourselves to have changed colour experiences by changing the colour of an object, what has actually happened is that we have changed colour experiences by changing the microphysical properties of the object; the presumed change in the categorical colour of the object is an epiphenomenon.

This problem arises because when you manipulate a colour you cannot but be manipulating a physical state. The variables are not independent. And we do not yet have a way of saying what the difference is between the case in which you are manipulating a colour by manipulating an underlying physical state, and the case in which you are directly manipulating the colour and only in so doing affecting the underlying physical state.

The issue depends on which set of variables it is right to use in describing the phenomena here. If the choice of a set of variables is arbitrary, then the issue has no substance. But in general the choice of a variable set does not seem to be arbitrary; we would usually think of it as one of the most difficult matters to address in finding how to characterize the causal functioning of a system.

I want to make a proposal about the general type of consideration we ought to be appealing to here, a proposal which is, I think, in line with the general spirit of an interventionist approach to causation. Here is a simple example to illustrate the idea. Suppose you are asked at what level you should characterize the causal functioning of a radio. You want to know whether the true causal structure is to be found at the level of a quantum-mechanical description of the whole set-up. So macroscopic matters such as the position of the volume control and whether the tuner has been set to a particular station are not themselves part of the causal structure; they are merely epiphenomena dependent on the underlying quantum-mechanical causal structure. Now it seems to me that an interventionist approach to causation has the materials to motivate the idea that we do find causal structure at the level of the macroscopic variables, such as the position of the volume control. An interventionist approach is not anthropocentric; it does not aim to characterize causation in terms of what humans can do. But it does aim to describe those objective features of our world that we exploit when we manipulate our surroundings. Now the point about the relation between, say, the position of the volume control and the loudness of the sound from the radio is this: under interventions on the position of the volume control, there is a correlation between each particular position of the volume control and each particular level of loudness. But there is more to it than that. There is a certain systematicity in this correlation under interventions: the level of loudness varies with the position of the control. Moreover, there is a very large statistical effect here. And, finally, the effect is specific: the position of the volume control selectively affects the loudness of the sound, it is not nearly so strongly correlated with any other outcome. These are objective features of the set-up, though they are of course the features we exploit in manipulating the controls. And I propose that if we can find a level of description, a collection of variables to use in characterizing a system, that has these features, then that constitutes the correctness of saying that the causal functioning of the system can be characterized in terms of those variables.

So one response to Locke's argument is simply to acknowledge the correctness of his point for the case of changing colour by pounding, or for a wide range of similar cases, such as the use of fire to scorch and thereby change the colour of an object. In these cases effects on colour do seem, even to common sense, to be by-products of broader systematic changes brought about by this kind of intervention. The point about pounding is that it is an effective systematic control specifically for such variables as motion. It is not an effective systematic control specifically of colour. So, if all interventions on colour were of this type, then we might accept that colour is not the right variable in terms of which to characterize the changes that mediate between an intervention on the object and subsequent changes in the colour experiences of those who see the thing.

In contrast, though, there is the whole broad class of paints and dyes, inks and other colourants, whose general systematic effect does seem to be to make changes specifically in the colours of objects, even though their operation is by no means universal: black dye will not make absolutely everything black, just as pounding will not affect the shape and movement of every object pounded. But the whole point of these substances is that they have large, systematic effects specifically on the colours of a variety of objects. It is not an appeal to magic to propose that we employ a set of variables characterizing the interventions here under which the use of black paint affected the object's colour directly. Of course, when the object was painted black, there will have been changes in the underlying microphysical structure of the object, on which the blackness supervenes. But that of itself does not show that the only causality here was at the level of the supervenience base. Our knowledge of the ordinary causes and effects of colour change, of the workings of paints and pigments and inks and dyes, is part of a common-sense 'colour theory', describing the large systematic upshots of interventions, which allows us to regard colours as categorical properties of objects, mediating between intervention on the object and the consequent changes specifically in the colour experiences of those who see the thing.

The criteria I am setting out here were foreshadowed in the medical statistician Hill's classic article giving criteria for the existence of a causal relation between an environmental hazard and a disease (Hill 1965). One criterion he gave was the 'dose-response' criterion:

> if the association is one which can reveal a biological gradient, or dose-response curve, then we should look most carefully for such evidence. For instance, the fact that the death rate from cancer of the lung rises linearly with the number of cigarettes smoked daily, adds a very great deal to the simpler evidence that cigarette smokers have a higher death rate than non-smokers. (1965: 298)

Similarly, the case for the causal efficacy of a drug is enhanced if we find not merely that recovery from illness is correlated with administration of the drug, but that the degree of recovery from illness is correlated with the amount of the drug administered. A second criterion is the sheer size of the correlation between the hazard and the disease: that is, the size of the ratio of the rate of contraction of the disease among those exposed to the hazard to the rate of contraction of the disease among those not exposed to the hazard. And the third of his criteria I want to mention here is the specificity of the correlation between the hazard and the disease.

Hill is explicit that he is not attempting to give an analysis of what causation is; these criteria, and the others that he gives, are intended as guides to when the practitioner has the right to conclude that there is not merely an association but a causal relation between two variables. It is because these remarks are not aimed at the analysis of what causation is that they may seem to be of merely practical, rather than philosophical, importance.

One aspect of Hill's points is that they suggest ways of diminishing the likelihood that the hazard is not the relevant variable; if we find systematicity, effectiveness and specificity in the correlation between the hazard and the disease, we diminish the likelihood that it is actually some other variable that is causing the disease. But there is another aspect to Hill's points, which we can bring out by asking whether it could be argued that smoking is not a cause of lung cancer, that both smoking and lung cancer are epiphenomena of the microphysical level at which we find the true causal relations.

As a medical statistician, Hill is approaching the question of causation from a broadly interventionist standpoint:

with the aims of occupational, and almost synonymously preventive, medicine in mind the decisive question is whether the frequency of the undesirable event B will be influenced by a change in the environmental feature A. (1965:295)

But the criteria he proposes are not asking merely whether some change or other can be effected by one or another intervention. His criteria are asking: how good are these variables as systematic ways of bringing about large changes in specifically these selected outcome measures?

It is certainly possible to have causation without the possibility of this kind of systematic control over the upshot. But we can nonetheless view Hill's criteria as giving us the beginning of a constitutive account of when it is right to use one set of variables rather than another in characterizing the causal functioning of a system. Suppose we find a correlation between an environmental hazard and a disease that meets Hill's criteria; for example, the correlation between smoking and lung cancer. It would be possible to insist that, nonetheless, the true causal structure here is to be found at the level of quantum mechanics. The relations between smoking and lung cancer, you might say, are merely epiphenomenal. But here it seems to me that Hill's criteria do have constitutive force. Since they show that intervention on smoking can be regarded as one of the variables providing for effective systematic control over the degree of lung cancer prevailing, there is no further question as to whether the true causal structure is to be found at some more basic level. Indeed, once we move to the quantum-mechanical level, we may well lose sight of any variables at all which would meet Hill's criteria for causation of lung cancer.

5 CAUSATION WITHOUT MECHANISMS: THE PSYCHOLOGICAL CASE

I want finally to put these remarks about error theories into a broader context. There is a general problem which arises whenever we have high-level classifications which supervene on phenomena at some lower level of description. Suppose we have two high-level variables, H1 and H2, and we suppose provisionally that H1 causes H2. Then whenever we have an instance of H1 we will have an instance of some lower-lever state L1, and whenever we have an instance of H2 we will have an instance of some lower-level state L2. The general problem is to explain the distinction between the case in which the causation is a high-level phenomenon, properly described at the level of the variables H1 and H2, and the case in which the causation is a low-level phenomenon, properly described at the level of L1 and L2.

In interventionist terms, the problem arises because when you intervene on a high-level state you cannot but be intervening on a lower-level state. When, in a particular case, we manipulate H1, we cannot but be manipulating the relevant L1. So we do not yet have a way of saying what the difference is between the case in which it is the manipulation of H1 that is causing H2, and the case in which it is the manipulation of L1 that is causing the difference in L2. This is familiar from the psychological case (cf., e.g., Kim 1998).

How does the approach I have been sketching bear on causation in psychology? Sometimes a change in a psychological state is evidently due to a change in a physiological state. For example, an aspirin may make a headache go away. This is like Locke's case in which pounding an almond changes its colour. But sometimes a change in a psychological state seems to be due to a change in another psychological state, as when a piece of good news makes my headache go away. This is like the case in which we manipulate the colour of an object by using paint or ink or dye. The trouble is that sometimes we are unsure which kind of case we are dealing with. Suppose I find that when I am worried I have trouble sleeping. Is this because the worry is causing insomnia, or is it rather that there is some neural arousal that is constituting my worrying, and that neural arousal is keeping me awake? To what principles should we be appealing in addressing this problem?

The interventionist account I sketched in §2 of itself provides no immediate way of answering this question. That approach simply assumes that we have already identified a suitable set of independent variables, and that the notion of an intervention is so carefully defined that if there is a change in the value of one variable when there is an intervention on another, that can only reflect a causal connection between the two variables. It does not immediately provide a way of addressing the question which of two non-independent variables, 'worry' or 'neural arousal', should be thought of as causing wakefulness.

I have, though, been proposing that there is a natural way of developing the interventionist approach so that this question is addressed. To characterize the causal functioning of a system, we have to find a set of variables in terms of which we can characterize interventions on the system. And we should aim to find a set of variables that maximizes the effectiveness, systematicity and specificity of the impacts of interventions on our outcome variables.

The mere fact that the mental is entirely constituted by the physical does not of itself mean that there will in general be any effective systematic variation specifically of mental variables as a result of change in physical variables. Continuous variation in an underlying physical variable might be accompanied by apparently random changes in which psychological state, if any, ensued. In contrast, systematic changes in the psychological content of the intervention might be accompanied by large and systematic changes specifically in the psychological content of the upshot. In that case we can mark the difference by saying that here it is the mental variable whose manipulation is responsible for the variation in the subsequent psychological state. I think that approach simply reflects scientific practice. Consider again the case of worry and insomnia. Should we say that the worry is causing the insomnia, or should we say that the neural arousal is causing the insomnia? If cognitive interventions on the worry have a large, systematic and specific effect on the insomnia we will say that the worry is the cause; if physiological interventions on the level of arousal have a systematic effect on the insomnia we will say that the arousal is the cause. It may also be that we will not have to choose: it seems entirely possible that insomnia should vary systematically with both worry and some purely physiological measure of arousal.

Finally, I want to end with one further remark on Locke's challenge. I have looked at just one element in the challenge: the problem of finding the right variable set to use. The other element is his appeal to a mechanistic view of causation. In effect, he is arguing, causation just is the transmission of motion by impulse. If we are to regard the pounding of an almond as causing change in colour, we have to suppose that there is nothing to the change in colour other than a change in certain motions. The colour we observe is not in fact the property we are acting on in an intervention. We would not now regard this form of mechanism about causation as tenable; there are plainly many causal interactions that do not consist merely of the transmission of motion by impulse. But it is not difficult to find more recent versions of mechanism about causation in terms of which it is easy to reformulate Locke's challenge. We can, for example, appeal to the proposal put forward by Dowe (2000), that causal interaction involves the exchange of conserved quantities. Since colour is not a conserved quantity, that is, a property subject to a conservation law (there is no law of the conservation of clear whiteness, for instance, unlike the situation with mass-energy, linear momentum or charge), it cannot figure in causal interactions. Therefore, the argument runs, we cannot be manipulating colour.

Notice, though, that the picture of high-level causation I have sketched makes no appeal to the notion of a mechanism; and it allows for the possibility of effects being produced by combinations of high-level and low-level variables. There may be cases of colour change which illustrate this kind of possibility; but there are certainly many possible cases to be found in psychiatry. Consider a recent finding, that an early episode of humiliation is one of the causes of later depression (Kendler et al. 2003). Not everyone is affected in this way by humiliation; some are resilient in the face of adversity. It may be that what constitutes resilience here is a normally functioning serotonin system; it may be that what constitutes vulnerability is an eccentricity in the serotonin system. And it may be that this physiological variable interacts with the psychological variable—humiliation—to produce depression, and that there is no further story to be told about any mechanism linking the physiological and the psychological variable. There may be no systematic account to be given of the physiological realization of humiliation.

Confronted with this possibility, it is natural to protest that there must be a mechanism linking the variables, humiliation and serotonin imbalance. But what mechanism could this be? It could not be a purely cognitive mechanism, because the serotonin imbalance is a biological phenomenon. We can make nothing of the idea of a 'mechanism' linking the experience of humiliation and this biological phenomenon—unless, of course, we think that we can give a reductive biological account of the experience of humiliation. And perhaps we can make something of the notion of a straightforwardly biological mechanism. Now, of course, biological reductionism may turn out to be correct. But in the present state of our knowledge, it is reckless to say that it must be correct. We could still have knowledge of the existence of a causal relation between humiliation, serotonin imbalance and later depression. The idea that the mere existence of a causal relation means there 'must' be a mechanism implies that we cannot recognize the causal relation without the reckless commitment to reductionism. We should rather let go of the apparently innocuous claim that there 'must' be a mechanism. We do not need any such commitment to acknowledge the truth of counterfactuals about what would happen to a system under interventions, where the variables characterizing the system are identified using the criteria I have indicated. And that is all we need to talk of causation.

REFERENCES

Dowe, Phil (2000), *Physical Causation* (Cambridge: Cambridge University Press).
Dummett, Michael (1973), *Frege: Philosophy of Language* (Oxford: Blackwell).
Geschwind, Norman and Fusillo, Michael (1997), 'Color-Naming Deficits in Association with Alexia', in Alex Byrne and David Hilbert (eds), *Readings on Color, Volume 2: The Science of Color* (Cambridge, Mass: MIT Press) 261–75.

Hill, Austin Bradford (1965), 'The Environment and Disease: Association or Causation?', *Proceedings of the Royal Society of Medicine* 58: 295–300.

Kendler, Kenneth S., Hettema, John M., Butera, Frank, Gardner, Charles O. and Prescott, Carol A. (2003), 'Life Event Dimensions of Loss, Humiliation, Entrapment, and Danger in the Prediction of Onsets of Major Depression and Generalized Anxiety', *Arch Gen Psychiatry* 60: 789–96.

Kim, Jaegwon (1998), *Mind in a Physical World* (Cambridge, Mass: MIT Press).

Locke, John (1975), *An Essay Concerning Human Understanding*, edited by P. H. Nidditch (Oxford: Oxford University Press).

Woodward, James (2003), *Making Things Happen: A Theory of Causal Explanation* (Oxford: Oxford University Press).

Woodward, James and Hitchcock, Christopher (2003), 'Explanatory Generalizations, Part 1: A Counterfactual Account', *Nous* 37: 1–24.

2

Perception and the Fall from Eden

David J. Chalmers

1   EDEN

In the Garden of Eden, we had unmediated contact with the world. We were directly acquainted with objects in the world and with their properties. Objects were presented to us without causal mediation, and properties were revealed to us in their true intrinsic glory.

When an apple in Eden looked red to us, the apple was gloriously, perfectly, and primitively *red*. There was no need for a long causal chain from the microphysics of the surface through air and brain to a contingently connected visual experience. Rather, the perfect redness of the apple was simply revealed to us. The qualitative redness in our experience derived entirely from the presentation of perfect redness in the world.

Eden was a world of perfect color. But then there was a Fall.

First, we ate from the Tree of Illusion. After this, objects sometimes seemed to have different colors and shapes at different times, even though there was reason to believe that the object itself had not changed. So the connection between visual experience and the world became contingent: we could no longer accept that visual experience always revealed the world exactly as it is.

Second, we ate from the Tree of Science. After this, we found that when we see an object, there is always a causal chain involving the transmission of light from

I owe a special debt to George Bealer for suggesting the central metaphor of this paper, in a memorable conversation in Chicago airport. In discussing whether perfect properties could be instantiated in any possible world, George said "Maybe that's how it was in Eden." I also owe a debt to Brad Thompson, whose exploration of a Fregean approach to phenomenal content in his dissertation helped to spark the line of thinking here. Conversations with John Hawthorne and Mark Johnston about primitivist views have also had a significant influence on the ideas here. I first presented this material at a conference on the ontology of color in Fribourg in November 2003, and comments from all of the participants there, especially Alex Byrne, Larry Hardin, Barry Maund, and Martine Nida-Rümelin were very helpful. Thanks also to audiences at the Universities of Nottingham, Virginia, and Arizona, and at conferences in Santa Barbara and in Florence. For their commentaries at these two conferences, I am grateful to Gideon Rosen, Susanna Siegel, and Aaron Zimmerman.

the object to the retina, and the transmission of electrical activity from the retina to the brain. This chain was triggered by microphysical properties whose connection to the qualities of our experience seemed entirely contingent. So there was no longer reason to believe in acquaintance with the glorious primitive properties of Eden, and there was no good reason to believe that objects in the world had these properties at all.

We no longer live in Eden. Perhaps Eden never existed, and perhaps it could not have existed. But Eden still plays a powerful role in our perceptual experience of the world. At some level, perception represents our world as an Edenic world, populated by perfect colors and shapes, with objects and properties that are revealed to us directly. And even though we have fallen from Eden, Eden still acts as a sort of ideal that regulates the content of our perceptual experience. Or so I will argue.

2 PHENOMENAL CONTENT

My project in this paper concerns the *phenomenal content* of perceptual experience. This notion can be defined in terms of the notions of *phenomenal character* and *representational content*.

The phenomenal character of a perceptual experience is what it is like to have that experience. Two perceptual experiences share their phenomenal character if what it is like to have one is the same as what it is like to have the other. We can say that in such a case, the experiences instantiate the same phenomenal properties. As I use the term "perceptual experience," it is true by definition that any perceptual experience has phenomenal character. As I use the term, it is not true by definition that every perceptual experience has an object in the external world: hallucinatory experiences count as perceptual experiences.

A representational content of a perceptual experience is a condition of satisfaction of the experience. I will take it for granted that perceptual experiences can be veridical or falsidical: they can represent the world correctly or incorrectly. Intuitively, perceptual illusions and hallucinations are falsidical, while non-illusory perceptual experiences of objects in the external world are veridical. And intuitively, a given experience will be either veridical or falsidical, depending on what the world is like. If so, we can say that an experience is associated with a condition of satisfaction. If and only if the world satisfies the condition, the experience will be veridical. For example, one might plausibly hold that an ordinary experience of a red square in front of one will be veridical roughly when there is a red square in front of one.

A *phenomenal content* of a perceptual experience is a representational content that is determined by the experience's phenomenal character. More precisely: a representational content C of a perceptual experience E is a phenomenal content if and only if necessarily, any experience with the phenomenal character of E has representational content C. Put this way, it is a substantive thesis that perceptual experiences have phenomenal content. But there is good reason to believe that they do. The basic reason has been articulated at length by Siewert (1998). It is plausible that perceptual experiences are assessable for accuracy, in virtue of their phenomenal character. Intuitively, by virtue of their phenomenal character, experiences present the world as being a certain way. My experience of a red square in front of me has a certain phenomenal character, and by virtue of this phenomenal character, the experience places a constraint on the world. The world can be such as to satisfy the constraint imposed by the phenomenal character of the experience, or such as to fail to satisfy the constraint. This is to say that the phenomenal character determines a condition of satisfaction for the experience, one that is shared by any experience with the same phenomenal character. This condition of satisfaction will be a phenomenal content.

The plausible thesis that perceptual experiences have phenomenal content leaves many other questions open. For example, the thesis is neutral on whether phenomenal character is prior (in some sense) to representational content, or vice versa. It is compatible with the thesis that phenomenal character is grounded in representational content (as held by Dretske 1995 and Tye 1995, among others), and it is compatible with the thesis that representational content is grounded in phenomenal character (as held by Searle 1990 and Horgan and Tienson 2002, among others).

The thesis also leaves open the nature of phenomenal content. On the face of it, there are many ways to associate representational contents with perceptual experience. For example, one might associate a perceptual experience with an object-involving content (the content that O is F, where O is the object of the experience), an existential property-involving content (for example, the content that there exists something in location L that is F), a content involving modes of presentation of these objects and properties (more on this shortly), and perhaps others.

My own view is that one should be a pluralist about representational content. It may be that experiences can be associated with contents of many different sorts by different relations: we can call such relations *content relations*. For example, there may be one content relation that associates experiences with object-involving contents, and another that associates experiences with existential contents. Each of the different sorts of content, and the corresponding content relations, may have a role to play for different explanatory purposes. On this view, there may not be such a thing as *the* representational content of a perceptual experience. Instead, a given experience may be associated with multiple representational contents via different content relations.

On the other hand, not all of these contents are equally plausible candidates to be *phenomenal* contents. Some of these contents seem to be such that they can vary independently of the phenomenal character of an experience. If so, they may be representational contents of the experience, but they are not phenomenal contents. More precisely, we can say that a given content relation is a *phenomenal content relation* when any two possible experiences with the same phenomenal character are related by the content relation to the same content. A phenomenal content relation relates a given experience to a phenomenal content of the experience. For ease of usage, I will speak of *the* phenomenal content of an experience, but we should leave open the possibility that there is more than one phenomenal content relation, so that a given experience can be associated with phenomenal contents of more than one sort. Later in the chapter I will explore this possibility in detail.

In this paper, I will focus on the question: what is the phenomenal content of a perceptual experience? This is a more constrained question than the corresponding question simply about representational content. But it is an important question to answer. On the face of it, the phenomenal content of an experience is an extremely important aspect of its representational content: it captures a way in which the world is presented in the *phenomenology* of the experience. One can reasonably expect that if we can understand phenomenal content, this will help us to understand the relationship between phenomenal character and representational content, and it may well help us to understand the nature of phenomenology itself.

In what follows, I will first consider and reject one hypothesis about phenomenal content (a Russellian hypothesis) and will argue for another hypothesis (a Fregean hypothesis). In doing so I will cover ground also covered in Chalmers 2004a, although in a slightly different way, so those familiar with that paper might just skim the next two sections. I will then raise some problems for the Fregean hypothesis, involving its phenomenological adequacy. I will argue that these problems are best handled by moving to a more refined view of phenomenal content, one that gives Edenic representation a key role.

3   RUSSELLIAN CONTENT

I will focus on the phenomenal content of visual experiences, and especially of experiences of color. I will take the canonical sort of color experience as an experience as of an object having a certain color at a certain location. Our experiences typically present objects to us as having a certain distribution of colors at different locations on their surfaces. A book might be presented to me as being certain shades of blue at some points on its surface and as being certain shades of red at other points. For simplicity, I will focus just on the experience of color at a specific point: for example, the experience of a book's being a specific shade of blue at a specific location on its surface. The conclusions generalize, however, and I will discuss the generalization later in the chapter.

What is the phenomenal content of such a color experience? That is, what sort of representational content is shared by all experiences with the same phenomenal character as the original experience?

A first attempt at an answer to this question might be the following: the experience represents object O (the book) as having color C (a specific shade of blue) at location L (a particular point in space). So one can associate the experience with the following condition of satisfaction: the experience is satisfied iff object O has color C at location L. This is an *object-involving* content: it involves a specific object O, and its satisfaction depends on the properties of O. We can say that in this case, the experience attributes a certain sort of color property to the object O.

It is plausible that experiences have contents of this sort. When a certain book appears red to us, there is a quite reasonable sense in which the experience will be satisfied iff the book in question is red at the relevant location. That is, satisfaction conditions for experiences can often be understood in terms of the instantiation of certain properties (such as redness) by certain objects (such as the book). In these cases, we can say that the experience *attributes* the property to the object.

It is implausible that this object-involving content is a phenomenal content, however. On the face of it, there might be an experience with the same phenomenal character as the original experience, directed at a quite different object O' (perhaps an experience that I could have when looking at a different copy of the same book, for example). And plausibly, there might be an experience with the same phenomenal character as the original experience, directed at no object at all (a hallucinatory experience, for example). These experiences could not have an object-involving content involving the original object O: the former experience will at best have a content involving a different object O', and the latter experience may have no object-involving content at all. If so, the object-involving content is not phenomenal content.[1]

---

[1] One sort of disjunctivism about perceptual experience (disjunctivism about phenomenology) denies that experiences directed at different objects could have the same phenomenology, and denies that a hallucinatory experience could have the same phenomenology as an experience of an external object. On this view, phenomenal content might be object-involving. I will assume that this view is false in what follows. Another variety of disjunctivism (disjunctivism about metaphysics) allows that a hallucinatory experience and an ordinary perceptual experience may share phenomenal character, but holds that they have a fundamentally distinct underlying metaphysical nature: one experience involves an object and one does not. I will be neutral about this view in what follows. A third variety (disjunctivism about content) allows that these experiences have the same phenomenology, but holds that they have different representational contents: for example, experiences of different objects will have different object-involving contents. Proponents of this view will agree that these object-involving contents are not phenomenal contents. They may deny that there is any phenomenal content, holding that the relevant experiences share no content, or they may accept that there is phenomenal content while holding that it is less fundamental than object-involving content. I am inclined to reject both varieties of disjunctivism about content, but I will not assume that they are false. In what follows I will in effect argue against the former view, but some of what I say may be compatible with the latter view.

A somewhat more plausible candidate for the phenomenal content of the experience is the following: the experience represents that there is an object that has color C at location L. This content is not object-involving: in effect, it is existentially quantified, so it does not build in any specific object. Unlike the object-involving content, this content can be possessed by experiences that are directed at different objects or at no object at all. The content is property-involving, however: in effect, it has a color property and a location property as its constituents. For the content to be a remotely viable candidate for phenomenal content, the location property cannot be an *absolute* location property: a phenomenally identical experience might be instantiated in a quite different location, and it is not plausible that this experience could attribute the same absolute location property as the original experience. Rather, the location property must be a *relative* location property: the property of being a certain distance in front of the perceiver at a certain angle, for example.

The contents discussed above are all Russellian contents, in that they are composed from objects and properties. The object-involving content can be seen as a certain structured complex of an object, a location property, and a color property, while the existential content can be seen as a structured complex involving an existential quantifier, a location property, and a color property. We can say that both of these contents involve the attribution of certain specific properties, although in one case the properties are attributed to specific objects, and in the other case to an unspecified object under an existential quantifier. Contents of this sort contrast with Fregean contents, composed from modes of presentation of objects and properties in the world, to be discussed shortly.

Let us say that the *Russellian hypothesis* holds that the phenomenal content of a perceptual experience is a sort of Russellian content. To assess this hypothesis, I will henceforth abstract away from issues involving the representation of objects, and will focus on the representation of properties. In particular, I will focus on the representation of color properties—or at least on the representation of properties by color experience. Later, I will discuss the representation of other properties.

On the Russellian hypothesis, the phenomenal content that is distinctively associated with color experience will be a Russellian property-involving content, involving the attribution of a property C. The Russellian hypothesis requires the *Russellian constraint*: all phenomenally identical color experiences attribute the same property to their object.

Strictly speaking, the Russellian hypothesis requires only that *globally* identical experiences attribute the same property to their objects, so that the property attributed may depend on the holistic character of a visual experience, including its spatial phenomenal character and its overall pattern of color phenomenal character. For simplicity, I will usually assume a view on which the property attributed depends on the *local* phenomenal character of the experience, so that any two experiences with the same local phenomenal character in respect of color will attribute the same property. Nothing important will depend on this assumption, however.

We can say two experiences that share their local phenomenal character instantiate the same local phenomenal properties. Local phenomenal properties include properties such as *phenomenal redness*: this is a property instantiated by all experiences that share a certain specific and determinate local phenomenal character, one that is often caused (in us) by seeing things with a certain specific shade of red. ("Phenomenal red$_{31}$-ness" might be a more apt label for a determinate property than "phenomenal redness", but I will use expressions of the latter sort for ease of usage.) Note that phenomenal redness (a property of experiences) will plausibly be distinct from ordinary redness, and from the property attributed by phenomenally red experiences.

If the phenomenal content of color experience is Russellian, what sort of properties does it attribute? Intuitively, these properties are color properties: a phenomenally red experience plausibly attributes redness, for example. I will not assume this in what follows, so that room is left open for views on which color experiences represent properties other than color properties. However, the natural hypotheses concerning the nature of the attributed properties correspond fairly closely to the standard range of options concerning the nature of color properties.

One might hold that the properties attributed are *physical* properties: something along the lines of a surface spectral reflectance. One might hold that the properties attributed are *dispositional* properties, involving the disposition to cause a certain sort of experience in appropriate conditions. One might hold that the properties attributed are *mental* properties of some sort: perhaps properties that are actually instantiated by one's experiences or by one's visual fields. Or one might hold that the properties instantiated are *primitive* properties: simple intrinsic qualities, of the sort that might have been instantiated in Eden.

Each of these views is a version of the Russellian hypothesis: we might call them *physicalist, dispositionalist, projectivist,* and *primitivist* versions of Russellianism about phenomenal content. (The projectivist and primitivist views correspond to what Shoemaker (1990) calls "literal" and "figurative" projectivism, except that I take primitivism to be neutral on whether the relevant properties are actually instantiated.) Each of these views is held by some philosophers. For example, the physicalist view is held by Tye (1995); the dispositionalist view is held by Shoemaker (2001); the projectivist view is held by Boghossian and Velleman (1989); and the primitivist view is held by Maund (1995).[2]

---

[2] The physicalist view is also held by Byrne and Hilbert (2003), Dretske (1995), and Lycan (1996). Versions of the dispositionalist view are also held by Egan (forthcoming) and Kriegel (2002). Versions of the primitivist view are also held by Campbell (1993), Holman (2002), Johnston (forthcoming), McGinn (1996), Thau (2002), and Wright (2003). See Stoljar (forthcoming) and Chalmers (2004a) for more discussion of these alternatives.

Each of these views has well-known problems. The physicalist view is incompatible with intuitions about spectrum inversion, according to which phenomenally identical color experiences could have represented quite different physical properties in different environments, and it also seems to be incompatible with the internalist intuition that phenomenal character does not constitutively depend on an individual's environment. The dispositionalist view is incompatible with the intuition that color experience attributes nonrelational properties, and also has serious difficulties in individuating the relevant dispositions so that phenomenally identical experiences always attribute the same dispositions. The projectivist and primitivist views suffer from the problem that it seems that the relevant properties are not actually instantiated by external objects, with the consequence that all color experience is illusory.

These problems have been discussed extensively elsewhere by others and by me (see Chalmers 2004a), so I will not dwell on them here. But one can summarize the problems with the following general argument against a Russellian view:

(1) Some phenomenally red experiences of ordinary objects are veridical.

(2) Necessarily, a phenomenally red experience of an object is veridical iff its object instantiates the property attributed by the experience.

(3) The properties attributed by color experiences are nonrelational properties.

(4) For any veridical phenomenally red experience of an ordinary object, it is possible that there is a falsidical phenomenally red experience of an object with the same nonrelational properties as the original object.

————————————————

(5) There is no property that is attributed by all possible phenomenally red experiences.

Here, premise (1) has obvious plausibility, and premise (2) is a natural part of any view on which experiences attribute properties. Premise (3) is grounded in the phenomenology of color experience, and premise (4) corresponds to a fairly weak inversion claim. In fact a version of (4) with a mere existential quantifier instead of a universal quantifier would suffice for the conclusion. But the universally quantified claim seems no less plausible. Take any veridical phenomenally red experience of an ordinary object: say, of an apple. Then it is plausible that there could be a community (one with a somewhat different visual apparatus, or with a somewhat different environment) in which apples of that sort normally cause phenomenally green experiences rather than phenomenally red experiences, and in which phenomenally red experiences are caused by objects of a quite different sort. In such a community, it might happen that on one occasion in unusual conditions, such an apple causes a phenomenally red experience. It is plausible that such an experience would not be veridical.

The conclusion follows straightforwardly from the premises: (1) and (4) entail that there are possible veridical and nonveridical phenomenally red experiences of objects with the same nonrelational properties. Conjoined with (2) and (3), one can conclude that there is no property attributed by both experiences. The conclusion entails that that there is no Russellian content that is shared by all phenomenally red experiences (given the natural assumption that if an experience has Russellian content, the property attributed by the experience is attributed by its Russellian content). The argument generalizes straightforwardly from phenomenal redness to any phenomenal property that can be possessed by veridical color experiences, including global phenomenal properties as well as local phenomenal properties. It follows that no veridical experience of an ordinary object has a Russellian phenomenal content. Given that there are veridical experiences of ordinary objects (premise (1)), it follows that the Russellian hypothesis about color experience is false.

One can strengthen the argument by noting that there is no requirement that the original and inverted communities perceive distinct apples. If we replace premises (1) and (4) by the premise that there can be phenomenally identical veridical and nonveridical experiences of the same object, then even without premise (3), it follows that there is no property that is attributed by all phenomenally red experiences. For there is no property that the apple simultaneously possesses and lacks: not even a relational or dispositional property.

(A possibility left open is that what is attributed is what we might call a "relational property radical": perhaps something like *normally causes phenomenally red experiences in*—, where the open place is to be filled by the subject of the experience (see Egan (forthcoming) for a view in this vicinity). We could say that different subjects attribute the same relational property radical, which determine different relational properties for different subjects. Of course, relational property radicals are not really properties, and this proposal is also subject to the usual phenomenological objections.)

Proponents of Russellian views will respond by denying one of the premises of the argument: depending on the view, they might deny premise (1), (3), or (4) of the original argument. This leads to a well-worn dialectic that I do not want to get into here. For now, I will just note that each of the premises enjoys strong intuitive support, and I will take this as strong prima facie reason to believe that the Russellian hypothesis is false.

If we accept premises (1)–(4), we are left with something like the following view. Color experiences attribute nonrelational properties, and these properties are sometimes instantiated by ordinary objects. The most plausible candidates for such properties are intrinsic physical properties, such as surface reflectance properties:[3] so our phenomenally red experiences might attribute a specific

---

[3] One might understand a surface reflectance property as a sort of dispositional property, involving dispositions to reflect certain sorts of light. If so, then the physical properties attributed by color experiences should probably be understood to be the categorical bases of surface reflectance

physical property, which we can call physical redness. On this view, color experiences have Russellian content that involve the attribution of these properties. However, it is possible that experiences with the same phenomenal character (perhaps in a different community) can have different Russellian contents of this sort, due to differences in the environment of the perceivers. So Russellian content is not phenomenal content.

4   FREGEAN CONTENT

If one thought that all content were Russellian content, one might conclude from the above that experiences (or at least color experiences) do not have phenomenal content. But this would require denying the strong intuition that experiences are assessable for accuracy in virtue of their phenomenal character. The alternative is to hold that phenomenal content is something other than Russellian content. There is a natural alternative: Fregean content.

Where Russellian content involves objects and properties, Fregean content involves modes of presentation of objects and properties. The idea is familiar from the philosophy of language. Utterances of "Hesperus is a planet" and "Phosphorus is a planet" have the same Russellian content (a content attributing planethood to Venus), but a Fregean view holds that they have different Fregean contents. The terms "Hesperus" and "Phosphorus" are associated with different modes of presentation of the planet Venus (different Fregean senses, for example), mirroring the difference in their associated cognitive roles. This difference in modes of presentation makes for a different Fregean content for the two utterances.

A natural view of Fregean modes of presentations holds that they are *conditions on extension*. The extension of an expression is something like an object or a property. The mode of presentation associated with an expression is a condition that an object or property must satisfy in order to qualify as the expression's extension. For a term such as "Hesperus," for example, one might plausibly hold that the associated mode of presentation is a condition that picks out the bright object at a certain position in the evening sky. For "Phosphorus," the mode of presentation might be a condition that picks out the bright object at a certain position in the morning sky. In the actual world, both conditions are satisfied by the planet Venus, so Venus is the extension of both expressions.

A pluralist view can allow that utterances have both Russellian and Fregean content, under two distinct content relations. An utterance of "Hesperus is Phosphorus" might be associated with both a Russellian content (holding that Venus is identical to itself) and a Fregean content (holding roughly that the

---

properties, rather than reflectance properties themselves. I will usually simply talk of reflectance properties in what follows, however.

bright object in the morning sky is identical to the bright object in the evening sky). Both of these contents (and the corresponding content relations) may be useful for different explanatory purposes: the former may be more relevant to evaluating the sentence in counterfactual circumstances, for example, while the latter may be more relevant to analyzing the sentence's epistemic role.

This model also applies to terms that refer to perceptible properties such as colors. For example, a color term such as "red" might refer to the same physical property as a physical term "P." Here, the two expressions will be associated with quite different cognitive roles: an utterance of "red is P" will be a cognitively significant claim. So there is reason to believe that the color term "red" has a Fregean content quite distinct from that of the physical expression "P," even though the two expressions have the same Russellian content.

At this point, it is natural to suggest that perceptual experiences, as well as linguistic expressions, have both Russellian and Fregean content. The Russellian content of a color experience will be the property attributed by the experience. If premises (1)–(3) of the earlier argument are correct, this will plausibly be an intrinsic physical property, such as a surface reflectance property: a phenomenally red experience may attribute physical redness, for example. The Fregean content will be a mode of presentation of that property. On the face of it, color experiences attribute colors under a distinctive mode of presentation (one quite distinct from a physical mode of presentation of the color, for example, and much closer to the mode of presentation associated with a color term). It is natural to suggest that this distinctive mode of presentation corresponds to a distinctive sort of Fregean content. This allows the attractive suggestion that where phenomenally identical experiences can have different Russellian contents, they will always have the same Fregean content. If so, Fregean content is phenomenal content.

What is the Fregean content associated with a color experience? It is a condition that a property must satisfy in order to be the property attributed by the experience. There is a natural candidate for such a condition. Let us assume, as before, that the property attributed by a phenomenally red experience is a physical property such as physical redness. Then one can naturally hold that the associated condition on this property is the following: it must be the property that normally causes phenomenally red experiences (in normal conditions for the perceiver). Plausibly, it is precisely because physical redness satisfies this condition that it is the property attributed by phenomenally red experiences. If so, this suggests that the Fregean content of such an experience is precisely this condition.

This Fregean content is a natural candidate for the phenomenal content associated with phenomenal redness. Certainly this content accommodates inversion scenarios quite straightforwardly. In an environment where phenomenally red experiences are normally caused by physically green things, such an experience will attribute physical greenness, so that its Russellian content differs from the Russellian content of a phenomenally red experience in our environment. But its Fregean content will be exactly the same: both are the condition that picks the property that normally causes phenomenally red experiences in the perceiver. (Here the perceiver will be picked out under an indexical mode of presentation that can be shared between two different perceivers; see the appendix (pp. 117–22) for a way to model this using centered worlds.) Due to differences in the environment, this common Fregean content yields distinct Russellian contents: the condition picks out physical redness in an ordinary environment, and physical greenness in the alternative environment. All this suggests that Fregean content is a plausible candidate to be phenomenal content.

The Fregean content of a given color experience can itself be seen as a condition of satisfaction. To a first approximation, the Fregean content of a phenomenally red experience will be satisfied when there is an object at the appropriate location relative to the perceiver that instantiates the property that normally causes phenomenally red experiences in the perceiver. To a second approximation, one might want to give a corresponding Fregean treatment to the attributed location property (as I will discuss later), and one might want to give a Fregean treatment to the object of the experience (for example, holding that the Russellian content of the experience is the specific object, and that the corresponding Fregean content is the condition that picks out the object that is causing the current experience). For now, I will abstract away from these matters and concentrate on that aspect of the content that is associated with color. But however we flesh out the details, this Fregean content will be a condition of satisfaction for the experience. If the perceiver's environment meets the condition, then the experience will be veridical; if it does not, the experience will be nonveridical.

The Fregean view of phenomenal content can be seen as combining aspects of a physicalist and dispositionalist view of the content of color experiences. As on the physicalist view, physical properties (such as surface properties) constitute the Russellian content of color experience, although on the Fregean view this content is not phenomenal content. And as on the dispositionalist view, dispositions to cause certain sorts of experiences are central to the phenomenal content of color experience, although on the Fregean view this content is not Russellian content. Instead, the disposition serves as a sort of Fregean mode of presentation for the physical property that is attributed by the experience.

Compared with the Russellian physicalist view of phenomenal content, the Fregean view has the advantage that it can accommodate inversion scenarios straightforwardly. It can also straightforwardly reconcile the environment-dependence of Russellian content with the environment-independence of phenomenology. There is good reason to think that Fregean content is a sort of *narrow* content, which depends only on the internal state of the individual and not on the environment (Chalmers 2002a). This allows us to combine the view that phenomenology is internally determined with the view that phenomenology is intrinsically representational. The sort of content that is intrinsic to phenomenology is (environment-independent) Fregean content. When situated in a particular environment, this yields a Russellian content.

Compared with the Russellian dispositionalist view, the Fregean view has the advantage that it can accommodate the intuition that experiences attribute nonrelational properties. Furthermore, putting the disposition in the mode of presentation removes worries about the individuation of the relevant dispositions: the idea of an indexical property is obscure, but there are already good reasons to believe in indexical modes of presentation. Finally, and importantly, the Fregean view can accommodate the strong intuition that things could have been as they perceptually seem to be, even had there been no observers.

Counterfactual judgments of this sort generally reflect Russellian content rather than Fregean contents (more generally, they reflect the second dimension in the two-dimensional framework rather than the first). So a view on which Russellian contents are dispositional does not respect these judgments, but a view on which Russellian contents are physical properties (picked out under a dispositional mode of presentation) delivers the intuitively correct results.

5 PHENOMENOLOGICAL ADEQUACY

The hypothesis that phenomenal content is Fregean content has many virtues. In particular, it seems to capture our intuitions about the environments in which an experience with a given phenomenal character will be veridical, yielding a condition of satisfaction that is determined by phenomenal character. Still, there remains a cluster of worries about the view.

This cluster of worries concerns what we might call the *phenomenological adequacy* of the view. Simply put, the worry is that Fregean content does not seem to adequately reflect the phenomenal character of an experience. In particular, one can argue that when we introspect and reflect on the way that the world is presented in the phenomenology of perceptual experience, the phenomenology seems to have properties that are in tension with the Fregean view of phenomenal content. These properties include the following:

Relationality. Intuitively, it seems to us that when we have an experience as of a colored object, there is a certain property (intuitively, a color property) that the object seems to have. And intuitively, it is natural to hold that the phenomenology of the experience alone suffices for it to seem that there is an object with that very property. That is, reflection on phenomenology suggests that there is an internal connection between phenomenology and certain properties that objects seem to have. One could summarize this by saying that the phenomenology of color experience seems to be *relational*: by virtue of its phenomenology, a specific color experience seems to relate us to a specific color property. If this point is correct, it suggests that color experiences have Russellian phenomenal content.

In a critical discussion of the Fregean view, Shoemaker (this volume, ch. 13) brings this point out by an appeal to the Moorean "transparency" intuition. According to this intuition, we attend to the phenomenal character of an experience by attending to the properties that objects in the world appear to have. An extension of this intuition suggests that we discern similarities and differences in phenomenal character by discerning similarities and differences in the properties that objects in the world seem to have. This suggests a strong connection between phenomenal character and Russellian content. Shoemaker says:

> the phenomenal character of veridical experiences of a given color can be different in different circumstances (e.g., different lighting conditions), and for creatures with different sorts of perceptual systems. So the same color will have to have a number of different modes of presentation associated with it. To say that this variation is only a variation in the *how* of perceptual representation, and in no way a variation in *what* is represented, seems to me at odds with the phenomenology. When the light-brown object in shadow and the dark-brown object not in shadow look the same to me, the sameness is experienced as being *out there*—and in such a case the perception can be perfectly veridical. Similarity in the presenting manifests itself in represented similarity in what is represented, and in the absence of perceptual illusion requires that there be similarity in what is represented. More generally, the best gloss on the Moorean transparency intuition is that the qualitative character that figures in the perception of the color of an object is experienced as in or on the perceived object (Shoemaker, this volume, pp. 461–80).

One can also bring out the point by appealing to an inversion scenario. Jack and Jill are phenomenal duplicates, but live in different environments. Jack's phenomenally green experiences are normally caused by objects with property X, while Jill's experiences are normally caused by objects with property Y. Shoemaker's point suggests that even if Jack's and Jill's experiences are associated with distinct properties (X and Y), there is a strong intuitive sense in which the objects look to be the same to Jack and to Jill. That is, the phenomenal similarity suggests that there is a common property (intuitively, a sort of greenness) such that the relevant objects look to have that property both to Jack and to Jill.

This intuitive point stands in tension with the Fregean view. The Fregean view entails that Jack's and Jill's experiences share a mode of presentation, but it does not entail that the experiences represent a common property. In fact, it suggests that Jack's and Jill's experiences represent distinct properties, X and Y. So it is difficult for the Fregean view to accommodate any internal connection between an experience's phenomenal character and the properties that it represents.

A related point is that phenomenologically, a color experience appears to represent an object as having a certain *specific* and *determinate* property. Intuitively, this specificity and determinacy is tied very closely to the specific and determinate phenomenal character of the experience. According to the Fregean view, while an experience may represent a specific and determinate property, its phenomenal character leaves the nature of this property wide open: the determinate property represented may depend on matters quite extrinsic to the phenomenology. This seems to conflict with a strong phenomenological intuition.

Simplicity: A second objection is that Fregean contents seem to be overly complex: one might say that they "overintellectualize" the content of an experience. According to this objection, the phenomenological structure of a visual experience is relatively simple: it represents certain objects as having color and shape properties, and so on. But one cannot find anything like "the normal cause of such-and-such experience" in the visual phenomenology. On the face of it, the "normal cause" relation is not phenomenologically present at all: it is something imposed after the fact by theorists, rather than directly reflecting the experience's phenomenology.

A related objection turns on the fact that Fregean contents require reference to *experiences*: properties are picked out as the normal cause of a certain type of experience, and objects might be picked out as the cause of a certain token experience. But one can object that the perceptual phenomenology does not (or at least, need not) involve representation of experiences: it need only involve representation of the world. This is another often-invoked aspect of the "transparency" of experiences: the phenomenology of perception usually seems to present the world directly, not in virtue of representation of any experiential intermediaries. Again, to invoke the representation of experience seems to overintellectualize the experience, by introducing complexity that is not apparent in the experience's phenomenology.

Internal unity: A final objection is that it seems that there can be internal unity among the contents of experiences that have quite different phenomenal character. For example, one can argue that there is an internal unity between the representation of space in visual and tactile experience, by virtue of which these are constrained to represent a common set of spatial properties. Phenomenologically, it seems that when an object looks flat and when it feels flat, it looks and feels to have the same property (flatness). This commonality seems to hold by virtue of an internal relationship between the phenomenology of visual and tactile experiences. It is arguable that something similar applies to experiences as of the same color in quite different lighting conditions. For example, experiences of a white object in shadow and out of shadow may have quite different phenomenal characters, but it is arguable that the experiences are internally related in a way so that both represent the object as being white.

This internal unity is not straightforwardly accommodated by a Fregean view (assuming that the Fregean view might also apply to experiences of space). One might think that because visual and tactile experiences of space are phenomenally quite different, they will be associated with quite different Fregean modes of presentation. One will represent the normal cause of certain visual experiences, and another will represent the normal cause of certain tactile experiences.

It might turn out that as a matter of contingent fact these normal causes coincide, so that the properties represented coincide, but nothing in the experiences themselves guarantees this. This stands in tension with the intuition above that there is an internal phenomenological connection between the tactile and visual representation of space, according to which these have common contents by virtue of their phenomenology. The same goes for the case of phenomenally different experiences as of the same color: the Fregean view suggests that these will have distinct modes of presentation that at best contingently pick out a common property, which stands in tension with the intuition that these experiences have common representational content by virtue of their phenomenology.

I do not think that any of these three objections—from relationality, simplicity, and internal unity—are knockdown objections to the Fregean view. For a start, all of them rest on phenomenological intuitions that could be disputed. I will not dispute them, however: I am inclined to give each of the intuitions some prima facie weight. But even if one takes the intuitions at face value, it is not clear that any of them entail that the Fregean view is false. Rather, I think all of them can be seen as pointing to a certain *incompleteness* in the Fregean view: the Fregean account so far is not a full story about the phenomenal content of experience. For a full story, the Fregean view needs to be supplemented.

The relationality objection, for example, suggests that there is a Russellian aspect to the phenomenal content of perceptual experience: that phenomenally identical experiences involve representation of some common property. The intuitions here are somewhat equivocal: in the Jack and Jill case, for example, at the same time as we have the intuition that some common property is phenomenologically represented (as a Russellian view of phenomenal content would suggest), we also have the intuition that different properties might be represented by virtue of distinct environmental connections (as a Fregean view of phenomenal content would suggest). If we are pluralists about content, these two intuitions need not contradict each other. Rather, they might be reconciled if we adopt a view on which there is both a Russellian and a Fregean aspect to the phenomenal content of experiences. The intuition here does not entail that Fregean content is not phenomenal content: rather, it suggests that Fregean content is not all there is to phenomenal content.

The force of the simplicity objection is somewhat unclear. Construed as an argument against Fregean phenomenal content, it turns on the tacit premise that the phenomenal content of an experience must have a structure that directly mirrors the phenomenological structure of the experience (or perhaps that it directly mirrors the way it seems to us on introspection that the world is perceptually presented). We might call this somewhat elusive idea the "mirroring constraint." A proponent of the Fregean view might reply simply that the mirroring constraint is an unreasonable constraint on an account of the phenomenal content of experience. As we have defined it, phenomenal content is content that supervenes on the phenomenal character of an experience, but there is nothing in this definition that requires a tighter connection than mere supervenience. And the simplicity objection does not give any reason to deny supervenience. So the Fregean may hold that unless one has an argument that supervenience of content on phenomenal character requires mirroring (or unless we redefine the notion of phenomenal content to build in the mirroring constraint), there is no objection to the claim that Fregean content is phenomenal content.

Still, the simplicity objection once again suggests a certain incompleteness in the Fregean view. One might reasonably hold that the supervenience of content on phenomenal character requires some sort of explanation. If there were a direct correspondence between the elements of the content and the elements of phenomenal character, this explanation would be much easier to give. As it is, the extra complexity of Fregean content (such as the invocation of causation and of experience) raises the question of how this complex content is connected to the simple experience. In particular, if one adopts a view on which phenomenal content is somehow grounded in the phenomenology of an experience, then one will need to tell a story about how a complex Fregean content can be grounded in a simple experience. And if one thinks that the phenomenology of an experience is grounded in its phenomenal content, then the same applies in reverse. So there is at least a significant explanatory question here.

Finally, the Fregean view could handle the internal unity objection by saying that visual and tactile experiences of space share a common phenomenal type (in effect, a crossmodal type), and it is this phenomenal type that is relevant to the Fregean mode of presentation of these experiences ("the property that normally causes experiences of type T"). If so, then the different experiences will be constrained to represent a common class of properties. One could likewise suggest that phenomenally distinct experiences of the same color (shadowed and unshadowed, for example) share a phenomenal type, with the same conclusion. This raises the question, however, of just how we assign the relevant phenomenal types. Any given experience belongs to many different phenomenal types, and the selection of the crossmodal phenomenal type (in the spatial case) or the phenomenal type shared by shadowed and unshadowed experiences (in the color case) may seem suspiciously ad hoc. At least, we need to fill in the Fregean view with an account of how the mode of presentation associated with a given experience is determined, by specifying a principled basis for the choice of a phenomenal type.

One can summarize the worries above by saying that as it stands, the Fregean view does not seem to fully reflect the *presentational phenomenology* of perceptual experience: the way that it seems to directly and immediately present certain objects and properties in the world. It is natural to hold that this presentational phenomenology is closely connected to the phenomenal content of experience. So, to make progress, we need to attend more closely to this presentational phenomenology, and to how it might be connected to phenomenal content.

6   BACK TO PRIMITIVISM

It is useful at this point to ask: what view of the content of perceptual experience is the most phenomenologically adequate? That is, if we were simply to aim to take the phenomenology of perceptual experience at face value, what account of content would we come up with? In particular, what view of the content of color experience best mirrors its presentational phenomenology?

Here, I think the answer is clear. The view of content that most directly mirrors the phenomenology of color experience is primitivism. Phenomenologically, it seems to us as if visual experience presents simple intrinsic qualities of objects in the world, spread out over the surface of the object. When I have a phenomenally red experience of an object, the object seems to be simply, primitively, *red*. The apparent redness does not seem to be a microphysical property, or a mental property, or a disposition, or an unspecified property that plays an appropriate causal role. Rather, it seems to be a simple qualitative property, with a distinctive sensuous nature. We might call this property perfect redness: the sort of property that might have been instantiated in Eden.

One might say: phenomenologically, it seems that visual experience presents the world to us as an Edenic world. Taking the phenomenology completely at face value, visual experience presents a world where perfect redness and perfect blueness are instantiated on the surface of objects, as they were in Eden. These are simple intrinsic qualities whose nature we seem to grasp fully in perceptual experience. For the world to be *exactly* the way that my phenomenology seems to present it as being, the world would have to be an Edenic world in which these properties are instantiated.

This suggests a view on which color experiences attribute primitive properties such as perfect redness and perfect blueness to objects. On this view, color experiences have a Russellian content involving the attribution of these primitive properties. Furthermore, this content is naturally taken to be phenomenal content. Intuitively, the nature of the primitive properties that are presented to one is fully determined by the phenomenology of the experience: if an experience attributes a primitive property, any phenomenally identical experience will attribute the same primitive property. So this view is a sort of Russellian primitivism about phenomenal content.

For all its virtues with respect to phenomenological adequacy, the Russellian primitivist view has a familiar problem. There is good reason to believe that the relevant primitive properties are not instantiated in our world. That is, there is good reason to believe that none of the objects we perceive are perfectly red or perfectly green. If this is correct, then the primitivist view entails that all color experiences are illusory.[4]

A first reason for doubting that these properties exist came when we ate from the Tree of Illusion. This made it clear that there is no necessary connection between primitive properties and perceptual experiences, and strongly suggested that if there is a connection, it is merely causal and contingent. And once we have accepted that one sometimes has phenomenally red experiences in the absence of perfect redness, it is natural to start to wonder whether the same goes for all of our phenomenally red experiences. This is a relatively weak reason, as the existence of illusions is compatible with the existence of veridical perception, but it is enough to generate initial doubts.

A second and stronger reason came when we ate from the Tree of Science. Science suggests that when we see a red object, our perception of the object is mediated by the reflection or radiation of light from the surface of the object to our eyes and then to our brains. The properties of the object that are responsible for the reflection or radiation of the light appear to be complex physical properties, such as surface spectral reflectances, ultimately grounded in microphysical configurations. Science does not reveal any primitive properties in the object, and furthermore, the hypothesis that objects have the relevant primitive properties seems quite unnecessary in order to explain color perception.

Still, someone might suggest that objects have the primitive properties all the same, perhaps supervening in some fashion in the microphysical properties of the object. In response, one might suggest that this picture will metaphysically complicate the world. It seems at least conceivable that objects with the relevant microphysical properties could fail to instantiate the relevant primitive properties. So it looks as if the relevant primitive properties are a significant addition to the world, over and above the microphysical supervenience base. A primitivist might respond in turn by denying that any metaphysical addition is involved (perhaps denying an inference from conceivability to metaphysical possibility), or by accepting that physicalism about ordinary objects is false.[5] But even if so, there is a remaining problem.

The third and strongest reason for doubting that primitive properties are instantiated stems from an elaboration of the inversion argument given earlier.[6] Take an ordinary object, such as a red apple. It is familiar from everyday

---

[4] In practice, primitivists are divided on this issue. For example, Holman, Maund, and Wright hold that the primitive properties are uninstantiated and that color experiences are illusory, while Campbell, Johnston, and McGinn hold that primitive properties are instantiated and that color experiences can be veridical.

[5] Among primitivists who think that the primitive properties are instantiated, Campbell and McGinn suggest that they metaphysically supervene on microphysical or dispositional properties, so that they are not a metaphysical addition in the strong sense, while Johnston seems willing to accept that they are a strong metaphysical addition.

[6] A version of this sort of argument is deployed by Edwards (1998) against Campbell's version of primitivism.

experience that such an object can cause phenomenally red experiences of the apple and (in some circumstances) can cause phenomenally green experiences of the apple, without any change in its intrinsic properties. It then seems that there is no obstacle to the existence of a community in which objects with the intrinsic properties of this apple *normally* cause phenomenally green experiences. We can even imagine that the very same apple normally causes phenomenally red experiences in one community and normally causes phenomenally green experiences in the other.

We can now ask: when a subject in the first community has a phenomenally red experience of the apple, and a subject in the second community has a phenomenally green experience of the apple, which of these experiences is veridical?

Intuitively, there is a case for saying that both experiences are veridical. But this is an unhappy answer for the primitivist. On the primitivist view, any phenomenally red experience attributes perfect redness, and any phenomenally green experience attributes perfect greenness. If both experiences are veridical, it follows that the apple instantiates both perfect redness and perfect greenness. The argument generalizes: for any phenomenal color, it seems that there is a community in which the apple normally causes experiences with that phenomenal color. Taking the current line, it will follow that the apple instantiates every perfect color! The choice of an apple was perfectly general here, so it seems to follow that every object instantiates every perfect color. It follows that no color experience of an object can be illusory with respect to color. Whatever the phenomenal color of the experience, the object will have the corresponding primitive property, so the experience will be veridical. This conclusion is perhaps even more counterintuitive than the conclusion that all color experiences are illusory.

A primitivist might suggest that one of the experiences is veridical and one of them is not. But this imposes an asymmetry on what otherwise seems to be a quite symmetrical situation. When a subject in one community has a phenomenally red experience of the apple and a subject in the other community has a phenomenally green experience of the apple, both subjects' perceptual mechanisms are functioning in the way that is normal for those communities. And the perceptual mechanisms themselves, involving light and brain, seem to be symmetrically well-functioning in both communities. Perhaps a primitivist can hold the line and assert that one of the experiences is veridical and one is falsidical, simply because the apple is perfectly red and it is not perfectly green. But this line leads to the conclusion that color experiences in one of the communities are *normally* falsidical (after all, objects like the apple normally cause phenomenally green experiences in that community) where corresponding experiences in the other community are normally veridical.

Apart from the unappealing asymmetry, this view yields a serious skeptical worry: it seems that we have little reason to believe that we are in a community that normally perceives veridically as opposed to falsidically. After all, nature and evolution will be indifferent between the two communities above. Evolutionary processes will be indifferent between perceivers in which apples produce phenomenally red experiences, perceivers in which apples produce phenomenally green experiences, and perceivers in which apples produce phenomenally blue experiences. Any such perceiver could easily come to exist through minor differences in environmental conditions or brain wiring. If we accept the reasoning above, only a very small subset of the class of such possible perceivers will normally have veridical experiences, and there is no particular reason to think that we are among them.

Once these options are ruled out, the reasonable conclusion is that neither experience is veridical: the apple is neither perfectly red nor perfectly green. Generalizing from this case, this reasoning suggests that primitive properties are not instantiated at all. I think that this is clearly the most reasonable view for a primitivist to take: on this view, experiences attribute primitive properties, but their objects never possess these properties.

Still, this view has the consequence that all color experiences are illusory. This is a counterintuitive conclusion, and runs counter to our usual judgments about the veridicality of experience. On the face of it, there is a significant difference between a phenomenally red experience of a red wall and a phenomenally red experience of a white wall that looks red because (unknown to the subject) it is bathed in red light. As we ordinarily classify experiences, the former is veridical and the latter is not. In classifying both experiences as falsidical, primitivism cannot respect this distinction.

7   PERFECT AND IMPERFECT VERIDICALITY

Here is where things stand. The Fregean view of phenomenal content seems to most accurately capture our judgments about veridicality, but it is not especially phenomenologically adequate. The primitivist view of phenomenal content is the most phenomenologically adequate view, but it yields implausible consequences about veridicality. For a way forward, what we need is an account that captures both the phenomenological virtues of the primitivist view and the truth-conditional virtues of the Fregean view. In what follows I will argue that such an account is available.

One can begin to motivate such a view with the following pair of intuitions:

(1)   For a color experience to be *perfectly veridical*—for it to be as veridical as it could be—its object would have to have perfect colors. The perfect veridicality of color experience would require that our world is an Edenic world, in which objects instantiate primitive color properties.

(2)   Even if the object of an experience lacks perfect colors, a color experience can be *imperfectly veridical*: veridical according to our ordinary standard

of veridicality. Even after the fall from Eden, our imperfect world has objects with properties that suffice to make our experiences veridical, by our ordinary standards.

This pair of intuitions is strongly supported, I think. The first is supported by the phenomenological observations in the previous section. If we were to take our experience *completely* at face value, we would accept that we were in a world where primitive properties such as perfect redness and perfect blueness are spread homogeneously over the surface of objects. The second is supported by our ordinary judgments about veridicality. When an ordinary white wall looks white to us, then even if it merely instantiates physical properties and not perfect whiteness, it is good enough to qualify as veridical by our ordinary standards.

These two intuitions need not be taken to contradict each other. Instead, they suggest that we possess two notions of satisfaction for an experience: perfect and imperfect veridicality. An experience can be imperfectly veridical, or veridical in the ordinary sense, without being perfectly veridical.

The terminology should not be taken to suggest that when an experience is imperfectly veridical, it is not really veridical. In fact, it is plausible that imperfect veridicality is the property that our ordinary term "veridicality" denotes. We speak truly when we say that a phenomenally red experience of an ordinary red object is veridical. It is just that the experience is not perfectly veridical. To capture this, one could also call imperfect veridicality "ordinary veridicality," or "veridicality simpliciter." Or one could use "veridical" for imperfect veridicality and "ultraveridical" for perfect veridicality. But I will usually stick to the terminology above.

Corresponding to these distinct notions of satisfaction, one will have distinct associated conditions of satisfaction. Imperfect veridicality will be associated with something like the Fregean condition of satisfaction discussed earlier: a phenomenally red experience will be perfectly veridical iff its object has the property that normally causes phenomenally red experiences. Perfect veridicality will be associated with the primitivist condition of satisfaction: a phenomenally red experience will be perfectly veridical iff its object instantiates perfect redness.

Imperfect and perfect veridicality can therefore be seen as associated with distinct *contents* of an experience. We might call the content associated with perfect veridicality the *Edenic content* of an experience, and the content associated with imperfect veridicality the *ordinary content* of the experience.

As we have already seen, our ordinary assessments of veridicality can be seen as associated with two contents in turn. For example, a phenomenally red experience has a Fregean content (satisfied iff its object has the property that normally causes phenomenally red experience) and a Russellian content (satisfied iff its object has physical redness). We might call these contents the *ordinary Fregean content* and the *ordinary Russellian content* of the experience.

One could also, in principle, associate assessments of perfect veridicality with both a Fregean and a Russellian content. But here the Fregean content is much the same as the Russellian content. The Russellian content involves the attribution of perfect redness: it is satisfied in a world iff the relevant object is perfectly red there. Unlike the ordinary Russellian content above, this content does not depend on how the subject's environment turns out. Regardless of how the environment turns out, the experience in question will attribute perfect redness. So there is no nontrivial dependence of the property attributed on the way the subject's environment turns out. It follows that the Edenic Fregean content of the experience (which captures the way that the perfect veridicality of the experience depends on the way the environment turns out) is satisfied iff the object of the experience has perfect redness. There may be some differences between the Edenic Fregean and Russellian contents here in the treatment of objects (as opposed to properties), and in the formal modeling (with worlds and centered worlds), but where the color-property aspect of the content is concerned, the contents behave in very similar ways. So for most purposes one can simply speak of the Edenic content of the experience, one that is satisfied iff a relevant object has perfect redness.[7]

So we have found three distinctive sorts of content associated with an experience: an Edenic content, an ordinary Fregean content, and an ordinary Russellian content. We have seen already that the ordinary Russellian content is not plausibly a phenomenal content: phenomenally identical experiences can have the same (ordinary) Russellian contents. However, for all we have said, both Edenic contents and ordinary Fregean contents are phenomenal contents. It is plausible that any phenomenally red experience will have the Fregean condition of satisfaction above (where satisfaction is understood as imperfect veridicality) and will have the primitivist condition of satisfaction above (where satisfaction is understood as perfect veridicality). So we have more than one phenomenal content for an experience, depending on the associated notion of satisfaction.

8 A TWO-STAGE VIEW OF PHENOMENAL CONTENT

Perfect and imperfect veridicality are not independent of each other. It is plausible to suggest that there is an intimate relation between the two, and that there is an intimate relation between the associated sorts of phenomenal content.

---

[7] In terms of the two-dimensional framework, one can say that phenomenally color properties (at the standard of perfect veridicality) are associated with the same primary and secondary intension. In this way they are reminiscent of expressions such as "consciousness", "philosopher," and "two," which also arguably have the same primary and secondary intensions. These terms can be seen as "semantically neutral" (Chalmers 2004b), as witnessed by the fact that their content does not seem to have the same sort of dependence on empirical discoveries about the environment as terms such as "water" and "Hesperus." One might say that perceptual representations of perfect redness are semantically neutral in an analogous way.

A natural picture of this relation suggests itself. A phenomenally red experience is perfectly veridical iff its object instantiates perfect redness. A phenomenally red experience is imperfectly veridical iff its object instantiates a property that *matches* perfect redness. Here, to match perfect redness is (roughly) to play the role that perfect redness plays in Eden. The key role played by perfect redness in Eden is that it normally brings about phenomenally red experiences. So a property matches perfect redness if it normally causes phenomenally red experiences. This yields a condition of satisfaction that mirrors the ordinary Fregean content above.

The notion of matching is what links imperfect veridicality to perfect veridicality. I will say more about this notion later, but one can motivate the idea as follows. For our experiences to be perfectly veridical, we would have to live in Eden. But we have undergone the fall from Eden: no primitive color properties are instantiated by objects in our world. So the best that objects in our world can do is to have properties that can play the role that primitive properties play in Eden. Of course no property instantiated in our world can play that role perfectly, but some can play it well enough, by virtue of normally bringing about phenomenally red experiences. Such a property might be called *imperfect redness*. In our world, imperfect redness is plausibly some sort of physical property, such as a surface spectral reflectance.

More generally, the following is a plausible thesis. If an experience is such that its perfect veridicality conditions require the instantiation of primitive property X, then the experience's imperfect veridicality conditions will require the instantiation of a property that matches X. As before, a property matches X (roughly) if it plays the role that X plays in Eden. The key role is causing experiences of the appropriate phenomenal type. In our world, these properties will typically be physical properties: the imperfect counterparts of X.

This relation suggests the following *two-stage* picture of the phenomenal content of experience. On this picture, the most fundamental sort of content of an experience is its Edenic content, which requires the instantiation of appropriate primitive properties. This content then determines the ordinary Fregean content of the experience: the experience is imperfectly veridical if its object has properties that match the properties attributed by the experience's Edenic content.[8]

----

[8] Aaron Zimmerman suggested that instead of associating an experience with two contents, we could associate an experience with a single graded content that has degrees of satisfaction: the content might be perfectly satisfied, imperfectly satisfied, and so on, depending on how the world turns out. A pluralist can allow that we can associate experiences with graded contents like these. However, this single graded content will lose some of the structure present in the dual contents: in particular, we cannot easily analyze it in terms of attribution of a property to objects in the environment, and the matching relation between Edenic and ordinary content will not easily be reflected in this account. So this picture will lose some of the explanatory structure that is present on the two-stage view.

On the two-stage view, the ordinary Fregean content of a phenomenally red experience will be satisfied (in an environment) iff a relevant object instantiates a property that matches perfect redness (in that environment). This ordinary Fregean content will itself be associated with an ordinary Russellian content: one that is satisfied iff the (actual) object of the experience has P, where P is the property that matches perfect redness in the environment of the original experience. On this view, all phenomenally red experiences will have the same Fregean content, but they may have different Russellian contents, depending on their environment.

Of course this Fregean content gives exactly the same results as the Fregean content discussed earlier: an object will instantiate a property that matches perfect redness iff it instantiates a property that normally causes phenomenally red experiences. But the two-stage view gives a more refined account of how this Fregean content is grounded, one that more clearly shows its roots in the phenomenology of the experience. The view also has the promise of being more phenomenologically adequate than the original Fregean view seemed to be, by giving a major role to the Edenic content that directly reflects the experience's phenomenology. The resulting view is a sort of semi-primitivist Fregeanism: a version of the Fregean view on which the Fregean content is grounded in a primitivist Edenic content.

On this view, Eden acts as a sort of regulative ideal in determining the content of our color experiences. Our world is not Eden, but our perceptual experience requires our world to match Eden as well as possible. Eden is central to the content of our experience: it is directly reflected in the perfect veridicality conditions of the experience, and it plays a key role in determining the ordinary veridicality conditions of our experiences.

One might put the two-stage view as follows: our experience *presents* an Edenic world, and thereby *represents* an ordinary world. We might say that the perfect veridicality conditions of the experience are its *presentational content*, and the imperfect veridicality conditions of the experience are its *representational content*. As pluralists we can allow that experiences have both sorts of content, with an intimate relation between them. Presentational content most directly reflects the phenomenology of an experience; representational content most directly reflects its intuitive conditions of satisfaction.

Because of this, the two-stage view yields natural answers to the objections to the Fregean view that were grounded in phenomenological adequacy. On the relationality objection: the two-stage view accommodates relationality by noting that there are certain specific and determinate properties—the perfect color properties—that are presented in virtue of the phenomenology of color experience. When Jack and Jill both have phenomenally green experiences in different environments, the two experiences have a common Edenic content, and so both are presented with perfect greenness. This captures the intuitive sense in which objects look to be the same to both Jack and Jill; at the same time, the level of ordinary Fregean and Russellian content captures the intuitive sense in which objects look to be different to both Jack and Jill. By acknowledging Edenic phenomenal content in addition to Fregean phenomenal content, we capture the sense in which perceptual phenomenology seems to be Russellian and relational.

On the simplicity objection: in the two-stage view, the simplicity of phenomenological structure is directly mirrored at the level of Edenic content. In Edenic content, there need be no reference to normal causes, and no reference to experiences: instead, simple properties are attributed directly. The residual question for the Fregean view concerned how a complex Fregean content might be grounded in simple phenomenology. The two-stage view begins to answer this question. A given experience is most directly associated with a simple Edenic content, and this Edenic content is then associated with a Fregean content by the invocation of the matching relation. There is still an explanatory question about just where the matching relation comes from, and how it might be grounded: I address this question later. But the two-stage view already gives us a skeleton around which we can build an explanatory connection between phenomenology and Fregean content.

On the internal unity objection: the two-stage view can accommodate the internal unity between visual and tactile experience of space by holding that the Edenic content of both visual and tactile experiences involve the attribution of perfect spatial properties (although the other perfect properties attributed by the experiences may differ). If so, then internal unity is present at the level of Edenic content. Further, the Fregean content of each will invoke the properties that match perfect spatial properties (in effect, the common typing of visual and spatial experiences is induced by the commonality in their Edenic content), and this common Fregean content will entail a common ordinary Russellian content. So the unity at the level of Edenic content will lead to unity at the level of ordinary content. Something similar applies to the case of representing the same color under different illumination; I will discuss this case in some detail shortly.

The two-stage view respects the insights of both the primitivist and the Fregean views in obvious ways. Like the original Fregean view, it can also respect certain key elements of dispositionalist and physicalist views. On the two-stage view, dispositions to cause relevant sorts of experiences still play a key role, not as the properties that are represented by experiences, but as a sort of reference-fixer for those properties. And the properties that are represented by the experience (at the standard of imperfect veridicality) are themselves plausibly physical properties, at least in the actual world. We might say that the view generates a broadly dispositionalist ordinary Fregean content and a broadly physicalist ordinary Russellian content.

9   EDEN AND EDENIC CONTENT

The view proposed raises many questions. In the remainder of this chapter I address some of these questions, and in doing so flesh out a number of aspects of the view. These include questions about Eden and Edenic content; about colors and color constancy; about matching and Fregean content; and about generalizing the model beyond the case of color. The order of these topics is arbitrary to some extent, so it is possible to skip to the topics that seem the most pressing.

What constraints are imposed by Edenic content?

A world with respect to which our visual experience is perfectly veridical is an *Edenic world*. (I defer until below the question of whether Edenic worlds are metaphysically possible.) It is natural to ask: what is the character of an Edenic world? A full answer to this question depends on a full analysis of the phenomenology of visual experience, which cannot be given here. But we can say a few things. As before, I will concentrate mostly on the aspects of phenomenology and representation associated with color, and will leave other aspects until later.

For any given experience, there will be many worlds with respect to which it is perfectly veridical. A visual experience—even a total visual experience corresponding to an entire visual field—typically makes quite limited claims on the world, and is neutral about the rest. For example, a visual experience typically presents things as being a certain way in a certain location, and is neutral about how things are outside that location. So, strictly speaking, in order to make an experience perfectly veridical, a world need merely be Edenic in certain relevant respects in a certain relatively limited area, and may be quite non-Edenic outside that area. Correspondingly, there will be a very large range of worlds that satisfy the relevant Edenic content. But here we can focus on what is *required* in order that the content be satisfied.

In a world that satisfies a typical Edenic content, primitive color properties such as perfect redness and perfect blueness are instantiated. Most often, visual phenomenology presents color as instantiated on the surface of objects, so an Edenic world will contain objects in which perfect colors are instantiated at certain locations on their surfaces. Strictly speaking, it will contain objects with certain perfect location-color properties: properties of having certain perfect colors at certain locations. Occasionally we have the phenomenology of volumes of color: as with certain transparent colored objects, for example, or perhaps with smoke and flames. In these cases, the corresponding Edenic world will have objects in which the relevant perfect colors are instantiated at locations throughout the relevant volume. It may be that sometimes we have the phenomenology of color not associated with objects at all: perhaps our experience of the sky is like this, just representing blueness at a certain distance in front of us.

If so, then a corresponding Edenic world will simply have perfect color qualities instantiated (by the world?) at relevant locations.[9]

From the fable at the beginning of the paper, one might infer that Edenic worlds must meet a number of further constraints: perceivers must be directly acquainted with objects and properties in those worlds, illusion must be impossible, and there must be no microphysical structure. On my view this is not quite right, however. Edenic content puts relatively simple constraints on the world, involving the instantiation of perfect properties by objects in the environment, and these further constraints are not part of Edenic content itself. Their relation to Edenic content is somewhat more subtle than this.

Perfect color properties are plausibly *intrinsic* color properties. By virtue of presenting an object as having a perfect color at a certain location, an experience does not seem to make claims about how things are outside that location. So, when an object is perfectly red in Eden, it is this way by virtue of its intrinsic nature. In particular, it seems that an object can be perfectly red without anyone experiencing the object as perfectly red. The phenomenology of color does not seem to be the phenomenology of properties that require a perceiver in order to be instantiated. (The phenomenology of pain is arguably different in this respect, as I will discuss later.) It seems coherent to suppose that there is a world in which perfect colors are instantiated, but in which there are no perceivers at all.

One *could* hold a view on which, for an experience to be perfectly veridical, a subject must perceive the relevant perfect colors. On such a view, the character of visual experience is such that in addition to representing the presence of colors, visual experiences also represent the *perception* of colors. If one held this view, one would hold that no such experience is perfectly veridical unless the relevant perfect colors are perceived by a subject (the subject at the center of the relevant centered world), perhaps by direct acquaintance.

I am inclined to think that the character of visual experience is not like this, however. The phenomenology of color vision clearly makes claims about objects in the world, but it does not obviously make claims about ourselves and our perceptual relation to these objects. As theorists who introspect and reflect on how our phenomenology seems, we can say that on reflection it seems to us (introspectively) as if we are acquainted with objects and properties in the world. But it is not obvious that perceptual phenomenology itself makes such a claim: to suggest that it does is arguably to overintellectualize perceptual experience. If perceptual experience does not make such claims, then the Edenic content of a visual experience will require that the relevant perfect properties are instantiated, but they will not require that we stand in any particular perceptual relation to those properties.

---

[9] Clark (2000) suggests that visual experience always involves the mere attribution of colors to locations rather than to objects. I find this suggestion phenomenologically implausible, but, if it is correct, one could accommodate it by saying that Edenic worlds involve the instantiation of perfect color qualities by locations (or the instantiation of perfect color-location properties by the world), without requiring any special relationship between these qualities and objects.

If this is correct, then in order to satisfy the Edenic content of an experience, a world must be Edenic in that perfect properties are instantiated within it, but it need not be a world in which we have not yet eaten from the Tree of Illusion. If an experience does not represent itself, it does not represent that it is non-illusory.

Likewise, a world that satisfies the Edenic content of an experience need not be one in which we have not yet eaten from the Tree of Science. The phenomenology of vision is arguably quite neutral on whether the world has the relevant scientific structure, as long as it also has primitive properties, and there is no obvious reason why a possible world could not have both.

To reinforce this view, we can note that the argument from the existence of illusions and of scientific structure to the nonexistence of perfect colors in our world was not a deductive argument. Rather, it was a sort of abductive argument: it undercut our reasons for accepting (instantiated) perfect colors, by suggesting that they are not needed to explain our visual experience. It remained *coherent* to suppose that primitive properties are instantiated in our world, but there was now good reason to reject the hypothesis as unnecessarily complex. On this view, eating from the Trees (by discovering the existence of illusions and scientific structure) did not directly contradict the Edenic contents of our experience, but it gave us good reason to believe that our world is not an Edenic world.

A more complete account of the Edenic content of color experience would require careful attention to all sorts of phenomenological details that I have largely ignored so far, such as the phenomenal representation of the distribution of colors in space, the fineness of grain of color representation, the different levels of detail of color experience in the foreground and background of a visual field, and so on. I cannot attend to all of this here, but as a case study, I will shortly pay attention to one such detail, the phenomenon of color constancy.

What is the character of Edenic perception?

Even if perceivers are not presented in the Edenic content of an experience, it is natural to speculate about how perception might work in an Edenic world. One way to put this is to ask: what sort of world maximally reflects how things seem to us *both perceptually and introspectively*? Even if perception makes no claims about our perceptual experiences and our perceptual relation to the world, introspection does. It seems to us, introspectively and perceptually, as if we stand in certain sorts of relation to the world. For this seeming to be maximally veridical, an Edenic world must contain subjects who stand in certain intimate relations to perfect properties in the world. We can call a world in which these seemings are maximally veridical a *pure Edenic world*.

Of course there are (possibly impure) Edenic worlds in which subjects perceive perfect colors via a mediated causal mechanism, at least to the extent that we perceive imperfect colors via such a mechanism in our world. But it is natural to think that this is not the best that they could do. It seems reasonable to hold that in Eden, subjects could have a sort of direct acquaintance with perfect colors. Perfect colors seem to be the sort of properties that are particularly apt for direct acquaintance, after all. And phenomenologically, there is something to be said for the claim that we seem to perceive colors directly. Certainly, there does not seem to be a mediating causal mechanism, and one could suggest more strongly that at least introspectively, there seems not to be a mediating causal mechanism.

It is natural to suggest that in the purest Edenic worlds, subjects do not perceive instances of perfect color by virtue of having color experiences that are distinct from but related to those instances. That would seem to require a contingent mediating connection. Instead, Edenic subjects perceive instances of perfect colors by standing in a direct perceptual relation to them: perhaps the relation of acquaintance. Edenic subjects still have color experiences: there is something it is like to be them. But their color experiences have their phenomenal character precisely by virtue of the perfect colors that the subject is acquainted with. It is natural to say that the experiences themselves are constituted by a direct perceptual relation to the relevant instances of perfect color in the environment.[10] We might say: in Eden, if not in our world, perceptual experience extends outside the head.

In the purest Edenic worlds, there are no illusions (if we take both introspection and perception to be maximally veridical, we conclude that things are just as they seem). In such a world, all color experience involves direct acquaintance with instances of perfect color in the environment. As soon as we eat from the Tree of Illusion, we have good reason to believe that we are not in such a world. But this need not cast us out of Eden entirely. There are somewhat less pure Edenic worlds in which there are illusions and hallucinations: perceivers sometimes have experiences as of perfect redness when the perceived object is perfectly blue, or when there is no object to be perceived. In these cases, the color experience cannot consist of a direct perceptual relation to an instance of perfect redness, as the subject stands in no such relation. Instead, it seems that the character of the experience is constituted independently of the properties of the perceived object.

In these impure Edenic worlds, an illusory or hallucinatory color experience involves a relevant relation to the property of perfect redness, without this relation being mediated by a relation to an instance of this property. (Something like this view is suggested as an account of hallucination in the actual world by Johnston 2004.) If so, then in such a world there may be phenomenally identical

[10] Is Edenic perception causal? Given that a perceptual experience consists of a relation of acquaintance with a perfect color property, is its character causally related to the perfect color property? This depends on subtle questions about the causation of relational properties by their relata. Compare: when a boy's first sibling is born, does this sibling cause the boy to be a brother? I am inclined to say yes, and to say the same thing about Edenic perception, holding that it involves a sort of unmediated causal relation. One could also say no, saying that this is a constitutive relation that is stronger than any causal relation. But even if so, there will at least be a counterfactual dependence of perceptual experience on perfect color properties in the world, by virtue of the constitutive relation.

experiences (say, veridical and falsidical phenomenally red experiences) whose underlying metaphysical nature is quite distinct: one is constituted by a perceptual relation to a property instance in the subject's environment, and one is not. This picture is reminiscent of that held by some disjunctivists about perceptual experience in our world. We might say that in Eden, if not in our world, a disjunctive view of the metaphysics of perceptual experience is correct.

Is Eden a possible world?

Eden does not exist, but could it have existed? That is, is there a possible world in which there are perfect colors? Could God, if he had so chosen, have created such a world?

I am not certain of the answer to this question. But I am inclined to say yes: there are Edenic possible worlds.

To start with, it seems that perceptual experience gives us some sort of grip on what it would be for an object to be perfectly red, or perfectly blue. It would have to be exactly like *that*, precisely as that object is presented to us as being in experience. It seems that we can use this grip to form concepts of qualities such as perfect redness and perfect blueness (I have been deploying these concepts throughout this paper). And there is no obvious incoherence in the idea that an object could be perfectly red, or perfectly blue. On the face of it we can conceive of such an object. So there is a prima facie case for believing that such an object is possible.

One can also reason as follows. There are good reasons to think that perfect redness is not instantiated in our world. But these reasons are empirical reasons, not a priori reasons. It was eating from the Tree of Illusion and the Tree of Science that led us to doubt that we live in an Edenic world. And eating from these Trees was an empirical process, based on empirical discoveries about the world. Before eating from these Trees, there was no special reason to doubt that our experience was perfectly veridical. In particular, it is hard to see how one could be led to the conclusion that perfect redness is not instantiated by a priori reasoning alone (although see below). So the hypothesis that our world is Edenic seems at least to be conceivable, and it is reasonable to suggest that it cannot be ruled out a priori.

I have argued elsewhere (Chalmers 2002b) that this sort of conceivability is a good guide to metaphysical possibility. In particular, there is good reason to believe that if a hypothesis is ideally negatively conceivable, in that it cannot be ruled out by idealized a priori reasoning, then there is a metaphysically possible world that verifies the hypothesis. And there is even better reason to believe that if a hypothesis is ideally positively conceivable, in that one can imagine a situation in which the hypothesis actually obtains (in a way that holds up on idealized a priori reflection), then there is a metaphysically possible world that verifies the hypothesis.

The hypothesis that our world is Edenic (that is, that perfect colors are instantiated in our world) seems to be at least prima facie negatively conceivable (it cannot easily be ruled out a priori) and prima facie positively conceivable (we can imagine that it actually obtains). Furthermore, it is not clear how this hypothesis could be undercut by further a priori reasoning. If it cannot, then the hypothesis is ideally (negatively and positively) conceivable. If so, and if the thesis above is correct, then there is a metaphysically possible world that verifies the hypothesis. Verification is a technical notion from two-dimensional semantics (verification goes with primary intensions, satisfaction with secondary intensions), but the technicalities do not matter too much in this case (the primary and secondary intensions of perfect color concepts are plausibly identical, so that if a world verifies the hypothesis that perfect colors are instantiated it also satisfies the hypothesis). So, if this reasoning is correct, one can simply say: it is metaphysically possible that perfect colors are instantiated.

One could resist the conclusion either by denying that the Edenic hypothesis is conceivable in the relevant senses, or by denying the connection between conceivability in the relevant senses and possibility. Speaking for myself, I am reasonably confident about the latter, but I am not certain about the former. I do not see any obvious way of ruling out the Edenic hypothesis a priori, but I cannot be sure that there is no such way. We will see later that in the case of pains, discussed below, there is arguably such a way to rule out the instantiation of perfect pains a priori. These considerations do not generalize to perfect colors, but they make salient the possibility that other considerations might. For now, I am inclined to think that an Edenic world is metaphysically possible, but I am not certain of this.

Is there a property of perfect redness?

If what I have said so far is right, there is no *instantiated* property of perfect redness, but it is natural to hold that perfect redness may be an uninstantiated property. It seems that we have a grip on such a property in experience: we grasp what it would be for an object to have the property of perfect redness. Certainly, if an Edenic world is metaphysically possible, then objects in those worlds will be perfectly red, and it seems reasonable to conclude that they have the property of perfect redness. And even if an Edenic world is metaphysically impossible, one might still hold that there is such a property: it is just a necessarily uninstantiated property (like the property of being a round square). These issues will interact with one's views on the metaphysics of properties to some extent: for example, if one thinks that properties are just sets of possible objects, or if one thinks that properties are very sparse relative to predicates, one might resist some of the reasoning here. But overall I think there is a good prima facie case for thinking that there is a property of perfect redness.

If there is no such property, or if there is no metaphysically possible Edenic world, then some of the details in this chapter might have to change. If there is no metaphysically possible Edenic world, one cannot model the conditions of satisfaction association with perfect veridicality using sets of (or functions over) metaphysically possible worlds. And if there is no property of perfect redness, one cannot say that there is a content that attributes this property to an object. But even if so, one could understand the contents in other terms. For example, one could understand Edenic contents in terms of sets of epistemically possible scenarios rather than metaphysically possible worlds. Or one could understand Edenic conditions of satisfaction using something like Fregean concepts rather than properties. One could also regard Eden as some sort of mere world-model, not yet a possible world, but one that plays a key role in determining the ordinary Fregean contents of perception, via the requirement that the actual world must match the world-model in various respects. In this fashion numerous key elements of the two-stage model of perceptual content could be preserved.

If there is a property of perfect redness, what sort of property is it? It is most natural to conceive of perfect redness as a sort of simple, irreducible quality, one that might be instantiated on the surface of objects in some possible world. Perfect color properties might not all be maximally simple. For example, they might be seen as a sort of composition from simpler perfect properties, such as certain perfect unique hues (so that a particular shade of perfect orange may be a composite of perfect redness and perfect yellowness to certain degrees, and a certain amount of perfect brightness). But the underlying properties are naturally held to be irreducible.

In particular, it is natural to hold that perfect colors are not reducible to physical properties. If one accepts the earlier arguments that perfect color properties are not instantiated in our world, this consequence follows naturally. But even if one thought that perfect color properties are instantiated in our world, one could still argue that they are irreducible to physical properties, by analogs of familiar arguments concerning phenomenal properties.[11] For example, one could argue that one can conceive of a physically identical world in which they are not instantiated, and infer that such a world is metaphysically possible. Or one could argue that someone without color vision could know all about the physical properties of objects without knowing about their perfect colors.

Still, it is at least coherent to hold a view on which experiences have Edenic content that represents the instantiation of perfect color properties, and to hold that as a matter of empirical fact, perfect color properties are identical to certain physical properties (such as surface reflectances). On this view, our *concepts* of perfect color properties may be simple and irreducible concepts, but they pick out the same properties as those picked out by certain physical properties. Such a

---

[11] Analog arguments of this sort are discussed in detail by Byrne (forthcoming). Byrne conceives these arguments as arguments for the irreducibility of color properties. I think the arguments work best as arguments for the irreducibility of perfect color properties.

view would be analogous to certain "type-B" materialist views about phenomenal properties, according to which phenomenal properties are empirically identical to certain physical properties, because simple phenomenal concepts pick out the same properties as certain physical concepts. On the resulting view, experiences could be seen to have a Russellian phenomenal content that represents the instantiation of certain physical properties (although the experience does not represent these properties *as* physical properties). On this sort of view, our experiences might be perfectly veridical even in a purely physical world. I do not find this view plausible myself: it is vulnerable to the usual objections to Russellian physicalist views based on inversion scenarios, for example (requiring either strong externalism about phenomenology or arbitrary asymmetries among inverted communities), and it is also subject to the conceivability arguments above. But I think that there is at least an interesting variety of Russellian physicalism about phenomenal content in the vicinity.[12]

One could likewise hold a view on which perfect color properties are empirically identical to certain dispositional properties; or one could hold a view on which perfect color properties are distinct from physical and dispositional properties, but on which they metaphysically supervene on such properties.[13] These views will be confronted with familiar problems: for example, the question of how to individuate the properties while still retaining plausible results about veridicality and illusion (for the view on which perfect colors are identical to or supervene on dispositional properties), and the questions of inversion and conceivability (for the view on which perfect colors supervene on intrinsic physical properties). But again, views of this sort are at least worth close attention.

Finally, it is possible to hold that perfect color properties are identical to certain mental properties, such as properties instantiated by one's visual field. This view agrees with the ordinary Edenic view that perfect colors are not instantiated by ordinary external objects, but holds that they are instantiated by certain mental objects (though they need not be represented *as* mental properties). The resulting view, a version of projectivism, does not suffer from the problems for the physicalist and dispositionalist views outlined above.[14] I am inclined to reject this view myself, because of familiar problems with holding that mental objects instantiate color properties or their analogs (Chisholm's (1942) "speckled hen" problem, for example), and because the view becomes particularly hard to accept when extending beyond the case of color (it is hard to

---

[12] The version of Russellian physicalism about phenomenal content advocated by Byrne and Hilbert (2003) may be particularly close to this view. This view contrasts with the physicalism about color advocated by Jackson 1996, according to which color properties are picked out as the properties that cause certain sorts of color experience. The latter view is more analogous to a "type-A" materialist view, in that it analyzes color concepts as concepts of properties that play a certain causal role.

[13] The views of Campbell (1993) and McGinn (1996) are at least closely related to the views on which perfect color properties supervene on intrinsic physical properties (for Campbell) and on dispositional properties (for McGinn).

[14] The projectivist view of color defended by Boghossian and Velleman (1989) seems to be compatible with an Edenic view on which the perfect color properties are instantiated by a visual field.

accept that mental objects instantiate perfect height, for example, of the sort that we represent in spatial experience). But the question of whether perfect properties might be instantiated in mental objects is at least well worth considering, and the corresponding version of projectivism might be able to accommodate many of the features of the two-stage view that I have been advocating.

For the remainder of this chapter, I will assume that perfect color properties are irreducible properties that are not instantiated in our world. But at least some aspects of the discussion may generalize to the other views I have outlined.

How can we represent perfect redness?

If perfect redness is never instantiated in our world, then we have never had contact with any instances of it. If so, one might wonder: how can perfect redness be represented in the content of our experiences?

Construed as an objection, this point turns on the tacit premise that representing a property requires contact with instances of it. In reply, one can note that we can certainly represent other uninstantiated properties (the property of being phlogistonated, Hume's missing shade of blue), and can even represent uninstantiable properties (being a round square). An opponent might suggest that these are complex properties whose representation derives from the representation of simpler properties, and so might suggest the modified premise that representing a *simple* property requires contact with instances of it. It is far from clear why we should accept this, however. For example, there seem to be perfectly coherent Humean views of causation on which we represent the simple property (or relation) of causation in our experience and in our thought, but in which there is no causation present in the world.

Certainly, there are cases in which representing a property crucially depends on contact with instances of it. But there are many cases of representation that do not work like this. One can plausibly represent the property of being a philosopher without being acquainted with any philosophers. The same goes for causation, on the Humean view above. One might divide representations into those that are subject to Twin Earth thought experiments (so that twins in a different environment would represent different properties), and those that are not. Representations in the first class (including especially the representation of natural kinds such as water) may have content that depends on instantiation of the relevant property in the environment. But representations in the second class (including perhaps representations of philosophers and causation, at least if this representation does not involve deference to a surrounding linguistic community) do not depend on instances of the property in this way. In these cases, representation of a property comes not from instances of that property in the environment, but rather from some sort of internal grasp of what it would take for something to instantiate the property. It is plausible that representation of perfect redness falls into this second class.

Of course to say this much is just to respond to the objection, and not to fully answer the question. The residual question concerns just *how* our mental states get to have a given Edenic content. I will not try to answer this question here. We do not yet have a good theory of how our mental states represent any properties at all, and the cases of "narrow" representation, such as the representation of philosophers and causation above, are particularly ill-understood. To properly answer these questions, and the analogous question about Edenic content, requires a theory of the roots of intentionality.

I would speculate, however, that the roots of Edenic content lie deep in the heart of phenomenology itself. Horgan and Tienson (2002) have suggested that there is a distinctive sort of "phenomenal intentionality" that is grounded in phenomenology, rather than being grounded in extrinsic causal connections. It is not unreasonable to suppose that Edenic content is a basic sort of phenomenal intentionality—perhaps even the most basic sort. This could be combined with a variety of views about the metaphysics of phenomenal intentionality. For example, one could hold that such intentionality is grounded in the projection of properties of certain mental objects, as on the projectivist view above. Or one could hold that the representation of Edenic content is even more primitive than this. If one is inclined to think that there is something irreducible about phenomenology, one might naturally hold that perceptual phenomenology simply consists in certain primitive relations to certain primitive properties: the presentation of perfect redness, for example. In any case, it is likely that understanding the roots of Edenic content will be closely tied to understanding the metaphysics of phenomenology.

10 COLORS AND COLOR CONSTANCY

What about color constancy?

Color constancy is the phenomenon wherein instances of the same color in the environment, when illuminated by quite different sorts of lighting so that they reflect different sorts of light, nevertheless seem to have the same color. A paradigmatic example is a shadow: when we see a surface that is partly in shadow, although there is something different about the appearance of the shadowed portion of the surface, it often does not seem to us as if the object has a different color in the shadowed portion. One might say: although there is a sense in which the shadowed and unshadowed portions look different, there is also a sense in which they look the same. Certainly, the shadowed and unshadowed portions produce phenomenally distinct experiences, but we often do not judge that the object has a different color in those areas.

To say this much is to stay neutral on the representational content of the relevant experience. But it is natural to wonder just how the content of such experiences should be analyzed. In particular, it is natural to wonder how the two-stage model can handle such contents. To address this question, one can ask as before: how would the world have to be, in order for experiences of this sort to be perfectly veridical? A definite answer to this question requires a close phenomenological analysis. I will not give a full analysis, but I will outline some options.

It is useful to focus on the case of shadows. As an example, we can take a white floor on which an object casts a crisp dark shadow. I will take it that there are visual cues indicating that a shadow is being cast, so that we judge that the floor is still white at the relevant point, though we also judge that it is in shadow. What is the content of this experience? How would the world have to be, in order for the experience to be perfectly veridical?

The answer depends on how we analyze the phenomenology of the experience. To start, one might take either a *simple* or a *complex* view of the phenomenology. On the simple view, the apparent sameness in color between the shadowed and unshadowed area is not present in visual phenomenology at all. Rather, the sameness is detected only at the level of visual judgment, or perhaps at the level of other perceptual mechanisms whose contents are not reflected in phenomenology. For simplicity, let us say it is at the level of visual judgment. On this view, the phenomenal character of the experience of the floor may be the same as the phenomenal character of a floor where the relevant portion of the floor is painted the relevant shade of gray, and in which the floor is under constant illumination; it might also be the same as in a case where the floor is in shadow in the relevant portion, but where there are no cues. (We can stipulate that the last two cases involve exactly the same retinal stimulation, so that there is not much doubt that the resulting experiences are phenomenally identical.) On the simple view, the original shadow case will differ merely in that relevant cues lead to a judgment of sameness in that case but not in the others. The simple view will say something similar about all cases of color constancy: the constancy is present at the level of judgment, not at the level of perceptual experience.

The simple view is naturally associated with a view on which the local phenomenology of color experience is three-dimensional: the relevant experiences can be arranged in a three-dimensional color solid that exhausts the relevant dimensions of variation. Or at least it will hold that if there are further dimensions of variation, then variations due to shadows, illumination, and so on are not among them. On this view, the local phenomenology of perceiving the shadow will be the same as the local phenomenology of veridically perceiving an unshadowed object that is a relevant shade of gray. It is natural to hold that the Edenic content of such an experience involves the attribution of perfect grayness. So, on this view, the perfect veridicality of a shadow experience will require the instantiation of the relevant shade of perfect grayness in the object of perception. If we accept the simple view, then if a shadow is cast in a pure Edenic world (one without illusion), the color of the object will change.

On the simple view, what are the imperfect veridicality conditions of such an experience? An experience of the shadow will be correct iff the floor instantiates a property that matches perfect grayness. A property matches perfect grayness, to a first approximation, if it normally causes phenomenally gray experiences. If we take it that there is a canonical normal condition that involves unshadowed light, then this property will be something like a certain specific surface reflectance that the shadowed area of the floor does not instantiate, so the experience will be (imperfectly) falsidical. If we allow that there is a wide range of normal conditions that includes both shadowed and unshadowed light, things are more complicated. I will discuss this complication further in the next section.

One other position compatible with the simple view holds that while the *local* phenomenology of seeing the partially shadowed floor is the same as the *local* phenomenology of seeing a partially gray floor without cues, the *global* phenomenology of the two cases is different (because of the difference in cues), and this difference in global phenomenology makes for a difference in conditions of veridicality. This view requires a certain anti-atomism about perceptual content: the veridicality conditions of an experience of a color at a location are not determined just by the local phenomenology associated with the location, but by the phenomenology of the entire visual experience. That is: two experiences can have the same local phenomenology but different local content, due to different global phenomenology. This view leads to a complicated further range of options about perceptual content, on some of which the shadow experience may end up being (imperfectly) veridical. These options end up roughly mirroring the options for the complex view that follows (which also postulates differences in local content, this time associated with differences in local phenomenology), so I will not discuss it further.

The alternative to the simple view is the *complex* view, on which the apparent sameness in color between the shadowed and unshadowed areas is present in some fashion in the visual phenomenology of seeing the floor. On this view, the experience of seeing the partially shadowed floor is phenomenally different from the experience of seeing a partially gray floor under uniform lighting, and the phenomenal difference is present in the visual phenomenology associated with the floor itself (and not merely in the experience of background cues). On this view, the presence or absence of cues makes a difference to the visual experience of the floor itself: one might say that the cues play a pre-experiential role and not just a pre-judgmental role.

This view is naturally associated with a view on which the local phenomenology of color experience is more than three-dimensional. For the sameness is accommodated in visual phenomenology; it is natural to hold that the color contents associated with the shadowed and unshadowed areas are in some respect the same. If local phenomenology were three-dimensional, and if differences in local content go along with differences in local phenomenology (the alternative that rejects this second thesis collapses into the anti-atomistic version of the simple view above), then this sameness in local content entails that the local phenomenology of seeing the shadowed and unshadowed white regions is exactly the same. That claim is not phenomenologically plausible. So the complex view suggests that the local phenomenology of seeing color has more than three relevant dimensions of variation, with correspondingly more dimensions of variation in representational content.

On this view, the shadowed and unshadowed area will be represented as being the same in some respect: intuitively, both will be represented as white. They will also be represented as being different in some respect: intuitively, one will be represented as being in shadow and one will not. And these respects of sameness and difference will both be present in the phenomenology. One can argue that this view is more phenomenologically attractive than the simple view, in allowing phenomenological and representational differences between seeing something as shadowed white and as unshadowed white, on the one hand, and between seeing something as shadowed white and as unshadowed gray, on the other. I am inclined to favor the complex view over the simple view for this reason, although I think that the correct characterization of the phenomenology is far from obvious and neither view is obviously correct or incorrect.

If the complex view is correct, what should we say about the Edenic content of an experience of shadowed white? Phenomenologically, such an experience seems to characterize the intrinsic properties of a surface: if one takes the experience completely at face value, there seems to be an intrinsic (although perhaps temporary) difference between the shadowed and unshadowed parts of the floor. So it is natural to say that the Edenic content of the experience attributes a complex intrinsic property to the floor. One might see this property as the conjunction of two intrinsic properties: roughly, perfect whiteness and perfect shadow. That is, the Edenic content presents the floor as being perfectly white, infused in the relevant areas with a perfect shadow. This conjunctive treatment of perfect shadowed white is not mandatory: one could see the property as a certain mode of perfect white, rather than as a conjunction of perfect white with an independent perfect shadow property. But the conjunctive proposal has a certain phenomenological plausibility, insofar as one can see differently colored areas as subject to the same sort of shadow.

On this view, perfect shadows are things that can come and go in Eden, while the perfect color of an object stays the same. When a perfect shadow is cast on a perfectly white object, the shadow is *on* the object in the sense that it affects the intrinsic nature of the object's surface. Of course there are different sorts of shadows, corresponding to different degrees of shadowing, each of which can come and go while an object's perfect color stays the same. Strictly speaking, it is best to talk of shadow properties instantiated at locations on objects, rather than talking of shadows: while we sometimes have the phenomenology of seeing shadows as objects, it is arguable that more often we do not.

One might worry that this view cannot adequately capture the dimension of sameness between shadowed white and unshadowed gray. There is a clear respect in which these experiences are phenomenally similar, and one might argue that this respect corresponds to a representational similarity: perhaps one could say that the objects of such experience seem the same with respect to superficial color, or something along those lines. The representational claim is not obviously mandatory here, but, if one accepts it, one might elaborate the Edenic model by saying that there is a respect in which any objects with perfect shadowed white and perfect unshadowed gray are similar to each other. One might say that both of these perfect properties entail perfect superficial grayness, for example. This might either be seen as a composite property, or simply as corresponding to another way of carving up the underlying multidimensional space.

What are the imperfect veridicality conditions of such an experience? Presumably an experience as of shadowed white is veridical iff its object has a property that matches perfect shadowed white; or, on the conjunctive treatment of shadowed white, iff it has a property that matches perfect white and a property that matches perfect shadow. The former is plausibly a physical property such as a certain surface reflectance (although see below). As for the latter, it will be a property that normally causes experiences as of the appropriate sort of shadow. It seems that no intrinsic property of surfaces is a good candidate here. Rather, the reasonable candidates are all relational: for example, the property of being subject to the occlusion of a light source to a relevant degree in the relevant area. This is a relational property rather than an intrinsic property, so it does not match the property of perfect shadow as well as it could. But with no intrinsic property being even a candidate, it seems that this property may match well enough. If so, then we can say the experience is imperfectly veridical iff the object has the relevant physical property (imperfect whiteness) and the relevant relational property (imperfect shadow). If it has one but not the other, one can say that the experience is imperfectly veridical in one respect but not the other.

One can extend something like this treatment to other cases of color constancy, and to cases of variation in illumination in general. One might hold that whenever there are relevant cues about illumination, these make a difference to the complex phenomenology of an experience with a corresponding difference in content. If the perceptual system is doing its job, then the object will be represented as having the same color, but it will also be represented as being different in some relevant respect, analogous to the presence or absence of shadows earlier. The difference in phenomenology seems to involve a difference in intrinsic (if temporary) properties, so the associated Edenic properties are intrinsic: one might call them perfect illumination properties (with the recognition that perfect illumination is intrinsic rather than extrinsic). There will plausibly be a complex space of such perfect illumination properties, perhaps a three-dimensional space, and a corresponding space of matching imperfect properties (which may once again be relational properties, such as the property of being illuminated by certain sorts of light). Once we consider color and illumination together, we will plausibly have at least a six-dimensional space of complex Edenic properties in the vicinity, and a corresponding space of imperfect physical/relational properties.

One might wonder about the experience of darkness. What happens in Eden, if darkness falls? I am inclined to say that darkness is in some respects like the experience of shadow, but more all-pervasive. In particular, as darkness falls, darkness seems to pervade the environment, present at every location. The whole space appears to become dark. Objects do not seem to change their colors, exactly, although the representation of their colors may become much less specific, and it eventually becomes absent altogether (as does the representation of objects, in pitch blackness). So it is natural to say: in Eden, when things become dark, perfect darkness is present throughout the relevant volume of space, intrinsically altering that volume, although it need not alter objects' colors. In Eden, when darkness falls, perfect darkness pervades.

What are imperfect colors?

The imperfect colors are the properties that match the perfect colors (in our world), and whose instantiation or non-instantiation makes our color experiences veridical or falsidical. Just which properties are these? So far, I have said that these are the intrinsic physical properties that serve as the normal cause of experiences with the corresponding phenomenal properties. A first approximation suggests that these may be certain surface reflectance properties, or, better, the categorical bases of the relevant surface reflectance dispositions. But there are some tricky issues.

One tricky issue, stressed by Hardin (1987), arises from the fact that there is no such thing as a canonical normal condition for the perception of colors. Instead there is a wide range of normal conditions, including bright sunlight, muted cloudy light, shaded light, and so on. For a given subject, the same object may cause experiences with different phenomenal characters in each of these conditions. So it is not obvious that there will be any specific physical property that can be singled out as the "normal cause" of a given phenomenal character property.[15]

How we handle this issue depends on whether we take the simple view or the complex view of color constancy. On the complex view, as long as the mechanisms of color constancy work reasonably well, then the same object may

---

[15] Hardin (1987) also stresses variations between normal perceivers, as well as variations in normal conditions. Variations between normal perceivers are no problem for the two-stage view, as matching is always relative to a subject, and it is the normal cause for a given subject that determines the Russellian content of a color experience. At worst, this sort of variation has the consequence that the Russellian content of phenomenally identical color experiences in different subjects may represent different physical properties.

cause experiences that are the same in certain key respects, while differing in other key respects. For example, a white object will cause an experience of shadowed white in shadowed conditions, and an experience of unshadowed white in unshadowed conditions. On the complex view in the previous section, the Edenic contents of these experiences attribute the same perfect color property (perfect whiteness) but different perfect illumination properties (perfect shadow and perfect unshadow). We can put this by saying that the experiences have the same phenomenal color property, and different phenomenal illumination properties. On this view, while a given object may trigger experiences with different phenomenal character in different conditions, these experiences will usually attribute the same phenomenal color (though different phenomenal illuminations), associated with the same perfect color property. So, on this view, the wide range of normal conditions is not incompatible with the existence of a reasonably specific property that typically causes experiences with the relevant phenomenal color (that is, experiences that attribute the relevant perfect color) across the range of normal conditions.

If we take the simple view of color constancy, the issue is more difficult. On this view, a white object may cause quite different experiences under bright and shadowed light: let us call them phenomenally white and phenomenally gray experiences. On this view, there is no relevant phenomenal property that is shared by such experiences: any sameness in content enters only at the level of judgment. On this view, a phenomenally gray experience may be caused by a white object in one condition and by a gray object in another condition, where both conditions are equally normal. So it appears that on the simple view there is no fine-grained intrinsic property that can serve as "the normal cause" of a phenomenally gray experience. (A similar issue could arise on the complex view, if it turns out that the mechanisms of color constancy are sufficiently unreliable.) And appealing to dispositional properties will not help, as the fine-grained dispositional properties of a white and a gray object differ as much as their intrinsic properties.

Here there are a number of possible reactions. One could hold that one condition (for example, bright midday sunlight) is singled out as normal. One could hold that the matching imperfect property is not an intrinsic or dispositional property of the object but a (transient) relational property, such as the property of (currently) causing phenomenally gray experiences, or the property of reflecting a certain sort of light, or the disjunction of being white under shadowed light, gray under unshadowed light, and so on. Or one could hold that it turns out empirically that no imperfect property matches perfect grayness, so that the (imperfect) Fregean content of such an experience determines no nontrivial Russellian content in the actual world (it is akin in certain respects to a sentence containing an empty description).

In my view the most plausible line for a proponent of the simple view to take is to hold that the normal cause of phenomenally gray experiences is a disjunctive or coarse-grained intrinsic property: one whose instances include white objects, gray objects, and any objects that cause phenomenally gray objects in some normal condition. On this view, a phenomenally gray experience of any such object will be veridical. This view has the advantage of capturing our intuitions that no such experience in reasonably normal conditions should be privileged over others, and that at least some of these experiences are veridical. The disadvantage of this view is that it suggests that the (imperfect) color properties attributed by color experiences are less fine-grained than one might have thought, and that in particular, a phenomenally gray and a phenomenally white experience do not attribute incompatible (imperfect) properties, even when they occur simultaneously. But on reflection, the consequence does not seem too bad: the incompatibility is still captured at the level of Edenic content, and if one takes the simple view and thinks of shadowed cases, it is reasonably intuitive that phenomenally gray and phenomenally white experiences might be compatible (for example, that both might veridically represent a white floor).[16]

Properties such as imperfect redness will be disjunctive in other respects. Color experience is most often caused by the reflection of light from objects, but it is also caused by the radiation of light from light sources, by the transmission of light from semi-transparent sources, and so on. The relevant cause of phenomenal color experiences in the first case will be something like a surface reflectance (or its categorical basis), but in other cases it will be something like a radiation profile (or its categorical basis). It seems reasonable to hold that color experiences of radiating objects and the like can be just as (imperfectly) veridical as those of reflecting objects. So imperfect redness is best seen as a disjunction of a range of reflectance properties, radiation properties, and other properties that can serve as the relevant basis.

What are colors?

What does this view say about the nature of colors? Philosophers argue about whether colors (such as redness) are best seen as physical properties, dispositional properties, mental properties, primitive properties, or something else. So far I have taken no stand on this matter. What view of colors does the two-stage view suggest?

It is reasonable to hold that much of the issue here is terminological. We can acknowledge a role for properties of each of these sorts. Once we understand the

---

[16] It might be objected that on this view, a phenomenally gray and white "striped" experience of an unstriped floor will be counterintuitively classified as veridical. This could be handled by saying that such an experience represents that the relevant areas are *differently* colored, a sort of relational color property. One could then say that the imperfect relation that best matches the relevant Edenic relation here is that of having different fine-grained surface reflectances, or something along those lines. Then the ordinary content of the experience will require that different fine-grained intrinsic properties are present in the relevant areas, but it will not take a precise stand on which fine-grained properties these are.

precise role that each plays, we understand the substantive issues in the vicinity, whichever of them we choose to call "color." That being said, the terminological issue is not wholly without content. There are certain core roles that we expect colors to play, and different properties are differently suited for the label "color" to the extent that they play more or fewer of these core roles.

On the two-stage view, the natural candidates to be called "colors" are perfect colors and imperfect colors. Both of these can be seen as playing one crucial role associated with colors: they are properties attributed in color experiences. Perfect colors are attributed in Edenic contents, and imperfect colors are attributed in ordinary contents. Perfect colors play certain further core roles that imperfect colors do not: we seem to be acquainted with their intrinsic nature in color experience, and the perfect colors arguably stand in relevant intrinsic structural relations to each other in a way that imperfect colors do not.

Still, perhaps the core role of colors is that they are the properties whose instantiation is relevant to the truth of ordinary color attributions. That is, an utterance of "that apple is red" will be true if and only if the apple instantiates redness. Furthermore, it is natural to hold that some apples really are red. The two-stage view is partly driven by the thesis that some ordinary color experiences are veridical (even if they are not perfectly veridical). It seems equally reasonable to hold that apples really are red (even if they are not perfectly red). If so, this suggests that redness is not perfect redness but imperfect redness.

So I am inclined to say that color terms, in their ordinary uses, designate imperfect color properties. Just which properties these are depends on how matching is understood, and to the extent that matching is somewhat indeterminate, the designation of color terms may be somewhat indeterminate. But I am inclined to think that our ordinary uses of color terms designate certain disjunctive physical properties, with properties such as surface reflectance properties among the disjuncts. The physical properties designated by ordinary color terms will be relatively coarse-grained, but there will be more fine-grained physical properties in the vicinity, which we might regard as the different shades of these colors.[17]

Of course, one can also reasonably use color terms to refer to Edenic properties ("perfect redness"), phenomenal properties ("phenomenal redness"), and

[17] If an advocate of the simple view of color constancy takes the line I suggested, on which experiences with specific phenomenal shades attribute relatively coarse-grained physical properties, then we will have three relevant sorts of physical properties. There will be highly coarse-grained properties (with some indeterminacy at the edges) that are the referents of terms such as "red"; there will be somewhat coarse-grained properties that are attributed by specific color experiences; and there will be fine-grained physical properties of which these coarse-grained properties can be seen as ranges or disjunctions. Probably the fine-grained properties are the best candidates to be called the "shades." The main costs are that we lose a tight correspondence between physical shades and phenomenal shades, and that there will not turn out to be a specific physical shade that qualifies as "unique red" (though there may still be unique phenomenal red, and unique perfect red). If we take the complex view of color constancy (and if the mechanisms of color constancy are sufficiently reliable), then these problems are avoided.

maybe to other properties as well. On this view, there are multiply interlocked families of properties: the perfect colors, the imperfect colors, possibly further families of imperfect colors associated with different notions of matching, and the phenomenal colors. As long as we understand the complex relationships between these families, and the roles that each can play, not much of real substance rests on the question which of these families is the true family of colors.

There is nothing especially original or distinctive about the view of the ontology of color that emerges from the two-stage view. In identifying colors (in the core sense) with physical properties, the resulting ontology of colors may be very similar to that of the physicalist about color. And the various families of color properties that are introduced may also be acknowledged by the primitivist. Although primitivists about color identify perfect color properties with the colors, they may also recognize that physical and dispositional properties play some of the roles of the colors. For example, Maund (1995) says that terms such as "red" refer in their core sense to the perfect colors (which he calls "virtual colors"), but also refer in an extended or metonymic sense to the physical properties that I have called imperfect colors. So the ontology recognized by this sort of primitivist view is not dissimilar to that recognized by the two-stage view.

What is distinctive about the two-stage view is not its associated ontology of colors but rather, its view of perceptual content. On the primitivist view, experiences have a single content (an Edenic content) that determines their veridicality. On the two-stage view, experiences have two layers of content, an Edenic content that reflects their phenomenology and a Fregean content that determines their veridicality. It is this two-layered view of content that is responsible for most of the explanatory power of the two-stage view.

Is this indirect realism?

One might worry that this view is a form of indirect realism about color perception. According to standard indirect realism, we perceive objects in the world only indirectly, by virtue of directly perceiving certain intermediate objects such as sense-data, which opponents see as a "veil of perception" that cuts off perceivers from the external world. The two-stage view I have outlined is certainly not a variety of standard indirect realism, as it does not invoke any intermediate objects as objects of perception. But one might worry that it is a form of indirect realism about the perception of *properties*. In particular, one might suggest that this is a view on which instantiated color properties (that is, imperfect color properties) are perceived only indirectly, by virtue of directly perceiving perfect color properties.

This objection invokes the relation of *perception* between subjects and properties. This relation is analogous to the relation of perception between subjects and objects: it is natural to say that when I veridically perceive a green square in the environment, I both perceive the square and perceive its greenness. So far in this paper, I have focused on the relation of perceptual representation, but not on the relation of perception. These seem to be different relations: one can perceptually represent an object or a property without perceiving it (in a hallucination, for example).

The standard view of the perceptual relation between subjects and objects holds that it is a *causal* relation: to perceive an object is roughly to have a perceptual experience that is appropriately caused by the object (and perhaps that has a phenomenal character that is appropriately related to the character of the object). The standard view of the perceptual relation between subjects and properties is presumably something similar: to perceive a property is roughly to have a perceptual experience whose phenomenal character is appropriately causally related to an instance of that property (and perhaps whose phenomenal character represents the instantiation of the property, or otherwise "matches" the property in some fashion).

If we adopt this standard view of the perceptual relation, there is no threat of indirect realism. In a typical veridical experience of a green object, the phenomenal character of my experience is causally related to the relevant instance of physical greenness, and represents the instantiation of physical greenness in its Russellian content. By contrast, the phenomenal character of my experience is not causally related to any instance of perfect greenness, as there are no such instances. So it seems that on the two-stage view, as much as on other views of perceptual experience, we perceive imperfect colors directly, and not by virtue of perceiving any other property.

It is true that on the two-stage view, perception is not as "direct" as perception could be. There is a sense in which perception in Eden is more direct than it is in our non-Edenic world. In Eden, perception works by direct acquaintance, and there need be no mediation between objects and properties perceived and a perceptual experience. In our world, there is complex causal mediation. This does not entail that our perception is *perceptually* mediated, though, as on the indirect realist view.

We might say that in Eden, an especially strong perceptual relation obtains, one that we might call *perfect perception*. Perfect perception of an object or property requires unmediated acquaintance with the object or the property, and perhaps also requires that the object or the property is itself a constituent of one's perceptual experience. By contrast, *imperfect perception* requires only the appropriate sort of causal connection to an object or a property. As before, it is plausible to suggest that if we took the deliverances of both perception and introspection fully at face value, we would conclude that we live in an Edenic world in which we perfectly perceive objects and properties in that world. But after the fall from Eden, there is no perfect perception; there is just imperfect perception.

We might call this view not *indirect realism* but *imperfect realism*. Our acquaintance with the world is not as direct as it would be in Eden, and perception does not reveal the intrinsic nature of things in the way that it does in Eden. But this is so for any causal theory of perception. Perception on the view I have outlined is no more and no less imperfect than on most causal theories. The idea of Eden just brings out the contrast, for all these theories, with the kind of perfect perception that we cannot have in our non-Edenic world. One might yearn for the kind of perfect contact with the world that we had in Eden, but after the fall, we have learned to live with the imperfection of perception.

11 MATCHING AND FREGEAN CONTENT

What is matching?

The notion of matching serves as the bridge between Edenic content and ordinary content. An experience is imperfectly veridical when its object has properties that match the perfect properties attributed by the experience. But what is it for a property to match a perfect property? To a first approximation, we can say that a property matches a given perfect property (for a given subject) if the property is the normal cause of the associated phenomenal property (in that subject). But this is clearly just a first approximation.

A basic constraint is that at most one imperfect property can match a given perfect property. Or at least, at most one imperfect property can match a perfect property for a subject at a time. Different imperfect properties can match the same perfect properties for different subjects, and probably for the same subject at widely separated times. (Strictly speaking, we should say that matching is a three- or four-place relation involving subjects and times, but I will usually leave the subject and the time in the background.) But we need at most one matching property for a subject at a time, in order that the ordinary Russellian content of an experience can attribute a property to its object. Of course it could be, for all we have said, that matching imperfect properties are often disjunctive properties, or determinable properties with many different determinates. And it may be that sometimes there is no imperfect property that matches a given perfect property.

Matching is best understood as a holistic relation. Rather than saying that imperfect redness is the property that normally causes phenomenal redness, one can say that the set of imperfect color properties is that three-dimensional manifold of properties that serves as the normal causal basis for the associated three-dimensional manifold of phenomenal color properties. This requires that there is a mapping from imperfect properties to phenomenal properties such that in many or most cases a given imperfect property will normally cause the associated phenomenal property, but this relation need not hold in all cases. If there are exceptions associated with certain imperfect properties in the manifold (such as Kripke's "killer yellow", a shade of yellow that always kills the perceiver if observed; or perhaps a Humean missing shade of blue that is never instantiated in our world for a lawful reason), this will not stop the manifold as a whole from matching, and the imperfect property will still be associated with a corresponding phenomenal property. When this mapping associates an imperfect property with a phenomenal property that attributes a given perfect property, we can say that the imperfect property matches the perfect property.

It will be clear that the notion of matching is a vague and messy one. One source of messiness arises from the issue discussed above: there is no precise delineation of the class of normal conditions. Even if there were such a delineation, there is no precise criterion for when a property causes an experience often enough in these conditions to count as its normal cause. Further, there is more to matching than normally causing an associated phenomenal property. We have seen that there are structural constraints, such as the constraint that imperfect color properties fall into the same sort of three-dimensional manifold as perfect color properties. There are also categorical constraints, such as the constraint that imperfect color properties be intrinsic properties if possible. And it is presumably desirable that (imperfect) color properties be properties that can stand in the sort of relations to (imperfect) spatial properties that perfect color properties stand in to perfect spatial properties.

One could attempt to encapsulate all these constraints and others in a full and precise definition of matching, but I am not optimistic about the prospects for such a definition, any more than I am for definitions of other philosophically important notions such as perception and knowledge. An alternative approach is simply to say: matching is that relation M such that, necessarily, an experience is imperfectly veridical iff its objects have properties that bear M to the properties attributed by its Edenic content. In effect, this notion exploits our relatively pretheoretical grip on imperfect veridicality, along with an independently grounded notion of Edenic content (explained in terms of perfect veridicality, say), to explicate the notion of matching.

Of course this explication does not say anything substantive about what matching involves. For a substantive characterization, one has to rely on our judgments about the (imperfect) veridicality and falsidicality of experiences. We do have such judgments, quite clear judgments in many cases. And it is plausible that we judge experiences to be veridical precisely when objects in the world instantiate certain properties, properties that correspond in some fashion to the perfect properties in the Edenic content of our experiences. Even if we cannot give a full account antecedently of what this correspondence consists of, there is good reason to believe that it is present, and one can say quite a lot about what it involves in specific cases, as we have done above. For example, it usually seems to require normal causation of an associated phenomenal property, and there are other constraints as suggested by various cases. As in the case of analyzing knowledge, there will probably be no straightforward articulation of necessary and sufficient constraints, but nevertheless the consideration of cases can help us to flesh out the constraints in the vicinity.

One might worry that this characterization taken together with the two-stage view will be circular. The two-stage view says that an experience is imperfectly veridical iff its objects have properties that match the relevant perfect properties. The characterization above says that matching is that relation M such that an experience is imperfectly veridical iff its objects have properties that bear M to the relevant perfect properties. There is no circularity, however. In the project of explication, we have a prior grip on the notion of imperfect veridicality, and we use this prior grip in order to explicate the notion of matching. Via this explication, we theoretically characterize a relation M. One can then use relation M for certain theoretical purposes, if one likes. At the very least, we can appeal to it in analyzing the relationship between imperfect and perfect conditions of veridicality. One might go further and hold that, metaphysically, for an experience to be imperfectly veridical is for its objects to bear M to the relevant perfect properties. Or one might hold that epistemically, our intuitive judgments about imperfect veridicality are mediated by a tacit prior grasp of M. I am cautious about making such further claims here, although I think there is something to them. But in any case, there is no more circularity here than in any other case where one uses a pretheoretical notion to help characterize a theoretical notion, which one then may use to help give a theoretical account of the pretheoretical notion.

Of course our judgments about (imperfect) veridicality are not always clear. There are many cases in which we are not sure what to say, or in which we are tugged in two different directions. Sometimes these judgments are cleared up on a certain amount of rational reflection, but sometimes they are not. When they cannot be cleared up in this way, the natural thing to say is that the relevant case is a vague case of imperfect veridicality. The vagueness of imperfect veridicality will give rise to a corresponding vagueness of matching: it will be vague whether the object in question instantiates a property that matches the relevant perfect property. There may be different ways of precisifying the notion of imperfect veridicality, which will give rise to corresponding precisifications of the notion of matching. But some vagueness and messiness in the notion of matching is just what we should expect, given the vagueness and messiness of imperfect veridicality.

Is Fregean content phenomenologically adequate?

Although the two-stage view has a clearer grounding in phenomenological structure than the original Fregean view, one might still worry about its phenomenological adequacy. The Edenic content of an experience (in which the two-stage content is grounded) seems to nicely mirror the structure of the phenomenology. But the imperfect Fregean content does not. In particular, there is nothing discernible in the phenomenology of visual experience that obviously corresponds to matching. Certainly, it is hard to see that there is any clear phenomenology of "normal causation" in a typical visual experience. And to the extent that matching is messier and more complex than a notion based on normal causation, it seems all the more distant from the phenomenology. For example, we have seen that matching can often be vague, as can the associated Fregean content. But the phenomenology itself need not be vague; or, if it is vague in some respects, it need not be vague in relevant respects. For example, it is plausibly vague in some cases whether an object has a property that matches perfect redness. But the associated phenomenally red experience may be quite precise, with the phenomenology of precisely presenting a specific property of the object. So one may ask, as we did before, whether this Fregean view is phenomenologically adequate.

Here, I think, one should concede that matching does not correspond directly to any element of the visual phenomenology. The phenomenology of visual experience is the same in our world and in Eden. The presentation of an Edenic world does not (or need not) involve attribution of normal causation and the like. So the phenomenology of ordinary visual experience does not (or need not) involve this either. Perhaps there are some experiences that present causal and dispositional relations, but it seems wrong to say that every ordinary color experience does this.

Where does matching come from, then? I think the answer is clear: it comes from the *inferential role* of visual experience. The content of a mental state need not be something that one can read off the intrinsic properties of its vehicles. There is good reason to believe that quite generally, mental content is tied to inferential role. This is especially so in the case of Fregean content, which was introduced by Frege to mirror the cognitive and inferential significance of thought and language. A belief that "Hesperus is Phosphorus" has a very different inferential role from a belief that "Hesperus is Hesperus," and this difference in inferential role is reflected in a difference in their inferential content. It is even possible to define the Fregean conditions of satisfaction of a belief partly in terms of the belief's inferential role, such as the conditions under which a subject will rationally accept or reject the belief, given information about the world (see Chalmers 2002a for such an account).

Beliefs are not the only mental states that have inferential roles. Perceptual experiences also have an inferential role, broadly understood. Just as one belief can serve as grounds for accepting or rejecting another belief, a perceptual experience can likewise serve as grounds for accepting or rejecting beliefs, and more generally for guiding our knowledge about the world. Most obviously, one can *endorse* a perceptual experience, yielding a perceptual belief about the character of one's environment, and that belief can be used to accept or reject other beliefs in turn. For example, when one has a phenomenally red experience as of an object in one's environment, this can be used as grounds for accepting a belief that there is a red object in front of one. One would not normally call this relation between experience and belief an "inference," but it can be seen as a sort of quasi-inferential relation.

Just as with belief, the inferential role of a perceptual experience can be analyzed in part by asking: when given information about how things are in the world, will a subject accept or reject the perceptual experience? That is, will they accept or reject the belief that things are as they perceptually seem to be? If one takes an example, such as a subject having a phenomenally red experience as of an object in front of them, one finds a specific pattern of judgments. If the subject discovers that there is really no object in front of her, she will reject the experience: things are not as they seem. If she discovers that there is an object in front of her but it has the sort of physical make-up that usually causes phenomenally green experiences (only causing phenomenally red experiences this time due to unusual lighting), then she will reject the experience: again, things are not as they seem. But if she discovers that the object in front of her has the sort of make-up that usually causes phenomenally red experiences, then she will accept the experience: at least in the relevant respect, things are as they seem.

In effect, the core inferential role of a perceptual experience is reflected in the pattern of judgments about veridicality and nonveridicality that the subject of such an experience makes, or, more strictly, in the pattern of judgments that they should rationally make. And we have already seen that this pattern of judgments closely corresponds to the Fregean content above. The pattern of judgments does not require that objects in the environment have any specific property, such as a surface reflectance, or even perfect redness. It requires only that the property be the property that plays the appropriate causal role. So as in the case of beliefs, this Fregean content closely mirrors the experience's inferential role.[18]

Here, we can respond to the charge of phenomenological adequacy by rejecting the claim that phenomenal content must precisely mirror phenomenological structure. Phenomenal content can equally be grounded in inferential role.

Of course, a proponent of the original Fregean view could have made the same response (as I did in response to a similar worry in Chalmers 2004a). So how is the two-stage view any better in this respect? To see the difference, recall where things stood at the end of section 5. It was not clear that the objections from phenomenological adequacy had any knockdown force, but they raised the issue of a serious explanatory incompleteness in the Fregean view. Fregean content is supposed to be a sort of phenomenal content, such that, necessarily, an experience with the same phenomenology has the same Fregean content. But the presentational phenomenology of visual experience does not simply wear its Fregean content on its sleeve. So there needs to be some explanatory story

---

[18] If someone is doubtful that experiences have Fregean content (perhaps holding that there is only Edenic phenomenal content and ordinary Russellian nonphenomenal content), it is this pattern of judgments about veridicality, and the corresponding inferential role, that gives the best reason to believe in it. There is no question that experiences are associated with this sort of pattern of judgments of veridicality, and there is no obstacle to our using this pattern to ground a notion of experiential content.

about how Fregean content is related to the phenomenology of the experience, and why it is that any experience with that phenomenology will have this Fregean content.

It is this explanatory story that the two-stage view provides. The presentational phenomenology of an experience immediately grounds an Edenic content. The Fregean content is grounded in the Edenic content by virtue of inferential role. The subject is immediately presented, in visual phenomenology, with an Edenic world. But a rational subject need not hold the world to an Edenic standard. In effect, a rational subject will use the Edenic phenomenology of a phenomenally red experience to ground the claim that the object in front of them is *red*, but she need not make strong claims about the intrinsic nature of redness. That is left open: if the subject discovers that objects with property P typically cause red experiences, then she will decide that those objects are red, and that if the original object has property P, then the original experience was veridical. In effect, the presentational phenomenology of the experience serves as direct ground for the first stage of the two-stage view (the Edenic content), and as indirect ground for the second stage (matching the Edenic content) by virtue of inferential role.

Is Fregean content phenomenal content?

Once we observe that ordinary Fregean content derives from inferential role, this may raise another worry: is Fregean content really *phenomenal* content? The mere fact that Fregean content does not completely mirror phenomenological structure here is no objection, as the definition of phenomenal content does not require this sort of mirroring. However, the definition does require that any experience with the same phenomenology has the same phenomenal content. And one may worry: if inferential role is extrinsic to phenomenology, could not two phenomenally identical experiences have different inferential roles, yielding distinct Fregean contents?

Of course, there is an obvious sense in which phenomenally identical experiences can have different inferential roles. For example, if I believe that red snakes are poisonous and you do not, then relevantly similar visual experiences in the two of us might produce quite different beliefs. But this difference in inferential role need not be a difference in the core aspect of inferential role that is relevant to defining Fregean content. This core aspect involves the subject's pattern of judgments of veridicality and nonveridicality associated with the experience. More precisely, it turns on whether the subject should rationally accept or reject the experience (that is, judge that things are or are not as they perceptually seem to be) when given relevantly complete information about the world. Two subjects may have the same pattern of judgments here despite different beliefs. For example, in the case above, both subjects may well have the same rational dispositions to accept or reject the experience, given full information.

Fregean content will be phenomenal content as long as the same experience rationalizes the same pattern of judgments, given relevant information, in all subjects. (Of course there may be differences in an associated *actual* pattern of judgments due to cognitive limitations, but a rational inferential role idealizes away from such limitations.) This will be the case as long as: (i) every phenomenally identical experience has the same Edenic content; (ii) every subject should rationally accept an experience, given relevant information, iff (according to that information) the relevant object has properties that match the properties attributed in the Edenic content; and (iii) the matching relation is the same for all subjects.

I think there is good reason to accept (i) and (ii). We have already seen that Edenic content is a sort of phenomenal content. I think, further, that the match-involving inferential role is rational for any subject with a perceptual experience. Such an experience presents a world with a certain distribution of Edenic properties, and rational judgments of veridicality should go with whether objects in the world have properties that match those properties. What is not so clear is whether one should accept (iii). We have already seen that the notion of matching is somewhat vague and imprecise. Could there not be subjects whose equally rational judgments invoke somewhat different matching relations, perhaps held to somewhat different standards in each case?

For example, one might suggest that before the fall from Eden, the inferential role of our experiences required a strict standard of matching. Perhaps an Edenic subject would judge an experience falsidical if they discovered that its object merely has an imperfect property that serves as its normal cause. However, there is good reason to hold that even our Edenic counterparts have dispositions such that *if* they were to discover that their world is non-Edenic, they would still judge their experiences to be (imperfectly) veridical when their objects have the relevant imperfect properties. After all, when we discovered that our world was non-Edenic, these were the judgments that we made. So there is reason to believe that Fregean inferential role is present even in Eden.

Still, one can ask whether there *could* be a rational subject (whether in Eden or outside) who has such a strict standard of matching that they will accept a phenomenally red experience only if the relevant object is perfectly red? If such a subject discovers that the world is non-Edenic, they will reject all their color experiences as falsidical. For such a subject, the relevant standard of matching would be the strict standard of identity: a property matches perfect redness iff it is perfect redness. Certainly there could be a subject that has an actual pattern of judgments like this. The relevant question is, could this pattern of judgments be as rational as the pattern of judgments that we have been discussing? The answer is not obvious.

Likewise, we can imagine subjects who make different judgments in difficult cases. For example, let us assume the simple view of color constancy. Then one subject might judge a phenomenally red experience to be veridical iff the relevant object has the property that causes such experiences in bright sunlight. Another subject might judge such an experience to be veridical iff the relevant object has any property in the range that might cause the experience in some normal condition. And another subject might judge that no such experience is veridical as there is no single specific property that plays the right role. The question then is: could these patterns of judgment be equally rational?

Finally, we can consider a possible difference between visual and olfactory experience. We do not usually judge olfactory experiences to be veridical or falsidical. We do not say that a rotten egg smell is veridical iff there is sulphur dioxide nearby and falsidical iff there is not, for example. This is not because the phenomenology of smell is not representational: intuitively, it seems to represent that certain smells are present in the world. It is just that we are not inclined to make judgments of veridicality and falsidicality; at best, we make judgments of misleadingness or otherwise. On the other hand, perhaps there could be subjects who make judgments of veridicality or falsidicality for phenomenally identical olfactory experiences. For example, one can imagine that if dogs could make judgments, this is what they would do! One could diagnose this by saying that for those subjects, but not for us, there are properties in the environment that match perfect smells. The question is: are both patterns of judgment equally rational?

It is possible to say no in all these cases. One might hold that one pattern of judgments in these cases is rational and that the others are not. For example, one could argue that in the first case there is some irrationality in holding the world to an Edenic standard, and that in the second case it is irrational to reject a color experience when its object has a property that normally causes that sort of experience.

One could also hold that in at least some of these cases, insofar as it is possible for corresponding experiences to rationalize different patterns of judgment, there will be a corresponding difference in the phenomenology. For example, in the third case above, one could suggest that the phenomenology of olfactory experience in dogs and humans differs: perhaps dogs have a more strongly presentational phenomenology of smell, for example. More generally, one might hold that certain differences in the character of presentational phenomenology might go along with differences in the associated standard of matching. In such cases, the existence of different rationalized patterns of judgment will be no obstacle to Fregean content serving as a sort of phenomenal content.

My own view is that it is not obvious that phenomenology underdetermines the standard of matching, but it is not obvious that it does not. Whether it does or not depends on difficult questions about the rational role of perception, and also about its presentational phenomenology, that I cannot adjudicate here. But I think that it is at least a live possibility that the standard of matching is underdetermined, and that there could be distinct equally rational patterns of judgment associated with the same sort of experience in different subjects.

If this is so, then what follows? One could say that the phenomenally identical experiences have distinct Fregean contents (in which case Fregean content is not phenomenal content), or one could say that they have the same highly indeterminate Fregean content (in which case imperfect veridicality is highly indeterminate). But I think that the best thing to say in this event is that these experiences have the same *unsaturated* Fregean content. This content is one that is satisfied iff the relevant object has properties that match the relevant primitive properties. However, the standard of matching is left unspecified by this unsaturated content, so the condition of satisfaction is in a certain sense incomplete. To yield a complete condition of satisfaction, the unsaturated content needs to be saturated by specifying a standard of matching. The resulting saturated Fregean content will yield a reasonably determinate condition of imperfect veridicality.

On this view, only unsaturated Fregean content, and not saturated Fregean content, will be phenomenal content.[19] This is a step back from the original view of Fregean content as phenomenal content, as an unsaturated Fregean content is not a complete condition of satisfaction. That is, it is not the sort of thing that is true or false absolutely in a scenario. Correspondingly, the unsaturated Fregean content of an experience does not determine whether or not the experience is imperfectly veridical in its environment. What determines imperfect veridicality is a saturated Fregean content, which is not fully determined by phenomenal character.

What determines saturated Fregean content, if not phenomenology? One natural answer is inferential role, here conceived as something that might vary independently of phenomenology. In the different subjects above, phenomenally identical experiences play different inferential roles, yielding different saturated Fregean contents. In effect, the different inferential roles in different subjects (as reflected in a pattern of veridicality judgments) determine different standards of matching. In this way phenomenology and inferential role together determine a saturated Fregean content, and a condition of imperfect veridicality.

An alternative suggestion is that saturated Fregean content is determined not by inferential role but by a *standard of assessment* that is extrinsic to the subject. On this view, in effect, one could evaluate the same experience as either veridical or nonveridical at different standards of assessment. We have already introduced dual standards of perfect and imperfect veridicality; on this view, there will be a

---

[19] Gideon Rosen suggested that for our counterparts on Psychedelic Earth, where experiences drift in a way that is completely unrelated to the environment (and where subjects know this), the experiences will have no inferential role at all, and so will not even have unsaturated Fregean content. However, it seems that if these subjects were to discover that the environment contains drifting properties that match the drifting experiences, they would then judge their experiences to be veridical. (It is precisely because they have discovered that there is no such match with the environment that they reject their experiences as a guide to the external world.) So it seems that these subjects still have the inferential disposition to endorse their experiences if they discover that the matching relation obtains. If so, this suggests that their experiences have Fregean content.

range of different standards in the vicinity of imperfect veridicality. This range of standards will correspond to a range of different standards of matching. To evaluate an experience with an unsaturated Fregean content, we must tacitly introduce a standard of matching. This standard will determine a saturated Fregean content, and according to this standard the experience will qualify as veridical or falsidical.

One can then say: our ordinary notion of veridicality tacitly invokes a certain standard of matching, one that is reasonably although not completely determinate. With this standard fixed, phenomenally identical experiences will have the same saturated Fregean contents. However, there might have been different evaluators with a slightly different notion of veridicality, corresponding to a different standard of matching. With that standard fixed, phenomenally identical experiences will also have the same saturated Fregean contents. But these contents will differ from those associated with our standard. One might say that, on this view, any given experience is associated with a whole range of (saturated) Fregean contents, depending on the corresponding notion of veridicality. Each of these Fregean contents could be seen as a sort of phenomenal content.

The two suggestions—according to which saturated content is determined by inferential role or by an external standard—yield somewhat different treatment of cases. Take a subject whose inferential role holds her experiences to the Edenic standard: upon discovering that the world is non-Edenic, she rationally rejects her perceptual experiences. On the former view, we will say that her experience is falsidical: it is her own rational inferential role that determines ordinary veridicality. On the latter view, we will say that her experience is veridical: it is our standards that determine the veridicality of an experience (according to the meaning of our term "veridical"). However, if she or someone sharing a similar standard were to say that her experience is "nonveridical," they would also be correct: they express a slightly different notion of satisfaction with their terms "veridical" and "nonveridical." On reflection I find the second suggestion somewhat more plausible and intuitive than the first, although the matter is far from obvious.

In any case, whichever view we take, one can say the following. The phenomenal character of an experience determines an Edenic phenomenal content, and it determines an unsaturated Fregean phenomenal content. According to the unsaturated phenomenal content, an experience is veridical iff the relevant object has properties that match the relevant Edenic properties. Once combined with a standard of matching, this unsaturated content determines a saturated Fregean content. This saturated Fregean content may or may not be phenomenal content, depending on what view one takes on the questions above. If one thinks that there is only one rational standard of matching associated with the phenomenal character of the experience, then the saturated Fregean content will be a phenomenal content. If one thinks that the associated standard of matching depends on a contingently associated inferential role in the subject, then the saturated Fregean content will not be a phenomenal content. If one thinks that the standard of matching is determined by an external standard of assessment, then the Fregean content will be a phenomenal content, but there will be a range of other Fregean contents associated with different standards of veridicality.

The choice between these three alternatives turns on difficult and subtle issues that I will not try to resolve here. But, in any case, we can be confident that phenomenal character determines Edenic content and unsaturated Fregean content. The status of saturated Fregean content as phenomenal content remains an open question.

12 BEYOND COLOR

I have concentrated on the content of color experience, but I think the two-stage model has much broader application. Here I will much more briefly discuss the extension to other aspects of perceptual experience.

Spatial experience

Apart from colors, the most salient properties attributed in visual experience are spatial properties. Does the two-stage model of phenomenal content generalize to these? I am inclined to think that it does.

One might think that spatial experience is more amenable to a straightforward Russellian treatment than color experience. But as Thompson (forthcoming) has argued, many of the same problems arise. A natural candidate for the Russellian content of spatial experiences involves the attribution of spatial properties such as that of being in a certain (absolute) location. But this content obviously cannot be phenomenal content, as a phenomenally identical experience could be had by a subject light-years away from that location. A natural next suggestion is a Russellian content involving the attribution of relative spatial properties (or relations, or relational property radicals) such as being 6 feet in front of the perceiver. But this cannot be phenomenal content either. In principle, a phenomenally identical experience could be had by a perceiver who is (and has always been) twice as big, in an environment where everything is twice as distant. Such an experience would not plausibly attribute the same relative spatial property; it would more plausibly attribute the relative property of being 12 feet away.

One might then move to more relativized spatial properties, such as the property of being twice as distant or twice as big as some other object. Or one might suggest that phenomenal content can at least attribute shape properties, such as being square or circular. But, as Thompson argues, similar problems arise. There could conceivably be an "El Greco" world in which everything is stretched ten times in one direction compared with our world, but in which structure and dynamics are otherwise isomorphic. In such an environment, phenomenally square experiences would normally be caused by (what we call) long and thin rectangles. Further, there is good reason to think that such experiences would be veridical: certainly, if we found that we inhabit a corner of the universe that is locally stretched in this fashion relative to the rest of the universe, we would not conclude that our spatial experiences are falsidical. Rather, the natural thing to say is that phenomenally square experiences attribute different properties in these environments: (what we call) squareness in one environment, and a certain sort of rectangularity in another.

A more extreme case along these lines is given by a Matrix scenario, in which phenomenally identical subjects have been hooked up for their lifetime to a computer simulation of the world. I have argued elsewhere (Chalmers 2003b) that such subjects are not massively deluded about the world. Their beliefs such as "there are tables," "I have hands," and "that is square" are true; it is just that the underlying metaphysics of their environment is not what they expect (in effect, it is an underlying computational metaphysics). The same can be argued for their perceptual experiences: their experiences as of red square objects are as veridical as ours. However, such experiences need not be of (what we would call) square objects: there need be nothing square inside the computer. At best, there are objects with some very different property: we might call this "virtual squareness." In any case, if phenomenally identical spatial experiences can be veridical in an environment that is spatially utterly unlike our own, this suggests that the phenomenal content of these experiences does not involve the attribution of ordinary spatial properties.

In this way, one can argue against Russellian views of spatial phenomenal content in ways that directly parallel our earlier arguments in the case of color experience. The natural alternative is a Fregean view of spatial phenomenal content. On this view, spatial experiences have Russellian content, attributing spatial properties and relations, but this content is not phenomenal content. Rather, phenomenal content involves a Fregean mode of presentation of spatial properties and relations: roughly, these are determined as that manifold of properties and relations that serves as the normal causal basis for the corresponding manifold of spatial experiences. On this view, the Fregean content of a spatial experience is one that will be satisfied if the object has a property that normally causes the relevant sort of spatial experience (or if it has a complex of properties each of which normally causes the relevant sort of spatial aspect of the experience). One can then raise worries about the phenomenological adequacy of this view, motivating a two-stage view of spatial phenomenal content.

On the two-stage view, spatial experiences have an Edenic content that attributes perfect spatial properties: perfect squareness, perfect rectangularity, and so on. Arguably, even an Edenic content does not attribute absolute spatial properties, but just relative properties. It is not clear that we have the phenomenology of being presented with absolute spatial properties, and one can make a case that even in Eden, there could be phenomenally identical veridical experiences at different locations. But we do have the phenomenology of being presented at least with absolute shapes, and relative distances. So the Edenic contents of our experience will attribute perfect properties of this sort. It is plausible that these properties are not instantiated in our world (though arguing this takes a bit more work than in the case of color). If not, then our experiences are not perfectly veridical.

Our spatial experiences may nevertheless be imperfectly veridical, by virtue of their objects instantiating imperfect spatial properties: those that match perfect spatial properties. These will be the properties that serve as the normal causal basis for our spatial experiences. Imperfect veridicality will be associated with a corresponding ordinary Fregean content, one that is satisfied iff relevant objects have properties that match the relevant perfect spatial properties. Phenomenally identical experiences will have the same Edenic contents, and the same ordinary Fregean contents (setting aside issues about standards of matching), but may have different ordinary Russellian contents, because different properties may match the relevant perfect properties in different environments.

The Matrix provides a good illustration. The subjects here do not have perfectly veridical experiences, but they have imperfectly veridical experiences, by virtue of the fact that relevant matching properties (virtual squareness and the like) are instantiated in their environment. So subjects in the Matrix may share Edenic spatial contents with us, and may share ordinary Fregean contents also, but they will have different ordinary Russellian contents.

Of course the two-stage model of spatial experience needs to be elaborated in numerous respects to handle all sorts of aspects of spatial content: for example, perspective, angle, size constancy, mirror reflections, and the like. But there is reason to think it can help explain certain phenomena. For example, it is better suited than the original Fregean view to accommodate internal connections between spatial representation in visual and tactile experience. On the original Fregean view, it might seem that there can be no internal connection, as the normal causes of visual spatial experience are not constrained to be the normal causes of tactile spatial experience. On the two-stage model, however, one can argue that the phenomenology entails that tactile and spatial experiences involve the attribution of common perfect spatial properties in their Edenic content. If so, then the matching imperfect properties will be constrained to be the same, thus grounding an internal connection between tactile and spatial experience.

It is a further question how this model should be extended to the representation of time and motion. I am inclined to say that the two-stage model can be extended to time as well as to space, though this turns on subtle issues about the metaphysics of time. A natural suggestion is that the Edenic content of temporal experience requires A-theoretic time, with some sort of true flow or passage. Our own universe may not instantiate these perfect temporal properties, but it may nevertheless instantiate matching B-theoretic properties (involving relative location in a four-dimensional "block universe") that are sufficient to make our temporal experiences imperfectly veridical, if not perfectly veridical. The representation of motion could be treated in a similar way.

One might go so far as to suggest that Eden is a world with classical Euclidean space, and an independent dimension of time, in which there is true passage and true change. Our own world is non-Euclidean, with time and space interdependent, and with pale shadows of perfect passage and change. On this view, Einstein's theory of spacetime was one more bite from the Tree of Science, and one more step in our fall from Eden.

The experience of objects

Our initial characterization of the Russellian contents of visual experience characterized them as having the following form: object O has color C at location L. In the case of color and location I have argued that this Russellian content is not phenomenal content, and have proposed a two-stage Fregean treatment instead. In the case of color, we have seen that the relevant Russellian content is also not plausibly phenomenal content. Does this mean that we should also give a two-stage Fregean treatment of the representation of objects?

A natural first suggestion is that experiences of objects have an Edenic content involving the representation of certain specific perfect objects: for example, perfect object O has perfect color C at perfect location L. However, this suggestion is implausible on reflection. In particular, it is implausible that the perfect veridicality of an experience of an object requires any particular Edenic object to be present. It seems that even in Eden, there could be two phenomenally identical experiences of different objects. The phenomenology of object experience seems to present us directly with objects, but it does not seem to acquaint us with their intrinsic nature in a sense over and above acquainting us with their colors, shapes, and so on. If it did, then the phenomenology of object experience would be quite different from what it is: experiences of different tennis balls would typically have quite different phenomenal characters, for example. But the experience of objects does not seem to be this way.[20]

Because of this, it is more natural to hold that even the Edenic content of object experience is existential. For example, one might hold that the Edenic content of an experience of a red sphere is satisfied iff there is a perfect sphere at the relevant location that is perfectly red. No specific object is required for the satisfaction of this content. On this view, Edenic content is not especially

---

[20] As in note 1, a disjunctivist view about phenomenology may hold that the phenomenology of experiences of different objects differs in precisely this way. Such a disjunctivist view might hold that the Edenic content (and perhaps the non-Edenic phenomenal content) of an experience is object-involving. On my view, however, reflection on Eden suggests that a "naive realist" view of perception does not require disjunctivism about phenomenology. In Eden, a sort of naive realism about perception is correct, but this entails only disjunctivism about the metaphysics of experience (as discussed in section 9), not disjunctivism about phenomenology.

different from ordinary content in the representation of objects, so the two-stage model has no special role to play.

Still, there may be a further role for the two-stage model to play. One might hold that a merely existential characterization of phenomenal content does not fully respect the directness of an experience of an object.[21] According to this objection, experience does not merely present that there *is* an object at a certain location with a certain color: it presents that *that* object is at a certain location with a certain color.

I think one might accommodate this suggestion without moving all the way to object-involving phenomenal contents, however. The phenomenology of perception does not seem to reveal the intrinsic haecceitistic natures of objects, but it does seem to present us with objects directly. To account for this, one can suggest that the experience of objects involves demonstrative modes of presentation.

In Eden, one is directly acquainted with objects, and no mediation is involved. One can simply demonstrate an object as *this* object, and acquaintance does the rest. This sort of reference is analogous to the unmediated way we refer to ourselves in our world, with "I," or perhaps to the unmediated way in which we ostend our conscious experiences. An Edenic content might correspondingly have the form [that is C at L], where "that" is a primitive demonstrative, C is a perfect color, and L is a perfect location. The demonstrative here does not build in the identity of the object, any more than the notion of "I" builds in a specific person: the same demonstrative could in principle refer to different objects, just as "I" can refer to different people. But neither is it associated with a substantive criterion of application. When the demonstrative has an object, it simply picks out the object directly, as *that* object. In the two-dimensional model, one could say: in Eden, one can refer directly to perceived objects as entities at the center of a centered world.

This Edenic content respects the direct presentational phenomenology of our experience of objects. But it is not clear that it has application outside Eden. In our world, we are not directly acquainted with objects outside ourselves: mediation is always involved. So our epistemic grip on objects is not as direct as it is in Eden, and the primitively demonstrative aspects of Edenic content are arguably not satisfied. Nevertheless, we stand in a weaker relevant relation to objects in our world: the relation of perception. One might say that by virtue of standing in this relation, the objectual aspects of our experience are *imperfectly satisfied*. There will be an associated condition of imperfect satisfaction. An object imperfectly satisfies the experience iff it is the object perceived with the experience: that is, if it is connected to the experience via an appropriate causal chain. One can think of this as a nonprimitive demonstrative condition of

---

[21] This sort of worry about the existential characterizations of perceptual content is canvassed by Campbell 2002 and Martin 2002. A demonstrative view of perceptual content is suggested by Burge 1991.

satisfaction: it comes with substantive requirements, but is grounded in a primitive connection to the experience itself. So, in effect, the objectual phenomenology of the experience can be perfectly or imperfectly satisfied: perfect satisfaction turns on primitive acquaintance, and imperfect satisfaction requires at least a mediated perceptual connection.

The imperfect satisfaction conditions of an experience can be seen as a sort of (ordinary) Fregean mode of presentation, picking out the object that the experience is appropriately connected to. The experience as a whole will be imperfectly veridical iff the object that is appropriately connected to the experience has properties that match the relevant perfect properties. On this view, the ordinary Fregean content of the experience will involve a connectedness condition of this sort, and it will determine in turn a Russellian content involving the relevant objects and its imperfect properties. Of course, the ordinary Fregean content is not a perfect mirror of the phenomenology: as usual, the phenomenology does not seem to involve reference to a causal condition, or reference to the subject's experience. But this is just what we expect: Edenic contents mirror the phenomenology, and associated Fregean contents capture veridicality conditions after the fall.

If one takes this view, one will class so-called "veridical hallucinations" (hallucinations that happen to mirror the environment in front of one) as not really veridical at all. In these cases there is no object that one is perceiving, so the Fregean content is not satisfied and an object-involving Russellian content is not determined. An alternative route to this result (Searle 1983; Siegel forthcoming) is to suggest that experiences have existential contents that attribute the relational property of being perceived with the relevant experience to the relevant object. Arguably, however, suggesting that this relational property is attributed along with color and location does not respect the subjunctive intuition that things could have been as they perceptually seem to be, even had there been no perceivers in the vicinity. By contrast, putting the perceptual requirement in the mode of presentation of the object allows this subjunctive intuition to be respected.

There is perhaps one other role for the two-stage model in the representation of objects. The phenomenology of vision seems to present a world that is carved into objects at its joints. One does not simply perceive a distribution of mass and color: one perceives objects on top of other objects, each of which may be articulated into objectual parts. Depending on one's metaphysical views, one may think that the world does not respect this articulation into objects. One might think that macroscopic objects do not exist in the world's basic ontology, or one might give their existence some highly deflationary treatment, on which their individuation is a matter of convention or conceptual scheme, or on which there is no deep fact of the matter about when there is an object or when there is not. But even if one's metaphysics is deflationary about objects, one's phenomenology is not. So perhaps, for our visual experiences to be perfectly veridical, there would have to be real, first-class, non-relative objects in the world.

One might say that in Eden, there are perfect objects. If our world's ontology does not have perfect objects, or at least if it does not have perfect objects corresponding to the apparent objects of ordinary perception, then our experiences are not perfectly veridical in this respect. But they may nevertheless be imperfectly veridical, by virtue of there being appropriately arranged matter in the environment, or by virtue of the environment's satisfying some other deflationary condition. Once again, Eden sets the standard, and our imperfect world can only match it.

Other sensory modalities

The two-stage model can naturally be extended from visual experience to auditory and tactile experience. The details of these extensions depend on a careful analysis of the phenomenology of these experiences, combined with analysis of judgments about veridicality. But there is reason to believe that the model outlined in the case of vision will apply.

The phenomenology of auditory experience, at a first approximation, seems to represent certain sounds as being present at certain locations. For example, in a musical experience, the phenomenology might suggest that a sound with a certain pitch, timbre, volume, and so on is being produced at a certain approximate location in front of me. As in the case of color, there are physical properties that one might plausibly identify with various pitch, timbre, and volume properties, and that one might hold to be attributed in an ordinary Russellian content. But these properties depend on the environment of the experience, and it seems that phenomenally identical experiences could have different Russellian contents of this sort. So one can move to a Fregean phenomenal content in these cases, and then, to respect phenomenological adequacy, hold that this content is grounded in the matching of an Edenic phenomenal content.

In Eden, one may hold, there are perfect sounds, with perfect middle-C pitch, perfect loudness, and so on. We grasp these simple intrinsic properties in our experience, but they are not instantiated in our world. Instead, in our world there are simply physical events such as air disturbances, with associated physical properties that match the Edenic properties. This is enough to make our auditory experiences imperfectly veridical, if not perfectly veridical.

Something similar goes for tactile experience. In Eden, objects may be perfectly smooth, or perfectly slimy, or perfectly velvety. These are intrinsic properties of objects or their surfaces, and we seem to be acquainted with these properties in our experience. But in our world there are just complex physical substitutes for these properties, such as imperfect sliminess and imperfect velvetiness. This is enough to satisfy the ordinary Fregean content of our tactile experiences, if not the Edenic content, and enough to make our tactile experiences imperfectly veridical.

Olfactory and gustatory experiences are trickier. The phenomenology of smell and taste seems to be representational. Intuitively, an olfactory experience represents that a certain smell is present in one's environment, perhaps in a certain broad location. A gustatory experience represents that something with a certain taste is in one's mouth or throat or on one's lips. But, at the same time, we do not usually assess experiences of smell and taste for veridicality, and the notion of an illusory olfactory or gustatory experience does not get a strong grip on us. Certainly, there can be smell experiences that are caused by properties that do not normally produce such experiences, and the same for taste experiences (imagine a rewiring of the connection between receptors and the brain, for example). But it does not seem natural to describe such experiences as illusions. It is slightly more natural to speak of olfactory and gustatory hallucinations, when an experience is generated for reasons quite independent of external objects. But the intuition is not strong.

Taste and smell differ in this way from hearing and touch. We certainly assess auditory experiences for veridicality, and speak of auditory illusions if there is not a sound being produced where there seems to be. This way of speaking is less common in the case of touch, as touch seems to be the most reliable of the sensory modalities, but we can nevertheless make good sense of the idea of a tactile illusion or hallucination. An object might feel smooth although it is not really smooth, or one might feel that an object is present when there is no object at all. In these cases we have no hesitation in classifying a tactile experience as falsidical. But in the case of taste and smell, one hesitates. I suspect that this is partly because we use taste and smell much less to gather information about our environment than we do hearing and touch, and partly (perhaps correspondingly) because the presentational element of their phenomenology is less striking.

Still, there is some presentational phenomenology in the experience of smell and taste. We seem to have some grip on intrinsic qualitative properties that are presented, although it is somewhat less obvious than in the case of vision that the phenomenology presents intrinsic properties of objects or of the environment as opposed to intrinsic qualities of experiences (or corresponding relational properties of objects and environment). Overall, though, I am inclined to say that olfactory and gustatory experiences have Edenic contents: the former presents perfect smells as being present in one's environment, and the latter presents perfect tastes as being instantiated in one's mouth.

It is the ordinary content of these experiences that is problematic. It is plausible that there are physical properties that normally cause the relevant olfactory and gustatory aspects of experiences, so one might think these would be the imperfect smells and tastes attributed in the ordinary content of these experiences. But because our assessments of veridicality are very unclear in these cases, it is likewise unclear whether these physical properties count as matching the relevant Edenic properties. In these cases, the standard for matching seems somewhat different from the case of vision and hearing, perhaps because of a difference in presentational phenomenology, or perhaps just because we apply a different standard because of different pragmatic purposes. So the status of ordinary Fregean and Russellian content in these cases is unclear. But we can nevertheless invoke Edenic content to help characterize the phenomenology.

Bodily sensations

What about bodily sensations, such as pain experiences, itches, hunger, and orgasms? On the face of it, these have a strong presentational phenomenology. The experience of pain, for example, seems to present a certain painful quality as being instantiated in part of one's body, such as one's ankle. The experience of an itch seems to present a certain itchy quality as being presented on one's skin. In the phenomenology, these qualities seem to have a highly distinctive intrinsic qualitative nature. So it is natural to hold that bodily sensations have an associated Edenic content, attributing Edenic properties such as perfect painfulness and perfect itchiness to locations in one's body.

There are two complications in this case. The first resembles the complication in the case of smell and taste. We do not generally assess bodily sensations for veridicality or falsidicality. Perhaps in an extreme case such as phantom limb pain, we are somewhat inclined to say there is some sort of falsidical pain hallucination. But we are not really inclined to speak of pain illusions, or of illusory itch experiences. If we did, we would probably be talking of a case where we mistake the phenomenal character of an experience, not where we mistake its object. As in the case of smell and taste, it seems that there are physical properties (such as tissue damage and the like) that normally cause the relevant experiences. But we are not especially inclined to say that when these properties are absent, an experience as of pain or as of an itch is falsidical. Even if there is no associated tissue damage, for example, we are not inclined to say that an intense pain experience is illusory. So the ordinary Fregean and Russellian content of these experiences seems somewhat unclear, in the same way as in the case of smell and taste.

A related complication concerns the Edenic content of bodily sensations. What are perfect pains like, in Eden? That is, what sort of properties need to be instantiated in one's body in order for a painful experience to be perfectly veridical? Here there are conflicting requirements. First, the properties seem to be intrinsic properties whose nature we grasp in experience. The phenomenology of pain in one's ankle seems to attribute a quality that is intrinsic to one's ankle. But second, the properties seem to have a strong connection to experience itself. Can one conceive of one's ankle being in perfect pain without anyone experiencing the pain? It is not clear that we can. In this respect the phenomenology of pain is quite different from the phenomenology of color, where we have no trouble conceiving of an object being perfectly colored even though no one ever experiences its color. But this seems strong to suggest that perfect pain is a relational property, as its instantiation places requirements on how things are outside the object in which it is instantiated.

Is the property of perfect pain intrinsic or relational? Neither answer is entirely comfortable. If perfect pain is an intrinsic property of an ankle, it seems that its instantiation should be independent of whether an experience is present. But it is not clear that unexperienced perfect pain is conceivable. But if perfect pain is a relational property, what relational property could it be: the property of causing a painful experience, or of having such-and-such intrinsic quality perceived in a painful experience? Neither of these seems apt to the phenomenology. Furthermore, the former seems to make too little a claim about what is going on in one's ankle, and the latter seems vulnerable to the objection that came up in the intrinsic case: we do not seem to have a grip on any relevant intrinsic quality here that we can conceive instantiated in the absence of a painful experience.

Perhaps the best answer is the following: perfect pain is an intrinsic property, but one whose instantiation entails the existence of an associated painful experience, or of associated phenomenal pain. We might think of it as an intrinsic property that, if instantiated, necessarily "broadcasts" further constraints on the world. In effect, it is an intrinsic property that stands in a necessary connection to distinct intrinsic properties of experience. In effect, it is a property whose instantiation brings about necessary connections between distinct existences.

If this property could be instantiated, problems would follow. It is not clear that there can be necessary connections between distinct existences of this sort. It seems plausible that for any conceivable or possible situation in which an intrinsic property is instantiated in one's ankle, it should be conceivable or possible that the property is instantiated in an arbitrarily different context. But it is not conceivable or possible that there is perfect pain without pain experience. The natural conclusion is that perfect pain cannot be instantiated: there is no possible world in which there is perfect pain, and on reflection it is not even conceivable that there is perfect pain. In effect, the instantiation of perfect pain places incoherent requirements on the world.

This does not entail that there is no property of perfect pain. There are other properties whose instantiation is impossible and inconceivable: that of being a round square, for example. One might hold that perfect pain is like this. On this view, one has a grip on the property of perfect pain, based on one's experience. But one does not need to eat from the Tree of Illusion or the Tree of Science to know that perfect pain is not instantiated: one can know this simply on sufficient reflection. Perhaps there can be matching intrinsic properties (without the relational constraint), or matching relational properties (without the intrinsic constraint), but no property can play both roles. Still, one may hold that the property exists, and one can hold that it is attributed in the Edenic content of our pain experiences.[22]

In effect, the Edenic content of pain sets a standard that is not just hard to meet, but impossible to meet. There are related instantiated properties, to be sure: that of causing painful experiences, for example, or having a certain sort of tissue damage. But because these fall so far short of playing the role of perfect pain (the former is not intrinsic, and the second has no strong connection to experience), one might suggest that they fail to match perfect pain. It is arguably because of this that we do not judge that the instantiation of these properties yields veridicality or falsidicality of pain experiences. The standard set by Eden is sufficiently high that there is little point holding the world to it.

What goes for pain goes also for other bodily sensations, such as the experience of itches, hunger, and orgasms. One finds the same combination in these cases: phenomenology seems to present an intrinsic property, but one that cannot be instantiated without a corresponding experience. The natural conclusion is that the perfect properties cannot be instantiated at all. One might suggest that this model applies in some other domains: for example, one might suggest that gustatory experiences present properties that cannot be instantiated except while being tasted, so to speak. If this were so, it could help to explain our reluctance to assess such experiences as veridical or falsidical. The phenomenology here is less clear than in the case of pain, and it is not obvious whether the claim of a necessary connection to experience is correct. But the analogy between the cases at least deserves attention.

It may be that some other Edenic properties that we have considered are not just uninstantiated but uninstantiable. For example, one might hold that perfect time (involving the flow of time, or a moving now) is incoherent, perhaps for McTaggartian reasons. Or if one is sufficiently deflationary about objects, one might hold that perfect objects cannot exist in any possible world. Nevertheless, the impossibility of satisfying these contents does not automatically stop them from acting as a regulative ideal. Here, the impossible might serve to regulate our experience of the actual.

High-level properties

One might try to extend this model beyond the representation of simple properties such as color and shape in experience, to the representation of high-level properties, such as that of being a duck, or being happy. It is plausible that representing such properties can make a difference to the phenomenology of experience (Siegel, this volume, ch.14). It is not clear that the phenomenal content of this sort of experience is easily analyzed using the two-stage model. One difficulty is that the deployment of *concepts* often plays a key role in such

---

[22] Adam Pautz explores an idea like this in forthcoming work.

experiences, and that the content of the experience is inherited from that of an associated concept rather than being determined by the two-stage model. When we see something as a book, or as a duck, for example, it is plausible that the associated phenomenal content is inherited from the content of our concept of a book or of a duck. And in these cases, we do not seem to have any grip on distinct perfect and imperfect veridicality conditions.

Still, there are a few cases where the two-stage model is at least tempting. For example, there is a phenomenology of moral experience, and it is arguable that moral properties such as being good or bad can be represented in perception. One might naturally suggest that for moral experiences to be perfectly veridical, relevant objects would have to have perfect moral properties: the sort that are objective, intrinsically motivating, and so on. But it is arguable that in our world (and perhaps in every possible world), no such properties are instantiated. If so, our moral experiences cannot be perfectly veridical. But there are various properties (including response-dependent properties, community-relative properties, and so on) that arguably match these properties well enough. If so, our moral experiences can be imperfectly veridical. There has been no perfect goodness since the fall from Eden, but we can at least be consoled by imperfect goodness in the world.

13 CONCLUSION

On the view I have presented, the most fundamental content of perceptual experience is its Edenic content. Other aspects of content such as ordinary Fregean and Russellian content can be seen as deriving from Edenic content, with the aid of the matching relation and the contribution of the environment. To understand the role of perceptual experience in representing the world, one needs to understand all these levels of content. But to understand the phenomenology of perceptual experience in its own right, understanding Edenic content is the key.

We have seen that the Edenic approach yields a very useful tool in doing phenomenology. To characterize the phenomenology of an experience, it is often helpful to characterize the sort of world in which that experience would be perfectly veridical. To do this, one sketches relevant aspects of the character of Eden. Doing this does not eliminate the need for thorough phenomenological investigation, and it does not solve the many associated hard methodological problems, but it at least provides an analytic tool that gives us some purchase in characterizing the contents of consciousness.

I am inclined to think that Edenic content may also give us an entry point for understanding the metaphysics of experience. I have said little in this paper about how it is possible for experiences to have Edenic contents, or about which of Edenic content or phenomenal character is the more fundamental. My suspicion is that neither is more fundamental than the other. It may be that perceptual experience is fundamentally equivalent to the presentation of an Edenic world. If so, then if we can understand how the presentation of an Edenic world is possible, then we will understand perceptual phenomenology.

APPENDIX: THE TWO-DIMENSIONAL ANALYSIS OF PERCEPTUAL CONTENT

The Fregean and Russellian content of perceptual experience can be modeled using the two-dimensional framework for the analysis of content. This analysis is not required in order to make use of the notions of Fregean and Russellian content (which can be understood intuitively as in the text), but it helps in order to make the use of these notions more precise, and in order to analyze certain subtleties that arise. It also can help us to shed light on the relationship between the content of perception and of belief.

In the linguistic version of the two-dimensional framework, expression tokens are associated with two intensions, or functions from possible worlds to extensions. The Fregean content of an expression is associated with a primary intension: a function from centered worlds to extensions, where a centered world is a world marked with a designated individual and a designated time (intuitively, these represent the perspective of the subject who utters the expression). The Russellian content of an expression is associated with a secondary intension: a function from (uncentered) possible worlds to extensions.

For example, the primary intension associated with "Hesperus" might be an intension that, in a given centered world, picks out the bright object that has been visible in the appropriate location in the evening sky around the center of that world. The secondary intension associated with "Hesperus" might be a function that picks out Venus in all worlds. Likewise, the primary intension associated with "Hesperus is Phosphorus" might be an intension that is true in a centered world iff the bright objects that have been visible at certain positions in the evening and morning skies around the center of that world are identical. The secondary intension associated with "Hesperus is Phosphorus" might be an intension that is true in a world iff Venus is Venus in that world.

This framework can be extended to the contents of mental states such as beliefs (Chalmers 2002a), and the discussion above suggests that it can also be extended to the contents of perceptual experiences. The Fregean content of a perceptual experience is associated with a primary intension. For example, the condition on extension associated with phenomenal redness can be modeled as a function from centered worlds to properties: in a given centered world, it picks out the property that normally causes phenomenally red experiences in the subject at the center of that world. The condition of satisfaction that is associated with a specific experience of a colored object can be represented as a function from centered worlds to truth-values: in a given centered world, it will be true iff there is a relevant object in the environment of the individual at the center that instantiates, at the relevant location relative to that individual, the property that normally causes phenomenally red experiences in that individual.

Likewise, the Russellian content of an experience is associated with a secondary intension. For example, the Russellian content associated with phenomenal redness can be seen as an intension that picks out physical redness in all worlds. And the Russellian condition of satisfaction that is associated with a specific phenomenally red experience of an object O might be seen as an intension that is true at a world iff object O is physically red in that world.

Why do I say that Fregean and Russellian contents are associated with primary and secondary intensions, rather than that they are primary and secondary intensions? This is because I want to leave open the possibility that these contents have a more fine-grained structure than functions from worlds to extensions. For example, it is reasonable to hold that the Russellian content of a perceptual experience is a structured proposition involving the attribution of certain properties to an object. Such a structured proposition determines a secondary intension, but it is not itself a secondary intension. Likewise, one might hold that the Fregean content of a perceptual experience is a structured complex made up of the Fregean contents of its associated aspects: the Fregean content associated with the color, and perhaps those associated with the object, the location, and other aspects of the experience. We might see this content as a structured intension, made up of the intensions associated with each aspect. This intension determines a function from centered worlds to truth-values, but it is not itself such a function.

It may also be that some specific aspects of experience have contents that are more fine-grained than intensions. For example, following Peacocke (1992), one might argue that when one sees an object as a square and then as a regular diamond, there is a phenomenological difference that corresponds to a difference in content (representing something as a square or a regular diamond) that cannot easily be modeled as a function from worlds to extensions. And perhaps one could make the case that there are some experiences that could not be veridical in any possible world: if so, their associated intension might be false in all worlds, but they might still intuitively have some nontrivial Fregean and Russellian contents. In these cases one might appeal to conditions on extension that are more fine-grained than functions from worlds to extensions (allowing substantial conditions that are impossible to satisfy, for example). Still, as before, these contents will at least determine associated intensions. In what follows the differences will not play a large role, so it will be useful to use primary and secondary intensions to analyze Fregean and Russellian contents.

In the two-dimensional analysis of belief and language, as I understand it, the two dimensions of content correspond to the evaluation of epistemic possibilities (ways the world might actually be, for all we know a priori) and subjunctive possibilities (ways the world might have been, but is not). The same goes for the analysis of perceptual experience.

Intuitively, a perceptual experience places a constraint on epistemically possible states of the world. For all I know a priori, there are many ways that the world could turn out to be. We can think of these ways as epistemic possibilities (in a broad sense), and we can model them using centered worlds. The same goes for the epistemic possibilities that confront a perceiver. For example, when I have a phenomenally red experience, it is epistemically possible that the object I am looking at has property P1 and that P1 normally causes phenomenally red experiences, and it is epistemically possible that the object I am looking at has property P2 and that P2 normally causes phenomenally red experiences. These two hypotheses correspond to different centered worlds W_1 and W_2. Intuitively, whether W_1 or W_2 turns out to be actual, my experience will be veridical. So we can say that W_1 and W_2 both verify the experience. On the other hand, there are worlds W_3 and W_4 where the object that the subject at the center is looking at has P1 and P2 (respectively), but in which that property normally causes phenomenally green experiences. Intuitively, if W_3 or W_4 turn out to be actual, my experience will be falsidical. So we can say that W_3 and W_4 both falsify the experience. These intuitions can be encapsulated in the claim that the primary intension of the experience is true in W_1 and W_2, but false in W_3 and W_4.

We can likewise evaluate perceptual experiences with respect to counterfactual circumstances, considered via subjunctive conditionals. If I have a phenomenally red experience directed at a red book B, then I can ask: if my eyes had been closed, but the book had still been present, would things have been as I (actually) perceive them to be? The intuitive answer is yes. Or I can ask: if the book had been present with the same intrinsic properties, but if I had been such that the book normally caused phenomenally green experiences in me, would things have been as I (actually) perceive them to be? The intuitions about this case are a bit less clear, but there is at least some intuition that the answer is yes. Intuitions of this sort suggest that with respect to counterfactual circumstances, the perceptual experience will be veridical (at least with respect to color) roughly iff the book B is (physically) red in those circumstances. This can be encapsulated by saying that the secondary intension of the experience is true in a world iff book B is red in that world.

One might even define the secondary intension of a perceptual experience in terms of these subjunctive conditionals. One can say that the secondary intension of an experience E is true at a world W iff: had W obtained, things would have been the way that they appear to be to the subject (actually) undergoing E. To the extent that our judgments about these subjunctive conditionals are not fully determinate, the corresponding secondary intension may not be fully determinate, but in any case the intension will capture some of our intuitions about content.

Defining the primary intension of a perceptual experience is not as straightforward. So far I have talked in an intuitive way of a condition on extension, and about the evaluation of epistemic possibilities, but this falls short of a definition. One could simply leave a notion here as basic, but it would be nice to do more. One thought is to appeal to indicative conditionals. For example, one could hold that the primary intension of an experience E is true in a centered world W iff: if the actual world is qualitatively like W (and if I am in the position of the person at the center of W at the time of W), then E is veridical. The trouble is that one may want to evaluate the experience at worlds where the experience is not itself present. It is not obviously part of the content of an experience E that E itself obtains: one may want to hold that the content largely constrains the external world. Furthermore, in the case of beliefs and utterances, there are good reasons not to define primary intensions in terms of conditionals that make explicit reference to whether a belief or utterance would be true as it occurs in some circumstance (see Chalmers 2004b), and these reasons plausibly extend to the case of perceptual experience. So it would be useful to have a definition that applies more broadly than this.

In the case of beliefs, one can define a primary intension in terms of the belief's inferential connections. In particular, one can say that the primary intension of belief B is true at a centered world W if there is an appropriate inferential connection between the hypothesis that W is actual and B. (The hypothesis that W is actual can be understood more strictly as the hypothesis that D is the case, where D is an appropriate canonical description of W.) One way of understanding the inferential connection is in terms of rational inference: if a subject were to accept that W is actual, ought they rationally to accept B? Another, arguably better way, is to understand it in terms of a priori entailment: if the subject accepts that W is actual, ought (idealized) a priori reasoning from there lead them to accept B?

A definition along these lines is not as straightforward in the case of perceptual experiences, as the notion of an inferential connection from an arbitrary hypothesis to a perceptual experience is not entirely clear. However, one can give such a definition by relying on certain inferential connections between perceptual experiences and beliefs that are somewhat clearer. In particular, we have a reasonable grip on what it is for a subject to *take an experience at face value*, yielding a perceptual belief. In such a case, we can say that the perceptual belief *endorses* the perceptual experience. Note that a belief that endorses a perceptual experience should be distinguished from a belief that the perceptual experience is true. The latter is a belief directed at the experience, but the former is a belief directed at the world.

The notion of endorsement is a primitive in the current account, but one can say some things to characterize it. Endorsement is a sort of truth-preserving inference between perception and belief: when a belief endorses a veridical experience, the belief will be true. This need not be true in reverse: that is, it can happen that a belief endorses a falsidical experience without itself being false. This can happen for a complex experience, for example, when intuitively the belief takes certain aspects of the experience at face value, and abstracts away from others. For example, a belief might endorse my current visual experience where color is concerned, and abstract away from shape. If my experience is veridical with respect to color but not to shape, the experience will be overall falsidical, but the endorsing belief will be veridical. On this conception, an endorsing belief may make fewer commitments than the experience that it endorses, but it cannot make any commitments that are not made by the experience that it endorses.

One can also introduce a notion of *complete endorsement*: a belief completely endorses an experience when it endorses that experience in all its aspects. Complete endorsement preserves both truth and falsity: when a belief endorses a falsidical experience, the belief will be false. For experiences of any complexity, it is not clear that we have the capacity to completely endorse them (as it is not clear that we can have beliefs with the relevant detail and complexity), but it seems that the notion is reasonable at least for simple experiences, and as an idealization in the case of complex experiences.

With these notions in place, we can use them in conjunction with the already defined notion of the primary intension of a belief to characterize the primary intension of a perceptual experience. One can say that the primary intension of an experience E is true at a centered world W iff the primary intension of any possible belief that endorses E is true at W. One could also appeal to complete endorsement here, simply equating the primary intension of a perceptual experience with that of a belief that completely endorses it, but the definition in terms of endorsement has fewer commitments. It does not require that complete endorsements exist for all perceptual experiences. Intuitively, it simply requires that for any aspect of a perceptual experience, there is some belief that endorses that aspect.

On the two-stage view, which has two different standards of veridicality for perceptual experience, this picture will be complicated slightly. We could say that just as there are two standards of veridicality for perceptual experiences, there are two standards of truth for perceptual beliefs: perfect and imperfect truth, say. On this model, endorsing a perfectly veridical experience will produce a perfectly true perceptual belief, and endorsing an imperfectly veridical experience will produce an imperfectly true belief. One could then associate a perceptual belief with two different primary intensions, corresponding to the standards of perfect and imperfect truth. These intensions will then ground two different primary intensions for an experience, corresponding to perfect and imperfect veridicality.

Alternatively, and perhaps more plausibly, one could say that there is just one standard of truth for beliefs, and two sorts of endorsement: perfect and imperfect endorsement, say. Intuitively, perfectly endorsing an experience requires holding that experience to the standard of perfect veridicality, while imperfectly endorsing it requires holding it only to the standard of imperfect veridicality. On this model, imperfectly endorsing an imperfectly (or perfectly) veridical experience will produce a true belief, perfectly endorsing a perfectly veridical experience will produce a true belief, but perfectly endorsing an imperfectly veridical experience may produce a false belief. On this model a belief will be associated with just one primary intension, but the two different endorsement relations will yield two different primary intensions for an experience. I will not choose between the two models here.

One might argue that there are representational aspects of perceptual experience that cannot be endorsed by any possible belief. For example, one might hold that extremely fleeting experiences, or experiences that are far outside attention, cannot be endorsed. Or one might argue that experiences in animals that lack concepts cannot be endorsed. I think in these cases one could make a case that it is at least *possible* for the experiences to be endorsed, perhaps assuming some idealization of the subject's actual cognitive capacity. But this is clearly a substantive issue and the answer is unclear. For this reason, the characterization above is probably best not regarded as a definition, but it is at least a useful characterization that gives reasonably precise results for a wide range of ordinary experiences.

A subtlety arises concerning the object-oriented aspect of the experience. If one holds (not implausibly) that the Russellian content of a non-hallucinatory experience involves the object of the experience, then there should be a corresponding element of the Fregean content of the experience that picks the object out. Here the natural suggestion is this: Fregean content picks out that object as the object that is causing (or that is appropriately perceptually connected to) the current experience. This suggests a primary intension that maps a centered world to the object causing (or perceptually connected to) the relevant experience of the subject at the center of the centered world. To model this, one may need to build in a marked experience to the center of the relevant centered worlds, as the subject at the center may have many experiences (this is something that one has to do in any case; see Chalmers 2002a, section 9). One can then say that the primary intension of a phenomenally red experience is true in a centered world if the object that causes (or is appropriately connected to) the marked experience at the center of that world has the property that normally causes phenomenally red experiences.

Once again, this characterization of the relevant intension is just a first approximation. A detailed account would require consideration of the complexities of color experience, and also would require an analysis of the Fregean contents of the experience of spatial location and perhaps of the object-oriented aspect of the experience. For example, one might hold that where an experience has a Russellian content involving a particular object, there is an associated Fregean content that picks out that object as the object that is causing the current experience. This would require a primary intension that maps a centered world to the object causing (or otherwise perceptually connected to) a relevant experience of the subject at the center of the centered world (see section 10.2 here).

I should note that there is no requirement that either Russellian content or Fregean content be *conceptual* content. That is, it is not required that to have an experience with a given Russellian or Fregean content, a subject must have concepts with corresponding content. Frege's own favored variety of content was a sort of conceptual content: Fregean senses were always grasped through the possession of corresponding concepts. But the Fregean contents discussed here need not be Fregean in that respect. Rather, they are Fregean in the sense that they involve modes of presentation of objects and properties in the world, whether or not these modes of presentation involve concepts.

My own view is that a subject can have perceptual experiences with quite determinate content even without possessing corresponding concepts. For example, one can have a color experience that represents a given shade even without possessing a concept of that shade. It is nevertheless plausible that such an experience possesses a Russellian content (attributing that shade to an object), and it also possesses a Fregean content (one that is true if the object appropriately related to the perceiver has the property that normally causes the relevant sort of experience). If so, these contents are nonconceptual contents: an experience can have such contents even if the subject lacks a concept of the relevant shade, lacks a concept of the relevant experience, and lacks a concept of "normally causes." I will not argue for this claim here, however, and it is inessential for the other claims in this chapter.

These nonconceptual Fregean contents need not themselves be a different sort of object from conceptual Fregean contents. For example, it could be that an experience as of a red object and a belief that completely endorses it have the same Fregean content. Instead, one might say that the Fregean content of perception involves a nonconceptual content *relation*: the relation that associates perceptual states with their Fregean contents is such that subjects need not possess the relevant concepts in order for their states to have the relevant content.[23] A pluralist about content can hold that there are both conceptual and nonconceptual content relations, but nonconceptual content relations are likely to be particularly useful in the analysis of perception.

---

[23] Heck (2000) distinguishes the "content view" of nonconceptual content (on which nonconceptual contents are objects quite distinct from conceptual contents) from the "state view" (on which nonconceptual contents are contents of nonconceptual states). One might call the conception suggested here the "relational view" of nonconceptual content. It is somewhat closer to the state view than to the content view, but it need not invoke the idea of a "conceptual state."

REFERENCES

Block, Ned (1990), "Inverted Earth," *Philosophical Perspectives*, 4: 53–79.

Boghossian, Paul and Velleman, J. David (1989), "Color as a Secondary Quality," *Mind*, 98: 81–103.

Burge, Tyler (1991), "Vision and Intentional Content," in Ernie Lepore and Robert van Gulick (eds), *John Searle and His Critics* (Oxford: Blackwell).

Byrne, Alex (2001), "Intentionalism Defended," *Philosophical Review*, 110: 199–240.

Byrne, Alex (forthcoming), "Color and the Mind–Body Problem," *Dialectica*.

Byrne, Alex and Hilbert, David (2003), "Color Realism and Color Science," *Behavioral and Brain Sciences*, 26: 3–21.

Campbell, John (1993), "A Simple View of Colour," in John Haldane and Crispin Wright (eds), *Reality, Representation, and Projection* (Oxford: Oxford University Press).

Campbell, John (2002), *Reference and Consciousness* (Oxford: Oxford University Press).

Chalmers, David J. (1996), *The Conscious Mind: In Search of a Fundamental Theory*, (Oxford: Oxford University Press).

Chalmers, David J. (2002a), "The Components of Content," in David J. Chalmers (ed.), *Philosophy of Mind: Classical and Contemporary Readings* (New York: Oxford University Press).

Chalmers, David J. (2002b), "Does Conceivability Entail Possibility?," in Tamar Gendler and John Hawthorne (eds), *Conceivability and Possibility* (Oxford: Oxford University Press).

Chalmers, David J. (2003a), "The Content and Epistemology of Phenomenal Belief," in Quentin Smith and Alexandr Jokic (eds), *Consciousness: New Philosophical Perspectives* (Oxford: Oxford University Press).

Chalmers, David J. (2003b), "The Matrix as Metaphysics," Philosophy section of *The Matrix* website, <http://consc.net/papers/matrix.html>.

Chalmers, David J. (2004a), "The Representational Character of Experience," in Brian Leiter (ed.), *The Future for Philosophy* (Oxford: Oxford University Press).

Chalmers, David J. (2004b), "Epistemic Two-Dimensional Semantics," *Philosophical Studies*, 118: 153–226.

Chisholm, Roderick (1942), "The Problem of the Speckled Hen," *Mind*, 204: 368–73.

Clark, Austen (2000), *A Theory of Sentience* (Oxford: Oxford University Press).

Dretske, Fred (1995), *Naturalizing the Mind* (Cambridge, Mass.: MIT Press).

Edwards, Jim (1998), "The Simple Theory of Colour and the Transparency of Sensory Experience," in Cynthia Macdonald, Barry Smith, and Crispin Wright (eds), *Knowing Our Own Minds: Essays on Self-Knowledge* (Oxford: Oxford University Press).

Egan, Andy (forthcoming), "Appearance Properties?," *Nous*.

Hardin, C. L. (1987), *Color for Philosophers* (Indianapolis: Hackett Publishing Company).

Harman, Gilbert (1990), "The Intrinsic Quality of Experience," *Philosophical Perspectives*, 4: 31–52.

Heck, Richard (2000), "Nonconceptual Content and the Space of Reasons," *Philosophical Review*, 109: 483–523.

Holman, Emmett (2002), "Color Eliminativism and Color Experience," *Pacific Philosophical Quarterly*, 83: 38–56.

Horgan, Terence and Tienson, John (2002), "The Intentionality of Phenomenology and the Phenomenology of Intentionality," in David J. Chalmers (ed.), *Philosophy of Mind: Classical and Contemporary Readings* (New York: Oxford University Press).

Jackson, Frank (1996), "The Primary Quality View of Color," *Philosophical Perspectives*, 10: 199–219.

Johnston, Mark (1992), "How to Speak of the Colors," *Philosophical Studies*, 68: 221–63.

Johnston, Mark (2004), "The Obscure Object of Hallucination," *Philosophical Studies*, 120: 113–83.

Johnston, Mark (forthcoming), *The Manifest.*

Kriegel, Uriah (2002), "Phenomenal Content," *Erkenntnis*, 57: 175–98.

Levine, Joseph (2003), "Experience and Representation," in Quentin Smith and Aleksander Jokic (eds), *Consciousness: New Philosophical Essays* (Oxford: Oxford University Press).

Lycan, William G. (1996), *Consciousness and Experience* (Cambridge, Mass.: MIT Press).

Lycan, William G. (2001), "The Case for Phenomenal Externalism," *Philosophical Perspectives*, 15: 17–35.

McGinn, Colin (1996), "Another Look at Color," *Journal of Philosophy*, 93: 537–53.

McLaughlin, Brian (2003), "Color, Consciousness, and Color Consciousness," in Quentin Smith and Aleksander Jokic (eds), *Consciousness: New Philosophical Essays* (Oxford: Oxford University Press).

Martin, M. G. F. (2002), "Particular Thoughts and Singular Thought," in Anthony O'Hear (ed.), *Logic, Thought, and Language* (Cambridge: Cambridge University Press).

Maund, J. Barry (1995), *Colours: Their Nature and Representation* (Cambridge: Cambridge University Press).

Peacocke, Christopher (1983), *Sense and Content: Experience, Thought, and Their Relations* (Oxford: Oxford University Press).

Peacocke, Christopher (1992), *A Study of Concepts* (Oxford: Oxford University Press).

Putnam, Hilary (1975), "The Meaning of 'Meaning,'" in *Mind, Language, and Reality* (Cambridge: Cambridge University Press).

Searle, John R. (1983), *Intentionality* (Cambridge: Cambridge University Press).

Searle, John R. (1990), "Consciousness, Explanatory Inversion, and Cognitive Science," *Behavioral and Brain Sciences*, 13: 585–95.

Shoemaker, Sydney (1990), "Qualities and Qualia: What's in the Mind?," *Philosophy and Phenomenological Research*, supplement, 50: 109–131.

Shoemaker, Sydney (1994), "Phenomenal Character," *Nous*, 28: 21–38.

Shoemaker, Sydney (2001), "Introspection and Phenomenal Character," in *Philosophical Topics*, reprinted in David J. Chalmers (ed.), *Philosophy of Mind: Classical and Contemporary Readings* (Oxford: Oxford University Press).

Siegel, Susanna (this volume), "Which Properties are Represented in Perception?," in Tamar Gendler and John Hawthorne (eds), *Perceptual Experience* (Oxford: Oxford University Press).

Siegel, Susanna (forthcoming), "Subject and Object in the Contents of Visual Experience."

Siewert, Charles (1998), *The Significance of Consciousness* (Princeton: Princeton University Press).

Stoljar, Daniel (forthcoming), "Consequences of Intentionalism," *Philosophical Studies*.

Thau, Michael (2002), *Consciousness and Cognition* (New York: Oxford University Press).

Thompson, Brad (2003), "The Nature of Phenomenal Content," Ph.D. dissertation, University of Arizona.

Thompson, Brad (forthcoming), "The Spatial Content of Visual Experience," <faculty.smu.edu/bthompso/spatialcontent.html>.

Tye, Michael (1995), *Ten Problems of Consciousness: A Representational Theory of the Phenomenal Mind* (Cambridge, Mass.: MIT Press).

Tye, Michael (2003), "Blurry Images, Double Vision, and Other Oddities: New Problems for Representationalism?," in Quentin Smith and Aleksander Jokic (eds), *Consciousness: New Philosophical Essays* (Oxford: Oxford University Press).

Wright, Wayne (2003), "Projectivist Representationalism and Color," *Philosophical Psychology*, 16: 515–33.

3

Is There a Perceptual Relation?

Tim Crane

1 INTRODUCTION

P. F. Strawson argued that 'mature sensible experience (in general) presents itself as . . . an *immediate* consciousness of the existence of things outside us' (1979: 97). He began his defence of this very natural idea by asking how someone might typically give a description of their current visual experience, and offered this example of such a description: 'I see the red light of the setting sun filtering through the black and thickly clustered branches of the elms; I see the dappled deer grazing in groups on the vivid green grass' (1979: 97). In other words, in describing experience, we tend to describe the objects of experience—the things which we experience—and the ways they are when we are experiencing them.

Some go further. According to Heidegger:

We never . . . originally and really perceive a throng of sensations, e.g., tones and noises, in the appearance of things . . . ; rather, we hear the storm whistling in the chimney, we hear the three-engine aeroplane, we hear the Mercedes in immediate distinction from the Volkswagen. Much closer to us than any sensations are the things themselves. We hear the door slam in the house, and never hear acoustic sensations or mere sounds. (1935: 156; quoted by Smith 2002: 105)

Whether or not we all want to agree with Heidegger that we have *immediate* consciousness of the difference between a Volkswagen and a Mercedes, many of us will agree with him that in normal perceptual experience the 'things themselves' seem much closer to us than a 'throng of sensations'. This does not by itself imply that we are not in *any* way aware of a throng of sensations in

Earlier versions of this chapter were presented at ELTE in Budapest, the University of York, the Joint Session of the Mind Association and the Aristotelian Society at Belfast in 2003, the University of Massachusetts at Amherst, Tufts University and the Centre for Subjectivity Research in Copenhagen. Thanks to the participants on these occasions, and especially to Alex Byrne, Stephen Everson, Katalin Farkas, Howard Robinson, Jonathan Schaffer, Susanna Siegel, Hong Yu Wong, Dan Zahavi and an anonymous referee for OUP for their comments. I am especially grateful to Tamar Gendler and John Hawthorne for their detailed and insightful comments on the penultimate version. This paper was written the support of a grant from the AHRB's Research Leave Scheme.

perceptual experience. Heidegger only says that we are not *originally and really* aware of them; even if the things themselves are 'closer' to us than sensations, this still implies that the sensations are somewhere to be found, so to speak, in the experiential neighbourhood. It is obvious that perceptual experience is sensory in a way in which thought is not, and a theory of perception has to make room for this.

Nonetheless, in recent years a number of philosophers have argued that *all* we are aware of in experience—and all we can be made aware of by introspecting an experience—are the 'things themselves': the everyday objects of experience and their properties. On this view, known as 'representationalism', introspection of a perceptual experience never reveals awareness of any properties of the experience itself or of what Heidegger calls a 'throng of sensations'. The opposing view holds that although we are aware in perceptual experience of things outside us, introspection of an experience can reveal awareness of properties of the experience itself. One reason someone might hold this is because they think experience always involves the instantiation of intrinsic, non-representational 'qualitative' properties, known as *qualia*.[1] I will call this view the 'qualia theory'. The qualia theory combines rejection of representationalism with an explanation of that rejection in terms of qualia.

Ned Block has called the dispute between representationalism and the qualia theory the 'greatest chasm in the philosophy of mind' (Block 1996: 19). The main purpose of this paper is to dispute this claim of Block's. I will argue that as far as the philosophy of perception is concerned, the dispute over the existence of qualia is not very significant at all. It may be that in other parts of philosophy of mind—for example, in the debate about the physicalistic reduction of consciousness—the existence of qualia is a chasm-creating question. (Actually, I doubt this too; but I will not argue for it in any detail here.[2]) My concern here is just with philosophical debates about perception: my claim will be that as far as the philosophy of perception is concerned, the question of qualia is not an important question.

---

[1] For defences of the qualia theory, see Peacocke (1983); Shoemaker (1990); Block (1996, 1997, and forthcoming). For defences of representationalism, see Harman (1990); Tye (1992, 1995, and 2000); Thau (2002); Hilbert and Kalderon (2000); Byrne (2001). Two important discussions which defend neither side as described here are Martin (2002) and Stoljar (forthcoming).

[2] But let me give a brief indication of my reasons for this doubt. Many people express the problem of consciousness in terms of the notion of qualia. Chalmers (1996) and Block (1996) put the problem in this way. Yet, while Block thinks there must be a naturalistic, physicalistic account of qualia, Chalmers thinks that there cannot be. So their dispute is not over the existence of qualia, but over whether they can be physicalistically explained. To this it may be said, as Byrne (2001) does, that if there were no qualia and if we therefore had a representational account of consciousness, this would be one step on the road to a physicalistic reduction of consciousness. But if this were the case, it would still be necessary to give a physicalistic explanation of why certain representations were conscious and others were not, and—'Higher-Order Thought' views notwithstanding—representationalist accounts of consciousness have made no more progress with this question than qualia-based accounts have with their parallel question. So it seems to me that in this case too, it is unlikely that the *existence* of qualia is the kind of issue in relation to which the real chasm develops.

The debate to which Block is referring is often discussed in terms of whether experience is 'transparent' or 'diaphanous'. But, as we shall see in section 2, whatever is correct in the idea of the transparency of experience cannot establish the truth of representationalism. In fact, it seems to me that it is relatively easy to show that representationalism is false. This rejection of representationalism does not touch the main problems of perception, although the *reasons* for the rejection point towards what these real problems are. Accordingly, in sections 3–5 of this paper, I will argue that there is a large chasm in the philosophy of perception, but that it is created by the dispute about whether experience is *relational*. It is this dispute—between 'intentionalists' and 'disjunctivists'—which contains the most recalcitrant problems of perception. The major theories of perception in contemporary analytic philosophy line up on either side of this dispute. I will argue that when seen in this context, the debate about the existence of qualia is a relatively minor side dispute among intentionalists, rather than a major chasm in the philosophy of perception.

My aim in demonstrating this is not simply negative. It is also an attempt to show what it means to say that perception is intentional, and therefore what the essence of an 'intentionalist' approach to perception is—something which I think has not been very well understood in recent philosophy of perception. A correct understanding of intentionalism about perception must derive from a correct understanding of the problems of perception. But before explaining this, I will begin with a few remarks about the transparency of experience.

2   TRANSPARENCY

What recent philosophers call the 'transparency' or 'diaphanousness' of experience is the idea that reflection on what it is like to have an experience does not reveal properties of experiences themselves, but only of their objects. As a number of writers have pointed out (Martin 2002; Siewert 2003: 18; Stoljar forthcoming), there are really two claims here: (i) we are aware of the objects of experience; and (ii) we are not aware of features of experiences themselves. In his expositions of the transparency idea, Michael Tye makes both claims. First, the positive claim about what we *are* aware of:

When one tries to focus on [an experience of blue] in introspection one cannot help but see right through it so that what one actually ends up attending to is the real colour blue. (Tye 1992: 160)

And, second, the negative claim about what we are *not* aware of:

When we introspect our experiences and feelings, we become aware of what it is like for us to undergo them. But we are not directly aware of those experiences and feelings; nor are we directly aware of qualities of experience. (Tye 2000: 51)

Plausible as these two claims might initially seem, I think it is easy to show that they are not true.

What is right about the first claim is that introspection does typically reveal the objects of perceptual experience, and that we typically describe our experiences in terms of these objects, as Strawson pointed out. But it does not follow from the fact that we typically describe our experience in this way, that in every case in which we introspect an experience of (e.g.) something blue, we 'see right through' to the real colour blue. For if this were so, then all introspectible experiences would involve relations to real objects and real instances of properties, like colours (assuming, for the sake of argument, that colours are real properties of external objects). But not all experiences do involve relations to real objects or property instances: one can have hallucinatory or otherwise deceptive experiences which involve no such relations.[3] So it cannot be true that in every case of perceptual experience 'the qualities to which we have direct access . . . are qualities of external things' (Tye 2000: 51).

Tye's response to this is to say that what one is aware of when hallucinating are 'specific aspects of the content of the experience'. And since he believes that one's state of mind when hallucinating is the same as when one is perceiving, this is what we are aware of when we introspect our perceptions as well as our hallucinations.

What is meant by the 'content of experience'? This is where we move into more specific areas of theories like his. Philosophers like Tye think that perception is a propositional attitude, and that, like belief, it has a content which is expressed by the 'that'-clause in ascriptions of perceptual experiences. The content of perception is therefore a proposition. Taking what Tye says literally, then, he is saying that in introspection we are aware of aspects of propositions. I will discuss this view in section 4 below. But notice here that we seemed already to have moved away from claims about what is obvious about perception: the immediate initial appeal of the idea that all we are aware of in perception are things like the wind in the chimney and the blue of the sea starts to crumble in our hands. If we are merely hallucinating something blue, then blueness is not instantiated at all. But that means that there is no instance of the real colour blue for us to be aware of in introspection. Even if we are aware of *the fact that our experience represents something blue*, this does not by itself mean that there is anything blue which we are aware of.

What about the second, negative, claim? It seems initially plausible that in normal perceptual experience one is not aware of features of one's experience. I started this paper with the observation that perceptual experience seems to be an awareness of the world, of the things themselves. So it might seem equally natural to say that in perceptual experience I am not aware of qualities of my

---

[3] I am putting to one side here (and in section 3) the view that in a hallucination we are aware of uninstantiated universals, a view defended by Johnston (2004). The view demands further discussion.

experience; I *have* the experience, and in *having* the experience, I become *aware* of the world.

But why should it *never* be true that one can be aware of qualities of one's experience? Is it impossible to take what J. J. Gibson once called the 'painterly attitude' to visual experience, and attend to the way the experience itself is, as opposed to the features of the things themselves? It may still be true in this kind of case that 'the public, mind-independent objects of perception and their features are not banished from one's attention just because one shifts one's interest from how things are in the environment to how things are experientially' (Martin 2002: 384). But this does not imply that one is *not* able to attend to how things are experientially.

Tye agrees with this; his view is that 'we attend to the external surfaces and qualities and thereby we are aware of something else, the "feel" of our experience' (2000: 51–2). You become aware of how your experience phenomenally is (its 'feel') by attending to what is represented. I think we should agree with Tye that this is often—or even usually—the case. But the next question is whether there is any situation in which you can become aware of how your experience is by attending to the experience *itself* rather than by attending to its objects (e.g., 'external surfaces and qualities'). For, after all, the question for a theory of perception is surely not how *often* we are aware of things of a certain kind, or (*pace* Kind 2003) how difficult it is to be aware of such things; the question is whether we are *ever* aware of things of that kind. So if we are ever directly aware of features of our experience which are not features of the objects of experience—or features which these objects are *represented as having*— then Tye's negative claim is false: we can be 'directly aware of qualities of experience'.

Brief reflection on some everyday phenomena seems to reveal many cases of such awareness. I remove my glasses and things seem blurry. Introspecting this experience, blurriness does certainly seem to be instantiated somewhere. But does it seem to be instantiated in the familiar objects of experience? Surely this need not be the case: it need not seem as if these objects are themselves blurry. When I say that 'everything seems blurry' I don't mean that it seems as if the things around me *are* blurry—any more than when I say that 'everything is dark in here' I mean that it seems as if the things around me *are* dark ('the chairs are dark, the table is dark...'). What I mean is that I am experiencing things in a blurry way. Isn't this a straightforward case of where one can be 'directly' aware of an aspect of one's experience which is not an aspect of the objects of experience? It is natural to say that I am aware of blurriness; but I am not aware of blurriness by being aware of any other properties; and blurriness does not seem to be a property of objects of experience.

Tye's response to cases like this appeals again to representation. He claims that there are cases when one experiences something *as* blurry, when one's visual experience 'comments inaccurately on boundaries': it 'says' that the boundaries of things are fuzzy (2000). We can concede that there are cases like this; but they are not relevant. The relevant case is one in which one experiences things *blurrily* without experiencing them *as* blurry. About this kind of case, Tye says that one 'simply loses information . . . one undergoes sensory representations that fail to specify where the boundaries and contours lie' (2000). In this kind of case, then, the experience does not 'say' incorrectly that things are blurry; it just fails to specify how things are in enough detail.

But how does this bear on the question of whether one can be 'directly aware of qualities of experience'? Let's accept that Tye is right that the experience underspecifies the perceived environment. The phenomenal upshot of this, everyone agrees, is that things are seen blurrily. So blurriness does seem to be a property of some kind, which does seem to be instantiated somewhere. Unlike when things are seen *as* blurry, it doesn't seem to be instantiated by the objects of experience. So what is wrong with saying that it is instantiated (in some way) in the experience itself? Moreover, since I do not have to make myself aware of blurriness by first making myself aware of other things—the awareness of blurriness comes along all together with the awareness of everything else—introspection of seeing blurrily does seem to reveal a case of being 'directly aware of qualities of experience' in an uncontroversial sense of that phrase.

Neither part of the transparency claim, then, is true without qualification. To be sure, it is generally true that the things we see directly are ordinary things and their properties: and in this sense we normally 'see through' experiences to the real-world objects and properties themselves. But if subjectively indistinguishable hallucinations are possible, then this is not always true. Likewise, it is generally true that we are not directly aware of properties of experiences themselves. But there also seem to be uncontroversial cases where we are, and it is not obvious why we should argue them away.

If representationalism is committed to the transparency theses, then it is false. But this fact does not itself imply the qualia theory. For the qualia theory as defined above is not simply the denial of representationalism; rather it denies representationalism *and* gives an explanation of this denial in terms of qualia (intrinsic, conscious, non-representational properties of experience).[4] I will return to the qualia theory in section 6.

Nonetheless, our brief investigation of transparency has brought to light two questions at the heart of the traditional philosophical debates about perception. Reflection on the positive transparency claim raises the question: how should we give an account of what we experience when we hallucinate something? And reflection on the negative transparency claim raises the question: how should we give an account of the properties which seem to be instantiated in experience when those properties are *not*—and do not even seem to be—properties of

---

[4] Sceptics about qualia will not find this definition of 'qualia' very illuminating; while I am sympathetic to this scepticism, I will assume this standard characterization in what follows for the sake of argument.

external objects? This second question leads us back to the argument from illusion; while the first leads us to the argument from hallucination.

3   THE PROBLEMS OF PERCEPTION

The traditional arguments from illusion and from hallucination deserve separate treatment. Some philosophers (occasionally following Austin 1962) have expressed scepticism about whether these arguments are still worth discussing. I will not target such scepticism directly, but instead I will rely on the recent defences of the arguments by Howard Robinson (1994) and A. D. Smith (2002).

First, the argument from illusion. An illusion here we can define with Smith as 'any perceptual situation in which a physical object is actually perceived, but in which that object perceptually appears other than it really is' (Smith 2002: 23). So illusion in this sense need not involve deception. The argument from illusion says that when one is subject to an illusion (in this sense) then one is experientially aware of something's having a quality, *F*, which the real object being perceived does not actually have. It is then argued that when one is experientially aware of something's having a sensory quality *F*, then there is something of which one is aware which does have quality *F* (this claim is what Robinson (1994: 32) calls the 'Phenomenal Principle'). Since the real object in question is, by hypothesis, not *F*, then it follows that one is not aware of this real object after all; or, if one is, one is aware of it only 'indirectly' and not in the direct, unmediated way in which we normally think we are aware of objects. Hence this normal belief—sometimes called 'naive realism' or 'direct realism'—is false. The standard traditional alternative to direct realism is the sense-datum theory, which says that the thing of which one is aware (or immediately or directly aware) is not a public physical object but an object (a 'sense-datum') whose existence depends on the existence of the experience. It is this object which has the quality *F* which the real object does not have.

The argument from illusion is often rejected because the Phenomenal Principle is rejected: why should it be that whenever anyone is aware of something as having a property, there *really is* something which has this property? This is not true for the case of belief or judgement, for example: that when someone consciously judges that something has a property, then there *is* something which has this property. Indeed, it is often said that perception, like belief, is a form of representation of the world, and it is not true of representations in general that when a representation represents that something has a property, there is something which does have that property. To claim that it must be otherwise in the case of perceptual experience is to beg the question in favour of sense-data.

Nonetheless, even if one rejects sense-data, one might hold that the quality *F* of which one is aware in having an illusory experience is not a quality of any object of experience, but is rather a quality of the experience itself. This is the essence of the 'abverbial' conception of experience (Chisholm 1957; Ducasse 1942). When one experiences a blue object, this is understood as experiencing bluely—where the adverb 'bluely' modifies, and therefore attributes a property to, the experience. The idea that perceptual experience involves this kind of property of experience resembles the central claim of the qualia theory. Like the adverbial theorist, the qualia theorist need not say that the quality predicated of an experience is the same *kind* of quality as the quality predicated of the object of experience. Instead they might say, with Peacocke (1983, ch. 1), that while objects are blue, regions of the visual field are blue', where being blue' is the way the visual field is when a blue object is perceived in normal circumstances. I will return to the relation between the adverbial theory and the qualia theory at the end of this paper.

The argument from hallucination can be formulated as follows. Perceptual experience in all five senses seems intuitively to be a relation to mind-independent objects of experience. But it seems possible for there to be an experience which seems just like a perception of a real mind-independent object but where there is no real mind-independent object being perceived. This is what we shall call a hallucination. If a hallucination is a mental state of the same fundamental kind as the perception, then it turns out that perceptual experience isn't a relation to a mind-independent object after all. The conclusion of this bit of the argument is that our pre-theoretical conception of perception as a relation to mind-independent objects must be wrong. So what should we say instead? A traditional answer again is that perception is instead a relation to sense-data, construed as mind-dependent entities (Broad 1923; Price 1932). This answer has been widely criticized and I will not add to these criticisms here.

But other answers are possible. One is to deny that perception is essentially a relation at all. Rather, perception is a representation of the world; and, as we saw above, it is not generally true that if X represents Y, then, Y must exist. So a perceptual representation need not essentially involve a relation to what it represents. This is the intentionalist conception of perception, which I will discuss in section 4 below. Another response to the argument is to deny that a perception and a subjectively indistinguishable hallucination are mental states or events of the same fundamental kind. Perception is a genuine relation to the world, but hallucination is a mere appearance or mere representation; and there is no more fundamental kind of mental state ('perceptual experience') to which they both belong. This is the disjunctivist conception of perception, to be discussed in section 5. The contrast between these two views is well described by John Campbell as the contrast between the 'Relational' and 'Representational' views of experience (Campbell 2002: 114–24).

Looked at from a sufficient distance, the arguments from illusion and hallucination have a similar form. They both present a conflict between an apparently manifest or obvious fact about perceptual experience, and a kind of perceptual error or misperception of the world. The apparently obvious fact is that experience seems to be a relation to its objects. From the subject's point of view, experience seems to be a kind of 'openness to the world': how things are in perceptual experience is partly determined by how things are with the objects of experience. And how things are in an experience is partly determined by how the objects of experience are at the time at which one is experiencing them. This seems an obvious apparent difference between perception and thought: what you can think about does not seem to be constrained, in general, by the existence and characteristics of the objects of thought; what you can perceive, however, does. (This point is not intended to presuppose internalism about thought; even if externalism were true, this contrast between perception and thought would stand.)[5]

The importance of this apparent relationality is especially obvious in the case of the argument from hallucination, which can be construed as a *reductio ad absurdum* of the idea that perception is a relation to mind-independent objects. But it is also implicit in the central premise of the argument from illusion, Robinson's Phenomenal Principle. Recall that this principle says that when a subject has a sensory experience as of something being *F*, then there is something which is *F* which the subject is experiencing. In other words, an experience of something's being *F* must be or involve a relation to an instantiation of *F*-ness. Faced with the apparent presence of *F*-ness even when the object perceived is not *F*, the sense-datum theorist says that *F*-ness is a property of a sense-datum. The adverbialist responds to this by saying that the experience has the property of being a sensing *F*-ly. This property is not *F*-ness: experiences of blue things are not themselves blue. But nonetheless even the adverbial theory holds that experience must be explained in terms of the instantiation of phenomenal mental properties of a certain kind.

Our reflections on the inadequacy of the transparency thesis led us back to the traditional problem of perception. The essence of this problem, it seems to me, is how to account for the apparent relationality of perception, given the possibility of illusion and hallucination. In other words, is there really a perceptual *relation*, as there seems to be? The three dominant theories respond to this in different ways: the sense-data theorist and the disjunctivist say that there is a perceptual relation, but while the sense-data theorist says that in cases of illusion and hallucination the relatum is not an ordinary mind-independent object, the disjunctivist says that genuine perception is a relation to ordinary mind-independent objects, but that there is no common fundamental kind of state—'perceptual experience'—present in cases of genuine perception, which is a relation to a mind-independent object, and illusion and hallucination, which are not. The intentionalist theory of perception in effect denies that perceptual

---

[5] Nor is the issue whether ordinary perceptual verbs, like 'sees that . . .' are factive. All participants to this dispute can agree with this, but this semantic point is independent of all the substantive issues raised by the problem of perception.

experience is a relation at all. In the next two sections I will consider this opposition between the intentionalist and disjunctivist theories of perception, before returning to the question of qualia in section 6.[6]

4   INTENTIONALITY

We saw that a natural response to the arguments from illusion and hallucination was to deny what Robinson calls the Phenomenal Principle. And the reason to deny it in the case of perceptual experience is because experience seems an obvious case of representation of the world, and principles like this are not generally true of representations. So we are not obliged to accept the Phenomenal Principle. To deny the Phenomenal Principle is to hold, then, that the existence of a perceptual experience does not entail the existence of its object. This implies straightforwardly that experiences are not relations to the objects of experience.[7]

It has traditionally been part of the concept of intentionality—the mind's directedness upon its objects—that the existence of an intentional state does not entail the existence of its object and that therefore intentionality is not a relation in the sense just specified (see Brentano 1995: 271–2; Husserl 2001: 216; Anscombe 1965). It is for this reason that I call the non-relational, representational conception of experience *intentionalism*. I will also assume, along with the philosophical orthodoxy, that if a condition or property is not relational then it is intrinsic. So intentionality in this traditional sense must be an intrinsic feature of mental states or acts. And intentionalism therefore says that the intentionality of perception is intrinsic to perceptual experiences themselves.

This traditional understanding of intentionality—that it is not a relation, and therefore an intrinsic feature of states of mind—has been obscured in recent discussion by a number of other ideas. One is externalism, which I will discuss below. Another is the fact that qualia are typically characterized as *intrinsic* features of states of mind, in contrast with intentional features which are then supposed to be relational. Intentional properties are sometimes said to be relational because intentionality is understood functionally, in terms of 'relations to other states of mind'. But in fact this is not an adequate understanding of functionalism—since many of these 'relations' are only dispositional in nature, and dispositions clearly are not relations to their manifestations—and it would in any case beg the question against a functionalist account of qualia, such as that presented by Shoemaker (1975).

---

[6] It will be obvious to anyone familiar with Mike Martin's work on perception (especially 2000, 2002, 2003) how much the discussion in this section is indebted to him.

[7] Assuming, of course, that the objects of hallucinations are not non-existent real objects. See Smith (2002: ch. 9) for an illuminating discussion of this kind of view.

Yet another reason why intentional properties are thought to be relational is that they are supposed to involve relations to 'intensional entities' such as propositions. In a recent paper, Daniel Stoljar introduces a thesis about the phenomenal character of experience which he calls the *relational thesis*: 'the phenomenal character of an experience is wholly determined by the objects that one is related to in having the experience'. Put this way, Stoljar's thesis sounds the same as Campbell's relational view of experience: 'the phenomenal character of your experience, as you look around the room, is constituted by the actual layout of the room itself' (2002: 116). But it turns out that Stoljar means something different, since the view he calls 'intentionalism' (which is in fact Tye's representationalism) holds this relational thesis too:

According to intentionalism . . . to have an experience is in effect to stand in a relation to some intentional object—say a property or proposition. . . . the relational thesis tells us that the phenomenal character of the experience is determined by features of the proposition or property that is the intentional object of the experience. (Stoljar forthcoming: section 2.5)

But we should distinguish the propositional content of an experience—the way it represents the world as being—from its intentional object. The intentional object of an intentional state or act is traditionally understood as what the intentional act is about or directed at. Hence the intentional object of a perceptual experience is *what it is that is experienced*. If I see a rabbit, the rabbit is the intentional object of my experience. My experience may also have the propositional content that there is a rabbit running through the field. But I do not see such propositional contents or propositions; I see rabbits and fields. For this reason, even if perceptual experience should be analysed in terms of relations to propositions, it is at best misleading and at worst absurd to say that these propositions are the intentional *objects* of experience in the normal understanding of this phrase.

In treating an intentional theory of perception as committed to what he calls the relational thesis—with 'object' understood to apply to propositions as well as ordinary objects—Stoljar conflates two ideas: relations to intentional objects and relations to propositions. If we are considering the special case of so-called 'singular' (or object-dependent) propositions, to be examined below, then it is natural to move from one to the other. But nonetheless the ideas are distinct: one could consistently deny that intentionality is a relation to intentional objects and yet maintain that it can involve relations to propositions of some kind. This might mean, for example, that intentional states have a structure which can be analysed in various ways. For instance, one can distinguish within a propositional attitude the attitude type (belief, hope, etc.) from the specific content of the attitude.[8]

---

[8] More generally, we can distinguish between what I call, following Searle (1983), intentional *mode* and intentional content (Crane 2001: 28–33). This is the distinction Husserl expresses as the distinction between intentional *quality* and intentional *matter* (Husserl 1900/1901: 233).

And one can hold this together with the denial that intentionality is essentially a relation to its objects. In the case of perception, this means that experiences are not essentially relations to the object of experience: *what is seen, touched, smelled, etc.* And since it would be absurd to think that a proposition is the object of an experience in this sense, the thesis that intentional states are 'relations to propositions' is consistent with the thesis that they are not relations to their objects. So an intentionalist theory of perception, on this understanding, says that perceptual representation is intrinsic to the perceptual state itself, that it represents the world, even if the state is one which can be analysed into its various components.[9]

Some philosophers, however, will deny that intentionality or representation is non-relational: externalists about intentionality or mental content will say that some intentionality is genuinely relational. They will say that some representations are relational and others are not. Hence they will say that some intentionality is relational and some is not. Of course, I cannot object to someone who decides to use the term 'intentionality' in this way; the important thing here is not which words one uses but which ideas and distinctions among ideas one is trying to express. Nonetheless, I doubt whether this is the most helpful way to use the terminology of intentionality in this context. For it seems to me extremely obscure how one of the fundamental characteristics of the mind (or, indeed, anything) could, in itself, be *sometimes* a relation, and sometimes not. But I will not address this issue directly here. Instead, I will briefly address the question of whether such a 'mixed' view of intentionality can properly accommodate the distinction I am drawing (to use Campbell's words) between relational and representational views of experience.

The mixed view says that this is best accommodated by the distinction between object-dependent and object-independent intentional contents or states. An object-dependent intentional state is one whose existence depends on the existence of a particular object; an object-independent state is one whose existence does not. So the idea is that a representational conception of experience must employ an object-independent conception of intentional states, and a

---

[9] This characterization of the intentionality of perception differs from that recently offered by Alex Byrne (2001). Byrne describes intentionalism about perception as the view that 'the propositional content of perceptual experiences in a particular modality (for example, vision) *determines* their phenomenal character. In other words: there can be no difference in phenomenal character without a difference in content' (Byrne 2001: section 2; see also Tye 2000: 45). Byrne takes intentionalism so characterized to be compatible with both a version of the sense-data theory and with disjunctivism (2001: 205, fn. 7, and end of section 1). This is because he thinks that these theories all hold that perception *has* a representational propositional content; they just differ over what the content exactly *concerns* or is *about*. Therefore the only non-intentional theories of perception are (a) the adverbial theory and (b) the qualia theory. This way of thinking is initially appealing: indeed, I accepted something like it myself in chapter 5 of Crane (2001); but I now think this way of thinking about perception misrepresents the essence of the intentional theory, since it does not make the significant distinction between the relational and representational views of experience.

relational conception must employ an object-dependent conception. However, the first of these claims is not true: as Burge (1991) has shown, a representational theory of perception can allow that particular episodes of perceiving are object-dependent in character. On Burge's theory, hallucination and perception have the same content, and hence are states of the same fundamental kind, even though the specific nature of a particular episode of perceiving may involve the existence of a particular object. We need to distinguish between what is true of the individual episode of perceiving and what is true of states belonging to the same fundamental kind (see Martin 2003 for a detailed defence of this distinction).

But even if the representational conception does not have to employ an object-independent conception of mental states, couldn't the essence of the relational conception be expressed by the idea of an object-*dependent* intentional state? The answer to this question is complex. First, it should be pointed out that the very idea of an object-dependent state of mind is not sufficient to account for genuine perception as the relational conception understands it. For object-dependent states of mind, if there are any such things, might be object-dependent for many reasons: maybe because they are essentially expressed using proper names; or maybe because they concern 'natural kinds'; or maybe because they exploit some causal link to the object of thought. In all of these cases, the existence of the particular state of mind is dependent on the existence of an object. But in none of them is the object present to the mind in the way that the relational conception says objects are present to the mind in perception. What is distinctive of this presence to the mind we find in perception? The defender of the mixed view may answer that what is distinctive of perception is that the specific kind of intentional act required is an act with a demonstrative content: thoughts with content of the form *that is F* or *that F is G*. The idea is then that the relational conception of perceptual experience will give an account of the object-dependent intentionality of perception in terms of the subject's capacity to have demonstrative thoughts about the objects perceived.

This is a plausible thing for the defender of the mixed view to say. But notice that it is making a claim about the distinctive content of perception depend on a claim about the distinctive kinds of demonstrative thoughts which perception makes available. As Campbell has argued, there is a more fundamental question: what is it for perception to make something available for thought in the first place? And here I think we get a better understanding of the sense in which perception is relational if we ask, not about the contents of thoughts based on perception, but about perception itself (see Campbell 2002). The fundamental idea behind the relational view of perception is that perception somehow makes the *world itself* manifest to the mind. To understand this idea better we should suspend this talk of object-dependent thoughts and try and locate the real heart of the relational conception of perceptual experience.

5 DISJUNCTIVISM

The theory which best accommodates the relational conception of perceptual experience is the disjunctivist theory. Disjunctivism is best seen as a response to the problem of hallucination which attempts to do justice to the fact that in genuine perception the objects of experience are present to the mind in a way in which they can never be in thought. In attempting to do justice to the sense in which the *world itself*—and not just a representation of it, even an object-dependent representation of it—is present to the mind in perception, disjunctivism proposes that different accounts should be given of genuine perception and hallucination. Disjunctivism makes the possibility of hallucination compatible with the relationality of perception by denying that the hallucination and the subjectively indistinguishable perception are states of the same fundamental psychological kind. The theory denies therefore that subjective indistinguishability of experiences is a sufficient for them to be of the same fundamental kind.

By denying this, disjunctivism does not deny that there is some true description under which both the perception, say, of a rabbit and a subjectively indistinguishable hallucination of a rabbit can fall. It is easy to provide such a true description: both experiences are *experiences which are subjectively indistinguishable from a perception of a rabbit*. Disjunctivists do not deny that there is such a true description. What they deny is that what *makes* it true that these two experiences are describable in this way is the presence of the *same specific kind of mental state* in the case of perception and hallucination. In the case of the perception, what makes it true that the description applies is that the experience is a perception of a rabbit; in the hallucinatory case, what makes it true that the description applies is that the experience is a hallucination of a rabbit. What the disjunctivist therefore rejects is what J. M. Hinton calls 'the doctrine of the "experience" as the common element in a given perception' and an indistinguishable hallucination (Hinton 1973: 71). The most specific common description of both states, then, is a merely *disjunctive* one: the perceptual appearance of a rabbit is *either* a genuine perception of a rabbit *or* a mere hallucination of a rabbit. Hence the theory's name.[10]

Disjunctivism is sometimes misunderstood, by its friends as well as by its enemies. In his endorsement of the theory, Putnam argues that its distinctive claim is 'that there is nothing literally in common' in perception and hallucination, 'that is, no identical quality' (1999: 152). But this cannot be right. For, as we have just observed, disjunctivists *do* say that there is something literally in common between a perception of an *X* and a hallucination of an *X*—each state is

[10] The theory was first proposed by Hinton (1973) and was later developed by P. F. Snowdon (1979), John McDowell (1982 and 1986) and M. G. F. Martin (2002, 2004). It has recently been endorsed by Hilary Putnam (1999) and Timothy Williamson (2000).

subjectively indistinguishable from a perception of an *X*—and to that extent they exhibit a common 'quality'. As McDowell says, 'the uncontentiously legitimate category of things that are the same across the different cases is the category of how things seem to the subject' (McDowell 1986: 157). But what the members of this category have in common is not that they are all the same kind of *experience*. It is rather that to be a member of this category, a state of mind merely has to satisfy a disjunctive condition of the kind described in the previous paragraph.[11]

Disjunctivists need not deny either that there is a common *physical* state—for example, a brain state—shared by the perceiver and the hallucinator. What they will deny is that the state of perceiving an object is identical with, or supervenes upon, this physical state. This is because perceiving an object is an essentially relational state, of which the object perceived is a constituent; so the perception is *constitutively dependent* on the object perceived. Whereas the intentionalist sees the qualities presented in perceptual experience as *represented*, the disjunctivist sees these qualities as *instantiated* in perception, and as merely represented in hallucination (Martin 2002: 392–5). This is why disjunctivists sometimes argue that only by treating qualities as instantiated in this way can we do justice to the sense in which perception is the *presentation* as opposed to the *representation* of the things perceived (see the discussion in Searle 1983: 45–6; and the commentary on this in McDowell 1994b). For this reason, it seems to me preferable not to say that the relationality of perception is best captured, according to this view, by a special kind of relational (or object-dependent) 'representational content'. Rather, the key idea is this: the phenomenal character of a genuine perception is determined by how the perceived world is.

The essence of the disjunctivist view, on the present understanding, is its attempt to preserve the genuine relationality of perception. As we saw at the beginning of this paper, that perceptual experience is a genuine relation to its objects seems at first like the most obvious fact about experience. It is easy to see how it lies behind Strawson's claim about our ordinary descriptions of experience, and behind the positive claim of the transparency thesis. So to preserve this relationality would be to preserve one of the central features of perception as we

[11] Putnam thinks, however, that there is an argument against the view that there is *anything* in common between perception and hallucination. Hallucinations are defined as states of mind which are subjectively indistinguishable from perceptions. But, he argues, subjective indistinguishability cannot define a condition for the identity of mental states since (as reflection on the so-called 'phenomenal sorites' shows) subjective indistinguishability is not transitive whereas identity must be (1999: 130). If Putnam's argument were sound, then it would show that there can be no common identical condition or state, defined simply in terms of subjective indistinguishability, in hallucination and perception. But, as we have seen, the existence of such a state or condition is a consequence of the definition of hallucination in this context; so everyone, disjunctivists included, must accept it. So there must be something wrong with Putnam's argument; for myself, I am persuaded by Graff (2001) that subjective indistinguishability is, contrary to widespread opinion, transitive.

experience it—part of the commonsense conception, if you like. Disjunctivists preserve this feature by denying something which is not (they claim) so obviously part of the common-sense conception of perception: that conscious states which are subjectively indistinguishable are states of the same fundamental, determinate or specific kind. So it is wrong to say, as Tye (2000) does, that disjunctivism can be rejected because it is contrary to common sense. Rather, the view is attempting to preserve what seems to be one of the most obvious or common-sense features of perception—its relationality—in the face of the challenge from the argument from hallucination. The price it pays for this is that it cannot count subjectively indistinguishable states of mind as states of the same fundamental kind, and therefore it imposes limits on what can be known about the nature of experience from the subjective perspective; in other words, limits on authoritative introspective self-knowledge (Martin 2003). These limits should not, however, come as a surprise to anyone tempted by externalist conceptions of the mind. For, despite the continued debate about the compatibility of externalism and authoritative 'self-knowledge', it is arguably part of the essence of externalism that it imposes limits on what can be known about the mind through introspection (Farkas 2003).

The intentionalist view also comes with a price. For it must deny that perceptual experience is a relation. When one does succeed in perceiving an object, one is related to it, of course; but this relation is not essential to the perceptual experience being of the fundamental kind that it is. In a certain sense, then, critics of intentionalism are right when they say that on the intentionalist view, perception 'falls short' of the world, and in this sense creates what Putnam calls an 'interface' between the mind and the world. The essence of perception—perceptual experience itself—does fall short of the world. But, according to the intentionalist, this is not something which should create any metaphysical or epistemological anxiety; it is simply a consequence of a general aspect of intentionality as traditionally conceived.

6   THE QUESTION OF QUALIA

Where does this discussion of the intentionalist and disjunctivist theories leave the question of qualia? To answer this question, I need to step back and recapitulate some of the points I have been trying to make here.

One reason we are provoked to offer a philosophical theory or account of some phenomenon is that the phenomenon is itself intrinsically puzzling, or because some argument is constructed to demonstrate that it is problematic or even impossible. So it is, I have argued, with philosophical theories of perception. The sense-data, intentionalist and disjunctivist theories of perception are attempts to answer the apparent contradictions found within the phenomena of perception when we consider certain actual or possible perceptual scenarios.

Without challenges like this, it is somewhat hard to see why we would need a philosophical theory of perception at all. I argued in section 2 that the transparency claims brought to light two questions: (i) how should we account for what we see when we see what isn't there? And (ii) how should we account for those properties instantiated in experience which are not properties of objects of experience? In section 3, I showed how these two questions lie behind the arguments from hallucination and illusion, and how the main theories of perception are best seen as responding to these problems. Sections 4 and 5 described in a bit more detail what the conflict between these theories of experience—the disjunctive and the intentionalist theories—really amounts to. I claim that the fundamental disagreement is about whether there is a perceptual relation.

Where does the qualia theory fit into this conception of the problems of perception? One possible place might seem to be that occupied by the adverbial theory. The adverbial theory says that when it seems that a perceived object is *F* even though it is not, the experience has the property of being a sensing *F*-ly. The theory can then use this account to answer the argument from hallucination: the objects one is aware of in hallucination are really modifications of one's own experience. Regardless of its plausibility, the adverbial theory is an intelligible response to the problems of perception as described here.

But today's qualia theory is not the adverbial theory. The qualia theory typically accepts that perception exhibits intentionality, that it has intentional content. But it holds that this cannot account for the entire phenomenal character of perceptual experience (Block 1996; Peacocke 1983: ch. 1). Hence it does not try to explain all aspects of what is given in experience in terms of qualia; only the 'qualitative' aspects. We need not embark on a discussion of what 'qualitative' means here; we need only observe that while it is often said that there are 'red qualia' or 'sour taste qualia', few qualia theorists these days will say there are tomato qualia or round qualia. The adverbial theory, on the other hand, *did* attempt to explain all aspects of what is given in experience in terms of properties of experience: this is because it was responding—however unsuccessfully—to the problems posed by the arguments from illusion and hallucination. Today's qualia theory, by contrast, does not seem to be a direct response to these problems.

It may be said here that this objection is purely *ad hominem*: even if today's qualia theory does not actually go all the way with the adverbial theory, what is stopping it from doing so? That is, why shouldn't the qualia theory attempt to explain *all* features of what it is like to have an experience in terms of intrinsic, non-intentional qualities of experience? The simple answer to this is that if it did this—and became a real adverbial theory—then it would cease to have any plausibility at all. There are familiar reasons why the adverbial theory is indefensible (see Jackson 1977) and their source can be traced back to the theory's failure to accommodate even the apparent relationality of perception (see Martin 1998; Crane 2000). So it is central to any plausibility the qualia theory has that it is not identical with the adverbial theory.

As it is normally formulated, then, the qualia theory is best seen as a form of the idea is that in addition to an experience's having representational content, the experience also has qualia. As explained in section 1, this claim is not simply the denial of representationalism. That is, it is not just the view that one can be aware of how one's experience is, as opposed to how the objects of experience are. I argued in section 2 that this view is very plausible, and that Tye's representationalism is therefore false. One can be aware, for example, that one is seeing something, and the fact that one is seeing something (as opposed to hearing it) is not itself a fact about the objects of one's experience (see Block forthcoming). Rather, it is an introspectible fact about the experience itself. The same is true of the case of seeing blurrily. However, these facts do not have to be understood in terms of the instantiation of intrinsic qualia. This is a further claim, which needs further argument.[12]

Disjunctivists and intentionalists should both deny Tye's representationalism for the reason just given. But since disjunctivists reject the idea that perceptual experience can be given an intrinsic qualitative characterization, they will accordingly reject the idea that experience involves qualia: the only characterization of a genuine, veridical, perceptual experience is a relational one; and the only experiential way of characterizing the hallucinatory experience is as a mental episode which is subjectively indistinguishable from a veridical experience. If there were qualia, then there would be a further common characterization of the perception and the hallucination in terms of their common intrinsic nature. Since the disjunctivist holds that there is no such thing, disjunctivists must reject qualia.

Philosopher's who reject Tye's intentionalism may still want to argue about whether there are qualia. But whatever the reasons on either side of this argument, they do not spring from the debates at the heart of the philosophy of perception, understood in terms of the traditional problems of illusion and hallucination. For adopting the qualia theory does not advance these debates, and nor does denying it. This is because these debates turn fundamentally on the question of whether there is a perceptual relation, and the qualia theory simply fails to engage with that question. Far from creating a chasm in the philosophy of perception, then, the question of qualia does not even make a small crevasse.

---

[12] To give an illustration of how you can deny representationalism while denying qualia: an intentionalist about perception might want to say that what one is aware of in these cases is something like the intentional *mode* (Crane 2001: 143–4) rather than visual field qualia like Peacocke's (1983) 'primed predicates'.

REFERENCES

Anscombe, G. E. M. (1965), 'The Intentionality of Sensation: A Grammatical Feature', in R. J. Butler (ed.), *Analytical Philosophy: First Series* (Oxford: Blackwell); reprinted in her *Metaphysics and the Philosophy of Mind: Collected Papers, Vol. II.* (Oxford: Blackwell); also in A. Noë and E. Thompson (eds) 2002.

Austin, J. L. (1962), *Sense and Sensibilia* (Oxford: Oxford University Press).

Block, Ned (1996), 'Mental Paint and Mental Latex', in E. Villanueva (ed.), *Philosophical Issues* 7 (Atascadero, Calif.: Ridgeview): 19–49.

Block, Ned (1997), 'Inverted Earth', in N. Block, O. Flanagan and G. Güzeldere (eds), *The Nature of Consciousness* (Cambridge, Mass.: MIT Press).

Block, Ned (forthcoming), 'Mental Paint', in M. Hahn and B. Ramberg (eds), *Others on Burge: 10 Essays with Responses from Tyler Burge* (Cambridge, Mass.: MIT Press).

Brentano, Franz (1995), *Psychology from an Empirical Standpoint*, transl. A. C. Rancurello, D. B. Terrell and R. McAlister; L. McAlister (ed.) (London: Routledge & Kegan Paul, 1973); reprinted with an introduction by Peter Simons (London: Routledge, 1995).

Broad, C. D. (1923), 'The Theory of Sensa', in R. J. Swartz 1965.

Burge, Tyler (1991), 'Vision and Intentional Content', in E. LePore and R. Van Gulick (eds), *John Searle and His Critics* (Oxford: Blackwell): 195–213.

Byrne, Alex (2001), 'Intentionalism Defended', *Philosophical Review* 110: 199–240.

Campbell, John (2002), 'Berkeley's Puzzle', in T. S. Gendler and J. Hawthorne (eds), *Conceivability and Possibility* (Oxford: Oxford University Press).

Campbell, John (2003), *Reference and Consciousness* (Oxford: Oxford University Press).

Chalmers, David (1996), *The Conscious Mind: In Search of a Fundamental Theory* (Oxford: Oxford University Press).

Chisholm, Roderick M. (1957), *Perceiving: A Philosophical Study* (Ithaca, NY: Cornell University Press).

Crane, Tim (ed.) (1992), *The Contents of Experience* (Cambridge: Cambridge University Press).

Crane, Tim (2000), 'The Origins of Qualia', in T. Crane and S. Patterson (2000).

Crane, Tim (2001), *Elements of Mind* (Oxford: Oxford University Press).

Crane, Tim and Sarah Patterson (eds) (2000), *History of the Mind–Body Problem* (London: Routledge).

Dancy, Jonathan (ed.) (1988), *Perceptual Knowledge* (Oxford: Oxford University Press).

Ducasse, C. J. (1942), 'Moore's Refutation of Idealism', in P. A. Schilpp (ed.), *The Philosophy of G. E. Moore* (Evanston, ILL: Library of Living Philosophers, now published by Open Court, La Salle, ILL).

Farkas, Katalin (2003), 'What is Externalism?', *Philosophical Studies* 112: 187–208.

Graff, Delia (2001), 'Phenomenal Continuua and the Sorites', *Mind* 110: 905–35.

Harman, Gilbert (1990), 'The Intrinsic Quality of Experience', in J. Tomberlin (ed.), *Philosophical Perspectives* 4 (Atascadero: Ridgeview); reprinted in N. T. Block, Ned, O. Flanagan and G. T. Güzeldere (eds) (1997) *The Nature of Consciousness: Philosophical Debates* (Cambridge, Mass.: MIT Press).

Heidegger, Martin (1935), 'The Origin of the Work of Art', in D. Farrell Krell (ed.) (trans.), *Martin Heidegger: Basic Writings* (New York: Harper and Row, 1977).

Hilbert, David R. and Kalderon, Mark Eli (2000), 'Color and the Inverted Spectrum', in S. Davis (ed.), *Color Perception: Philosophical, Psychological, Artistic and Computational Perspectives* (New York and Oxford: Oxford University Press).

Hinton, J. M. (1973), *Experiences* (Oxford: Clarendon Press).

Husserl, Edmund [1901] (2001), *Logical Investigations*, transl. J. N. Findlay; Dermot Moran (ed.) (London: Ruutledge).

Jackson, Frank (1977), *Perception: A Representative Theory* (Cambridge: Cambridge University Press).

Johnston, Mark (2004), 'The Obscure Object of Hallucination', *Philosophical Studies* 120: 113–83.

Kind, Amy (2003), 'What's So Transparent about Transparency?', *Philosophical Studies* 115: 225–44.

Loar, Brian (2002), 'Transparent Experience', in A. Jokic and Q.Smith (eds), *Consciousness: New Philosophical Perspectives* (Oxford: Oxford University Press).

McDowell, John (1982), 'Criteria, Defeasibility & Knowledge', *Proceedings of the British Academy 1982*: 455–79; reprinted in J. Dancy (ed.) (1988).

McDowell, John (1986), 'Singular Thought and the Extent of Inner Space', in P. Pettit and J. McDowell (eds) (1986); reprinted in McDowell (1998).

McDowell, John (1994a), *Mind and World* (Cambridge, Mass.: Harvard University Press).

McDowell, John (1994b), 'The Content of Perceptual Experience', *Philosophical Quarterly* 44: 190–205; reprinted in A. Noë and E. Thompson (eds) (2002).

McDowell, John (1998), *Meaning, Knowledge and Reality* (Cambridge, Mass.: Harvard University Press).

Martin, M. G. F. (1995), 'Perceptual Content', in S. Guttenplan (ed.), *A Companion to the Philosophy of Mind* (Oxford: Blackwell).

Martin, M. G. F. (1998), 'Setting Things before the Mind', in A. O'Hear (ed.), *Contemporary Issues in the Philosophy of Mind* (Cambridge: Cambridge University Press).

Martin, M. G. F. (2000), 'Beyond Dispute: Sense-Data, Intentionality and the Mind–Body Problem', in T. Crane and S. Patterson (eds) (2000).

Martin, M. G. F. (2002), 'The Transparency of Experience', *Mind and Language* 17: 376–425.

Martin, M. G. F. (2003), 'Particular Thoughts and Singular Thought', in A. O'Hear (ed.), *Thought and Language* (Cambridge: Cambridge University Press).

Martin, M.G. F. (2004), 'The Limits of Self-Awareness', *Philosophical Studies* 120: 37–89.

Noë, Alva and Thompson Evan, (eds.) (2002), *Vision and Mind: Selected Readings in the Philosophy of Perception* (Cambridge, Mass.: MIT Press).

Peacocke, Christopher (1983), *Sense and Content* (Oxford: Oxford University Press).

Pettit, Philip and McDowell, John (eds) (1986), *Subject, Thought and Context* (Oxford: Clarendon Press).

Pitcher, George (1970), *A Theory of Perception* (Princeton: Princeton University Press).

Price, H. H. (1932), *Perception* (London: Methuen).

Putnam, Hilary (1999), *The Threefold Cord* (New York: Columbia University Press).

Robinson, Howard (1994), *Perception* (London: Routledge).

Searle, John (1983), *Intentionality* (Cambridge: Cambridge University Press).

Shoemaker, Sydney (1975), 'Functionalism and Qualia', *Philosophical Studies* 27: 291–315.

Shoemaker, Sydney (1990), 'Qualities and Qualia: What's in the Mind?', *Philosophy and Phenomenological Research* 50, Supplement: 109–31.

Siewert, Charles (2003), 'Is Experience Transparent?', *Philosophical Studies* 117: 15–41.

Smith, A. D. (2002), *The Problem of Perception* (Cambridge, Mass.: Harvard University Press).

Snowdon, P. F. (1979–80), 'Perception, Vision and Causation', *Proceedings of the Aristotelian Society* 81: 175–92.

Snowdon, P. F. (1990), 'The Objects of Perceptual Experience', *Proceedings of the Aristotelian Society Supplementary* 64: 121–50

Stoljar, Daniel (forthcoming), 'The Argument from Diaphanousness', *Canadian Journal of Philosophy*.

Strawson, P. F. (1979), 'Perception and Its Objects', in G. Macdonald (ed.), *Perception and Identity: Essays Presented to A. J. Ayer with His Replies* (London: Macmillan); page references to reprint in A. Noë and E. Thompson (eds) (2002).

Swartz, R. J. (1965), *Perceiving, Sensing and Knowing* (Los Angeles and Berkeley: University of California Press).

Thau, Michael (2002), *Consciousness and Cognition* (Oxford: Oxford University Press).

Tye, Michael (1992), 'Visual Qualia and Visual Content' in T. Crane (ed.) (1992).

Tye, Michael (1995), *Ten Problems of Consciousness: A Representational Theory of the Phenomenal Mind* (Cambridge, Mass.: MIT Press).

Tye, Michael (2000), *Consciousness, Color and Content* (Cambridge, Mass.: MIT Press).

Williamson, Timothy (2000), *Knowledge and Its Limits* (Oxford: Oxford University Press).

4

Perception without Awareness

Fred Dretske

> We appear to be on the horns of a dilemma with respect to the criteria for
> consciousness. Phenomenological criteria are valid by definition but do not
> appear to be scientific by the usual yardsticks. Behavioral criteria are
> scientific by definition but are not necessarily valid.
>
> Stephen Palmer, *Vision Science: Photons to Phenomenology*, p. 629

Unknown to Sarah, her neighbor, a person she sees every day, is a spy. When she
sees him, therefore, she sees him without awareness of either the fact that he is a
spy or the fact that she sees a spy. Why, then, isn't the existence of perception
without awareness (or, as some call it, *implicit* or *subliminal* perception)
a familiar piece of common sense rather than a contentious issue in psychology?[1]
It isn't only spies. We see armadillos, galvanometers, cancerous growths,
divorcees, and poison ivy without realizing we are seeing any such thing. Most
(all?) things can be, and often are (when seen at a distance or in bad light), seen
without awareness of what is being seen and, therefore, without awareness that
one is seeing something of that sort. Why, then, is there disagreement about
unconscious perception? Isn't perception without awareness the rule rather than
a disputed exception to the rule?

I deliberately misrepresent what perception without awareness is supposed to
be in order to emphasize an important preliminary point—the difference
between awareness of a stimulus (an object of some sort) and awareness of facts
about it—including the fact that one is aware of it. When in the course of
ordinary affairs S sees a spy without realizing he is a spy, S, though not aware that
he is a spy and, therefore, not aware that she sees a spy, is nonetheless aware of
the spy. She sees him. She just doesn't know he is a spy. She can point at him and

Thanks to Tamar Gendler, Güven Güzeldere, Peter Graham, John Hawthorne, Ram Neta, and
Mark Phelan for helpful comments and criticisms. I also received useful feedback from members of
the philosophy department at California State University at Northridge.

[1] See Holender (1986) and commentaries; also Dixon (1981), especially ch. 9, for an account of
the sometimes acrimonious debate.

ask, "Who is that?" This is perception with awareness because S, though not aware of certain facts, is aware of the stimulus, her neighbor, the spy. Ignorance of the fact that one is seeing a spy does not impair one's vision of the spy, and it is lack of awareness of it, the spy, the stimulus, not the fact that he is a spy or the fact that one sees a spy, that constitutes perception without awareness.

Perception without awareness, unconscious perception, is therefore to be understood as perception of some object without awareness (consciousness[2]) of that object. Is this possible? Isn't perception defined as a kind of awareness? It is in some dictionaries. *Webster's Ninth New Collegiate Dictionary* tells us that perception is "awareness of the elements of the environment through physical sensation." If this is what it means to perceive the elements around one, then perception of these elements without awareness of them is like a bachelor getting divorced. It can't happen.

The scientific debate about unconscious perception is nourished by a variety of unusual—sometimes quite extraordinary—phenomena that are seldom encountered in ordinary affairs. We will look at some of these later, but, for now, it suffices to say that in deciding how to describe these results, scientists have found it necessary to distinguish different ways of perceiving x. If the way one person obtains visually mediated information about x is strikingly different from the way another person does it, then it proves useful to classify these as different ways of perceiving x. One distinction that has developed over the years is that between a conscious (supraliminal, explicit) and an unconscious (subliminal, implicit) perception of a stimulus: perception of x with awareness and perception of x without awareness of x. This sounds strange to ordinary ears—at least it does to mine—but the visual/cognitive deficits this language is used to mark are strange enough, or so it seems to many investigators, to justify these unusual descriptions. They have convinced many scientists that perception without awareness is a valid and useful concept. My purpose here is to look at these scientific studies for the purpose of learning what they reveal about consciousness. If psychologists can really identify something that deserves to be called perception without awareness, they must have an operational grasp on not only what it takes to perceive something, but on what it takes to be conscious of it. If this is really so, philosophers have something to learn from them; if not about what consciousness is, then about what it does.

1   PERCEPTION

If we are going to find a situation that deserves to be called perception of x without awareness of x we need to first agree about a test for perception (call it T_p) and a

---

[2] I think my usage is fairly standard but, to forestall misunderstandings, I take *awareness* (of a stimulus) and *consciousness* (of a stimulus) to be synonymous. I sometimes speak of being *consciously*

test for awareness (call it T_a) in which satisfaction of the first, though compatible with, does not require satisfaction of the second.

Many psychologists take transmission of information from x to S as an acceptable T_p. S saw x, despite not realizing it, despite denying she saw anything at all, if during the time she was exposed to x, S received information about x. If S's behavior is only (plausibly) explicable by assuming she was getting information about the F-ness (orientation, shape, color, location) of the stimulus, then, although not aware that she perceived it, S must have gotten information about it. S therefore perceived it. Kanwisher's (2001: 90) description of perception as the extraction of perceptual information from a stimulus, without assumption about whether or not this information is experienced consciously, is typical.

Is this really a test? Is it a way of telling whether or not S perceived x? S can get (extract, receive) information about a stimulus and never use this information in any overt way. It might be stored for later use and lost ("forgotten") before it can be used. Or maybe we haven't yet devised appropriately sensitive ways to show that S received information about x. If exposure to x makes a revealing difference in S's behavior, we can be sure S perceived x, but if there is no difference in S's behavior, we cannot conclude she didn't perceive x. Failure to manifest P is not a manifestation of not-P.

This problem can, perhaps, be minimized by remembering that we seek only a positive test, a behavioral sufficient condition, for perception. A behavioral necessary condition isn't really needed. If we can show that S got information about x—and sometimes this is perfectly obvious in S's behavior (if, for example, S describes x in glorious detail)—then even if it is sometimes difficult or impossible to show that S didn't receive information about x, we have what we need—a way of showing that S perceived x. All we need, in addition, to show that S perceived x without awareness is a test for awareness of x that S can fail while demonstrably getting information about x.

A more serious problem concerns the kind of information, the receipt of which should count as perceptual. We don't want to include every reaction by S to x that carries information about x. People have quite distinctive allergic reactions to ragweed. Do these people, for that reason alone, perceive the ragweed? The rash on my leg carries information about my recent contact with or proximity to poison ivy. Should this physiological reaction to poison ivy count as perception of the plant? Human hair is a fairly sensitive indicator of relative humidity. Its length changes in regular and repeatable ways as the humidity varies. Do we perceive (with our hair, as it were) changes in humidity? If so, unconscious perception is a commonplace, not really worth special attention by psychologists and philosophers.

aware of an object, but, given my usage, this is a redundancy. I also use vision (seeing x) as my chief example of perception (and perceptual awareness), but what I say is intended to apply to all sense modalities.

As these examples indicate, information about x may be deemed necessary, but if we trust common-sense judgments, it should not be taken as sufficient for perception. Something besides information about x is needed for perception of x. What might this be? Some will be quick to say *awareness* of x, a *conscious* experience of x, exactly the thing that is missing in the above examples. The reason allergic reactions to ragweed don't count as perception of ragweed is because they don't involve a conscious experience of ragweed. The physiological reaction carries information about the ragweed, yes, but it doesn't make one aware of the ragweed. So it isn't perception.

This move, at this stage of the game, would definitely settle matters: perception without awareness is impossible because awareness of x, a conscious experience of x, is required to make the receipt of information about x a perception of x. There are, however, other options. We might concede that experiences of some kind or other are necessary for perception, but following Carruthers (2000: 147–79) allow for the possibility of unconscious experiences.[3] If we take this route, though, we should be ready to say what, besides carrying information about x, makes an internal state of S an experience of x? If a state needn't be conscious to be an experience, and allergic reactions to ragweed are not to count as experiences of ragweed, what additional properties of information-bearing states make them experiences of x? This is by no means an easy question to answer, but, guided by the way we conceive of conscious experiences of external objects, two additional requirements can be imposed: (1) the information in these states should be available for the control and guidance of action (if the experience is unconscious, of course, the actor need not be aware of this influence); and (2) the information should be extracted from stimulation (as it is with conscious experiences) by accredited receptor systems.[4] If information about x is extracted from light by the photosensitive pigment of the retina, for instance, and this information is available for the control or modification of behavior (reaching, pointing, grasping, identifying, describing), then the state (activity, event) carrying this information is a visual experience of x. Whether or not it is a conscious experience is a separate question. What these two additional conditions give us is the following: E is a visual (auditory, etc.) experience of x in S if E carries information about x, the information is extracted from light by photoreceptors in S's eyes (from sound by acoustic

---

[3] Causal theories of perception (e.g., Grice 1961; Lewis 1980) typically portray perception of objects in terms of a causal relation between the object perceived and some perceptual experience of the perceiver. If experiences are necessarily conscious, then, of course, causal theories are incompatible with unconscious perception. One can keep the causal condition while conceding the possibility of unconscious perception only by acknowledging the possibility of unconscious experiences.

[4] What is "accredited" is pretty much up for grabs, of course, but one thing it is meant to suggest is that it is a receptor system that, given normal continuation, sometimes at least, gives rise to *conscious* experiences. For obvious (to those who know the literature) reasons I do not include neural *pathways* (e.g., dorsal vs. ventral in the case of vision) in "accredited receptor system."

receptors in S's ears, etc.), and this information is directly[5] available for control of S's actions. Allergic reactions to ragweed don't count as perceptions (experiences) of ragweed because the information they carry fails to meet at least one—probably both—of these added constraints. The information isn't extracted by an accredited receptor system, and even if it is (according to some more liberal interpretation of "receptor system"), this information is not directly available for the control and guidance of S's behavior. So, although S receives information about ragweed, she does not perceive it—not even unconsciously.

Even with the additional qualifications to come in a moment (see below), this "test" for perception of an object is not going to withstand philosophical scrutiny—too many loose ends and philosophically troublesome qualifiers. Nonetheless, I propose to adopt it here. As I read the literature, this test comes reasonably close to the usage of people involved in this research while remaining tolerably close to ordinary language—close enough, perhaps, to justify using words like *see* and *hear* for what is being described. We could, I suppose, use subscripts to distinguish this special usage—if it is, indeed, a special usage—but as long as we keep clearly in mind what we are describing with these perceptual terms, confusion can, I hope, be avoided.

There is, however, another respect in which even if information arrives over an accredited sensory channel and influences a person's behavior, this is not enough for perception. I receive information about the Middle East, about continued violence in that part of the world, not by seeing that part of the world, but by reading a newspaper in my living room. I don't have to see my gas tank to get information about it—that it is almost empty—through my eyes. What I actually see is the gas gauge, not the gas tank. Perception typically provides us with information about all sorts of objects we don't perceive. That is what instruments, radio, television, and newspapers (not to mention spies and informants) are for. They provide information about things we do not, perhaps cannot, ourselves perceive.

What is needed here, of course, is some principled distinction between direct and indirect perception. The rough idea is that if information about x is obtained by getting information about y where $y \neq x$ (e.g., a measuring instrument, a newspaper, a pilot light), then as long as y is not a proper part of x, perception of x is not direct. It is indirect. If the information you get about x is embedded in information you get in a direct way about y, then it is y you perceive. You may come to know about and react to x, but it is y you see, hear, or smell. The information I get about the Middle East from the newspaper is derived or indirect information—information delivered via information about the

---

[5] The "directly" is needed here because S's allergic reaction to x might, for instance, result in an itch that S feels or a skin rash that S sees. Feeling the itch or seeing the rash might lead to behavior—scratching or heading to the medicine chest—but in this case the information about x has been re-embodied (re-coded) in an acceptable experiential form. The information in the physiological reaction that gives rise to the itch or the rash is not *directly* available.

newspaper—that the headlines *say* there is continued violence in that part of the world. Information obtained about objects directly in front of us is presumably not indirect in this way. When I read the newspaper in normal conditions, I see the newspaper not simply because I get information about it (I could get that by looking at a photocopy), but because the information I obtain about it is not embedded in information I get about some more proximal object.[6]

I will not try to supply the required definition of *direct* perception. It would take us too far afield. I simply assume a satisfactory account is available. If my own account (Dretske 1981) is deemed unsatisfactory (Haugeland 1996 thinks it is), the reader is free to supply his or her own. If perception—conscious or unconscious—of physical objects (newspapers, gas gauges, people) is deemed possible, some such account must be presupposed.

Finally, a word about *how much* information one must receive (in a direct way) about x in order to perceive x: it needn't be much. Some information is necessary, but it needn't be enough to identify x. One can, after all, see a gadzit at a distance in poor light. It looks the same as a variety of non-gadzits look at this distance and in this light—like a small speck on the horizon. About the only information one gets in these conditions is information about its location. One can point at it. One can keep one's eye on it. One sees Venus in the night sky. It looks like a bright star. Without special instruments, information about the planet is not sufficient to identify it as a planet, not enough to distinguish it from a star. Nonetheless, one still gets information about it; information about its relative location in the night sky. In these circumstances, that is enough— enough, that is, to see it. In other circumstances (examining a bug under a microscope) one gets information about details of x without necessarily getting information about where x is (though one might know, on other grounds, where it is—in the lab, on the slide).

Pulling these ideas together, then, the proposed test for perception looks like this:

T_p: S perceives x = S has a perceptual experience (in our special inclusive sense) that provides (in a direct way) information about x.

From a scientific standpoint, one of the merits of T_p is that it does not require or presuppose consciousness. So it avoids the vexing issues we are trying to defer until §2. It leaves open the possibility of perceiving something unconsciously— without awareness of it. Whether that is really possible depends, of course, on whether an acceptable test for awareness can be formulated that makes awareness

---

[6] In Dretske (1981: 155–68) I argue that it is a mistake to think that information about physical objects (the gas gauge, the newspaper) is always indirect—carried by information we receive about (even) more proximal objects (retinal images? sense-data?). The suggested restriction on the way the information about x must be received (i.e., directly) in order for x to be perceived does not, I argue, preclude perception of familiar objects and events.

of x something more than perception of x and, therefore, something possibly absent when a subject perceives x.

2 CONSCIOUS AWARENESS

"Much of the long-standing controversial status of the study of unconscious processing revolves around the lack of a general consensus as to what constitutes an adequate operational definition of conscious awareness" (Reingold and Toth 1996: 159). An operational definition (at least an operationally useful necessary condition) of conscious awareness (of a stimulus) is our next topic. What can plausibly be used as a test for awareness of x that can fail when (according to T_p) x is perceived?

As already seen (spy example), we cannot use the fact that S does not believe[7] she sees an F (or believes she does not see an F), and therefore sincerely reports not seeing an F, to show that S is not consciously aware of an F. S might not know what Fs are. She might be confused or just not know about the existence (or prevalence) of Fs and, therefore, believe (and say) she is not aware of one when she is, without realizing it, staring one in the face. Or the F that S sees may be so far away, or exposed so briefly, or in such bad light, that it is impossible for S to tell (identify) what it is. That doesn't mean she isn't aware of an F. It only means she doesn't know what it is she is aware of.

More promising than identification or recognition is *detection* of a stimulus. To detect an F one doesn't have to know it is an F. One has only to be able to tell the difference (distinguish or discriminate) between it (the F) being there (wherever one is looking) and its not being there. One doesn't even have to be able to discriminate between Fs and non-Fs. Even if S doesn't believe in extraterrestrials and, as a result, refuses to believe she is seeing one (they look like large dandelions) in her front yard, S will be able to tell the difference between seeing one there ("Look at that huge dandelion!") and not seeing one there ("It's gone now"). If S can, in this way, tell the difference between the presence and absence of extraterrestrials (she needn't be able to tell the difference between extraterrestrials and dandelions), then, no matter what she thinks they are, she can detect them. So, on a detection test of awareness, S is aware of extra-terrestrials in her yard whether or not she knows (believes, judges, thinks) she is. She sees them consciously—with awareness. If, on the other hand, their presence makes no difference to S (they may, like electrons, be very tiny or move around

---

[7] I include a subject's judgments (beliefs, knowledge, thoughts) as a legitimate part of a test for awareness because I assume, for convenience, sincerity (subjects believe what they say), and cooperation (subjects say what they believe relevant). In my way of proceeding, then, a judgment (that P) is equivalent to a report (that P), a more or less obvious piece of behavior. If readers find this objectionable, substitute "report" for "belief" and make the corresponding adjustment in the evidential status (less direct and, therefore, less reliable) of the test result.

too fast to be detected), then, even when they completely surround her, she isn't aware of them. If she nevertheless gets information about them (directly), if she (in our extended sense) experiences them, then, according to T_p she perceives them without awareness. Her perception of them is unconscious, subliminal, or implicit.

But how do we tell whether S can distinguish (discriminate, tell the difference) between x's presence and its absence? Do we leave this up to S? If S sincerely says she can't tell the difference between the presence and absence of x, if, according to S, things look the same to her whether x is there or not, does that settle the matter? Why? Why should we leave this up to S? Maybe she really can "tell" the difference (and we could show this if we found the right way to probe S), but she doesn't realize she can. Maybe her standards for seeing something are too demanding. Maybe she is biased in some way or isn't able or doesn't like to report things she sees in her left visual field.

We are now entering murky territory, territory in which there is a divergence of opinion amongst psychologists about what appropriate criteria are. We can't say, simply, that S can discriminate x's presence from its absence—hence, detect x—if x's presence makes *a* difference to S because this is equivalent to equating detection with perception of x. Making *a* difference to S is just a way of describing S as getting information about the presence of x. We may, in the end, want to declare unconscious perception a theoretical impossibility, but this seems too quick.

Many scientists prefer a *subjective* criterion for detection, a test in which S's judgments and consequent reports about what she (consciously[8]) experiences or perceives (when they reflect a genuine power to detect the stimulus) define what S consciously experiences. Cheesman and Merikle (1984, 1986) clearly opt for this test in establishing subliminal perception: if a subject, asked to say whether anything is present, believes she is just guessing, then the stimulus is below S's subjective threshold of consciousness. S isn't conscious of the stimulus, whether or not she is getting information about it. Of those stimuli S perceives, she is conscious of the ones she believes she is conscious of and not conscious of those she thinks she isn't. Restricting matters to stimuli S perceives[9] in location L (on the screen, in her left visual field, to the right of fixation point), we can express this subjective (superscript "s") test for awareness (subscript "a") as:

^sT_a: If S thinks (sincerely says) she is aware of x in L, she is aware of x; if she thinks (sincerely says) she isn't aware of anything in L, she isn't aware of x.

---

[8] We have to add this qualification because, given our awareness-neutral test for perception (namely, T_p), S might believe she perceives x in this sense by being *told* she perceives x. Blind-sighters, in fact, come to believe they perceive objects in this sense in this way. This, clearly, isn't enough to become consciously aware of the things perceived.

[9] Unless S perceives x (gets *some* information from x), questions about S's awareness of x don't arise. If S gets no information about x, S cannot be aware of x.

Two important clarifications:

(1) ${}^s T_a$ is expressed not as a single condition necessary and sufficient for awareness, but as a dual sufficient condition: one sufficient for awareness, the other for lack of awareness. There is no proposed equivalence between awareness of a stimulus and thinking you are aware of it, for good reason. We do not want to say of someone who perceives x that she is conscious of x if *and only if* she believes (sincerely reports) she perceives x. That would make a judgment that you perceive x into a necessary condition for awareness of x. It isn't. Human infants and a great many animals, I am assuming, are conscious of things around them.[10] They see, hear, and smell things in the same conscious way you and I do, but they do not (need not be able to) think or say that they are aware of them. They are conscious, yes, but, lacking conceptual sophistication, they do not think they are. Nor do they think they are not. They don't have thoughts on this topic. There is awareness, but no *acknowledged* awareness. Acknowledgment, though, isn't necessary for awareness. That is a level of understanding you don't need in order to be aware of things.

Consider my dog, Fido. When Fido sees food in his bowl in what (I am assuming) is a fully conscious way, he may know there is food in his bowl. He may even be trained to "report" (by barking, say) to this effect, but unless the conceptual prowess of animals is vastly underestimated, Fido doesn't think (judge, know) that he sees, doesn't think he is conscious of, doesn't believe he experiences, food in his bowl. That is what *I* think. I believe this as a result of Fido's behavior (wagging his tail, eating from the bowl, barking), but that isn't what Fido thinks.[11] All Fido thinks, if he thinks anything at all, is that there is food in his bowl. That doesn't mean he's not aware of food in his bowl. Fido's impoverished intellectual life doesn't mean he is perceptually deficient. It doesn't mean he isn't aware of his food. He just doesn't know he is aware of it. So ${}^s T_a$ doesn't tell us anything about Fido. Fido satisfies neither the sufficient condition

[10] Not everyone accepts this (see Carruthers 1989, 2000: ch. 7), but I think it is widely enough accepted to justify assuming it here without further argument.

[11] In a series of experiments Logothetis (1998) trained monkeys to, as it were, "report" on their own experiences. Different stimuli were presented to each eye and the monkeys were trained to report on which stimulus they experienced. Under these conditions (binocular rivalry) human subjects report experiencing not a superposition of the two images, but an alternating sequence—first, say, vertical stripes (presented to the left eye), then horizontal stripes (presented to the right eye). A monkey's "reports" also alternate in this way. I think, however, it would be a mistake to treat these "reports" as reports about the monkey's experience. Unlike human subjects who understand the difference between x, the object of experience, and their experience of it, a monkey only reports on *what* it experiences—"vertical" vs. "horizontal" stripes—not *that* it is experiencing these different things. We assume that when a monkey reports the presence of a stimulus, he is aware of the stimulus in something like the way we are. We assume, that is, that the monkey would not be able to report "vertical" lines unless he was aware of them, but this (the fact that the monkey is aware of vertical stripes) is an inference we make about what it takes for an animal to report "vertical stripes." It should not be confused with what the animal is reporting—much less judging, believing, or knowing.

for awareness of food in his bowl nor the condition for the absence of awareness. If we want to know whether Fido is conscious of the food in his bowl (we already infer from his behavior that he perceives it), we would have to use some other test. The same is true for humans (e.g., one-year olds) before they understand what it means to perceive something (hence, are unable to judge and report that they are or are not aware of things). The inapplicability of ^sT_a to very young children and animals, however, does not mean that it is not a suitable test for those of us who know what it means to be aware of things. All it means is that we should understand the test to be of limited scope. It is designed for subjects who understand and can make judgments about not only the objects they are aware of, but their awareness of them.

(2) For awareness of x, ^sT_a requires (as part of the sufficient condition for awareness) more than perception of x. It requires that the information (necessary for perception of x) be embodied, specifically, in S's beliefs or judgments about whether she is aware, whether she perceives, x. S might perceive x and, according to ^sT_a, *not* be aware of x because the information (necessary for perception) fails to produce a belief, a judgment, that she is aware of something. It is not enough that S believes (or says) that there is something (which turns out to be x) in L in order to be aware of x. According to ^sT_a, S must actually judge (and be prepared to say) that she *perceives* it. We shall, in a moment, look at an *objective* test for awareness, ^oT_a, that requires, for awareness of x, merely that S reliably judge or say whether x is present. This objective test for awareness of x is a test a subject can satisfy while believing she perceives absolutely nothing at all. ^sT_a is stronger. It requires that the subject not only reliably "say" a stimulus is present when it is present (Fido can do this much by barking), but think she is aware of it (Fido, I assume, can't do this).

Scientists have objected to ^sT_a on the grounds that it places on the individual subject the responsibility for establishing the criterion of awareness. (Eriksen 1959, 1960: 292; Underwood and Bright 1996: 4; Merikle 1984). It transfers responsibility for defining awareness (saying when a subject is aware of x) from the investigator to the subject of investigation.

factors unrelated to awareness, such as demand characteristics and preconceived biases, may lead subjects to adopt a conservative response criterion and report null perceptual awareness even under conditions in which conscious perceptual information is available. Response bias represents a threat not only to the validity of the subjective report measure of awareness, but also to its reliability. In particular, variability in response criteria makes it difficult to compare reports of null subjective confidence across-subjects, or within-subjects across conditions. (Reingold and Toth 1996: 162)

Such considerations led Eriksen (1959, 1960) to reject a subjective test as an adequate measure of awareness. He suggested, instead, that awareness be operationally defined in terms of performance on tasks that are independent of the subject's judgments about what she is or is not aware of. He urged the use of a forced-choice discrimination measure. Don't ask S whether she is aware of x or, if you do, don't take her word for it. If S doesn't think she can tell whether x is present, if she professes being unable to see anything at all (hence, according to ^sT_a, being aware of nothing at all), she is asked ("forced") to choose anyway: is there something there or not? If S thinks she can't see anything, she is urged to guess. It turns out in some conditions that subjects who say and think they are guessing are nonetheless able to "tell" (in a statistically significant way) whether x is there. Their "guesses" are more often right than wrong. In a sense, then, these subjects are detecting x when they do not believe they can—even when they believe they can't. If we adopt this *objective* measure of awareness, ^oT_a, subjects can be conscious of a stimulus while thinking and sincerely saying they are aware of absolutely nothing at all. They are no longer authorities on whether they are conscious of something.

This is called an objective test of awareness because the results are independent of what subjects *think* they are aware of. S may think (and say) she sees absolutely nothing in location L (thus being unaware of x in location L by ^sT_a) and, yet, have her choices (she thinks of them as mere guesses) about whether something is present significantly affected by the presence of x. The objective test is obviously less demanding than ^sT_a. If we use the objective test, it turns out that S is aware of more than she would be under the subjective test. If the objective test for awareness is used, perception without awareness still occurs (see Boornstein 1992: 193–4, for a summary), but it occurs less often and is harder to demonstrate experimentally.

Reingold and Merikle (1988, 1990) have argued that the validity of this objective test (as a test for *awareness*) depends on the plausibility of assuming that only stimuli that S is aware of actually influence her discriminative responses.[12] If stimuli S is not aware of can affect S's decisions about whether x is present in an objective test for awareness, the objective test is not really a test for awareness. We don't want a test for S's awareness of x to allow things that S isn't aware of to affect the results that indicate awareness. Otherwise S needn't be aware of x to be counted, by such a test, as being aware of x. We want the test to be *exclusive* or *pure*, to admit only factors that a subject, in some recognizable sense, is conscious of. This, though, is an exclusiveness, a purity, there is no assurance an objective test satisfies. Why infer that S is conscious of x in any recognizable pre-theoretic sense just because S's decisions about whether x is present are affected by x if S's decisions (choices, guesses) about whether x is present can be affected by things S isn't (in any recognizable pre-theoretic sense) aware of?

Reingold and Toth (1996: 163) think this a "devastating problem for an objective test of awareness." It certainly seems to be a problem. It has pushed people otherwise sympathetic with objective methods back toward a subjective criterion of awareness, back towards something like ^sT_a. Many—and, as I read

---

[12] This is called the *exclusiveness assumption* or (Jacoby 1991) the *process-purity* assumption.

the literature, *most*—scientists and philosophers feel that, even with its problems, $^{s}T_a$ comes closer than any objective measure in capturing something like our ordinary, common-sense, idea of what it takes to be consciously aware of something.[13] As a result of such widespread agreement, a subject's judgments (and, if they make them, sincere reports) on what she is (or is not) aware of remain the standard measure of consciousness in scientific studies of consciousness.

The use of the subjective test, $^{s}T_a$, is not only supported by raw conviction about what we mean to be talking about when we talk about awareness of a stimulus (namely, something subjects *are* authoritative about), it is also confirmed by a variety of theoretical approaches to the study of consciousness. I mention only two:

(1) Higher-Order Thought (HOT) theories of consciousness (Armstrong 1968; Carruthers 1989, 2000; Dennett 1978; Lycan 1987, 1992; Rosenthal 1986, 1990, 1991) maintain that S's experience of x is conscious if and only if, at some higher level, S is aware that she is having the experience. Lower-order mental states (e.g., S's perceptual experience of x) become conscious (making perception of x conscious) by becoming the object of a higher-order thought. This theoretical orientation makes it natural—indeed, almost unavoidable—to use $^{s}T_a$ as a behavioral test for consciousness. What *makes* an experience conscious is thinking you are having it; so if you think you are not having an experience of x, that you are not seeing x, you can't (unless you contradict yourself) be having a *conscious* experience of x.

(2) Global Access Theories of consciousness (Baars 1988) identify conscious processes with those whose informational content is accessible to a wide variety of output systems. If the only output (response, reaction) a given piece of information controls is direction of a person's gaze or size of the pupils in her eyes, then that information is not *globally* accessible—hence, not conscious. But if the information is also available to control a variety of bodily movements— e.g. where S points, where S looks, what S says—then this information is globally accessible and, therefore, conscious. If this is one's view about what makes information conscious, then $^{s}T_a$ is a natural test for consciousness. If S doesn't think (hence, is not prepared to say) she is aware of something in location L, the presence of something in location L is information that, even if S receives it (and thus perceives x), is, arguably at least, not globally (enough) accessible to qualify as conscious.

I will, in the next section, question $^{s}T_a$'s validity, but for now, and for these reasons, I tentatively accept it as the standard measure of awareness. If we use it,

---

[13] A small sample: Kanwisher 2001: 101, n. 2, Cheesman and Merikle 1986: 344, 363; Dehaene and Naccache 2001: 6; Dienes and Perner 1996: 231; Merikle, Smilek, and Eastwood 2001: 125; Underwood 1996: vi; Potter 1999: 41; Dixon 1981: 187.

then, together with T_p, there are a variety of experimental results that indicate the existence—indeed, prevalence (in certain unusual cases)—of unconscious or implicit perception. Today, perhaps the best-known of these is blindsight (Pöppel, Held, and Frost 1973; Weiskrantz 1997), a condition in which patients with a partial "blindness" due to lesions in the visual cortex report seeing nothing in their blind field (thus, according to ^sT_a, lacking awareness of the objects that are there) while obtaining information about them (as revealed by forced choice). Such accurate performance (indicating the receipt of information) accompanied by lack of awareness has been identified in many categories of neuropsychological impairment (for instance, *numbsense,* a tactile analog of blindsight: Rossetti, Rode, and Boisson 2001). Unless there are reasons for rejecting either T_p or ^sT_a, then, the existence of perception without awareness—unconscious, subliminal, or implicit perception—is an established scientific fact.

3 VALIDITY OF ^sT_a

Is ^sT_a a reasonable test for awareness? For lack of awareness? It says, in effect, that belief that one is not aware of anything is to be treated as infallible. If you believe you are not aware of anything, you can't be wrong since believing this is sufficient for not being aware of anything. We have already seen that most such beliefs are fallible. Beliefs that I am not (visually) aware of a spy or an extra-terrestrial are obviously fallible: I can see them and think I'm not. It isn't just specific kinds of things: spies, extraterrestrials, and poison ivy. I can believe I'm seeing absolutely nothing at all on the CRT monitor (I think and say that the screen is completely blank) and be mistaken. I confusedly think the figures I (consciously) see on the screen are figments of my own overactive imagination.[14] If "something" on a CRT means "something physical" (what else could it mean?), why can't I be aware of something there and believe I'm not?

What we are asking, remember, is not merely whether *perception* of something can occur without awareness of it, but whether *conscious* perception can occur alongside a belief that one is aware of nothing. If the reader feels that this is simply not possible, well and good. For them ^sT_a will be close to a definitional truth. It captures part of what they mean in describing someone as aware of a

---

[14] Cheves West Perky (1958) induced subjects to believe that the colored shapes they were seeing (carefully projected on the wall by Perky) were actually their own imaginative constructions. They saw things on L (the wall) that they didn't believe existed on L (they thought the "images" they were conscious of were in their own mind).

Skeptics tell me that Perky's experiments have not been successfully replicated. I assume here that failure to replicate an experiment is not a demonstration—experimental or otherwise—that the results of these experiments are invalid or otherwise unworthy of credence. It depends on why the experiments haven't been replicated. How many people tried? Some experiments are terribly hard to perform. If we can think that things in our own mind (e.g., hallucinatory images) are, in fact, real objects, why shouldn't it be possible to think that real objects are in our own mind?

stimulus, as consciously perceiving something. But others—I confess to being one of them—are not so sure. So it is at least worth looking at some of the unusual cases that challenge the validity of ^sT_a.

A Split Brains

The corpus collosum is a large tract of fibers connecting the two cerebral hemispheres. When it is cut (to relieve epileptic seizures), the two hemispheres can no longer communicate with each other and patients reveal (under careful experimental tests) remarkable deficits relating to the perceptual, cognitive, and linguistic functions housed in the two hemispheres. Here is an example from Palmer:

A split-brain patient, N.G., was presented with a fixation point in the middle of a screen. Once she fixated it, a picture of a cup was briefly flashed to the right of the dot [information goes to left hemisphere where linguistic functions reside: FD]. She was asked what she saw, and she replied, "A cup." On the next trial, a spoon was flashed to the left of the dot [this information goes to the right hemisphere where linguistic functions are largely absent: FD]. Again she was asked what she saw, but this time she replied, "Nothing." She was then asked to reach under the screen with her left hand [behavior of left hand controlled by right hemisphere: FD] and pick out the object that had just been shown in her left visual field but without being able to see the objects. She reached under and felt each object, finally holding up the spoon. When she was asked what she was holding, she replied, "A pencil" [verbal behavior controlled by left hemisphere: FD]. (1999: 631)

N.G. was receiving information (in the right hemisphere) about the spoon—that it was a spoon. How else can we explain her ability (this is no lucky guess; she consistently gets it right) to pick it out (with her left hand). So N.G. must (T_p) see the spoon. But is she aware of it? Does she have the same kind of experience of it—i.e., a conscious experience—as occurs when she reports seeing a cup in her right visual field? Well, if she is aware of the spoon, and we take her word for what she believes, she certainly doesn't believe, and in this sense is not aware, that she is aware of it. If we take her verbal report as an honest and reliable expression of what she believes, then we are forced to conclude that N.G. believes she does not see a spoon on the left. She believes she sees *nothing* in that part of her visual field (left of fixation point). So, according to ^sT_a, she is not conscious of the spoon: a striking instance of perception without awareness.

But why take this as an instance of perception without awareness rather than a striking counterexample to ^sT_a? Why not say that N.G. (or maybe the right hemisphere of N.G.'s brain) is conscious of the spoon, but because of a severed corpus collosum this information is not being transmitted to the speech centers on the left in charge of reporting whether she is, and, if so, what is being perceived? Normal subjects detect and name objects in the left visual field because, after initially projecting to the right hemisphere, information is relayed via the corpus collosum to the left hemisphere where the stimulus can then be named and described. N.G.'s commisurotomy (severance of the corpus collosum) makes this communication about the existence of conscious experience (in the right hemisphere) impossible, but why should that be taken to mean that there is no conscious experience there? Wouldn't that be like concluding that nothing is happening in Foggyville simply because a storm that knocks out communication facilities prevents our getting news of the events occurring there? Why not conclude with Palmer (1999: 632) that the most likely explanation of N.G.'s behavior is that each hemisphere is conscious of the object projected to it, but only the left hemisphere is able to talk about it? The right hemisphere has conscious experiences. It just can't say (and think?) so.

If this is the way we interpret this extraordinary situation, then ^sT_a is not a valid test of awareness. N.G. is having (in the right hemisphere) a conscious experience of a spoon despite believing (if we take her report as an expression of what she believes) she is aware of nothing at all.

It may be objected, though, that in these special circumstances we are no longer entitled to accept what is reported as an accurate indication of what is believed. Once we split the person into cerebral hemispheres with distinct streams of conscious experience, as we are now doing, we ought also split the person into distinct loci of judgment or belief: a left hemisphere capable of judging and talking about the experiences it is having (as evidenced by the person's ability to report seeing a cup when the cup is in the right visual field) and a right hemisphere that, even if capable of making such judgments, is incapable of expressing them verbally. If we do this, then we do not have a violation of ^sT_a. N.G.'s right hemisphere (in contrast to N.G.) does not judge (at least we have no evidence that it judges) that it is not aware of anything. N.G.'s right hemisphere may be like a human infant or an animal—aware of things but unable to report that it is (when it is) or that it isn't (when it isn't). We can take N.G.'s choice of a spoon with the left hand as a way of non-verbally reporting that there was, earlier, a spoon on the left, but this isn't yet a report that she was *aware* of a spoon (or anything else) on the left, and it is this report, a report (judgment) that she was aware of something on the left, that ^sT_a requires for awareness of the spoon on the left (see footnote 11). If we proceed in this way, ^sT_a renders no verdict on whether N.G.'s right hemisphere is conscious of anything just as it is silent on whether dogs and turtles are aware of things. We cannot say, at least not on the basis of T_p and ^sT_a, whether this is perception with or without awareness. It is perception, yes: the right hemisphere is getting information (presumably in a direct way) about the spoon through the eyes and this information is controlling N.G.'s (left-handed) behavior. There is a visual experience (in our extended sense) in the right hemisphere, then, but is this experience conscious? ^sT_a does not tell us. It renders no decision about whether awareness is present in a location (the right hemisphere) where (as far as we can tell) no relevant judgments are occurring.

Whether split brains constitute a violation of ^sT_a, then, depends on how one interprets the experiments. Is this to be understood as a person being conscious (with her right hemisphere) of a stimulus while believing (according to her verbal report) she is not aware of anything? If so, we have a violation of ^sT_a. Or is it a person's right cerebral hemisphere being conscious of a stimulus while (as far as we can tell) not believing that it is (or that it isn't)? If so, there is no violation of ^sT_a. Or is it, rather, a person's right cerebral hemisphere being conscious of a stimulus while at the same time judging that it is (as manifested in the person's left-handed behavior) but simply being unable to express this judgment in verbal form. If so, we have only an apparent violation of ^sT_a. How are we to choose between these interpretations? I don't know. Maybe it is best to wait to see if anything else can be said against ^sT_a.

B Change Blindness

Change blindness refers to the inability of subjects to detect visible—sometimes quite prominent—differences. If the change (producing these differences) occurs when the subject can't see it (e.g., during an eye saccade) or during a suitable distraction (e.g., a mud splat), the differences produced by this change are sometimes hard to detect. Pictures of people standing around a jet airplane differ in a certain obvious (once you notice it) way: one picture has one of the jet engines (a prominent part of the picture) missing. Shown these pictures in alternating sequence (with a suitable intervening mask) subjects have trouble seeing the difference.

To have a familiar sort of example to focus on, suppose S looks at a scene in which there are seven people gathered around a table. Each person is clearly visible. S gazes at the scene for several seconds, runs her eye over (and, in the process, foveates[15]) each person at the table, but pays no particular attention to any of them. She then looks away. While S is looking away, an additional person—call him Sam—joins the group. Sam is clearly visible. There are now eight visible people. When S looks back, she doesn't notice any difference. Having no reason to suspect that a change has occurred, S thinks she is looking at the same group of people. When asked whether she sees a difference in the scene between the first and the second observation, S says, "No."

This is an example of change blindness—a clearly visible difference that S doesn't see. At least she doesn't believe she sees it. The question we need to ask is whether this is a genuine case of blindness. Did S actually see Sam on the second occasion (without noticing him) and, if so, was this conscious or unconscious perception? If S was consciously aware of Sam, she was clearly not aware (of the fact) that she was aware of him (or, indeed, of anything additional),

---

[15] To foveate means to bring the image of each person on to the fovea (the sensitive part) of the retina.

but that, remember, is not the question. The question is not whether S is aware of *the fact* that she is aware of something different on the second occasion, but whether she is aware of the additional stimulus, Sam, on the second occasion. We are not interested in what *facts* S is aware of. We are asking what *objects* she is aware of.

It seems reasonable to say—at least it seems like a possible thing to say—that S not only saw Sam, but that her experience of him was of the same kind, a conscious experience, as was her experience of the other seven people. She was aware of Sam in the same way she was aware of each of the other seven people around the table. She was aware of the person who made a difference without being aware (realizing, noticing, or believing) that there was this difference. This is object awareness (of Sam, a member of the group) without fact awareness (that there is a difference in the group)—conscious perception of a stimulus without knowledge or realization that it is occurring. It would be completely arbitrary to say that S consciously sees only the same seven people she saw the first time and that, therefore, her perception of Sam, the new member of the group, is unconscious, subliminal, or implicit. Why just Sam? Why not each of the other seven people at the table? Or, despite S's protests (she thinks she saw, maybe, a half dozen people), S isn't aware of *any* people at the table?[16]

It seems more plausible to say that, on the second occasion, S perceived Sam in the same way S perceived every other person in the scene, the same way S perceived all seven people on the first occasion—namely, consciously. S's experience on the second occasion was different from what it was on the first occasion, and the experience, on both occasions, was conscious. S just didn't notice (hence, remains ignorant of and, therefore, fails to report on) the difference. One can be conscious of the objects that constitute a visible difference and not be conscious of the fact that one is conscious of them.[17] If this is, indeed, the correct way to describe this situation, then ^sT_a is not a valid test of awareness. S is aware of an additional stimulus object—Sam—on the second occasion, something that makes a difference to what she consciously experiences, that she is not aware (does not realize) she is aware of. S believes there is no difference.

---

[16] This is basically the argument I gave in Dretske (1993) for the conclusion that, contrary to higher-order theories of consciousness, one need not be aware of differences in one's experiences for these differences to be conscious differences. Also, see Dretske (forthcoming) and the distinction between epistemic and non-epistemic perception in Dretske (1969). The difference between object awareness (of objects that make a difference) and fact awareness (that there is a difference) is, I think, a more perspicuous way of putting the distinction between *phenomenal* and *access* consciousness (Block 1995). In other words, I agree with Nicholas Humphrey (1995) that the sensation/perception distinction is—or it *should be*—the primary distinction. See Block (2001) for a similar treatment of change blindness.

[17] One must be careful to distinguish: (1) awareness of the difference, which, in my idiolect anyway, implies awareness of the fact that there is a difference; and (2) awareness of an object—in this case Sam—that makes or constitutes the difference. S can be aware of Sam, the object that constitutes the difference, without being aware (in the factive sense) of the difference that Sam makes.

S believes that there is *not* another person at the table and, therefore, that she is not aware of another figure. She believes her (conscious) experience, at least with respect to the number of figures she sees, is the same. She is wrong. Contrary to ^sT_a, S's beliefs and sincere reports about her own conscious experiences are mistaken.[18]

This conclusion doesn't mean that a person is always conscious of *all* the elements in a complex display. All it means is that one can be consciously aware of more than one realizes. If S looks (for several seconds) at seven hundred people in a room, seven thousand in a parade, or seventy thousand in a football stadium, she is unlikely to see everyone even if they are all clearly visible from her vantage point. The subjective impression of seeing hundreds, perhaps even thousands, of distinct elements, is (or may often be) an illusion.[19] These other (other than the ones attended to) objects may no more be seen (consciously or unconsciously) than are those objects whose image projects to the blind spot on the retina of a stationary eye (Dennett 1991). Maybe this is so; maybe it isn't. This is an empirical question. It depends, surely, on how much information about these objects one actually gets, and it is important to remember in this regard that not much information is needed to see an object. Information about color, for instance, is clearly not necessary or we wouldn't be able to see things at dusk. Information about an object's shape isn't necessary. Things of different shape can look pretty much the same shape at 600 yards, at acute angles, and when one isn't wearing one's glasses. That doesn't prevent their being seen. All that is really needed to see x is enough information about x to enable one to point at x and ask, "What is that?" If you get this much information about x, you see x, and, it seems reasonable to say (given that you can point at x and ask, "What is that?") that this is perception *with* awareness.[20] Our question about whether S is conscious of Sam, then, might be put this way: when S looks the second time, is her experience of the group such that she could have wondered "Who is *that*?" where

---

[18] Hurley (1998: 156–7) has an interesting discussion of the possibility of miscounting the points on a star-shaped after-image. If this is possible, and I don't see why it isn't, it makes the same point I am trying to make in the text—that it is possible for there to be differences in (the elements of) conscious experience of which we are not (fact) aware.

[19] Contrary to what O'Regan and Noë (2001) suggest, the real question about change blindness is not whether one sees (or is aware of) *everything* in a complex scene (surely not!), but whether one can see (and be aware of) more of the elements, *more* of the detail, than one realizes. If there is anything (not *everything*, but *anything*) one can be aware of without realizing one is aware of it, then blindness to differences (failure to realize, notice, or believe that there is a difference) shows absolutely nothing, by itself, about what objects one is aware of. Change blindness is blindness to facts (a cognitive deficit), not necessarily (although it may sometimes be explained by) blindness to objects (a visual deficit). Although failure to see an object can explain why one doesn't notice it, there are other explanations. I am aware of nothing in the change-blindness literature (other than an implicit acceptance of ^sT_a—the criterion now in question) that shows that the cognitive failures they exhibit (not noticing differences that are plainly visible) are produced by a failure to consciously see the objects and/or features that make up these differences.

[20] Brewer (1999: 44–5) and Campbell (2002: 133) argue (and I agree with them) that demonstrative reference requires awareness of that to which reference is made.

"*that*" refers to Sam? Since this seems clearly possible with other members of the group, why not for Sam? If it is so for Sam, then her perception of Sam is conscious perception even when she insists she sees no difference.

If this is the correct way to think about change blindness, at least some instances of change blindness, then what change blindness shows is that sometimes—perhaps often—we do not notice some of the things we are consciously aware of. It shows that conscious experiences of the world are sometimes richer, more variegated, more textured, than the judgments one ends up making on their basis. It shows that "change blindness" might more correctly be described as a kind of "change amnesia" (Wolfe 1999: 74–5), an inability to retain (for judgment and report) information that is consciously registered at the perceptual level. It shows (Potter 1999: 35) that only some of the information consciously registered is still available when the time for action (e.g., reporting what is seen) arrives. It shows that ^sT_a is not a valid test for awareness of a stimulus.

C Attentional Deficits: Unilateral Neglect and Extinction

Unilateral spatial neglect is a relatively common and disabling neurological disorder after unilateral brain damage. It is characterized by a lack of awareness for sensory events located towards the contralesional side of space (e.g., towards the left following a right lesion), together with a loss of the orienting behaviors, exploratory search and other actions that would normally be directed toward that side. Neglect patients often behave as if half of their world no longer exists. In daily life, they may be oblivious to objects and people on the neglected side of the room, may eat from only one side of their plate, read from only one end of a newspaper page, and make-up or shave only one side of their face. (Driver and Vuilleumier 2001a : 40)

In *extinction*, unlike full-blown neglect, a patient can see and report on objects on either side of the visual field without difficulty if these objects are shown one at a time. If shown two objects at once, though, one on the good side and one on the bad side, they will report seeing only the one on the good side. Experiences of objects on the good side *extinguish* experiences of objects on the bad side.

If we use ^sT_a as our criterion for when a subject is conscious of a stimulus, then, since neglect patients insist they are not conscious of the objects they neglect (Driver and Vuilleumier 2001a: 45) we must conclude with Palmer (1999: 637) that even if (according to T_p) neglected objects are perceived (there is evidence that they are[21]) they are not consciously perceived. The question we are asking now, though, is whether this is the right conclusion to draw. Could it be that these people are conscious of objects they say they don't see?

---

[21] For example, when shown otherwise identical pictures of a house, one of which has flames coming from the left side of the house, neglect patients will deny seeing any difference in the pictures, but they will consistently "prefer" the picture of the house that isn't burning (Palmer 1999: 637)—thus indicating that they are getting information about that part of the house (the left side) that they neglect.

The reason one may be suspicious of the conclusion that patients are not aware of objects they neglect is that, unlike blindsight where there is damage to the primary visual cortex, many of the neural pathways normally associated with conscious perception (including primary sensory areas) remain intact in neglect patients (Driver and Vuilleumier 2001a: 45). Furthermore, unlike blindsight, some neglect patients can report an isolated light wherever it appears in the visual field on either the good side or the bad side. What they can't do is report it on the left when there are (as there usually are in daily life) competing objects that "extinguish" it on the right. Nonetheless, despite the absence of report (and, presumably, belief) fMRI studies show that these extinguished objects on the left continue to activate the primary visual cortex and early extrastriate visual areas of the brain's right hemisphere in a manner similar to objects (when there is no competition from objects on the right) consciously seen on the left. As a result, Driver and Vuilleumier (2001a: 66) are left wondering how these patients can possibly fail to be aware of the objects they neglect.[22]

There is, furthermore, substantial processing of information from "extinguished" objects beyond the primary visual cortex. Patients who report seeing nothing on the left can nonetheless make accurate judgments (they think they are guesses) about similarities and differences between objects presented simultaneously on the left and the right (Driver 1996: 200; Rafel and Robertson 1995). When asked to report where objects appear (on the left, right, or both sides) right-parietal patients (who extinguish on the left) report seeing nothing on the left, but when they are asked to count these same stimuli (are you seeing a total of one, two, or four objects?), some patients had no difficulty including the extinguished objects on the left in the reported total (Vuilleumier and Rafel: 1999). We could, in accordance with T_p and ^sT_a, describe these exploits as striking cases of perception (subjects are clearly getting information about extinguished stimuli) without awareness (i.e., while thinking and saying they don't see them), but the question now being asked is whether this is the *best* way to describe these results. Why not say, instead, that, contrary to ^sT_a, these subjects consciously experience objects on the left, but, like certain cases of change blindness, do not realize (notice, believe) they are experiencing them and, hence, do not report it. Neglect and extinction, after all, are typically classified as impairments of attention, and one can see things, consciously see things, one doesn't attend to in any ordinary sense of "attention."[23] That, at least, is a

---

[22] It is known, by the way, that information from unattended (therefore, unnoticed and unreported) stimuli is often processed to a very high degree (Shapiro and Luck 1999; Kanwisher, Yin, and Wojciulik 1999; Potter 1999). Beck and colleagues (2001: 649) report finding face-specific activity in the brain when subjects are "blind" to ("unaware of" according to ^sT_a) the change this activity signifies, indicating that, in some sense, the brain is registering changes that subjects report no experience of. Also see Shiffrin, et al. (1996: 226) discussion of the "flanker" effect.

[23] It is not uncommon, for instance, to say such things as: "I saw a lot of people (trees, animals, etc.), but I only paid attention to the one that was acting funny." Significantly, Driver and Vuilleumier (2001b: 116) report that many researchers have attempted to resolve these paradoxical

possible interpretation our discussion of change blindness suggests. On this way of describing things, neglect patients are conscious of objects on the left. They just cannot attend to them in the way required for judgment and report. Their attention is directed only to objects on the right. Since objects in unattended regions cannot be reported (Dehaene and Naccache 2001: 8; Mack and Rock 1998), that would explain why they do not report seeing them. Besides an unshakable commitment to ^sT_a, why take the further step of denying awareness of these objects?

This way of describing the results is not mandatory, of course, but we are not now looking for the way these patients *must* be described. We are asking how *best* to describe them. Since discussion of both split brains and change blindness has opened up the possibility—indeed (in the case of change blindness) the plausibility—that people are aware of things they believe they are not aware of, this seems like an available option in the case of neglect also.

4 AN ALTERNATIVE TEST: INTENTIONAL ACTION

If we forsake ^sT_a, though, what takes its place? If we cannot rely on a subject's sincere reports about her own conscious experience, what can we appeal to? This isn't just a problem for the study of consciousness in others. It isn't just a problem of other minds. Giving up ^sT_a seems to create an epistemological problem about one's own conscious experience.

Blindsight may provide a clue. Blindsighters perceive things (in our T_p sense) without (unless told) realizing they perceive them. They normally believe they do not perceive objects in their scotoma (the "blind" portion of their visual field). They also exhibit striking cognitive and behavioral deficits with respect to these objects. If forced to guess or choose, they can more often than not correctly "say" whether x is vertical, blue, or moving (thereby exhibiting perception of x), but they seem unable to exploit these facts in order to initiate spontaneous behavior. Saying (or believing) that x is vertical is not for them what it is for us, those of us who are conscious of x, something they are motivated or have reason to say. If they are cooperative, then, when asked to guess, they have reason to say something, but they do not, as we do, have reason to say vertical rather than horizontal. This suggests that perception of x with awareness might be distinguished from perception without awareness on the basis of the rational motivation for responses to x.

Something like this reasoning has led a number of investigators (e.g., Marcel 1983b: 238–41; Dehaene and Naccache 2001; Flanagan 1991: 11;

results by proposing that the deficits exhibited in neglect and extinction may be more "attentional" than "sensory." Given that everyone agrees that subjects are perceiving (getting information about) the stimuli they neglect, I take this to be a way of saying that subjects might be conscious of neglected stimuli without attending to them in a way sufficient for report.

Hurley 1998: chapter 4; Clark 2001; Milner and Goodale 1995; Goodale and Milner 2004; Van Gulick 1994) to view conscious awareness as, somehow, bound up with or manifested in rational agency. The idea, roughly, is that sensory information comes in different forms (and, perhaps, via different causal pathways): (1) in a form that makes it available for fixation of belief, rational planning, and choice—this is conscious experience; and (2) in a form that, although not available for planning, decision-making, and the grounding of judgment (and report), can be used to control and tweak behaviors that have been rationally selected on other grounds. In the first form information helps determine what we choose to do (and, therefore, our purpose in doing what we do) and what we believe. It has a reason-giving, a motivational, role. In the second form information, though not available as a reason to do (or believe) anything, and hence not available as a motivational factor, helps determine how we do whatever we (with or without reasons) choose to do (Clark 2001; Jacob and Jeannerod 2003). This kind of picture also lies behind efforts by Dretske (1981, 1995), Evans (1982), and Tye (1995), to conceive of conscious perceptual experience as that part of incoming information available to cognitive centers for fixation of belief (reasons to believe) and goal selection (reasons to do).

To make this kind of picture plausible, especially if it is to be couched in terms of reasons, we have to carefully distinguish explanatory reasons, the reasons *why* S does A or believes P, from justifying reasons, S's reasons *for* doing A or believing P, the reasons S (if able) might give to justify doing A or believing P. Explanatory reasons are those facts that explain, or help explain, why something happens—including why people (or animals) do (or believe) the things they do. As such, explanatory reasons have to be true. Heavy rainfall can't explain why Sarah takes her umbrella if, in fact, it isn't raining. If it isn't raining, *that* can't be the explanation, the reason *why* she takes her umbrella. Justifying reasons, on the other hand, needn't be true. Even if it isn't raining, that it is raining can be S's justification, the reason she has and the reason she gives, for taking her umbrella. If she (justifiably) thinks it is raining, or if it sounds to her like it is raining, that it is raining can be the reason she has—and certainly the reason she gives—for taking her umbrella whether or not it is raining.

Explanatory reasons have to be true; justifying reasons needn't be true. Justifying reasons needn't be true because a justifying reason (as I am using the term here,[24]) unlike an explanatory reason, is the way the world, in either

---

[24] I should register here a small departure from an account of reasons with which I am sympathetic. Basically I agree with Dancy (2000; also see Dancy, Wallace, Darwall, et al. 2003) and Moran (2001: 128) that S's reason (for taking her umbrella, for instance) is the fact that it is raining, not the fact that S sees (or believes) that it is raining. It is what S perceives or thinks (that it is raining), the *content* of her perceptual or cognitive state, not her perceiving or thinking that it is raining, that is her reason. Believing that it is raining may be necessary for the fact that it is raining to be her reason (it, so to speak, *enables* the fact that it is raining to be S's reason), but believing that it is raining is not, thereby, her (justifying) reason.

thought or experience, is represented to be. Since things do not have to be the way they are represented, since things are sometimes misrepresented, that it is raining can be S's reason for taking her umbrella even when it isn't raining. This "fact" (in scare quotes to indicate putative fact), qualifies as a reason for S to take her umbrella, even when it isn't raining, even when it isn't a fact, because from S's point of view it is represented as fact, as though it were true. It is, therefore, something whose falsity in no way diminishes an agent's rationality. From the agent's standpoint, a putative fact that is represented, in either thought or experience, to be a fact is, for purposes of both justification and motivation, as good as a real fact. A sunny day disqualifies the putative fact that it is raining as an explanation of anything, and therefore disqualifies it as the reason *why* S takes her umbrella, but it doesn't disqualify it as the reason S has, and gives, *for* taking her umbrella.

Although we cannot use what S believes—that it is raining—to explain why S believes P or does A when it isn't raining, we can use the fact that she believes it is raining or the fact that it sounds (looks, smells) like it is raining in our explanations of why S takes her umbrella. We can do this because unlike the putative fact *that it is raining*, that she believes it, or that it sounds that way to her are genuine facts. She does believe it. It does sound that way to her. So although what she believes (that it is raining) cannot be the (explanatory) reason why she takes her umbrella, that she believes it is raining can be.[25]

So much for the distinction between explanation and justification, the difference between reasons why S did A and S's reasons for doing A. To see how it plays out in an example more relevant to present concerns, and to anticipate its eventual use in a criterion for consciousness, consider the following situation. A subject in a psychological experiment is told to press the right button if the target, x, is vertical, the left button if it is horizontal. On the first trial S presses the right button. When asked why she pressed the right button, S (puzzled by the question since x is plainly visible to everyone) says, "Because x was vertical."

What about false beliefs? What if S takes her umbrella because she mistakenly thinks it is raining? Since S would still (given what she thinks) *give* as her reason the "fact" that it is raining, this "fact" is still, in my sense, a justifying reason. As I read Dancy, he would deny that this is a reason. Under normal conditions (i.e., when use of an umbrella is to protect one from rain) one has no reason to take an umbrella when it isn't raining no matter what one happens to think. One might think one has a reason, but one doesn't. Whether or not Dancy is right about this (I think there is a sense of "reason" in which he is), I merely note that I am using the notion of a (justifying) reason more inclusively—as what is believed or experienced whether or not what is represented as true is true. In my sense, that it is raining can be S's reason for taking her umbrella even when it isn't raining. If she thinks it is raining, or it sounds like it is raining, and S takes her umbrella, in part, because things seem this way to her, then that it is raining is (among) her (justifying) reason(s) for taking her umbrella.

[25] On a causal theory of knowledge, when S knows it is raining, her belief that it is raining is caused by the rain. In this special case, then, justifying reasons are (remote) causes of behavior. S's reason for taking her umbrella—that it is raining—is the cause of her belief that it is raining, and the belief (causally) explains why she takes her umbrella.

Given her instructions, and being a cooperative subject, that was her reason, her justification, for pushing the right button. On the next set of trials exposure time is reduced. S is instructed as before: press the right button if x is vertical, the left if it is horizontal. S protests that she can no longer see x. She is asked to guess. She presses the right button. When asked why she pressed the right button, she says impatiently that it was just a guess. She had no reason. As she understands her instructions, she doesn't need a reason. She was, after all, instructed to guess and, for guessing purposes, one button is as good as the other. If we are convinced (by, say, a history of correct guesses at this exposure time) that S, despite her failure to realize it, perceives x (is receiving information about x in some primary way) we have, according to ^sT_a, a case of perception (of x) without awareness (of x). Although x's orientation is obviously influencing S's guesses (why else is she right so often?) its vertical orientation is clearly not S's justification or reason for pushing the right button. She doesn't have a reason for pushing the right (as opposed to the left) button. She is just guessing.[26] That is why she wouldn't venture a judgment unless "forced." That x is vertical, or that she perceives it to be vertical, may be the explanation of *why* she pushes the right button, but S herself has no reason, no justifying reason, for pushing the right button or, if she does (e.g., I like to do things with my right hand), her reasons are not related to x's orientation.

Using our two tests, T_p and ^sT_a, we have here a case of perception without awareness. We also have explanation in the absence of justification. There exist, in what S perceives, reasons why she pushes the right button without there being, in what she perceives, reasons for pushing the right button. This is suggestive. The obvious thought is that, perhaps, what constitutes a lack of awareness is not a *belief* that nothing is perceived—a failure, that is, of ^sT_a, a test we have already found reasons to question—but the absence of justifying reasons. This is the idea that I will try to develop in the remainder of this chapter.

Aside from the differences between explanatory and justifying reasons already described, there is another striking difference: although F (some fact) can explain why S does A without S being aware of F, F cannot justify S in doing A unless S is aware of F. Justifying reasons, unlike explanatory reasons, are facts (or, in the

---

[26] Hurley (1998: 148) puts the same point in terms of intentions:

When you guess on cue about a stimulus you are not conscious of, you guess intentionally. But information about the very stimulus in question does not feature in the content of your intentional guess in the same way it does when you intentionally report a stimulus you are conscious of, or when you act on it spontaneously. If information is conscious, you can report or act spontaneously on it: you can have the background intention to push the lever if, say, a light flashes, and you can then push it intentionally just because the light has flashed. More generally, if information is conscious then you can form an intention whose content is provided in part by that information and act on it just for the reason that information provides. Conscious information is available as an effective reason for acting. This is not the case when you can only guess on cue; the information in question does not activate your intention, or provide your reason for acting intentionally. You do not have intentional access to the information you can only respond to by guessing on cue.

case of justifying reasons, putative facts[27]) that one is necessarily conscious of. If S isn't aware that it is raining, the fact that it is raining cannot be her reason for saying or thinking that it is raining. It can't be her reason for taking her umbrella. That it is raining might still explain why (in a forced-choice situation) S says it is raining. It might be the reason *why* she takes her umbrella. But it can't be S's reason *for* taking her umbrella—not if she is unaware of this fact.

If we combine this fact—the fact that one is necessarily aware of justifying reasons—with the plausible assumption that for those who perceive x, awareness of facts about x requires awareness of x itself, we get the following sufficient condition for awareness of a stimulus: S is consciously aware of x if for some action A or belief P the fact (or putative fact) that x is F is S's (justifying) reason for doing A or believing P. Conscious perception of x, perception of x with awareness of x, occurs when information (necessary for perception of x) becomes S's justification for belief or action. Call this principle J.

Notice, first, that although ^sT_a and J render the same verdict in many cases, they render it for quite different reasons. J is, or at least it is intended to be, less demanding than ^sT_a. J does not require, as does ^sT_a, that a subject believe she perceives x in order to be aware of x. All J requires is that information about x (that it is vertical, say) be S's justifying reason for doing (or believing) something, and this might be true of someone—a child or an animal, say—who lacks an understanding of what it means to be conscious and who cannot, therefore, satisfy ^sT_a. As long as the animal or child can do things *for reasons*, as long as it can be motivated to act by having reasons to act, we can have grounds (according to J) for inferring that it is conscious of x even though it cannot think it is. If we are convinced that Fido, who just saw the cat run up this tree, has reasons for barking under this tree, and we are convinced, moreover, that his reason is that this is the tree (he saw) the cat run up, then J tells us that Fido was conscious of the cat when it ran up this tree. As long as information about the cat—that it ran up this tree—is Fido's reason for barking here, Fido must not only have seen the cat run up this tree (and be acting on this information), but must have been aware of the cat when it ran up the tree. This is perception with awareness. J delivers this verdict for animals that lack an understanding of what it means to see things and, therefore, cannot (as required by ^sT_a) judge themselves aware of a cat.

As this example is intended to illustrate, J does not require of the fact, F (S's reason for doing A), that S believe (think, know, judge) that F. Belief, and the concepts it requires, isn't necessary. Maybe, as some philosophers think, Fido is incapable of having beliefs about cats and trees. If they are right, dogs don't

---

[27] I hereafter concentrate on facts, the content of *true* beliefs and *veridical* experiences. I will, therefore, drop the distracting "or putative fact." It is to be understood, however, that S's justifying reasons need not be true. In the ideal situation, S's justifying reason (that it is raining, for instance) will be the content of a true belief, a belief that is part of the explanatory reason why S behaves the way she does (takes her umbrella or says that it is raining), but things aren't always optimal.

think. They don't make judgments. If reasons for action, reasons for doing A, have to be states that deploy concepts, then, if these philosophers are right, dogs don't have reasons for the things they do. That doesn't mean they are not conscious, that they aren't aware of things. Fido might still see a cat run up a tree, but, lacking concepts, he couldn't see *that* (hence, know and believe that) a cat ran up the tree. If these philosophers are right (I don't think they are, but I set aside that quarrel for now), Fido is not barking under the tree because he thinks a cat ran up this tree. He is *caused* to bark there, yes. There are reasons *why* he barks there, yes. But he doesn't have reasons (a justification) *for* barking there. Not if justification requires belief. According to J, however, we can neatly avoid this deflationary (to animals) result without settling questions about the conceptual prowess of animals. Even if dogs lack concepts (and, therefore, beliefs) they can still have reasons for the things they do. Sense experience, if understood (at least in part) in representational terms, in terms that allow it to misrepresent surroundings, is enough. To have a reason for barking here, it is enough if Fido saw a cat run up the tree (one can do this without believing that a cat ran up the tree and without having the concepts *cat, tree,* and *ran up*). If Fido saw this happen, and Fido's visual experience of this event represents it, in some phenomenal sense, as a cat running up this tree (or simply as something moving up something else), then that a cat (something) ran up (moved up) this tree (something else) can be the dog's reason for barking here. Fido needn't be able to conceptually represent what he saw as a cat running up a tree to have a reason, in what he saw—a cat running up a tree—for barking under the tree.[28]

If one has certain intuitions (see the discussion in §3) J also seems to do better than ^sT_a with split brains. Using ^sT_a we concluded that a commisurotomy patient who saw a spoon on the left was unconscious of it. Although N.G. picked out the spoon with her left hand, indicating thereby receipt of information about it, she denied seeing anything on the left. So, according to ^sT_a, she was not aware of it. We found reason to question this verdict. Maybe there is, in the right hemisphere, a conscious experience of the spoon (there certainly is in the left hemisphere when she sees something on the right) without a judgment or report of this experience being possible because the hemispheres are separated. J justifies this result. It seems reasonable to say that the subject has a reason for picking out (with her left hand) the spoon. Selecting the spoon (as opposed to a knife or a cup) was not just a guess, a forced choice, or a random act. She carefully felt these objects before making her choice. If her choice is rational, something she has a reason to do, then although S may be incapable of verbally communicating her

---

[28] For a broadly compatible view of experience, and the possibility of there being reasons in experience without the experiences requiring (on the part of the person having the experience) the concepts we use in expressing or describing their content, see Peacocke's (1992) notion of *scenario content* (roughly, the non-conceptual content of a perceptual experience). Seeing a square (in the right conditions) can give S a perceptual reason to believe it is a square even if S doesn't know what a square is and cannot, therefore, exploit that reason in coming to judge that it is a square.

reasons to us, it seems right to say that S's justification for picking out the spoon was that it (the object she saw earlier) was represented—certainly in experience and maybe even in both experience and thought—as a spoon. That it was a spoon or that she saw a spoon is, therefore, her reason for choosing a spoon. If that is her reason, J tells us she was conscious of the spoon. Contrary to the verdict of ^sT_a, this is perception of a stimulus with awareness of the stimulus by someone who believes (if we take what she says as an honest expression of what she believes) she is aware of nothing.

If we use J as a test (at least a sufficient condition) for a subject's awareness of a stimulus, we have a condition that, unlike ^sT_a, not only yields acceptable results when applied to animals, young children, and split-brain patients, but a test that explains why ^sT_a, despite its drawbacks, is such an intuitively appealing test and why, in many cases, it works as well as it does. For if S is conscious of x according to ^sT_a, S will also be conscious of x according to the weaker, less demanding, condition J since the actions and perceptual judgments of cooperative subjects (the only ones we are considering here) will be reasonable, judgments and actions for which there will be (justifying) reasons. S's justification for thinking and saying she saw something in L will be—what else?—facts about the object she saw in L and this will include the fact that she saw it. So a subject conscious of x according to ^sT_a will also be conscious of x according to J. But not (as Fido and split brains indicate) vice versa. This suggests that maybe J is doing the heavy lifting. If S satisfies ^sT_a, S must be conscious of x, yes, but not because she thinks she is conscious of x (Fido can be conscious of x without thinking he is) but because a fact about x (that she sees it) is the subject's reason for thinking she sees x, a reason she cannot have, according to J, without being conscious of x.

There are, however, problems with J that I have been ignoring. Aside from the fact that J is not really a genuine test (how, for instance, can one tell whether Fido has a *justifying* reason for barking under the tree) J expresses a sufficient, not a necessary, condition for awareness. We cannot use it, therefore, to establish what we set out to establish—conditions in which a person perceives x but is *not* aware of x. We can be certain that S is aware of x if S has, as her reason for doing A (or believing P), information about x, but if she doesn't do anything that has a fact about x as her reason, J is completely silent on the question of whether S is conscious of x. She might be or she might not be. S might be aware of the vertical stripes, but the fact that they are vertical may not be relevant to any of S's current plans or projects. There is nothing S is doing, or plans to do, or wants to do, for which their verticality is relevant. If we wanted to find out whether S was aware of these (vertical) stripes, we would have to arrange for S to do something for which their orientation was relevant. If S is cooperative, we could simply ask her whether x is vertical and assume that, if she gets it right (and isn't just guessing) the fact that x is vertical is her reason for saying it is vertical. With animals and uncooperative subjects the task is harder. If S does nothing that has information about x as her justification, however, given only J, we are left to speculate about whether S is conscious of x. J is of no help. It certainly doesn't tell us that S is *not* aware of x.

To rectify this problem (it may be just papering over the problem) and secure a necessary condition for awareness we need to say that S is aware of x if and only if information about x is *available* to S as a reason. It is the availability of information for rationalizing and motivating intentional action (even if one is not capable of such action—e.g., paralyzed or buried in cement), not its actual use, that makes it conscious. We need something like the following (superscript "r" standing for a *reason* test):

> $^{r}T_a$: S is aware of $X = S$ perceives X, and information about X is available to S as a reason (justification) for doing what she wants (chooses, decides) to do.

Securing a condition for awareness that is both sufficient *and* necessary comes at a price. How do we tell what information is *available* to S? To use an example from earlier, if S sees eight people around the table this time, but only seven people the first time, is information about Sam, the additional person, available to S if S denies seeing any difference? If S is really conscious of Sam without realizing it, how could we show that information about Sam is nonetheless available to her as a reason for doing or believing something when she denies seeing a difference? If this information is really available to her, S certainly isn't accessing it in answering questions about whether she sees a difference.

Demonstrating that this information is available might take experimental ingenuity, but, with the help of a little hindsight, one can imagine ways it might be done. We might, for instance, adapt Sperling's (1960) (also see Averbach and Coriell, 1961; Averbach and Sperling 1961) partial report technique for determining what information is in a perceptual experience of a complex stimulus. In Sperling's experiments subjects are briefly shown (50 milliseconds) a set of letters, as shown in Figure 1.

At this short exposure time, when asked to report as many letters as they can (the "whole report" condition), subjects identify at most four letters, no matter how many letters are in the array. So if we took the number of letters they could identify as the number of letters they were aware of, we would have to conclude that, when exposed for 50 milliseconds to an array of nine letters, subjects were

T   D   A

S   R   N

F   Z   B

Fig. 1. The set of letters shown in Sperling's experiments.

aware of, at most, four of them. Nonetheless, when asked[29], *after removal of the stimulus*, to identify the letters in only a single row (the "partial report" condition) subjects could often identify every letter in the row no matter which row they were asked about. In the partial report condition, then, subjects could identify *any* letter in the entire set despite being able to identify, at most, only four letters in the full report condition. This is not a case of attention being drawn to the queried row since the signal for which row to report occurs *after* removal of the stimulus. There is no longer anything out there (where the stimulus was) for their attention to be drawn to. Rather, subjects extract this information from what they describe as a conscious but rapidly fading image ("icon") that persists for a short time after removal of the stimulus. They use the information embodied in this conscious experience to identify letters in a stimulus that is no longer physically present. Sperling (1960: 20) concludes that: "A calculation of the information available to the Ss for their partial reports indicates that between two and three times more information is available for partial reports than for whole reports." If more information is available than subjects can use, Sperling continues, they must choose a part to remember. In doing so, they choose a part to forget (1960: 23). Although this information is lost before being used, this information is nonetheless there, available to a subject (as revealed by the partial reports), in conscious experience, at the time (and shortly thereafter) the letters are seen. It is there, available as a reason to do (say) one thing rather than another. Sperling's brilliance consists of his finding the circumstances—partial rather than full report—in which information about each letter (though not information about all letters) could be used as a reason.

If we interpret these results as showing that subjects are perceptually conscious of more letters than they can (with such brief exposure) identify, that there is more information in their conscious experience of the letter-array than they can (in a "full report" mode) cognitively process and report on, we might use a similar procedure to demonstrate that a subject allegedly "blind" to differences is actually aware of the objects (e.g., Sam) that constitute the difference. After seeing the second (eight-member) group, but before the "icon" (conscious experience) fades, a subject might be prompted by an arrow pointing at the position (formerly) occupied by Sam and asked, "Was anyone standing here?" If the answer is "Yes," it seems reasonable to conclude that the subject was, at the time she was looking at this group, consciously aware of Sam. If the same is true of the other seven people (this could be tested in the same way), we can conclude from this collection of "partial" reports that S was aware of all seven people on the first occasion, all eight on the second, but unaware (in full-report mode, as it were) that there was a difference in the number of people she was aware of. The

---

[29] Subjects were "asked" this after removal of the stimulus by a distinctive tone (a different tone for each row) that signaled which row they were to report.

availability of reasons and, thus (according to $^\Gamma T_a$), the difference in S's conscious experiences, is revealed by the "partial" reports, but not by the "full" or "whole" report. S cannot say, in full-report mode, whether there are differences in the scene, but by concentrating on parts of the scene, we get the kind of difference in response that $^\Gamma T_a$ takes to be symptomatic of a conscious difference.

This, as I say, is only one possibility. There may be other ways of probing subjects to find out what they consciously experience. If we use $^\Gamma T_a$ as our guide, the way to go about determining what subjects are consciously aware of is not by asking them. Many of them (animals and infants) can't tell you. And of those who can tell you (adult human beings), many don't know. There is, often enough, too much going on in there (e.g., change blindness) for them to be very reliable about all that is going on in there. The way to proceed is, rather, by looking, in the most varied possible conditions, at what an agent finds it reasonable to do, at what, therefore, given suitable desires and circumstances, the agent is motivated to do. It is this information that most reliably indicates, and is the most accurate test of, how much of the world is being consciously experienced.

REFERENCES

Akins, Kathleen. (1996), *Perception* (Oxford; Oxford University Press).

Armstrong, David M. (1968), *A Materialist Theory of the Mind* (London: Routledge).

Averbach, E. and Coriell, A. S. (1961), "Short-term Memory in Vision," *Bell System Technical Journal* 40: 309–28.

Averbach, E. and Sperling, G. (1961), "Short Term Storage of Information in Vision" in C. Cherry (ed.), *Information Theory* (London: Butterworth): 196–211.

Baars, Bernard. J. (1988), *A Cognitive Theory of Consciousness* (Cambridge: Cambridge University Press).

Beck, D. M., Rees, G., Frith, C. D., and Lavie, N. (2001), "Neural Correlates of Change Detection and Change Blindness," *Nature Neuroscience* 4(6): 645–50.

Block, Ned. (1995), "On a Confusion about a Function of Consciousness," *Behavioral and Brain Sciences* 18.2; reprinted in N. Block, O. Flanagan and G. Güzeldere (eds) (1997).

Block, Ned. (2001), "Paradox and Cross Purpose in Recent Work on Consciousness," in S. Dehaene (ed.) (2001): 197–219.

Block, Ned, Flanagan, Owen and Güzeldere, Güven. (eds) (1997), *The Nature of Consciousness* (Cambridge, Mass.: MIT Press).

Boornstein, R. F. (1992), "Subliminal Mere Exposure Affects," in R. F. Boornstein and T. S. Pittman (1992): 191–210.

Boornstein, R. F. and Pittman, T. S. (eds) (1992), *Perception without Awareness: Cognitive, Clinical, and Social Perspectives* (New York: Guilford Press).

Brewer, Bill. (1999), *Perception and Reason* (Oxford: Oxford University Press).

Campbell, John. (2002), *Reference and Consciousness* (Oxford: Oxford University Press).

Carruthers, Peter. (1989), "Brute Experience," *Journal of Philosophy* 86: 258-69.

Carruthers, Peter. (2000), *Phenomenal Consciousness* (Cambridge: Cambridge University Press).

Cheesman, J. and Merikle, P. (1984), "Priming with and without Awareness," *Perception and Psychophysics* 36: 387–95.

Cheesman, J. and Merikle, P. (1986), "Distinguishing Conscious from Unconscious Perceptual Processes," *Canadian Journal of Psychology* 40: 343–67.

Clark, Andy. (2001), "Visual Experience and Motor Action: Are the Bonds too Tight?," *Philosophical Review* 110: 495–519.

Coltheart, Veronika (ed.) (1999a), *Fleeting Memories* (Cambridge, Mass.: MIT Press).

Coltheart, Veronika (1999b), "Introduction: Perceiving and Remembering Brief Visual Stimuli," in V. Coltheart (ed.) (1999a): 1–12.

Coltheart, Veronika (1999c), "Fleeting Memories: Summary and Conclusions," in V. Coltheart (ed.) (1999a): 239–60.

Dancy, Jonathan. (2000), *Practical Reality* (Oxford: Oxford University Press).

Dancy, Jonathan, Darwall, Stephen., Wallace, R. Jay, et al. (2003), Book Symposium on *Practical Reality, in Philosophy and Phenomenological Research* 67: 412–90.

Dehaene, Stanislas (ed.) (2001), *The Cognitive Neuroscience of Consciousness* (Cambridge, Mass.: MIT Press).

Dehanene, S. and Naccache, L. (2001), "Towards a Cognitive Neuroscience of Consciousness: Basic Evidence and a Workspace Framework," Dehaene (2001): 1–37.

Dennett, Daniel. (1978), "Toward a Cognitive Theory of Consciousness," in C. Savage (ed.), *Minnesota Studies in the Philosophy of Science, Volume* 9 (Minneapolis, Minn.: University of Minnesota Press).

Dennett, Daniel. (1991), *Consciousness Explained* (Cambridge, Mass.: MIT Press).

Dienes, Z, and Perner, Joseph. (1996), "Implicit Knowledge in People and Connectionist Networks," in G. Underwood (ed.) (1996): 227–55.

Dixon, Norman F. (1981), *Preconscious Processing* (New York: John Wiley and Sons).

Dorfman, J., Shames, V. A., and Kihlstrom, J. F. (1996), "Intuition, Incubation, and Insight: Implicit Cognition in Problem Solving," in G. Underwood (ed.) (1996): 257–96.

Dretske, Fred. (1969), *Seeing and Knowing* (Chicago: University of Chicago Press).

Dretske, Fred. (1981), *Knowledge and the Flow of Information* (Cambridge, Mass: MIT Press).

Dretske, Fred. (1993), "Conscious Experience," *Mind* 102: 1–21.

Dretske, Fred. (1995), *Naturalizing the Mind* (Cambridge, Mass.: MIT Press).

Dretske, Fred. (2004), "Change Blindness," *Philosophical Studies* 120: 1–18.

Driver, J. (1996), "What can Visual Neglect and Extinction Reveal about the Extent of 'Preattentive' Processing?," in Kramer, et al. (eds) (1996): 193–224.

Driver, J. and Vuilleumier, P. (2001a), "Perceptual Awareness and Its Loss in Unilateral Neglect and Extinction", in S. Dehaene, and L. Naccache (eds) (2001): 39–88.

Driver, J. and Vuilleumier, P. (2001b), "Unconscious Processing in Neglect and Extinction," in B. Gelder, E. Haan, and C. Heywood (eds) (2001): 107–39.

Eriksen, C. W. (1959), "Unconscious Processes," in M. R. Jones (ed.), *Nebraska Symposium on Motivation, 1958* (Lincoln: University of Nebraska Press): 169–227.

Eriksen, C. W. (1960), "Discrimination and Learning without Awareness: A Methodological Survey and Evaluation," *Psychological Review* 67: 279–300.

Eriksen, C. W. (1990), "Attentional Search of the Visual Field," in D. Brogan (ed.), *Visual Search* (New York: Taylor & Francis): 3–19.

Evans, G. (1982), *Varieties of Reference* (Oxford: Clarendon Press).

Flanagan, Owen (1991), *The Science of the Mind*, Second Edition (Cambridge, Mass.: MIT Press).

Gelder, Beatrice, Haan, Edward, and Heywood, Charles (eds) (2001), *Out of Mind: Varieties of Unconscious Processes* (Oxford: Oxford University Press).

Goodale, Melvin and Milner, David (2004), *Sight Unseen* (Oxford: Oxford University Press).

Grice, H. P. (1961), "The Causal Theory of Perception," *Proceedings of the Aristotelian Society*, Supplementary volume 35: 121–52.

Haugeland, John. (1996), "Direct Perception," in K. Akins (ed.) (1996).

Holender, D. (1986), "Semantic Activation without Conscious Identification in Dichotic Listening, Parafoveal Vision, and Visual Masking: A Survey and Appraisal," *Behavior and Brain Sciences* 9: 1–23.

Humphrey, N. (1995), "Blocking out the Distinction between Sensation and Perception: Superblindsight and the Case of Helen," *Behavioral and Brain Science* 18: 257–58.

Hurley, Susan. (1994), "Unity and Objectivity," in C. Peacocke (ed.), *Objectivity, Simulation and the Unity of Consciousness, Proceedings of the British Academy* 83 (Oxford: Oxford University Press): 49–77.

Hurley, Susan. (1998), *Consciousness in Action* (Cambridge, Mass.: Harvard University Press).

Jacob, Pierre and Jeannerod, Marc (2003), *Ways of Seeing: The Scope and Limits of Visual Cognition* (Oxford: Oxford University Press).

Jacob, L. L. (1991), "A Process Disassociation Framework: Separating Automatic from Intentional Uses of Memory," *Journal of Memory and Language* 30: 513–40.

Kanwisher, N. (2001), "Neural Events and Perceptual Awareness," in S. Dehaene and L.Naccache (eds) (2001): 89–113.

Kanwisher, N., Yin, C., and Wojciulik, E. (1999), "Repetition Blindness for Pictures: Evidence for the Rapid Computation of Abstract Visual Descriptions," in V. Coltheart (ed.) (1999a): 119–50.

Kramer, A. F., Coles, M. G. H., and Logan, G. D. (eds) (1996), *Convergent Operations in the Study of Visual Selective Attention* (Washington, DC: APA Press).

Kunst-Wilson, W. R. and Zajonc, R. B. (1980), "Affective Discriminations of Stimuli that Cannot be Recognized," *Science* 207: 557–8.

Lewis, David. (1980), "Veridical Hallucination and Prosthetic Vision," *Australasian Journal of Philosophy* 58: 239–49.

Logothetis, N. K. (1998), "Single Units and Conscious Vision," *Proceedings of the Royal Society of London, Series B* 353: 1801–18.

Lycan, William. (1987), *Consciousness*. (Cambridge, Mass.: MIT Press).

Lycan, William. (1992), "Uncertain Materialism and Lockean Introspection," *Behavioral and Brain Sciences* 15: 216–17.

Mack, Arien and Rock, Irvin (1998), *Inattentional Blindness* (Cambridge, Mass.: MIT Press).

Marcel, A. J. (1980), "Conscious and Preconscious Recognition of Polysemous Words: Locating the Selective Effects of Prior Verbal Context," in R. S. Nickerson (ed.), *Attention and Performance VIII* (Hillsdale, NJ: Erlbaum): 435–57.

Marcel, A. J. (1983a), "Conscious and Unconscious Perception: Experiments on Visual Masking and Word Recognition," *Cognitive Psychology* 15: 197–237.

Marcel, A. J. (1983b), "Conscious and Unconscious Perception: An Approach to the Relations between Phenomenal Experience and Perceptual Processes," *Cognitive Psychology* 15: 238–300.

Merikle, P. (1984), "Toward a Definition of Awareness," *Bulletin of the Psychonomic Society* 22: 449–50.

Merikle, P. (1992), "Perception without Awareness: Critical Issues," *American Psychologist* 47: 792–5.

Merikle, P. and Reingold, E. M. (1992), "Measuring Unconscious Perceptual Processes," in R. F. Boornstein and T. S. Pittman (eds) (1992): 55–80.

Merikle, P., Smilek, D., and Eastwood, J. D. (2001), "Perception without Awareness," in S. Dehaene (ed.) (2001): 115–34.

Milner, David and Goodale, Melvyn (1995), *The Visual Brain in Action* (Oxford: Oxford University Press).

Moran, Richard. (2001), *Authority and Estrangement: An Essay on Self-Knowledge* (Princeton: Princeton University Press).

O'Regan, J. Kevin and Noë, Alva (2001), "A Sensorimotor Account of Vision and Visual Consciousness," *Behavioral and Brain Sciences* 24: 939–1031.

Palmer, Stephen E. (1999), *Vision Science: Photons to Phenomenology* (Cambridge, Mass.: MIT Press/A Bradford Book).

Peacocke, Christopher. (1992), *A Study of Concepts* (Cambridge, Mass.: MIT Press).

Perky, C. W. (1958), "An Experimental Study of Imagination," in C. Beardslee and M. Wertheimer (eds) (1958), *Readings in Perception* (Princeton: Princeton University Press).

Pöppel, E., Held, R. and Frost, D. (1973), "Residual Visual Function after Brain Wounds Involving the Central Visual Pathways in Man," *Nature* 243: 295–96.

Potter, M. C. (1999), "Understanding Sentences and Scenes: The Role of Conceptual Short Term Memory," in V. Coltheart (ed.) (1999a): 13–46.

Rafel, R. and Robertson, L. (1995), "The Neurology of Visual Attention," in M. S. Gazzaniga (ed.), *The Cognitive Neurosciences* (Cambridge, Mass.: MIT Press): 625–48.

Reingold, E. M. and Merikle, P. M. (1988), "Using Direct and Indirect Measures to Study Perception without Awareness," *Perception and Psychophysics* 44: 563–75.

Reingold, E. M. and Merikle, P. M. (1990), "On the Inter-relatedness of Theory and Measurement in the Study of Unconscious Processes," *Mind and Language* 5: 9–28.

Reingold, E. M. and Toth, J. P. (1996), "Process Dissociations versus Task Dissociations: A Controversy in Progress," in G. Underwood (1996): 159–202.

Rosenthal, David. (1986), "Two Concepts of Consciousness," *Philosophical Studies* 94: 329–59.

Rosenthal, David. (1990), "A Theory of Consciousness," *Report No. 40, Research Group on Mind and Brain* (Bielefeld, Germany: University of Bielefeld).

Rosenthal, David. (1991), "The Independence of Consciousness and Sensory Quality," in E. Villanueva (ed.), *Consciousness* (Atascadero, Calif.: Ridgeview Publishing Co.).

Rossetti, Y., Rode, G., and Boisson, D. (2001), "Numbsense: A Case Study and Implications," in B. Gelder, E. Haan, and C. Heywood (eds) (2001): 265–92.

Shapiro, K. L, and Luck, S. J. (1999), "The Attentional Blink: A Front-end Mechanism for Fleeting Memories," in V. Coltheart (ed.) (1999a): 95–118.

Shiffrin, R. M., Diller, D., and Cohen, A. (1996), "Processing Visual Information in Unattended Location," in A. F. Kramer, et al. (eds) (1996): 225–46.

Sperling, G. (1960), "The Information available in Brief Visual Presentations," *Psychological Monographs* 74: 1–29.

Tye, M. (1995), *Ten Problems of Consciousness* (Cambridge, Mass.: MIT Press).

Underwood, Geoffrey. (ed.) (1996), *Implicit Cognition* (Oxford: Oxford University Press).

Underwood, G. and Bright J. E. H. (1996), "Cognition with and without Awarenes," in G. Underwood (ed.) (1996): 1–40.

Van Gulick, Robert. (1994), "Deficit Sudies and the Function of Phenomenal Consciousness," in G. Graham and L. Stephens (eds), *Philosophical Psychology* (Cambridge, Mass.: MIT Press): 25–50

Vuilleumier, P. and Rafal, R. (1999), "Both Means More Than Two: Localizing and Counting in Patients with Visuospatial Neglect," *Nature Neuroscience* 2: 783–84.

Weiskrantz, Lawrence (1997), *Consciousness Lost and Found: a Neuropsychological Exploration* (New York: Oxford University Press).

Wolfe, J. M. (1999), "Inattentional Amnesia," in V. Coltheart (ed.) (1999a): 71–94.

Wolfe, J. M., Klempen, N., and Dahlen, K. (2000), "Postattentive Vision," *Journal of Experimental Psychology: Human Perception and Performance* 26: 693–716.

5

Experience and Knowledge

Anil Gupta

I INTRODUCTION

The question I wish to address in this essay is: what is the contribution of experience to knowledge? We suffer experiences and, as a result, acquire bits of knowledge about the world. Consider an ordinary example: I walk into a room full of people, I have a particular experience, and I come to know that Fred is wearing a red tie. My experience makes a causal contribution to my knowledge. It is an important causal factor in the process that produces in me the belief that Fred is wearing a red tie—or at least it is plausible to suppose so. There is another sort of contribution of experience, however, and it is this that concerns me here: experience somehow contributes to the *rationality* of belief.[1] My belief about Fred's tie is rational, and the source of its rationality is, in part, my experience. But what exactly is the contribution of experience here? How does the experience help make the belief rational? The following terminology will prove useful. Let us say that the *given* in an experience is the total rational contribution of that experi-ence.[2] Then the question before us is: what is it that is given in an experience?

This essay is drawn from a book I am writing on empiricism and experience, where the ideas sketched here receive a fuller treatment. I have presented these ideas in talks given at Oxford, Pittsburgh, Davis, Waterloo, Brown, and Boulder; and, in a more extended way, in my Fall 2002 seminar at the University of Pittsburgh. I learned something from each occasion, and for this I wish to thank the participants. I have also benefited from discussions with a number of friends, students, and colleagues—including George Bealer, Nuel Belnap, Bob Brandom, Bill Brewer, Joe Camp, Bill Demopoulos, John McDowell, José Martínez-Fernández, John Morrison, Karen Neander, Kevin Scharp, Susanna Schellenberg, Ernest Sosa, and Mark Wilson. I wish to thank the editors of this volume, Tamar Szabó Gendler and John Hawthorne, as well as two anonymous referees, for their valuable comments. Especial thanks are due to Chris Hill, with whom I have enjoyed e-mail exchanges and several long conversations on the ideas of this chapter.

[1] There are philosophers who deny that experience makes any rational or normative contribu-tion to knowledge. Donald Davidson, for example, has written, "No doubt meaning and know-ledge depend on experience, and experience ultimately on sensation. But this is the 'depend' of causality, not of evidence or justification" (2001: 146). John McDowell (1994: Lecture I) has stressed, against Davidson, the normative role of experience.

[2] Sometimes the expression "the given in experience" is used in a more narrow and philosophically loaded way. It is used to talk about the immediate contents of experience—things such as ideas,

This question about the given and experience is essentially *logical* in character. We know many things about the world: that sugar is sweet, that the earth moves, that there are black holes, and so on. Call this body of propositions that we know *K*. Now *K* bears some relationship to the experiences we have suffered. There is something *X* that is given in our experiences, and this *X* bears some logical relationship to *K*—a relationship that contributes to the rationality of our acceptance of *K*. What is this *X*? And what is its logical relationship to *K*? More fundamentally still: what is the general logical character of *X*? Is *X* a totality of propositions, or properties, or objects, or something altogether different? In this essay, I want to put forward an account of the logical character of *X*—an account that is suggested by the logic of interdependent concepts that Nuel Belnap and I have developed.[3] To make sense of the given in experience, it turns out, we need to make sense of certain interdependencies. So tools that are useful in dealing with the logic of interdependent concepts prove to be useful in dealing with the logic of experience also.

It is a central thesis of empiricism that the materials for our knowledge are all supplied by experience. This thesis has a psychological dimension: our possession of concepts and our states of knowledge have causal origins in our experiences. Thus interpreted, the thesis may or may not be true—its status can be settled only by an empirical inquiry. The empiricist thesis has a logical dimension as well: the rationality of our concepts and of our knowledge claims issues entirely from experience. It is this logical reading of the thesis that I shall, henceforth, understand by the term "empiricism." Whether empiricism so understood is true depends crucially on the account of the given. For it claims, essentially, that the given in experience logically forces our body of knowledge *K*. I must confess to being partial to empiricism. I wish for an account of the given on which it would be strong enough to force *K*. This is what I say I *wish* for, not what I am setting out to provide in this essay. Empiricism is not easily sustained, and any inquiry into it must be long and difficult. My aim in this essay is to provide a highly idealized and simplified account of the given, one for which it is not utterly absurd to suppose that it might sustain empiricism.

II TWO CONSTRAINTS

It may appear at first sight that our question about the given has an easy, commonsensical answer. Consider again the experience I had when I walked into the room full of people. The given in this experience, it may be said, just consists of the ordinary judgments of perception—judgments such as that Fred is

---

impressions, and sense-data—and the immediately available propositions about them. See Alan H. Goldman (1992). One can deny the existence of the given in this narrow sense, as I wish to, and yet insist—as I shall—that experience makes a rational contribution to knowledge.

[3] See Gupta and Belnap (1993). For a brief sketch of the theory, see Gupta (1988–9).

wearing a red tie, that he is standing next to a woman, that there are many people in the room, and so on. If this kind of naive answer were right, a good part of modern philosophy would deserve to be thrown in the trash bin. But it is not right. The answer fails to respect two vital constraints on any account of the given:

The Equivalence Constraint. The given in subjectively identical experiences is the same;

and

The Reliability Constraint. The given in an experience never contains a false judgment (i.e., false proposition).

It is easy to see that the naive account fails to respect the two constraints. Let e be the experience I had when I walked into the room. Let e' be an experience subjectively identical to e', but one that is non-veridical. Perhaps e is a dream experience, or perhaps e' is caused by an optical illusion, or perhaps by some chemicals I have ingested. Anyhow, the Equivalence constraint demands that the given in e and e' must be the same. Hence, on the naive account, the given in e' must consist of the same ordinary judgments of perception as those assigned to e'. But this violates the Reliability constraint, for the given thus assigned to e' contains a false judgment.[4]

Let me offer a brief defense of the two constraints. Let me first take up the Equivalence constraint. This says that the given in subjectively identical experiences must be the same, that such experiences must make the same rational contribution to knowledge. The constraint focuses on *subjectively* identical experiences, for our interest is in the contribution of experience *from the viewpoint of the experiencing subject.* We want to understand the enrichment that a particular experience entails (or should entail) in the cognitive life of the subject—not in the cognitive life of an external observer prying into the subject.

---

[4] The argument assumes the existence of a pair of subjectively identical experiences. This assumption can be avoided by moving to a modal version of the argument. We read the two constraints modally, as holding not just of actual experiences but also of possible experiences. And now we can deduce the desired conclusion from the mere possibility of certain subjectively identical experiences.

Let us note that the non-modal argument above yields only the conclusion that the given does not *always* consist of ordinary judgments of perception. It does not establish that the given *never* consists of such judgments. To gain the stronger conclusion from the non-modal premises we need a hefty existence assumption: that for every veridical experience there is a subjectively identical non-veridical experience. Again, a modal argument dispenses with this assumption in favor of a corresponding claim about possible experiences.

In general, existence assumptions about subjectively identical experiences can be eliminated, in arguments that concern us, by moving to modalized readings of the Equivalence and Reliability constraints. It is simpler to work with the non-modal readings, however, and so I shall freely make various existence assumptions in the course of my exposition. These assumptions are all dispensable. (The practice of assuming—and even affirming—the existence of subjectively identical experiences is common in the epistemological literature. For an example, see the fourth "heading" in the extract from Cicero's *Academica* in n. 6.).

Differences in subjectively identical experiences—no matter how large from an external viewpoint—make not an iota of difference to the rational evolution of the subject's view of the world. Suppose that, when I walked into the room full of people, my epistemic state was of the sort that we take to be normal. I believed—and was justified in believing—that I was awake, that my sense-organs were functioning normally, and so on. The experience e I suffered on entering the room entitled me to believe that Fred was wearing a red tie. Now suppose that my friends had played a visual trick on me. On entering the room, I suffered an experience e' subjectively identical to e even though Fred was not wearing a red tie. Because of the trickery, my belief about Fred's tie would be false. But it would be no less *rational* than in the original case. The differences between e and e' are great—one is veridical and the other is not. Nonetheless, the differences between them are immaterial from my epistemic viewpoint. The two experiences should have the same impact on the rational evolution of my beliefs. In short, their rational contributions must be the same.[5]

Imagine two similar and ideally rational beings that are subjected throughout their existence to subjectively identical series of experiences. If the Equivalence constraint were false then the two beings might end up having different views of the world. For, some of the corresponding elements in the two series of experiences may yield different givens, which in turn may entail differences in the views of the two rational beings. It is a virtue of the Equivalence constraint that it eliminates this possibility. The constraint guarantees that similar rational beings suffering subjectively identical experiences will have the same view of the world.[6]

Let me now turn to the Reliability constraint. This constraint requires that the given in an experience should not contain a false proposition. Note that the constraint is purely negative in character. It does not require the inclusion of

---

[5] If I am a brain in a vat, my beliefs about the world are false but they are not thereby irrational. Consider a related example: an evil demon can so arrange things around me that much of my view of the world is false. But this does not entail that he has made me irrational. To bring this about, the evil demon will have to manipulate not just my environment but things internal to me.

[6] The Equivalence constraint, or one of its near neighbors, has been on the epistemological scene from ancient times on. For example, Cicero (106–43 BCE) gives in his *Academica* (2.83) the following skeptical argument against the Stoic notion of "cognitive impression." Cicero attributes this argument to the New Academy of Arcesilaus (315–240 BCE).

There are four headings to prove there is nothing which can be known, cognized or grasped, which is the subject of this whole controversy. The first of these is that some false impression does exist. The second, that it is not cognitive. The third, that *impressions between which there is no difference cannot be such that some are cognitive and others not.* The fourth, that no true impression arises from sensation which does not have alongside it another impression no different from it which is not cognitive. Everyone accepts the second and third of these headings. (Long and Sedley, 1987: 40J; my italics)

The third "heading," italicized above, seems to me to be a neighbor of the Equivalence constraint.

Another neighbor of the Equivalence constraint is in play in the widely discussed Argument from Illusion. See, for instance, Bill Brewer's formulation of the argument (1999: 13–14).

true propositions; it merely excludes false propositions from the given. Now, the principal doubt attaching to this constraint issues from the thought that the constraint cannot be met, that it is just too strong. This doubt can be dispelled only by a positive theory of experience, one that is plausible and also satisfies the constraint—this is the burden of the constructive part of the present essay. Let me for now gesture in the direction of three motivating considerations in favor of the constraint.

The first consideration is that the Reliability constraint is consistent with the *un*reliability of our ordinary judgments of perception. From the phenomenological point of view, ordinary judgments of perception are not the given in an experience. The given in my experience of, say, looking at a ripe tomato does not contain judgments such as "That is a tomato," "That tomato is red," and "I am seeing a tomato." It is plain on reflection that my visual experience, when considered in isolation, does not entitle me to the judgment that the object before me is a tomato. Tomatoes are solids, they have a distinctive inner structure, they have a distinctive origin (they are fruits of a certain kind of plant), and so on. But there is nothing in my visual experience that tells me that the object before me is not hollow. Or that it is not a nature-less, three-dimensional surface. Or that it did not spontaneously come into being a few minutes ago. We need to exercise care in constructing an account of the given. We must not put elements into it whose source is not experience. Ordinary perceptual judgments are shaped, in part, by our beliefs; they do not belong in the given.[7] These judgments can be erroneous, but we should not hastily conclude that the given can be erroneous.

The second consideration is that experience is passive, and it is always a good policy not to assign fault to the passive. If during a walk in a forest I bump my head on a low branch of a tree, it is better that I assume responsibility (and change my ways) than that I pin the blame on the tree. The tree is passive. It is bound to be the way it is, given the circumstances; and it is useless to blame it for my sore head. Similarly, if having suffered an experience, I acquire a false perceptual belief, it is better that I assume responsibility (and change my manner of "reading" experience) than that I pin blame on the experience. The experience is bound to be the way it is, given the circumstances; and it is useless to blame it for my false belief. The best remedy for false perceptual beliefs is to change *oneself*, not the hope that experience will change its ways.

When I have what is called a "misleading" experience, experience has *done* nothing to mislead me. The fault, if any, lies with *me* and *my* beliefs—beliefs for which *I* am responsible. When on a foggy day I take a pillar to be a man, it is not my visual experience that tells me that there is a man before me; the experience is

---

[7] Similarly, if the content of an experience is shaped by belief and other cognitive states, then it too cannot be the given in the experience. Susanna Siegel argues in her contribution to this volume (ch. 14) that the antecedent holds of some visual experiences.

ill-equipped to do such a thing. *I* form the belief that there is a man. *I* read the experience as indicating the presence of a man. I could have the same visual experience but without the disposition to falsely conclude that there is a man. And here it is not as if I have to resist the prodding of experience that there is a man before me. A misleading experience is not like a liar. It is not even like an innocent misinformer. Liars and misinformers *say* things, and their lies and misinformation cast doubt on their character. Misleading experiences do not cast any doubt on the character of experience. In a misleading experience I am misled, but it is not experience that does the misleading. Experience remains innocent.

The third, and final, consideration in favor of the Reliability constraint is this: only skeptics and rationalists can comfortably abandon this constraint, but not empiricists, who view experience as vested with the highest epistemic authority. If experience sometimes lies—if the given in experience sometimes contains false propositions—how does one correct the resulting error? Skeptics can comfortably hold that there is no way of doing so. Rationalists can comfortably appeal to one of the substantive principles that they deem to be truths supplied by reason. But what can empiricists say? That the error is corrected through considerations of coherence, the coherence of the totality of experiential judgments? The notion of coherence that is invoked here cannot be purely logical, since, from the logical point of view, even false judgments yield coherent wholes; they even yield coherent wholes that are maximal.[8] But if coherence is substantive, whence does it derive its authority? The empiricists are in danger of positing a sixth sense, the sense of coherence, as the ultimate seat of epistemic authority. And their differences from the rationalists now appear to be merely verbal: rationalists call this sixth sense *reason*.[9]

III CARTESIAN CONCEPTIONS OF EXPERIENCE

It may be objected that the two constraints, though plausible individually, have intolerable consequences when they are taken together. The constraints imply that the given in an experience never contains judgments about ordinary objects.[10] It follows, the objection continues, that only judgments about what is

---

[8] I am assuming that a proposition that is given in experience is not self-contradictory.

[9] The Reliability constraint too has an established position in the history of epistemology. It is, for instance, a crucial ingredient in George Berkeley's argument for his claim that only ideas are immediately perceived by sense. This argument, which receives an extended treatment in Berkeley's *Three Dialogues between Hylas and Philonous* (1713), is an ancestor of the Argument from Illusion. Note that a version of the Reliability constraint is explicitly invoked by Philonous (Luce and Jessop edition, 1948: 238; Dancy edition, 1998: 121).

[10] For, by the Reliability constraint, a non-veridical experience cannot yield judgments about ordinary objects. Hence, by the Equivalence constraint, a veridical experience cannot do so either. See n. 4.

common to subjectively identical experiences can be in the given. That is, the given can contain only judgments about the subjective character of experience. The constraints thus lead us to deny our common-sense conception of experience in favor of a *Cartesian* conception. We no longer think of experience as acquainting us with ordinary objects and some of their properties and relations (e.g., "ball" and "touches"). Instead, we are forced to think of it as acquainting us with a special subjective realm—special objects such as sense-data and their subjective qualities and relations ("orange" and "is next to"). Under the Cartesian conception, experience entitles us only to thin judgments about the subjective realm (e.g., "An orange round sense-datum is next to a yellow round one"), not to ordinary judgments of perception (e.g., "An orange ball is touching a yellow one").[11]

The objection continues: "The two constraints burden us with the epistemological problem of the external world. We now need to provide a rational justification for our ordinary judgments of perception, and this requires us to somehow bridge the gulf between the subjective given and the objective judgments. The burden thus imposed is great even for the rationalists: it is not easy to find bridging principles that can plausibly be regarded as truths of reason. For the empiricists, the burden is unbearable. The materials supplied by experience on the Cartesian conceptions are too thin and ephemeral to support a solid and enduring world. The only hope for empiricists to escape the clutches of skepticism is to embrace idealism or its twentieth-century descendant, phenomenalism—neither of which has proved to be viable. In short, the two constraints throw us back into the morass of Cartesian conceptions and their intractable problems, a morass from which twentieth-century epistemology has, with difficulty, extricated us."

It seems to me that it is a virtue of modern epistemology—the epistemology of Descartes, Locke, Berkeley, Hume, and others—that it respects the two constraints, that it insists that the given does not consist of ordinary judgments of perception, and that it recognizes that there is *a* problem about our knowledge of the external world. Our ordinary judgments of perception are, of course, familiar and—*pace* the skeptic—rational. We are right to accept them in our day-to-day affairs. However, familiarity does not preclude theoretical perplexity. A mountain range may be familiar; nonetheless it is a good question how it came to be. The rationality of our ordinary judgments of perception is familiar; still, it is a good question how these judgments come to be rational. If experience accounts for their rationality, what is it that is given in experience and what is its logical link with the ordinary judgments of perception? I think it is a virtue of modern epistemology that it recognizes an important theoretical problem.

---

[11] Several different Cartesian conceptions of experience are to be found in the philosophical literature. In my exposition, I will use the terminology of sense-datum theories, but I do not mean to suggest that these are the only Cartesian conceptions, or that they are the best ones.

I admit that the modern philosophers, despite all their ingenuity, do not provide a satisfactory solution to the problem. I admit also that the roots of the difficulties lie in the Cartesian conceptions of experience: the epistemological problem is insoluble once such a conception is accepted. But these difficulties, I want to insist, should not be pinned on the two constraints. The constraints do not force a Cartesian conception upon us. There is another idea in play in the argument above for Cartesian conceptions—an idea that is almost invisible because it is so natural. The idea is that *the given in experience is propositional*. A Cartesian conception is inevitable once the two constraints are joined with this natural idea—but not otherwise. It is this natural idea that we should look upon with suspicion. The deeper roots of the modern difficulties, I want to argue, lie here.[12]

It may appear that the idea of the propositional given is not only natural but also inevitable. Experience can serve as a rational constraint on knowledge, it may be said, only if the given bears such logical relations as "entailment," "consistency," etc., with the contents of our knowledge claims. But such relations hold only between propositions. So, it is argued, experience can exercise rational constraint only if the given is propositional: a denial of the propositional given is a denial of the given altogether. Thus there appear to be only two choices: either accept the propositional given or accept the idea that experience makes no rational contribution to our knowledge.[13] My principal claim is that this is a false dilemma. I will argue that experience can exercise a rational constraint even though the given is not propositional. We can preserve the two constraints *and* the rational contribution of experience without falling into a Cartesian conception.

IV   THE HYPOTHETICAL GIVEN

Let us return to an ordinary, everyday type of situation. Say I am walking along a street, I turn a corner, and I am surprised to find myself in front of a large wall, light green in color. I have a certain type of experience and I take myself to know a few things that I did not know before. I am prepared to assert—and I take myself to be entitled to assert—that there is a wall before me, that it is light green in color, that it lies around the corner from such-and-such a street, and so on. Only a fool or a philosopher would question my entitlement—the former for poor and silly reasons; the latter for deep and subtle ones. The latter insists that

---

[12] As I see it, classical empiricism is entirely natural: it is a product of legitimate constraints and the natural idea that the given is propositional. If we wish to call classical empiricism into question, we should call the natural idea into question.

Note that the idea of a propositional given is assumed not only by the advocates of classical empiricism but also by its most prominent critics, for instance, Willard V. Quine and Wilfrid Sellars.   [13] See Brewer (1999: ch. 5).

my entitlement does not lie solely in the experience itself. An ideal rational being subjected only to that experience would not be in a position to make the assertions that I am prepared to make.[14] This is a fair point. Still, the following is beyond doubt: *given* my concepts, conceptions, and beliefs—in short, given my *view*—at the time of the experience, I am perfectly entitled to perceptual judgments such as "there is a light green wall before me." The entitlement claimed here is only hypothetical: assuming that I am justified in my view, I am justified in my perceptual judgments. This is perfectly compatible with the philosopher's point that my experience by itself does not provide justification for my perceptual judgments, for the experience by itself does not provide a justification for the view I bring to bear on it. The philosopher is not questioning the idea of conditional entitlement: given that I have the experience and given that I am entitled to my view, it follows that I am entitled to my perceptual judgments. This is something that only a fool would question. The philosopher's point is that the move from the conditional entitlement to a categorical entitlement requires a *prior* entitlement to my view. And here there is a serious problem: how can I be entitled to a view if my only entitlement to perceptual judgments is thus conditional?

Let us leave this troublesome problem to one side for the moment and focus on the point of agreement, which we may represent schematically thus:

(1) View + Experience → Perceptual Judgments.

In the above example, when I turned the corner and was confronted by the wall, I had a certain view—that is, I had certain concepts such as "wall" and "light green," I had the ordinary conception of street corners and walls, and I had certain beliefs such as that my eyes are functioning properly, the lighting is normal, and so on. Once I bring this view to my experience, I am entitled to certain perceptual judgments—judgments such as, "There is a light green wall before me." Now, I can take the same experience and consider it under a different view. I can, for example, consider it under a view like the earlier one, but with the belief that a certain disease has tinged my eye lenses yellow and things that look green to me are actually blue. Considered under this view, the experience does not entitle me to the perceptual judgment "There is a light green wall before me," but to the contrary judgment "There is a blue wall before me." So, the same experience when conjoined with different views can yield different perceptual judgments.

Let us observe that an experience and a view may entitle me to false perceptual judgments. In the previous example, my belief about my eye lenses may be

---

[14] Compare this with the following remark of Philonous in Berkeley's *Three Dialogues*:
[T]hose things alone are actually and strictly perceived by any sense, which would have been perceived, in case that same sense had then been first conferred on us (Luce and Jessop edition, 1948: 204; Dancy edition, 1998: 90).

false—my eyes may be perfectly fine—and I may in fact be standing before a light green wall. Nevertheless, given my view, I am entitled to the false judgment "There is a blue wall before me." Furthermore, the perceptual judgments can even be radically false: the same view, the same experience, but I am dreaming. I remain entitled to judge that the wall I am seeing is blue, but now there is no such wall. Similar examples show that perceptual judgments can also be vague and confused. The general point is that perceptual judgments are liable to reflect the defects of the views we bring to bear on experience. They are not pristine truths built from clear and distinct concepts.

Experience yields judgments even when conjoined with extraordinary views. Consider a *Cartesian view*: I am a mind that has direct awareness of itself and its own sense-data, concepts, and thoughts; it does not have direct awareness of physical objects such as walls—these are mere logical constructions or posits from sense-data.[15] When I conjoin my experience with the Cartesian view, I am entitled to perceptual judgments such as "A light green sense-datum fills my entire visual field" and "I sense a colored sense-datum." A variant of the Cartesian view is the *neutral-monist* view.[16] This view holds that there is direct awareness of sense-data, concepts, etc., but not of the self. The self is as much a logical construct or posit as physical objects. Under the neutral-monist view, my experience yields judgments such as "Lo! A light green sense-datum."

In summary: an experience when combined with a view yields judgments. The view may be ordinary or extraordinary, it may be clear or confused, and it may be true or utterly false—in each case experience yields judgments. These judgments themselves can be of varying character, ranging from ordinary, clear, and true to extraordinary, confused, and utterly false. The character of the judgment depends in part on experience and in part on the view that is brought to bear on it. This observation would not, I think, be disputed by philosophers, no matter how skeptical their disposition.

Our views depend upon perceptual judgments and, as we have seen, these judgments in turn depend upon the views.[17] Now, one strategy—the classical strategy—for extracting the contribution of experience from this circle of interdependence is through a process of filtration: filter out all views and judgments about which there is any doubt and uncertainty. The pure residue, consisting of propositions that are absolutely certain, is what experience contributes to knowledge; this is the given in experience. This strategy is forced upon us if we insist that the given is propositional in form. If, however, we are willing to abandon the idea of a propositional given, then a natural alternative presents itself. We can forego the process of filtration and we can say simply that the

---

[15] This provides only a hint of the contents of the Cartesian view. It should not be treated as a complete description. If it were a complete description, the view would not yield any judgments under any experience.   [16] See James (1912); Russell (1918).

[17] Sellars' remarks (1956: §36) that we must reject the idea that observational knowledge "stands on its own feet." (I do not endorse argument Sellars's in §36, however.)

contribution of experience is hypothetical in character: it yields judgments only when conjoined with a view. The logical category of the contribution of experience is not that of proposition but that of *function*. Let e be an experience and let Γ_e be the logical contribution of e—the *given of* e. Then the suggestion is that Γ_e is a function that takes views v as inputs and yields classes of judgments $\Gamma_e(v)$ as outputs.[18] An experience does not yield absolute entitlement to any judgments. It yields at best only conditional entitlements: given such-and-such a view, one is entitled to so-and-so judgments. An experience taken in isolation does not pronounce on how things are. It tells us only how to fill out a view—any view. It adds just a little bit of color and a little bit of detail to the view.

V   A COMPARISON

The character of the given in experience is in some respects parallel to that of an argument-form (e.g., *modus ponens*). An argument-form draws a connection between premises and conclusions. Similarly, the given draws a connection between views and perceptual judgments. Suppose the argument-form rules that the following is valid:

$P_1, \ldots, P_n$, therefore, C.

Then it imposes a rational constraint on an individual who believes the premises $P_1, \ldots, P_n$. In most cases the constraint is met simply by adding the conclusion C to the individual's beliefs—but not in all cases. Sometimes the constraint requires that one modify one's attitude towards the premises—as, for example, when one is shown that one's premises are logically incoherent. The situation is similar with the rational constraint imposed by experience. Suppose that an experience e yields, when conjoined with a view v, a class of judgments that contains Q. Let us represent this as follows:

(2) $Q \in \Gamma_e(v)$.

Suppose further that we have a rational being who holds the view v and suffers the experience e. This being has to cope with the rational constraint expressed in (2). In most cases the constraint is met simply by accepting Q, but in some cases it may require a modification of the view v. I shall sometimes read (2) as

---

[18] Strictly speaking I should let $\Gamma_e(v)$ be a vague class, since it can be indeterminate whether a judgment belongs to $\Gamma_e(v)$. For example, the experience one sometimes has of the sky around the setting Sun can leave it indeterminate whether one is entitled to the judgment "The part of the sky over there by the Sun is orange." Furthermore, I should let $\Gamma_e(v)$ carry information about the degrees of confidence that one is entitled to have in perceptual judgments. An experience and a view may entitle one to have greater confidence in some perceptual judgments than in others. These complications can be neglected, I think, at this stage of our inquiry. I will continue to think of $\Gamma_e(v)$ as a class of judgments.

saying that the experience *e* and the view *v entail* the judgment *Q*.[19] The present point, then, is that the character of this entailment is similar to that of logical entailment: it does not always yield entitlement. A rational being that holds the view *v* and suffers the experience *e* is not automatically entitled by (2) to assert *Q*. Constraint (2) forces the rational being to adjust its view *v in light of Q* (and the other judgments in $\Gamma_e(v)$). Most often this is achieved simply by adding *Q* to *v*. But sometimes it requires a substantial revision of the original view *v* to a new view *v'*. It is possible that *v'* does not sustain the judgment *Q*—it may even be that *e* and *v'* entail the negation of *Q*. In such a case, the total effect of *e* and *v* is to preclude entitlement to *Q*.[20]

There are, of course, important differences between argument-forms and the given in experience. *First*, an argument-form has no new information to add to the premisses: the content of the conclusion of a valid argument is already contained in that of the premisses. The situation with experience is radically different: the content of perceptual judgments is not already to be found in the view. Perceptual judgments enrich and, sometimes, disturb the view. A view *v* may be coherent and yet may become incoherent when the judgments $\Gamma_e(v)$ entailed by *e* are added to it.

Second, valid argument-forms do not yield conclusions for all possible premisses. *Modus ponens*, for instance, does not yield any conclusion if it is fed the premisses "*P* or *Q*" and *P*. Experience, on the other hand, yields perceptual judgments for *all* views. I will not consider anything to be a view unless it yields at least some perceptual judgments for each and every experience. This constraint is weak, since "I smell something unusual," "I hear something," and "Lo! Blue!" count as perceptual judgments.

Third, with argument-forms, the premisses and the conclusions belong to the same logical category, namely, proposition. Not so with the given in experience. A view is not a proposition or a judgment. A view contains judgments (example: "I am wearing glasses that are tinted yellow"). But it cannot be identified with a conjunction (or other complex) built out of judgments. Having a view is not the same thing as having an attitude of belief (or acceptance) towards a complex of propositions. No belief, no matter how complex, can by itself prompt me to respond—or make it rational for me to respond—to *this particular* experience that I am having right now with the judgment "There is a beige monitor before me." Even if I have a belief such as "Experiences having *these* qualities signal the presence of beige monitors," there is still a gap to be bridged before I can judge "There is a beige monitor before me." I need to judge of *this particular*

---

[19] If the view *v* is clear from the context, I will sometimes say that *e* entails *Q*. Another reading of (2) that I will use—and have used—is "*e* and *v* yield *Q*."

[20] The terminology of "perceptual judgment" suggests entitlement, and the suggestion is harmless in most situations. But it is important to stress that there is not always an entitlement to perceptual judgments—at least on the understanding of "perceptual judgment" that I shall adopt in this essay.

experience that it has *these* qualities. And belief alone cannot prompt me—nor make it rational for me—to do so.[21]

Views cannot be identified, then, with judgments. However, as we have already seen, views do have judgments as constituent parts. Hence, evaluative concepts that we apply to judgments—e.g., the concepts "true," "false," "reasonable," and "confused"—can also be applied to views. A view may be said to be false, for instance, if any judgments contained in it are false; it may be said to be true if the constituent judgments are all true. Note, though, that there may be dimensions of evaluation of views that make no sense for judgments.

The account of the given in experience that I am proposing is built on the scheme:

(3) View v + Experience e → Perceptual Judgments $\Gamma_e(v)$.

I have noted that perceptual judgments do not bring with them entitlement: a rational being that holds the view v and suffers the experience e is not always entitled to affirm the judgments $\Gamma_e(v)$. There is another point about perceptual judgments that is important to note: there is no absolute demarcation of judgments that are perceptual from those that are not. The demarcation of the perceptual can shift as one shifts one's view. The shift can be large, as for example when we shift from our ordinary, common-sense view to a sense-datum view. On the former view judgments such as "There is a light green wall before me" count as perceptual, while on the latter view only judgments such as "I am presented with a light green sense-datum" do so. The shift can be small and subtle, as for example when we shift from one ordinary view to another. My judgment "I saw Fred enter the bank" may count as perceptual in the context of an inquiry from Fred's son about Fred's whereabouts, but may fail to count as perceptual in the context of an inquiry from Fred's lawyer at Fred's trial. This shift will occur if the views in play in the two situations are relevantly different. Suppose, for example, that Fred's lawyer has established that at the time in question someone else entered the bank and that this person can easily be mistaken for Fred. Now, with this information at hand, I can no longer insist that my judgment "I saw Fred enter the bank" is perceptual. On the other hand, in the context of the inquiry from Fred's son, where the information provided by

[21] Some readers may have wondered why the hypothetical given proposed above is not perfectly consistent with the idea of a propositional given. It may be suggested that one can take the given in an experience e to consist of the conjunction of propositions of the form:

$v \rightarrow Q$,

where v is an arbitrary view and $Q \in \Gamma_e(v)$. The observation just made points to one difficulty with this suggestion. Since v is not a proposition, there is no proposition of the form $v \rightarrow Q$. There is another difficulty worth noting. The suggestion preserves the letter of the propositional given while abandoning its spirit. It associates a proposition with an experience, but this proposition cannot be manifested in the experience. The experience does not acquaint a subject with the constituents of the given proposition. So the suggestion preserves the idea of the propositional given but only by abandoning the entire conception of experience in which the idea is embedded.

Fred's lawyer is unavailable, my judgment counts as perceptual. The shifting demarcation of the perceptual from the non-perceptual is not a problem for our account of the given in experience. The account does not rest on a prior, absolute demarcation of the perceptual. It needs only a *relative* demarcation—a demarcation that may shift with view. Scheme (3) should be understood along the lines of (4):

(4) View v + Experience $e \rightarrow$ Judgments $\Gamma_e(v)$ that are deemed perceptual by the view v.

Let us observe that the present account of the given has little difficulty in meeting the Equivalence and Reliability constraints. The Equivalence constraint is met by imposing the following natural requirement on Γ_e. If e and e' are subjectively identical experiences then Γ_e and $\Gamma_{e'}$ are identical. Thus, as we have already noted, a dream experience entails the same perceptual judgments as a subjectively identical waking experience.

Furthermore, on the present account, the given never yields a false proposition, since it never yields any propositions at all. Hence, the Reliability constraint is met—at least in letter. I think the constraint is met in spirit as well. The parallel between the given and argument-form is helpful here. A valid argument-form is perfectly reliable in the sense that *if* the premises are true *then* the conclusion is bound to be true. To object that the form is not reliable because the conclusions are sometimes false is to misunderstand the nature of argument-forms. Similarly, to object that an experience e is unreliable because the judgments $\Gamma_e(v)$ are sometimes false is to misunderstand the nature of experience. The reliability of e consists in this: *if* the view v is correct *then* the judgments $\Gamma_e(v)$ are true. The falsity of $\Gamma_e(v)$ does not impugn the reliability of e. The question of the reliability of experience (and, derivatively, of the senses) is often construed as a question about the truth and falsehood of the deliverances of experience (and the senses). But this construal rests on a category mistake. The deliverances of experience are not the kinds of things that can be true or false. Experience is reliable in the only sense that matters. It is the best and our most perfect guide to knowledge of the world. But experience does not guide by providing us with pristine truths. Its mode of operation is different.

Observe that the present account presupposes no relations of "acquaintance," "direct sensing," and such of Cartesian conceptions. Indeed, it presupposes nothing about the nature of the self and its relation to the world. Such presuppositions are proper to *views* and are confined to them. They do not sully the given.

We are part way towards our goal: to preserve the two constraints and the rational contribution of experience and at the same time evade commitment to Cartesian conceptions of experience.

VI TRANSITION TO THE CATEGORICAL

The given, on the present account, is in one respect even thinner than on Cartesian conceptions. On these conceptions, an experience entitles one to at least *some* judgments, lightweight though they may be. On the present account, however, an experience yields no entitlements whatsoever. Even the lightweight judgments of the Cartesian conceptions (e.g., "I am sensing an orange sense-datum") have, on the present account, at most a conditional entitlement: *if* the Cartesian conception in question is justified *then* so is the subjective perceptual judgment. This raises a natural and important question: how is the hypothetical given of the present account substantial? It is plain that experience makes it irrational for us to believe many things—for example, that the tides are caused by giant turtles. This irrationality is categorical, not conditional. But if the given in an experience is invariably conditional in nature, how can experience impose categorical rational requirements on us?

Even though the given, on the present account, is thin in one respect, there is another respect in which it is thick—and it is this that we need to exploit to gain categorical requirements from conditional ones. The given in an experience yields judgments for *all* views, including views that are false and confused. Intuitively: experience speaks—it guides us—even when we bring to it a false and confused view. But experience has no vocabulary of its own. It uses the vocabulary of the view that we bring to bear on it. The judgments an experience issues may thus be false and confused; still, these judgments guide the rational evolution of the view. Just as bitter poisons can heal the body, similarly, false and confused judgments can guide an erroneous view towards truth. This is the peculiar power of experience: it can guide a misconceived view out of its misconception using only the misconceived resources. Traditional accounts neglect this important dimension of experience.

Imagine a *ra*tional, *ima*ginative, and *ex*periencing being—a *raimex*, for short—that holds a view v and that suffers an experience e. The experience will yield perceptual judgments $\Gamma_e(v)$ and will induce the being to change her view. Let

$\rho_e(v) = $ the result of revising v in light of the judgments $\Gamma_e(v)$.

Experience e can be viewed, then, as exerting a rational force that moves a raimex to shift her view from v to $\rho_e(v)$. Imagine now that our raimex is subjected to a sequence of experiences of which e is the first member and e', e'', e''', . . . are the subsequent members. Let E be this sequence. That is,

$E = <e, e', e'', \ldots>.$

Plainly the raimex's view will undergo an evolution under the impacts of e, e', e'', etc. The being began with the view v. Under the impact of e, the view v is transformed to $\rho_e(v)$. Now, under the impact of e', this new view $\rho_e(v)$ will in turn be transformed. The being will come to hold the view $\rho_{e'}(\rho_e(v))$. The impact of e'' will result in yet another change in view. The experiences in E will thus force the being to run successively through the views in the sequence:

$$<v, \rho_e(v), \rho_{e'}(\rho_e(v)), \rho_{e''}(\rho_{e'}(\rho_e(v))), \ldots >.$$

Let us call this sequence *the revision sequence generated by E and v*.[22] For any sequence S, let $l(S)$ be the length of S and let S_n be the value of S at the n-th stage. For example, if S is the sequence

$$< v, v^*, v', v\# >$$

then $l(S) = 4$, $S_0 = v$, and $S_3 = v\#$. For simplicity, I shall consider only sequences of experiences that are finite in length, though the notions introduced below can apply also to ω-long sequences.

A raimex suffering experiences may go through a series of views that are all fundamentally the same. It can happen that the effect of the experiences is to add only details to a view without entailing any fundamental shifts. This is not the only possibility, however: experience can result in radical shifts in view. The most spectacular examples of such shifts are to be found in the sciences, where the cumulative force of the experience of generations of humans is brought into play. Here is a simplified example. One can imagine an ancient civilization systematically measuring distances between cities. It discovers that the straight distance between a city X and a city Y, directly north of X, is 3,000 stadia and that between X and a city Z, directly east of X, is 4,000 stadia. But it discovers that the straight distance between Y and Z is significantly less than the expected 5,000 stadia. We can imagine that the civilization discovers similar anomalies for other cities, and the combined weight of empirical evidence results in a fundamental revision of its view: from the view that the earth is flat to the view that it is spherical.[23] Pythagoras, it is believed, was the first to have proclaimed the sphericity of the earth, but his reasons are not known.[24] I am purposely making the example fictional.

Consider the impact of the sequence of experiences E on two distinct views v and v'. Let the resulting revision sequences be, respectively, V and V'. It is possible that V and V' converge in the sense of the following definition.

V and V' *converge* iff there is a stage after which the views in V' and V' are virtually identical—more precisely, iff $l(V) = l(V')$ and there is a number $p < l(V)$ such that for all numbers $n < l(V)$, if $n \geq p$ then V_n and V'_n are virtually identical in the sense explained below.

---

[22] This is, of course, a highly idealized account of revision sequences that are generated by experiences. It is an idealization to treat $\rho_e(v)$ as a unique view rather than as a family of views together with a plausibility ordering. It is yet another idealization to treat experience as impacting in discrete chunks. Further, the important bearing of action on experience is neglected in the present sketchy treatment. See also n. 18.

[23] We have here a simple illustration of how judgments formulated in a misconceived vocabulary can guide a view out of a fundamental misconception.   [24] See Heath (1932).

Consider again the example of my turning the street corner and finding myself before a large, light green wall. I can bring to bear the following two distinct views on my experience: first, the ordinary view in which I take everything to be normal—call this view v—and, second, the ordinary view in which I take my eye-lenses to be tinged yellow by disease and in which I believe that things that look green to me are actually blue—call this view v'. Imagine that after experiencing the wall, I undergo a series of experiences with color charts in an optometrist's office. It is easy to imagine that, as a result of these experiences, there is convergence in the sequences of views generated by v and v'. The experiences can easily force me to revise v' and to conclude that my eyes are normal after all, that they were not diseased, and that the wall I faced was in fact light green. Two rational beings that suffer the experiences that I suffered and that begin respectively with the views v and v' will, after a time, have virtually identical views. Their views will differ slightly because of their different histories. One will believe, correctly, that she had taken the wall to be blue, while the other will have no such belief. But, setting aside the minor differences caused by the differences in their initial views, their later views will be identical. They will believe the same things about the wall and about the functioning of their eyes. It is this sort of relation between views that I wish to mark by calling them *virtually identical*.

We can pictorially represent convergence as shown in Figure 1. The virtual identity of the stages of V and V' is here represented by the identity of the corresponding points.

Let us observe that two sequences V and V' generated by E can converge, even though they begin with views that are fundamentally different. We have seen in the wall example above a situation in which two variants of our ordinary view converge under the guidance of experience. The point now is that convergence can occur even if we begin with views that are fundamentally different. Consider an extraordinary view that takes dream experiences and waking experiences to be on par. Both types of experiences, according to this view, yield perceptual judgments of equal authority; both reveal features of one and the

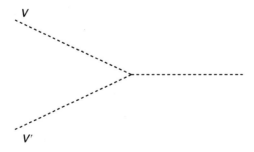

Fig. 1. Convergence of two sequences.

same reality. Such a view might be sustained by a course of experience. But, equally, a course of experience is easily imagined that will make it converge to our ordinary view.

A raimex, being imaginative, can consider the effects of experiences E on *all* views. Let us allow the possibility that some of the views can a priori be ruled to be unacceptable starting points of revision—this possibility will play an important role below. Then, *the revision process for E*—in symbols, Π_E—may be defined as the totality of revision sequences generated by E and *acceptable* initial views. That is,

> V belongs to Π_E iff there is an acceptable initial view v such that V is generated by E and v.

Let us define the convergence of revision processes thus:

> Π_E is *convergent* iff there is a number $p < l(E)$ such that, for all numbers $n < l(E)$ and all sequences V and V' that belong to Π_E, if $n \geq p$ then V_n and V'_n are virtually identical; the least such p *is the convergence point of* Π_E. A process that is not convergent will be said to be *divergent*.[25]

In a convergent process, the revisions of all acceptable initial views end up being virtually identical with one another. A convergent process may be pictured as shown in Figure 2.

It is useful to define the notion of *the totality of surviving views for E at stage n*—in symbols, $\sigma_E(n)$—, where $n < l(E)$:

> v belongs to $\sigma_E(n)$ iff, for some V in Π_E, $v = V_n$.

Suppose experiences E generate a revision process that has p as its point of convergence. Let n be any stage of revision higher than p. Then, at stage n, all surviving views must be virtually identical. They must contain the same basic account of the self and the world and, furthermore, they must agree on numerous details as well. At stage n, our raimex has no obligation to accept the judgments on which the surviving views differ, but she does have an obligation to accept the massive core on which the views agree. *Convergent processes generate absolute rational obligations; indeed, they dictate a particular conception of the self and the world.*[26] The hypothetical given is compatible therefore with the idea that experience imposes unconditional—even substantial—rational requirements on us.[27]

---

[25] The notions of convergence defined here and above take into account the possibility that the sequence of experiences is ω-long.

[26] Note that E can generate rational obligations even when its revision process fails to be convergent. For, at a stage n, a rational being has an obligation to accept all that is common to the surviving views $\sigma_E(n)$. And views that are fundamentally different may agree on some factual propositions.

[27] Experiences taken individually yield only conditional constraints of rationality since for any experience e, the views in the range of ρ_e have little in common. Still, when individual experiences are strung together, the resulting sequences can give rise to unconditional demands of rationality.

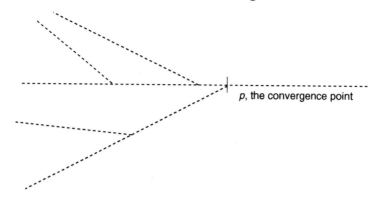

Fig. 2. A convergent process.

Let E be a sequence of experiences $<e_i>$ of length m. Then, the *given of E*, Γ_E, is the sequence of the givens yielded by the experiences in E; that is,

$$\Gamma_E = <\Gamma_{e_i}>_{i < m}$$

The crucial logical relationship between the given Γ_E and a body of propositions B may be defined thus:

> Γ_E *converges to* B iff B is a constituent of all the views that survive the revision process generated by E—that is, iff B is a constituent of all views in $\sigma_E(n)$, where $l(E) = n + 1$.

On the traditional account, the given is a collection of propositions and it bears such relations as "implication" and "confirmation" to beliefs that are justified by experience. In contrast, on the present account, the given is hypothetical in character—the given in E is Γ_E—and the logical relation it bears to beliefs justified by experience is that of convergence.

VII SOLIPSISM

I have argued that a hypothetical given is consistent with the idea that experience imposes unconditional rational requirements on us. But it may be objected that this is so only when "consistency" is understood in a broad and highly abstract sense. Once ordinary facts are taken into account, it may be said, consistency is bound to fail. For consider our ordinary experience under the following solipsist view:

> There are two sorts of things in the world, minds and sense-data. The Self is the only mind in the world, and it has direct awareness of all the sense-data

that exist at a moment. The present experience yields perceptual judgments such as that the Self is directly aware of an orange oval sense-datum [belonging to the coaster on the desk], and that it is directly aware of a soft whirring auditory sense-datum [of the hard drive of the computer], and . . .

The revision process generated by ordinary experience, the objection continues, is bound to be divergent. A rational being that holds the solipsist view will affirm the existence of different sense-data from moment to moment but would never move beyond sense-data. (There is an assumption here that the philosophical tradition provides ample proof of: solipsist foundations are insufficient for any claims about the external world.) Hence, with the solipsist view in play, our ordinary experience does not converge to our objective conception of the world. We are back in the old epistemological predicament, unable to provide any rational justification for our ordinary way of conceiving the world.

The response to this objection is that solipsism is not an acceptable initial view; hence, solipsism is never a threat to the convergence of the revision process. Solipsism has this peculiar immutability: irrespective of the sequences of experiences that impact it, the solipsist view is never undermined. It does not evolve into a different view; it remains fixed.[28] The world can be structured in all sorts of different ways. Things in the world, including the self, can have a variety of different natures and can bear a variety of different relationships to each other. But solipsism is blind to all the possibilities. It is unable to pick up clues from experience to adjust itself—to bring itself more in alignment with the way the world is. No matter what the structure of the world, no matter what the experience, solipsism remains the same rigid view. Solipsism is an unacceptable starting point of revision because it is closed and insensitive. No immutable view is an acceptable initial view.[29] We cannot gag the messenger and then wail about our ignorance.

It is useful to distinguish two kinds of rationality, one narrow and the other broad. Individuals are rational in the narrow sense iff they respect the constraints of logic and experience. That is, they ensure that their views conform to the principles of logic and evolve in the manner dictated by experience. Individuals are rational in the broad sense iff they respect the constraints not only of logic and experience, but also of imagination. That is, they take full account of the available *possibilities* in forming their views. A lunatic can be rational in the narrow sense: he starts from a crazy and closed view, he pays attention to logic

---

[28] Of course, the solipsist view does change in the sense that new sense-datum judgments are added to it. The present point is that the solipsist conception of the self and sense-data remains fixed, irrespective of experience.

[29] Note that immutable views are excluded only as *starting points* of revision, not as possible *outcomes*. In ruling solipsism to be an unacceptable initial view, we are not ruling out the possibility that solipsism is true nor that it might sometimes be rational to believe it to be true. Hence, the exclusion does not violate the empiricist maxim that reason has no special insight into the nature of the world.

and experience to the last nitpicky detail, but he is never budged from his view. (Philosophy—alas!—is fertile ground for such lunatics.) We can try desperately to refute the lunatic but shall fail. And our failure does not reflect on our own rationality. Granted, it is an ideal of rationality that beings with radically different views can, through discourse and experiment, reach consensus.[30] But the ideal does not include rational lunatics and their closed views. A solipsist is a rational lunatic. The fact that we cannot bring him around to our view using only logic and experience casts no doubt on the rationality of our view. To talk a solipsist out of his view we need to appeal to his imagination, to his sense—if he has it—of the different possible views and of different possible arrangements of things in the world.

A solipsist enjoys a special sort of immunity, an immunity that philosophers often covet: an immunity from refutation. Traditional epistemology regards this immunity to be a virtue—a virtue of such import that solipsist perceptual judgments are seen as lying at the very foundations of knowledge. Thus arises the traditional project to show how our knowledge of the external world could be built on these slender foundations. The present approach, in contrast, regards the immunity as a grave defect—a defect so great that solipsism deserves to be ruled out as a starting point of revision. This, it seems to me, is an advantage. Solipsism belongs in the problem box of empirical knowledge, not its solutions box. It does not deserve a place of honor at the foundations of knowledge; it deserves instead to be excluded and ignored.

In order to reject solipsism, we do not need to entertain such strong theses as that it is meaningless or that it violates some rule of language. We can reject solipsism on the basis of its dynamical behavior: the way solipsism evolves under the pressure of experience. The rejection of solipsism consists of two stages. First, the dynamical behavior entitles us to rule solipsism out as an acceptable initial view. Second, the actual course of our experience entitles us to deny solipsism altogether, for all views that survive the revision process are contrary to solipsism.

VIII   CONCLUDING REMARKS

The distinguishing feature of the account I am recommending is that it takes seriously the interdependence of views and perceptual judgments. The rationality of a view depends upon the rationality of perceptual judgments, and the

---

[30] Charles Sanders Peirce noted the importance of convergence. He wrote in §IV of his essay "How to Make Our Ideas Clear":

Different minds may set out with the most antagonistic views, but the progress of investigation carries them by a force outside of themselves to one and the same conclusion. ... No modification of the point of view taken, no selection of other facts for study, no natural bent of mind even, can enable a man to escape the predestinate opinion. This great law is embodied in the conception of truth and reality. (1878: 138–9)

rationality of perceptual judgments depends in turn upon the rationality of the view. Traditional accounts of experience and knowledge try to break this circle. The present account, in contrast, leaves the circle intact and goes on to exploit it. It is this that dictates the main components of the present account: (i) that the given in experience is hypothetical in character; (ii) that the transition to the categorical is made via a revision process; and (iii) that the logical relationship between the given and experiential knowledge is that of convergence. Wherever there is interdependence, one finds the same structure: revision rules, revision processes, and convergence. One finds this structure in the theory of interdependent definitions—which was my own starting point in developing the present account—as well as in, for example, numerical approximations and in Bayesianism. Once one takes the interdependence seriously, the structure of the account of experience and knowledge is fixed. There are no alternatives.

It is an attractive feature of the present account—in particular, of the hypothetical given—that it yields an advantage in dealing with the skeptics. The skeptics base their argument on the idea that human reason and experience are too weak to justify any substantial knowledge of the external world.[31] They delight in sketching out possibilities in which our experience is the same as our actual experience but the world is radically different: perhaps solipsism is true, or perhaps I am a brain in a vat, or perhaps I am deceived by an evil demon, or . . . . Now, on the propositional conception of the given, the skeptical possibilities thin out the materials supplied by experience. And the skeptics have little difficulty in reaching their desired conclusion, for these materials are now too meager to build up our knowledge of the external world. The propositional given makes things easy—a little too easy—for the skeptics: the weird skeptical possibilities suffice to undermine our common-sense view of the world. If, however, we accept the idea of the hypothetical given, then the skeptical conclusion is not so easily reached. The skeptical possibilities no longer thin out the given in experience. If anything, they highlight its thickness: experience yields judgments even under the extraordinary possibilities envisioned by the skeptics. To establish the skeptical conclusion, under the present account, one needs to show divergence—that is, one needs to show that the revision process for ordinary experience diverges—and this is a harder task.[32] Solipsism and the evil demon hypothesis, for instance, suffice to thin out the propositional given. But they do not show divergence, since they are not acceptable initial views. The present

---

[31] The sixth mode of skepticism in Book I of Sextus Empiricus's *Outlines of Scepticism* contains the following argument:

So because of admixtures our senses do not grasp what external existing objects are accurately like. But our intellect does not do so either, especially since its guides, the senses, fail it. . . . According to this mode too, therefore, we see that we cannot say anything about the nature of external existing objects, and are forced to suspend judgement. (Annas and Barnes 2000: I.127–8)

This argument contains a remarkable anticipation of the modern problem of the external world.

[32] More explicitly, one would need to show that there is an acceptable initial view under which ordinary experience does not converge to our common-sense view.

account imposes a greater burden on the skeptic, and to my eyes a burdened skeptic makes a pleasing sight.

Another attractive feature of the present account is that it makes the debate between rationalism and empiricism less one-sided. On the propositional conception, with its thin given, rationalism wins the debate hands down. The propositional conception burdens the poor empiricist with the impossible task of building the external world from a thinned-out given. The rationalist's task is easy: to show that a substantial contribution of reason is essential if we are to justify our knowledge of the world. It is no wonder that, in the modern period, rationalism is seen as the only viable alternative to skepticism. To be a coherent empiricist is to be a skeptic. The propositional given masks the virtues of empiricism and makes it a thoroughly unattractive idea.

In contrast, with the hypothetical given, empiricism gains a fighting chance. The issue between empiricism and rationalism is now this. Rationalism insists—and empiricism denies—that convergence must fail unless the revision process is constrained by some substantial a priori truths. In this debate, the burden on rationalism is to produce such truths. The burden on empiricism is to articulate a rich conception of the acceptability of initial views—a conception that is both a priori and yet is powerful enough to ensure convergence. This debate reflects the traditional disagreement between rationalism and empiricism: rationalism insists—and empiricism denies—that reason has the capacity to provide us with a substantial insight into the nature of the world and, furthermore, that this insight is essential if we are to justify our knowledge. But, unlike the traditional debate, rationalism is not now assured of an easy victory. Empiricism, under the present account, has available not only a richer conception of experience. It has available a richer conception of reason. Empiricism can insist, as usual, that there is no a priori insight into the nature or structure of the world. But this does not entail a commitment to the traditional empiricist idea that the contribution of reason is merely formal and logical. Reason has, in the present account, a substantial role to play: that of ruling on the acceptability of initial views. The acceptability of an initial view depends upon the dynamical behavior of the view under possible streams of experience, and this is something that can be determined a priori—it is the proper domain of reason. So, even though reason yields no substantial *truths*, it can make a substantial contribution to our knowledge. In particular, it can enable us to rule out certain coherent views (e.g., solipsism). The present proposal thus provides empiricism with resources that make it more robust and credible.

Experience, I have argued, is not an informant. It does not reveal little truths about the world—truths that can then be used to build up the edifice of knowledge. Experience taken in isolation is mute. It speaks—it guides us—only when a view is brought to bear on it. Furthermore, experience can serve as a guide not just for the gods with their one true view of the world. It can serve as a guide to us mortals with all our various misconceptions about the world. The richness of the contribution of experience is to be found not in the truths that it delivers, but in the range of views that it can guide towards the truth.

REFERENCES

Annas, Julia and Barnes, Jonathan (eds) (2000), *Sextus Empiricus. Outlines of Scepticism* (Cambridge: Cambridge University Press).

Berkeley, George (1713), *Three Dialogues between Hylas and Philonous*, in A. A. Luce and T. E. Jessop (eds), *The Works of George Berkeley, Bishop of Cloyne* (London: Thomas Nelson and Sons, 1948–57), reprinted in J. Dancy (ed.), Oxford Philosophical Texts series (Oxford: Oxford University Press, 1998).

Brewer, Bill (1999), *Perception and Reason* (Oxford: Clarendon Press).

Davidson, Donald (1983; with Afterthoughts, 1987), "A Coherence Theory of Truth and Knowledge," reprinted in *Subjective, Intersubjective, Objective* (Oxford: Clarendon Press): 137–53.

Goldman, Alan H. (1992), "The Given," in J. Dancy and E. Sosa (eds), *A Companion to Epistemology* (Oxford: Blackwell).

Gupta, Anil (1988–9), "Remarks on Definitions and the Concept of Truth," *Proceedings of the Aristotelian Society* 89: 227–46.

Gupta, Anil and Belnap, Nuel (1993), *The Revision Theory of Truth* (Cambridge, Mass.: MIT Press).

Heath, Thomas L. (1932), *Greek Astronomy* (New York: Dover Publications, 1991).

James, William (1912), *Essays in Radical Empiricism* (Lincoln: University of Nebraska Press, 1996).

Long, Anthony A. and Sedley, David N. (1987), *The Hellenistic Philosophers: Vol. 1. Translations of the Principal Sources with Philosophical Commentary* (Cambridge: Cambridge University Press).

McDowell, John (1994), *Mind and World* (Cambridge, Mass: Harvard University Press).

Peirce, Charles S. (1878), "How to Make Our Ideas Clear," page references are to the reprint in Nathan Houser and Christian Kloesel (eds), *The Essential Peirce: Selected Philosophical Writings*, vol. I (Bloomington: Indiana University Press, 1992).

Russell, Bertrand (1918), *The Philosophy of Logical Atomism* (Chicago: Open Court, 1985).

Sellars, Wilfred (1956), *Empiricism and the Philosophy of Mind* (Cambridge, Mass.: Harvard University Press, 1997).

6

Active Perception and Perceiving Action: The Shared Circuits Model

Susan Hurley

ABSTRACT

Recently research on imitation and its role in social cognition has been flourishing across various disciplines. After briefly reviewing these developments under the headings of behavior, subpersonal mechanisms, and functions of imitation, I advance the *shared circuits model*. This model of subpersonal functional architecture describes a unified framework relating control, imitation, and simulation. It has explanatory and heuristic value in providing a context for predictions and further questions at both higher, personal and lower, neural levels, while avoiding over-simple or a priori assumptions of isomorphism between the subpersonal and personal levels. A striking aspect of the model is the way it connects a shared information space for action and perception with a shared information space for self and other, while at the same time illustrating how the distinctions between self and other, and between the possible and the actual, can be overlaid on these shared information spaces. In this model information about intentional agents in the subpersonal 'first-person plural', which does not distinguish or infer between self and others, is prior to the self/ other distinction. The shared circuits model also illustrates a horizontally modular architecture: it avoids the common conception of perception and action as separate and peripheral to central cognition. Rather, it views perception and action as dynamically co-enabled and shows how cognitively significant resources, such as distinctions between self and other and between possible and

For comments on earlier drafts of this material and related discussions, I am grateful to John Bargh, Jeremy Butterfield, Nancy Cartwright, John Cummins, Chris Frith, Vittorio Gallese, Tamar Gendler, Philip Gerrans, Robert Gordon, Jeffrey Gray, Rick Grush, Celia Heyes, Marco Iacoboni, Andrew Meltzoff, Alva Noë, Hanna Pickard, Joëlle Proust, Nicholas Rawlins, Rosalined Ridley, Simon Saunders, Nick Shea, Evan Thompson, and the members of various audiences on occasions when I have delivered this material. I am also grateful to Nick Chater for his ready agreement to my drawing on material I drafted for Hurley and Chater (2005b), and to Tom Stone of MIT Press.

actual actions, and information for action understanding and planning, might emerge from the information space that action and perception share.

INTRODUCTION

This article develops the implications of a view of perception as essentially active, which I and others have been developing[1], for the perception of action.

Some substantive stage setting may be useful. Elsewhere (1998, 2001) I have identified a conception of the mind I dubbed "the classical sandwich," which is widespread across both philosophy and the empirical sciences of the mind. The classical sandwich conception regards perception as input from the world to the mind, action as output from the mind to the world, and cognition as sandwiched in between. Central cognition, on this view, is where all the conceptually structured general purpose thinking happens: perceptual information is assessed in light of standing beliefs and goals, deliberative and inferential processing occurs, action plans are formulated and sent on for execution. I have argued that the mind isn't *necessarily* structured in this vertically modular way, and that there is growing evidence that it is not *actually* so structured.[2] Instead, perception and action can be understood as sharing information-processing resources in specific domains and as dynamically co-enabled in interaction with the environment, rather than as separate buffers around all-purpose central cognition. Cognitive resources and structure can emerge, layer by layer, from the shared information spaces that enable perception and action. Such horizontally modular structure may be able to do significant parts (I don't claim *all*) of the work that the classical sandwich conception assigned to central cognition. In this chapter I provide a detailed view of how this promise might be made good in the realm of the perception of action and associated social cognition.

Some methodological stage-setting may also be helpful. My arguments are in the style of philosophy of science[3] rather than philosophy of mind, focusing on empirical research and subpersonal functional architecture rather than personal-level experience. Subpersonal processing can provide information that enables personal level processes even though there is no simple isomorphism between the levels. This paper examines philosophical issues that emerge organically from empirical work, rather than importing an independent philosophical agenda from traditional philosophy of mind and applying it to empirical work. This style of philosophizing aims to complement rather than to challenge or

---

[1] See, for example, Hurley (1998, 2001); O'Regan and Noë (2001a, 2001b, 2001c); Hurley and Noë (2003).

[2] As well as Hurley (1998, 2001) and the references cited there, see Brooks (1999) and Noë (2004).

[3] Think of my approach as analogous to philosophy of physics rather than to metaphysics. Thanks here to Nancy Cartwright for discussion.

displace traditional philosophical approaches; it can usefully be labelled "natural philosophy".

In this chapter I do two things. First, I review recent developments in the cognitive and neuro-sciences concerning imitation.[4] Imitation is still often thought of as a cognitively undemanding form of behavior. But, since Thorndike (1898) showed that many animals could learn through trial-and-error but could not imitate, scientists have come to regard imitative learning as more cognitively demanding than individual trial and error learning. Recent work across various sciences argues that imitation is a rare ability that is fundamentally linked to characteristically human forms of intelligence, in particular to language, culture, and the ability to understand other minds.[5] This burgeoning body of work has important implications for our understanding of ourselves, both individually and socially. Imitation is not just an important factor in human development, but also has pervasive influence throughout adulthood, in ways we are just starting to understand. Here, I review why imitation is currently a topic of such intense research interest, under three headings: behavior, subpersonal mechanisms, and functions.

Second, I suggest a model that draws some of these threads of work on imitation together: the *shared circuits model*.[6] It includes elements suggested by various researchers, contributes further elements, and unifies these in a distinctive way. It describes a unified subpersonal functional architecture for control, imitation, and simulation, in five stages or layers. It is put forward as an explanatory and heuristic general framework, which raises further empirical and philosophical questions.

PART I AN OVERVIEW OF IMITATION

A Behavior

Imitation may be presumed to require at least *copying* in a generic sense: the observer's perception of the model's behavior causes the observer's own similar behavior, in some way such that the similarity between the observed behavior and the observer's behavior plays a role, though not necessarily at a conscious level, in generating the observer's behavior. Even copying in this generic sense raises issues about the mechanisms in play; but I postpone discussion of these and focus first on how imitative behavior is identified, and on its distribution across animals, children, and adults.

---

[4] Drawing on Hurley and Chater (2005a; 2005b), with revisions.

[5] See, for example, Arbib (2005); Arbib and Rizzolatti (1997); Gallese (2001, 2005); Gallese and Goldman (1998); Gordon (1995b); Iacoboni (2005); Meltzoff (2005); Rizzolatti and Arbib (1998, 1999); Tomasello (1999); Stamenov and Gallese (2002); Whiten et al. (2005); Williams et al. (2001).   [6] Drawing on Hurley (2005a), with revisions.

Imitation needs to be distinguished from other forms of social learning that may look superficially similar.[7] The most restrictive understanding of true imitation requires that a novel action be learned by observing another do it, and, in addition to novelty, requires an instrumental or means/ends structure: you copy the other's means of achieving her goal, not just her goal, or just her movements. Imitation in this sense should be contrasted with stimulus enhancement, goal emulation, and response priming. In *stimulus enhancement* another's action draws your attention to a stimulus that triggers an innate or previously learned response; you do not thereby learn a novel action by observing the other. In *emulation*,[8] by contrast, you observe another achieving a goal in a certain way, find that goal attractive and attempt to achieve it yourself by whatever means. Individual trial-and-error learning may then lead you to the other's means of achieving the goal. A further contrast is with mere *response priming*, as in flocking behavior or contagious yawning, in which bodily movements are copied, but not as a learned means to a goal.

Goal emulation and response priming can be thought of as providing the ends and means components, respectively, of full-fledged imitation. However, the distinction between ends and means is not absolute; ends and means can be more or less distal or proximal, which can make for misunderstandings in discussions of whether ends or means or both are copied and hence of whether imitation or emulation is present (see Voelkl and Huber 2000: 196, 201). A movement may be the proximal means to achieving a bodily posture, which could be regarded as the proximal end of the movement (see Graziano et al. 2002: 354–5); but the posture may in turn be regarded as a means to achieving some effect on an external object or member of the social group, which may be a more distal end. We can understand more complex forms of imitation in terms of a structured sequence and/or hierarchy of means/ends relationships, in which one acquires a goal, learns how to achieve it by achieving several subgoals, learns how to achieve the subgoals by certain means, and so on.

1 Animals

Studies of social learning in animals often focus on distinguishing true imitation from other superficially similar behaviors. Stimulus enhancement, goal emulation and response priming are certainly found in nonhuman animals. Careful experiments are needed to obtain evidence of imitation in a more restricted sense. For this purpose, the *two-action* experimental paradigm has become the

---

[7] The concept of "true imitation" is contested, owing in part to the different theoretical aims and methodologies of those concerned with imitation. See and cf. Byrne (2005); Heyes (1996, 2001); Rizzolatti (2005). What matters for present purposes is not what deserves this label, but that relevant distinctions be recognized.

[8] "Emulation" in the sense well established in social learning theory (see Call and Carpenter 2002; Tomasello 1999) should be distinguished from the quite independent sense of the same term as used by Rick Grush (1995, 2004). I use "emulation" here in the social learning theory sense, not Grush's sense.

tool of choice.[9] Suppose two models illustrate two different means of obtaining the same attractive result; one group of animals observes one model, while the other observes the other model. Will the observer animals tend differentially to copy the specific method they have seen demonstrated? If not—if the animals' choices of method do not reflect the specific method they have seen modeled, say, because animals in both groups converge on one method despite the different methods observed—they may be displaying mere goal emulation plus trial-and-error learning, or stimulus enhancement, rather than imitative learning.

The difference between copying the ends of action and copying the means of action is important for understanding the phylogeny of the capacities for imitation and for understanding observed actions by others. For example, consider the view that understanding events as the purposive acts of other intentional agents precedes imitation phylogenetically (Rizzolatti 2005). This view faces an objection: many animals are able to replicate movements, but it would be implausible to attribute action understanding to them all. Recall that in response priming, observing a movement primes the same movement by the animal, independently of any understanding of the goal of the movement (as in the flocking of birds). But in response to this objection it has been suggested that such low-level copying of movements could be present without high-level mirroring of goals, or vice versa (Rizzolatti 2005); moreover, while imitative learning requires both of these capacities, either can be present without imitation. Action understanding requires the capacity to mirror goals, which is found in monkeys who have not shown genuine imitative learning. Thus action understanding, along with response priming and goal emulation, can precede genuine imitative learning. The latter would require the interplay of copying of both the ends and the means of action that is found in human beings. The phylogenetically rare capacity for imitative learning is arguably linked to the flexible recombinant means/ends structure of intentional action: the ability to use a given movement for different ends and pursue a given end by a variety of means (Tomasello 1999).

It has proved remarkably difficult to find evidence of true imitation in non-human animals.[10] While early fieldwork with chimps appeared to provide evidence of their imitative abilities, critics challenged this interpretation effectively, and many subsequent experimental studies reported a lack of chimp imitation. For a long while sceptics who regarded the capacity for imitation as exclusively human had the upper hand. For example, in 1993, Tomasello, Kruger, and Ratner found no convincing evidence of imitative learning in nonhuman animals, and proposed that the understanding of behavior as

---

[9] See, for example, Nagell et al. (1993); Call and Tomasello (1994); see and cf. Voelkl and Huber (2000) for further refinements.

[10] See and cf. Byrne (1995); Galef (1988, 1998, 2005); Heyes and Galef (1996); Tomasello and Call (1997); Voelkl and Huber (2000); Zentall (2001).

goal-directed or intentional distinguishes human social learning from social learning in other species. On this view, while human beings can either imitate observed means or choose other means to emulate observed goals, other animals do not distinguish means and goals in this way. Rather, animals can copy movements without understanding their relevance to goals, or can learn about the affordances of objects by observing action on them. In neither case, the claim was, do other animals learn about the intentional, means/end structure of the observed action.

But a new consensus is now emerging, as a result of painstaking work to show imitation in some great apes and monkeys,[11] dolphins (Herman 2002), and birds such as parrots[12] and others.[13] Continuities are being described along a spectrum from the capacities of other social animals to the characteristically human, interrelated capacities for imitation, mindreading, and language.[14]

For example, innovative experiments have extended the two-action method by employing "artificial fruits," which can be opened in various ways to obtain a treat. These reveal that chimps may imitate with respect to one aspect of a modeled task and emulate for another, while children tend to imitate both aspects, even when the method imitated is inefficient. These experiments suggest that chimps imitate selectively, according to their appraisal of the significance of a particular aspect of the modeled task for achieving their goal, and that children are more likely than chimps to imitate obviously futile movements.[15]

2 Children

Indeed, children are "imitation machines," with strong conventional and conformist tendencies.[16] While children do not always imitate unselectively and there are cases where they emulate goals (Gergely et al. 2002), children have a greater tendency than chimps to imitate rather than to emulate when the method imitated is transparently inefficient (Tomasello 1999, 29–30). For example, after seeing a demonstrator use a rake inefficiently, prongs down, to pull in a treat, two-year-old children do the same; they almost never turn the rake over and use it more efficiently, edge down, instead. By contrast, chimps given a parallel demonstration tend to turn the rake over (Nagell et al. 1993; cf. Povinelli 2000, ch.6, where chimps are not permitted trials and errors with rake orientations; thanks here to Rosalind Ridley).

One explanation of these strong imitative tendencies of children is that in young children the perception of behavior tends to be enacted automatically in

[11] See Whiten et al. (2005); Voelkl and Huber (2000).

[12] See Pepperberg (1999, 2002, 2005).

[13] Hunt and Gray (2003); see and cf. Weir et al. (2002); Akins and Zentall (1996, 1998); Akins et al. (2002).   [14] Tomasello (1999); Arbib (2005).

[15] See Whiten (2002), Whiten et al. (1996); Whiten et al. (2005); see also Nagell et al. (1993); Call and Tomasello (1994); Galef (2005); cf. Heyes (1998); Tomasello and Carpenter (2005); Harris and Want (2005); Gergely et al. 2002.   [16] Meltzoff (2005); Tomasello (1999), 159.

imitative behavior (in a broad sense that includes copying of bodily movements), unless actively inhibited. Inhibition is a function of frontal areas of the brain, but babies and very young children do not yet have a well-developed frontal function or capacity to inhibit imitative tendencies (Kinsbourne 2005).

Imitative behavior appears to play important roles in human development (see in particular the section on mindreading below). Various imitative and related behaviors are acquired at stages throughout human infancy and development (Meltzoff 2005). Infants from 6 weeks to 14 months recognize that they are being imitated,[17] but only older infants act in ways that apparently purposively test whether they are being imitated. Since only people can imitate systematically, an ability to recognize being imitated provides a means of recognizing that an entity is a person. By 14 months, infants imitate a modeled novel act after a week's delay: for example, they turn on a light by touching a touch-sensitive light panel with their foreheads instead of their hands, differentially copying the novel means modeled as well as the result.[18] They do not turn the light on in this odd way unless they have seen the model do it first. By 15 to 18 months, infants recognize the underlying goal of an unsuccessful act they see modeled, and produce it, using various means: after seeing an adult try but fail to pull a dumbbell apart in her hands, they succeed in pulling it apart using knees as well as hands. However, they do not pick up the goals of failed "attempts" from similar movements by inanimate devices, which suggests that young children perceive or understand agents and non-agents quite differently.[19]

3 Adults

Adults with damage to certain frontal areas of the brain also imitate uninhibitedly.[20] Such "imitation syndrome" patients persistently imitate gestures that the experimenter makes, although they have not been instructed to do so, even when these are socially unacceptable or odd, such as putting on eyeglasses when already wearing glasses. But the human tendency to imitate is not confined to the young and the brain-damaged. While normal adults are usually able to inhibit overt imitation selectively (and it is adaptive to do so), overt imitation can be regarded as just the disinhibited tip of the iceberg of continual covert, inhibited imitation. Such covert imitation may reflect a basic motivation of human beings, adults as well as children, to interact synchronously or entrain with one another, which is a mechanism of affiliation as well as of social perception and learning (Kinsbourne 2005).

Despite inhibition, the underlying tendency to imitate remains and can readily be revealed or released. A number of experiments show how action can be spontaneously induced or modulated by the perception of similar action.

---

[17] With differential activation of right inferior parietal lobe; see Decety and Chaminade (2005).
[18] Meltzoff (1988, 2005); cf. Gergely et al. 2002.
[19] See Meltzoff (1988, 1995, 1996, 2005); Meltzoff and Moore, (1977, 1999a, b).
[20] Lhermitte et al. (1986); Lhermitte (1986).

Similarity between stimulus and response affects responses. For example, normal adult subjects, instructed to point to their nose when they heard the word "nose" or to point to a lamp when they heard the word "lamp," performed perfectly while watching the experimenter model the required performance, but made mistakes when they observed the experimenter doing something else: they tended to copy what they saw done rather than to follow the instruction heard. (See Prinz 1990; Eidelberg 1929). In imitative interference paradigms, both the initiation and selection of gestures are faster when participants are primed by perception of similar gestures or of their results or goals, even if such primes are logically irrelevant to their task. Induction paradigms examine when spontaneous movements are induced by actions you actually perceive (*perceptual induction*, or involuntary imitation) or by actions you would like to perceive (*intentional induction*, as when moviegoers or sports fans in their seats make gestures they'd like to see made). Both types of induction are found, and are modulated by various contextual factors. Interestingly, perceptual induction can in some cases depend on background beliefs about whether what is perceived is the result of agency or rather generated by a computer, or on whether one's action is understood as part of a coordinated collective action by more than one person. (See W. Prinz 2005.) Thus, perception has effects on action that, even when they are automatic, can also have cognitive depth, in that they depend on the way participants understand what they are perceiving and doing.

In considering the way observed action or external visual or verbal representations of action can control action, it is useful to distinguish between the imitation of *specific observed behaviors*, which may be facilitated by shared representations of our own acts and observed acts, and what has been called *the chameleon effect*, where *complex patterns of behavior* are induced. Demonstrations of the chameleon effect show that we automatically tend to assimilate our behavior to our social environment: modeled or represented personality traits and stereotypes tend automatically to activate corresponding behavior in us.[21] This tendency arguably acts as "social glue," leading people to coordinate actions, to interact more smoothly, and to like each other. (See Dijksterhuis 2005; Chartrand and Bargh 1999).

In an experiment involving a specific observed behavior, normal adult subjects who interact in an unrelated task with someone who rubs her foot rub their own feet significantly more; transferred to another partner who touches his face, subjects start to touch their faces instead. Other experiments involve complex patterns of behavior, traits, or stereotypes, which may be primed by representations rather than perceptions of behavior. For example, normal adult participants have been primed by exposure to stimuli associated with traits (such as hostility, rudeness, or politeness) or with stereotypes (such as elderly persons,

---

[21] Bargh (2005) comments on the striking similarities between imitation syndrome patients and normal college students who display the chameleon effect.

college professors, or soccer hooligans). Hostility-primed participants are found to deliver more intense "shocks" than control participants in subsequent, ostensibly unrelated experiments based on Milgram's (1963) classic shock experiments. Rudeness-primed participants spontaneously behave more rudely, and politeness-primed participants more politely, than control participants, in subsequent, ostensibly unrelated interactions with experimenters. Youthful participants subliminally primed with words associated with the elderly, such as "grey," "bingo," or "sentimental," subsequently walk more slowly, perform worse on memory tasks, and express more conservative attitudes than similar-aged control participants. Perhaps most strikingly of all, college professor-primed participants perform better and soccer hooligan-primed participants perform worse than control participants on a subsequent, ostensibly unrelated, general knowledge quiz. That is, some participants were asked before doing the multiple-choice test to do some ostensibly unrelated exercises about college professors, while a control group was not. The participants primed by thinking about this stereotype, generally associated with intelligence, got significantly higher scores. In another session different participants were given an unrelated exercise about soccer hooligans, while a control group was not. The participants primed by thinking about this stereotype, generally associated with lack of intelligence, got significantly lower scores.[22] (See Dijksterhuis and van Knippenberg 1998; Dijksterhuis 2005.)

Such priming results are very robust: they hold across a wide range of verbal and visual primes and induced behavior, across dozens of different stereotypes and general traits, and using a variety of different priming methods, when primes are presented subliminally as well as when participants are conscious of them. Whether the subjects are conscious of the primes or not, they are unaware of any influence or correlation between the primes and their behavior. These results show that exposure to traits and stereotypes elicits general patterns of behavior and attitudes, and influences the ways in which behavior is performed. These influences are rapid, automatic, and unconscious, apply both to ends and to means, and do not depend on the subjects' volition or on their having a relevant independent goal that would rationalize their primed behavior. Imitation in this broad sense is our default social behavior, which needs to be specifically inhibited or overridden. Just thinking about or perceiving a certain kind of action auto-matically increases, in ways of which participants are unaware, the likelihood of engaging in that general type of behavior oneself (Dijkstershuis 2005). It is difficult for subjects in these experiments to accept that these broad imitative influences apply to themselves: both because they are unconscious and auto-matic, so people are not aware of them, and because such external influences threaten their conception of themselves as being in conscious control of their

---

[22] Priming with specific exemplars (e.g., Albert Einstein) produces contrast or comparison effects, while priming with a generic category (e.g., scientists) produces assimilation effects.

own behavior (Bargh 1999). Nevertheless, these influences are often inhibited, for example, by goals that make conflicting demands: elderly-primed participants do not walk more slowly if they have an independent need to hurry.

B   Mechanisms

I now turn to examining the subpersonal mechanisms that might enable and explain imitative behavior.

1   The Correspondence Problem

The generic idea of copying perceived behavior appears to require the solution to a difficult *correspondence problem* (Nehaniv and Dautenhahn 2002): how is perceived action by another agent translated into similar performance by the observer? When I imitate your hand movements at least I can see my own hands, even though my visual perspective on the two actions is different. But when I imitate your facial gestures, I cannot see my own face. How is the mapping from perception to similar behavior achieved? What information and mechanisms are needed to solve this problem?

Evidence that newborns and infants under one month old imitate facial gestures, even though they cannot see their own faces, suggests that there are at least some innate, supramodal correspondences between action and perception of similar action.[23] However, this would leave room for acquisition of further correspondences as imitative abilities develop. And skeptics about newborn imitation may also be skeptical about innate correspondences (Heyes 2005).

It has been argued by Cecilia Heyes that imitation does not require innate correspondences between perception and similar action. Rather, these could be acquired, in the right environment, through general-purpose associative learning mechanisms whereby neurons that fire together, wire together. The needed sensorimotor associations could be acquired through both direct and indirect routes. Direct sensorimotor associations could be formed when someone watches her own hand gesture, for example. But this won't work when the agent cannot perceive her own actions, as in facial gestures. Here, the association could be mediated by a third item, such as a mirror, an action word, or a stimulus that evokes the same behavior in the actor and in other agents the actor observes. Moreover, adult imitation of infants is common, and can perform the associative function of a mirror. In effect, the associative mechanism that enables imitation can extend into the cultural environment. Novel acts can be learned by observing another agent perform an unfamiliar sequence of familiar act elements, where

[23] Meltzoff (1988 through 2005); Meltzoff and Moore (1977 through 2000). Developmental psychologist Moshe Anisfeld (1979 through 2005), Anisfeld et al. (2001) represents a minority, including also Cecilia Heyes and Susan Jones, who remain skeptical of evidence for very early and newborn imitation.

each perception of an act element already has a motor association, resulting in a new sequence of motor elements that become linked through repetition to give rise to a novel act. On this view, imitation can emerge from the interaction between organisms with general purpose associative-learning mechanisms and certain cultural environments. (See Heyes 2001, 2005.)

2 Common Coding

Evidence of infant imitation has been explained in terms of a shared information space for perception and action: proprioceptive feedback from the infant's own acts are compared and matched to an observed target act, where these are coded in common, supramodal terms (Meltzoff and Moore 1977). An innate common code could initially code for relations among bodily organs such as lips and tongue, and develop through experience of body babbling toward more dynamic, complex, and abstract coding (Meltzoff and Moore 1997). But a common code might also be acquired, along the lines suggested by Heyes (see her 2005, which discusses how the innateness and common coding issues are related; see also Part II below).

Evidence of the normal adult tendency to imitate and the reaction time advantage of imitative tasks has also been explained in terms of common coding of perception and action (see W. Prinz 2005). This would enable and facilitate imitation, by avoiding the correspondence problem and the need for translation between unrelated input and output codes to solve it. The common coding of perception and action has been associated with what William James called *ideomotor theory*, according to which every representation of movement awakes in some degree the movement that it represents. In particular, a representation of observed movement by another agent tends inherently to produce a similar movement by the observer, and has priming effects even when movements do not break through overtly. The regular concurrence of action with perceived effects enables the prediction of the effects of an action[24] and the selection of action, given an intention to produce certain effects[25] (Greenwald 1970, 1972). As a result, representation of a regular effect of action, whether proximal or distal, acquires the power to evoke similar action, if not inhibited.

Support for these ideas can be found from various further sources. Neurophysiologists have shown that observing a particular action primes precisely the muscles that would be needed to perform the same action (Fadiga et al. 1995, 2002). Watching an action sequence speeds up your own performance of the same sequence; merely imagining a skilled performance, in sport or music, improves your own performance: constitutes a kind of practicing, as many athletes and musicians know.[26] Similar ideas have been applied to the perception

---

[24] As in a forward model or efference copy; see the section on mirror neurons, below.
[25] As in an inverse model; see the section on mirror neurons, below.
[26] Pascuale-Leone (2001); Jeannerod (1997), 117, 119–22.

and experience of emotion. Simulation theorist Robert Gordon argues that it takes a special containing mechanism to keep the emotion-recognition process from reverting to emotional contagion; this mechanism is not fail-safe. If simulation theory is right, he holds, only a thin line separates one's own mental life from one's representation of the mental life of another; off-line representations of other people have an inherent tendency to go on-line.[27]

3 Mirror Neurons

Common-coding theories characterize the subpersonal architecture that enables imitation in functional terms. But how might this architecture be realized neurally? What kind of neural architecture and processing would enable and explain imitative and related behaviors? The recent discovery of mirror neurons seems relevant here.

Certain neurons appear to constitute a direct link between perception and action in that their firing correlates with specific perceptions as well as specific actions. Some of these, *canonical neurons,* can be thought of as reflecting affordances (in Gibson's sense, 1986): they fire when a certain type of action is performed, but are also triggered when objects that afford such actions are perceived. Others, *mirror neurons,* fire when a certain type of action is performed, but also when another agent is observed doing the same type of action.[28] That is, mirror neurons are sensitive both to others' actions and to equivalent actions of one's own; they do not register the difference between one's own action and similar actions by others. They can be very specifically tuned. For example, certain cells fire when a monkey sees the experimenter bring food to her own mouth with her own hand *or* when the monkey brings food to his own mouth (even in the dark, so that the monkey cannot see his hand).

The function of mirror neurons in relation to imitation is a matter of intense current interest. When mirror neurons were discovered, it was tempting to suggest that they enable imitation by avoiding the correspondence problem: if the same neurons code for perceived action and matching performance, it may seem that no neural translation is needed. But things are not quite that simple. Giacomo Rizzolatti, one of the discoverers of mirror neurons, holds that imitation requires both the ability to understand another agent's action and the ability to replicate it. On his view, recall, action understanding precedes imitation phylogenetically and is subserved by mirror systems, which are necessary but not sufficient for imitation. Rizzolatti suggests that the motor resonance set up by mirror neurons makes action observation meaningful by linking it to the observer's own potential actions. (See Rizzolatti 2005).[29]

---

[27] Gordon (1995b); see also Adolphs (2002).

[28] For surveys, see Rizzolatti (2005); Iacoboni (2005); Stamenov and Gallese (2002).

[29] Psychologist Paul Harris (in discussion, Royaumont conference, 2002) has suggested an experimental assessment of the extent to which mirror neurons subserve action understanding in monkeys. Monkey mirror neurons fire when the monkey reaches for an apple, or when she sees the

Mirror neurons were discovered in monkeys by single-cell recording; evidence for human mirror systems includes brain-imaging work, as well as demonstrations that observing another agent act primes the muscles the observer would need to do the same thing. Rizzolatti describes mirror neurons in frontal areas of monkeys' brains as part of a neural circuit that also includes parietal and visual areas. A similar circuit in human beings, he suggests, constitutes a control system, in which an intended imitative movement is compared to an observed target movement, enabling imitative learning.[30] In monkeys, mirror neurons appear to code for the goals of performed or observed actions. For example, a monkey mirror neuron may fire, then the monkey reaches for an apple or sees another reach for it, even if a screen has come down to hide the apple. However, if the monkey has first seen that that there is nothing behind the screen, observation of the same reaching movement toward a spot behind the same screen will not activate that neuron (Rizzolatti 2005). In contrast, the human mirror system extends also to the specific movements that are the means to achieving goals. As we saw, this difference between mirroring the ends of action and mirroring the means of action is important for the argument that action understanding precedes imitation phylogenetically. If seeing someone reach for an apple produces motor activation associated with the same goal in the observer (though not necessarily associated with the same movements in the observer), that could provide information about the goal-directness of the observed action, but would not necessarily provide information for imitative learning, that is, about how to achieve the goal by means of the observed movements.

Human brain-imaging studies suggest a division of labor within the mirror system: that frontal areas of the mirror system code for the ends or goals of action, and parietal areas for movements and means. To enable imitation, both areas generate motor signals relating to a planned imitative action for comparison with the observed action; the motor plan is then adjusted until a match is

experimenter reach for the apple. The same mirror neurons also fire when the monkey sees a screen come down in front of the apple, so that it is no longer visible, and then sees the experimenter's hand reach behind the screen to where the apple is hidden. But they do not fire when the monkey first sees that there is no apple, and then comes down and the monkey sees the experimenter's hand reach behind the screen in the same way. The mirror neurons, that is, appear to code for the goal of the action. Harris suggests a variation that would address how insightfully the monkey attributes goals to others. Suppose the monkey and experimenter look at a nut, and see the screen come down in front of it. Then the experimenter leaves the room. The monkey is permitted to remove the nut. Now the experimenter returns and the monkey sees the experimenter reach behind the screen for the nut, which the monkey knows is no longer there. Will the monkey's mirror neuron for reaching for the nut fire? If so, this would suggest that the monkey attributes the goal of reaching for the nut to the experimenter, who "doesn't know" that the nut is no longer there. Or will it not fire, because the nut is not there? Does the mirror neuron, that is, code for the *intended goal* of the observed action, or merely its result? Note that even chimps fail nonverbal false belief tests; see and cf. Call and Tomasello (1999); Call et al. (2000); cf. Hare et al. (2000, 2001). For discussion, see Hurley (2003a).

[30] Rizzolatti (2005). Others postulate similar control systems, though they differ on details: e.g., Rizzolatti locates the comparator site in PF, while Marco Iacoboni (2005) locates it in STS.

obtained. This neural architecture for imitation has been compared with current ideas about functional architectures for instrumental motor control, which combine inverse and forward models. *Inverse models* estimate what motor plan is needed to reach a certain goal from a given state of affairs. They can be adjusted by comparison with real feedback from motor activity, but this is slow. It is often more efficient to use real feedback to train *forward models*, which take copies of motor plans as input and simulate or predict their consequences. Forward models can then be used with inverse models to control goal-directed behavior more efficiently. In particular, forward models can predict the consequences of a planned imitative action for comparison with the observed action, so that the motor plan can be adjusted until a match is obtained (see Iacoboni 2005).

In sum, mirror neurons are arguably necessary, though not sufficient, for full-fledged imitation. They were discovered in macaque monkeys, but while these monkeys can emulate, they have not been shown to be able to imitate in the strict sense.[31] In these monkeys, the mirror system appears to code for the ends rather than the means of action. In human beings, in contrast, the mirror system has instrumental structure: some parts of it code for the goals of actions; others for specific movements that are the means used to achieve goals. It has been suggested that the human mirror system can be used to imitate and not just to emulate because it codes for means as well as ends, unlike the macaque's. Various suggestions have been made about the way in which mirror neurons may contribute to subpersonal comparator control circuits.

C   Functions

There is also intense current interest in whether mirror neurons can shed light on the possible functions of imitation in relation to other distinctively human capacities, such as the capacities for language, and for identifying with others and understanding the mental states that motivate the actions of others. The greatest differences between chimp and human brains are precisely in the significant expansion of the areas around the Sylvian fissure that subserve imitation, language, and the understanding of action (Iacoboni 2005). This is indeed where mirror neurons are concentrated. The relationships among this trio of capacities—for language, mindreading, and imitation—are of fundamental importance for understanding the transition of human infants to adult persons. Does the development of either language or mindreading depend on imitation? If so, at what levels of description and in what senses of "depend?" Or does dependence run the other way, or both ways, dynamically? The answers are controversial, and may of course differ for language and mindreading. A further controversy, about whether mindreading is best understood as theorizing about other minds or as simulating them, is also relevant here. How does the

---

[31] But see Voelkl and Huber (2000) for evidence of imitation in marmosets.

theory-simulation controversy bear on the relationships between imitation and mindreading, or vice versa?

It is arguable that imitation has other important functions as well, in human life and culture. I shall survey various ideas about the possible functions of imitation under four headings: language, the ratchet effect and cultural evolution, cooperation, and mindreading.[32] My treatment of the first three possible functions of imitation will be very brief; they are an important context for the shared circuits model I go on to develop and help to suggest some of its broader relevance in understanding what is distinctive about human minds. The mindreading function will be discussed at greater length, since it is more directly relevant to the shared circuits model.

1 Language

Intriguingly, mirror neurons that code for the goals of action in human beings are found in Broca's area,[33] one of the primary language areas of the brain. This area is among those activated in humans when imitative tasks are performed. Transient virtual "lesions" to Broca's area created by transcranial magnetic stimulation interfere with imitative tasks.[34] Now, a broadly nativist view of language could motivate a kind of protectiveness about Broca's area as the best candidate for an innate language module in the brain.[35] However, the discovery that Broca's area is occupied by the mirror system and has an essential role in imitation has underscored questions about how language acquisition might exploit imitative learning mechanisms rather than (or in addition to) expressing innate linguistic knowledge,[36] and has generated new arguments about how language might depend on the capacity for imitation, either in evolutionary or developmental timeframes.[37]

What are the key features of imitation and the human mirror system that language might build on or exploit? First, I suggest, flexible, articulated relations between means and ends in imitative learning could be an evolutionary precursor of the arbitrary relations between symbols and what they refer to. Second, as Iacoboni (2005) and Arbib (2002, and 2005) argue in different ways, the mirror system provides a common code for the actions of self and other, and thus for language production and perception; by enabling intersubjective action

[32] This discussion of possible functions of imitation is not intended to be exhaustive. For discussion of the function of imitation in moral development, see J. Prinz (2005).

[33] Or the homologue thereof in monkeys; they are also found in other areas, e.g., frontal area 6.

[34] Iacoboni (2005); see also Heiser et al. (2003).

[35] A remark to this effect was made by Marco Iacoboni at the Royaumont conference (2002) on imitation; see his (2005).

[36] See also Heyes (2005) on how the mirror properties of neurons might be acquired.

[37] Arbib (2002) and (2005); Arbib and Rizzolatti (1997); Iacoboni (2005); Rizzolatti and Arbib (1998, 1999); Stamenov and Gallese (2002). On language and imitation/social learning more generally, see: Baldwin (1995); Christiansen (1994, 2005); Christiansen et al. (2002); Deacon (1997); Tomasello (1999) on establishing shared reference to an object through joint attention, established by gaze following and role-reversal imitation.

understanding, the mirror system may be the basis for the intersubjective "parity" or sharing of meaning that is essential to language. Third, as Arbib suggests, the flexible recombinant structure of ends and means in imitation may be a precursor of recombinant grammatical structure in language.[38] Fourth, as Richard Byrne suggests, the problem of finding recombinant units of action in apparently smooth streams of bodily movement has many parallels with the problem of finding linguistic units such as words in the apparently continuous acoustic stream of speech. Skilled action has a modular structure that facilitates flexible recombinant function. Byrne describes how patterns of organization of action might be learned imitatively (*program level imitation*), despite variation in implementational details, by means of a mirror mechanism combined with a behavior parsing mechanism that would recognize the boundaries of behavior modules. Behavior parsing capacities may be an important precursor to more sophisticated human abilities for high-level perception of an underlying structure of intentions and causes in the surface flux of experience (see Byrne 2005). It is tempting also to regard behavior parsing and the recombinant structure of program-level imitation as precursors of syntactic parsing and the recombinant structure of language.

2 The Ratchet Effect and Cultural Evolution

Why might evolution favor neural structures that enable or facilitate response priming, emulation, and imitation? Suppose variations in the behavioral traits of adults that are not genetically heritable slightly favor some members of a given generation over others, so that some reproduce successfully and others do not. Their offspring may benefit if they can acquire the behavioral traits of their successful parents through response priming, emulation, and imitation, as well as through genetic inheritance. A young creature that tends to copy its parents will tend to pick up the nonheritable behaviors of creatures that have survived long enough to reproduce, and tend to form associations between such behaviors and the environmental conditions in which they are appropriate. Depending on how costly or error-prone individual learning is, imitation may contribute more to genetic fitness.

If full-fledged imitation, as opposed to response priming and goal emulation, requires mirror circuits for means and ends to be wired together in the right way, it may be a more difficult trick for evolution to pull off, and so rarer—as indeed it is. But wouldn't this rare development actually be a maladaptive handicap? Recall that children seem to be at a disadvantage (at least in the short run) compared to chimps in two-action paradigms, because children have a greater tendency to imitate even inefficient models while chimps have a greater tendency to emulate and find a more efficient means to achieve an attractive goal.[39]

---

[38] Cf. Iacoboni (2005) for a different view of how evolution leads from action recognition through imitation to language.   [39] Nagell et al. (1993); Whiten et al. (2005).

Despite the short-term disadvantages of imitating with such determination, could it be adaptive in the long run?

The ratchet effect (Tomasello 1999) explains how it might be. Occasionally, gifted or lucky individuals may have rare insights or discover novel means of achieving goals, which would not be rediscovered readily by independent trial-and-error learning. Without imitation, they would be lost; imitation preserves and spreads these discoveries around, making them available to all as a platform for further developments. Once the capacity for imitation has evolved genetically, imitation provides, via the ratchet effect, a mechanism that drives cultural and technological transmission, accumulation and evolution. A similar point is made by meme theory. *Memes* are units of cultural evolution analogous in some respects to genes; both are replicators that evolve through a process of imperfect copying under selective pressure. Memes are understood to be whatever is copied by imitation, the transmission mechanism that makes memetic evolution possible, so imitation is fundamental to meme theory. While genetic adaptations may explain the emergence of the capacity for imitation in the first place, once imitation is on the scene, meme theory explains cultural evolution in terms of the comparative reproductive success of memes themselves rather than the comparative reproductive success of genes. Various accounts have been given of the ways in which culture and life co-evolve, and of how cultural evolution can drive genetic evolution, as well as vice versa.[40]

4   Cooperation

As well as being subject to automatic imitative influences, human beings often deliberately select a pattern of behavior to imitate because it is associated with certain traits and stereotypes, even if they do not themselves actually partake of the relevant traits or stereotypes. This can be benign and contribute to moral development (see J. Prinz 2005); perhaps I can become virtuous, as Aristotle suggested, by behaving like a virtuous person. But, like automatic imitation, deliberate selective imitation does not always operate benignly.

The ability to turn imitation on and off selectively can be a Machiavellian social advantage:[41] for example, by imitating the behavioral signs used by a group of cooperators to identify members, you may be able to obtain the benefits of cooperation from others, but then inhibit your own cooperative behavior before it comes time to reciprocate. That is, a group of cooperators may develop shared

---

[40] See and cf. Baldwin (1896); Dawkins (1976/1989); Boyd and Richerson (1982, 1985), Blackmore (1999, 2000, 2001); Dennett (1995); Deacon (1997); Hurley and Chater (2005b, part 4). The reproductive success of memes can depend on feedback effects that operate via their information content, or on content-independent tendencies, such as a tendency to copy the most frequent memes, or those associated with the highest-status people; see Boyd and Richerson (1985); Henrich and Boyd (1998); Henrich and Gil-White (2001). Harris and Want (2005) argue it is capacity for selective imitation rather than for imitation per se that underwrites the ratchet effect and the explosive development of complex tool forms in the upper Paleolithic.

[41] On Machiavellian intelligence, see Byrne and Whiten (1988); Whiten and Byrne (1997).

behaviors by means of which members identify one another as cooperators and exclude noncooperators from freeriding. Noncooperators may then selectively imitate such behaviors in order to induce cooperative behavior from group members, and then fail to return cooperative behavior, thus deceptively obtaining the benefits of cooperation without paying the costs. So-called *greenbeard genes* could produce genetically determined analogues of such imitative freeriding (see Dawkins 1982: 149). But the evolution of a general capacity for flexible selective imitation would make it possible to get the advantages of freeriding without the need to evolve genes for specific behaviors.

How can the potential benefits of cooperation be achieved despite the ubiquitous threat of freeriding? Certain solutions to collective action problems in effect require being able to recognize and identify with others' mental states. For example, John Howard's (1988) Mirror Strategy for one-off Prisoners' Dilemmas provides a simple if self-referential rule: cooperate with any others you encounter who act on this very same rule. This rule has been implemented computationally and shown to outperform defection even where the same players do not meet repeatedly (when players do play one another repeatedly, it is well known that various strategies, such as Tit-for-Tat, can outperform Defection).

Notice a striking property:[42] mirror strategists need to detect the way one another think (their "programs," or methods of choice, or mental states such as intentions), not just to observe one another's behavior. Which choices the cooperators should make are not determined until it is known whether relevant other agents are cooperators, so cooperation must be conditioned not on the choices of others but their methods of choice. Of course, it may be difficult to detect methods of choice with perfect reliability, especially given incentives to obtain the benefits of cooperation without paying the costs by deceptive mimicry of the signals by which cooperators identify one another. Such imitative freeriding could be expected in turn to prompt more sophisticated and insightful methods of detecting the true methods of choice behind possibly deceptive behavioral signals. An arms race would result between insightful recognition of true methods of choice and deceptive mimicry of behavior patterns associated with methods of choice.

These observations suggest a hypothesis about the function of "mindreading"[43] in solving collective action problems. Psychologists ask: what is the functional difference between genuine mindreading and smart behavior-reading

---

[42] Which also applies to Regan's (1980) proposal for solving coordination problems.

[43] I prefer the term "mindreading" to "theory of mind," when used generically to indicate abilities to discern, understand and/or identify with the mental states of others. The two major substantive theories of how mindreading is done are theory-theory and simulation theory; "theory of mind" used generically is liable to be confused with theory-theory or to imply that theory-theory occupies the whole field.

(Whiten 1996)? Many of the social problems animals face can be solved merely in terms of behavior–circumstance correlations and corresponding behavioral predictions, without the need to postulate mediating mental states.[44] And, after all, it might be said, all we ever "really observe" is behavior in environments; we infer mental states from this. However, mindreaders do not merely keep track of the behavior of other agents, but also understand other agents in terms of their mental states. Mindreaders can attribute intentions to others even when their acts do not carry out their intentions; they can attribute beliefs to others even when those beliefs are false. Mindreading is something that human children only learn to do gradually; for example, children under four do not generally attribute false beliefs to others. Moreover, the capacity for mindreading is characteristically human; evidence for mindreading in nonhuman animals is scarce and controversial.[45] What problem-solving pressures are addressed by going beyond the mere tracking of behavior-circumstance correlations to attribute mental states to explain observed behavior?

I suggest that this question is illuminated by being put in the context of the problem of how to obtain the benefits of cooperation, and in particular the way identifying others as cooperators may require recognizing and identifying with their mental states. As indicated, at least some solutions to problems of cooperation and coordination require more than merely tracking the behavior of others, in part because of the way behavior is subject to deceptive imitation. If cooperators need to know whether others have the mental processes of a cooperator before they can determine what cooperators will do, as in Howard's Mirror Strategy, they must rely on more than unmediated associations between circumstances and behavior. Such solutions require the understanding of others in terms of the mental states that generate their behavior, such as intentions to cooperate with other cooperators. Moreover, participants in such collective action would have to be not just mindreaders, but also to be able to identify, more or less reliably, other mindreaders. In order to counter the invasion of collective cooperative units by ever more sophisticated deceptive imitation that obtains the benefits of cooperation without paying the cost, recognition of other cooperators would be driven progressively further away from merely detecting surface behavior-circumstance correlations toward the detection of underlying mental variables, or mindreading. Capacities for mimicry might in turn be expected to become more subtle and mentalistic. Mindreading and intersubjective identification may result from such an arms race.[46]

---

[44] See and cf. Heyes (1998); Povinelli (1996; forthcoming); Heyes and Dickinson (1993); Call and Tomasello (1999).

[45] See and cf. Davies and Stone (1995a, 1995b); Carruthers and Smith (1996); Heyes (1998); Hare et al. (2000, 2001); Povinelli (forthcoming); Tomasello and Call (forthcoming).

[46] See Hurley (2005b) for an extended version of the argument of this section; see also Hurley (2003b).

5 Mindreading

Human beings are distinctive among animals in both their strong tendency to imitate and their skill at understanding other minds. I've explained how, in the presence of imitation, mindreading might emerge from an arms race between cooperation and deception. What more can be said about the possible functions of imitation in relation to mindreading?

As already indicated, a hypothesis gaining support among scientists and philosophers is that mirror systems are part of the mechanism for understanding observed actions by intersubjective identification with others, for empathy and for simulation.[47] When you see someone do something, your own motor system is primed to imitate, even if imitation is inhibited or taken "off-line": simulation can be regarded as off-line copying. This enables you to regard yourself and others as similar, to identify with others, and to understand the motivation of others' actions in a means/ends structured way. Extensions of the human mirror system provide a plausible neural basis for emotional understanding and empathy.[48] Within this broad intellectual development, however, it is useful to distinguish several different positions. Here, I compare those of neuroscientist Gallese, developmental psychologist Meltzoff, philosopher Gordon, and developmental psychologist/primatologist Tomasello.

Gallese's *shared manifold hypothesis* proposes that the mirror system has a general role in enabling empathy. The mirror system develops out of the way biological control systems model interactions between organisms and their environments. Mirror systems are the neural basis of a primitive intersubjective information space or shared manifold, which is prior to self/other distinctions both phylogenetically and ontogenetically but is preserved in human adults. This view softens the contrast between adult human mindreading and mere responses to others' behavior as found in other social animals. The shared manifold underwrites automatic intersubjective identifications not just across different perceptual modalities and action, but also for sensations and emotions. There is evidence, for example, of mirror mechanisms for pain and disgust; and hearing an expression of anger increases the activation of muscles used to express anger (see Gallese 2001, 2005).

Meltzoff (2005) draws on his work on early imitation to argue that early imitation and its enabling mechanisms beget the understanding of other agents, rather than the other way round. In Meltzoff's view, the ability to understand

---

[47] See, e.g, Gallese (2001, 2005); Gallese and Goldman (1998); Gordon (1995a, 1995b); Goldman (2005), discussing autistic subjects' deficiency at imitation in early years; Williams et al. (2001) on mirror neurons as basis for imitation and mindreading and autism as a deficit in an ontogenetic cascade. Consider also the finding of Chartrand and Bargh (1999), experiment 3, that those high in dispositional empathy imitated more than those low in empathy. Thanks here to John Bargh.

[48] As argued in various ways by Gallese (2005); Meltzoff (2005); Rizzolatti (2005); Iacoboni (2005); Decety and Chaminade (2005); see also Adolphs (2002).

other minds has innate foundations, but develops in stages. Imitation plays a critical role in his arguments for a middle ground between Fodorian nativism and Piagetian theory. Infants have a primitive ability to recognize being imitated and to imitate, hence to recognize people as different from other things and to recognize equivalences between the acts of self and other. The initial bridge between self and other provides a basis for privileged access to people that we do not have to other things, which is developed in an early three-stage process. First, own acts are linked to others' similar acts supramodally, as evidenced by newborn imitation of others' facial acts. Second, own acts of certain kinds are linked bi-directionally to own mental states of certain kinds, through learning. Third, others' similar acts are linked to others' similar mental states. This process gets mindreading started on understanding agency and the mental states most directly associated with it: desires, intentions, perceptions, and emotions. Meltzoff emphasizes that the ability to understand other minds is not all or nothing.[49] Understanding mental states further from action, such as false beliefs, comes later, with further development.

This early three-stage process is not conceived as a matter of formal reasoning, but rather of processing the other as "like me." On the one hand, Meltzoff is often interpreted as viewing mindreading in terms of theoretical inferences from first-person mind-behavior links to similar third-person links, in an updating of classical arguments from analogy.[50] There are indeed clear elements of first-to-third-person inference in his view of how mindreading develops. As he expresses it, "the crux of the idea is that infants may use their own intentional actions as a framework for interpreting the intentional actions of others" (2005: 75). For example, 12-months old infants follow the "gaze" of a model significantly less when the model's eyes are closed than when they are open, but do not similarly refrain from following the "gaze" of blindfolded models until they are given first-person experience with blindfolds. But, on the other hand, the initial self–other linkage Meltzoff postulates, expressed in newborn imitation, is via a supramodal common code for observed and observer's acts, which is direct and noninferential (see Meltzoff and Moore 1997). On a graded view of mindreading such as this, the role of theoretical inference from the first to the third person in mindreading can enter at later stages and increase significantly with development.

Thus, while Meltzoff's approach to mindreading is usually viewed as a version of the "theory theory" rather than the simulation theory of mindreading, it has elements of both approaches. The *theory theory* approach to mindreading regards common-sense psychology as a kind of proto-scientific theory, in which knowledge is represented in the form of laws about mental states and behavior;

[49] The same point can be made for other animals; see Tomasello (1999) on levels of mindreading ability.

[50] Goldman's important version of simulation theory, which space does not permit me to discuss here, shares this first-to-third-person aspect. See his (1989, 1992, 2005).

to the degree that these are not known innately, they are discovered by testing hypotheses against evidence. People's specific mental states and behaviors are inferred from other mental states and behaviors by means of such laws. No copying is involved. By contrast, *simulation theories* understand mindreading to start with the mindreader taking someone else's perspective and generating pretend mental or behavioral states that match the other person's. These are not made the object of theoretical inference, but rather are used as inputs to the simulator's own psychological processes, including decision-making processes, while these are held "off-line," producing simulated mental states and behavior as output. The simulated outputs are then assigned to the other person; these may be predicted behaviors by the other, or mental states of the other that explain his observed behaviors. Such simulation is an extension of practical abilities rather than a theoretical exercise: the simulator copies the states of the other and uses the copies in her own decision-making equipment, instead of making inferences about the other based on laws.[51]

Meltzoff's three-stage process can be restated in explicitly theory-theory terms, as follows. At stage one, the innate equivalence between my own acts and others' acts (exploited by early imitation and recognition of being imitated) makes it possible to recognize that some acts (by myself) are similar to other acts (by another). At stage two, first person experience provides laws that link one's own acts and own mental states. At stage three, it is inferred that another's act that is similar to mine is lawfully linked to the other's mental states in the same way that my act is lawfully linked to my mental states. As Meltzoff points out (personal communication), there is no inference from the first person to the third person at stage one of this account; the initial bridge between self and other expressed in imitation and recognition of being imitated is bi-directional. However, an inference from the first person to the third person does enter as we proceed through stages two and three of this account: it resembles traditional arguments from analogy in inferring laws linking third-person acts and mental states from laws linking first-person acts and mental states.

By contrast, Gordon's radical version of simulation theory explicitly rejects the first-to-third-person direction of explanation in understanding other minds and offers a different view of the link between imitation and mindreading.[52] In what he calls "constitutive mirroring," a copied motor pattern is part of the very

---

[51] Within this broad theory/simulation contrast, many finer distinctions have rightly been drawn, among various versions, levels of description, and aims within each category. For some of these, and challenges to the distinction, see Davies and Stone (1995a, 1995b); Carruthers and Smith (1996). See also Millikan (2005), who distinguishes ontological, ontogenetic, and epistemological questions about thoughts of other minds, on which theory-theory and simulation theory may differ.

[52] See Gordon (1986, 1995a, 1995b, 1996, 2002, 2005). Note that it is a mistake to associate simulation theories too closely with the first-to-third-person arguments from analogy (Gordon's view is a counterexample) or theory-theories with rejection of this type of argument (Meltzoff's view is a counterexample). The theory vs. simulation distinction cuts across acceptance or rejection of the first-to-third-person direction of explanation.

perception of the other person's action in the first place, although the motor pattern may be inhibited and thus not produce overt movement. Gordon finds constitutive mirroring in Gallese's account of the primitive intersubjective 'we' space, the basis of empathy that implicitly expresses the *similarity* of self and other rather than their *distinctness*.[53] Gordon proposes that when constitutive mirroring imposes first-person phenomena, a process of analysis-by-synthesis occurs in which the other's observed behavior and the self's matching response— part of the very perception of the other's behavior—become intelligible together, in the same process. For example, when I see you reach to pick up the ringing phone, your act and my matching response are made sense of together, within a scheme of reasons that is part of the fundamental commonality of persons. Thus, as he puts it, I don't infer from the first to the third person, but rather multiply the first person (2005).

Gordon argues that the first-to-third-person inference in Meltzoff's account is problematic, not because it attributes *similarity* to one's own and others' acts or experiences, but because it requires that they be *identified* and *distinguished*. In the first stage of Meltzoff's account, the similarity between acts of self and other is supposed to be established by their innate equivalence, which is exploited by early imitation; this stage may involve constitutive mirroring, as in Gallese's primitive shared manifold. But the second and third stages of Meltzoff's account, where the analogical inference occurs, requires that self and other also be distinguished: if this kind of act *of mine* is linked to *my* mental states of a certain kind, then a similar (as established in stage one) kind of act *by another person* is also linked to *her* mental states of a similar kind. But, Gordon objects, if I cannot distinguish *a* from *b*, I cannot make an analogical inference from *a* to *b*. While such an inference may sometimes be a feature of mature imitative mirroring, Gordon regards it as beyond the capacities of infants (2005).

However, a standard charge against pure simulation theories of mindreading has been that they lack the resources to explain how mature mindreaders distinguish and identify different people and keep track of which actions and mental states are whose. Gordon suggests that multiple first persons are distinguished and tracked in the process of making them intelligible as persons, to avoid incoherence and disunity under the common scheme of reasons.[54] Mental states that do not make sense together are assigned to different persons. But can this be done in pure simulation mode, with no overlay of theory and inference? Simulation is supposed to be the off-line use of practical abilities, in contrast with theorizing about actions. But what exactly is the difference between interpreting an action to make sense of it and theorizing about it? When I use practical reason off-line in mindreading, I don't formulate normative laws from

[53] Gallese understands empathy to involve not the recognition of others as bodies endowed with minds, but rather the assumption of a common scheme of reasons by reference to which persons, self and others alike, are intelligible. Gallese (2005); see and cf. Strawson (1959, 1966).

[54] See also and cf. Hurley (1989, 1998: part 1).

which I make inferences; rather, I activate my own normative and deliberative dispositions. As Millikan might put it (see her 2005), my thought about another's action is not wholly separate from my entertaining that action.

A suggestion worth considering here is this: the fundamental *similarity between self and other* may best be understood not in terms of theorizing, but rather in terms of simulation (as in Gordon's constitutive mirroring, Gallese's shared manifold, the innate self/other equivalence exploited by early imitation, on Meltzoff's view, and my layer 3, below). Such primitive intersubjectivity may persist into adulthood and remain an essential aspect of mature empathy and mindreading, as Gallese suggests. But as mindreading develops it also employs a *self/other distinction*, as when the older child attributes to the other false beliefs, different from her own, or distinguishes imitating from being imitated.[55] More generally, mature mindreading requires the ability to distinguish, identify, and track multiple other persons and to assign acts and mental states to them in a process of interpretation. The full range of distinctions and identifications mature mindreading requires may indeed require theoretical and inferential resources, even while the simulative foundation remains essential.

Gallese, Meltzoff, and Gordon stress the contribution of imitation to understanding other agents.[56] By contrast, Tomasello and Carpenter, like Rizzolatti, emphasize the contribution of action understanding to imitation and the ways in which imitative learning depends on intention reading. Tomasello and Carpenter (2005) argue that paradigms recently developed with children (see especially Meltzoff 1995) have made a clearer distinction between imitative learning and other forms of social learning than the two-action method does. In these paradigms, the modeled action is unsuccessful or accidental. If the observer copies what was intended even though it was not shown, as opposed to only the observed movements or the observed though unintended result, that suggests the observer does understand the intentional structure of the observed action. Tomasello and Carpenter argue that, in demonstrations of imitative learning in which the modeled behavior is the same and only the modeled intention varies across conditions, the ability to read intentions is needed to explain what is copied. Given the results from the various imitation paradigms, they regard it as most parsimonious to assume that children use their understanding of intentions to imitate.

How then should we view the relationship between imitation and mindreading? On some views, action understanding precedes imitation and

---

[55] Decety and Chaminade (2005) invoke single-cell, imaging, and behavioral evidence in support of the shared neural coding of action and the perception of action in a mirror system. They regard such automatic motor resonance as a necessary basis for intersubjectivity in action understanding and emotional empathy. However, they focus not on the intersubjective space that precedes the self/other distinction, but rather on the characteristically human self/other distinction, and the way it is imposed on what is common to the representation of self and other. They report imaging experiments that probe the neural bases of the self/other distinction and reveal the relevance of left–right lateralization.   [56] As does Goldman (2005).

full-fledged imitative learning, with intentional, means/ends structure, depends on intention reading.[57] On other views, imitation underwrites early mindreading abilities.[58] Are these views in tension?

Not necessarily. In order to appreciate their potential compatibility, however, it is important to distinguish various stages or levels in both imitation and mindreading and the ways these could build on one another dynamically, in evolutionary and developmental processes. Recall Rizzolatti's argument that action understanding precedes imitation in evolution, which distinguishes the mirroring of movements (in response priming), from the mirroring of goals (in emulation), and from genuine imitative learning with flexible intentional structure relating observed means to observed results. He suggests that the capacity to copy observed results via mirror systems may underwrite phylogenetically early understanding of action in terms of goals and intentions, which in turn is needed for phylogenetically later imitative learning with intentional structure, in which the mirroring of means and of ends are linked flexibly in the larger mirror circuit characteristic of human beings (2005). Recall also earlier suggestions that recognition of a fundamental self/other similarity via simulation (as in Gallese's primitive shared manifold, Meltzoff's innate self-other equivalence, and Gordon's constitutive mirroring) may precede developmentally the registration of a self-other distinction, and more generally precede the inferential, interpretative abilities drawn on in more advanced mindreading to identify and distinguish multiple persons and to keep track of which mental states go with which persons. Thus, very early imitation may express registration of a fundamental self/other similarity, while the distinctive human capacity for imitative learning with its flexible means/ends structure in turn contributes to the development of the self/other distinction and of more advanced mindreading skills.

PART II THE SHARED CIRCUITS MODEL

I've now reached the second half of this essay, in which I want to draw together some of the threads of work on imitation surveyed above, by putting forward unified functional architecture for control, imitation, and simulation. Various researchers at the currently buzzing intersection of work on these processes have suggested that they are closely connected or even co-constituted.[59] There is

---

[57] Rizzolatti (2005); Tomasello and Carpenter (2005).

[58] Gallese (2005); Meltzoff (2005); Gordon (2005); Goldman (2005).

[59] See and cf. Frith et al. (2000); Gallese (2000, 2005); Gerrans (forthcoming); Gordon (2002); Grush (1995, 2004); Iacoboni (2005); Jeannerod (1997, 2001); Meltzoff (2005); Oztop and Arbib (2002); Arbib et al. (2000); Proust (2003); Rizzolatti (2005); Wolpert et al. (2003); Gallese and Goldman (1998); Blakemore and Decety (2001).

something intuitively right and important here, yet the suggested relationships are often partial or expressed in one of several overlapping technical jargons that may be inaccessible to those in other disciplines who are interested in essentially the same issues. At this point it is worth exposing the substantive issues clearly in a way that cuts across disciplinary boundaries. Here, I put forward in plain terms a unified framework that makes the relationships among the mechanisms that enable control, imitation, and simulation explicit. Many of the phenomena discussed above can be located and understood by reference to this framework. I call it the *shared circuits model*. It can be regarded as a descendant of the common-coding hypothesis about perception and action, though it describes commonality in terms of the functional dynamics rather than the coding of perception and action. It is also closely related to Gallese's shared manifold hypothesis, though it situates elements of Gallese's views explicitly within an overall framework.

Philosophers distinguish the attribution of contentful actions and mental states to persons from subpersonal descriptions of information being processed and passed between subsystems (Dennett 1969). The mental lives of persons depend on and are enabled by subpersonal information processes, though the latter need not correspond directly to people's conscious mental processes or reasons (McDowell 1994). Subpersonal processes can be described functionally, or in terms of their neural implementations. Two related types of question arise about personal/subpersonal relations: 1) How are specific personal-level capacities *in fact* enabled by subpersonal-level processes? 2) What kinds of subpersonal processes could *possibly* do the enabling work? For example, are there isomorphism constraints between the levels? Views about latter questions can influence answers to the former.

The shared circuits model addresses the second type of question about social cognition, using subpersonal resources associated with an active perception/ embodied cognition approach and without assuming interlevel isomorphism. The shared circuits model is a mid-level model of subpersonal functional architecture, cast at a level of description between those of neural implementation and of the personal level of conscious perception and intentional action.[60] While it may be too early to claim definitive empirical support for this particular specification, it may nevertheless have explanatory and heuristic value in providing a context for observations and questions at both higher and lower levels, while avoiding over-simple or a priori assumptions of isomorphism between subpersonal and personal-level descriptions. Some of the work I've surveyed does not keep clear track of distinctions between neural, functional subpersonal, and personal levels of description. While the boundaries between these levels are not wholly opaque, it will conduce to clarity and progress to recognize distinctions

---

[60] Read "animal level" for "personal level" where appropriate; for a defense of this move, see Hurley (2003a).

between levels, and to frame issues about interlevel relations, more explicitly. Looking downward from the functional shared circuits architecture, we can ask whether there is evidence that particular neural circuits implement parts of it. Looking upward, we can ask what its behavioral and cognitive implications are. If information about self and other is processed subpersonally along the lines suggested by the shared circuits model, what implications might that have for the role and uses of such information at the personal level? For example, if intersubjective information is prior, at the subpersonal level, to information that differentiates self and other, does this have any implications about the basis of our personal-level knowledge of other minds? Unfulfilled predictions, implausible consequences, or incompatible neural circuitry could lead either away from the general idea of shared circuits for control, imitation, and simulation, or to a better specification of those shared circuits.

I draw attention as I proceed to some striking aspects of the shared circuits model. In particular, this model connects a shared information space for action and perception with a shared information space for self and other, while at the same time illustrating how the distinctions between self and other, and between the possible and the actual, can be imposed on these shared information spaces. In this model, information in the subpersonal version of the first-person plural, without distinction or inference between self and other, is prior to the self/other distinction. Moreover, the shared circuits model avoids the classical sandwich and illustrates a horizontally modular architecture.[61] It conceives of perception and action as dynamically co-enabled and shows how cognitively significant resources, such as the self/other and possible/actual distinctions, and information for action understanding and planning, can emerge from the information space that perception and action share.

The shared circuits model describes a subpersonal functional architecture in five major stages or—better—layers.[62] Some of these could be further expanded into different sublayers. Multiple instances of the shared circuits structure could be linked together into a network of such shared circuits, for hierarchical yet flexible control permitting decomposition and recombination of elements. Further questions arise about how the specific layers might map onto phylogenetic or ontogenetic stages. The layers are described heuristically, in an intuitive order reflecting increasing complexity, but this order does not represent a universal order of evolution, development, or learning. Rather, the layers of the model provide generic, adaptable tools for framing for specific hypotheses. (For example, layer 2 can be combined with layer 4 as well as with layer 3, as I shall explain below.)

---

[61] See Hurley (1998, 2001) for arguments against the input–output picture of perception as input from the world to the mind and action as output from the mind to the world, with cognition sandwiched in between.

[62] The allusion to Brooksian subsumption architecture is intentional—another expression of what I call horizontal modularity. See Brooks (1999).

A key feature of the shared circuits model is this subpersonal progression:

- predictive simulation of the observable effects of movement, which enables improvement in instrumental motor control
- mirroring of observed action
- simulation of the internal causes of observed movement, which enables understanding of the observed actions of others as intentional.

This progression allows us to understand how the shared space for perception and action can be the basis of a shared intersubjective space and of the self/other and possible/actual distinctions. Whether this theoretical model describes paths of evolution, development, and/or learning is a further question. In work in progress I consider how it can be adapted to the perception of emotion and emotional understanding.

"Simulation" here has a generic sense applying both to simulation of effects (in predictive forward models) and of causes (in mirroring). It implies that the same processes that can generate or result from actual action ("on-line") are used to generate related information by producing a disengaged ("off-line") version of an associated effect or cause. Simulation *uses* certain processes to generate related information, rather than *theorizing about* them in separate meta-processes.

First Layer: Basic Adaptive Feedback Control

The first layer constitutes a simple adaptive control system for general purpose motor control, which can usefully be compared to a thermostat. The elements of this are (see Figure 1):

(1) a target or reference signal (such as desired room temperature, in the case of the thermostat);

(2) an input signal (such as actual room temperature), which is the joint result of (3) and (5);

(3) exogenous events in the environment (such as nightfall);

(4) a comparator, which determines whether the target and input signals match and the degree of any mismatch or error (e.g., the room is still 5 degrees below the desired temperature);

(5) the output of the control system, (such as the level of heat output) which is determined by comparison between target and input signals (e.g., heat output is turned up if the room temperature is measured to be below the thermostat setting);

(6) a feedback loop, by which output has effects on the succeeding input signal (e.g., actual room temperature rises).

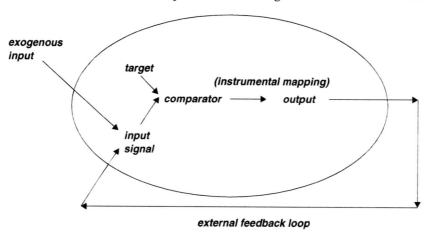

Fig. 1. First layer: basic adaptive feedback control.

Consider the function that takes the system from target, in the context of actual input, to instrumental output.[63] I'll call this the *instrumental mapping*: in effect, it maps goal to means, or specifies the means that will be used to approach the target, in given circumstances. The feedback loop at this layer is relatively slow, since it operates in real time (e.g., the room takes a while to warm up after the heat has been turned up). In organisms, this is input to the system that results from the organism's own activity,[64] in contrast with input to the system resulting from exogenous events.[65] Feedback from the organism's own activity includes, for example, visual and proprioceptive inputs resulting from movements of its own hands, or movement through space, or manipulation of objects. Inputs from events originating in the external environment, both inanimate and animate, would include visual inputs resulting from movements by other creatures in a social group.

This kind of feedback control system is *adaptive* because it adjusts itself to changing environmental conditions and compensates for exogenous disturbances: in the presence of different exogenous events, different output is needed to achieve the target. The control process is cyclical and dynamic; it does not have discrete steps or a nonarbitrary start or finish. Input is as much an effect as a cause of output. Information about inputs is not segregated from information about outputs; the dynamic relations among inputs and outputs are critical for control. This feature will be preserved as further layers are added; to the extent that perception and action are enabled by a system with this basic feature, they share a fundamental information space (see Hurley 1998, 2001).

---

[63] An "inverse model," in engineering terminology.   [64] "Reafference."
[65] "Exafference."

Layer 2: Predictive Simulation of Effects Added to On-line Feedback Control

An inner loop is now added, which maps a copy of the output signal directly onto the 'expected' input signal, or means to results.[66] Over time an association is established between copied output and subsequent input, so that in effect a copy of the motor output signals comes to evoke the associated input signal. It can then operate as a simulation of feedback, to predict the consequences of output on input during on-going action (see Figure 2; new aspects are italicized).

This process provides a general purpose improvement in the on-line functioning of the instrumental motor control system, because the system no longer needs to wait for output to produce actual feedback effects. Rather, the system can bypass relatively slow processes by learning and then anticipating the likely effects of output on input. For example, a temperature control system with this feature doesn't need to wait for the room actually to heat up to a certain level when the heat output is increased by a certain amount; it can predict that this will happen and can adjust its output accordingly. A *simulation* of the expected effects of the system's output speeds up the control process and smoothes the appropriate behavioral trajectory. In the case of a significant mismatch between real and simulated input, a local switch can default back to actual feedback control while the predictive simulation is further fine-tuned to improve its subsequent predictions.[67] This simulation is low level, in the sense that it can perform its speeding and smoothing control functions without the system needing to monitor continuously or to access globally whether it is using actual or simulated feedback.

Recall that the order of the layers is heuristic and does not necessarily represent the order of evolution, development, or learning. For example, in the learning of particular tasks, layer 2's forward models may be acquired from feedback, enabling motor prediction, before layer 1's instrumental mappings are acquired, enabling motor control.[68] One does not necessarily have to be pursuing a goal in order to learn to predict the sensory consequences of movement, even if it is natural to conceive of such prediction of feedback in an instrumental context.

Notice, however, that a system that includes predicted feedback from the organism's own movements in addition to actual feedback has the resources to track the distinction between information about events in the world and information about goal-directed activity originating in the organism, that is, its behavior. When the train I am on pulls out of the station, I register movement relative to the train on the next platform, but this does not necessarily give me information about whether my train or the train on the next platform has begun

---

[66] In organisms this mapping is often understood in terms of *efference copy* (or *corollary discharge*); in engineering it is referred to as a *forward model*.

[67] See Grush (2004) on how Kalman filters combine real and simulated input continuously, and recall that Grush's sense of "emulation" is very different from the sense used in the summary above; see Wolpert and Kawato (1998); Haruno et al. (2001); Wolpert et al. (2003); on the mosaic model and selection among different forward models.

[68] Flanagan et al. (2003); here I am indebted to comments from Marco Iacoboni.

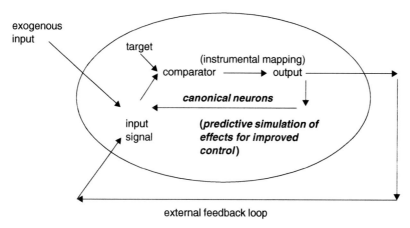

Fig. 2. Second layer: predictive simulation of effects for improved control.

to move. Comparison of predicted feedback from action with actual input gives an organism the resources to resolve an analogous subpersonal ambiguity, and hence provides information about the distinction between activity by the self and activity by the world.[69] This information could provide part of the basis for the personal-level distinction between action and perception, which on this view would emerge from a shared information space and processing resources. Note that information for the action/perception distinction is prior to and more general than information for the self/other distinction (see layers 3 and 4 below). In this sense there are more and less fundamental layers of information about self.

At this point it could be predicted that cells that mediate the association between copies of motor signals and actual input signals might come to have both motor and sensory fields. Suppose an animal typically acts in a certain way on the perceived affordances of a certain kind of object: eating a certain kind of food in a certain way, for example. There will be associations between copies of the motor signals for the eating movements and a multimodal class of inputs associated with such objects and the eating of them. Any cells that mediate this association might thus have both sensory and motor fields that between them capture information about the affordances of the objects in question. *Canonical neurons* are candidates for such predicted sensorimotor affordance neurons.[70]

Layer 3: Mirroring for Priming, Emulation, and Imitation

Now consider how the system described so far would apply to movements that produce visual feedback for their agent, as when a creature watches his own hand

---

[69] For discussion of this familiar point, and references, see Hurley (1998), 140–1 and passim. "Self" here does not entail "person," but is neutral between persons and other animals.

[70] Rizzolatti (2005); Iacoboni (2005); Gallese (2005).

movements. (The contrast here is with movements such as facial expressions: while they produce proprioceptive feedback, the creature cannot normally see his own facial expressions.) As the creature watches his own hand movements, an association is formed between copies of motor signals for such movements and visual feedback from such movements. Here it could be predicted that cells that mediate this association might have matching sensory and motor fields. If the first creature watches another creature perform hand movements of the same kind and he receives similar visual inputs, these will also activate his sensorimotor matching neurons with their motor fields. The sensory fields of such matching neurons cannot tell the difference between his own actions of this kind and similar actions by others; they will fire when he does something or observes someone else do the same thing. *Mirror neurons* are of course candidates for such predicted matching sensorimotor neurons, and provide a potential neural implementation of the kind of primitive blended intersubjective information space described by Gallese in terms of a shared manifold and by Gordon in terms of constitutive mirroring (though more work is needed on how the mirror properties of individual neurons function in a neural mirror network or system). Note the intimate relationship between the sharing of circuits for action and perception and for self and other: the blended intersubjective information space is a specification of and presupposes the generic blended sensorimotor information space.

Assume now that the sensorimotor matching association is bi-directional. Then, as well as copies of motor signals predictively simulating input signals, as described so far, input signals can also evoke motor signals. That is, assume that the predictive simulation can run in reverse.[71] The result would be *mirroring*: motor priming or copying at some level or levels (see Figure 3). "Mirroring" is used here in a functional sense, to describe a default behavioral tendency produced by observing similar behavior; it can be overridden or inhibited (see layer 4). Functional mirroring depends on implementation by neural mirroring mechanisms. If a particular shared circuit controls details of movement,[72] a predicted result would be mirroring of similar movement: motor priming. If the circuit instead controls the result of movement,[73] rather than the detailed movements that are the means to these results, a predicted result would be mirroring of goals: emulation. If shared circuits for both motor means and results are themselves flexibly associated so that they can function instrumentally together, they would enable full-fledged imitation in which means as well as ends are copied (as revealed by the two-action methodology for identifying imitation). Such full-fledged imitation would be predicted to be rarer than either response

---

[71] See and cf. Gallese and Goldman (1998); Blakemore and Decety (2001).

[72] As in Rizzolatti's *low-level resonance* (2005).

[73] As in Rizzolatti's *high-level resonance*, for example, in the monkeys in whom mirror neurons were discovered.

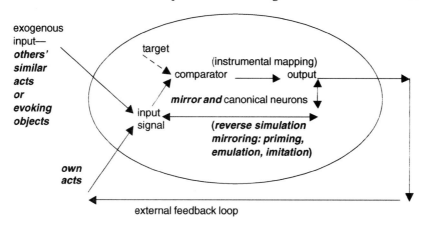

Fig. 3. Third layer: mirroring for priming, emulation, imitation.

priming or emulation separately, since it would require circuits for both means and ends, appropriately linked together. And indeed it is rarer.

Instrumental mappings and reverse simulation mirroring (henceforth: *mirroring*, for short) both go from input signals to output. The distinction between them is functional (the neural paths that perform these functions might overlap). An instrumental mapping functions instrumentally (!), to bring about a goal by matching input to a target within a comparator system. Mirroring does not in itself have this instrumental function.[74] The priming of my own action by observing someone else's similar action is rather a by-product of the presence of the predictive simulation, which functions at layer 2 to improve the functioning of the control system. However, this priming may in due course be exapted for other functions, such as those associated with imitation and simulation for action understanding. The neural mechanism by which such reverse functionality might be acquired is a matter of speculation.[75]

Circuits with this mirroring aspect could function in a variety of useful ways to capture information about the instrumental structure of action. If seeing someone move in a way that produces a result generates motor activation associated with a similar *goal* for the observer (though not necessarily associated with the same *movements* in the observer), that could provide information for action understanding, about the goal-directness of the observed action. If seeing someone move in a way that produces a result also generates motor activation associated with the same *movements* in the observer, that could provide information for imitative learning, that is, about how to achieve the goal by means of the observed movements. Such circuits could be linked to enable

---

[74] See and cf. Peterson and Trapold (1982).
[75] See and cf. Heyes (2005) on cells that fire together and wire together.

understanding that observed movements are the means to a subgoal, which is in turn the means to a further goal, and so on; or to enable imitative learning of how to achieve a goal by achieving a more proximal goal, and so on. Again, the distinction between ends and means is not absolute; movements can be the means to other movements, which are in turn the means to something else. Such linked circuits could generate behavioral building blocks or modules that could be strung together in program level imitation, of sequences (Byrne, 2005) or of hierarchical structures (Whiten et al. 2005). They could allow an infant to form three-way associations between observed behavior by its parents (who have survived to reproduce, so may have adaptive behaviors not all of which are heritable), observed circumstances in which its parents perform such behavior, and its own similar behavior. Such associations could drive contextual imitation: act like that, when the environment is like this (Byrne, 2005).

Note that the sensorimotor affordance associations described in the second layer (mediated by canonical neurons?) could also be bilateral. If so, observation of an object that affords some type of action would be predicted to prime the type of action afforded.[76]

So far, the reverse simulation and mirroring account does not explain copying of movements that cannot be seen by their agents. How can a correspondence be established between one's own acts and similar acts by others, when there is no feedback from the organism's own actions in the same modality as its observations of others' acts? For example, a creature receives visual input when observing another's facial expressions, but normally only receives proprioceptive, not visual, feedback from its own facial expressions. How can these be compared and matched across modalities? How then can an association be established between my seeing another's facial expression and my making a similar expression myself? One answer is that some such supramodal correspondences are innate (Meltzoff, 2005). Another is that they are acquired in a variety of ways, through experience with mirrors, or with being imitated (Heyes, 2005).

The shared circuits model is compatible with these suggestions; it has no commitments about whether such opaque correspondences are innate, acquired, or both. It also naturally accommodates another suggestion: that *stimulus enhancement* can establish associations between one's own and others' similar acts in such cases. Suppose a social creature repeatedly visually observes others' actions of a certain type, and its attention is thereby drawn to the characteristic objects of such actions. Such stimulus enhancement repeatedly evokes in the observer an innate or otherwise acquired response to those objects. As a result, an association is formed between visual observations of others' actions and one's own similar action. This is not initially imitation or any kind of copying; the object independently evokes others' and one's own acts. But while the link is

---

[76] See and cf. Lhermitte's utilization syndrome patients; Lhermitte (1983, 1986); Lhermitte et al. (1986).

initially indirect, nevertheless an association between own and others' acts may be established. Cells that mediate this association may acquire mirror properties such that subsequently merely observing another's act comes to prime similar action by the observer. In this way mere stimulus enhancement may develop into copying, and an indirect stimulus enhancement link into a direct sensorimotor matching link. This suggestion about how opaque correspondences could be established is similar to one Heyes (2005) makes about the mediating role of words, but it applies to stimulus enhancement in general.[77]

Layer 4: Simulative Mirroring for Action Understanding with Monitored Output Inhibition

Next consider the possibility that a creature might observe another's act, which primes a similar act in the usual way, yet its own action is inhibited so that the observed behavior is not actually copied. In effect, the output of the mirroring function is taken "off-line" prior to motor output. Since observing the other's act is still associated with motor priming even when copying is inhibited, such observation could be interpreted as providing the observer with simulated information about the intentional character of the observed act. Such simulation for action understanding is off-line copying. But now what is being simulated are not effects, but causes. Instead of predicting the feedback that results from action, we now have simulation of the motor signals that would generate feedback similar to what is observed. Applied to emulation circuits that control the result of movement, the simulation would provide information about the goal to which the other's movement is directed, or the instrumental structure of the action. The ability to pick up the information that another's movement is directed toward a certain goal can be regarded as enabling an early stage in understanding other agents and hence other minds (see Figure 4).

Although it uses the same circuit in reverse, simulation for action understanding can function at a higher level than the predictive simulation for speeding and smoothing on-line control described in layer 2.[78] Recall that the basic functions of predictive simulation in on-line control do not require the system to monitor continuously whether it is relying on actual or predicted feedback, though it should be able to switch between them as needed. In other words, as long as the predictive simulation works well and there is no significant

---

[77] Heyes' ASL model (2005) claims that visual and motor representations are linked according to the same Hebbian principles whether or not the movement can be seen by its agent. The only difference is that in the case where it can be seen, self-observation will lead to the formation of links between movements that are the same from a third-party perspective. What I'm regarding here as stimulus enhancement could be regarded as acquired equivalence learning. The ASL model cites words as examples of the kind of stimuli that could act as the "third term" in acquired equivalence learning, but acknowledges that, as in most experiments on acquired equivalence in animals, the third term is often a non-linguistic stimulus. Thanks here to Cecilia Heyes.

[78] By "control" here, I refer to the overall function of the control system, not merely to that of the instrumental mapping component.

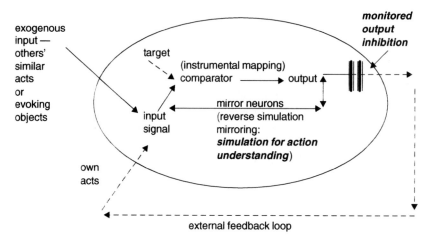

Fig. 4. Fourth layer: simulative mirroring for action understanding with monitored output inhibition.

mismatch in retrospect, the system does not need to know that it is using the predictive simulation to improve its own functioning; the distinction between actual and simulated feedback does not here have global significance for the system.

In contrast, for simulation flexibly to subserve, as needed, understanding as opposed to copying an action, the system has to monitor the distinction between states in which the system's output is inhibited and states in which it is not; this distinction *is* of global significance. While we have seen that copying can have many beneficial functions, unselective overt copying of an action can in some circumstances have disastrous results for the observer. So the capacity selectively to inhibit overt copying is also adaptive, and should be expected to develop. Moreover, the system needs to keep track of whether the action it is "entertaining" is merely simulated, for purposes of understanding another's behavior, or under execution, since these in general have quite different consequences and make quite different demands on subsequent behavior. Information about whether a movement is another's or one's own thus comes to overlay the primitive blended intersubjective manifold. Information about the distinction between self and other in this way emerges. Keep in mind, however, that this model is described at the level of subpersonal information; while subpersonal information is enabling, it is a further question how it is used at the personal level.

In particular, the shared intersubjective space—subpersonal information about instrumental actions in the first-person plural, in a form that does not distinguish or infer between self and others—is prior to the self/other distinction. Subpersonal processing of information about other agents is a matter of simulated recentering of the information processing that enables intentional action, rather than of inference from first-person information to third-person information. At the level of subpersonal information, the problem of "knowledge" of other minds is reconfigured: it is neither one of starting from information about the self and constructing a bridge across a gulf to information about other persons, nor one of starting from information about other persons and from the resources it provides somehow generating information about the self. The shared circuits model gives concrete if subpersonal form to the interdependence and parity of information about self and other minds.

Again, it is a further question how these subpersonal relations are reflected at the personal level. Do they give any support to a parallel priority of the first-person plural at the personal level? How should "priority" indeed be understood in this question: as a question about development, or about the structure of mature understanding of other persons, and what is the relation between these? Can personal-level understanding and knowledge of other minds be non-inferentially based on or enabled by reliable subpersonal information? Is there any reason, conceptual or empirical, to believe that the problem of knowledge of other minds is similarly reconfigured at the personal level, so that it is neither one of starting from the first-person perspective and constructing a bridge across a gulf to the third-person, nor one of starting from the third person perspective and from the resources it provides somehow creating the first-person perspective? Careful further thought is needed here. We should not simply help ourselves to an isomorphic projection from the subpersonal to the personal levels, but nor should we assume that the structure of subpersonal information processing has no implications for the personal level.

One way of responding to these issues is suggested by the affinities between the shared circuits model and Gordon's version of simulation theory.[79] In Gordon's felicitous phrase, constitutive mirroring *multiplies the first person*, through a process of making sense of observed behavior and the self's matching response together, under a common scheme of reasons, a process that assigns incoherent mental states to different persons (2005). While the shared circuits model offers a subpersonal description in which first-person plural information is prior to the self/other distinction, Gordon's account of the multiplication of the first person under a scheme of reasons is more ambitious in linking subpersonal constitutive mirroring to personal-level understanding of other minds.[80]

---

[79] See especially Gordon (1995a, 56, 58, 68; 2002; 2005).

[80] Gordon appeals to *ascent routines* to explain how simulation can underwrite mindreading without depending on inference from the first to the third person, as other versions of simulation theory do (see Gordon 1995a, 2005; compare Gallese and Goldman 1998). When I use an ascent routine, I answer a meta-question about my own or another's mental states by looking at the world; ascent routines are as well suited in principle to answering questions about another's mental states as about one's own. For example, to answer a question about whether I believe *p*, I consider whether *p* is true; to answer a question about whether another believes *p*, I perform an egocentric shift and

Finally, note that layers 2 and 4 could combine functionally also, independently of mirroring. Simulative predictions at layer 2 improve on-line control of actual action. We've seen that for this function it isn't essential that the system monitor whether it is currently using actual or simulated feedback, as long as the target is achieved. But simulative predictions of results could also function off-line, with actual motor output inhibited. Multiple simulative predictions could provide information about the results of alternative possible actions, rather than anticipating results for ongoing action. The simulated results of alternative possible actions could be compared with a target prior to actual action, providing information about which produces the closest match. Such information could enable decision-theoretic intelligence, instrumental deliberation, and planning. However, enabling these further capacities would require not just comparing the simulated results of different possible acts with a target, but also monitoring whether motor output is inhibited, so that the distinction between possible and actual actions is tracked. Layer 4's added capacity for monitored inhibition provides a basis for this distinction: simulated results given output inhibition would provide information about possible actions; simulated results without output inhibition would provide information about actual actions. So, multiple predictive simulations could provide information about the consequences of alternative actions by the agent, while monitoring of output inhibition could provide information that such actions are possible rather than actual.

Whether or how subpersonal informational structures described above correspond to the personal-level sense of being able to do otherwise, or of empathy with others' goals, or of being the agent of an action, are further questions. The present point is to show how aspects of the personal level could be informationally enabled by subpersonal resources described by the shared circuits model. The actual/possible and self/other distinctions are necessary (if not sufficient) for much explicit theorizing and for aspects of the normativity and intersubjectivity that characterize the personal level. Understanding how information for these distinctions can arise subpersonally helps to understand how subpersonal processes can enable the personal level. The shared circuits model explains how these two distinctions could have a common informational basis in monitoring of motor inhibition; in this way, theoretical informational resources can arise from practical.

---

imaginatively recenter myself to the other's perspective, and then again consider whether *p* is true. Similarly, for questions about what I or another perceive or intend: I look out at the world and the reasons it provides, though in the case of others having first transformed myself imaginatively. Note that on this view, to answer questions about what I or others believe, perceive, or intend, someone must first have the ability to perceive and act in the world. There is here another parallel, between Gordon's conception of ascent routines and the first aspect of the shared circuits model I have noted in the text: the way a shared intersubjective space is distilled out of and simulatively employs the shared perception/action information space.

Layer 5: Counterfactual Input Simulation for Strategic Deliberation and Planning

Finally, the system can be taken off-line on the input side as well as the output side (Figure 5). Monitored simulation of inputs to control systems equipped with simulative prediction and mirroring functions can provide a distinction between others' actual and possible acts. Counterfactual inputs can now simulate different possible acts by others and their results. This social extension of counterfactual information combined with simulation of different possible acts by self and their results provides information needed to track how the results of various possible acts by others may in turn result from various possible acts of one's own, and vice versa. This combination of functions provides enabling information for strategic or "Machiavellian" social intelligence, game-theoretic deliberation, coordination and cooperation (see Hurley, 2005b, on *mirror heuristics*). These simulative informational resources for instrumental and strategic functions may in turn provide a practical foundation for capacities to manipulate counterfactual information and modes of counterfactual theorizing more generally.

At this level, the demands of differentiating and tracking interacting means/ends relations for multiple other agents and multiple possible acts are acute. Meeting these demands, and further demands in differentiating the epistemic states of multiple others, may well require the simulative informational basis for understanding other agents to be supplemented by language-dependent theorizing capacities. Mindreading, like social learning and instrumental control, is a graded phenomenon, not all or nothing (Tomasello 1999). Capacities for

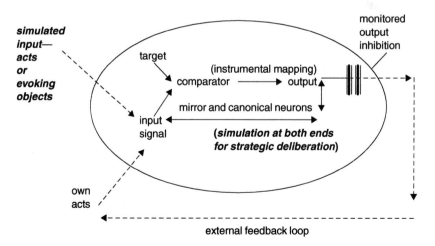

Fig. 5. Fifth layer: counterfactual input simulation for strategic deliberation and planning.

interpretative theorizing about others may build on the fundamental simulative self/other distinction to fine-tune differentiations and identifications of multiple other intentional agents. The shared circuits model allows that simulation and theorizing may both be needed for mature mindreading with all the bells and whistles, though it describes the foundations of mindreading in terms of simulative mirroring of means/ends relations.

Concluding Remarks

The shared circuits model provides a unified subpersonal architecture relating control, imitation, and simulation at a middle level of description: a functional level above that of neural implementation but below that of the normatively constrained and/or conscious personal level. We can now step back from the details to see the broad outline: The feedback effects of certain motor outputs, such as visual inputs that result from certain movements, are predicted via simulation; such prediction can benefit on-line instrumental control. Mirroring reverses this predictive simulation, so that observation of movements of a certain kind by another induces in the observer motor output that would typically cause such movements. While copying can be beneficial, the capacity to inhibit actual copying is also adaptive. Monitored inhibition of overt copying while the causes of observed behavior are nevertheless simulated provides information to enable action understanding. The progression is from simulation of effects through mirroring to simulation of causes.

Hand in hand with this building up of mechanisms goes the building up of a subpersonal informational structure that stands in an *enabling* relation to various aspects of the personal level (see and cf. McDowell 1994). Such enabling subpersonal information is *not* necessarily the conscious basis, or the reason for, or sufficient for actions or judgments by the person (or animal). Nevertheless, what people can do depends on and is enabled by subpersonal informational resources. Figure 6 displays the way subpersonal informational resources described in the shared circuits model (outside the bold box) could be drawn on to enable various personal-level distinctions and capacities (inside the bold box).

At the lower levels, simulative prediction of effects within an instrumental control system provides information that enables actions to be distinguished from perceptions. In this sense, the action/perception distinction is informationally fundamental; but this is not yet information for a full-fledged self/world distinction, since information is not yet present about either the similarity or the distinction between the actions of self and of others.

At the higher levels, the mirroring of actions provides information about the instrumental structure of action in the subpersonal first-person plural: one's own intentional acts and others' are gathered together (for simplicity, this is not depicted separately in Figure 6). Then, simulative mirroring with monitored

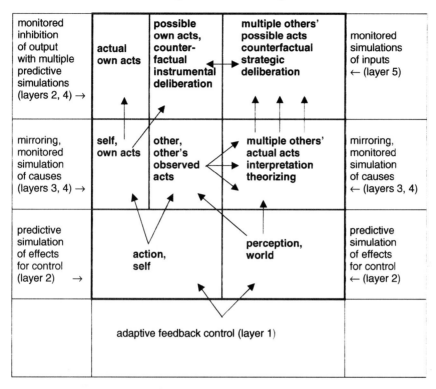

Fig. 6. Structure of enabling subpersonal informational resources.

inhibition of copying overlays a basic self/other distinction on intersubjective information about intentional action, providing information for the active perception of the actions of others. The self/other distinction is thus at its informational base a distinction between self and others as intentional agents, i.e, the agents of instrumentally structured actions. Independently of mirroring, simulative prediction for improved control combined with monitored inhibition of output makes available information about the results of alternative possible acts by the agent and the distinction between actual and possible acts, providing counterfactual information that can enable instrumental deliberation. Finally, monitored simulation of inputs adds counterfactual information about the results of possible acts by others, enabling strategic deliberation. Capacities for interpretation and theorizing may build on the fundamental simulative resources for action understanding and the self/other distinction, to fine-tune differentiations and identifications of multiple other intentional agents and the interactions of their and one's own multiple possible actions.

In considering how the shared circuits subpersonal functional architecture might map onto the neural and personal levels, care is needed to avoid over-simple interlevel projections and isomorphism assumptions. Here, the model may play a useful heuristic role even if it proves to be wrong in details. For example, looking down to the level of neural implementation, we can ask: where might the postulated comparators be located?[81] Are shared circuits for the results of action found in prefrontal areas while those for detailed movements are in parietal areas? Does the model bear any relationship to the distinction between ventral and dorsal processing streams? Does it cast any light on the presence and function of mirror neurons in Broca's area and their relation to linguistic capacities? I have sketched the dynamics of the shared circuits model in cybernetic terms, but if neural implementations can be found, their interactive behavior through time could be represented as the evolution of a phase space in the manner of dynamical systems theory, and its attractor structure investigated.

Looking up to the personal level, we can ask: What behavioral and cognitive predictions does the model provide? Intentional agents achieve their goals by means that can be given successively finer specifications, related by an asym-metrical "do x by doing y" relation: for example, I turn on the light by flipping the switch by moving my fingers. If we envisage a series of spectra with control of the ultimate result or goal of action at one extreme, and control of detailed fine movements that are the means to the result at the other extreme, then the shared circuits model could apply at successive linked points along such spectra. Thus the means outputted to the target of one circuit could be the target of the next circuit. A network of such linked circuits could enable hierarchical control of action while permitting the flexible decomposition and recombination of goals and means. What relationship might such recombinant flexibility have to the recombinant flexibility characteristic of language? What does the model suggest about the functional relationships among three distinctive human capacities, for imitation, mindreading, and language?[82] The shared circuits model has a cybernetic rather than a conceptual structure, yet it may provide informational resources for sophisticated cognitive abilities usually understood to display conceptual structure, such as the abilities to deceive and to cooperate, to interpret other minds, to use language, to deliberate and plan, and to reason instrumentally and counterfactually. The model thus has a bearing on issues about whether the subpersonal resources on which conceptual abilities depend must themselves have conceptual structure. What implications might it have for the issue of whether simulation approaches to mindreading require an inference

---

[81] PF? STS? Compare Rizzolatti (2005) and Iacoboni (2005).
[82] Cf. Rizzolatti and Arbib (1998); Iacoboni (2005); Meltzoff (2005).

from the first to the third person? What constraints does the model suggest on the relationships among various personal-level distinctions: between action and perception, between self and other, between the actual and the possible? Comparator structures play a prominent role in both the shared circuits model and in various recent approaches to consciousness; does this suggest any particular way of linking theories of consciousness and social cognition, or of updating social theories of consciousness?[83] Can the model play any role in distinguishing conscious and unconscious mental states and processes? How might the model be extended to include the perception of facial expression and the emotional mirroring postulated by various researchers?[84] Might the layers of the model usefully be mapped onto evolutionary or developmental stages, in theorizing the imitative and mindreading abilities of other animals or children?

I conclude by summarizing the shared circuits model. Theories about the control, imitative, and simulative functions of the mirror system, and evidence from imitation studies for ideomotor and common-coding theories, suggest that perception and action share a fundamental information space that is preserved as higher cognitive capacities and distinctions are built on it. The distinction between results and the means to those results, essential to goal-directed, perceptually-guided intentional action as well as to imitative learning, emerges as a flexible articulation of this shared processing. But perception remains fundamentally active, in a way that challenges orthodox views of perception and action as separately constituted and hence of perception as motivationally inert. The intersubjectivity characteristic of human beings, their distinctive capacity to understand and empathize with one another, emerges as a specialization of active perception: I perceive your action by means that engage my own potential for similar action, thus enabling me to understand, or to imitate, your action. Shared processing of the actions of other and self is a special aspect of the shared processing of perception and action. Within this informational structure, it is not so much that intersubjectivity bridges a self/other gap as that the self/other distinction is imposed on the fundamental information space that self and other share. At the subpersonal level, the problem of "knowledge" of other minds is reconfigured: it is neither one of starting from information about the self and constructing an inferential bridge across a gulf to information about other persons, nor one of starting from information about other persons and from the resources it provides somehow generating information about the self. Whether this subpersonal informational structure has implications for the epistemology of other minds at the personal level is a matter for further argument. Simulation theories of mindreading can be right about shared processing for self and other

---

[83] See and cf. Hesslow (2002); Frith et al. (2000); Gray (2004); Jeannerod (1997); Milner and Goodale (1995: 64).

[84] I have work in progress on this question. See Rizzolatti (2005), Gallese (2005); Iacoboni (2005); Decety and Chaminade (2005); see also Hesslow (2002), which I am grateful to John Cummins for drawing to my attention.

with respect to this fundamental intersubjectivity, even if more advanced aspects of mindreading require theorizing, in ways enabled by language.

I have emphasized three noteworthy aspects of the shared circuits model. First, it distils a shared intersubjective space (enabling imitation, intersubjective empathy, and action understanding) from a shared information space for action and perception (understood in terms of control processes). Second, it illustrates how the distinctions between perception and action, between self and other, and between the actual and the possible can be imposed on these shared information spaces. These informational distinctions play important roles in enabling the mental life characteristic of persons. In particular, the shared intersubjective space for information about intentional agents in the subpersonal 'first-person plural' is prior to the self/other distinction. The shared circuits model gives concrete form to the interdependence and parity of information about self and other minds. Finally, the shared circuits model avoids the classical sandwich and illustrates an alternative *horizontally modular* architecture.[85] On this view, perception and action are dynamically co-enabled and cognitively significant resources—such as the self/other and possible/actual distinctions, and information for action understanding and planning—emerge from the information space that perception and action share.

[85] Hurley (1998, 2001); see also Brooks (1999).

REFERENCES

Adolphs, Ralph. (2002), "Recognizing emotion from facial expressions: Psychological and neurological mechanisms," *Behavioral and Cognitive Neuroscience Reviews* 1: 21–61.

Akins, C. and Zentall, T. (1996), "Imitative learning in male Japanese quail (*Conturnix japonica*) using the two-action method," *Journal of Comparative Psychology* 110: 316–20.

Akins, C. and Zentall, T. (1998), "Imitation in Japanese quail: The role of reinforcement of demonstrator responding," *Psychonomic Bulletin & Review* 5: 694–7.

Akins, C., Klein, E., and Zentall, T. (2002), "Imitative learning in Japanese quail (*Conturnix japonica*) using the bidirectional control procedure," *Animal Learning & Behavior* 30: 275–81.

Anisfeld, Moshe. (1979), "Interpreting 'imitative' responses in early infancy," *Science* 205: 214–15.

Anisfeld, Moshe. (1984), *Language Development from Birth to Three* (Hillsdale, NJ: Erlbaum).

Anisfeld, Moshe. (1991), "Neonatal imitation," *Developmental Review* 11: 60–97.

Anisfeld, Moshe. (1996), "Only tongue protrusion modeling is matched by neonates," *Developmental Review* 16: 149–61.

Anisfeld, Moshe. (2005), "No compelling evidence to dispute Piaget's timetable of the development of representational imitation in infancy," in S. Hurley and N. Chater (eds) (2005a): vol. 2, 107–31.

Anisfeld, M., Turkewitz, G., Rose, S., Rosenberg, F., Sheiber, F., Couturier-Fagan, D., Ger, J., and Sommer, I. (2001), "No compelling evidence that newborns imitate oral gestures," *Infancy* 2: 111–22.

Arbib, Michael. (2002), "The mirror system, imitation, and the evolution of language," in K. Dautenhahn and C. Nehaniv (eds) (2002), *Imitation in Animals and Artifacts*: 229–80.

Arbib, Michael (2005), "From monkey-like action recognition to human language: an evolutionary framework for neurolinguistics, behavioral and brain sciences," *Behavioral and Brain Sciences* 28: 105–124.

Arbib, M., Billard, A., Iacoboni, M., and Oztop, E. (2000), "Synthetic brain imaging: grasping, mirror neurons and imitation," *Neural Networks* 13: 975–97.

Arbib, M. and Rizzolatti, G. (1997), "Neural expectations: a possible evolutionary path from manual skills to language," *Communication and Cognition* 29: 393–424; reprinted in P. van Loocke (ed.) (1999), *The Nature of Concepts: Evolution, Structure, and Representation* (London: Routledge): 128–54.

Baldwin, D. (1995), "Understanding the link between joint attention and language," in C. Moore and P. Dunham (eds), *Joint Attention: Its Origin and Role in Development* (Hillsdale, NJ: Erlbaum): 131–58.

Baldwin, J. (1896), "A new factor in evolution," *American Naturalist* 30: 441–51, 536–53.

Bargh, John. (1997), "The automaticity of everyday life," in R. Wyer (ed.), *Advances in Social Cognition*, vol. 10 (Mahwah, NJ: Erlbaum): 1–61.

Bargh, John. (1999), "The most powerful manipulative messages are hiding in plain sight," *The Chronicle of Higher Education* (January 29): B6.

Bargh, John. (2005), "Bypassing the will: towards demystifying the nonconscious control of social behavior," in R. Hassin, J. Uleman, and J. Bargh (eds), *The New Unconscious* (New York: Oxford University Press).

Bargh, J. and Chartrand, T. (1999), "The unbearable automaticity of being," *American Psychologist* 54 (7)(July): 462–79.

Bargh, J., Chen, M., and Burrows, L. (1996), "The automaticity of social behavior: direct effects of trait concept and stereotype activation on action," *Journal of Personality and Social Psychology* 71: 230–44.

Bargh, J., Gollwitzer, P., Lee-Chai, A., Barndollar, K., and Trötschel, R. (2001), "The automated will: nonconscious activation and pursuit of behavioral goals," *Journal of Personality and Social Psychology* 81: 1014–27.

Bavelas, J., Black, A., Lemery, C., and Mullett, J. (1987), "Motor mimicry as primitive empathy," in N. Eisenberg and J. Strayer (eds), *Empathy and Its Development* (Cambridge: Cambridge University Press): 317–38.

Bekkering, H. and Wohlschläger, A. (2002), "Action perception and imitation: a tutorial," in W. Prinz and B. Hommel (eds), *Attention & performance XIX. Common Mechanisms in Perception and Action* (Oxford: Oxford University Press): 294–314.

Blackmore, Susan. (1999), *The Meme Machine* (Oxford: Oxford University Press).

Blackmore, Susan. (2000), "The meme's eye view," in R. Aunger (ed.), *Darwinizing Culture: The Status of Memetics as a Science* (Oxford and New York: Oxford University Press): 25–42.

Blackmore, Susan. (2001), "Evolution and memes: the human brain as a selective imitation device," *Cybernetics and Systems* 32: 225–55.

Blakemore, S. and Decety, J. (2001), "From the perception of action to the understanding of intention," *Nature Reviews Neuroscience* 2: 561–7.

Boyd, R. and Richerson, P. (1982), "Cultural transmission and the evolution of cooperative behavior," *Human Ecology* 10: 325–51.

Boyd, Robert and Richerson, Peter. (1985), *Culture and the Evolutionary Process* (Chicago: University of Chicago Press).

Boyd, R. and Richerson, P. (2000), "Memes: universal acid or a better mousetrap?," in R. Aunger (ed.), *Darwinizing Culture: The Status of Memetics as a Science* (Oxford and New York: Oxford University Press): 143–62.

Brass, M. (1999), "Imitation and ideomotor compatibility" (unpublished dissertation, University of Munich, Germany).

Brass, M., Bekkering, H., and Prinz, W. (2001), "Movement observation affects movement execution in a simple response task," *Acta Psychologica* 106: 3–22.

Brooks, Rodney. (1999), *Cambrian Intelligence* (Cambridge, Mass.: MIT Press).

Byrne, Richard. (1995), *The Thinking Ape: Evolutionary Origins of Intelligence* (Oxford: Oxford University Press).

Byrne, Richard. (1998), "Imitation: the contributions of priming and program-level copying," in S. Braten, (ed.), *Intersubjective Communication and Emotion in Early Ontogeny* (Cambridge: Cambridge University Press): 228–44.

Byrne, Richard. (1999), "Imitation without intentionality. Using string parsing to copy the organization of behavior," *Animal Cognition* 2: 63–72.

Byrne, Richard. (2002a), "Imitation of complex novel actions: what does the evidence from animals mean?," *Advances in the Study of Behavior* 31: 77–105.

Byrne, Richard. (2002b), "Seeing actions as hierarchically organized structures: great ape manual skills," in A. Meltzoff and W. Prinz (eds) (2001): 122–40.

Byrne, Richard. (2005), "Detecting, understanding, and explaining animal imitation," in S. Hurley and N. Chater (eds) (2005a): vol. 1, 225–42.

Byrne, R. and Russon, A. (1998), "Learning by imitation: a hierarchical approach," *Behavioral and Brain Sciences* 21: 667–721.

Byrne, Richard and Whiten, Andrew (eds) (1988), *Machiavellian Intelligence: Social Expertise and the Evolution of Intellect in Monkeys, Apes and Humans* (Oxford: Oxford University Press).

Call, J. and Carpenter, M. (2002), "Three sources of information in social learning," in K. Dautenhahn and C. Nehaniv (eds) (2002): 211–28.

Call, J., Agnetta, B., and Tomasello, M. (2000), "Social cues that chimpanzees do and do not use to find hidden objects," *Animal Cognition* 3: 23–34.

Call, J. and Tomasello, M. (1994), "The social learning of too use by orangutans (Pongo pygmaeus)," *Human Evolution* 9: 297–313.

Call, J. and Tomasello, M. (1999), "A nonverbal theory of mind test: the performance of children and apes," *Child Development* 70: 381–95.

Carpenter, M., Akhtar, N., and Tomasello, M. (1998), "Fourteen- through 18-month-old infants differentially imitate intentional and accidental actions," *Infant Behavior & Development* 21: 315–30.

Carpenter, M., Call, J., and Tomasello, M. (forthcoming), "Understanding 'prior intentions' enables 2-year-olds to imitatively learn a complex task," *Child Development.*

Carpenter, M., Tomasello, M., and Savage-Rumbaugh, S. (1995), "Joint attention and imitative learning in children, chimpanzees, and enculturated chimpanzees," *Social Development* 4: 217–37.

Carruthers, Peter and Smith, Peter (eds) (1996), *Theories of Theories of Mind* (Cambridge: Cambridge University Press).

Chartrand, T. and Bargh, J. (1999), "The chameleon effect: the perception-behavior link and social interaction," *Journal of Personality and Social Psychology* 76: 893–910.

Chartrand, T., Maddux, W., and Lakin, J. (2005), "Beyond the perception-behavior link: the ubiquitous utility and motivational moderators of nonconscious mimicry," in R. Hassin, J. Uleman and J. Bargh (eds), *The New Unconscious.* (New York: Oxford University Press).

Christiansen, Morten. (1994), "Infinite languages, finite minds: connectionism, learning and linguistic structure" (Unpublished Ph.D. dissertation. University of Edinburgh).

Christiansen, Morten. (2005), "On the relation between language and (mimetic) culture," in S. Hurley and N. Chater (eds) (2005a): vol. 2, 391–6.

Christiansen, M., Dale, R., Ellefson, M., and Conway, C. (2002), "The role of sequential learning in language evolution: computational and experimental studies," in A. Cangelosi and D. Parisi (eds), *Simulating the Evolution of Language* (London: Springer-Verlag), 165–87.

Craighero, L., Buccino, G., and Rizzolatti, G. (2002), "Speech listening specifically modulates the excitability of tongue muscles: a TMS study," *European Journal of Neuroscience* 15: 399–402.

Dautenhahn, Kirsten and Nehaniv, Chrystopher L. (eds) (2002), *Imitation in Animals and Artifacts.* (Cambridge, Mass.: MIT Press).

Davies, Martin and Stone, Tony. (eds)(1995a), *Folk Psychology* (Oxford: Blackwell).

Davies, Martin and Stone, Tony. (eds)(1995b) *Mental Simulation* (Oxford: Blackwell).

Dawkins, Richard. (1976/1989), *The Selfish Gene* (Oxford: Oxford University Press).

Dawkins, Richard. (1982), *The Extended Phenotype* (Oxford: Oxford University Press).

Deacon, Terence. (1997), *The Symbolic Species: The Coevolution of Language and the Human Brain* (London: Penguin Books; New York: Norton).

Decety, Jean. (2002), "Neurophysiological evidence for simulation of action," in J. Dokic and J. Proust (eds), *Simulation and Knowledge of Action* (Philadelphia: Benjamins Publishing Company): 53–72.

Decety, J. and Chaminade, T. (2003), "Neural correlates of feeling sympathy," *Neuropsychologia* 41(2): 127–38.

Decety, J. and Chaminade, T. (2005), "The neurophysiology of imitation and inter-subjectivity," in S. Hurley and N. Chater (eds) (2005a): vol. 1, 119–40.

Decety, J. and Grèzes, J. (1999), "Neural mechanisms subserving the perception of human actions," *Trends in Cognitive Sciences* 3: 172–8.

Decety, J., Grèzes, J., Costes, N., Perani, D., Jeannerod, M., Procyk, E., Grassi, F., and Fazio, F. (1997), " 'Brain activity during observation of action,' Influence of action content and subject's strategy," *Brain* 120: 1763–77.

Dennett, Daniel. (1969), *Content and Consciousness* (London: Routledge).

Dennett, Daniel. (1995), *Darwin's Dangerous Idea: Evolution and the Meanings of Life.* (New York: Simon & Schuster; London: Penguin).

Dijksterhuis, Ap. (2005), "Why we are social animals: the high road to imitation as social glue," in S. Hurley and N. Chater (eds) (2005a): vol. 2, 207–20.

Dijksterhuis, A. and Bargh, J. (2001), "The perception–behavior expressway: automatic effects of social perception on social behavior," *Advances in Experimental Social Psychology* 33, 1–40.

Dijksterhuis, A. and van Knippenberg, A. (1998), "The relation between perception and behavior or how to win a game of Trivial Pursuit," *Journal of Personality and Social Psychology* 74: 865–77.

Eidelberg, L. (1929), "Experimenteller beitrag zum Mechanismus der Imitationsbewewung," *Jahresbucher fur Psychiatrie und Neurologie* 45: 170–3.

Fadiga, L., Craighero, L., Buccino, G., and Rizzolatti, G. (2002), "Speech listening specifically modulates the excitability of tongue muscles: a TMS study," *European Journal of Neuroscience* 15: 399–402.

Fadiga, L., Fogassi, L., Pavesi, G., and Rizzolatti, G. (1995), "Motor facilitation during action observation: a magnetic stimulation study," *Journal of Neurophysiology* 73: 2608–11.

Flanagan, J., Vetter, P., Johanson, R., and Wolpert, D. (2003), "Prediction precedes control in motor learning," *Current Biology* 13: 146–50.

Frith C., Blakemore S., and Wolpert D. (2000), "Abnormalities in the awareness and control of action," *Philosophical Transactions of the Royal Society* B, Biological Sciences, 355: 1771–88.

Galef, Bennett. (1988), "Imitation in animals: history, definition and interpretation of data from the psychological laboratory," in T. Zentall and B. Galef (eds), *Social Learning: Psychological and Biological Perspectives* (Hillsdale, NJ: Erlbaum): 3–28.

Galef, Bennett. (1998), "Recent progress in the study of imitation and social learning in animals," in M. Sabourin, F. Craik and M. Roberts (eds), *Advances in Psychological Science, Vol. 2: Biological and Cognitive Aspects* (Hove, Sussex: Psychological Press): 275–9.

Galef, Bennett. (2005), "Breathing new life into the study of animal imitation: what and when do chimpanzees imitate?," in S., Hurley and N. Chater (eds) (2005a): vol.1 295–7.

Gallese, Vittorio. (2000), "The inner sense of action: agency and motor representations," *Journal of Consciousness Studies* 7(10): 23–40.

Gallese, Vittorio. (2001), "The 'shared manifold' hypothesis: from mirror neurons to empathy," *Journal of Consciousness Studies* 8: 33–50.

Gallese, Vittorio. (2003), "The manifold nature of interpersonal relations: the quest for a common mechanism," *Philosophical Transactions of the Royal Society of London* 358: 517–28.

Gallese, Vittorio. (2005), " 'Being like me': self–other identity, mirror neurons and empathy," in S. Hurley and N. Chater (eds) (2005a): vol. 1, 101–18.

Gallese, V. and Goldman, A. (1998), "Mirror neurons and the simulation theory of mind-reading," *Trends in Cognitive Sciences* 2: 493–501.

Gergely, G., Bekkering, H., and Király, I. (2002), "Rational imitation in preverbal infants," *Nature* 415: 755.

Gerrans, Phillip (forthcoming), *The Measure of Madness: Philosophy and Cognitive Neuropsychiatry* (Cambridge, Mass.: MIT Press).

Gibson, James. (1986), *The Ecological Approach to Visual Perception* (Hillsdale, N.J.: Lawrence Erlbaum Associates).

Gil-White, Francisco. (2005), "Common misunderstandings of memes (and genes). The promise and the limits of the genetic analogy to cultural transmission processes," in S. Hurley and N. Chater (eds) (2005a): vol. 2, 317–38.

Goldman, Alvin. (1989), "Interpretation psychologized," *Mind and Language* 4: 161–85.

Goldman, Alvin. (1992), "In defense of the simulation theory," *Mind and Language* 7: 104–19.

Goldman, Alvin. (2005), "Imitation, mind-reading, and simulation," in S. Hurley and N. Chater (eds) (2005a): vol. 2, 79–93.

Gordon, Robert. (1986), "Folk psychology as simulation," *Mind and Language* 1: 159–71.

Gordon, Robert. (1995a), "Simulation without introspection or inference from me to you," in M. Davies and T. Stone (eds) (1995b): 53–67.

Gordon, Robert. (1995b), "Sympathy, simulation and the impartial spectator," *Ethics* 105: 727–42.

Gordon, Robert. (1996), " 'Radical' simulationism," in P. Carruthers and P. Smith (eds.) (1996): 11–21.

Gordon, Robert. (2002), "Simulation and reason explanation: the radical view," *Special Issue of Philosophical Topics* 29.

Gordon, Robert. (2005), "Intentional agents like myself," in S. Hurley and N. Chater (eds) (2005a): vol. 2, 95–106.

Gray, Jeffrey (2004), *Consciousness: Creeping up on the Hard Problem* (Oxford: Oxford University Press).

Graziano, M., Taylor, C., Moore, T., and Cooke, D. (2002), "The cortical control of movement revisited," *Neuron* 36: 349–62.

Greenwald, A. (1970), "Sensory feedback mechanisms in performance control: with special reference to the ideo-motor mechanism," *Psychological Review* 77: 73–99.

Greenwald, A. (1972), "On doing two things at once: time sharing as a function of ideomotor compatibility," *Journal of Experimental Psychology* 94: 52–7.

Grush, Rick (1995), *Emulation and Cognition* (Doctoral dissertation, Department of Philosophy, University of California at San Diego).

Grush, Rick (2004), "The emulation theory of representation: motor control, imagery, and perception," *Behavioral and Brain Sciences* 27: 377–42.

Hare, B., Call, J., Agnetta, B., and Tomasello, M. (2000), "Chimpanzees know what conspecifics do and do not see," *Animal Behaviour* 59: 771–85.

Hare, B., Call, J., and Tomasello, M. (2001), "Do chimpanzees know what conspecifics know and do not know?," *Animal Behaviour* 61: 139–51.

Hari, R., Forss, N., Avikainen, S., Kirveskari, E., Salenius, S., and Rizzolatti, G. (1998), "Activation of human primary motor cortex during action observation: a neuro-magnetic study," *Proceedings National Academy of Science, USA* 95: 15061–5.

Harris, P. and Want, S. (2005), "On learning what not to do: the emergence of selective imitation in young children's tool use," in S. Hurley and N. Chater (eds) (2005a): vol. 2, 148–62.

Haruno, M., Wolpert, D., and Kawato, M. (2001), "Mosaic model for sensorimotor learning and control," *Neural Computation* 13: 2201–20.

Heiser, M., Iacoboni, M., Maeda, F., Marcus, J., and Mazziotta, J. C. (2003), "The essential role of Broca's area in imitation," *European Journal of Neuroscience* 17: 1123–8.

Henrich, J. and Boyd R. (1998), "The evolution of conformist transmission and the emergence of between-group differences," *Evolution and Human Behavior* 19: 215–41.

Henrich, J. and Gil-White F. (2001), "The evolution of prestige: freely conferred status as a mechanism for enhancing the benefits of cultural transmission," *Evolution and Human Behavior* 22: 165–96.

Herman, Louis. (2002), "Vocal, social, and self-imitation by bottlenosed dolphins," in K. Dautenhahn and C. Nehaniv (eds) (2002): 63–106.

Hesslow, Germund. (2002), "Conscious thought as simulation of behaviour and perception," *Trends in Cognitive Sciences* 6: 242–7.

Heyes, Cecelia. (1993), "Imitation, culture and cognition," *Animal Behaviour* 46: 999–1010.

Heyes, Cecelia. (1996), "Genuine imitation?," in C. Heyes and B. Galef Jr. (eds) (1996): 371–89.

Heyes, Cecelia. (1998), "Theory of mind in nonhuman primates," *Behavioral and Brain Sciences* 21: 101–14.

Heyes, Cecelia. (2001), "Causes and consequences of imitation," *Trends in Cognitive Sciences* 5: 253–61.

Heyes, Cecelia. (2005), "Imitation by association," in S. Hurley and N. Chater (eds) (2005a): vol. 1, 157–76.

Heyes, C. and Dickinson, A. (1993), "The intentionality of animal action," in M. Davies and G. Humphreys (eds), *Consciousness* (Oxford: Blackwell).

Heyes, Cecilia and Galef, C. Bennett (eds). (1996), *Social Learning in Animals: The Roots of Culture* (San Diego: Academic Press).

Howard, John. (1988), "Co-operation in the prisoner's dilemma," *Theory and Decision* 24: 203–13.

Hunt, G. and Gray, R. (2003), "Diversification and cumulative evolution in New Caledonian crow tool manufacture," *Proceedings of the Royal Society London B* 270, 867–74 (DOI 10.1098/rspb.2002.22 99).

Hurley, S. L. (1989), *Natural Reasons* (New York: Oxford University Press).

Hurley, S. L. (1998), *Consciousness in Action* (Cambridg, Mass.: Harvard University Press).

Hurley, Susan. (2001), "Perception and action: alternative views," *Synthese* 291: 3–40.

Hurley, Susan. (2003a), "Animal action in the space of reasons," *Mind and Language* 18: 231–56. Susan Hurley and Matthew Nudds (eds), (2006)(Oxford: Oxford University Press).

Hurley, Susan. (2003b), "The limits of individualism are not the limits of rationality," *Behavioral and Brain Sciences* 26 (2): 164–5.

Hurley, Susan. (2005a), "The shared circuits hypothesis: a unified functional architecture for control, imitation, and simulation," in S. Hurley and N. Chater (eds), (2005a) vol. 1, 176–93.

Hurley, Susan. (2005b), "Social heuristics that make us smarter," *Philosophical Psychology* 18: 585–611.

Hurley, Susan. and Chater, Nick. (eds) (2005a), *Perspectives on Imitation: From Neuroscience to Social Science*, 2 vol (Cambridge, Mass.: MIT Press).

Hurley, Susan. and Chater, Nick. (2005b), "The importance of imitation," in S. Hurley and N. Chater (eds) (2005a): vol 1. 1–52.

Hurley, Susan and Noë, Alva. (2003), "Neural plasticity and consciousness," *Biology and Philosophy* 18: 131–68.

Hurley, Susan and Nudds, Matthew (eds), (2006), *Rational Animals?* (Oxford: Oxford University Press).

Iacoboni, Marco. (2005), "Understanding others: imitation, language, empathy," in S. Hurley and N. Chater (2005a): vol. 1, 77–99.

Iacoboni, M., Woods, R., Brass, M., Bekkering, H., Mazziotta, J., and Rizzolatti, G. (1999), "Cortical mechanisms of human imitation," *Science* 286: 2526–8.

James, William. (1890), *Principles of Psychology* (New York: Holt).

Jeannerod, Marc. (1997), *The Cognitive Neuroscience of Action* (Oxford: Blackwell).

Jeannerod, Marc. (2001), "Neural simulation of action: A unifying mechanism for motor cognition," *Neuroimage* 14: S103-S109.

Kinsbourne, Marcel. (2005), "Imitation as entrainment: brain mechanisms and social consequences," in S. Hurley and N. Chater (eds) (2005a): vol. 2, 163–72.

Lhermitte, F. (1983), " 'Utilization behaviour' and its relation to lesions of the frontal lobes," *Brain* 106: 237–55.

Lhermitte, F. (1986), "Human autonomy and the frontal lobes, Part II," *Annals of Neurology* 19: 335–43.

Lhermitte, F., Pillon, B., and Serdaru, M. (1986), "Human autonomy and the frontal lobes, Part I," *Annals of Neurology* 19: 326–34.

McDowell, John.(1994), "The content of perceptual experience," *Philosophical Quarterly* 44: 190–205.

Meltzoff, Andrew. (1988), "Infant imitation after a 1-week delay: long-term memory for novel acts and multiple stimuli," *Developmental Psychology* 24: 470–6.

Meltzoff, Andrew. (1990), "Foundations for developing a concept of self: the role of imitation in relating self to other and the value of social mirroring, social modeling, and self practice in infancy," in D. Cicchetti and M. Beeghly (eds), *The Self in Transition: Infancy to Childhood* (Chicago: University of Chicago Press): 139–64.

Meltzoff, Andrew. (1995), "Understanding of the intentions of others: re-enactment of intended acts by 18-month-old children," *Developmental Psychology* 31: 838–50.

Meltzoff, Andrew. (1996), "The human infant as imitative generalist: a 20-year progress report on infant imitation with implications for comparative psychology," in C. Heyes and Bagalef (eds) (1996): 347–70.

Meltzoff, Andrew. (1999), "Origins of theory of mind, cognition, and communication," *Journal of Communication Disorders* 32: 251–69.

Meltzoff, Andrew. (2002a), "Elements of a developmental theory of imitation," in A. Meltzoff and W. Prinz (eds) (2001):19–41.

Meltzoff, Andrew. (2002b), "Imitation as a mechanism of social cognition: origins of empathy, theory of mind, and the representation of action," in U. Goswami (ed.), *Handbook of Childhood Cognitive Development* (Oxford: Blackwell): 6–25.

Meltzoff, Andrew. (2005), "Imitation and other minds: the 'like me' hypothesis," in S. Hurley and N. Chater (eds) (2005a): vol. 2, 55–77

Meltzoff, A. and Decety, J. (2003), "What imitation tells us about social cognition: a rapproachment between developmental psychology and cognitive neuroscience," *Philosophical Transactions of the Royal Society B* 358: 491–500.

Meltzoff, A. and Moore, M. (1977), "Imitation of facial and manual gestures by human neonates," *Science* 198: 75–8.

Meltzoff, A. and Moore, M. (1979), "Note responding to Anisfeld, Masters, and Jacobson and Kagan's comments on Meltzoff and Moore (1977)," *Science* 205: 217–19.

Meltzoff, A. and Moore, M. (1983a), "Imitation of facial and manual gestures by human neonates," *Science* 198: 75–8.

Meltzoff, A. and Moore, M. (1983b), "Newborn infants imitate adult facial gestures," *Child Development* 54: 702–9.

Meltzoff, A. and Moore, M. (1983c), "The origins of imitation in infancy: paradigm, phenomena, and theories," in L. Lipsitt and C. Rovee-Collier (eds), *Advances in Infancy Research*, vol. 2 (Norwood, NJ: Ablex): 265–301.

Meltzoff, A. and Moore, M. (1989), "Imitation in newborn infants: exploring the range of gestures imitated and the underlying mechanisms," *Developmental Psychology* 25: 954–62.

Meltzoff, A. and Moore, M. (1992), "Early imitation within a functional framework: the importance of person identity, movement, and development," *Infant Behavior and Development* 15: 479–505.

Meltzoff, A. and Moore, M. (1994), "Imitation, memory, and the representation of persons," *Infant Behavior and Development* 17: 83–99.

Meltzoff, A. and Moore, M. (1995), "Infants' understanding of people and things: from body imitation to folk psychology," in J. Bermúdez, A. Marcel and N. Eilan (eds) *Body and the Self* (Cambridge, Mass: MIT Press): 43–69.

Meltzoff, A. and Moore, M. (1997), "Explaining facial imitation: a theoretical model," *Early Development and Parenting* 6: 179–92.

Meltzoff, A. and Moore, M. (1998), "Infant intersubjectivity: broadening the dialogue to include imitation, identity and intention," in S. Braten (ed.), *Intersubjective Communication and Emotion in Early Ontogeny* (Cambridge: Cambridge University Press): 47–62.

Meltzoff, A. and Moore, M. (1999a), "Persons and representations: why infant imitation is important for theories of human development," in J. Nadel and G. Butterworth (eds), *Imitation in Infancy. Cambridge Studies in Cognitive and Perceptual Development* (Cambridge: Cambridge University Press): 9–35.

Meltzoff, A. and Moore, M. (1999b), "Resolving the debate about early imitation," in A. Slater and D. Muir (eds.), *The Blackwell Reader in Development Psychology* (Malden, Mass.: Blackwell): 151–5.

Meltzoff, A. and Moore, M. (2000), "Resolving the debate about early imitation," in D. Muir (ed.), *Infant Development: The Essential Readings* (Malden, Mass.: Blackwell): 167–81.

Meltzoff, A. and Prinz, W., (eds) (2001), *The Imitative Mind: Development, Evolution, and Brain Bases* (Cambridge: Cambridge University Press).

Milgram, S. (1963), "Behavioral study of obedience," *Journal of Abnormal and Social Psychology* 67: 371–8.

Millikan, Ruth. (2005), "Some reflections on the simulation theory–theory theory debate," in S. Hurley and N. Chater (eds) (2005a): vol. 2, 182–8

Millikan, Ruth. (2006), "Styles of rationality," in S. Hurley and M. Nudds, (eds) (2006).

Milner, A. David and Goodale, Melvyn (1995), *The Visual Brain in Action* (Oxford: Oxford University Press).

Nadel, Jacqueline and Butterworth, George (1999), *Imitation in Infancy* (Cambridge: Cambridge University Press).

Nagell, K., Olguin, R., and Tomasello, M. (1993), "Processes of social learning in the tool use of chimpanzees (*Pan troglodytes*) and human children (*Homo sapiens*)," *Journal of Comparative Psychology* 107: 174–86.

Nehaniv, C. and Dautenhahn, K. (2002), "The correspondence problem," in K. Dautenhahn and C. Nehaniv (eds) (2002): 42–61.

O'Regan, Kevin and Noë, Alva. (2001a), "A sensorimotor account of vision and visual consciousness," *Behavioral and Brain Sciences* 24: 883–917.

O'Regan, Kevin and Noë, Alva. (2001b), "Acting out our sensory experience," *Behavioral and Brain Sciences* 24: 955–75.

O'Regan, Kevin and Noë, Alva. (2001c), "What it is like to see: a sensorimotor theory of perceptual experience," *Synthese* 129: 79–103.

Oztop, E. and Arbib, M. (2002), "Schema design and implementation of the grasp-related mirror neuron system," *Biological Cybernetics* 87:116–40.

Pascual-Leone, A. (2001), "The brain that plays music and is changed by it," *Annals of the New York Academy of Sciences* 930: 315–29.

Pepperberg, Irene. (1999). *The Alex Studies: Cognitive and Communicative Studies on Grey Parrots* (Cambridge, Mass.: Harvard University Press).

Pepperberg, Irene. (2002), "Allospecific referential speech acquisition in grey parrots (*psittacus erithacus*): evidence for multiple levels of avian vocal imitation," in K. Dautenhahn and C. Nehaniv (eds) (2002): 109–31.

Pepperberg, Irene. (2005), "Insights into vocal imitation in grey parrots (*Psittacus erithacus*)," in S. Hurley and N. Chater (eds) (2005a): vol. 1, 243–62.

Peterson, G. and Trapold, M. (1982), "Expectancy mediation of concurrent conditional discriminations," *American Journal of Psychology* 95: 571–80.

Povinelli, Daniel. (1996), "Chimpanzee theory of mind?," in P. Carruthers and P. Smith (eds) (1996): 293–329.

Povinelli, Daniel. (2000), *Folk Physics for Apes* (Oxford: Oxford University Press).

Povinelli, Daniel and Vonk, Jennifer. (2006), "We don't need a microscope to explore the chimpanzee's mind," in S. Hurley and M. Nudds (eds) (2006).

Povinelli, D. and Giambrone, S. (1999), "Inferring other minds: failure of the argument by analogy," *Philosophical Topics* 27: 167–201.

Preston, S. and de Waal, F. (forthcoming), "Empathy: its ultimate and proximate bases," *Behavioral and Brain Sciences*.

Prinz, Jesse. (2005), "Imitation and moral development," in S. Hurley and N. Chater (eds) (2005a): vol. 2, 267–82.

Prinz, Wolfgang. (1984), "Modes of linkage between perception and action," in W. Prinz and A. F. Sanders (eds), *Cognition and Motor Processes* (Berlin & Heidelberg: Springer): 185–93.

Prinz, Wolfgang. (1987), "Ideomotor action," in H. Heuer and A. Sanders (eds), *Perspectives on Perception and Action* (Hillsdale, NJ: Erlbaum): 47–76.

Prinz, Wolfgang. (1990), "A common-coding approach to perception and action," in O. Neumann and W. Prinz (eds), *Relationships between Perception and Action: Current Approaches* (Berlin and New York: Springer): 167–201.

Prinz, Wolfgang. (1997), "Perception and action planning," *European Journal of Cognitive Psychology* 9: 129–54.

Prinz, Wolfgang. (2001), "Experimental approaches to imitation," in A. Meltzoff and W. Prinz (eds) (2001): 143–62.

Prinz, Wolfgang. (2005), "An ideomotor approach to imitation," in S. Hurley and N. Chater (eds) (2005a): vol. 1, 141–56.

Proust, Joelle. (2003), "Thinking of oneself as the same," *Consciousness and Cognition* 12: 495–509.

Regan, Donald. (1980), *Utilitarianism and Co-operation* (Oxford: Clarendon Press).

Rizzolatti, Giacomo. (2005), "The mirror neuron system and imitation," in S. Hurley and N. Chater (eds) (2005a): vol. 1, 55–76.

Rizzolatti, G. and Arbib, M. (1998), "Language within our grasp," *Trends in Neuroscience* 21: 188–94.

Rizzolatti, G. and Arbib, M. (1999), "From grasping to speech: imitation might provide a missing link: reply," *Trends in Neuroscience* 22: 152.

Rizzolatti, G., Camarda, R., Fogassi, M., Gentilucci, M., Luppino, G., and Matelli, M. (1988), "Functional organization of inferior area 6 in the macaque monkey: II. Area F5 and the control of distal movements," *Experimental Brain Research* 71: 491–507.

Rizzolatti, G., Fadiga, L., Fogassi, L., and Gallese, V. (2002), "From mirror neurons to imitation: facts and speculations," in A. Meltzoff and W. Prinz (eds) (2001): 247–66.

Stamenov, Maxim and Gallese, Vittorio (eds). (2002), *Mirror Neurons and the Evolution of Brain and Language* (Amsterdam/Philadelphia: John Benjamins).

Strawson, P. F. (1959), *Individuals* (London: Methuen).

Strawson, P. F. (1966), *The Bounds of Sense* (London: Methuen).

Thorndike, E. (1898), "Animal intelligence: an experimental study of the associative process in animals," *Psychological Review and Monograph* 2: 551–3.

Tomasello, Michael. (1996), "Do apes ape?,", in C. Heyes and B. Galef (eds) (1996): 319–46.

Tomasello, Michael. (1998), "Emulation learning and cultural learning," *Behavioral and Brain Sciences* 21: 703–4.

Tomasello, Michael. (1999), *The Cultural Origins of Human Cognition* (Cambridge, Mass.: Harvard University Press).

Tomasello, Michael and Call, Josep (1997), *Primate Cognition* (Oxford: Oxford University Press).

Tomasello, M. and Call, J. (2006), "Do chimpanzees know what others see–or only what they are looking at?," in S. Hurley and M. Nudds (eds) (2006).

Tomasello, M. and Carpenter, M. (2005), "Intention-reading and imitative learning," in S. Hurley and N. Chater (eds) (2005a): vol. 2, 133–48.

Tomasello, M., Kruger, A. and Ratner, H. (1993), "Cultural learning," *Behavioral and Brain Sciences* 16: 495–552.

Voelkl, B. and Huber, L. (2000), "True imitation in marmosets," *Animal Behaviour* 60: 195–202.

Want, Stephen and Harris, Paul. (2001), "Learning from other people's mistakes: causal understanding in learning to use a tool," *Child Development* 72: 431–43.

Weir, A., Chappell, J., and Kacelnik, A. (2002), "Shaping of hooks in New Caledonain crows," *Science* 297: 981.

Whiten, Andrew. (1996), "When does smart behaviour-reading become mind-reading?," in P. Carruthers and P. Smith (eds) (1996): 277–92.

Whiten, Andrew (2002), "Imitation of sequential and hierarchical structure in action," in K. Dautenhahn and C. Nehaniv (eds), *Imiation in Animals and Artifacts* (Cambridge, Mass.: MIT Press), 191–209.

Whiten, Andrew and Byrne, Richard, (eds) (1997), *Machiavellian Intelligence II: Extensions and Evaluations* (Cambridge: Cambridge University Press).

Whiten, A., Custance, D., Gomez, J., Teixidor, P. and Bard, K. (1996), "Imitative learning of artificial fruit processing in children (*Homo sapiens*) and chimpanzees (*Pan troglodytes*)," *Journal of Comparative Psychology* 110: 3–14.

Whiten, A., Horner, V., and Marshall-Pescini, S. (2005), "Selective imitation in child and chimpanzee: A window on the construal of others' actions," in S. Hurley and N. Chater (eds) (2005a): vol. 1, 263–83.

Williams, J., Whiten, A., Suddendorf, T., and Perrett, D. (2001), "Imitation, mirror neurons and autism," *Neuroscience and Biobehavioral Reviews* 25: 287–95.

Wohlschläger, A., Gattis, M., and Bekkering, H. (forthcoming), "Action generation and action perception in imitation: An instantiation of the ideomotor principle," *The Philosophical Transactions of the Royal Society*.

Wolpert, Daniel. (1997), "Computational approaches to motor control," *Trends in Cognitive Sciences* 1: 209–16.

Wolpert, D. and Kawato, M. (1998), "Multiple paired forward and inverse models for motor control," *Neural Networks* 11: 1317–29.

Wolpert, D., Doya, K., and Kawato, M. (2003), "A unifying computational framework for motor control and social interaction," *Philosophical Transactions of the Royal Society of London, B* 358: 593–602.

Wolpert, D., Ghahramani, Z., and Jordan, M. (1995), "An internal model for sensor-imotor integration," *Science* 269: 1880–2.

Zentall, Thomas. (2001), "Imitation and other forms of social learning in animals: evidence, function, and mechanisms," *Cybernetics and Systems* 32: 53–96.

7

Better than Mere Knowledge? The Function of Sensory Awareness

Mark Johnston

Here I develop a certain sort of analogy between perception and digestion. Once we understand how sensory perception takes in items in the environment and "digests" them mentally, certain forms of skepticism loosen their grip on us. In order to appreciate the philosophical content of the analogy between perception and digestion, we need to work towards a new understanding of the function of sensory awareness.

Contemporary philosophy has no good answer to the question: what is the function of sensory awareness as opposed to immediate perceptual judgment? Because we lack the right answer, we have failed to finish off modern skepticism and the pernicious picture of the mind as a realm of private items.

THE WALLPAPER VIEW

A standard, but I think quite bad, answer to the question as to the function of sensory awareness is that sensory awareness provides us with sensations, raw feels or "qualia," items understood as: (a) *subjective*, in being ontologically dependent on the individual mind that is enjoying them; (b) *qualitative*, in that it makes sense both to ask what it is like to enjoy them, and, in a sense to be refined; (c) *mere accompaniments* of immediate perceptual judgment. Call the position that combines (a)–(c) "The Wallpaper View."

To get a feel for the import of that View consider a case in which one sees the moon as full, and so forms the immediate, which is to say *non-inferential*, judgment that the moon is full. According to the Wallpaper View, when sensing prompts one to make the immediate judgment that the moon is full, one typically is enjoying certain qualitative mental items that are perspective-determined

Thanks to the editors, Tamar Gendler and John Hawthorne, for their comments on an earlier draft.

mental counterparts of the moon's color and shape. These qualia are mere accompaniments of the immediate perceptual judgment that the moon is full in the sense that there is no *positive* epistemic connection between them and the process that issues in that immediate judgment.

The qualification—"no *positive* epistemic connection"—is meant to allow that the Wallpaper View can make sense of the *negative* epistemic impact of the loss or fading or inversion of qualia for a subject used to enjoying qualia: to wit, rational hesitancy in immediately forming such judgments as the judgment that the moon is full. For a subject used to enjoying sensory qualia, the loss or fading or inversion of qualia should be an alarm bell, a warning that things are far from normal. That certainly can have epistemic significance; in particular, it can provide a ground for withholding beliefs about the scene before the eyes, and, more generally, for withholding beliefs about the scenarios before the senses.

Nevertheless, what the Wallpaper View cannot explain is why subjects forever devoid of qualia, and so devoid of sensory experience as the View construes it, would *thereby* lack a license to immediately form beliefs about the scenarios before the senses, beliefs such as the belief that the moon is full. For the View has it that such immediate perceptual beliefs are not themselves *licensed, warranted, or justified* by any operation on the qualitative deliverances of sensory experience.

The Wallpaper View can consistently allow that typically the immediate perceptual judgment that the moon is full arises as a result of a reliable causal process in which the subject's qualia play a particular causal role. But an equally *reliable* process in which qualia play no causal role seems readily imaginable, and genuinely possible. It is the reliability of the two processes generating the judgment that the moon is full, plus perhaps the absence of evidence to the contrary, that confers warrant or justification on the judgment. So the Wallpaper View implies that a subject's judgment could have these epistemic properties even if his accompanying qualia are absent, or idiosyncratic, or faded, or faint, or systematically reversed with respect to the qualia enjoyed by all others.

Thus, on the Wallpaper View, when it comes to the epistemic status of immediate perceptual judgment, the deliverances of sensory awareness may be compared to the wallpaper or to the background music during a dinner. Neither the wallpaper nor the *tafelmusic* mediate a diner's ingestion of food, even if the diner might stop eating were the wallpaper to peel suddenly or the music to change volume abruptly. The Wallpaper View of the deliverances of sensory awareness makes sensory awareness a curious sideshow, a mere provider of sensation alongside the epistemically interesting perceptual act.

Even those who deny that our sensory experience is graced by qualia can be found endorsing the view that there could be no positive epistemic connection between sensory experience and immediate perceptual judgment or belief. This is often done by the solemn invocation of very general conceptual points that only a blunderer could have failed to notice. So Donald Davidson claims,

"Nothing can count as a reason for holding a belief except another belief,"[1] and follows up with these remarks:

the relation between a sensation and a belief cannot be logical since sensations are not beliefs or other propositional attitudes. What then is the relation? The answer I think is obvious: the relation is causal. Sensations cause some beliefs and in this sense are the basis or ground of those beliefs. But a causal explanation of a belief does not show how or why the belief is justified.[2]

There is no reason to suppose that Davidson thinks of the having of sensations as the enjoying of qualia. But, even so, he envisages no positive epistemic role for "sensations" to play.

The Wallpaper View, and this more general denial of the epistemic significance of "sensations," can both be understood as reactions against another bad view of the function of sensory awareness. On this other bad view, often suggested by classical formulations of the Sense Datum Theory, the structured qualia that sensory awareness provides are indeed supposed to be the epistemic bases for our most immediate perceptual judgments. The catastrophic upshot is that our immediate perceptual judgments, which concern how things in the environment stand, leap far beyond their sources or grounds, which are nothing more than private mental items. Someone who makes the immediate perceptual judgment that the moon is full typically knows that it is. How could he know this if his evidence was simply his enjoying a sense datum or structured quale?

Some once answered: By way of an argument to the best explanation of his sense data understood as evidence.[3] But we now know that this cannot be so. In the case at hand, where the subject makes the immediate judgment that the moon is full, the subject's immediate evidence is supposed to be his enjoying a "moonish" sense datum. The subject's being in that state is an effect, and any explanation of it in terms of external causes will be shaky and conjectural, because massively underdetermined by the effect being explained. Nor is it clear how, merely by drawing on one's "moonish" sense data, one can be in a position to consider the environment-involving hypotheses (e.g. thoughts about the moon, its rough and ready distance, and its illumination by the already set sun) that are supposed to explain the occurrence of one's "moonish" sense data. It is not just that sensation, as standardly conceived, is epistemically barren. So conceived, sensation is also unable to provide the rich, environment-involving contents which we immediately judge.

The view that sensory awareness plays no positive role in determining the epistemic status of immediate perceptual belief can thus be construed as a

---

[1] "A Coherence Theory of Truth and Knowledge," in *Truth and Interpretation*, ed. E. LePore and B. McGlauchlin (Oxford: Blackwell, 1986): p. 310.   [2] Ibid., p. 311.

[3] For classical statements of the view of sense data as epistemic starting points, see H. H. Price, *Perception* (London: Methuen, 1932) and A. J. Ayer, *The Problem of Knowledge* (Harmondsworth: Penguin, 1970).

strategic retreat from these epistemological failures of the classical Sense Datum Theory.

The view that sensory awareness plays no positive epistemic role, sometimes combined with the more specific Wallpaper View, frequently operates as a powerful structuring assumption in discussions of sensory awareness. The psychologist Nicholas Humphrey makes the Wallpaper View the centerpiece of his engaging popular work *A History of the Mind*.[4] David Chalmers in *The Conscious Mind* systematically deploys talk of qualia, and of qualia-free variants of us known as "Zombies" in order to make the world less safe for Materialism. In the course of this, he takes the Wallpaper View as a fixed point to argue from.[5] He supposes that although Zombies enjoy no qualia, have no conscious sensory awareness at all on his favored picture of what conscious awareness comes to, these Zombies could still immediately know more or less what we immediately know concerning the world around us. After all, the unfortunate Zombies could still form immediate perceptual beliefs as a result of a reliable process. Why regard them as less endowed than we are with immediate perceptual knowledge?[6]

The same structuring assumption is often found in discussions of two other philosophical inventions: inverted spectra and radical blindsight. Play along with talk of qualia for a moment, and suppose that when you look at the flag of Germany you enjoy qualia of just the same sort as I enjoy when I look at a similarly patterned flag whose constituent colors are green, blue, and white. Even though we have entirely different sensory deliverances, the Wallpaper View has the incredible consequence that we can both immediately know just by looking that a given German flag is red, yellow, and black. For, consistent with our spectrum inversion relative to each other, it could be that we are each wired up in such a way as to reliably form the true immediate judgment that such flags are red, yellow, and black. The qualia difference is again treated as a difference in mere mental accompaniments, as if, from the epistemic point of view, it amounted to no more than a difference in our respective bodily sensations, or in what music we happened to be recalling in our respective mental ears.

---

[4] *A History of Mind* (New York: Harper Perennial Books, 1993).

[5] *The Conscious Mind* (New York: Oxford University Press, 1996); see, for example, p. 182:

True, it may not be especially worrying that [sensory] consciousness is explanatorily irrelevant to our first-order phenomenal judgments, such as "That is a red thing". It is reasonable that these should be explained purely in terms of perception and other psychological processes; after all, the judgments in question are not directly concerned with conscious experience, but with the state of the world.

[6] In more recent, unpublished work David Chalmers has attempted to find a way of denying what is in effect the Wallpaper View consistent with his conception of "conscious" sensory awareness as the presentation of qualia. The key idea is that qualia partly individuate certain concepts that figure in immediate perceptual judgment by entering in as constituent parts, so that the content of what is immediately judged is nuanced by what qualia we happen to enjoy. See below for a brief discussion of this sort of proposal. In his paper in this volume (ch. 2), Chalmers presents a further sophistication in his view about the content of perceptual experience.

This can't be right. If external things are colored, then their colors must be tightly connected to the distinctive qualities which visual awareness alone reveals. Our immediate perceptual judgments about the colors of items in the environment do not systematically prescind from the qualities of surfaces ostensibly presented in sensory experience. Instead those judgments seem to predicate *those very sensed qualities* of environmental items. So it is hard to make clear how two subjects with inconsistent qualitative visual presentations could both be right in their immediate beliefs about the color of the relevant stripe in the flag. Each might of course be prompted by his immediate belief to make the same true *public language statement* about the color of the flag. But each can't be right in the way they pre-linguistically take the world to be. The qualities predicated of objects in immediate perceptual judgment must be closely tied to the qualities which sensory awareness reveals. (That is to put it mildly: the close tie seems to be identity; we often judge things to be just the way the senses present them as being.) The Wallpaper View leaves this tie mysterious.

The Wallpaper View also fails to account for a defect in radical blindsight, an imagined extension of surprising actual cases where patients, who honestly take themselves to be blind, nevertheless upon prompting make systematically correct "guesses" about the objects presented out of reach but before their eyes. Interpreted in terms of the qualia view of sensory awareness, the story is supposed to be that although a blindseer has little or no visual qualia and so honestly counts himself blind, the epistemic channel remains open. When activated by patterns of retinal stimulation this channel still gives reliable information about the scene before the eyes. So the blindseer can have knowledge, albeit hesitant knowledge, of such propositions as that there is a spoon before him. This application of the Wallpaper View implies that being blind in the sense of enjoying no visual sensory awareness is consistent with knowing more or less what we know by sight.

It can't be right. For suppose we ask a blindseer alleged to know that there is a spoon before him, *which* spoon is before him? He might wave his finger in the direction of the spoon and say "That spoon, of course." But if he has no sensory awareness he has no immediate idea of which spoon he is talking about, even if at some sub-personal level a channel of information remains open. In the absence of any sensory awareness of the spoon he cannot have a singular demonstrative thought about that spoon. The spoon is not present to him; not available as a topic of thought and talk, except by way of a merely descriptive connection. The blindseer may be canny enough to pick the spoon out descriptively as "the spoon that my reliably caused belief was about, whichever spoon that is" or something of that sort. But such an attributive definite description gives the game away; the blindseer has no spoon present to him, no spoon available for direct demonstration and so for direct demonstrative thought. All of the blindseer's immediate beliefs would thus differ from ours in having an inevitably non-singular or general structure. He cannot know the singular demonstrative propositions we know. So, after all, it must be that sensory awareness somehow facilitates singular demonstrative judgment concerning items in the environment. The Wallpaper View leaves this fact mysterious.

This constraint, that sensory awareness must facilitate singular demonstrative judgment, works against one attempt to deny the Wallpaper View while remaining faithful to the conception of sensory awareness as the presentation of mental qualia. The leading idea is to tie immediate perceptual knowledge to the enjoying of a sense datum or structured quale, by insisting that qualia partly individuate certain concepts figuring in immediate perceptual judgment. So on this account, when my qualia-reversed counterpart and I both describe the same stripe in the German flag as yellow, behind our common true statement in our common public language, we have different immediate perceptual judgments. His immediate judgment predicates of the stripe in the flag something that depends essentially on the qualia he is enjoying. My immediate judgment predicates of the stripe in the flag something that depends essentially on the different qualia I am enjoying. Thanks to our differing qualia we are not making the same immediate pre-linguistic judgment about the flag. Pre-linguistically, we are not taking the flag to be the same way.

Without pressing for the details of just how it could be that wholly subjective qualia might partly individuate concepts of the objective qualities of external things—concepts of their real external colors, shapes, sounds, smells, etc.—it should be clear that the account at hand does nothing to help explain how it is that sensory awareness facilitates singular demonstrative thought about such external things. How does enjoying a structured quale caused by the stripe in the flag in any way make available *the stripe in the flag* as an object of direct demonstration? Certainly to suppose that the subject enjoying the structured quale had appeal to any such mental descriptions as "the cause of this distinctive quale" would lack psychological realism, and would provide at most for *radically indirect* and *indeterminate* reference to items in the environment. Moreover, in such a scheme, the qualia are simply providing a peg to tie down indirect descriptive reference; other non-qualitative effects such as distinctive thoughts could play the same role. A theorist might build in a side-reference to accompanying qualia in his account of the content of immediate perceptual judgment, but this in itself goes no way towards explaining how sensory awareness provides for the world-involving demonstrative character of much of our immediate perceptual judgment.

Our question as to the function of sensory awareness thus divides into two questions. How does sensory awareness function so as to make available external items as objects of immediate demonstration, consequently introducing them as new topics for thought and talk? And how does sensory awareness function so as at least partly ground what is then judged or predicated of such items?

SOME UNSATISFACTORY ANSWERS

Some attempt to finesse the second question by identifying sensory awareness with immediate perceptual judgment, or by making it wholly derivative upon such judgment. Thus David Armstrong once held that sensory awareness is no more than the acquisition of immediate perceptual belief. As first formulated, this account of sensory awareness seemed to fall to the following counter-example: when I am visually aware of an oar half submerged in water the oar appears separated, but I do not believe, and am not disposed to believe, that the oar is separated. The suggestion of David Armstrong and George Pitcher was that such cases show that sensory experience is the acquisition of a *possibly suppressed* disposition to believe things about the scene before the eyes.[7]

As against this, the acquisition of a disposition to believe or judge is only a regular effect of sensory awareness. It is possible that the cause may occur without the usual effect, so that the acquisition of a disposition to believe is not even a necessary condition of sensory awareness. Nor is the acquisition of a disposition *sufficient* for sensory awareness. One could acquire a (suppressed) disposition to believe, e.g., that the scene before the eyes is poorly lit, in ways that bypassed sensory experience; sudden depression, hypnotism, and so on. One could have one's eyes closed all the time, and so not be having any relevant sensory experience of the scene, let alone of its being poorly lit.

The same points apply to those who might be tempted to develop a suggestion of David Lewis and Lawrence Nemirow, and treat visual awareness as the acquisition of an ability to imagine seeing the scene. The acquisition of such an ability is a common *effect* of visual awareness, but effects cannot be identified with causes. The causes might not produce the effects that are being offered as part of their analysis. For example, transpose the Lewis/Nemirow account of visual experience to olfactory experience, where our capacities to image a scenario containing scents we have previously experienced is extremely impoverished. Here it is clear that smelling a scent is one thing, while the ability to imagine an olfactory scenario containing that scent is quite another. Though the chemists at Estée Lauder may be better at this, I can often recognize familiar scents, but I cannot imagine them. My "mind's nose" is blind, as it were. (And even when it comes to recognition of scents, I can recognize many fewer scents that I can smell.)

Returning to the visual case, the ability to image a scene, like a disposition to believe that a scene is thus and so, could come about in some bizarre way that bypassed sensory awareness. So we are left with the question: what then is sensory awareness and why does it typically confer such abilities and dispositions on subjects?

---

[7] George Pitcher, *Perception* (Princeton: Princeton University Press, 1976), pp. 92–3; Armstrong, *A Materialist Theory of Mind* (London: Routledge and Kegan Paul, 1968), pp. 222–3.

Moreover, we have made no progress on the question of how the acquisition of an ability to imagine a scenario before the senses enables subjects to make original demonstrative reference to items in the scenarios before the senses. The Lewis/Nemirow account of sensory experience is no better placed to answer this question than the Armstrong/Pitcher account was.

Let us now turn to a more promising account of sensory awareness, albeit one with some real difficulties.

SENSING AS A FACT-DIRECTED ATTITUDE

The Sense Datum Theory, along with its cousin the Adverbial View, which trades in an act/object account of sensory experience in favor of subjective manners of sensing, share the assumption that it is the function of the external senses to provide *sensation*, where sensation is understood as something "inner" or wholly subjective.[8] This is not just the dominant philosophical understanding of sensation; it is also dominant in empirical psychology.

One diagnosis of why the picture is dominant in empirical psychology might be that as we understand more and more about the sub-personal processing of information in the brain's visual system the more indirect it seems to be. Indeed, it appears that Humpty Dumpty is broken up and reassembled, in the sense that information about color and shape are separated in one part of the visual system and then recombined in another part. So the supposed sensations of colored shapes produced by the visual system are then naturally construed as the next local event *caused* by complex information processing going on in the brain. So these sensations are "inner" in the sense of not being individuated in terms of the items in the environment that they represent.

The thing to notice is that this common route to the idea of the senses as delivering sensations involves a substantial philosophical inference from sub-personal information processing to the intentionality of sensory experience. For example, there is no need to suppose that sensing is the next local event *caused* by

---

[8] The view that the deliverances of the senses are akin to bodily sensations, qualitative effects produced in us by external causes, is vividly expressed by Galileo in *The Assayer* (1623). Galileo writes:

A piece of paper or a feather drawn lightly over any part of our bodies performs intrinsically the same operations of moving and touching, but by touching the eye, the nose, or the upper lip it excites in us an almost intolerable titillation, even though elsewhere it is scarcely felt. This titillation belongs entirely to us and not to the feather; if the live and sensitive body were removed it would remain no more than a mere word. I believe that no more solid existence belongs to many qualities which we have come to attribute to physical bodies—tastes, odors, colors and many more. (From the Stillman Drake translation published as *Discoveries and Opinions of Galileo* (Doubleday Anchor, 1957), pp. 274–5)

The crucial and horrible idea that was to wreak so much havoc in modern philosophy is that the deliverances of the senses should be compared to bodily sensations or "titillations." Cardinal Bellarmine had the right culprit on the wrong charge.

complex information processing going on in the brain. Sensing external objects could be a process which is *constituted* by the long causal process which includes the energy coming from the object sensed, the activation of the internal senses, and the sub-personal processing in the brain's sensory systems. Thus, consistent with the indirection of sub-personal processing of visual information, we may understand the deliverances of the senses as intentional acts partly individuated in terms of the items in the environment that they present.

In philosophy, the dominant picture of the senses providing "inner" sensations at least has a natural opponent, which treats sensing as the formation of a certain sort of "fact-directed" attitude; that is, an attitude directed at facts, where these are understood as the components of the scenarios before the senses.

On such a Fact-Directed Attitude View there is a *sui generis* attitude of sensing, or perhaps many such attitudes, each corresponding to a particular sense—visually sensing that p, sensing by touch that p, and so on. In each of these cases the attitudes are relations between subjects and facts, where the facts in question lie in one or another scenario before the subject's senses.

Let's concentrate on the visual case. The attitude or act of visually sensing that there is a spoon before me is not the attitude of judging that there is a spoon before me, for, as long as I merely sense that there is a spoon before me, I am as yet uncommitted as to how the world stands. Often enough, I *do* go on to judge what I sense. The very thing sensed is then something I judge to be true. And I thereby make a commitment as to how the world stands. So the relation between sensing and judgment is all too easy to state: Often I sense that so and so is the case and then I judge what I sense, namely, that so and so is the case.

How then, on the Fact-Directed Attitude View, does sensory awareness help confer the status of knowledge on immediate perceptual judgment? Well, what is sensed—the content of the attitude of sensing—is a non-subjective worldly item, namely, a fact, e.g., that there is a spoon over by the alarm clock. This fact is, as it were, "merely taken in" by the sensing of it, and judgment goes beyond sensing not in the content judged, but just in the attitude taken up toward that content. As a result of judging that p one becomes committed to its being the case that p. But, since one has sensed the fact that p, then it is the case that p, and one's immediate perceptual judgment is true. So an immediate perceptual judgment has a strong prima facie claim to be knowledge, because typically it will have been reliably formed in the presence of its sensed truthmaker; a fact, which sensing just takes in. The prima facie claim might be defeated if the subject making the judgment either possess or should possess evidence against his judgment. And it might be defeated if the method of judging what one senses is unreliable in the kind of case at hand. Still, when we consider immediate perceptual judgment as a kind of mental act, we can say that when our immediate perceptual judgments are judgments of what we have sensed they typically constitute knowledge of what is judged.

The Fact-Directed Attitude View of sensing seems to me to be a move in the direction of the truth about sensing.[9] There remain however a number of difficulties, one of which entirely disables the View.

The first difficulty is that the View models sensory awareness as a relation to a fact. That is, after all, the non-metaphorical core of its attractive claim that sensory awareness is not the enjoying of subjective mental items merely accompanying immediate perceptual belief, but is rather a primary form of "openness to reality." This inevitably raises the question of how illusion and hallucination are to be accommodated.

It may help to make the distinction between hallucination and illusion in a somewhat stipulative fashion. In illusion there is a spatio-temporal particular which sensory awareness somehow gets wrong, as when the oar in the water seems separated. When one suffers a sensory illusion one senses an external particular, but one wrongly senses it as having some feature which it does not have. By contrast, in hallucination, as I shall understand it, it is not that there is a relevant external particular that one misperceives. Instead, the whole experience is out of kilter with the real objects before the senses, as when, in a pitch-black room, one hallucinates lights. Illusion and hallucination seem to be kinds, albeit defective kinds, of sensory awareness. Yet they cannot be represented as relations to facts about external objects.

Is it, upon reflection, a mistake to think of illusion and hallucination as kinds of sensory awareness? It might be said that they are no more kinds of sensory awareness than a fake duck is a kind of duck. In that spirit, a theorist might treat visual hallucination and illusion as merely apparent seeing or, as John McDowell puts it, "ostensible seeing that is not in fact seeing."[10] That way lies Disjunctivism about sensing, with its badly impoverished treatment of hallucination, something I have discussed in detail elsewhere.[11] But this may seem not to be the decisive issue, for one can contemplate an adjustment according to which sensing is a propositional attitude, usually directed at facts or true propositions. In the case of illusion or hallucination, however, some part of the propositional content of the experience is false. (More will be said about this sort of adjustment below.)

The decisive problem with the Fact-Directed Attitude View is that it does not earn the right to the metaphor of the senses taking in *concrete* reality. According to the View, the relation between what we sense and what we sometimes go on to judge is particularly intimate. It is identity. If the sensed scene is simple enough we can visually sense that p and then judge that p; here the very same item is sensed and judged. The objects of judgment are bearers of truth-values, and

---

[9] I hesitate in making the unqualified attribution, but I do take this to be the backbone of John McDowell's much more subtle and detailed account in *Mind and World* (Cambridge, Mass.: Harvard University Press, 1994).

[10] John McDowell, "The Woodbridge Lectures," *Journal of Philosophy*, 95, 1997: 483 passim.

[11] "The Obscure Object of Hallucination," *Philosophical Studies* 120: 113–83, 2004.

when their subject matter is contingent those bearers can be either true or false. Since the truth about the scene before the eyes is mostly contingent, most perceptual judgments are directed at truth-value bearers that might have been false. *But concrete reality does not consist of items that could have been false.* Concrete reality consists of items whose existence accounts for the truth of what is contingently true and for the falsity of what is contingently false.

I can feel the hardness of the seat beneath me, but the hardness of the seat is not a bearer of a truth-value. It is a truthmaker; something that makes bearers of truth-value take on one or the other truth-value.

The metaphysical theme that concrete reality does not consist of items that could be false comports with the picture of concrete reality that emerges from the examination of our simplest sensory reports. We report primitive acts of sensing as relations to objects, stuff, events, and states. These items are not themselves truth-value bearers. That is, there is a kind of sensory awareness which is reported not by way of citing propositional or even fact-directed attitudes, but rather by direct object constructions involving "saw," "heard," "tasted," etc., as in:

Uri saw the spoon.
Jane smelt the coffee.
Sam heard Sutherland's vocal acrobatics.
Mary tasted the astringency of the calvados.

That is not to deny that in ordinary language we also report people as seeing *that* there is a spoon to the right of them, where the reported relation of seeing seems to take a true proposition, i.e., that there is a spoon to the right of them, as its relatum. However, such reports seem to be viable only when the subject has done more than *simply seeing* the object in question in its location. It would be wrong to report someone as seeing that there is a spoon to his right if he did not notice the spoon, say, because he was focusing on another part of his visual field. Yet, as Fred Dretske pointed out years ago, it does seem entirely right to say that someone might see a spoon in the corner of his visual field and not notice or attend to it. I am seeing many things on my desk at this moment, even though I am only attending to the computer screen.

The acts of sensory awareness reported above are most naturally understood as directed not at facts, but at spatio-temporal particulars; that is, objects, or stuff of some kind, or events, or states of some sort. Although the reports of such acts are consistent with the supposition, they do not entail that the subject is attending to what he or she is sensing. Nor do they entail that the subject has an ability to judge that the corresponding proposition, e.g., that a spoon exists, that Joan Sutherland is engaging in vocal acrobatics, that calvados is astringent, holds. Such non-fact-directed sensing seems a basic form of sensing that we share with infants and animals. Accordingly, if we are to get real insight into the nature of sensory awareness, then we should enquire into the relation between *non-fact-directed* sensing and immediate perceptual judgment. We can then determine if the fact-directed attitude of sensing *that* such and such is the case plays any distinctive role in the explanation, or whether it actually falls into two parts, namely, sensing things and then immediately judging that they are such and so.

FULLY VERIDICAL ILLUSION: IS SENSING THAT P MORE BASIC?

Only if sensing that p is the more basic attitude, an attitude in terms of which we can explain reports of "non-fact-directed" sensing, can the Fact-Directed Attitude View be an adequate account of sensing.

What follows is a new argument to the effect that we need to recognize a class of sensings of spatio-temporal particulars that are not reducible to attitudes directed at propositions or to attitudes directed at facts. The argument will be that there are cases of "fully veridical illusion"; cases in which the subject is suffering an illusion even though there is no falsity in the propositions which would capture the content of his visual experience. The illusion consists of the subject failing to be aware of some state or event that makes true the propositions in question.

If there are such cases, then sensing cannot be modeled simply as a relation to facts or propositions. The standard assumption in the philosophy of mind to the effect that the mental consists of propositional attitudes and acts of awareness of qualia—the assumption that frames the debate over the adequacy of Functionalism, just to take one example—will emerge as seriously incomplete.

To get to the cases in question, it is best first to go by way of some approximations which miss the mark, in order to convey the novel idea of fully veridical illusion.

Consider the familiar Muller-Lyer illusion, in which a line with "wings" on both ends is presented above another line that is "arrow-headed" on both ends. If the two lines are the same length then the winged line will look longer than the arrowed line. That is the content of the illusion. *However, it is very difficult to get two lines that are exactly the same length.* I would therefore bet that in the vast majority of presentations of the Muller-Lyer illusion the lines are not the same length. So I would guess that in about half of these cases the line that looks longer *is longer*. The subject is nonetheless suffering an illusion.

Here there *is* a false proposition which is plausibly taken to be part of the content of the subject's visual experience—part of how things seem to the subject to be. After all, the subject's visual experience suggests that the winged line is longer than the arrowed line *by a certain amount*. Thanks to the lengthening effect of the wings on the top line, the subject is misled; the top line is not longer *by that amount*.

But now suppose that the relevant Muller-Lyer illusion is presented not by way of lines but by way of wires suspended in space. As before, the top, winged wire is longer than the bottom, arrowed wire by a certain amount. But now the top wire is slightly twisted or rotated so that its left-hand side is further away from the viewing subject than its right-hand side. The subject does not notice this. A propositional report which captured how the scene seemed to him to be would not include the proposition that the top wire is slightly rotated relative to the bottom wire; nor need such a report include its denial. His visual experience just expresses no "view" on this; it just leaves open the exact orientation of the top wire relative to the bottom wire.

As the reader has no doubt guessed by now, we will stipulate that the illusory shortening effects of differential orientation more or less exactly compensate for the lengthening effects of the wing/arrow contrast. So the top wire looks to be longer than the bottom *by just the amount that it is longer*. Still, the subject is enjoying an experience with illusory elements; two, in fact. There is the Muller-Lyer illusion and the illusory effects of unnoticed differential orientation. *Yet there need be no false proposition that captures the content of the subject's experience.*

He is nonetheless a victim of an illusion because he does not see a crucial item in the scene before the eyes, namely, the relational state of the winged wire being longer than the arrowed wire by the relevant amount. That item is crucial because it is the relevant truthmaker for the proposition that the winged wire is longer than the arrowed wire by the relevant amount, a proposition that his visual experience *does* pronounce upon. His visual experience is in this sense failed or defective, even though it encourages a wholly correct belief about how things are in the scene before the eyes. His visual experience does not disclose the truthmakers for the relevant belief. (That, I think, is why the subject should not be said to see that the winged wire is longer than the arrowed wire by the relevant amount.)

The obvious objection will be that the subject's experience must include some definite "view" about the orientation of the wires. The proposition that captures that "view" will be false. Hence, even in the twisted variant of the Muller-Lyer illusion, the illusory nature of the experience can be modeled in terms of a relation to a false proposition.

Consider then a second case in which a subject is enjoying two illusions, which for a moment entirely offset each other. Suppose two twins are of the same height. Still, the first looks taller than the second because the second is wearing a football jumper with horizontal blue and white stripes. It so happens that the two twins are also walking around in an Ames room, a room whose height is artificially compressed in one corner, so that people as they approach that corner look increasing taller than they are. The subject is looking at the twins walking around the Ames room. The subject is enjoying many illusions as to their relative height. Sometimes the one looks taller than the other, sometimes vice versa. But there are some pairs of positions in the room where the illusory effects of the horizontal stripes exactly offset the illusory effects of the Ames room. Call these pairs of positions "sweet spots." Obviously their location is a relative matter; it crucially depends on the position of the observing subject.

Suppose, after adopting various positions in the room, the twins occupy sweet spots for a moment. The subject has been enjoying two sorts of height-illusion throughout, and there is no reason to think that he ceases to be subject to both of them at that moment. But the two height illusions are now exactly offsetting each other. There need be nothing in the so-called "content of the subject's visual experience" that is false. That is, there need be no proposition which his visual experience supports, or presents as true, which is in fact not true. The twins look to him to be exactly the same height. He could thus be visually entertaining the true so-called "singular" proposition to the effect that *those* twins are the same height.

Moreover, the subject need not be "visually entertaining" any false proposition about the scene before his eyes. His visual experience, considered as a conscious presentation of the scene, may be taking no very determinate view about the slope of the ceiling relative to the floor. The deviation from the normal relation required to cancel the shortening effects of the horizontal jumper could be quite subtle, and not itself visually salient. The exact slope of the ceiling relative to the floor in a room we look into is something we often do not see, even though our visual system is processing quite detailed information about such things, in order to get clues as to relative height.

What then is the illusory element in the subject's experience at the crucial moment? In what sense is the subject not taking in the reality that is the scene before his eyes? My suggestion is that he is not visually aware of a relational state of the twins, namely, their sameness in height. There is a sense in which that relational state is not revealed by, but is actually "occluded" by, his visual experience. The subject is out of touch with this aspect of reality.

To get an initial grip on that suggestion, consider the more familiar case of so-called "veridical hallucination." Macbeth might hallucinate a dagger in the air at a relative distance and orientation, a distance and orientation at which there actually happens to be an exactly matching real dagger hanging by an invisible thread. The hallucination "occludes" the real dagger in this sense: it is because he is hallucinating a dagger over there that he does not see the real dagger over there. (Imagine the situation physiologically; his visual cortex gets into a state because of stimulation coming from somewhere other than the sensory nerves.) He has a deviant visual experience, which just happens to match the scene. He is not seeing the dagger, even though his visual experience supports the proposition that there is a dagger of just the right sort there. So Macbeth's visual experience is defective though *fully veridical*, i.e., unimpeachable in propositional terms. Even though Macbeth's experience encourages wholly correct beliefs about how things are in the scene before his eyes, beliefs such as that there is *a real dagger there*, it does not disclose the truthmakers for the relevant beliefs. That is, Macbeth is not visually aware of *the (real) dagger's being there*, a condition of the dagger that makes true the proposition that the dagger is there.

Similarly, the subject looking at the twins in the Ames room is not visually aware of the sameness of height of the twins, and remains unaware of this relational state of the twins even when they occupy sweet spots. So the subject's visual experience is defective though *fully veridical*, i.e., unimpeachable in propositional terms. Even though the subject's experience encourages wholly correct beliefs about how things are in the scene before his eyes, beliefs such as that the twins are the same height, it does not disclose the relevant truthmakers for such beliefs.

In the case of veridical hallucination, we are not inclined to say that Macbeth *sees that* there is a dagger there. The case of veridical hallucination shows that this is not because it is false that there is a dagger there. Nor is this because Macbeth lacks the justified belief that there is a dagger there. (His hallucination may be fully convincing.) Macbeth does not see that there is a dagger there because he is not visually aware of the dagger. This last attitude is not a relation to a fact or a proposition. But it must be invoked as part of the explanation of why Macbeth cannot be assigned certain attitudes to propositions. This suggests the object-directed attitude is more basic than the propositional attitude of seeing that p.

In the case of veridical illusion, we are not inclined to say that the subject *sees that* the twins are the same height. The case of veridical illusion shows that this is not because it is false that the twins are the same height; nor is this because the subject lacks the justified belief that they are the same height. (He may look into the room only at the crucial moment and find his experience fully convincing.) The subject does not see that the twins are the same height because he is not visually aware of the crucial relational state, their sameness in height. This last attitude is not a relation to a fact or a proposition. But it must be invoked as part of the explanation of why the subject cannot be assigned certain attitudes to propositions. This suggests the state-directed attitude is more basic than the propositional attitudes.

There is a temptation to suggest that the reason why the subject is not properly said to see that the twins are the same height is that he does not know that they are the same height. That temptation is to be resisted, not because the subject does know that they are the same height, but because the suggestion misconstrues the relation between seeing that p and knowing that p. The suggestion requires that seeing that p entails knowing that p. *If* that were so, then the best way of understanding that entailment would be to treat it as like the entailment between something being red and it being colored. Seeing that p would be a determinate of the determinable, knowing that p; it would be just one specific way of knowing that p. We do not *explain* the absence of a determinate by citing the absence of its determinable. So, also, we do not explain the subject's failing to see that the twins are the same height by citing the fact that he does not know that they are the same height.

THE COUNTERFACTUAL STRATEGY

Some friends of a purely propositional account of sensing may try to explain the defect in veridical hallucination and veridical illusion in counterfactual terms. They may suggest that although the propositional content of the subject's experience is fully true in veridical hallucination and veridical illusion, none-theless the propositional content is not counterfactually robust, in the sense that it would not vary systematically were the scene to so vary. So the content of Macbeth's experience would be that there is a dagger over there, even if the real dagger moved. We need not appeal to non-fact-directed attitudes to explain the relevant defects; it is the lack of robustness of the content of propositional attitudes under counterfactual variation that is the ground of veridical hallu-cination and illusion.

Such counterfactual accounts of hallucination and illusion run foul of the fact that sensing in general, and seeing in particular, can be quite adventitious. A subject can see an object without any illusion or hallucination entering in, even if the subject would lose a grip on the object's nature were the object to undergo a small intrinsic change. For one thing, it could be the case that the small intrinsic change would set off catastrophic effects in his visual system. For another, there may be higher-order mental processes operating in the subject that would pro-duce visual hallucination if the scene changed slightly.

So consider the prudish psychotic who is forced to walk down the main corridor of a bordello. He walks head down looking at the Persian carpet before him. If he were to turn his head slightly and see into the adjoining rooms then he would be confronted with scenes which profoundly affronted his sensibility. In fact he would not see those scenes, for hallucination of something much less threatening would set in. Surely that is consistent with his seeing the Persian carpet and its details. So, also, he could be seeing the Persian carpet and its details even if the following counterfactual held: if the details were to take on certain suggestive shapes (to change intrinsically in that way) then he would defensively hallucinate the old details. So seeing is compatible with a lack of counterfactual robustness in the content of visual experience, both with respect to changes of the scene and changes in the items seen.

On the other side of the ledger, a subject's illusions can also be highly adventitious; it could well be the case that he would suddenly see the object of his illusory experience *perfectly* if that object were to undergo any small change. This kind of case will occur when the illusion is a delicate matter depending on small details of the relative position of subject and object.

When you see something as it is, usually you will continue to see it as it is, even if it changes slightly, or you change your position slightly. The consequence of that ordinary fact is that the propositional content of your visual experience is usually counterfactually robust. This ordinary fact about object-directed attitudes is what makes the relevant counterfactuals true in the usual case. So we should not expect to analyze a subject's seeing an item as it is, or more generally a subject's sensing an item as it is, in terms of the counterfactual robustness of the truth of the propositions which capture how some part of the world seems to the subject to be. Here, as elsewhere, the counterfactuals hold because of the "factuals" that are the targets of the proposed counterfactual analysis.

SEARLE'S POSITION

Given that there are cases of veridical hallucination, why do we need to struggle our way through the cases of veridical *illusion* in order to make the point that sensory experience is not primarily propositional? The answer lies in the availability of a position like that of John Searle's, as developed in his book *Intentionality*.[12] Searle would deny that there are cases of veridical hallucination, i.e., cases in which the propositional content of a hallucination is true to the scene before the eyes. This is because he regards the propositional content of sensory experience as in a certain way "self-referential." So, according to Searle, the content of Macbeth's hallucinatory visual experience includes something like this:

> That there is a dagger over there, some of whose features are playing a standard role in causing this very experience.

This kind of propositional content is false even when there is a real dagger in just the place where Macbeth is hallucinating a dagger. No features of the real dagger (no states of the real dagger) are causing the hallucinatory experience. So, given Searle's position, it seems we *can* say what is defective about veridical hallucination in terms of the falsity of some proposition that captures part of the content of visual experience.

But this kind of self-reference doesn't help in the case of veridical illusion. For the content

> That there are twins over there some of whose features are playing a standard role in causing this very experience.

is true throughout the period when the twins are meandering around the Ames room. And it is true when they occupy sweet spots.

To extend Searle's strategy to the case of veridical illusion, so that the defect in veridical illusion can be captured in propositional terms, we would need to construe the content of visual experience as including something as complex and strong as the following:

> That there are twins over there which this experience represents in these ways F1.... Fn and for each of the Fi the corresponding Fi-ness of the twins is

[12] *Intentionality* (Cambridge: Cambridge University Press, 1983), pp. 66–71.

playing a standard role in causing the experience to be an experience to the effect that the twins are Fi.

So construed, the experience of the subject at the crucial moment will have a false propositional content, for the twins being the same in height will presumably not then be playing a standard causal role in causing the experience to be an experience to the effect that the twins are the same height. The presence of the two illusions will somehow mean that everything is not standard with respect to the causing of the experience to be an experience as of the twins being the same in height. So there is a propositionalist fix, even in the case of veridical illusion.

Here is a point at which philosophical judgment comes in. Doesn't the claim that the contents of our experiences are so complexly choreographed in such delicate patterns of causal dependence amount to simply reading into the content of experience whatever needs to be said to save the propositionalist construal?

Speaking for myself, when I look at the complexity of the supposed content, I am pretty confident that the intentionality of sensory experience is not to be comfortably captured in purely propositionalist terms. We should at least look elsewhere to see if there is some other way of capturing the intentionality of sensory experience.

OBJECTIONS CONSIDERED

Of course, there is the argumentative option of insisting that at the crucial moment in the Ames room, when the twins occupy sweet spots, the two illusions do not just offset each other, but cancel each other out, so that there then is nothing illusory about the subject's experience.

Let's distinguish two versions of this idea. One is acceptable to me and the other isn't. The first version is just this: "veridical illusion" is a solecism, a contradiction in terms. When the propositional content associated with a visual experience is fully true to the scene before the eyes there is no point in calling the visual experience "illusory." I accept that, or almost all of that. I only persist in talking of "veridical illusion" to highlight certain cases which show us something about the logic of perception. Compare the philosophical use of the term "veridical hallucination."

The second version of the idea is that at the crucial moment in the Ames room the defects associated with the two sorts of illusion are no longer present, so that there is nothing defective about the subject's visual experience. This I deny. Even at the crucial moment the subject is not visually aware of the sameness of the twin's height. This is the best explanation of why we are not prepared to say that the subject *sees that* the twins are the same in height.

Let me present another case. There is an interesting empirical conjecture about color vision in the barely illuminated dark; that is, in situations where you can still see, but only because of the operation of the rods, which specialize in such conditions of low illumination. The conjecture is that although the rods provide only monochromatic visual information, in the barely illuminated dark we do see some colors outside the black/gray/white scale. Those colors are seen as poorly illuminated reds, greens, blues, and so on. So far this is not controversial. The more controversial conjecture is that this seeing of color in the dark is memory based, as if visual memory was "coloring in" the visual experience of familiar objects.

The conjecture implies that when you look into your own car in the dark you see the upholstery as the color it is, albeit poorly illuminated. It also implies that when you look into a stranger's car you see the upholstery as some shade of gray. I understand that a famous psychologist has personally tested this prediction and finds it to be true, at least on dark Scottish nights. (Fortunately, he was not arrested by the Edinburgh police for peering into the cars of strangers at night.)

Suppose the conjecture is true. And let us leave the (in my view perfectly good) rhetoric of "veridical illusion" to one side. Still, I want to say that when your visual experience correctly presents your own upholstery as red and as poorly illuminated, there is something defective about your visual experience. You are not visually aware of the relevant state of the upholstery, namely, the redness of the upholstery. Memory is filling red in.

Notice that vision could not generally involve this kind of memory. (If it did, one could maintain that this was just how ordinary non-defective seeing actually turns out to work.) We need to have seen some of the colors of things for this kind of color memory to be available to operate. So, considering just the visual system, it is not operating as it usually does to disclose the color states of objects in the dark. There is a partly reliable, partly unreliable back-up cognitive process that is making up for some of the defects of vision in the dark.

We can dramatize the unreliable element and its effects on what is seen by imaging an experimenter repainting objects familiar to you in their complementary colors, leaving only one or two as they were. Your memory now systematically misleads as to the colors of the familiar objects. Even in the couple of cases where it fills in the right colors, the thing to say is that you are not seeing the colors of the couple of objects in question. It is because this crucial state-directed attitude is not in place that we will also resist saying that you do not see that such an object is red, even if it is red and your visual experience presents it as red.

This is all I claim for the cases of "veridical illusion." They suggest that, when it comes to experience, object- or stuff- or state- or event-directed attitudes are more basic than the corresponding propositional attitudes.

Much more can be said about such cases, *pro et contra*. I simply want to take away from this discussion a certain hint about sensory experience, a hint which I shall expand upon in the remainder of this paper. *What is distinctive about non-hallucinatory and non-illusory sensory experience is that it presents the truthmakers for the propositions that we immediately judge true on the basis of sensory experience.*

That is, the function of sensory experience is not to provide accompanying qualia, or to present facts about the scenarios before the senses, or to present propositions that might state the facts about such scenarios. The function of sensory experience is to present truthmakers for the immediate judgments we make about the scenarios we are sensing. Recognizing this is an important part of explaining why those judgments constitute knowledge, or perhaps better put, something at least as good as, and maybe even better than, what is ordinarily called "knowledge."

SENSING TRUTHMAKERS

The argument from veridical illusion generalizes against all accounts that recognize only propositional acts of sensing. No plausible purely propositionalist account of sensing is adequate to impeach—to capture what is not sensed in— cases of veridical hallucination and veridical illusion. For this reason, a purely propositionalist account will misconstrue the nature of sensory intentionality, its distinctive directedness to items in the scenarios before the senses. For the most basic sensory acts are directed at spatio-temporal particulars, items that are not facts and not propositions.

So the suggestion is that the function of sensory awareness is not to provide accompanying sensation, nor to deliver ready-made facts, but rather to make present the sensible truthmakers out of which our immediate perceptual judgments are formed. For this suggestion to even seem viable it is important to recognize that truthmakers for judgments need not be facts. A truthmaker for a judgment is something whose existence guarantees the truth of the judgment. More exactly, if *t* is a truthmaker for the judgment that p then it is necessary that if *t* exists, then the proposition that p is true.[13] So Frege—an object—is a truthmaker for the judgment that Frege exists. Frege's prejudice—an obtaining state or condition of Frege's character—is a truthmaker for the judgment that Frege is prejudiced. Frege's mocking of Wittgenstein's fledgling ideas—a particular event—is a truthmaker for the judgment that Frege is mocking Wittgenstein's fledgling ideas.

[13] To be *more* precise we would have to recognize that this merely modal account of truthmaking is intuitively inadequate: Intuitively, the singleton of Socrates is not the truthmaker for the proposition that Socrates exists. We may proceed in a different way in order to characterize the truthmakers for judgments. In the world, properties, relations, and kinds are *exemplified* by objects and stuff (and properties, relations, and kinds). In *judgment*, properties, relations, and membership in kinds are *predicated* of the same items. A truthmaker for a judgment could thus be thought of as the worldly item that mimics the propositional structure of the judgment in this way: where the judgment unifies its elements by predication, the truthmaker unifies those elements by exemplification. So Frege's past prejudice would be the truthmaker for the judgment that Frege was prejudiced.

Now we are in a position to address our second question, about sensing and demonstration. Start with the notion that the senses provide neither sensations nor qualia, but awareness of environmental particulars—objects, stuffs, states, and events. One distinctive consequence of such awareness of an environmental particular is this: By turning our attention toward the particular of which we are aware we then have *it*, and not merely some quale it has produced or some mode of presentation of it, isolated as a topic or subject for further thought and judgment. Attention to the deliverances of sensory awareness is in this way the most fecund source of new topics for thought and judgment.

Where then does the predicative element in thought and judgment come from? In many cases it too is something of which one is immediately aware. Indeed, it is distinctive of what I have been calling immediate perceptual judgment that what one judges or predicates of an item is some feature of which one is also aware. So, when I taste the astringency of the calvados, I am not only aware of the calvados—a certain liquid in my mouth—but I am also aware of its astringency. This astringency is a completely determinate or fully specific quality, which I am in a position to take the calvados to have, i.e., to judge or predicate of the calvados. If I do so, I have moved from sensing the fully specific astringency of the calvados to judging that the calvados is astringent in that very specific way, a way which language is a rough and ready means for describing. (The predicate "is astringent" is inevitably a determinable predicate covering a host of more determinate forms of astringency. Perhaps we never limn in descriptive language the full specificity of the sensible qualities of which we are aware.) The full specificity of the predicable element in my immediate pre-linguistic judgment is a sign that my judgment has in a certain way *not gone beyond* what I was aware of in being aware of the astringency of the calvados. This is an important clue when it comes to the relation between sensory awareness and immediate perceptual judgment.

Let us continue to work with the simplest case: a subject/predicate judgment, arguably the characteristic form of immediate perceptual judgment. Our clue suggests that one's immediate perceptual judgment can be the predication of some sensed feature of some sensed item, where the item's having the feature, that state or condition of the item, is something of which one is directly aware. The immediate judgment is true if the item isolated by attention has the pre-dicated feature isolated from the state by selective attention. So if one senses the item's having the feature, and then abstracts the feature, and then predicates it of the item, one will have *rearranged* the elements of a state into a proposition which one is immediately judging. The proposition in question will be one which has the sensed state as its truthmaker. Moreover, the very elements that make up the proposition derive from that sensed truthmaker. So the judgment is guaranteed to be true because of its origin. The origin is sensory awareness of a spatio-temporal particular, not sensory awareness of a fact.

Of course, we are here exploiting a certain intimate connection between states and events on the one hand, and facts or true propositions on the other. The connection is so intimate that it has been mistaken for identity. Yet there is difference between such things as the snubnosedness of Socrates—a certain state or condition of Socrates—and the true proposition that Socrates is snubnosed. The first is a spatio-temporal particular that could be the object of sight or touch, while the second is proposition, something which could be judged to be true. There is an enormous amount to be said for and against this distinction, but here I can only hope to exhibit one advantage of parsing reality this way. The snubnosedness of Socrates—something we can immediately sense—is a truth-maker for the proposition that Socrates is snubnosed, something his cohorts could have immediately judged true. In this way what is sensed can make true what is immediately judged on the basis of sensing. And what is immediately judged can be a proposition whose elements are abstracted out of what is sensed. Hence the claim that our immediate perceptual judgments are *made out of* their sensed truthmakers.

As with states, so also with events: for example, a particular chiding of Socrates by Xantippe. This is a truthmaker for the proposition that Xantippe chided Socrates, and of course for a host of weaker propositions entailed by it. The event could have been witnessed and the witness could have immediately judged that the one chided the other. Once again, the proposition judged could be made out of the elements contained in its sensed truthmaker.[14]

A schematic description may help to convey the general idea of how sensory awareness of states and events can generate judgments whose truth is guaranteed by the very origins of those judgments. In the typical case I sense—am aware of—a host of states and events, a host of exemplifications of properties by objects and quantities of stuff (the snubnosedness of Socrates, or the astringency of the calvados). From this typically enormous range of exemplifications, I attend to the F-ness of a particular object (or of some stuff). As it happens, I have an ability to predicate F-ness of an object (or quantity of stuff) when I am sensing and attending to an exemplification of F-ness by that object (or quantity of stuff). Although this ability operates relatively automatically, I also have the ability to

---

[14] The point of distinguishing states and events is simply to respect the observation that events essentially involve changes in objects or stuffs and perhaps places. Some have suggested that everything we call a state essentially involves some changes, however slow. If so, this is no great matter; events and states are exemplifications of properties by particulars, they make true propositions to the effect that the particulars in question exemplify the properties in question, and all the weaker propositions implied by these propositions.

There is more of an issue about how to press sensed objects and quantities of stuff into the role of truthmakers for immediate judgment. It is a nice question as to whether you can barely sense an object (or some stuff) without sensing some state of it or some event in which it is implicated. This is not the question whether all seeing is seeing that such and such is the case, but the related question of whether the objects of awareness are primarily events and states of substantial objects and quantities of stuff. Fortunately, to illustrate the view I have in mind we need not settle this issue here; we can stick with the sensed states and events for illustrative purposes.

inhibit it, if judging so is irrelevant to me, or if there is significant evidence to the contrary which I possess. When the ability in question is deployed I predicate F-ness of an object (or quantity of stuff) when I am attending to an exemplification of F-ness by that object (or quantity of stuff).

My judgment does not go beyond its truthmaker, which sensory experience has made manifest. Its truth is thus guaranteed by its origins. This is how immediate perceptual judgments often have the status of knowledge. There is no evidence from which they are inferred; instead they are reliably formed out of awareness of their truthmaker, often in the absence of any evidence to the contrary.

Recall our two questions as to the function of sensory awareness. How does sensory awareness function so as to make available external items as objects of immediate demonstration, consequently introducing them as new topics for thought and talk? And how does sensory awareness function so as at least partly ground what is then judged or predicated of such items?

The implied answer to our two questions concerning the function of sensory awareness can now be explicitly set out. Sensory awareness discloses the truthmakers of our immediate perceptual judgments. Those truthmakers are external spatio-temporal particulars, which sensory awareness makes available for immediate demonstration. The structural elements (objects, stuff, their qualities, and the relations in which they stand) in those truthmakers are then recombined in immediate judgment. So the truthmakers which sensory awareness discloses also provide the contents of immediate perceptual judgment.

So, in short, the function of sensory awareness is to disclose items which are both *truthmakers* and *content providers* for our immediate perceptual judgments.

THE ROLE OF "CONCEPTS"

The abilities to attend to a sensed event or state and to predicate some property there exemplified may be more or less innate, as with attending to a startling bang, or inevitably learned, as with noticing a tell at poker or a fork in chess. In order to attend to, or even to be aware of, certain items and certain features one may need considerable conceptual sophistication, considerable training of attention and thought, so that thoughts which predicate F-ness arise systematically from attention to sensed exemplifications of F-ness. There is a sophisticated sensing illustrated by what Wittgenstein called "seeing as," which enormously expands the range of things that can be sensed and immediately judged. We should certainly not think that only simple qualities are able to be predicated on the strength of awareness of their exemplifications. Among other things, this mistake entails that the content of immediate perceptual judgment is extremely minimal, so that immediate perceptual knowledge would be without any significant foundational role. The "content" of sensory awareness is not a propositional content, but is rather a host of interconnected exemplifications of properties, relations, and kinds. That "content" is *pre-predicative* in the sense that awareness of it need involve no predication, no judgment that such and such is the case, nor any proto-judgment implicitly deploying the concepts on which the corresponding explicit judgment depends. This is dramatized by the already mentioned fact that I often see things, say, in the periphery of my visual field, which I do not even notice. I do not identify them as any kind of thing. I am not aware that I have seen them. My only access to the fact that I have seen them might be an inference from the fact that they were there to be seen in an area that was in fact scanned by my gaze. Not only can I see without noticing what I see, but I can also see without noticing that I am seeing. Like David Armstrong's dazed truck driver, I can realize that I must have visually taken in the last stretch of road even though mentally I was completely elsewhere. Human animals often negotiate their environment by such dumb inattentive gazing. Not only is seeing not necessarily believing, it need not even involve appreciating what is seen.[15]

Moreover, my tendency to make a proto-judgment may be at odds with what I am actually seeing. I can see an opaque surface while wrongly seeing it as transparent, as when I am taken in by a *trompe l'oeil* of a window onto a garden scene. I can also see an opaque surface whether or not I have the concept of opacity. It is not in general true that to see an F I need see it as an F. Likewise, in order to see an F I need not conceptualize, classify, or think of it as an F. This is the sense in which visual experience can be *conceptually undemanding*.

This truth is entirely consistent with the fact that just which exemplifications in the sensed field one can be immediately aware of depends importantly upon one's conceptual sophistication. You can't be immediately aware of someone's bluffing in poker unless you understand something of the rules and point of poker. Being aware of your opponent's bluffing depends upon a pattern of directed attention and visual search into the changing scene, and this is the manifestation of an ability which is practically inseparable from the inevitably conceptual understanding of poker. Conceptual sophistication helps us to use our senses to *mine* the scene, or more generally the scenario before the senses, for relevant exemplifications—his bluffing, her raising, your having a busted straight.

So, although the animals sense, and although some of what *we* sense requires little if any in the way of deploying our conceptual sophistication, the totality of what we sense, and so the totality of the truthmaking exemplifications with which we are presented, is immensely richer thanks to our conceptual sophistication.

To admit this is crucially not to grant that *the exemplifications themselves are the product of an antecedent synthesis under concepts*. In the poker game, the

---

[15] It is Fred Dretske, more than anyone else, who has forcefully argued this point. See *Seeing and Knowing* (Chicago: University of Chicago Press, 1969); "Seeing, Believing and Knowing" in *Visual Cognition and Action*, eds Daniel Osherson, Stephen Kosslyn and John Hollerbach (Cambridge, Mass.: MIT Press, 1990).

scene—the manifest acts of the poker players—needs no synthesis or assembly; *it already has all the intrinsic order and structure required of a game of poker.* Conceptually refined sensing does not *constitute* its objects. It is just that having certain concepts requires certain abilities, and that among these abilities are characteristic refinements of the capacity to sense what is there in the environment anyway. Hence, although conceptual sophistication helps us to search and mine a sensed field for exemplifications that could not be manifest without that sophistication, the Kant of the *Critique of Pure Reason* goes too far when he says at A79/B104–5

> The very same function which gives unity to the various representations in a judgment also gives unity to a mere synthesis of various representations in an intuition.

The ability to mine the sensed field by an appropriate sensory search, and thus allow certain objects, stuff, events, or states—a forced stalemate in three, say—to come into view, can be essentially dependent on the capacity to make certain judgments. But it is not yet an actualization of that very capacity. Still less is the object of sensory awareness, none other than the objective scenario before the senses, in need of unification by that capacity.

So what Wilfred Sellars once called the "this-suches" which sensory awareness immediately reveals are none other than environmental objects, stuff, states, and events; not proto-judgments as Sellars himself seems to have supposed.[16] Accordingly, sensory awareness is "presentational" not representational. If sensory awareness were representational, we would inevitably face the skeptical question of how we could know that the human style of representation is not entirely

---

[16] *Science and Metaphysics* (London: Routledge and Kegan Paul, 1967), pp. 3–7. For an opposing view of the objects of sensory awareness, see John McDowell, "The Woodbridge Lectures," 1997, op. cit. (n. 11). Here, for example, is McDowell assimilating *seeing* to *seeing that . . .*, an assimilation which is so helpful in making seeing seem conceptual and representational in his very strong sense:

> Here the fact that, say, "cube" figures in a specification of the content of an intuition—the intuition represents its object as that red *cube*—reflects the fact that for one to be the subject of such intuition is in part for there to be actualized in one's sensory consciousness the very same conceptual capacity—possession of the concept of a cube—whose exercise would partly determine the predicative element in the content of a judgment whose content we could specify, . . . in the form of "That is a red cube." In fact, the actualization of the relevant conceptual capacity in the intuition is an actualization of it in a conceptual occurrence whose content is so to speak, judgment shaped, namely a seeing (a seeing that . . .) whose content is that there is a red cube *there.* . . . This seeing that . . . , in describing which we explicitly place an expression for the concept in question in predicative position, is the very same conceptual occurrence—an actualization of the very same conceptual capacities with the same logical togetherness—as the intuition. (p. 461)

But the "logical togetherness" of the property of being a cube and the cube is not the same in the sensed exemplification and the judgment. Instantiation is one thing; predication is another. Treating sensing or intuition as representational obscures this difference, so that McDowell is led to say:

> An actualization of the capacity to have objects come into view is itself already an actualization of the capacity to have occur in one's life occurrences with the sort of content that judgments have, not just an element in that actualization. (p. 463)

idiosyncratic relative to the intrinsic natures of things.[17] And it would be a very good question, deeply embarrassing to the whole enterprise of knowledge; since to leave it unanswered is to leave upon the possibility that our sensibility and understanding have always been, in effect, virtual reality machines, presenting us with no more than the idiosyncratic subjective effects that external items induce in us.

Once we have the option that the senses present objective truthmakers, Kant's first synthesis—the synthesis of intuition—begins to seem thoroughly retrograde from the epistemic point of view. For it trades in modern skepticism about knowledge for the more profound ancient skepticism concerning the very possibility of acquaintance with the intrinsic natures of external things. Both forms of skepticism can be met if we can vindicate the idea that immediate judgment is directly adapted to a structure of some items in the environment, items *selectively made present, but not synthesized,* by our "sensibility," our distinctive capacities for sensory awareness. Hence the interest of trying to understand how it could be that sensory awareness presents the environmental truthmakers out of which immediate perceptual judgments are made.

THE IDEA OF AN "INNER" SENSE

The proposed model of a judgment formed out of its sensed truthmaker has application beyond the external sensory case. I can have immediate knowledge, knowledge of how things stand without inference from any evidence, of my own mental acts. So among the things I can be aware of—as one might misleadingly put it, be aware of "by introspection"—is *my tasting* the astringency of the calvados. This is an event, my exemplifying a certain property. It is an event that I can be aware of and can attend to. Now, I do have an ability to predicate tasting the astringency of the calvados of myself while I am aware of and attending to my exemplification of that property. When this ability is deployed I have predicated the property of tasting the astringency of the calvados of myself. And I have done this while I am attending to an exemplification by me of that property. My judgment does not go beyond its truthmaker, which higher-order awareness has made manifest. Its truth is thus guaranteed by its origins. In this way, so long as there are no defeaters in play, I can have genuine self-knowledge *without evidence.* That is, as far as I can tell, the legitimate extent of the analogy between outer and "inner" sensing.

---

[17] As Richard Rorty famously put it: how could we know that we are "successfully representing according to Nature's own conventions of representation?" See *Philosophy and the Mirror of Nature* (Princeton: Princeton University Press, 1979), p. 298. The trick is to reject Rorty's fundamental conceit. The senses are indeed not pure or correct representers, not "mirrors of nature." They are inevitably selective open windows on certain aspects of the objective environment.

THE CONNECTION WITH SKEPTICISM CONCERNING THE SENSES

The proposed model of sensory awareness providing the truthmakers for immediate perceptual judgment helps us to mount a fitting response to modern skepticism with regard to the senses' capacity to provide knowledge of the external world. The right way with such skepticism is not try to meet the skeptic on his own terms, by giving a proof from neutral premises of the conclusion that we are almost always sensing an external world rather than systematically hallucinating. We should rather aim to articulate a position that shows why the skeptic's terms are at least optional, and perhaps even unreasonable.

Yet so long as our sensory starting points are taken to be items "in our own minds," be they qualia or narrowly supervening propositional contents, one can only agree with the skeptic's suggestion that the environment-characterizing contents of our immediate perceptual judgments are conjectural, and neglect a host of equally good alternatives left open by our entertaining such subjective mental items. Then it does seem that sensory awareness plays no positive epistemic role, as on the Wallpaper View. Moreover, the familiar attempts to treat the skeptical alternatives as irrelevant or properly neglected will just seem self-serving if items in our mind are the bases for our judgments about our external environment. For then those judgments would be as massively under-supported as David Hume supposed. Our sensory "impressions" would be mere qualitative effects or inner representational symptoms produced in us by external causes. Any ampliative inference from the symptoms to some specific world-diagnosis would be inevitably shaky and conjectural. This is a telling result, which no amount of contemporary epistemological sophistication has been able to overcome.

It is the terms of the debate that need to be transformed. Suppose that the function of sensory awareness is not to provide sensation. ("Visual sensations" would, by the ordinary grammar of the expression, have to be something akin to bodily sensation, something like feelings in our eyes.) Suppose instead that the function of sensory awareness is to present objects, quantities of stuff, states, and events, all objectively *there* in the environment. Given reliable abilities to attend, abstract, and predicate, many of our immediate perceptual judgments will be reliably formed out of their sensed truthmakers, and will therefore amount to straightforward knowledge of how things stand in our environment (at least in the absence of evidence to the contrary). This is why immediate perceptual judgment is suited to play a foundational role with respect to other judgments. It can support them because it is typically knowledge, not mere plausible conjecture. This is also why immediate perceptual judgment is suited to play a criterial role with respect to other judgments. It can provide the test against which we decisively reject them because it is typically knowledge, not mere plausible conjecture.

The familiar refrain from the skeptical chorus re-enters at this point: "Ah, but doesn't the problem of alternatives resurface? After all, you admit that sensory awareness can malfunction, as in illusion or hallucination. For any veridical sensory awareness you take yourself to be having couldn't you have a hallucination qualitatively identical with it? Isn't it therefore the case that your present sensory deliverances are compatible with the assumption that you are hallucinating, and hence that you have no way of telling the difference?"

One advantage of the present proposal is that it enables us to highlight just what is mistaken in this all too familiar pattern of argument. Yes, sensory awareness can malfunction, as in hallucination or illusion. Yes, at least in principle, for any veridical experience one enjoys there could be a hallucination that one could not distinguish from it. *But no, it doesn't follow that my present sensory deliverances are compatible with the assumption that I am hallucinating.* My sensory deliverances are disclosures of sensible truthmakers, and not the neutral starting points I would share with someone who is constantly hallucinating or dreaming. Veridical sensory awareness is not a relation to something which one could be directly aware of even if one were hallucinating or dreaming. The view that it is simply reiterates the subjectivist picture of sensing that we have taken so much trouble to set aside.

The skeptic about our knowledge of the external world makes great play with the following conceit: things can be set up so that a subject *can't tell the difference* between seeing and hallucination. That seems right, at least in the sense that there could be a subjectively seamless transition between one's seeing a spoon on a table and one's hallucinating a spoon on a table. *But here is the nub of the matter: this doesn't entail that when one is seeing a spoon on the table one does not know one is seeing a spoon as opposed to hallucinating a spoon. When I am seeing a spoon on the table I can easily know that I am seeing a spoon on the table. I can know it in the same kind of direct way as I know that there is a spoon on the table. I attend to an event or state, and then form the appropriate judgment out of it.*

In the little opera of modern skepticism, a false subjectivist picture of so-called inner perception walks hand in hand with a false subjectivist picture of outer perception. Corresponding to the subjectivism that treats the deliverances of sensory awareness as akin to bodily sensations, there is the subjectivism that treats the awareness of one's own mental acts as akin to the introspection of bodily sensations. Suppose one sees the spoon, and by so-called "inner perception" one becomes aware of one's seeing of the spoon. The false subjectivist picture of inner perception has it that awareness of one's seeing the spoon is directed at a mental common factor that could be there whether one was hallucinating a spoon or seeing the spoon.

There is a different way of thinking of so-called inner perception. Knowledge of one's own mental acts is like perception in being immediate judgment made out of the very objects of awareness which are the truthmakers for the judgments in question. Among the things I can be aware of are my own mental acts, for example, my seeing the spoon on the table. Such mental acts are events, which like environmental events can be objects of my awareness. If I attend to this act and attend to the property of being a seeing by me of a spoon on the table, and then predicate the property I have attended to, then my higher-order judgment that I am seeing the spoon on the table will have been made out of its present truthmakers. My higher-order judgment that I am seeing the spoon on the table stands to my higher-order awareness of my seeing the spoon on the table in just the way that immediate perceptual judgment stands to sensory awareness.

Of course, the skeptic can press his case at the next level. He can suggest that my higher-order judgment could not be knowledge because my seeing the spoon on the table could be subjectively indistinguishable from a case of my hallucinating a spoon on the table. Here again, the skeptic insinuates the old idea that all I really have to work with in awareness—be it sensory awareness or higher-order awareness—is some mental common factor present both in the case of my seeing and in the indistinguishable case of my hallucinating.

The present account of awareness rejects the idea that the objects of awareness are *exhausted by* the factors in common between veridical and qualitatively indistinguishable falsidical acts of awareness.[18] Given that, the proper response to the skeptic is to point out that if I am seeing the spoon on the table, then my epistemic starting points are the presence of the spoon on the table and my seeing the spoon on the table. I am not at some neutral point that requires that I have some further evidence against the claim that I am hallucinating. I know without evidence that I am seeing. Neither the senses, nor higher-order awareness of mental acts, provide evidence for immediate judgment. They provide awareness of the truthmakers out of which the relevant judgments are formed.[19]

---

[18] For a detailed defense of this claim, see "The Obscure Object of Hallucination," 2004, op. cit., n. 12.

[19] Doesn't this account imply direct realism, and so is it not refuted by that absurd implication? I should confess that I regard the standard reaction to direct realism as itself a little naive. I believe that the arguments against direct realism from the vagueness and explanatory incompleteness of what is manifest to the senses, from the variation in appearances across animal species and from illusion are, all of them, bad arguments. But what I have said so far is compatible with other pictures of the mind's place in nature. One such picture, an essentially Kantian picture, is that sensible objects, states, and events are themselves phenomenal, that they have been "prepped" or synthesized by antecedent aspects of our sensory and conceptual endowment. For all I have said so far, phenomenal objects, states, and events could be the truthmakers for the propositions we immediately judge. The environment could be phenomenal. In the end, I would reject such a Kantianism because it depends on a transcendental conception of the antecedent structuring activity that issues in sensible objects, states, and events. I take it to be vividly absurd to suppose that such a transcendental apparatus is in play when it comes to the simpler animals that also have sensory awareness of items in their environment.

Kant in the A-deduction recognizes three syntheses: (i) the synthesis of intuition in apprehension; (ii) the synthesis of reproduction in imagination; and (iii) the synthesis of intuition in judgment. The strategy for the direct realist is to try to mimic the effect of the first two syntheses by way of two ideas: first, that the environment is multi-structured and multi-qualified *anyway*; second, that our sensibility, like any other, is inevitably selective, making only some ranges of quality and structure manifest.

The skeptic may now be tempted to take a new tack. Instead of maintaining that I do not *know* that I am seeing a spoon on the table, he may now maintain that I am *not* seeing a spoon on the table. But this is a rather absurd dogmatic claim with nothing in particular to recommend it. Certainly the skeptic is no longer doing what David Hume so engagingly did. He is not drawing reasonable inferences from a subjectivist picture of sensory awareness. He is just making odd claims about what is the case.

To summarize: in the face of familiar skepticism about our sensory access to the external world, the right thing to say is that if I am seeing a spoon on the table, and judge accordingly, then I typically know there is a spoon on the table. Moreover, if I am seeing a spoon on the table, and make the judgment that I am seeing a spoon on the table, then I typically know that I am seeing a spoon on the table. I typically know these things because the judgments in question are reliably formed from their respective truthmakers, which awareness makes manifest.

But, again, we should not obscure the main point here by disputes over words. I can imagine someone not wanting to call such judgments "knowledge," even when the subject does not possess and should not posses evidence against the judgment in question.[20]

My point is really that what we get from sensory experience is better than what is ordinarily called "knowledge." When one makes one's judgments out of their sensed truthmakers, the mind's response to reality is wholly adequate. The elements that make up the sensed truthmakers are abstracted and recombined in the corresponding judgment. A sliver of reality has been adequately *digested* in judgment. Give me that, and the interest of modern skepticism, if not its letter, is deflated. Grant the present description of the function of sensory awareness, and epistemic skepticism to the effect that our immediate perceptual judgments are not secure enough to ground the other judgments that are based on them must then take the form of skepticism about whether we have ever *sensed* external items and digested them in judgment in the way described. That form of skepticism is strongly analogous to skepticism as to whether we have ever *eaten* external items and digested them in the more familiar way. It is coherent, but whacky.

Isn't that, after all, how epistemic skepticism actually strikes us? It is part of the appeal of the "digestive realism" about sensing defended here that it helps anatomize the way in which modern epistemic skepticism is "strained and ridiculous," as David Hume famously put it.

---

[20] So if, by a clever plot, which no one can be reasonably expected to have seen through, almost all apparent calvados is fake calvados and I am one of the lucky few who gets to taste real calvados and appreciate its astringency, then my judgment that the calvados is astringent may not count as knowledge, even though I would have sensed by taste that the calvados is astringent. Still, I have adequately digested reality in my immediate judgment. That judgment *is* suited to play a foundational role with respect to the rest of what I judge.

REFERENCES

Armstrong, D. M. (1968), *A Materialist Theory of Mind* (London: Routledge and Kegan Paul).

Ayer, A. J. (1970), *The Problem of Knowledge* (Harmondsworth: Penguin).

Chalmers, David (1996), *The Conscious Mind* (New York: Oxford University Press).

Davidson, Donald (1986), "A Coherence Theory of Truth and Knowledge," in Ernest LePore (ed.), *Truth and Interpretation: Perspectives on the Philosophy of Donald Davidson* (Oxford: Blackwell): 307–19.

Dretske, Fred (1969), *Seeing and Knowing* (Chicago: University of Chicago Press).

Dretske, Fred (1990), "Seeing, Believing and Knowing," in Daniel Osherson, Stephen Kosslyn, and John Hollerbach (eds), *Visual Cognition and Action* (Cambridge, Mass.: MIT Press).

Galilei, Galileo [1623] (1957), *The Assayer*, in Stillman Drake (trans.), *Discoveries and Opinions of Galileo* (New York: Doubleday Anchor).

Humphrey, Nicholas (1993), *A History of Mind* (New York: Harper Perennial Books).

Johnston, Mark (2004), "The Obscure Object of Hallucination," *Philosophical Studies* 120: 113–83.

Lewis, David (1988), "What Experience Teaches," in *Proceedings of the Russellian Society* (Sydney: University of Sydney); reprinted in William Lycan (ed.) (1990): 499–518.

Lycan, William (1990), *Mind and Cognition* (Oxford: Blackwell).

McDowell, John (1994), *Mind and World* (Cambridge, Mass.: Harvard University Press).

McDowell, John (1997), "The Woodbridge Lectures," *Journal of Philosophy* 95: 431–91.

Nemirow, Lawrence (1990), "Physicalism and the Cognitive Role of Acquaintance," in William Lycan (ed.) (1990): 490–9.

Pitcher, George (1976), *Perception* (Princeton: Princeton University Press).

Price, H. H. (1932), *Perception* (London: Methuen).

Rorty, Richard (1979), *Philosophy and the Mirror of Nature* (Princeton: Princeton University Press).

Searle, John (1983), *Intentionality* (Cambridge: Cambridge University Press).

Sellars, Wilfred (1967), *Science and Metaphysics* (London: Routledge and Kegan Paul).

8

The Experience of Left and Right

Geoffrey Lee

A transcendental argument is an argument of the form 'Experience has feature F. If experience has feature F, then the external world has feature G. So the external world has feature G.' Kant and others have attempted to use arguments of this form to argue against sceptics about the existence of the external world.[1] In this chapter I'm not going to argue against any sceptics, but I'm going to show you how certain very plausible assumptions about experience can lead to surprising conclusions about how certain experiences are *physically realized*. In particular, you'll see how to travel transcendentally from facts about experience to facts about the *spatial* properties of the brain.[2]

But to get that far will take us a while. To begin with, let me remind you of the frequently discussed possibility of 'spectrum inversion'.[3] The familiar hypothesis is that the qualitative character of your colour experience might differ systematically from mine. So, for example, when I see a red object, my colour experience might be qualitatively like yours is when you see a green object, and vice versa. Further, it is claimed, since there is a (non-trivial) isomorphism from the colour-space on to itself that preserves all the basic qualitative similarities and differences between colours, this could occur without resultant differences in our (ordinary) behaviour. It is this supposed symmetry that is meant to allow for the possibility of non-manifest spectrum inversion.

The starting point for my discussion is the idea of qualitative inversion with respect to another perceived feature of the local environment—its left/right

I would like to thank the following people for helpful and inspiring comments and discussion: Ned Block, David Chalmers, Shamik Dasgupta, Tamar Szabó Gendler, John Hawthorne, Rory Madden, Chris Peacocke, Derek Parfit, Adam Pautz, Richard Price, Carlos Schafer, Sydney Shoemaker, Declan Smithies, Sebastian Watzl, and two anonymous referees (you know who you are).

[1] Or, our knowledge thereof. Transcendental arguments typically have conclusions like 'there is an external world', or 'I am not a brain in a vat', rather than, e.g., 'I know that there is an external world'.

[2] Martin Davies (1992) has attempted to run a similar kind of argument, in his case from armchair considerations to the conclusion that there is a Language of Thought.

[3] For a classic discussion, see Shoemaker (1982).

orientation about the viewer.[4] The idea is that there could be intra- or inter-subjective inversion with respect to the 'reflective orientation of the world', so that the way things appear to you when actually on the right is the way they appear to me when actually on the left, and vice versa.[5] It should be less controversial that there is a symmetrical structure to the qualitative space of left–right experience. This symmetry can be exploited to generate a different kind of experiential inversion hypothesis.

So, for example, when you look in a mirror, the apparent reflective orientation of the world gets inverted with respect to vision. Writing appears backwards, a chair that is on the left-hand side of the room appears on the right-hand side, and so on. Of course it's normally quite easy to tell that you are looking in a mirror. For example, one important cue is that items apparently in the mirror world appear to change position systematically with a change in position of the subject, in a way that would not occur if they were instead being viewed through a transparent pane of glass.

But although such cues exist when this inverting effect is produced by mirrors, perhaps experience could be left/right inverted in such a way that no such cues exist. (In order for this to occur without behaviourally manifest consequences, *all* the senses would need to be suitably inverted, not just vision.[6])

So, to be explicit, when I say things like 'the possibility of reflective inversion' in this chapter, I mean the following:

> *The Inversion Hypothesis:* There could be a subject exactly like me in his classi-ficatory and discriminatory dispositions, and in his ability to navigate the world, but who is such that, when under normal conditions he is presented with a particular external stimulus, he has experiences that are left/right inverted with respect to those that I would have under normal conditions, when presented with the same stimulus.

I will call the experiences of someone who is thus inverted with respect to me '(non-manifest) mirrored experiences' and I will refer to such a person as being '(non-manifestly) mirror-inverted'. (I will omit the parentheticals unless context requires their inclusion.)

The point of considering this hypothesis rather than the usual colour inversion hypothesis is that we will be led to certain surprising results already alluded to, results that do not have obvious analogues in the colour case. So what I am

---

[4] After completing this paper, I discovered that Susan Hurley has a related discussion of left/right inversion in her (1998)—see, in particular, ch. 8.

[5] I should note the related idea of up/down inversion, although I think it's much harder to make sense of non-manifest up/down inversion than left/right inversion. Interestingly, on at least one way of spelling out what up/down inversion would amount to, it is just the same thing as left/right inversion.

[6] Note that there also has to be an inversion of the causal relationships between (narrowly construed) intentions to move and bodily action if the experientially inverted subject is to suc-cessfully navigate the space around her.

interested in is not just the truth of Inversion Hypothesis (although I will present some arguments for it), but also certain other results about left/right experience that will be uncovered as we proceed. Moreover, the case of left/right inversion can be used to make most of the same points that the inverted spectrum example is frequently used to make, but less controversially. It also has the interesting feature that left and right are *spatial* relations and not sensory qualities—this means that certain ways of characterizing the inversion phenomenon that appeal to the specifically *sensory* nature of colours will not be available in this case.

But before entering the main discussion, I need to show that non-manifest mirrored experiences are at least prima facie conceivable (they are definitely quite hard to imagine).

THE CONCEIVABILITY OF MIRRORED EXPERIENCES

I have found that when some people consider the hypothesis of mirror inversion, they doubt whether there could be a coherent train of mirrored experiences. Perhaps the world could look inverted if I were just gazing in one direction, but could inverted experiences be consistently produced if I started to move around? Let me explain what these experiences would be like with the following example (the example will also serve as a basis for later considerations).

Take the layout of objects, floors, ceilings and walls in my apartment. It is obviously possible that an exact mirror image of my apartment could be constructed, and mirror-image versions of all the objects inside be put in appropriate counterpart locations. Furthermore, it seems obvious that if you were to wander into this mirror apartment, things would look very different from the way they would look if you wandered into my actual apartment.

Note that this mirror apartment would look like a reflection of my apartment viewed from any counterpart position within the apartment at any counterpart angle. It is an elementary result of geometry that the mirror image of a figure that results from reflecting it through any one chosen plane can be mapped on to the mirror image that results from choosing any other plane as the reflecting plane, just using rotation and linear movement operations. Thus whatever plane we chose to reflect the apartment through, the mirror apartment we would construct as a result would be intrinsically the same.

We can use this set-up to describe the experience of an individual who is mirror inverted.[7] The character of *his* experience as he walks through the door into my *actual* apartment would be the *same* as the character of *your* experience as you walk through the door into the *mirror* apartment. As he moves along any

---

[7] Likewise, one might explain the colour inverted spectrum hypothesis by saying that your experiences might be just like the ones that I would have if I were in an environment exactly like this except that all the colours of the external objects had been systematically switched.

path through my apartment, his experience is the same as yours would be if you traced the mirror path around the mirror apartment. And, given the simple geometrical point made in the previous paragraph, we can see that at every stage in this path, his experience would be a 'mirror' of the experience you would be having in your counterpart journey.

This description of an inverted subject's experience is not restricted to vision. For example, the qualitative character of the overall experience he would have if he stood in the middle of the apartment and turned around clockwise in a complete circle would match the one you would have if you stood in the middle of the mirror apartment and turned anticlockwise in a complete circle. Here it's not just the visual experience that would feel the same, but also the proprioceptive experience and action awareness associated with turning the body. Or, to take another example, if someone were to throw a ball at him that hit his left elbow, he would have an experience qualitatively the same as the one you would have if a similarly thrown ball were to hit your right elbow. Likewise with sounds, smells, tastes, etc. A triumphant peal of bells coming from the left would sound to this subject the way it would to you coming from the right; a bitter crystal dissolving on the left side of the tongue would feel like it would to you dissolving on the right side, and so on.

I will now consider some interesting arguments designed to show how mirrored experiences might be *physically realized*. These will serve to show that, on certain assumptions, the Inversion Hypothesis is true.

MIRROR MEN

Consider first the following puzzle. Take the brain of a subject who is in the midst of a train of conscious experiences. Suppose we also had another subject's brain that was exactly like the brain of this subject, except that the matter was arranged in a mirror image.[8] The question is: could there be any difference between the experiences being had by the two subjects? A closely related question is the following: suppose it were possible to physically reflect your brain in the middle of a course of experiences, but hold all the other physical facts about the brain constant. Would there be any difference between the experiences that ensue and the ones you would have had if your brain hadn't been flipped? (We should avoid being seduced here by a misguided picture of experience as involving a super-rigid homunculus gazing at an intra-skullular cinema screen that would be inverted by the flipping.)

The answers we can give to these questions are constrained by the view we take of the metaphysics of left and right. Let me briefly sketch the main views.

---

[8] There are certain difficulties that arise with this idea to do with the possibility of laws of nature that are sensitive to the left/right distinction. They will be dealt with later.

Consider a left glove. There are two basic views about what makes it left-handed. According to one view, call it 'absolutism', what makes a glove left or right is its possession of an intrinsic shape property of 'right glovedness' or 'left glovedness'. On this view there is an intrinsic difference between a left glove and a right glove, and every glove has one of these two reflective properties.

The other view, call it 'relationism', is rather more subtle. On this view, there is no intrinsic non-relational difference between a left glove and a right glove. All there really is, is the relation of congruence—that is, the relation that two gloves stand in when they are of the same glovedness. There are no intrinsic properties such as 'left glovedness' and 'right glovedness', so a left glove and right glove are intrinsically the same.

Of course, the absolutist and relationist both agree that the congruence relation exists; what is affirmed by the absolutist and denied by the relationist is that when two gloves stand in that relation their so doing is *grounded* by a difference in intrinsic properties. According to absolutism every glove has an intrinsic reflective property, either 'left glovedness' or 'right glovedness', and relations of congruence are supervenient on the distribution of these intrinsic properties. According to relationism there are only reflective *relations* between gloves, which are not grounded on the objects having any intrinsic reflective properties.

A closely related distinction is between those who think there are inter-world facts about congruence, and those who do not. For example, Kant mentions a world containing a single lonely hand.[9] Is there any fact of the matter about whether it is a left hand or a right hand? If you think that facts about inter-world sameness and difference depend only on the distribution of properties and relations *within* worlds, then you will think that there could only be such a fact of the matter if absolutism were true. Similarly, a relationist is likely to hold that there is no real difference between any two worlds that purportedly differ only in that one is arranged as a mirror image of the other. Strictly speaking, there is no contradiction in a relationist *not* saying this, but that would commit him to the view that there are brute modal facts that do not supervene on the distribution of non-modal facts.

Whether you are an absolutist or a relationist makes a difference to how you answer my questions about the experiences of incongruently brained subjects. For if you are a relationist, then you hold the position that two incongruous counterpart brains are intrinsically identical. If you also suppose that the character of experience supervenes on the intrinsic character of the brain, then you are forced into the position that the experiences being had by the owners of the different brains are the same. If you are an absolutist, then you think there is an intrinsic difference between the brains. So the same supervenience claim does not commit you to saying that the experiences in the two subjects are the same. The

---

[9] See Kant (1991) for his classic 1768 discussion of this point.

answer you give to these questions then depends on whether you believe that intrinsic reflective properties could be part of the minimal base of physical properties that determine the experiences being had by the owner of the brain.

The same kinds of questions arise even if you considerably weaken the supervenience claim, as some philosophers with externalist tastes are wont to do. Suppose, for example, that you only claim that the qualitative character of experience supervenes on the intrinsic character of the whole subject and his local environment (so, in particular, this intrinsic character includes relations between the subject and the objects that he is experiencing). You can then compare this set-up with an incongruous counterpart of the set-up, involving the subject and his environment laid out in a mirror image. Again, if you are a relationist, you will be committed to the view that the experiences being had in the two places are the same.

THE RELATIONIST ARGUMENT

Keeping these points in mind, I will now present a more complex argument that bears more directly to the question of whether inter-subjective reflective inversion of experiences is possible. I'll call this the 'Relationist Argument'. I'll call it that because it's supposed to show that if relationism is true then the Inversion Hypothesis is true. A bit later on we will consider what happens if we suppose absolutism to be true.

So let us take relationism as a premise. The Relationist Argument again considers the difference between the experiences of a subject and a mirror-image copy of this subject, although this time it's the *whole* physical subject we will be considering, not just a brain. Another difference is that we will only assume that the subjects are incongruous immediately *prior* to the stimulation that causes the experiences that we will compare. To anticipate, the conclusion of the argument is that a subject who was *initially* a physical reflection of you (your mirror twin) would, when presented with the same stimulus as you, have an experience that was inverted with respect to yours.

The gist of the Relationist Argument is as follows. If we were to reflectively invert the whole world around you the subject, then it seems like that would make a big difference to its appearance. For example, if you were about to read a sign that said 'MIT', then if we reflected the whole world around you, the sign would instead read 'TIM'. But if we are relationists, then there is no real difference between reflecting the world around you, and reflecting you the subject, holding the world constant. So we can conclude that if we made a mirror copy of you, he or she would have experiences like those you would have if the world around you were flipped over.

The Relationist Argument can be illustrated with a 'toy model' of how experience might depend on the physical realm. Imagine a group of subjects whose heads are painted red on the left side and white on the right side. These striped subjects are able to have experiences just like ours. But what happens when such a subject experiences an environment is that an image of the scene in front of them is literally imprinted on their forehead. So if a bed is on the subject's left, and a kite on his right, then the bed will imprint on their red side, and the kite on their white side. And the experiences the subject has of any scene obey the following rule: which experiences the subject has supervenes on the layout of the imprinted image with respect to the red and white portions of their head.

So suppose we have one of these red and white beasts, and let us christen him 'Striped Lefty'. Compare the imprinted pattern that Striped Lefty would get of this 'bed and kite' stimulus with the pattern that would result from him being exposed to the incongruent counterpart of the stimulus. Had the environment been arranged mirrorwise, Striped Lefty would have instead ended up with a kite image imprinted on his red side and a bed image imprinted on his white side.

Note that due to the asymmetrical distribution of colour on Striped Lefty's head, this second pattern on his forehead is neither identical to, nor the incongruous counterpart of, the pattern caused by the first stimulus; this time the bed image is white and the kite image is red. Indeed, that is just what we require if his experience of the mirrored stimulus is to be different from that of the original stimulus and we are assuming relationism.

Now suppose we build a mirror-image counterpart of Striped Lefty, as he was prior to being imprinted. Let us christen this new beast 'Striped Righty'. Striped Righty starts off life with the right side of his head red, and the left side of his head white. If we expose him to the 'bed on left, kite on right' stimulus, then he will end up with a bed image imprinted on his white side, and a kite image imprinted on his red side. In other words, he will end up in a state that is physically a mirror image of the state Striped Lefty was in when we exposed him to the opposite 'kite on left, bed on right' stimulus. But if we are relationists, this is exactly the same physical state. So it follows that Striped Righty's experience of the 'bed on left, kite on right' stimulus is the same as Striped Lefty's experience of the 'kite on left, bed on right' stimulus. And the same is true of any other stimulus and its incongruent counterpart. In other words, Striped Righty is experientially mirror inverted with respect to Striped Lefty.

Note that the physical state Striped Righty goes into when presented with any stimulus is neither identical to, nor the incongruous counterpart of, the state Striped Lefty goes into when presented with the same stimulus. So there is no contradiction here in holding that relationism is true and that Striped Righty and Striped Lefty would have mirror-inverted experiences of the same stimulus. (We *would* be in trouble, however, if both sides of Striped Lefty's head were the *same* colour to begin with; more on that shortly.)

The argument seems to work just as well if we consider instead the actual supervenience base for experience rather than the red/white image imprinting model. So suppose this time that we have just a normal human being, who we'll christen 'Simple Lefty' (or 'Lefty' for short). Suppose at t1, Lefty has his eyes closed[10] and is about to view my apartment, and that at t2 the apartment viewing begins. Let 'Simple Righty' ('Righty' for short) be a mirror image copy of Lefty at t1.

The following statement is surely true:

(A) Suppose at t2 Lefty is viewing my apartment as it actually is. Then it is true that if the apartment had been laid out in a mirror image of the way it is actually laid out, his experience of it would have been reflectively inverted with respect to the experience he is actually having of it.

Now suppose that we are relationists about left and right. We might think that the following two hypotheses are really the same, in so far as the physical layout of the respective universes is concerned.[11]

(1) At t2, Lefty has just opened his eyes, and is standing gazing at the *reflected* version of my apartment, with the whole physical universe around the apartment also reflected.

(2) At t2, Righty has just opened his eyes, and is standing gazing at my apartment, as it *actually* is, from the perspective equivalent to the one Lefty is gazing from in scenario (1).

Add in the third scenario:

(3) At t2, Lefty has just opened his eyes, and is standing gazing at my apartment, as it *actually* is, from the same perspective as in (2).

Add in a fairly weak supervenience claim:

(WS): The qualitative character of a subject's experiences supervenes on the layout of physical properties of the whole universe.

We can now argue that the Inversion Hypothesis is true. It follows from (A), (WS) and the physical sameness of (1) and (2) that the experiences had in (2) and (3) are mirror-inverted with respect to each other. But they are experiences of exactly the same environment from the same perspective (and we can stipulate that conditions are quite normal). So we seem to have established at least one possible case of inter-subjective reflective inversion. Therefore, if relationism is true, then the Inversion Hypothesis is true.

The argument gives a physical sufficient condition for a mirrorwise difference in experiences—an individual who is initially a physical mirror duplicate of another individual will have experiences that are left/right inverted with respect to that individual. This is a strict sufficient condition. If we found individuals whose brain structure appeared to be built roughly in a mirror image to that

---

[10] Or, better, he is in a state of total sensory deprivation.

[11] Here we can ignore the possibility of haecceitistic differences between objects.

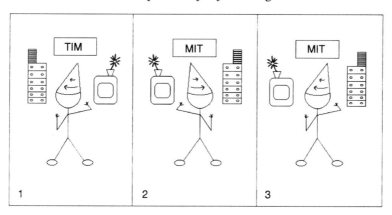

Fig. 1. Three hypotheses.

found in normal humans, that might be thought by a proponent of the Relationist Argument to be empirical evidence that they were experientially left/right inverted. (And indeed I am told that this is the situation with certain left-handed people.)

As I set it up, the Relationist Argument assumes relationism. In fact it is obvious that we could weaken this assumption to: 'if there are absolute reflective facts, then they are irrelevant in the determination of experience', and the argument would be equally good. So, if you're an absolutist, you can still consistently use the Relationist Argument, as long as you don't think absolute reflective facts are part of what determines experience.

INVERSION AND FUNCTIONAL EQUIVALENCE

An objection to the Relationist Argument which I should mention straight away is as follows: the complaint is that this could not be a genuine case of 'inverted qualia', because at the time when they are having inverted experiences of the same stimulus, Lefty and Righty are in physically quite different states (they are no longer merely incongruent), and so might be functionally quite different. But aren't inverted qualia cases supposed to be examples of functionally identical subjects who nevertheless have different qualia?[12]

The issues here are similar to those that arise in the case of colour, so I will be brief. My reply to this point is that we must distinguish different levels at which two subjects might be functionally alike. The conventional inverted spectrum scenario is normally only presented with a commitment to the subjects being functionally the same at the common-sense level of classification, discrimination, navigation and so forth. Such functional sameness is compatible with the

[12] Ned Block, David Chalmers, and an anonymous referee all stressed this point to me.

subjects being functionally distinct at some deeper level on which the difference in qualia depends. So, for example, Shoemaker advertises himself as a proponent of the possibility of inverted qualia, even though he is a physicalist, and a functionalist about *all* physical properties.

Now I would claim that if the Relationist Argument goes through, Lefty and Righty are *relevantly* functionally alike, so should count as an example of inverted qualia. Righty's basic sensorimotor capacities are the same as Lefty's; for example, it is *not* the case that if Righty attempts to reach for an object on the left, he will reach to the right—he will succeed in basic navigation just as well as Lefty. Having said this, I should admit that there may be some functional differences at a fairly common-sense level, like the ability to interact with familiar asymmetrical stimuli such as writing and remembered environments. These things would indeed look strange at first to Righty. But it's hard to believe that once Righty learned to adapt to these phenomena, and so became functionally the same as Lefty with respect to them, that would make him qualitatively left/right inverted with respect to his former self. Such abilities are very plausibly irrelevant to the orientation of our experiences—for example, people who have trouble remembering how to unlock their front door, surely can have normal left/right experiences. The case of memory of familiar environments is perhaps more controversial, and you might be tempted to conclude that Righty's inversion just consists in his finding these places to be different from how he remembers them. I think that would be a mistake too, although it would take us too far astray to argue the case in detail here. (A few suggestions are provided in the footnote below.)[13] But my main interest is with certain consequences of the Relationist Argument that follow whether or not this should be classified as a genuine case of inverted qualia, as that is normally understood.

Below we will see what happens if you think that absolute reflective facts exist and *are* relevant to what experiences we have. But first I want to point out one interesting and paradoxical-seeming consequence of the Relationist Argument.

SYMMETRICAL OBSERVERS

The conclusion of the Relationist Argument was that if we were to construct a molecule-for-molecule physical duplicate of Lefty at the time when his eyes are

---

[13] The position would have to be that experiencing an environment as having one orientation rather than another consists of an input representation being compared with memory (the congruence relations being calculated, and so forth). Against this, it seems plausible that: (1) someone would have different experiences of incongruent stimuli even without stored information about his environment, for example, if he were a baby or an amnesiac; (2) the visual processing on which the basic spatial content of experience depends does not involve a 'top down' memory component of this kind, but is wholly 'bottom up'; and (3) if left/right determinate experience requires memory in this way, then your first experiences could not be left/right determinate—but then how could memories formed from them serve as a basis for the left/right determinacy of later experiences?

closed, but arrange the matter in an exact mirror image of the way it is organized in his actual body, the resulting mirror twin would, on opening his eyes, have experiences that were reflectively inverted with respect to Lefty's. However, this result raises the following puzzle: what if Lefty happened to be constructed symmetrically?[14] In particular, what if his brain, the organ responsible for his experiences, was constructed symmetrically? On the face of it, there seems to be no reason why such a design could not be totally adequate for this organism to achieve everything we actually achieve. Let us suppose that we have such a symmetrical beast, and let us christen him 'Simple Simon' ('Simon' for short).

The problem now raised is that if we were to produce a mirror twin of Simon, he would be in all intrinsic respects physically the same as Simon. So, provided we are assuming that some reasonable kind of mental/physical supervenience thesis is true, we would expect Simon to have the *same* kinds of experiences in the same situations as his mirror twin. (In particular, if we consider Simon and mirror Simon gazing at a scene from the same perspective at t2, having had their eyes shut at t1, then, since they are intrinsically the same at t1, they'll still be intrinsically the same at t2.) But if we were to assume that symmetrical Simon's experiences depend on the world in much the same way that ours do, then we are also led by the Relationist Argument to conclude that they would be *different* from his mirror twin's. So the assumptions of the Relationist Argument seem to lead to a contradiction.

To clarify, note that Simon is only assumed to be symmetrical immediately *prior* to being imprinted with experiences. Of course, once the river of experiences starts flowing we would probably expect asymmetries to appear in the brain, perhaps depending on how the brain is constructed. For example, you might expect an experience of an asymmetrical landscape to require an asymmetrical pattern of electronic activity in the brain. The point is that if Simon is *initially* symmetrical, then *at the time of experience* he will be an exact mirror duplicate of the way he would have been had the environment been arranged mirrorwise. The puzzle is that if we suppose that absolute reflective facts are irrelevant to determining experiences, then Simon would have the same experiences whether the environment was arranged one way or the other.

In terms of our 'toy model' for experience, the situation is like one where both sides of our imaginary subject's head are painted the same colour. If that were the case, then his forehead would end up in the same state (up to incongruence) whichever of two incongruent stimuli we showed him. So he would have qualitatively the same experiences of the two stimuli.

Clearly, the only thing that someone who wishes to endorse the Relationist Argument can do to avoid contradiction is to bite the bullet and say that Simon has the same experiences of incongruent environments. We could describe this consequence as 'geometrical symmetry entails experiential symmetry'. Someone

---

[14] Again, there is a problem here with asymmetrical laws of nature, which I will discuss later.

is *experientially symmetrical*[15] if her (veridical) experiences of incongruous environments are the same. Another way of putting this consequence is that asymmetrical experiences are necessarily underwritten by an initial asymmetry in the subject's brain. And I think that if this were true, that would be quite surprising.

Even if we can't imagine from the inside being experientially symmetric, it seems there is nothing obviously incoherent about the idea, even if it is quite puzzling. For example, Rory Madden described to me how when he was a child he was puzzled by the idea of colour blindness. If someone can't tell the difference between green and red, but their colour discriminations are otherwise normal, surely this means that their experiences of both red and green things must either be both like a normal person's red experiences, or both like a normal person's green experiences. And then of course the puzzle is: which is it? But, as he concluded, evidently the answer to this puzzle is that they are neither— the colour-blind person's experiences are just less determinate than ours with respect to colour. And similarly with symmetric experiences—even though we can't imagine seeing an environment without seeing it as oriented reflectively one way or the other, it seems at least prima facie possible that someone else's experiences could just be less determinate than ours in this respect. (To approximate to what their experiences would be like, try imagining having two visual fields, one oriented one way, and one the other. Or, even better, try imagining having a patchwork of *infinitely* many visual fields arranged so they alternate spatially in orientation.[16] (The key thing is to not make the mistake of thinking that symmetrical experiences would be like our experiences of symmetrical environments.))

So there is sufficient reason for not dismissing the idea of experiential symmetry offhand. However you might wonder whether it's really true that symmetrical Simon would have these experiences. There are two kinds of strategy for casting doubt on this. First, you might simply attack the specific argument we have for this claim, for example, by supposing that absolute reflective facts exist and are part of what determines our experiences. Second, you might argue that the conclusion is false on independent grounds, hence casting doubt on the original argument. I'll first discuss a worry of the latter kind.

As I mentioned briefly above, it seems offhand that a brain whose initial design (i.e., prior to experience) was symmetrical could potentially achieve anything that our brains can achieve. There is no *obvious* reason for supposing that this design would necessitate any limitation on the range of psychological features that the brain could support. It therefore seems bizarre to suppose that this brain could not produce left/right experiences anything like ours.

An important example of a psychological feature that Simon clearly could have, the existence of which jars with the view that his experiences would be

---

[15] This bit of terminology was suggested to me by Ned Block.
[16] Thanks to John Hawthorne for suggesting the infinite version of the 'multiple visual fields' idea.

symmetrical, is the following: it seems like Simon could perfectly well intentionally move towards an object on his right, and it be true that had the object been on his left he would have moved instead to the left to reach the object. So Simon's perceptual system could be quite capable of sustaining the normal kinds of dependence between a bodily action and the location of the target of that action. But you might wonder whether that fact is consistent with the claim that the experience of the object would be the same whether the object was on the left or the right.[17]

You could respond to this as follows. First, it has to be admitted that there is after all at least one important psychological limitation that is imposed by symmetry. This is that an initially symmetrical person like Simon could not make any *classificatory* distinctions between things on the left and on the right.[18] If you ask Simon to say which side of his visual field an object is in, left or right, then he could not tell you. Equally, if you presented him with a word containing only symmetrical letters like 'TIM' he could not tell you whether it said 'TIM' or 'MIT'. This is because we would expect the only physical difference between Simon and his behaviour with respect to incongruous stimuli to be itself just incongruence.[19] But it seems like such classificatory differences would require more than just incongruence. It seems that in order to make such a classificatory distinction there would have to be a left–right asymmetry in the brain that was exploited to distinguish the two stimuli, in a way somewhat analogous to the way a lock picks out a key.

Does this show that Simon has symmetrical experiences? Probably not. On the face of it, experiencing a difference between left and right, and being able to classify that difference are two quite different things. For example, being able to *say* whether an object is on the left or right is a skill that is surprisingly difficult to acquire. But we would not take a lack of such classificatory skills in a child to be evidence that her experiences were not left/right determinate. So, if there is strong connection between the content of experience and the ability of the subject or the brain to classify information, that is something that is unobvious and must be argued for. (Perhaps one way of articulating the debate over whether experience could have non-conceptual contents would be in terms of this distinction between content and classification.)

Indeed, doubt about such a connection is cast by the point about Simon's actions. The fact that Simon would walk in the correct direction to reach an object whether it is on the left or right suggests that there can be evidence that supports the attribution of a left/right distinction to the subject's experience that does not involve him *classifying* that difference.

---

[17] A closely related point is that there is a sense in which incongruous subjects are functionally different—their dispositions to move either to the left or right, for example, are different, so the 'output clauses' given in the functional characterization of their mental states would be different. This might be thought sufficient for a difference in their experiences. (Also, see discussion on p. 309–11). [18] I am grateful to Ned Block for pointing this out to me.
[19] Again, modulo the effects of asymmetrical laws of nature, which I will discuss on p. 311–12.

The relationist might respond to that point by saying that the two situations of the object being on the right or the left could only relevantly differ if there was some asymmetry in the subject's body prior to experience. For example, he will say that the difference between a subject being embedded in an environment as opposed to its incongruent counterpart, is not that the two environments are intrinsically different, rather that they differ in their relations to the subject's body. But these relations only differ if the subject is left/right asymmetrical prior to experience. Otherwise the two scenarios are really the same, and so there is no difference in behaviour that needs explaining. (This response seems to me sufficient to remove much of the force of this observation.)

A final point about Simon is that unlike a colour-blind subject, it is plausible that he might be able respond differentially to *successive* presentations of congruent or incongruent stimuli.[20] For example, if you showed him 'MIT' *followed* by 'TIM', he could tell that the second stimulus was different, and he would say that his second experience was qualitatively different from his first. This is so, even though on the relationist view, had he been shown the opposite sequence of stimuli ('TIM' then 'MIT'), he would have had qualitatively the same sequence of experiences. Now it seems that we must say that the second experience is asymmetrical, otherwise we risk scepticism about whether *our* experiences are asymmetrical.[21] But then it seems surprising to claim that the first experience was not also asymmetrical. Indeed, the problems seem to start even earlier. To what extent is it coherent to speak of the 'first experience'? (How long did it last?) And, even supposing that there is such a thing, how could it introduce the required asymmetry into Simon's brain? For, if we suppose (as I suggested in n. 13) that the basic spatial content of experience depends only on 'bottom up' processing, and not on memory, then one might expect the relevant part of the brain to 'reset' itself prior to each new train of experience. This view of the processing, combined with relationism, would result in the view that each new train of Simon's experience would be symmetrical, even though Simon would be able to discriminate between incongruent stimuli, and would think that his experiences of them were different. In light of this, the relationist may be forced into the view mentioned in n. 13, that the existence of the left/right content of experience depends on memory.[22] This seems to be a fairly forceful consideration against the view.

I now move on to consideration of what happens if we reject the main premise of the Relationist Argument, and suppose that absolutism is true.

---

[20] Not every symmetrical being would necessarily have this capacity. But there seems to be nothing about symmetry to *prevent* you from having such a capacity.

[21] If Simon's subsequent experiences were *not* asymmetrical, he would still think that they were. But then how would we know that we were not in the same position as Simon?

[22] If this is right, then perhaps the relationist should reject my claim that adjusting to asymmetrical stimuli like writing and remembered environments would not invert Righty's experiences. This would weaken the sense in which Righty could be said to be non-manifestly inverted.

WHAT THE ABSOLUTIST MIGHT SAY

The main premise of the Relationist Argument is that the experiences had in perfectly incongruent scenarios are qualitatively the same (at least with respect to left/right orientation). For example, it was claimed that the experiences had by Lefty in scenario (1), and the experiences being had by Righty in scenario (2), would feel the same. Now, as I have already remarked, an absolutist about the left/right orientation of space could accept this premise, and so could accept the conclusions of the Relationist Argument, provided they don't think that the intrinsic difference that they believe exists between incongruent counterpart scenarios is relevant to determining the reflective character of any experiences being had in those scenarios. On the other hand, they could also *reject* the main premise of the argument, by insisting that this intrinsic difference *does* make a relevant experiential difference.

If there is an intrinsic physical difference between scenario (1) and scenario (2), then global supervenience alone will not tell us anything about the relationship between the experiences in the two scenarios—supervenience is compatible with the experiences being completely different. However, it is reasonable to assume that both subjects are correctly perceiving the spatial layout of the objects in the same amount of detail (perhaps modulo the reflective orientation of the objects in space—we can leave open the possibility that one of the subjects is perceiving this incorrectly). Given this assumption, we can intelligibly compare the reflective orientation of their experiences—either it is the same or it is different. The main premise of the Relationist Argument is that it is the same, because the experiential facts do not depend in any way on absolute spatial facts (if there are any at all). The most plausible alternative[23] to this relationist view would be to hold that in general the orientation of experiences being had in perfectly incongruent scenarios like (1) and (2) is *different*—that is, the experiences are *opposite* in orientation.

I will call this view *Absolutism* with a capital 'A'. (Note that to be consistent with global supervenience, this view requires that absolute reflective facts exist and that orientation of our experiences depends on them.)

We can illustrate the Absolutist view by considering again the case of incongruent counterpart brains. Would the owners of these brains have experiences that feel the same? Provided that the Absolutist thinks that the qualitative character of experience supervenes narrowly on the intrinsic state of the brain, the Absolutist's view is that the experiences had by the owners of these two brains are *opposite in* their reflective character, because the brains are identical except for the intrinsic reflective difference between them.

---

[23] Strictly speaking, you could also hold the view that in *some* pairs of cases like (1) and (2) the orientation is the same, and in some pairs of cases it is different. Most of my discussion of Absolutism will also apply to this view, which suffers further difficulties I will not discuss.

But, even if he does not assume any narrow supervenience hypothesis, the Absolutist can still say, for example, that the experiences being had by Lefty in scenario (1) and Righty in scenario (2) are relevantly different because the two scenarios are perfectly incongruent, both with respect to the intrinsic set-up of the observers *and* their environments. And that is one way to block the Relationist Argument.

It is interesting to note that it would follow from Absolutism that Righty and Lefty would have the *same* experiences of actual stimuli, and so would not be reflectively inverted with respect to each other after all. For example, according to Absolutism, when Righty sees 'MIT' he is experientially inverted with respect to Lefty seeing 'TIM'; so if we show them both 'TIM', they will have the same experience of it.

I will shortly assess the plausibility of holding this Absolutist position. But let us first ask: where would an Absolutist stand on whether the Inversion Hypothesis is true? The answer depends on what kind of supervenience thesis about the qualitative character of experience he thinks is true. If he thinks that what it's like for the subject depends only on what's going on in the subject's brain (the 'narrow supervenience' view), then he should think that inversion is possible. If he thinks that a more external dependence holds, then he might reasonably think that inversion is not possible.

As I have just remarked, on the narrow supervenience view, the Absolutist is committed to the view that the owners of incongruent conscious brains will be having mirrorwise different experiences. And now it's not that hard to see how you could set things up so the states of two such brains would be caused by the same external stimuli under normal circumstances, so that inversion is possible.

For example, we could take Righty, and literally cross over all the neural wiring in his body leading from brain to sensory neurons at the surface. For example, we would reroute the neural connection that goes from left thumb-tip to brain so that it goes from right thumb-tip to brain, and so forth. We could also similarly rewire all the motor neurons, so that he could move around successfully. Once rewired this way and given a particular stimulus, what would happen in his brain during experience would be physically a mirror image of what would happen in Lefty's brain given the same stimulus.[24] So if it is true that brainwise physical inversion (at the time of experience) entails experiential inversion, as we are now assuming, then 'doctored Righty' is experientially mirror inverted with respect to Lefty.

Suppose we thought instead that certain external facts *are* part of the minimal base of facts on which the qualitative character of experience supervenes, so that narrow supervenience is false. If the Inversion Hypothesis is true, then there could be inverted experiences caused by the same stimulus under normal conditions. But the stipulation of same stimulus and normal conditions might mean that the

---

[24] Again, modulo asymmetrical physical laws, which I will discuss shortly.

relevant *external facts* are the same, depending on which ones we are putting in the supervenience base. So the Absolutist externalist could argue that two subjects under these conditions must be having reflectively the *same* experiences. So the externalist Absolutist could argue that inversion is impossible.

If we are absolutists (small 'a'), then it is certainly plausible that such externalism is the correct view about the left/right *content* of experience. For example, you might think that if an experience of an object that presents it as 'phenomenally left' is also caused under normal circumstances by the object being actually on the left, then the experience represents it as on the left. (For the relationist, the story about content might be more complicated—unfortunately, I can't get into that here.) If something like that is right about the left/right content of experience, then there is one interesting brand of Absolutist externalism that can be viewed as saying that what it's like to see something as on the left is exhausted by the fact that it is being represented as on the left. That may sound plausible until we consider the possibility of left/right inversion. If inversion is possible, then content externalism could mean that inverted subjects' experiences have the *same* spatial contents, even though they are phenomenally different with respect to left/right presentation.

It's worth noting how much this kind of Absolutist externalist view of the qualitative character of spatial experience jars with the unreflective view most people would take. It would imply that it is possible for two subjects to be in the same brain state, and both be having veridical experiences, but nonetheless for the qualitative character of their experiences be different. That would be the situation, for example, if we compared Righty viewing one environment with 'doctored Righty' (as defined three paragraphs above) viewing the incongruous counterpart of that environment. Since the environments are incongruous and we can assume that both subjects are having veridical experiences with absolute left/right content, their experiences must differ in content, and hence, according to this view, also in qualitative character.[25] But their brain states are identical.

I expect some people will take this view, but its metaphysical oddness should be acknowledged. The question of what the qualitative character of experience supervenes on is surely at least partly an *empirical* matter; but I take it that our common-sense empirical view is that sameness of the most proximate stimulus can be sufficient for sameness of qualitative character, so that the more distal facts could not be part of the minimal supervenience base. It would be a remarkable discovery if that turned out to be false.

The externalist view is sometimes motivated by the thought that experiences are *relational* states of affairs, and not simply monadic properties of subjects, where the relata are subjects and local states of affairs like a layout of words on a page being read, or an apartment being viewed. Since the same relation cannot

---

[25] I'm assuming here that this theorist is allowing that there can be a qualitative difference between seeing something on the left and seeing it on the right. That might be left open by my characterization of the view above.

hold both in a case of veridical experience and a case of hallucination, these experiences must be different, the thought continues, even if the intrinsic brain states involved are the same. But to conclude from this that these experiences would be *qualitatively* different seems to me to be a non-sequitur—there is evidently no reason why experiences that involve relations to different states of affairs should not *feel* the same to the subjects having them. Equally, you might even think that being experientially related to the *same* state of affairs could feel different to different subjects. So it is evidently quite consistent to hold a narrow view of the supervenience of qualitative character along with a relational view of experience in *this* sense.[26]

So much for Absolutism and the Inversion Hypothesis. We now need to ask: could Absolutism really be true?

The idea that these absolute spatial properties could make any difference to experience might plausibly be thought as absurd as the idea that if the whole universe suddenly spun around 180 degrees in absolute space that could determine some change in our experience. This intuition can be brought out especially strongly if we consider the fact that reflection is not a mathematical operation of a substantially different kind from rotation or linear translation. In fact, it can be shown that reflection is just an *instance* of a linear translation and rotation, albeit through a higher dimension.[27] Hence it would not be inaccurate to say that the difference between a subject gazing at my apartment and a mirror-image copy of the subject gazing at the mirror apartment is merely a difference in the *orientation* of the two environments (the subject included as part of the environment). But how could a mere difference in the orientation of the subject and his environment constitutively determine a difference in experience, even if these orientations could be thought of in absolutist terms? Again, we would strongly resist this idea if the orientation in question was, for example, just the location and direction of the subject and his environment in 3D space.[28]

---

[26] A different 'relational' position about experience (see, for example, Johnston 2004) is one that insists that the qualitative character of the experience is exhausted by and uniquely correlated with the structured array of properties and relations one is related to in having the experience (rather than the more concrete particulars and states of affairs). But that is not necessarily incompatible with narrow supervenience, especially if one thinks that you can be acquainted with such an array in having an hallucination. Is this position correct? It would be *close* to being the right view if it could be argued that whenever one's experience has a certain sensory quality, such as that involved in seeing a red object, one is ipso facto experientially related to a correlative secondary property such as redness. But if one thinks of a case like left/right inversion, it is clear that sometimes one can motivate the idea that experience has some qualitative aspect, without it being in any way natural to think of tokenings of that quality as involving the subject being experientially related to some secondary property.

[27] See Van Cleve (1991) for discussion of this point, which was originally made by the mathematician Moebius—see Moebius (1991).

[28] Perhaps if absolutism is true then a change in orientation might be *causally* sufficient for a change in experience, but that is obviously not to the point. The present claim would have to be that there would be a change in experience, even if all the other physical facts were held constant (even if that is nomologically impossible).

I would suggest that if we think that reflection is a significantly different kind of operation from these other spatial operations like rotation, that is because it appears to us that the difference we experience between incongruent objects is of a different kind from that we experience between, say, mutually rotated qualitatively identical objects. But when we just look formally at these operations, the intuition this appearance suggests is not supported—and it should be clear by now that we do not need to bring in some magic difference in the operations to explain these experiential facts. It could be that the right way to think about it is that seeing a difference between incongruent objects is a bit like seeing exactly similar congruent objects, but from different sides, i.e., in situations where our *relations* to the objects differ, not the objects themselves.

Another very different objection to the Absolutist view is that it is inconsistent with certain ways of being a *functionalist* about experience. Absolute spatial facts are facts that on many views could differ across worlds without any relevant difference in the causal profiles of those worlds.[29] So, for example, you might think that if absolutism (small 'a') is true, then there is a world just like our world except that it is arranged in a mirror image. The Absolutist is committed to the view that the experiences being had by your counterpart in that world are quite different from your experiences, even though all the functional facts in these two worlds are the same.[30]

Another way of bringing out this point is to consider a thought experiment by Ned Block, as updated by Arnold Zuboff.[31] It seems that in principle we could remove each of your brain cells one by one and fit each removed cell and the adjacent cells with minute radio transmitters that were capable of ensuring that the cells continued to fire exactly as and when they would if still embedded in the ordinary way. It is very hard to see how this could make any difference to the experiences had by the subject.[32] This suggests that we could in principle put the cells of your brain in any spatial arrangement that we fancied without this affecting how your experiences ensued, the relevant functional organization being preserved by the operation.

If this is right, then the spatial arrangement of the brain seems irrelevant to the determination of experience after all. For example, if we were to take Lefty and doctored Righty, and explode their brains *à la* Block/Zuboff, we would end up with the same system of transmitters connected to the body in the same way. So, if the intuition generated by the Block/Zuboff experiment is correct, then the

[29] That would not be allowed for on a 'causal essentialist' view like Shoemaker's (1980), however.

[30] Actually not *all* functionalists need say this—if we consider 'local' functional characterizations of you and your counterpart, with input and output clauses that are allowed to mention absolute spatial properties, then we could get different characterizations for you both. We only get in trouble if we 'Ramsify' out over the input and output clauses also.

[31] See Block (1980) and Zuboff (1981).

[32] Admittedly, Block's original thought experiment was designed to provoke the opposite intuition.

absolute spatial difference between Lefty's and doctored Righty's brains, whilst undergoing counterpart experiences, could not make any difference to those experiences. So Absolutism is false.

You could try making a similar point about the supposed requirement of asymmetry that was established from the premises of the Relationist Argument. You might think you could apply the Block/Zuboff technique to any normal subject to render him temporarily *symmetrical*, and his subsequent experiences would still differentiate between incongruent stimuli. (I am unsure about whether this objection to a relationist position could be made to work, but it's interesting to contemplate.[33])

The Absolutist might respond as follows. Suppose we take a complete description of our universe, and then 'Ramsify' over it, replacing all the property and relation names with variables, except those that refer to the causal relation. Is it really plausible that if we bleach out everything in this way, including even terms for *spatial* properties and relations, we'll end up with a description that completely determines which experiences are occurring? We wouldn't think that if we 'Ramsifyed out', even over the causal relation as well, so that the description of the universe was completely formal. So what's so special about the causal relation?[34] For example, we can imagine a computer simulation of the actual world that satisfies the same Ramsey description, but does not literally contain the same distribution of spatial properties. And it is at least not obvious that running such a simulation would produce real experiences. So, viewed from an abstract standpoint, it is not particularly compelling that spatial properties could not be relevant to the determination of experience.

Similarly, a Block/Zuboff exploded brain shares a certain Ramsey characterization with a normal brain—they are in a certain way functionally the same, even though they can massively differ in their spatial properties. Unlike in the case of functionally equivalent universes, the functional equivalence here is only at a relatively macroscopic level—the brains are not functionally the same at the level of fundamental particles, for example. And the brain is not a causally closed system, so the relevant functional description may be in terms of substantially specified sensory inputs and behavioural outputs; and there are other related differences like the fact that only a normal brain can be stroked or stamped on. But these differences can hardly make all the difference. Unless we

---

[33] Suppose, for example, that having an experience of a certain stimulus involves a sequence of synchronous neuron firings, each synchronous firing involving 10,000 neurons. Suppose that had the experience been of an incongruent stimulus, there would have been a completely different sequence of synchronous firings, each synchronous firing instead involving 9,800 neurons. Then there will be no way to set things up using the Block/Zuboff technique so that the pattern of neural firings would be the same up to incongruence whichever stimulus is presented. However, in order for the point to go through, only *one* possible case is required, so this consideration is far from decisive. It is unclear, however, how one would establish the existence of such a case. (One suggestion, made to me by Tamar Szabó Gendler, would be to try making replacements in a way that was not one–one.)   [34] John Hawthorne (2001) makes this kind of point.

are externalists who think that the only spatial facts that matter to experience are those external to the brain, then if we think that it is dubious whether the spatial properties really are irrelevant in the universe case, we should probably think the same about this more localized version.

ASYMMETRICAL LAWS OF NATURE

So much for considerations for and against the view that absolute reflective properties are relevant to experience. One final issue that is opened up by supposing absolutism (small 'a') is that natural laws might be sensitive to the left/right distinction.[35] So, for example, it might be a law that all fundamental particles are shaped like left gloves.[36] This would be relevant to our discussion if it meant that making perfect mirror-image copies of objects is *physically impossible*, since both the Relationist Argument and the Absolutist considerations for intra-world inversion relied on the idea that such things *are* possible (remember that an absolutist can run the Relationist Argument.) Similarly, it might mean that making a perfectly *symmetrical* object like Simon is physically impossible. Finally, it would also be relevant if it meant that systems that start off as incongruent counterparts do not necessarily evolve in the same way. For example, I assumed earlier that if you show symmetrical Simon a certain stimulus, then the state he would go into would be the incongruent counterpart of the state that he would have gone into had he been shown an incongruent counterpart stimulus. If the laws are asymmetrical, this counterfactual claim might not be correct.

These impossibilities are worrying because we might be forced to locate these thought experiments in worlds with different natural laws to ours, worlds where perhaps we should not even be confident that left/right experiences are possible at all. One response would be to claim that only relatively macroscopic mirroring is required for the thought experiments to run, because experiential facts depend only on properties at some relatively coarse level of grain, such as

[35] It is very plausible that there could only be such laws if absolutism was true. Otherwise the only way the asymmetry could be created by a law of nature would be if a canonical formulation of the law made explicit reference to a sample asymmetrical object, and then fixed the asymmetry universally using the congruence relation. It would surely be very surprising if a law looked like that, since we do not think that fundamental laws mention particular objects.

[36] It turns out that the empirical evidence suggests, somewhat surprisingly, that the universe is indeed ruled asymmetrically in this way. So there is empirical evidence that absolutism is true. Changing the reflective parity of an atom would change the charge of the particles that constitute it, transubstantiating it from matter into anti-matter. And the laws governing matter and anti-matter are rather different (although I am told that an invariance does exist if we consider the trio of variables: charge, reflective parity, and time. So one could still hold a more complex form of relationism, consistently with these observations). In particular, given laws governing the interaction of matter and anti-matter, if you produced a mirror-image copy of an object it would disappear in a flash of energy before it had the chance to have any experiences.

neural properties. These coarser properties could presumably be laid out in a mirror image even if the fundamental properties couldn't be.

But the problem with this is that what experience supervenes on is an empirical matter, and so it's not clear why we should trust these intuitions, given that they do not appear to be backed up by any empirical evidence.[37] We would do better to just insist on running our arguments in worlds where the laws of nature are not of this kind. If an opponent were to press the complaint that we have no reason to suppose left/right experience is possible in these symmetrically ruled worlds, we can throw down the following challenge. If these experiences are not possible in such worlds, then that must be because there is some physical property required for left/right experience that can only be instantiated in worlds that are ruled asymmetrically. But at first blush that is just an extreme example of an 'initial asymmetry' requirement.[38] So it is hard to see how a position about left/right experience distinct from those we have already considered could be generated from bringing these laws into play.

Certainly more discussion is needed of this issue. It's not obvious in what sense having such an asymmetrically profiled property would have to make you *spatially* asymmetrical, so the position may be slightly different from the one generated by the Relationist Argument. There may also be an interesting way of denying Inversion by taking such a line—it could be claimed that the property required for having experiences with one phenomenal orientation could not be instantiated in the same universe as the property required for having experiences with the other orientation, since the instantiation of these properties requires different causal laws. (Without further argument, such a position strikes me as rather implausible, but it does represent an epistemically possible way things might be.)

TRANSCENDENTAL INFERENCES

If I have been successful, the argument so far should have convinced you of the following: that however we look at it, there are some interesting connections between the *geometrical* properties of the world, and the *experiential* properties that are instantiated in the world. And these connections seem to have been established on an a priori basis given only some very slim assumptions about the nature of experience.

We can summarize these findings as follows: if absolute reflective properties do not affect the qualitative character of experience, then the experiences being

---

[37] It's worth noting here that authors such as Penrose have claimed that facts at a deep level could be relevant to experience, so clearly not everyone shares the intuition that only relatively macroscopic features of the world are relevant to experience.

[38] Notice that it wouldn't be a version of Absolutism, because there can be absolute reflective facts in symmetrically ruled worlds.

had in perfectly incongruent scenarios are qualitatively the same. It follows from this that a subject who started life as a mirror image of you, but who received the same stimuli as you, would subsequently be experientially inverted with respect to you; and this shows that experiential asymmetry requires a prior *physical* asymmetry in the subject. On the other hand, if conversely Absolutism is true, then the experiences being had in perfectly incongruent scenarios are reflectively opposite, and so the qualitative character of experience depends in a certain way on the absolute spatial facts. Furthermore, the truth of the Inversion Hypothesis is entailed by Absolutism, provided narrow supervenience obtains. If it does not obtain, it is left open by Absolutism whether the Inversion Hypothesis is true. In sum, whichever way we look, there seem to be tight connections between the spatial properties of the subject (or on an externalist view, the subject and/or his environment) and the associated experiential properties.

It's certainly surprising that we could have discovered all this a priori from a few extremely uncontroversial assumptions about experience. Could I really work out, just sitting here, that my brain is asymmetrical? Perhaps if you take an externalist line such as the following—that the spatial character of the experience is inherited from the spatial properties of the things experienced—then you shouldn't find it surprising how easily a connection between space and experience is established. (This might be evidence in favour of the externalist view.) But even the externalist is faced with the possibility that we have an armchair argument to the conclusion that either Absolutism is true, or the surprising consequences of the Relationist Argument follow. And that disjunctive conclusion alone is surprising as a candidate for armchair accessibility.

To decide whether we really have acquired such knowledge from our armchairs, and if so what kind of knowledge it is (is it empirically defeatable, for example?), would require a long discussion about epistemology which is beyond the scope of this chapter. But, at first blush, the argument seems to proceed from known premises using moves that are warrant transferring. So the burden of proof appears to be on the person who thinks that the argument is not knowledge conferring.

CLIMAX AND CONCLUSION

I have now looked at the competing ways of drawing out the connections between the spatial properties of brains and the left/right character of experiences, and suggested some considerations for and against different ways of thinking about the problem.

Now for the climax of the paper. One of the following pictures of left–right experience must be correct, even though each is in its own way quite bizarre. We have, in short, what Aristotle called an 'aporia'—a choice of views, none of which seem true, accompanied by knowledge that one of them is. So, by way of a summary, here are the main contenders ((III), (IV) and (V) simply result from denying assumptions made in the paper until this point):

The Five Options

(I) To say that if there are non-relational reflective properties, then they are irrelevant in determining experiences, and hence to accept that a physically symmetrical individual like Simon would be experientially symmetrical.

(II) To be an absolutist about the reflective orientation of the world, and claim that this orientation would be sufficient to determine a difference in the subject's experiences in our various cases.

(III) To deny that there is ever any qualitative difference between a veridical experience of an environment and its mirror image by the same subject.

(IV) To deny the supervenience of experiential properties on physical properties.

The fifth option is to endorse what Shoemaker calls the 'Frege-Schlick' hypothesis.

(V) To deny that there are any inter-personal, inter-world, or inter-temporal facts about the sameness and difference of the qualitative character of experiences.

Of the five, options (III) and (IV) are the least plausible. Option (III) requires the barefaced denial of an apparently incontestable feature of experience. And— unless it is tantamount to commitment to a free-floating realm of experience largely independent of the physical world—it is unclear that (IV) really helps, for, even if the physical to mental dependencies are merely nomological, it appears we could run the same arguments considering the *causal* basis for experience instead of the supervenience base.

What about (V), the Frege-Schlick view? The view is motivated by the thought that what makes particular experiences the same or different is simply how a subject would classify them if confronted with them; this immediately rules out inter-subjective comparisons of experiences.[39] But, to me, simple examples from everyday life seem sufficient to establish that such comparisons *are* possible, so the view seems like a last resort. Others disagree, however,[40] so perhaps the view warrants further investigation.

This leaves us with (I) and (II). I argued that (I) entails that inter-subjective reflective inversion is possible, although we were left with some doubts about that.[41] Option (II) less controversially entails this, provided we assume that the qualitative character of experience supervenes on the intrinsic set-up of the

---

[39] Although see Shoemaker (1982) for an attempt to hold on to this thought without accepting the Frege-Schlick view.   [40] For a recent dissenter, see Stalnaker (1998).

[41] See in particular n. 22, and the surrounding discussion.

observer's brain. (If we reject that assumption, we get the 'externalist Absolutist' view that I have mentioned, which is compatible with denying the possibility of inversion.)

I think that these views are the only serious contenders. Each brings surprising consequences about the physical basis of experience, yet one of them must be true. Which way should we go?

REFERENCES

Block, Ned (1980), 'Troubles with Functionalism', in Ned Block (ed.), *Readings in Philosophy of Psychology, Volume 1* (Cambridge, Mass.: Harvard University Press): 268–305.

Davies, Martin (1992), 'Auntie's Own Argument for the Language of Thought', in J. Ezquerro and J. M. Larrazabal (eds), *Cognition, Semantics and Philosophy: Proceedings of the First International Colloquium on Cognitive Science* (Dordrecht: Kluwer Academic Publishers): 235–71.

Hawthorne, John (2001), 'Causal Structuralism', *Philosophical Perspectives 15: Metaphysics* (Oxford: Blackwell): 361–79.

Hurley, Susan (1998), *Consciousness in Action* (Cambridge, Mass.: Harvard University Press).

Johnston, Mark (2004), 'The Obscure Object of Hallucination', *Philosophical Studies* 120: 113–83.

Kant, Immanuel (1991), 'On the First Ground of the Distinction of Regions in Space', in James Van Cleve and Robert E. Fredericks (eds), *The Philosophy of Right and Left: Incongruent Counterparts and the Nature of Space* (Boston: Kluwer Academic Publishers): 27–35.

Moebius, August Ferdinand (1991), 'On Higher Space', in James Van Cleve and Robert E. Fredericks (eds), *The Philosophy of Right and Left: Incongruent Counterparts and the Nature of Space* (Boston: Kluwer Academic Publishers): 39–43.

Shoemaker, Sydney (1980), 'Causality and Properties', in Peter van Inwagen (ed.), *Time and Cause* (Dordrecht: D. Reidel): 228–54.

Shoemaker, Sydney (1982), 'The Inverted Spectrum', *Journal of Philosophy* 79: 357–81.

Stalnaker, Robert (1998), 'Comparing Qualia Across Persons', *The Philosophy of Sydney Shoemaker, Philosophical Topics 26* (Denver, Colorado : Philosophical Topics Inc.): 385–404.

Van Cleve, James (1991), 'Left, Right, and Higher Dimensions', in James Van Cleve and Robert E. Frederick (eds), *The Philosophy of Right and Left: Incongruent Counterparts and the Nature of Space* (Boston: Kluwer Academic Publishers): 203–35.

Zuboff, Arnold (1981), 'The Story of a Brain', in Douglas R. Hofstadter and Daniel C. Dennett (eds), *The Mind's I: Fantasies and Reflections on Self and Soul* (New York: Basic Books): 202–13.

9

Phenomenal Impressions

Eric Lormand

In normal perceptual experiences, it is as if we cannot introspect any special phenomenal properties, but only normal environmental properties, such as the colors and shapes of seen objects. Call this the impression—veridical or illusory—of "transparency." In normal imaginative experiences, it is as if we can introspect special phenomenal objects with normal environmental properties, such as colored and shaped visual likenesses of environmental objects, in our minds. Call this the impression—veridical or illusory—of "images." After describing the scope of these impressions (part 1), my aim is to give a psychological explanation of them (part 2) and to draw from this explanation a positive theory of phenomenal experience (part 3).

1 A DESCRIPTION OF THE IMPRESSIONS

The strongest impression of images is in normal imagination, while the strongest impression of transparency is in normal perception. Since the relevant issues are most familiar in the visual modality, I introduce images with reference to normal visual imagination (section 1.1) and transparency with reference to normal visual perception (section 1.2). Then I argue that the patterns exemplified there are common to other forms of experience: degraded visual perception; upgraded visual imagination; nonvisual imagination and perception; thought; and bodily sensation (section 1.3).

1.1 Images in Visual Imagination

Jean-Paul Sartre claims in *The Psychology of Imagination* that when we imagine things visually, and attempt to introspect this activity, we are subject to an "illusion of immanence":

We believed, without giving the matter any thought, that the image was *in* consciousness.... We pictured consciousness as a place peopled with small likenesses and these likenesses were the images. No doubt but that this misconception arises from our habit of thinking in space and in terms of space. This we shall call: *the illusion of immanence*. . . . It is also the point of view of common sense. When I say that "I have an image" of Peter, it is believed that I now have a certain picture of Peter in my consciousness. (1940: 4–6)

Such likenesses, however faint, can seem to be essential to imagination—for instance, they can seem to be what distinguishes imagining a banana from merely *conceiving* of a banana, and even from merely conceiving of the *look* of a banana. We do sometimes describe what it is like to have introspectible visual-imaginative experiences as if in having them we are aware of phenomenal denizens of an inner mental world: we say we "form" images of a banana or a building, and we even accept instructions to "flip" them or "rotate" them. Call such alleged mental likenesses "phenomenal objects." Why do we talk as if in introspecting some experiences we introspect phenomenal objects?

One possibility is that we talk this way because it is accurate—maybe we *do* introspect what are *in fact* visual images in a strict and literal sense, mental likenesses of imagined physical objects, entities with some of the same perceptible properties as what's imagined. On this account banana images are yellow and curved just as bananas are and just as (perhaps faded) pictures of bananas are. But a search for such banana likenesses is unlikely to be fruitful. In "forming an image of a banana" there is nothing obvious in one's brain or body or (causally relevant) environment that is literally yellow like a banana or curved like a banana. It will not help to appeal to mind/body dualism in locating visual likenesses, since presumably items made of a nonphysical substance cannot literally have color and shape at all. The best bet for a defender of immanence would be to suppose that likenesses are arcane: that they exist in the brain, body, or environment but are unknown to current scientific theory (Jackson, 1977: 101–4). The only alternative is to be an "eliminativist" about literal visual images, to deny they exist. My explanation of the image impression, in part 2, will be of use to the eliminativist, explaining why we speak of images even if they don't exist. But even if there *are* literal mental likenesses, some account must be given of how we are sensitive to them in experience. So my explanation of how and why we (mis)represent likenesses may be of use in either case.

We cannot explain the image impression simply by giving the ordinary word "image" a more cautious interpretation than the literal "likeness" one. For example, an eliminativist about mental likenesses may accept that there are mental events or states or objects that *represent* bananas without being visually *like* bananas—just as (a use of) the phrase "yellow, curved banana" represents yellowness and curvature without being yellow or curved. Some philosophers propose that visual images *are* these representational mental entities—in effect, that the phrase "a mental image" refers to an event of imaginatively *experiencing* (see Tye, 1995: 84–7; also, less clearly, Sartre, 1940: 6–8), or refers to a distinctive "symbol structure" housed in the brain (see Block, 1983: 506–7). On such views we are literally correct when we say we have images; in this chapter I take no stand on this issue. My focus is on the *residual* task of explaining why we speak as if there are mental *likenesses*, why we speak as if there are mental entities with perceptible properties, such as yellowness and curvature, even if these are in fact merely possessed by the ordinary physical objects we imagine, if anything at all.[1]

The most common eliminativist strategy for explaining talk of mental likenesses is to attribute them to a kind of *looseness* in ordinary practices of reporting experiences. Ned Block pursues this strategy by pointing out that "it is easy to slip into ascribing to representations the properties of what they represent": the phrase "a nude painting" may be used for a painting *of* nudity, and "a loud oscilloscope reading" may be used for an oscilloscope reading *of* loudness (1983: 515–18). On this view it is taken to be no surprise that people loosely describe images (experiencings, symbol structures) *of* color and shape as themselves *being* colored and shaped, and so no surprise that in loose talk they treat them as likenesses. Similarly, Michael Tye says that our talk of colored and shaped visual images is part of a "much broader usage" on which "we save breath by speaking as if the representations themselves have the properties of the things they represent" (1995: 107).

This explanation of phenomenal-object claims is overcharitable, much too tidy. While we are not genuinely tempted to think that a painting is literally nude or literally a tree, we are normally very tempted to think that mental images are literally colored and literally shaped. To explain the latter temptation by comparison with the former alleged temptation is to miss what is distinctively powerful about the latter. We say that banana images *look* yellow and curved. By contrast, we don't normally say that a "nude" painting looks nude or that a "loud" oscilloscope reading sounds loud. Another indication that this explanation is too weak is that we do not talk in imagistic ways about *arbitrary* representational mental phenomena, such as propositional attitudes. We don't speak as if our beliefs *that bananas are curved and yellow* are themselves curved or yellow, nor do we talk this way about our desires *to eat curved yellow bananas*. Yet this is what one should expect on the "loose talk" view. If it saves breath to speak of yellow banana-images rather than images of yellow bananas (relieving the burden of saying "of"), wouldn't it save *more* breath to speak of yellow banana-beliefs rather than "beliefs that bananas are yellow" (yielding the life-prolonging benefits of avoiding "that" and "are")?[2]

---

[1] Of course, if mental images are objects such as symbol structures, and these objects are in the brain, then they have color and shape just as written words do. But they will not often have the colors and shapes we attribute to them, to say the least.

[2] Block has suggested (in personal communication) that, just as we are tempted to think of images as colored and shaped, so we are tempted to think that beliefs can be powerful and sharp. However, in the image impression, there is a *systematic* correlation between properties a state represents (of environmental entities) and properties it seems to have. The impression of images as colored and shaped is causally related to the fact that they (or the associated imaginative states, at

It is more plausible to suppose that in speaking of colored and shaped mental images people are trying to express their imaginative experiences—or perhaps their most natural beliefs about their experiences—sincerely, strictly, and literally. On this account the experiences or beliefs *represent* that there are images with color and shape, even if there are no such things. This takes more seriously Sartre's idea that we are under an *illusion* (or hallucination), or a mistaken impression. We need to explain how we (mistakenly or not) come to be subject to such an impression. Is the impression a (mis)*con*ception, as Sartre thinks, or is it more like a (mis)*per*ception? Does the root cause involve certain mental habits regarding *space*, as Sartre also thinks, or something else? What is the exact content of the impression? Does it serve some purpose, or is it merely a side-effect of other processes? These are questions I address in part 2. But first I want to intensify the problem by introducing a second, largely complementary, phenomenal impression, and by arguing that the image impression has far greater extent than visual imagination.

1.2   Transparency in Visual Perception

G. E. Moore claims in "The Refutation of Idealism" that when we perceive things visually, and attempt to introspect this activity, we are subject to a misleading impression of "diaphanousness":

> [T]he moment we try to fix our attention upon consciousness and to see *what*, distinctively, it is, it seems to vanish: it seems as if we had before us a mere emptiness. When we try to introspect the sensation of blue, all we can see is the blue: the other element is as if it were diaphanous. Yet it *can* be distinguished if we look attentively enough, and if we know that there is something to look for. (1903: 450)

Moore is trying to explain why it might be natural for certain idealist philosophers to confuse experiences with environmental objects. His explanation is that when one tries to attend, say, to a visual experience of a blueberry, one normally "sees through" the experience to the blueberry itself; it is as if experience is transparent.[3] When one tries to describe what *seeing* the berry is like, one typically describes what the *berry* is like (or looks like). This point is strengthened by the fact that all the seen features—blueness, ellipticity, motion,

least) represent color and shape, whether this impression is a genuine confusion, or merely loose or ambiguous talk, or veridical. Our talk of beliefs being powerful or sharp, in contrast, is not systematically related to their representation of powerfulness or sharpness. I may have a powerful belief that John is weak, or a weak belief that John is powerful, or a sharp belief that John is dull, or a dull belief that John is sharp. When there is a match between the properties of a belief and the properties of its subject matter (e.g., a powerful belief that John is powerful) this is a coincidence.

[3] Sometimes "transparent" is used for "completely and/or infallibly known," as when it is sometimes alleged that Descartes thinks the mind is "transparent to itself." In the present discussion, in contrast, "transparent" implies "presenting no appearance of its own"; if Moore is right, this makes experiences especially *difficult* to know.

etc.—are naturally experienced as "stuck on" seen objects and the environment, in at least three respects. The features seem to be:

Nonintervening: We intuitively "locate" features *at* the distal objects and places we visually attend to in order best to detect them—colors and shapes do not seem to travel through the air from seen objects to us, and spatial relations among seen objects seem to be out "among" the objects.

Experience-free: We do not see features as being *relations* to seeing. We intuitively seem to be mere spectators of them rather than participants in them.

Objectively possessed: We also do not see features in any other way as being *dependent* on seeing. We intuitively seem to discover them rather than to create or maintain them.

Otherwise, presumably, we would naturally describe some properties (or relations) of objects partly in terms of properties (or relations) of experience or intervening entities, and there would not be an impression of transparency.[4] This is in contrast with the impression of images in visual imagination, where the phenomenal objects and their apparent features seem to be subjective, experience-laden, and intervening between us and imagined objects. Why does it sometimes seem difficult to introspect properties of visual perception or intervening entities, as opposed to visually perceived objects?

In fact Moore insists that we have only an initial difficulty, since experience is not *quite* transparent. We can introspect that experiences have some distinctive properties, namely, that they *represent* features of objects. We introspect that the experience is "an awareness of blue" (1903: 449), and this representational property distinguishes experiences from blueberries.[5] So, according to Moore, sensations may be distinguished from physical objects introspectively, by their being awarenesses, despite the initial impression of "mere emptiness." This point does not render the impression of transparency psychologically uninteresting, although it does complicate discussion of it. In introspective reports about a visual experience we do sometimes talk as if the only properties we notice are (i) objective, experience-free, nonintervening features of seen objects, together with (ii) relations of representing these objective, experience-free, nonintervening features.[6] It will be useful to have a term for these two kinds of properties—I will

---

[4] We do experience objects and the environment as bearing certain relations to our *bodies*—if not to our *experiences*—especially spatial relations of distance and direction. These introduce special complications, and have prominence in what follows.

[5] Assuming, of course, that berries don't represent *themselves*. Though this implicit assumption is very plausible—as plausible as anti-idealism, anyway—its deniability is what keeps Moore from having a "refutation" of the sensation/object confusion he considers.

[6] Moore claims that introspectible representational relations are quite generic ones of "awareness," "just that which we mean in every case by 'knowing' " (1903: 449). To keep sight of this claim long enough to consider alternatives, the second category of objectual properties—i.e. (ii)—includes

call them "objectual" properties. So the question becomes: why do we talk as if in introspecting visual-perceptual experience we introspect only objectual properties?

One possibility is that we talk this way because it is accurate—maybe we *do* introspect what are *in fact* only objective, experience-free, nonintervening features of seen objects, and our representing these features.[7] On this account the only introspectible properties of seeing a blueberry are the relations of *representing* stuck-on features of the blueberry; all other properties "introspected" are stuck-on properties of the berry itself, not phenomenal properties of the experience, or features intervening between the berry and the experience. But a search for such blueberry-experience properties is likely to be fruitful. Consider seeing the particular ellipticity of a blueberry from various angles and distances. Though the berry can appear invariantly ellipsoidal in all these experiences, there is also a sense in which the berry appears differently in each case; one is introspectively sensitive, in ordinary terms, to the differences among the multiple "looks" of a particular unchanging shape. Perhaps surprisingly, given the connotations of the term "look," such shape-looks are subject to an impression of transparency, for they do *seem* to be stuck on seen objects, in the three respects mentioned above. As one moves around an object, although one is sensitive to multiple looks of its shape, it does not seem to one that the shape *changes*, and more importantly it does not seem to one as if by moving one *brings about* new looks in the way one brings about new spatial relations to the object. Rather, it seems that, from *here*, one can discover that the object has *this* objective look—stuck on one side of it, say—while from *there*, one can discover that the object has *that* objective look—stuck on another side of it.[8] The game is afoot when

only bare or generic relations of representing, and not more specific "ways" of representing. For each member of (i), there is a single member of (ii), namely, the generic relation of representing that member of (i). It *seems* that Moore underestimates introspection, since one typically introspects that one is *seeing* as opposed to feeling, hearing, or merely knowing. Even more specifically, one is typically introspectively sensitive to whether one sees in a *degraded* fashion, as in unfocused or doubled vision. But, as I will explain below (see n. 11), there is room to try to explain *ways* of representing as simply *more* representing: perhaps introspection of *representing F in a certain way* is introspection of *representing F together with representing G*.

[7] Here, and throughout this paper, when I speak of introspecting (/perceiving/experiencing/ . . .) a property (/relation) this is a convenient shorthand for introspecting the *having* of the property by some object(s). I do not assume (or deny) that we can see universals in addition to particular objects, events, and facts. I also do not assume that this requires introspecting the object *as* having the property. Just as one can perceive an object *as* a different object, so one can introspect the having of a property *as* the having of a different property. Even when it is agreed that we introspect an object *as* having an objective, experience-free, nonintervening property, this is what allows for the question of whether we do so in part because we introspect what is *in fact* a subjective or experience-laden or intervening property.

[8] This impression that looks are stuck on seen objects is strong enough to seep into our non-perceptual, "offline" thinking. If we were somehow to come to believe that Martians visually discriminate spheres as well as we do, but receive from them what are to us (say) cube-looks, it would be difficult to shake the intuitive idea that they see spheres *wrongly*. Similarly, if we were to discover that bats or porpoises discriminate ellipticity by senses other than our own, it would be

we ask: what properties or relations *are* such looks, and how are we sensitive to them?[9]

The differences among looks do not seem to be explainable as *obvious* objectual differences, since multiple looks can all be of the same invariant objectual shape. The best bet for a defender of transparency would be to suppose that looks are more arcane combinations of properties that are in fact stuck on seen objects, and that in introspection we are aware at best of such objectual combinations, and our representing them.[10] The only alternative is to deny literal transparency, to explain looks partly in terms of introspectible properties that are not *in fact* stuck on seen objects—such as *spatial relations* between perceivers and seen objects, or properties of *proximal stimuli* interposed between perceivers and seen objects, or *phenomenal properties* of visual experiences. My explanation of the transparency impression, in part 2, will be of use to the defender of introspectible nonobjectual looks, explaining why we speak as if they are objectual, even if they aren't. But even if looks are all objectual, some account must be given of how we are sensitive to them in experience. So my explanation of how and why we (mis)represent looks as objectual may be of use in either case.

---

difficult to shake the intuitive and somewhat envious idea that they are sensitive to an objectively stuck-on aspect of ellipticity that is hidden from us.

⁹ One possibility is to suppose that looks are not genuine properties or relations of anything at all, although then it would be difficult to explain how our (various) perceptual experiences come to (mis)represent them. The difficulties are buried deeply in the theory of mental content and can only be summarized here. Plausible theories involve some distinction between representationally simple and complex states (events, data structures, experiences, etc.). A *complex* state type may well never apply to anything—for instance, a complex state representing the *coinstantiation* of golden color and mountainous shape and size. This is because its content depends not on what *it* applies to but on what its representational *parts* apply to—simpler perceptual-state types about golden color, mountainous shapes, and mountainous sizes. The same account cannot be extended to *simple* perceptual-state types, however. On most accounts the content of a simple perceptual-state type is partly fixed by the properties it applies to, so there cannot be a contentful simple perceptual-state type that never applies to anything (or, a least, there cannot be more than one such content). If there are no looks-properties at all, anywhere, then a perceptual state can be *as of* looks only if it is a representational complex out of other (perceptual) states that do apply to real properties. But it is a mystery which component states and associated (perceptible) properties would "add up" to a look.

¹⁰ As an illustration of the arcaneness involved in defending literal transparency, consider a case described by Christopher Peacocke in the course of an argument for the existence of phenomenal properties of experience. He asks one to consider seeing two same-sized trees, at varying distances from one along a straight road stretching to the horizon:

Your experience represents these objects as being of the same physical height and other dimensions. . . . Yet there is also some sense in which the nearer tree occupies more of your visual field than the more distant tree. This is as much a feature of your experience itself as is its representing the trees as being the same height. The experience can possess this feature without your having any concept of the feature or of the visual field: you simply enjoy an experience which has the feature. . . . (1983: 12)

Tye considers various substitutes for Peacocke's phenomenal properties, only one of which is (arguably) objectual: "it visually appears to me that if the trees were moved into line, the nearer one would completely obscure the other but not vice versa" (1992: 173). Possibly, but, since trees rarely prance around, it would be odd for Tye's visual system continually to speculate about what might happen if they did.

Although looks seem to be stuck on objects, rightly or wrongly, they also seem to be *monomodal*, to be detectable only through a single sense modality—in this case, of course, vision. We intuitively think that a blind perceiver, though perhaps sensitive by touch to the ellipticity of a berry, is insensitive to related stuck-on features of the berry—its ellipticity-looks. The same is true for ellipticity-"feels": in feeling the ellipticity of a berry, using various body parts and motions, we are sensitive to multiple feels of what is nonetheless experienced as an invariant shape. And we intuitively think that a numb perceiver might be sensitive by sight to a berry's ellipticity without being sensitive to such ellipticity-feels. Arguably, our sensitivity to the overall differences among looks and feels of the same shape helps explain the *ease* with which we can typically determine not only the shape but whether we're seeing or feeling it, and whether we are seeing it in an unfocused or doubled fashion (see n. 6). Introspectively, at least, degree of focus and degree of convergence are treated more naturally as features of one's experience than as objectual features of seen objects. This applies even to nondegraded vision, when one is introspectively sensitive to the contrasting fact that the seeing is *non*blurred and *non*double.[11]

I have used experiences of a primary property, shape, in initiating a search for nonobjectual introspection, but the same structure holds for visual experiences of alleged secondary qualities, such as colors. Our visual systems respond to complex spectral-reflectance features of seen surfaces (also spectral-radiance features, but I will simplify), in isolation and in comparison with neighboring surfaces. These reflectance features are objective, experience-free, nonintervening, and in principle detectable not only by vision but also by other modalities; a being could in principle detect spectral reflectance properties by a highly sensitive version of touch, for example. Yet in visual experience the objective world

---

[11] What is required is an explanation of how one introspects that an experience *is* visual, and how one introspects what degree of degradation it has. It would be difficult, even if not impossible, to explain this by appeal only to introspection of objectual properties. Seeings and other kinds of experiences do normally represent different objective features of objects—e.g., vision has a greater "bandwidth" or "field size" than touch, and vision unlike touch represents spectral reflectance and brightness, while touch unlike vision represents warmth and firmness. It might be suggested then that we introspect whether we are seeing shape (vs. feeling shape) by introspecting bandwidth, or by introspecting whether we are representing reflectance or warmth as well. But it is unlikely that seeings and nonseeings *must* differ in objectual content, and unlikely that such differences explain the ease with which one can introspectively distinguish these experiences. Consider someone with limited bandwidth vision, who therefore sees shape by scanning borders in the way one feels shape by running a finger around borders, and who can detect reflectance via touch (say, by distinctive itch-like sensations) and warmth via sight (say, by distinctive aura-like sensations). There is every reason to suppose such a subject would be able to distinguish seeing from feeling shape, as easily as we can. Likewise, it would be difficult to maintain that blurred or doubled seeings must represent different features of objects than nonblurred or nondoubled seeings. For instance, if one looks at a berry and voluntarily crosses one's eyes slightly, this does not engender a visual illusion that there are two overlapping berries, or one berry in two overlapping places—as might be the case if crossing one's eyes sometimes yielded *four* "images." Rather, vision "controls" for the crossed eyes in much the same way that it controls for voluntary head movements, so that objects do not look to move when one moves one's head.

does not *seem* to be populated only with spectral reflectances, but with fully clothed reflectance-*looks*, to which a blind reflectance-feeler could be insensitive. Compared with shape-looks, reflectance-looks do not vary much as we move around objects; however, they do vary with certain changes in ambient lighting even though the seen objects do not seem to change color. I take no stand in this paper about whether *colors* are "primary" spectral reflectances, or "secondary" dispositions to cause reflectance-looks, or (certain preferred) reflectance-looks themselves, or combinations of the above, or something else entirely. My emphasis is on the fact that in introspecting normal, diaphanous, vision it is not as if we perceive our images or experiences, or in any other way perceive properties as mediating between ourselves and ordinary objects, and so reflectance-looks—whether or not they *are* colors—are intuitively taken to be stuck on ordinary perceived objects, without relation to our experiences.

In normal vision, then, we speak as if looks are stuck on objects, as if introspectively we find only objectual properties. But there is no direct inference from the fact that we introspect a property as objectual to the conclusion that it is in fact objectual (see n. 7). This inference is plausible, but only unless and until there is a good account of why introspection should go wrong on these counts.

As with the impression of images, it should not be plausible that Moore's claims about diaphanousness are grounded only in ordinary loose talk. We would not "save breath" by "slipping into" speaking as if seen objects objectively have the properties and relations we introspect seeings or intervening entities as having. It is more plausible to suppose that in speaking only of objectual properties people are trying to express their perceptual experiences—or perhaps their most natural beliefs about their experiences—sincerely, strictly, and literally. On this account the experiences or beliefs *represent* properties only as objectual, even if some of these properties are nonobjectual. We are under an impression of transparency, whether due to (mis)conception or (mis)perception or both. The distinctiveness of transparency-talk is another indication of this: our propositional attitudes do not engender such talk, contrary to what would be expected if we were merely given to speaking loosely. When we are introspectively sensitive to the strength or rationality of a belief about a blueberry, or a desire for a blueberry, we don't speak as if the blueberry itself is strong or rational.[12]

1.3   The Impressions in Other Phenomenal Experiences

Although Sartre and Moore focus almost entirely on normal visual imagination and perception, the impressions of images and transparency seem important to

---

[12] Block has suggested (in personal communication) that just as we are tempted to think that a surface can have a phenomenal property, such as a round look, so we are tempted to think a bunch of ink marks can, like beliefs, be muddled, convincing, or important. However, in the transparency impression, there is a *systematic* (e.g., causally generated) correlation between the varying

what it is like to have many other kinds of experiences. The pattern constituting the image impression, which generalizes beyond normal visual imagination, is that normal environmental properties and relations are experienced (rightly or wrongly) as if they were possessed by mental or intervening objects. The pattern constituting the transparency impression, which generalizes beyond normal visual perception, is that mental or intervening properties and relations are experienced (rightly or wrongly) as if they were possessed by normal environmental objects. In this section I catalog impressions of images in nonvisual imagination and degraded perception (such as afterimaging), then impressions of transparency in nonvisual perception and upgraded imagination (such as dreaming), and finally I turn to hybrid cases, including bodily sensation and pain experiences. My purpose is to give what introspective support I can to the "data" I seek to explain in part 2, so that it stands independent of the theory presented there, and also to lay some ground for the conjecture in part 3 that the impressions are necessarily present in all (and only) phenomenal experiences.[13]

Perhaps the clearest nonvisual home of the image impression is auditory imagination. Daniel Dennett remarks that we are less inclined to "strike up the little band in the brain" for audition than we are to "set up the movie screen" for vision (1969: 133), but the two cases are more parallel than this would allow. In auditory imagination we may not be inclined *visually* to imagine a band, but equally in visual imagination we are little inclined *auditorily* to imagine a soundtrack. In auditory imagination there seem to be likenesses of environmental sounds just as in visual imagination there seem to be likenesses of environmental surfaces. When one imagines hearing a foghorn, or when one

properties/relations of a perceptual state and the varying objectual looks an environmental object seems to have. But our talk of ink marks being muddled, convincing, or important is not systematically related to our ink-mark-beliefs being muddled, convincing, or important. I may have an unmuddled belief that the ink marks are muddled, an unconvincing belief that the ink marks are convincing, an unimportant belief that the ink marks are important, and so on. When there is a match between the properties of the ink marks and the properties of the belief (e.g., a muddled belief that the ink marks are muddled) this is a coincidence.

One class of exceptions arises from the properties of being *convincing-to-me* and *important-to-me*. Perhaps one does think the ink marks are convincing-to-one because one has a belief about the ink marks that is convincing-to-one. Even if so, this wouldn't be a potentially illusory impression but instead would be a fully proper inference. "Convincing-to-one" here means something like "causes one to believe persistently," and "important-to-one" here means something like "causes one to dwell persistently." Typically, if the ink marks cause a belief that causes one to believe or dwell persistently, then the ink marks *do* (indirectly) cause one to believe or dwell persistently.

There is another key difference between the transparency impression and these temptations regarding beliefs. In the transparency impression, there are properties we are tempted to think that environmental entities have *instead* of mental entities. But, in Block's examples, we are tempted to think the properties are had by ink marks *in addition* to beliefs. This is a symptom of a genuine impression rather than mere ambiguity or loose talk.

[13] Although I abbreviate the discussion in this section as much as the stakes allow, I fear the details may be annoying for some readers whose introspective verdicts seem to disagree with mine, and may be tedious for some readers whose introspection seems to come up dry on these matters. Such readers may skip to part 2 at any point, weighing the proposals there primarily against the "data" of visual experience.

plays a song in one's head, one often seems to produce a faint or ghostly "mental sound," typically in the cranial auditorium between and slightly above one's ears. A similar auditory impression of word-likenesses occurs when one "hears oneself think." Though we are genuinely tempted to think that these likenesses have volume or pitch, this impression is often weak and faint compared to ordinary hearing of genuine sounds, just as visual images only weakly or faintly "look" colored and shaped. Similarly, if one imagines oneself lifting a glass of wine, then smelling and tasting the wine, one seems to produce mental likenesses (nonvisual ones, of course) in the vicinity of one's fingers, nose, and mouth. The glass likeness seems to feel cool, moist, and even curved, and the wine likenesses seem to smell and taste (say) woody and recessive, although all these impressions are faint compared with their perceptual counterparts. And, of course, even if there are no objects in one's body, brain, environment, or soul with the relevant volume, texture, odor, or flavor, there are image impressions of such entities.

Is the image impression restricted to cases of *imagination*, whether visual or nonvisual? It plays little or no role in normal, seemingly transparent, perception.[14] However, it seems to arise in some cases of *degraded* perception. Consider lucid impressions of vision such as afterimages, floating spots, and the fireworks displays that begin when we close our eyes. In some sense it looks as though there are such faint or ghostly items with color and shape, even if there are no such phenomenal objects, and as in the case of imagination we are rarely wholly convinced by this impression. Nonvisual lucid impressions, such as ringing in one's ears, or aftertastes, also provide good examples of the image impression.

Switch now to transparency. My "primary" illustration of this impression in the previous section concerns varying looks of an unchanging shape, and their contrast with varying feels of the same shape, which in effect illustrates the impression in both visual and tactile perception of primary properties. Feels as well as looks seem objectively stuck on objects, discovered rather than created or participated in. The structure of my "secondary" visual illustration of the transparency impression, for color-relevant reflectances and reflectance-looks, carries over to nonvisual experiences of alleged secondary qualities, such as flavors, odors, noises, and degrees of warmth. In these experiences, our perceptual

---

[14] There are hints of differences among the perceptual modalities in the strength of the image impression. In addition to hearing and smelling ordinary physical objects, we normally seem to hear sounds and smell smells as distinct entities, perhaps to some extent experienced as mental or experience-dependent. They seem to leave noisy or odorous objects, and travel through the air to us. The effect is slight, I admit, but by contrast we *clearly* do not see looks or feel feels as entities distinct from ordinary physical objects—looks do not seem to move to us, and we do not seem to remove feels from tangible objects. This contrast may be evidence that the image impression is weakly present in normal hearing and smell experiences. (It also displays a respect in which, for perception if not for imagination, we are *more* inclined to "strike up a little band" than to "set up a movie screen," contra Dennett.) I am unsure on which side of this fence tastes sit. We do seem to remove tastes from (say) an apple, but this may simply be the (tactile) sense of removing apple pieces from the apple. However, I think some sense of taste-transfer persists when one merely holds an apple to one's tongue, or merely lets a piece of apple rest on one's tongue.

systems respond to complex objective features of molecules and air waves. Yet, intuitively, more features seem to comprise the experienced portions of the objective world—not only the structure and motion of air waves and molecules, but fully clothed *appearances*: air-wave-*sounds* (for noises), molecular-*feels* (for warmth), molecular-*tastes* (for flavors), and molecular-*smells* (for odors). The genuinely objective features of air waves and molecules can in principle be detected using modalities other than the ones we naturally use, but we intuitively suspect that such modalities could well "miss" the sounds, tastes, feels, and smells we "detect" as being stuck in the environment. As with colors, I am not concerned with the metaphysical question of what noises, degrees of warmth, flavors, and odors *are*—primary features of air waves and molecules, secondary dispositions to cause the relevant appearances, (certain preferred) appearances themselves, combinations of these, or something else entirely. I am interested in the independent psychological claim that even if these appearances to which we are sensitive are partly dependent on the nonobjectual properties and relations of experience, we do not experience them as if they were.

As far as the transparency impression is concerned, what goes for normal perception goes for *mis*perception, as in the case of (ordinary) perceptual illusions as well as (nonlucid) hallucinations. Even though in these experiences there may be no relevant perceived object or feature, it is not as if we perceive an image instead—what it is like to misperceive that something is yellow is introspectively no (or little) different from what it is like to perceive that something is yellow, but introspectively quite distinct from what it is like to imagine that something is yellow. All the properties we represent in misperception are represented *as* objectual, even appearance properties that may depend nonobjectually on experience. Likewise, just as the image impression seeps into degraded perception, the transparency impression reaches into upgraded imaginings, especially nonlucid dreams. At least when we are not half-aware introspectively that we are dreaming, we do not seem to experience mental objects, and all the dreamed features seem discovered, stuck on objects independently of the experience.

The image and transparency impressions are normally complementary—each is strongest in experiences in which the other is weakest.[15] Yet there are experiences in which the two coexist or at least seem to oscillate as if in a futile

---

[15] In imagination it does seem introspectively that images have not only (say) shape but shape-looks, which is *one* aspect of the transparency impression. But the key aspect of the transparency impression is missing, since the images do not seem to have shape-looks (nor even shape, nor even existence) *independently of experience*. A complication arises from the fact that typically, in imagining a banana, not only the image but the *banana* is represented as having shape-looks. Does this amount to the transparency impression? No, because we need to distinguish between *declarative* representation and *fitless* representation. Declarative states such as beliefs or perceptions purport to be *true* of their subject matter; they have "mind-to-world direction of fit" (Searle, 1983). Fitless states such as pretending or idly entertaining a proposition, in contrast, may mismatch the world without being in epistemic need of revision. As I mean the term, an "impression" arises only for declarative representation, not for fitless representation. In imagining a banana the image is declaratively (but weakly) represented, while the banana is merely fitlessly represented.

conflict. When one crosses or presses one's eyes more than slightly, squints, or tries someone else's strong corrective lenses (or removes one's own), it can become difficult to describe, intuitively, what kind of objects one seems to see— environmental objects, or mental images? I think the best introspective description is that sometimes one seems to see both, whether simultaneously or in alternation. Lucid dreams present a similarly mixed case.

I think that bodily-sensational experiences yield another unstable hybridization of images and transparency. In this as in other respects, proprioception does not easily fit molds of either perception or imagination. The image impression enters into experiences of pressure, warmth, or limb-position insofar as we are tempted to take there to be "sensations" that are themselves pressing, warm, or located in our limbs—mental likenesses of pressing, warm, physical objects in our limbs. Similarly, in each tickle or itch experience one represents parts of one's body as being "rubbed" or "prickled" with very specific intensities, directions, speeds, and contact-point sizes. Often, there seems to be a mental "tickle" or "itch" that itself seems to be moving and pressing in these ways. Such reification seems automatic and nearly irresistible, at least when the experienced features are restrictively localized or pointlike rather than diffuse or pervasive. When the features are experienced as diffuse, it is easier to attribute them to ordinary body parts, which unlike reified sensation-objects are not experienced as mental. I think this is why when we feel (diffuse) fatigue we don't easily speak of *fatigues* (Dennett, 1978: xix–xx), although when we feel (pointlike) tingling we easily speak of *tingles*. Similarly, when we feel all warm and fuzzy it is easier to reify (pointlike) "fuzzies" than (diffuse) "warmies," or one big body-shaped "warmy." I think the presence or absence of reification is not merely verbal but has systematic and robust consequences for what the experience is like. Features attributed to reified mental likenesses most naturally seem to be experience-dependent, to be incapable of persisting unfelt. They typically seem to be "activated" rather than discovered when we attend in their direction.[16]

Features attributed to body parts are easier (though not quite *easy*) to experience as objective, discoverable:

As I pace back and forth in my room I find that I frequently pause in front of the window. Asking myself why, it suddenly dawns on me that I am quite cold, and that my pauses have been due to the succoring warmth of the sun's rays. (Hill, 1991: 119)

---

[16] The term "activation" is due to Christopher Hill (1991: 121–2). He cites Walter Pillsbury's (1908) description:

If you will attend fixedly for a few moments to any point on the external skin, you will find coming into consciousness a number of itching, tingling, or prickling sensations which you had not previously noticed, and would in all probability not have observed were it not for the increased attention to that part of the body.

In such a case, as Hill says, "one experiences the birth" of the sensations rather than experiencing a mere "increase in prominence" of them.

In such a case when we imagine what has been succoring, we imagine that all along our bodies must have had a kind of warm *feel* that we can discover; the features we would be sensitive to merely in *seeing* high molecular agitation would not succor at all. To the limited extent that this "feel" seems to be possessed by our body parts, discoverable as afflicting us from there, proprioception can subject us to an impression of transparency, in addition to the more common image impression.[17]

As usual, pain experience presents special difficulties. In pain experience it seems to us that *something* is going on in various parts of our bodies. We often speak of *pains* as subjective objects felt in our bodies, which is *one* aspect of the image impression. But a stronger requirement must be met for the image impression to be present. We must feel the pains as if they were subjective *likenesses*; we must feel them as *having* features that are in fact had only by normal physical objects. What features, then, do pain experiences represent? The details matter in relation to to the presence or absence of the image impression. On some views, for example, pain experiences represent *damagedness* or *disturbance*—but these properties don't engender image impressions, since we don't suppose our *pains* are damaged or disturbed. In fact, however, we never have pain experiences that represent merely an unspecific damage or disturbance. In pain experiences we represent parts of our bodies in specific ways that we try to express as "throbbing" or "burning," or as being "stabbed," "pounded," "pinched," "pulled," and so on. The image impression in such cases makes it also seem that there is a pain-object that itself throbs, burns, stabs, pounds, or is at the limb.[18]

With somewhat more hesitation, I think that pain experiences can also breed the impression of transparency. This claim has been disputed by Paul Boghossian and David Velleman. Although they defend the view that visual appearances are projected onto seen objects, they reject such projectivism about pain feelings, on the grounds that we don't feel the painfulness of a pinprick as existing objectively in the pin (1989: 95). They are of course right about the pin, but the general pattern of projection from the mental to the nonmental is

---

[17] Hill provides a second example of a feature less diffuse than warmth: "I find myself scratching one of my legs and come to realize that I am doing so for a reason—the leg is itching" (1991: 119). I do not find this as compelling as warmth as an illustration of apparent objectivity. But what *does* seem striking is Hill's use of the reification-unladen phrase "the leg is itching." In trying to describe a case of itching without clear awareness, it is noticeably more apt to say "the leg was itching all along" than to say, with reification, "there was an itch in the leg all along."

[18] Furthermore, given such specific contents, it is doubtful that pain experiences must also represent the body as being disturbed or damaged in some more abstract sense. To have various pain experiences, for example, one needn't experience anything common to them (contra Armstrong, 1968: 314). I doubt that there is anything common and distinctive to what it is like to have arbitrary physical pain experiences, but, even if there is, recognition of it requires one to have not merely the pain experiences but also sophisticated introspective, conceptual, and memory capacities. For similar reasons, I doubt that a pain experience must represent *that there is a pain experience* (rather than *that there is burning here* or *that there is stabbing there*, etc.). Representing something *as* pain requires more introspective or conceptual resources than *feeling* pain.

apparent even in some pain experiences. We do sometimes feel aspects of painfulness as belonging to our *body parts*. Which aspects? Ones we may clumsily try to describe as burningness and throbbingness, for example. Burningness and throbbingness are perfectly objectual properties, like shape, open both to being seen and to being felt, but the appearance properties we try to express strike us as burningness-*feels* and throbbingness-*feels*, not open to being seen. These experience-dependent appearance-properties, nevertheless, often feel stuck in our arms, in our teeth, discovered as afflicting us from there.

For these feels to generate a transparency impression, a stronger requirement must be met: it must be that they introspectively seem stuck on our body parts *independently* of experience. This would be doubtful if it required there to be *achings* in the absence of experience, since (rightly or wrongly) many people recoil at that idea. But in a burning-pain experience the *burning* (and burningness-feel) can seem to exist independently of experience, even if when it is not experienced there is no *aching*. The aching plausibly includes some sort of *aversion* to the burning, which requires experience of the burning in addition to the apparently objective burning itself.[19] So the transparency impression does not require that *hurting* should seem independent of experience. It only requires (say) that burning and throbbing (clothed in their multiple feels) seem to belong to body parts objectively, in the same way that warmth (clothed in warmth-feels) can seem discoverable in one's body. To the extent that people can have pain experiences without experientially or introspectively reifying their pains as the objects with these features, they invite instead the transparency impression. This extent is limited: in burning-pain experience does one typically feel one's *skin* as burning, or does one feel pain sensation-objects *at* one's skin as burning, or both (simultaneously or in alternation)? I vote "both"; some cases introspectively seem mixed in the way degraded vision does.

Some will object that feeling one's skin as burning and feeling pains at one's skin as burning are not distinct experiences at all, and perhaps they are right, but I hesitate. The experiences may differ in noticeable ways that differently spell *relief*.

The process we naturally describe as "attending to a pain" can provide a kind of relief from *distress*, even though if anything it tends to increase the intensity of the uncomfortable features we naturally describe as "burning," "throbbing," and so on. Dennett proposes that by "studying" pains we "find, as it were, no room left to *mind* them" (1978: 206). Perhaps this is part of the right explanation, but we do not know how much room minding requires; certainly studying *atrocities* leaves plenty of room, and extra reason, to mind *them*. Dennett advances a

---

[19] Similarly, itching (in one sense) may require *annoyance* at (and therefore experience of) prickling, and being tickled (in one sense) may require *amusement* at (and therefore experience of) rubbing. In this way prickling-feels and rubbing-feels in one's body parts may seem to have a life of their own independent of experience, even if it does not seem that one can itch or tickle without experience.

second hypothesis, according to which the attention dampens signals from the body, but this forgets that the feelings of throbbingness, etc, remain vivid. The effect is unlike analgesia or local anesthesia.

I would like to suggest a sense in which attending to a pain may bring about *reasons* not to mind the pain, even though the uncomfortable properties are felt at least as vividly as before attending to the pain. Perhaps one of the reasons attending well to a pain brings relief from distress is that it causes or strengthens *reattribution* of properties like burning and throbbing from body parts (skin, toe, lower back, etc.) to reified pain-objects. We may naturally *worry* about the condition of our body parts—damage to which threatens health and life, more than we worry about the condition of our (alleged) pain-objects—mere mental *likenesses* of burning and throbbing objects, likenesses that are not even *apparently* damageable. Also, concentrating on pain-objects rather than body parts moves the pain experience in the direction of imagination, of apparent experience-dependence, rather than perception, which may be reassuring in itself, alleviating a sense of helplessness or passivity. Finally, to the extent that the image impression correlates with features represented as *pointlike* rather than *diffuse*, reifying a pain may tend to keep it from seeming to *expand*, alleviating a source of panic.

These speculations could be tested, perhaps, by comparing distress after instructing subjects in an "image" condition to "attend to the *aches* that come from your tooth," and instructing subjects in another "transparency" condition to "attend to how your *tooth* aches." Although both involve attending, I would predict greater relief in the first condition. A significant difference in either direction would, however, be some evidence that the experiences are distinct, and that pain experience can yield transparency impressions as well as image impressions.

2   AN EXPLANATION OF THE IMPRESSIONS

The eliminativist about phenomenal objects of experiences would do well to explain the allegedly illusory impression of their presence (e.g., in normal imagination), and the noneliminativist about phenomenal properties of experience would do well to explain the allegedly illusory impression of their absence (e.g., in normal perception). While many philosophers of mind lament the impression of images—William Lycan (1987) calls it the "Banana Peel" too often used to slip up materialist theories of consciousness—few existing theories of phenomenal experience attempt to explain how or why we have it. And while many have tried to make use of the impression of transparency—Moore wields it against idealism, and others try to argue from it that we "project" colors and odors onto the dull objective world—I know of no theories that attempt to explain how or why we are subject to it. I propose that the two impressions would be explained if there is a certain kind of introspection that produces inner perceptions, given some widespread and natural assumptions about perception and attention (section 2.1). To play this explanatory role such inner perception should be *involved* in experience (rather than added to experience or directed at it from outside), and this helps insulate inner perception from some of the main objections it faces (section 2.2). Finally, I argue against some possible rival accounts of the impressions (section 2.3).

2.1 Binding in Perception and Introspection

The image and transparency impressions are both impressions engendered by *introspection* and *attention*, in some sense, as they relate to phenomenal experience. Sartre claims that an image "is describable only by an act of the second degree in which attention is turned away from the object and directed at the manner in which the object is given" (1940: 3), while Moore, as quoted earlier, holds that transparency is noticed when we "try to introspect" a sensation or "try to fix attention upon consciousness" (1903: 450). It is likely that to explain the impressions we will need a substantive understanding of the relations among introspection, attention, and experience. I begin with some fairly uncontroversial assumptions about these relations.

There are very many theories of introspection, some of which may be genuine rivals, and some of which may describe compatible processes that should each go by the name of "introspection". I will develop an account of *one* kind of introspection (perhaps coexisting with others) that I think is especially relevant to explaining our two impressions of phenomenal experience; for now, call this "E-introspection" ("E" for "experience"). I assume that E-introspection is an "indicative" process in the sense that it produces some sort of psychological states (events, data structures, etc.—let's just use "state" broadly) that have a *subject matter* and *purport* to be true or accurate about that subject matter. I do not begin with finer assumptions about whether E-introspection produces *beliefs* or else *perceptions* (or judgments, or hypotheses, etc.), and I do not make assumptions about whether these products are conscious, or whether they are complete or infallible or reliable about their subject matter. I do assume that the subject matter of these introspective products can include features of psychological states involved in phenomenal experiences. Finally, I assume at least some of these introspected states have their *own* subject matter, typically regarding experienced physical objects.

Call the states produced by E-introspection "I-states", since they are typically inner-directed (or about one's own mental states); similarly, call E-introspec*ted* states "O-states", since they are typically outer-directed (or about things other than one's own mental states, such as tables, trees, and one's body). (The "O" may also express their status as representational "objects" of E-introspection.) For instance, on this view, E-introspection regarding a perceptual or imaginative

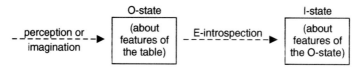

Fig. 1. Structure of E-introspection.

experience of a table would involve at least the following structure (where the dashed arrows signify causation that is typically present but not strictly required):[20]

What features of O-states are represented by I-states? Here I will be quite noncommittal, since the details will not be crucial to the explanation of the impressions. I-states may be about intrinsic features of O-states, such as neural structure, or about extrinsic features of O-states, such as their causal relations to other mental states (including other O-states), to sense organs, or to environmental stimuli. What *does* matter to the impressions is that all such features are "mental" or "mental-like": they are "experience-dependent" at least in the sense of being dependent on the existence of O-states; they are normally imperceptible by others because they are partly or wholly realized in one's head; yet one is sensitive to them in a kind of introspection.[21] In contrast, I assume O-states typically represent wholly experience-free features of environmental stimuli, such as shape, motion, and reflectance.[22] The features represented by I-states serve as the looks, feels, and other varying appearances of these environmental stimuli.

Now switch from introspection to attention. Attention is focused on some subject matter when a state representing it is given greater *priority* than "rival" states in processing—in producing further states about (or behavior toward) the subject matter, or in identifying it in the first place. There is also typically a *strengthening* of the state representing the subject matter, and a weakening of

---

[20] There is a "reflexive" view of introspection according to which an experience represents itself (perhaps in addition to representing other things); this view is championed by Brentano (1874), and is widespread in phenomenology. On a reflexive account I-states and O-states would be identical, but I mean that to be consistent with my discussion and my use of the following diagrams. Partisans may simply think of the E-introspection arrow as looping back to its source, affecting what content the O-state has, and making the O-state into a combined O-state/I-state.

[21] I do not assume (or deny) that I-states involve complex *concepts* of neural structure or of psychological function; another possibility is that they respond to specific neural or psychological features in more primitive ways, just as in perception one may be sensitive to wavelengths or molecular motion without having concepts of waves or molecules. If despite this point a reader objects to the very idea that we can be sensitive introspectively to neural or psychological features, it would be fine with me for present purposes if that reader takes I-states to represent "qualia" of O-states, somehow thought to be distinct from neural features and causal relations. It would also be fine for readers to identify qualia with the E-introspectible neural or causal features, or with the representing of them, or to deny the existence of qualia altogether.

[22] This assumption coheres with psychophysical claims about the contents of many states of perceptual systems. It is also necessary in order to avoid simply taking for granted the impression of transparency—complete with representation (as objectual) of nonobjectual mental properties—without explaining this impression.

rival states, in dimensions such as conviction and salience. The process of attention direction is not always completely subject to willful control; one may *try* to attend to a subject matter but fail because rival states remain strong or prioritized. I also assume that O-states and I-states are typically rivals. So when attention is (successfully) directed outwardly, O-states are typically stronger than I-states and are processed with greater priority; they have greater influence for identification of objects and for inferential and behavioral treatment of them. When attention is (successfully) directed inwardly, the reverse is true—I-states are stronger than and have priority over O-states. The latter point can be difficult to keep straight. What it is for attention to be focused *on* an O-state is not for the O-state itself to be strengthened or given priority, but for an accompanying state *about* it to be strengthened and prioritized (i.e., an I-state). This parallels the external case—what it is for attention to be focused *on* a table is not (absurdly) for the table itself to be strengthened or prioritized, but for an accompanying state about it to be strengthened and given priority (i.e., an O-state).

What does all this have to do with the impressions of images and transparency? The impressions may spring from a certain kind of (con)fusion of O-states and accompanying I-states. (Think "confusion" if an impression is illusory, and "fusion" if it's veridical.) O-states and I-states represent features that may not *in fact* be had by the same things (typically, O-states represent features of environmental objects and I-states represent features of O-states).[23] The (con)fusion I postulate is that these states attribute these features to the *same* objects, or, in other words, that the states operate as if they are about the same objects. For example, suppose a perceptual or imaginative O-state represents something (say, a table) as being square and as reflecting predominantly long-wave (red) light. Also, suppose the O-state is itself E-introspected as having certain structural or functional features Q and R. On the view I propose, the O-state and I-state represent the *bearer* of these features in a unified way, as if by using the same variable, name, or dummy constant (say, "x"):

In a moment I will try to explain why there might well be this (con)fusion involving O-states and I-states; for reasons to be explained below, call it the "binding (con)fusion." First, I want to indicate how such a (con)fusion *would*, if it existed, yield a unified explanation of the image and transparency impressions. The parameter that varies between these impressions is whether attention is directed outwardly (at the perceived or imagined object) or inwardly (at the perception or imagination of the object).

The transparency impression occurs most easily in introspecting normal perception or nonlucid dreams, when O-states rather than I-states are strengthened and given priority in object identification—that is, when attention is focused on the environmental objects that O-states are about. In introspecting

---

[23] If the O-state and I-state are identical, as on the reflexive view of n. 21, the single combined state represents both sorts of features—features of environmental objects and features of the combined state—and the (con)fusion to be described exists between these two sorts of features.

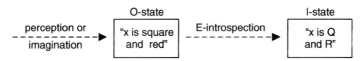

Fig. 2. Binding confusion in E-introspection.

a visual perception of a red square one identifies the object of the experience most saliently as something environmental—e.g., as something square and (objectively) red—and adjusts one's inferential and behavioral dispositions toward it accordingly. Since the salient properties are environmental (and publicly perceptible), the object seems environmental (and publicly perceptible). Given E-introspection, there is also weak and inattentive representing of mental (or at least normally publicly inaccessible) properties Q and R. What would the binding (con)fusion generate in this context? The weakened and subsidiary I-states would be treated as applying to the (alleged) environmental objects themselves. We would weakly represent the red square as having Q and R—a "projection" of experience-dependent properties of the O-state itself as *appearances* belonging to the environmental, public object. The transparency impression would be explained as an attentive identification of the (environmental) objects O-states represent, and an inattentive attribution that they have the (mental) properties I-states represent. The resulting impression would be of features that are had by experiences, or had by objects in relation to experiences (Q and R, in the example) as being stuck on environmental objects.[24]

Conversely, the image impression occurs most easily in introspecting some forms of perceptual imagination or abnormal perception, when I-states rather than O-states are strengthened and given priority—that is, when attention is focused on the mental entities that I-states are about (namely, the O-states).[25] In introspecting a visual-imaginative experience one identifies the object of the experience most saliently as something *mental*—e.g., as something Q and R— and adjusts one's inferential and behavioral dispositions toward it accordingly (typically, by dampening them). Since the salient properties are mental (and publicly inaccessible), the object seems mental (and publicly inaccessible).[26]

---

[24] When one perceives a table as square by sight and touch, for example, one has O-states in both sight and touch that represent the squareness. But these O-states have different structural or relational properties, so their accompanying I-states should represent different features. This can explain why the *look* of squareness is different from the *feel* of squareness, even though the squareness represented is one-and-the-same, and why we are *sensitive* to this difference in experience. The difference is a matter of differences in the features represented by I-states in sight and touch, a difference in something mental even if not in the square thing. Nevertheless, square-looks and square-feels typically *seem* objectively stuck on the external square things in diaphanous experience, since these looks and feels are (rightly or wrongly) "bound" to the square things.

[25] This is the point at which it can be difficult to keep straight the relations between attention and strengthening described three paragraphs earlier.

[26] I will have more to say in section 2.3 about the sense in which "mentality" can enter into the content of the impressions.

Given the weakened, inattentive, O-states about red-reflectance and squareness, what would the binding (con)fusion yield? The mental object would weakly be represented as being square and red—as *imagistic*. The image impression would be explained as an attentive identification of the (mental) objects I-states represent, and an inattentive attribution that they have the (environmental) properties O-states represent. The resulting impression would be of features that are had by environmental objects (squareness and red-reflectance, in the example) *as* being subjectively had by mental objects, such as images or pains.

On this account, to the limited extent that it is possible to shift attention between perception and introspection, it should be possible to shift between the transparency impression and the image impression. I think this is what we find. This is why wicked philosophy instructors can convince beginning students that all they ever really see are their images—*if* they sit still in an uneventful room, attending to their experience rather than to the world. And to the extent that attention cannot normally be *divided* between perceptions and introspections, the transparency and image impressions should normally be alternatives, as in fact they are.

The explanation of the image and transparency impressions contains three main components:

(1) There is a binding (con)fusion between states representing objectual features of ordinary perceived objects, and states representing other features.

(2) These latter states include I-states produced by a (perhaps distinctive) kind of introspection, E-introspection, of the former states (O-states).

(3) There is attentive rivalry for strength and priority between the two kinds of states.

(1) and (2) are meant to explain what is common to the impressions, while (3) is meant to explain how they diverge. I have not given direct reasons to believe (1)–(3). Of course, some indirect reason is provided by the very fact that *if* they were true they *would* help explain the impressions. The significance of this will become clearer given the failures of alternative explanations (see section 2.3). But a fully convincing argument that (1)–(3) *are* true and *do* explain the impressions would require more direct scientific evidence. As a step in that direction, let me try to explain why there might well be a binding (con)fusion between O-states and I-states (even if the resulting impressions are illusory).

First, one must understand a certain feature of normal outer-directed perception (whether experiential or subliminal, conscious or unconscious). Various sensory "transducers"—small portions of sense organs such as retinal cells, tactile receptors, and auditory follicles—each produce in different areas of the brain what Dennett (1991) calls "multiple drafts" (states, events, data structures, etc.) bearing information or misinformation about many properties of stimuli (e.g., sudden discontinuities of brightness, ratios of spectral reflectance, shapes, motions, etc.). This creates what is known in perception research as the "binding problem": how does a perceptual system keep track of which properties belong to which perceived objects? As usually raised in the cognitive neuroscience of vision, the problem is a *book-keeping* one: given that the visual system produces, in *different* areas of the brain, drafts representing color, motion, orientation, shape, and so on, what neural or functional "stamp" does vision give to these separate drafts when the features are seen as coinstantiated? There are various proposals for this stamp of coinstantiation in vision; the most influential is that in spatially separate visual drafts representing features as coinstantiated, the neurons involved fire, repeatedly, in synchrony.[27] What seems seldom noticed is that finding such a stamp of coinstantiation can solve only *half* the problem about coinstantiation. The remainder of the problem is this: whatever a perceptual system uses as a *stamp* of coinstantiation, what does it use as a *symptom* of coinstantiation? How does a perceptual system determine *which* features to stamp as coinstantiated? I suggest what seems obvious: whatever other symptoms may be used, one extremely plausible and reliable method for determining coinstantiation is to treat drafts caused by the same *transducers* (at a moment) as applying to the same object. If a blue-representing draft and a circle-representing draft have one set of transducers as a common cause, while a red-representing draft and a square-representing draft have a different set of transducers as a common cause, then it is an excellent bet that one is seeing a blue circle and a red square, rather than a red circle and a blue square. Call this "common-connection binding."[28]

Now, if some of these perceptual drafts (or O-states) are E-introspectible, common-connection binding could also apply to I-states about them. An I-state caused by an O-state is of course indirectly caused by the same transducers as the O-state. If common-connection binding extends to the products of E-introspection, this would explain the presence of a binding (con)fusion

---

[27] These proposals are meant to account for binding *within* a single sense modality; polymodal detection of coinstantiation presumably presupposes monomodal detection of coinstantiation, and involves the subsequent application of more elaborate detection mechanisms. They also seem to be meant only to account for binding of *monadic* properties rather than relations—should a draft about a relation between a circle and a square, such as *contact*, be stamped like the circularity-drafts, or like the squareness-drafts—(although perhaps the theory can be extended suitably)? For an extension to consciousness of results about binding, see Crick and Koch (1990).

[28] The effective common cause need not be transducers, exactly. For example, the primary visual cortex processes information from the retina *before* drafts about color, shape, motion, etc., are distributed to their own separate regions of secondary visual cortex. Since cells in primary visual cortex are functionally and spatially arranged in a "map" mirroring that of the retinal transducers, a good symptom of coinstantiation for various drafts in secondary cortex would be whether they have as common cause the same cell assemblies in primary cortex. This is important for applying common-connection binding to visual imagination, which involves primary cortex but not retinal transducers. As another complication, perhaps in imagination primary cortical activity is an *effect* rather than a cause of the relevant drafts, so for generality I use the phrase "common-connection binding" rather than "common-*cause* binding." For simplicity, however, I will continue to focus on causation by transducers.

between O-states and I-states, which is in turn the proposed key to explaining the phenomenal impressions. In other words, on this account the price of solving the binding problem for perceived properties of physical objects is that E-introspected properties of perceptual drafts are bound along with them. The impressions of images and transparency are side-effects of a valuable perceptual strategy understandably overextended to E-introspection.

Pending a more powerful and simple explanation of the impressions (see section 2.3), I believe that this outcome—that common-connection binding applies to E-introspection—gives both support and meaning to one version of the traditional doctrine that there are "inner perceptions." I will end this section by describing why I believe this.

Common-connection binding is generally reliable only for a very restricted range of representational states. For example, the reliance upon *retinal* transducers in binding should be restricted only to *visual* states, narrowly delimited, not to judgments (or beliefs) generally, even if they *happen* to be caused by vision. The judgments caused by a single set of transducers (at a moment) may differ *arbitrarily* in subject matter: some bit of retinal activity at a moment may (distinctively help) cause me to judge that there's a *bee* nearby, or that *I* am going to be stung, or that *the lake* would be a good place to hide, or that *Mickey Mantle* would have been proud of the way I'm swinging this stick, and so on. Since all these judgments attribute properties to *different* objects, common-connection binding cannot be in use for them. For a given perceptual system, we should expect common-connection binding to apply only to representational states that *belong* to that perceptual system, in the sense that their subject matter is fixed *solely* through the system, rather than through other perceptual modalities or through inferential relations to "central" judgment and belief. So if the impressions are to be explained in the manner of (1)–(3) above, via binding (con)fusions that extend to the products of a kind of E-introspection, then we should expect this E-introspection to produce states that *themselves* belong to perceptual systems. E-introspection of O-states in the visual system should produce I-states that function as parts of the visual system, explaining why they would be "(con)fused" with visual O-states.

This gives a strong sense in which the products of E-introspection are *perceptual*. On this account, rather than being states of a distinctive inner faculty, I-states are states of the various outer-perceptual systems, and so count as visual, auditory, or other perceptual states, with minimal violence to the proper use of these terms. Although there are outer sense organs that produce outer perceptions, there need not be inner sense organs that produce inner perceptions. Once I-states are produced, in whatever way, they are *processed* like outer perceptions, as further states in particular sense modalities. For example, visual I-states help to produce visual beliefs, help to control visuomotor skills, and are not introspectively distinguished in kind from visual O-states. They may qualify as perceptual due to their *use*, even if not due to their *origin* (since there are no inner eyes and ears). By virtue of producing such perceptual outputs, the process of E-introspection may rightly be called "inner perception" or "inner sense," *however* the process is structured internally.[29]

2.2   Inner (Mis)perceptions in Phenomenal Experience

For both scientific and everyday purposes we try roughly to distinguish *perceptual* impressions from *judgments*. Typically, when in error the two require different sorts of home remedies: broad rationalistic appeals to evidence or authority or prudence may work against the latter, while having little or no effect on the former; narrow animalistic strategies such as squinting or moving around or refocusing attention may work against the former, while having little or no effect on the latter. There is also typically a difference in self-control: knowing that a particular judgment is in error typically enables one to cease the judgment, while knowing that a perceptual experience is illusory typically does not enable one to cease the experience. There is much controversy about whether and how to draw a distinction between perception and judgment, and I do not wish to delve into this controversy here. The distinction is perhaps especially difficult to draw in the realm of imagination, which often involves purposeful and cognitive influences on systems normally used for perception. What I wish to argue is that the image and transparency impressions bear the hallmarks of the *clearest* cases of familiar perceptual impressions, whatever the facts may be about borderline cases.

We most naturally speak as if the impressions of image and transparency govern how things *appear* rather than how they are merely judged to be. In the image impression, there seem to be visual images, afterimages, and closed-eye fireworks that *look* purple and round, thoughts and ringings-in-the-ear that *sound* faint or high-pitched, and tactile images and pains that *feel* dull or in motion. This claim is supported by the fact that when we have image impressions about (say) visual experiences, we only have them with regard to visible properties, *very* strictly delimited: we are tempted to think that our images of yellow bananas are banana-shaped and yellow, but not slippery or imported, and not genuine bananas. Similarly, in the impression of transparency, we seem to see and not merely to judge circularity-looks as opposed to circularity-feels, we seem to hear and not merely to judge air-wave-appearances, and so on. Also, like familiar perceptual impressions, image and transparency impressions persist virtually unchanged even when we come to believe they are illusory. The perceptual *temptations* to believe in colored and shaped images remain even when one is convinced by argument that no such things exist. The perceptual temptations to take shape-appearances and color-appearances as objective persist even

---

[29] There are many philosophical objections to inner perception, some of which I address in the next section. Elsewhere (1994, MS) I also defend inner perception from Dennett's (1991) criticisms of the "Cartesian Theater," and from other influential objections.

when we know better—even when we resist *judging* that they are independent of our experiential faculties. The impressions therefore seem to be *built into* phenomenal experience, due to some components of our perceptual systems—or some strictly perceptual components of our imaginative systems—rather than *juxtaposed with* experience by our highly "cognitively penetrable" systems of judgment.

The binding-(con)fusion account from the previous section can explain how the impressions are built into perceptual experience itself, on the additional assumption that *E-introspection* is built into phenomenal experience.[30] This would explain, for example, why one seems to experience and not merely to judge that there are subjective images and objective appearances. Nevertheless, even if the image and transparency impressions are illusory they would not render the *entire* content of experience illusory. On this proposal a perceptual experience involves both outer perceptions (O-states about shapes, reflectances, etc.) and inner perceptions (I-states about some structural or functional properties of perceptions). A visual-perceptual experience can be both veridical about objective red-reflectance and squareness (represented by O-states) and illusory about objective reflectance-looks and shape-looks (represented by I-states). A visual-imaginative experience can be both veridical about subjective reflectance-looks and shape-looks (represented by I-states), and illusory about subjective red-reflectance and squareness (represented by O-states). Furthermore, in each case the allegedly illusory content is borne by *weak* and *background* states, while the strong, prioritized states bear the (potentially) veridical content. So the image and transparency impressions, even if they are illusions, need not be much of a threat to one's pride or one's hide.

Independently of explaining the impressions, perhaps the main reason for postulating an (E-)introspective component to experience is that this can provide part of an explanation of the (sharp or vague) distinction between normal, conscious, phenomenal, perceptual *experience* and unconscious, non-phenomenal, nonexperiential perception. Arguably there are perceptual states without experience, in subliminal perception, "blindsight," and "early" states in processing in the retina, lateral geniculate nucleus, and (perhaps) primary visual cortex.[31] We conceive of these as perceptual without assuming they are

---

[30] Of course, not everything that goes by the name of "introspection" is fit to play a role within experience—for example, it is implausible that ongoing experiences involve deliberate, active, theory-laden soul-searching, resulting in the application of complex concepts of oneself and one's mental states. Experiences come and go in too large a quantity, in too small a time, and in the mental lives of too primitive creatures, to require such elaborate self-access. E-introspection is a better fit for experience, because it produces states within perceptual systems narrowly delimited. As for the *mechanism* by which such inner perceptions may be produced, all I assume is that it is passive and psychologically "inexpensive" enough to be involved in ongoing experiences.

[31] In subliminal perception and blindsight subjects come to represent things by looking, despite denying—sincerely, and without hypochondria—that they have relevant visual experiences (see Weiskrantz, 1988). I believe this denial is plausible on its own, although it is of course controversial in some circles. Perhaps a fuller argument that experience is missing would show that these states

experiential—and so we speak of subliminal *perception*, blind*sight*, primary *visual* cortex, and so on. Unconscious perception of a table is like conscious perception of a table in generating mental states about the table—states akin to O-states— but seems unlike conscious perception precisely in the absence of even primitive introspective awareness of these states—in the absence of I-states.[32] The claim that there can be perceptions wholly lacking in consciousness and phenomenal properties helps to insulate inner perception (and E-introspection) from its two most influential philosophical objections. It is ironic that these objections concern images and transparency, which I have used in indirect *support* of inner perception.

The objection concerning images stems from the (wholly proper) denial of "sense data"—immanent phenomenal objects interposed between physical objects and one's perceptions of physical objects. The worry is that accepting inner perception (especially as part of perceptual experience) would involve accepting that one at best perceives outer objects *indirectly* through inner perceptions of phenomenal objects in one's own mind (see, for example, Harman, 1990). My response is that a properly formulated inner-perception model of experience is not committed to sense data. Inner perceptions needn't be directed at entities *interposed* between objects and one's perceptions of them—the causal chain in perceiving a table needn't proceed from the table to an introspection and then to a perception of the table. Rather, on a more natural view, the causal chain goes directly from the table to a perception of the table (an O-state), and *then* (in cases in which the table-perception is not merely subliminal) to an introspection of the perception of the table (an I-state). Both outer perception and inner perception are "direct" in the sense of not requiring mediation by further perceptions.

The objection concerning transparency begins by drawing out an alleged commitment of inner perception: since each outer-perceptual modality (seeing, hearing, etc.) makes its own distinctive contribution to what experience is like, an additional modality of inner perception should be expected to make *its* own contribution, to change what it is like. The alleged problem with this commitment, given apparent transparency, is that what it is like to introspect a

lack the allegedly troublesome second-order features associated with experience. These states do not involve mental features that even *seem* (rightly or wrongly) to be directly or reliably introspectible, private, ineffable, unanalyzable, intrinsic, irreducible to functional or representational relations, or mysterious in function.

[32] Many philosophers single out "direct influence on beliefs and desires," rather than inner perception, as the key missing element of subliminal perception, blindsight, and early perceptual states. I agree that this is *a* missing element, but argue elsewhere (2004) that such influence is insufficient for phenomenal experience. Attitudes and moods have such influence, but (I argue) are not phenomenal experiences. Similarly, in (imaginary) "superblindsight" cases blindsight subjects are trained to "guess" (or hypothesize) automatically about the stimuli in blindsight regions, and grow to trust these hypotheses. The influence on beliefs and desires could be as direct as that of normal visual experience (I argue) without there being any visual experience. As with attitudes and moods, superblindsight states would be "for" a person but not "like something" for the person.

perceptual experience seems simply borrowed from what it is like to have the experience itself (perhaps the best statement of this problem is in Rosenthal, 1990). When one tries to attend to features of normal experiences, one normally "sees through" the experiences to outer objects. So a fundamental disanalogy between outer perception and alleged inner "perception" is that the former but not the latter has its own phenomenology or perceptual quality. This is reason to think that inner perception cannot explain introspection of ongoing phenomenal experiences. My response is based on the idea that inner perception (E-introspection) is *involved* in phenomenal experience from the start. Contrary to the objection, outer perceptual modalities are not in themselves sufficient for phenomenal experience, which is how there can be states of perception it is like *nothing* to have (perhaps retinal states, wholly subliminal states, blindsight, etc.). Rather, on the present account, inner perception helps *convert* ordinary nonphenomenal outer perceptions into phenomenally conscious "experiences." Instead of *borrowing* phenomenal qualities from an outer perception, as the transparency objection alleges, inner perception would help *generate* these qualities together with (otherwise nonphenomenal) outer perception. This explains why inner perception doesn't add further qualia to an outer-perceptual experience: inner perception has *already* made its phenomenal contribution for there to be an outer experience with phenomenal properties in the first place.

What specific phenomenal contributions *could* E-introspection make to experience? I remain noncommittal about which properties and relations of O-states are represented by E-introspection, but it is worthwhile to explore some possibilities. E-introspectible *intrinsic* features of an O-state may include features specific to its hardware realization—such as the rough number of neurons that realize it, or their rough average rates of firing—or more abstract "syntactic" features. E-introspectible relations among O-states—those that can't be reduced to their intrinsic features—may include certain of their functional relations and perhaps even their spatial relations in the brain. These are the sorts of properties that we might expect E-introspective processes to detect with some reliability. Let me illustrate how I take such E-introspections to enter into perceptual experiences.

First, consider cases of double vision or blurred vision. Typically, we are sensitive to the doubleness or blurriness of such experiences, though this is difficult to explain as mere sensitivity to objectual properties—objective features of environmental surfaces together with the generic relation of representing them (see n. 11). My suggestion is that we are sensitive to doubleness or blurriness because we E-introspect relevant *nonobjectual* structural or functional properties of our O-states. In double vision, we may E-introspect of two O-states (say, two matching perceptions of an edge) that they *are* two in number—this is not itself an objectual property, but a kind of relation between the O-states. In blurred vision, we may E-introspect of a certain O-state (say, a perception of an edge) that it is in a causal relation with an unusual set of other O-states (say, perceptions that line up poorly in the retinotopic maps in primary visual cortex—see n. 29). In normal focal vision, by contrast, we are typically sensitive to the *non*doubleness and *non*blurriness of our experience. This could be explained by our E-introspection of related structural features of O-states. We detect of an O-state of an edge that it has no distinct matching O-state, and that it is in a causal relation to a "lined-up" set of other O-states.

Also, consider Peacocke's case of the two trees (see n. 10). Peacocke argues that "you simply enjoy an experience which has the feature" of different sizes-in-the-visual-field. However, it is not simply that the experience "has" this visual-field feature, in the way it might "have" the feature of being realized in, say, molecules. In addition, one is normally *sensitive* to an experience's visual-field features (in a way one is not normally sensitive to its being realized in molecules). An E-introspection account can explain the visual-field differences in Peacocke's two experiences, as well as one's sensitivity to these features, as follows: compared with O-states about the distant tree, O-states about the nearer tree are realized by (or causally connected to) many more O-states in retinotopic maps in the early visual system. This is just the sort of relation to which E-introspections may be sensitive.

2.3 Alternative Explanations of the Impressions

The common root of the impressions of images and transparency, on the account I have offered, consists of the following:

(1) There is a binding (con)fusion between states representing objectual features of ordinary perceived objects, and states representing other features.

(2) These latter states include I-states produced by a (perhaps distinctive) kind of introspection, E-introspection, of the former states (O-states).

I divide the two claims in this way because it is tempting to maintain the first without the second. The core of the binding-(con)fusion explanation of the impressions can in principle work independently of the alleged role of E-introspection (inner perception). The most important feature of E-introspection, for purposes of explaining the transparency impression, is that it is sensitive to *nonobjectual* properties: properties (e.g., neural or functional ones) that relate many-to-one with perceived objectual features (e.g., shape), in the way that looks and feels and appearances generally do. It is the fact that I-states represent nonobjectual features that generates an *illusion* of transparency when I-states are treated as O-states through the binding (con)fusion. And the most important feature of E-introspection, for purposes of explaining why there *is* a binding (con)fusion in the first place, is that it could plausibly be subject to common-connection binding—the strategy of treating perceptual states caused by the same transducer (at a moment) as about the same object. But the transparency impression might be explained with a similar binding (con)fusion, also due to common-connection binding, *without* I-states. There are two other natural *nonintrospective* candidates for states representing nonobjectual properties: (a) states representing transduced proximal *stimuli* that vary while distal properties remain constant, and that vary across sense modalities; and (b) states representing causal or spatial *relations* between ourselves and experienced objects. These two possibilities need not be rivals to one another (or to inner perception); some cases of transparency may be of one sort, others of another sort. But they do require separate comment.

States early in the perceptual process clearly show sensitivity to transduced proximal stimuli. On virtually all detailed theories of normal vision, for example, cell-firings in each retina cause (or constitute) states representing the amount of incoming light of various wavelengths at various points near each eye, which cause states representing sudden discontinuities of incoming brightness, which cause further proximally representing states, and, eventually, familiarly conscious visual experiences. Some may not wish to say these early states "represent," but the label doesn't matter here so much as the states themselves (which might be said to "protorepresent" instead). What matters for explaining transparency is that the properties they respond to are vision-specific, at least given *our* other sensory modalities. One has no nonretinal perceptual way to detect the proximal properties affecting one's retina. If these proximal properties are the properties we call *looks*, this might explain why (we think) we can't be sensitive to looks in any way other than vision.[33] It is very tempting to try to explain transparency via a binding-(con)fusion involving these states—to hold that proximal stimulus properties are confusedly bound onto distal objects. For one thing, proximally representing states and distally representing states share transducers as common causes, just as distally representing states and inner perceptions of them would. For another thing, we already know *that* there are proximally (proto)representing states, and we already understand well *why* there are. The same cannot be said for inner perceptions!

Nevertheless, early-visual states about proximal stimuli are unlikely to figure directly in phenomenally conscious experiences, and so are unlikely to be the states crucially relevant to the transparency impression. Retinal cells are active even in cases of subliminal visual perception and blindsight. Also, since our familiar visual experiences are not continually like double images, there seems to be nothing phenomenal about our separate left-eye-caused and right-eye-caused

[33] These proximal properties may even seem "private" in the sense that other people normally cannot see one's proximal visual stimuli. Even though we can both see the moon, and I can see your eyes, I cannot see the light entering your eyes from the moon—that light does not reflect to me in a way my vision can separate from surrounding light. At best, if you let me, I can see the moon's reflection *in* your eyes; but what your retinas "see" is the moon's reflection *to* your eyes.

I doubt, however, that the pattern displayed by retinal stimuli generalizes to all our proximal stimulus properties. Even if I cannot feel the light that enters my eyes, I can see the surface that presses my skin. Why on this account would pressure-feels seem invisible?

early visual states themselves. Normal visual experience clearly involves stereoptical states representing distal properties, but only dubiously involves monoptical states representing proximal stimulus properties. It is also unclear why, unlike inner perceptions, proximally representing states would be attentive *rivals* for distally representing states, rather than each of them calling upon independent attentional resources: proximally representing states must have strength and processing priority in order for distally representing states to acquire their own strength and processing priority. Without the rivalry appropriate for generating apparent transparency rather than apparent images, there would be no explanation on this view for why consciously we seem not to see arrays of incoming brightnesses, i.e., for why our intuitively conscious experiences do not represent distant objects as being behind two splotches of light near our eyes (nor, in monocular vision, one splotch). So in the end I do not think there is much prospect for identifying proximal stimulus properties with the "looks" we experience as stuck on distal objects.

Although we clearly have perceptual states (proto)representing proximal stimuli, it is less clear that there are many perceptual states (proto)representing the obtaining of *relations* between ourselves and perceived objects. Our retinal cells may be sensitive to the proximal brightness and wavelength patterns that *result* from (and vary with) our spatial relations to the moon, but they don't seem to be *about* our having relations to the moon. In part this is because they are not about the moon, and in part this is because they are not about us. Psychophysicists have not yet identified any retinal cells whose receptive fields include either the moon or the self. But at some point in the perceptual process *distance* and *direction* become viable perceptible candidates: we can see or hear how near we are to something along which line, and these relations can vary while the object does not look or sound like it pivots, travels, changes volume, and so on. Despite this, such spatial relations do not seem relevant to explaining "looks" and "feels," because they are not even apparently restricted by sense modality. One can see, feel, hear, and even sometimes smell how far one (or another) is from an object, and in what direction. Also, like states representing proximal stimuli, states representing spatial relations seem to lack the attentive rivalry relations they would need to explain the impressions. Just as it is not taxing to attend simultaneously to the shape and color of an object, so it is easy to attend simultaneously to the shape and distance of the object. So if the binding-(con)fusion and attentive rivalry are to be operative, all or most of the work of explaining the transparency impression seems to fall to inner perception.

Most attempts to explain the image impression, unlike my own, turn on the role of *space* in imagery. Sartre's first step toward a diagnosis of the image impression, quoted in section 1.1, blames "our habit of thinking in space" for our "misconception" of images. Even in advance of the details, this is an unpromising direction for developing a space-based explanation. To the extent that we have a relevant *general* "habit" of spatial thinking, we should display this habit even when we think of beliefs and desires about color and shape, and so we should be subject to the impressions that these attitudes are colored and shaped. But we are not. There must be something *more specific* to imagination that explains why the impression is so tempting in this realm. *If* space is at the root of the impression, it is likely to be due to spatial *perception* rather than spatial *thinking*. Georges Rey pursues an explanation of the image impression along these lines:

[P]eople tend to reify the objects of their thought. In the [movies], there are rapidly moving celluloid images that cause certain illusions . . . not of an object in real space, but in some peculiar space on the screen; and in the case of qualia, there are . . . illusions of corresponding properties, properties that appear to exist not in the ordinary world, but in some "internal" world of the mind. . . .

[P]redicates [or predicative states] released by the visual module . . . [are] parameterized for relative position in at least two dimensions. . . . [S]ince real length and width and color seem to persist in real space, it is difficult to resist the impression that "phenomenal length, width, color" persist in mental space. . . .

[H]owever, [we have] no reason to take any of these reifications seriously. (1992: 309)

Even if we agree with Rey that we should not accept the tempting reifications of mental objects, we should not agree with him (and with Sartre) that *spatial* oddities create the temptations, inclining us to view images as "phenomenal" or mental, or otherwise quirkily, unlike normal perceptible objects.

Someone might seek to explain the apparent quirkiness of images by their appearing *nonspatial* or at least (with Rey) by their appearing in *nonphysical* space. But visual images do appear spatial—we speak of their shapes, directions, sizes, and so on. Perhaps surprisingly, images also appear to be in the *same* physical space as ordinary physical objects. We represent spatial relations between afterimages and perceived objects; closed-eye fireworks seem to be on or near the backs of our eyelids; the products of visual imagination seem to float around just inside of our eyes; other kinds of images seem to be in our cranial auditoriums, fingers, noses, and mouths; and ringing-in-the-ears seems to be in the ears. The quirkiness of images cannot be explained by their appearing in our bodies or heads, either. Some objects perceived as being in our heads and bodies lack the quirkiness of images (e.g., teeth, and pieces of apple being swallowed), and some alleged images seem to be outside of our heads and bodies (e.g., some visual afterimages, and the feeling of a surface through a held stick or wand).[34] Regardless of their apparent locations, there seems to be something *ghostly* about how images appear, which needs describing and explaining. The apparent ghostliness of visual images is also not a matter of apparent flatness, since not all of them seem flat; instead, one seems to be able to rotate them in depth. All of

---

[34] Dennett only slightly hyperbolizes that "it seems as if some of your nerve endings were in the wand," since "you feel the . . . surfaces at the tip of the wand" and "[i]t takes a special, and largely ineffectual, effort to attend to the way the stick feels at your fingertips" (1991: 47).

these points weigh against attempts to explain the image impression in spatial terms as Rey and Sartre do.[35]

Temporal fleetingness does not explain the apparent ghostliness of images any more than spatial oddities do, since some ghostly images persist, and since some ordinary fleeting objects (e.g., lightning, weak soap bubbles) are not ghostly in any way that tempts us to take them as mental. Although the spatiotemporal quirks require explanation, they do not seem essential to the image impression. Likewise, a feeling of having willed or created an image is not necessary—we have no such feelings in cases of lucid hallucinations (afterimages, ringing-in-the-ears, aftertastes), bodily sensations, or of being haunted by unwanted imagery.

Although I do not think weird space is the key to images, I agree with Rey that the image impression stems from deep features of perception. I think the most general way in which images appear quirkily unlike perceived physical objects has to do with *monomodality*. The features represented by I-states in a given perceptual system are monomodal in the sense that they are normally detectable only by that system—not by other senses and not by other perceivers. For this reason we have no natural dispositions to "test" I-states against the verdicts of other senses or other perceivers.[36] This contrasts with our visual O-states about (say) shape, which we are disposed to test against tactile states, and it even contrasts with our visual O-states about color-reflectance, which we are disposed to test against (reports of) the visual states of others. In imagination, O-states about such *polymodal* properties are weakened and given low priority in processing. Given this, a perceptual system primarily (mis)identifies images in terms of the monomodal properties represented by stronger, prioritized I-states. Even though visual images weakly appear to have shape and color-reflectance, then, we find ourselves without a readiness to investigate visual images by other senses or other perceivers.

Consider, in contrast, the sense in which normal perception represents objects as nonghostly. Ordinary physical objects, as opposed to ghosts and visual images,

---

[35] Even if early visual states represent only two dimensions (Rey says "at least" two), this doesn't mean that they represent properties or objects as being at *no* depth from one (and in that sense, perhaps, internal or mental); more plausibly, these predications represent them as being at depths *to be determined*, by later processes such as stereopsis. Furthermore, it is doubtful that monocular, pre-stereopsis 2D-representing states, of the sort Rey mentions, directly underwrite the image impression. When we stare with both eyes at a light, then turn away, we don't have two mismatching afterimages (though even in primary visual cortex we have two mismatching 2D-representing states, realized in cells that receive input only from a single eye). Also, as far as I know, there is no evidence that in imagination one activates states that are (in perception) monocular or otherwise prior to processing of depth cues, and this is unlikely since visual images do not typically seem flat (2D). Finally, even if all these points could be addressed, there is little chance that 2D-representing states also figure in the image impression in other modalities, explaining what seems phenomenal about thoughts, pains, smells, etc.

[36] It is probably technologically possible now to overcome this normal monomodality by peering into someone's brain, but this is not a possibility that has shaped or would shape the perceptual distinctions or the intuitive judgments we make.

are *tangible* as well as visible. When we seem to see a table, we expect to be able to touch it, but when we seem to see a ghost or visual image, we expect not to be able to touch it.[37] Apparent intangibility cannot capture the ghostliness of all images, since bodily sensations and tactile images do appear tangible—we seem to feel them in our bodies. Nevertheless, when we seem to feel a pain or a tactile image, we expect not to be able to see it, though we expect visibility when we seem to feel a table. When we undergo auditory image impressions, we do not expect to see, feel, smell, or taste the images, nor do we expect others to hear them; similarly, in the grip of other image impressions, we expect only to *feel* our alleged tactile images and pains, we expect only to *taste* our alleged gustatory images, and we expect only to *smell* our alleged olfactory images. We also take allegedly visible images to be untouchable, untasteable, and unsmellable, like allegedly visible ghosts, and even to be inaudible.[38] The content of the image impression is better explained by general features of inner perception than by general features of spatial perception or judgment.

3 AN EXPLANATION OF PHENOMENALITY?

Consider the following conjecture:

> *IT hypothesis*: For there to be something it is like for a creature C to have a state s (event, process, data structure, . . .), it is necessary and sufficient that s engenders for C (veridical or illusory) impressions of images or transparency.

I cannot properly defend this conjecture here; at a minimum, to do so would require an extended philosophical scouring for and wrangling about

---

[37] Thus Macbeth (Act II, Scene I) tries to ask, of a certain unresponsive implement of destruction:

Art thou not, fatal vision, sensible/To feeling as to sight? or art thou but / A dagger of the mind, a false creation, / Proceeding from the heat-oppressed brain? / . . . / Mine eyes are made the fools o' the other senses, / Or else worth all the rest: I see thee still; /.

[38] Ghosts at least do us the courtesy of making noise, so there is some room to wonder whether visual images are similarly audible, but in this respect I think visual images are even more ghostly than ghosts. We can informally test this claim. Arrange to see and hear an environmental object, say, a passing car. In such a case, you hear the sound as being at the same place as what you see, or at least as coming from there. (By the reports of mystical visionaries, such a coincidence also appears when one allegedly sees and hears a ghost.) Next, try to see and hear a mental image. Close your eyes and form a visual image of a passing car, and imagine hearing it as it moves. Does the auditory image appear in the same place as the visual image? With care, I think, you will notice that they do not seem to coincide spatially. The visual image seems to be near your eyes, while the auditory image seems to be near your ears, or seems to fill the top of your head between your ears. You can of course get yourself to think that the imagined sound comes from the visual image, but I don't think you can hear the sound (even with your mind's ear) as coming from the visual image, in the way that you can hear a sound as coming from a car (or a ghost).

counterexamples. What I can do is to indicate why I do not think there are likely to be any clear counterexamples, and, more positively, to indicate some of what I take the IT hypothesis to explain.

In part 1 I argued that the impressions are engendered in all of the following kinds of experiences, which I take to be the *most clear* cases of phenomenal experiences, of states it is like something to have:

(i) clearly conscious perceptual experiences, such as tastings and visual experiences;

(ii) clearly conscious bodily-sensational experiences, such as pain, tickle, and itch experiences;

(iii) clearly conscious imaginative experiences, such as those of one's own actions or perceptions; and

(iv) clearly conscious thinking experiences, as in streams (or trains) of thought in words or in images.

Call these the "Qualitative Quartet". The impression as of objective looks and feels is rife in normal perception, upgraded imagination, and diffuse bodily sensation. The impression as of subjective likenesses is most at home in normal imagination, degraded perception, thought, and nondiffuse bodily sensation. Although I proceeded by giving examples, the examples seem arbitrary: my claim is not simply that *some* members of each of the four categories display the impressions, but that *all* members of each of the categories do.

If true, this result would be very startling given that the Quartet seems to be a hodge-podge sampling of mental phenomena. Even ignoring the wide variations within each group, there are obvious differences among the groups—perceptual and bodily-sensational experiences largely impinge on us, while imaginative and thinking experiences are largely under our control; perceptual, imaginative, and thinking experiences clearly have representational content (we perceive, imagine, or think *about* things), while bodily-sensational experiences at least *seem* not to (we don't seem to hurt or itch or tickle about anything); perceptual and ima-ginative experiences seem largely pictorial, while thinking experiences seem largely linguistic and bodily-sensational experiences seem neither, and so on. Given this heterogeneity, it is extremely striking that the impressions seem common to all the Quartet states, especially given that the impressions can themselves be explained in a unified fashion.

Of course, all Quartet experiences are conscious in some sense, but con-sciousness is not what they have *distinctively* in common. There are other conscious mental states that, I believe, can be made out as clearly nonphenomenal—such as conscious moods and conscious propositional attitudes (beliefs, desires, emo-tions, etc.). While there is often something it is like *when* we have a conscious mood or attitude, I argue elsewhere (1996), on grounds independent of the present paper, that this is not due to the mood or attitude itself but due to coexisting Quartet experiences. Conscious moods and attitudes are not themselves phenomenal.[39] They also fail to engender the image or transparency impressions. In contrast with the image impression, we do not typically seem to perceive our moods, or propositional attitudes, clothed in properties normally possessed only by environmental objects. It does not *look* as though blue moods and beliefs about blueness are blue, but it does (weakly) look as though blue images are blue. And, in contrast with the transparency impression, we do not systematically project properties of moods and attitudes onto their causes or objects. A prolonged depressed mood caused by a loss, and a strong understandable preference against the loss, do not make the loss itself seem prolonged or depressed or strong or understandable.

My conclusion is that there is a surprisingly robust correlation between the impressions and the *clear* cases of phenomenal experiences, the mental states being such that there is clearly something it is like for one to have them. This correlation in clear cases would make sense on the IT hypothesis. If trouble is lurking, it is most likely in the space of *unclear* cases, including nonintrospectible Quartet-like states,[40] Quartet-like states in animals and

---

[39] In what sense are they conscious if they are not themselves phenomenal? In (1996) I defend the following conjecture, meant to explain nonphenomenal consciousness in terms of a more fundamental or ("primary") phenomenal consciousness (or "p-consciousness"):

P-primacy hypothesis: If C has a conscious state *s* that is not itself p-conscious, *s*'s being conscious consists partly or wholly in C's thinking p-consciously about *s*, or at least in C's having p-conscious symptoms of *s* that dispose C without further observation or theorizing to think p-consciously about *s*.

("Thinking p-consciously" means having phenomenal thoughts in the sense of Quartet states (iv), not merely wholly unconscious and nonphenomenal higher-order beliefs of the sort that figure in so-called higher-order "thought" theories of consciousness—see Rosenthal, 1990.) The p-primacy hypothesis allows that states can be *phenomenally* conscious even if we don't have (dispositions to) thoughts about them. A mood or attitude needs an accompanying thought or symptom to be (nonphenomenally) conscious, but the thought or symptom can be (phenomenally) conscious without a *second* accompanying thought or symptom.

In this way, a state can be phenomenally conscious even though we do not form any sort of higher-order thoughts or judgments about it. This is not to deny that phenomenally conscious states require *some* reflection in "inner awareness"; indeed, according to the account offered in part 2, a state is a phenomenally conscious experience only if it involves an inner perception. I hold that one can innerly perceive a state without forming thoughts or judgments about it, just as one can outerly perceive an apple without forming thoughts or judgments about it.

In the terms of this chapter, I would say that moods and attitudes are conscious in virtue of being introspectible in *some* sense—thought about, where these thoughts are themselves phenomenal—but that unlike genuinely phenomenal states they are not E-introspectible (representable by inner perceptions).

Block (1995) has argued that states may be "access conscious" in a sense that requires neither phenomenality nor introspectibility—roughly, a state is access-conscious if it is available for widespread rational influence in one's mind. I am unconvinced that this is more than a stipulative, technical sense of "conscious," but I see no harm in being relaxed about these matters.

[40] My view is that these states do not generate either image or transparency impressions (even unconsciously). One who subliminally perceives a blue circle is precisely one who forms an outer perception of blue-reflectance and circularity without being sensitive to *appearances* of blue-reflectance or circularity. And one who unconsciously thinks of a solution to a problem is precisely one who does so without thought-*images* (as of inner talking or reading, as of visualizing, etc.). If

babies,[41] and Quartet-like states in robots, not to mention all the purer products of philosophical imagination.

Many people would dare to claim that no possible robot could have even a shred of phenomenal experience. I think there are good but necessarily long-winded grounds to resist this claim, grounds concerning the claim's invitation to a kind of skepticism about one's own phenomenal experience, but I cannot pursue the matter here (see, for example, Rey, 1986, 1992; Chalmers, 1996, ch. 7). My concern is with the upshot of the conjecture, assuming robot experience is at least possible.[42]

I rest then with the more cautious conclusion that the impressions are among the things a good theory of phenomenal experience must explain. Some theorists

the "necessity" half of the IT hypothesis is correct, these states should not be phenomenal; there should be nothing it is like to have unconscious perceptions and thoughts. This is controversial (see Lloyd, 1989), though I believe it is plausible (see n. 32).

[41] The requirements for the impressions are psychologically minimal. In my view animals and babies can have perceptual impressions of subjective likenesses and objective looks and feels, even if they do not have propositional attitudes, self-concepts and concepts of mental states, rational inference, language, etc. While also controversial, I think it is a virtue of the "sufficiency" half of the IT hypothesis that it could extend qualitative perceptual experiences and bodily sensations to animals and babies (without necessarily extending it to plants, rocks, thermostats, or our own unconscious, early-stage, perceptual subsystems).

[42] The "sufficiency" half of the IT hypothesis does not yield the result that *existing* computers have phenomenal experience. They may have (crude, unconscious) attitudes of some sort, and they may have (crude, unconscious) outer perceptions (e.g., of keyboard states), but they do not have inner perceptions and associated binding (con)fusions of the sort that generate the image and transparency impressions. To the extent that my explanation of the phenomenal impressions works, however, robots subject to the impressions should be within practical reach. If the sufficiency claim is right, phenomenally conscious robots are also within practical reach. This is understandably dubious given the existing state of robots, and also given the way we imagine designing more sophisticated robots. We imagine them with more and better attitudes and outer perceptions—we connect them to TV cameras and to contact detectors rather than merely to keyboards, and we increase their inferential and linguistic capacities—and we rightly judge that doing so will not generate any phenomenal experience.

Crucially, we normally do not imagine going out of our way to give robots (illusory) impression-producing inner perceptions and binding (con)fusions. To be fair, we must consider a robot that not only visually represents the polymodal properties of polymodal objects, but visually represents the monomodal visual appearances of these properties, and visually represents monomodal images as having all these properties. I can think of little that would be better evidence that something has a phenomenal visual field. This is especially so if the representing of monomodal objects and properties resists trivializing explanations. The imagined robot should represent monomodal objects and properties by having inner perceptions of them, not merely by conceiving of them, or by relying on outside testimony about them, or by confabulating them, or by a hardwired disposition, upon representing that *x* is G, to add that "a phenomenal *x* is phenomenally *G*." It is all too easy to imagine any of *that* going on while things are all dark inside for the robot.

A few stronger psychological requirements can be extracted from my discussion of the impressions. In addition to keeping track of perceived properties, the robot would need perceptually to *identify* objects by their properties, to represent properties separately perceivable as coinstantiated in distinctive combinations. It would also need to be sensitive perceptually to a *distinction* between the monomodal and the polymodal. Perhaps this requires multiple perceptual modalities with dispositions to query each other for some (polymodal) but not other (monomodal) perceived properties.

think it is in principle impossible to provide a satisfactory explanation of phenomenal experience; regardless of whether they are right, the best unified explanations of the phenomenal impressions are likely to be the best hopes we have even for the beginnings of an explanation of phenomenal experience. I maintain that binding (con)fusions, especially as applied to inner perceptions, provide the best account going.

REFERENCES

Armstrong, David. 1968. *A Materialist Theory of the Mind*, London: Routledge and Kegan Paul.

Block, Ned. 1983. "Mental Pictures and Cognitive Science," *Philosophical Review*, 92: 499–542.

Block, Ned. 1990. "Inverted Earth," *Philosophical Perspectives*, 4: 53–79.

Block, Ned. 1995. "On a Confusion about a Function of Consciousness," *Behavioral and Brain Sciences*, 18: 227–87.

Boghossian, Paul and Velleman, David. 1989. "Colour as a Secondary Quality," *Mind*, 98: 81–103.

Brentano, Franz. 1874. *Psychology from an Empirical Standpoint*, trans. 1973 by A. Rancurello et al., London: Routledge and Kegan Paul.

Chalmers, David. 1996. *The Conscious Mind*, Oxford: Oxford University Press.

Crick, Francis and Koch, Christof. 1990. "Towards a Neurobiological Theory of Consciousness," *Seminars in the Neurosciences*, 2: 263–75.

Dennett, Daniel. 1969. *Content and Consciousness*, London: Routledge and Kegan Paul.

Dennett, Daniel. 1978. *Brainstorms*, Montgomery, VT: Bradford Books.

Dennett, Daniel. 1991. *Consciousness Explained*, Boston: Little, Brown.

Harman, Gilbert. 1990. "The Intrinsic Qualities of Experience," *Philosophical Perspectives*, 4: 31–52.

Hill, Christopher. 1991. *Sensations*, Cambridge: Cambridge University Press.

Lloyd, Dan. 1989. *Simple Minds*, Cambridge, Mass.: MIT Press.

Jackson, Frank. 1977. *Perception*, Cambridge: Cambridge University Press.

Lormand, Eric. 1994. "*Qualia!* (Now Showing at a Theater Near You)," *Philosophical Topics*, 22: 127–56.

Lormand, Eric. 1996. "Nonphenomenal Consciousness," *Nous*, 30: 242–61.

Lormand, Eric. forthcoming. "The Explanatory Stopgap," *Philosophical Review*.

Lormand, Eric. MS. "Inner Sense until Proven Guilty," <http://www.umich.edu/~lormand/phil/cons>

Lycan, William. 1987. *Consciousness*, Cambridge, Mass.: MIT Press.

Moore, George. 1903. "The Refutation of Idealism," *Mind*, 12: 433–53.

Peacocke, Christopher. 1983. *Sense and Content*, Oxford: Clarendon Press.

Pillsbury, Walter. 1908. *Attention*, New York: Macmillan.

Rey, Georges. 1986. "A Question about Consciousness," in H. Otto and J. Tuedio (eds), *Perspectives on Mind*, Dordrecht: D. Reidel, 5–24.

Rey, Georges. 1992. "Sensational Sentences Switched," *Philosophical Studies*, 68: 289–319.

Rosenthal, David. 1990. "A Theory of Consciousness," ZIF Report 40, Bielefeld: Center for Interdisciplinary Research.

Sartre, Jean-Paul. 1940. *The Psychology of Imagination*, trans. 1948 (anon.), New York: Philosophical Library.

Searle, John. 1983. *Intentionality*, Cambridge: Cambridge University Press.

Tye, Michael. 1992. "Visual Qualia and Visual Content," in T. Crane (ed.), *The Contents of Experience*, Cambridge: Cambridge University Press.

Tye, Michael. 1995. *Ten Problems of Consciousness*, Cambridge, Mass.: MIT Press.

Weiskrantz, Lawrence. 1988. "Some Contributions of Neuropsychology of Vision and Memory to the Problem of Consciousness" in A. Marcel and E. Bisiatch (eds.), *Consciousness in Contemporary Science*, Oxford: Oxford University Press, 183–99.

10

On Being Alienated

M. G. F. Martin

Disjunctivism about perceptual appearances, as I conceive of it, is a theory which seeks to preserve a naive realist conception of veridical perception in the light of the challenge from the argument from hallucination. The naive realist claims that some sensory experiences are relations to mind-independent objects. That is to say, taking experiences to be episodes or events, the naive realist supposes that some such episodes have as constituents mind-independent objects. In turn, the disjunctivist claims that in a case of veridical perception like this very kind of experience that you now have, the experiential episode you enjoy is of a kind which could not be occurring were you having an hallucination. The common strategy of arguments from hallucination set out to show that certain things are true of hallucinations, and hence must be true of perceptions. For example, it is argued that hallucinations must have non-physical objects of awareness, or that such states are not relations to anything at all, but are at best seeming relations to objects. In insisting that veridical perceptual experience is of a distinct kind from hallucination, the disjunctivist denies that any of these conceptions of hallucination challenges our conception of veridical perceptions as relations to mind-independent objects.

More specifically, I assume that the disjunctivist advocates Naive Realism because they think that this position best articulates how sensory experience seems to us to be just through reflection. If the disjunctivist is correct in this contention, then anyone who accepts the conclusion of the argument from hallucination must also accept that the nature of sensory experience is other than

This paper was originally conceived as a contribution to a conference on disjunctivism organized by Marcus Willaschek and Tim Crane in March 2004. Charles Travis provided commentary on that occasion; a version was also presented to the NYU workshop in Florence in June 2004, with Alex Byrne and Susanna Siegel commenting. I wish to thank all three for their comments. Versions were also presented to a seminar in Harvard, to the Wittgenstein workshop in Chicago, and to a conference on self-knowledge in Amiens. I am grateful to audiences at all events. I have also benefited from discussion of this material with Dave Chalmers, Jim Conant, Tim Crane, Tamar Szabó Gendler, Mark Eli Kalderon, Michael Kremer, Véronique Munoz-Dardé, Chris Peacocke, and Paul Snowdon.

it seems to us to be. In turn, one may complain that any such error theory is liable to lead to sceptical consequences. A Humean scepticism about the senses launches a challenge about our knowledge of the world through questioning the conception we have of what sense experience is, and how it can provide knowledge of the world. If the conception one has of how one knows something is falsified, then one's claim to that knowledge can seem to be undermined. We seem to be cut off from the world through lacking the kind of contact with it that we supposed ourselves to have.

Note that this sceptical problem is not the same as the more familiar scepticism with regard to the external world associated with the *Meditations*. The Cartesian sceptical challenge can be formulated on the basis that it is conceivable that one should be in a situation which seemed, from the perspective one then occupied, to be no different from this situation, even if in that circumstance one cannot know anything about the world because one has been deprived of the conditions necessary for perceiving and coming to know how things are around one. The challenge then made is for one to demonstrate to the challenger's or one's own satisfaction that one does not occupy this situation. The initial hypothesis does not require that one make any assumption about the nature of perceptual experiences, and in particular does not require that one assume that the very same experiential episodes could occur in hallucination as in perception. It would be a mistake, therefore, to suppose that advocating disjunctivism might address directly this kind of problem. The disjunctivist is not concerned with Cartesian scepticism, but rather concerned to defend a common understanding we have of perceptual contact with the world, and hence a naive understanding of how we are in a position to know about and think of the kinds of objects that we perceive and track through the use of our senses. Disjunctivism so conceived is reactive: it blocks a line of argument which would threaten to show we have no knowledge of the empirical world because we lack the kind of perceptual access to it we supposed ourselves to have. This need not be intended to answer Descartes's challenge, so the proposal should not be assessed by how well or badly it does that.

Now, one might doubt that this sketch offers a coherent motivation for disjunctivism. For example, one might suppose that some form of intentional theory of perception, which emphasizes the idea that we can think of our perceptual experiences as representational states about or directed on the world, is as well placed to articulate our common-sense conception of perceiving as Naive Realism. Alternatively, one might question what kind of consequence rejecting such a common-sense conception of experience would have for our understanding of our knowledge of, and reference to, the things around us in the environment: so an error theory of perception is quite acceptable. But, in the context of this chapter, I would like the reader to assume that only Naive Realism correctly captures the common-sense conception of perception; and that rejecting common sense leads to scepticism. For I suspect that there are many philosophers who are inclined to think that even if the disjunctivist could establish these concerns as a serious motivation for the doctrine, still the theory itself would be unacceptable because of the consequences the theory has elsewhere in our conception of the mind; namely, in relation to the character of sensory experience and our awareness of that character.

What I want to do here is to try and articulate somewhat more the kind of gut resistance to disjunctivism that many feel (of course, I may be rather too sympathetic to the project to succeed in doing this). Indeed, the aim here is to try and locate as best I can what should be the most fundamental point of disagreement between a disjunctivist position and any of the alternatives. From a disjunctivist perspective, resistance to the account will be based on a false picture, either of sensory experience, or of the kind of knowledge we have of it. If we can locate the place of most fundamental disagreement, the disjunctivist will then be better placed to try and offer an explanation of why it should seem so counterintuitive even if true.

In the bulk of the chapter I will be taken up with identifying and elaborating the fundamental disagreements here. They will turn on the possibility according to the disjunctivist that someone should be a certain way experientially simply by virtue of their situation being indiscriminable through reflection from veridical perception. This seems to describe a situation, according to the opposing intuition, in which phenomenal consciousness itself has been left out of the picture. In the first part of the chapter, though, I aim to present in a compact form what I take to be the fundamental commitments of disjunctivism. In this part I précis and slightly revise material I expand on elsewhere.[1] I then turn to the formulation of this worry about the seeming absence of phenomenal consciousness and its relation to older concerns about absent qualia. In turn this raises questions about the role of higher-order perspectives in characterizing disjunctivism. I aim to sketch opposing models of how phenomenal consciousness and self-awareness fit together. In the brief, final section I connect these different models to different reactions to external world scepticism.

PART ONE

1

We can see the distinctive content of disjunctivism about the theory of perception as comprising three basic commitments.[2] As I will argue, the

---

[1] The bulk of this section is an extremely compressed discussion of the first few sections of Martin (2004) and, beyond that, ch. 3 and ch. 8 of *Uncovering Appearances* (in preparation).

[2] The disjunctive theory of appearances (such labelling, I think, is due to Howard Robinson 1985), is first propounded by Michael Hinton (1967), and elaborated further by him (1973); the view was then defended further by Paul Snowdon (1980–1, 1990); and separately by John

commitment which seems most clearly counter-intuitive is the third of these, and our discussion for much of the rest of this paper will focus on what is and is not involved in this final commitment. I'll spell out each of the commitments in turn, setting each in the context of motivations for it, and exploring some of the consequences, aiming to show that the third and most problematic commitment flows from the motivations associated with more familiar elements of disjunctivism.

The first commitment reflects the antecedent acceptance of Naive Realism. Taking as our starting point one of entirely veridical perception, a visual perception, say, of a white picket fence as the thing it is, the disjunctivist's first claim is:

(I) No instance of the specific kind of experience I have now, when seeing the white picket fence for what it is, could occur were I not to perceive such a mind-independent object as this.

We should understand this claim as the rejection of what McDowell calls, 'the highest common factor' view of sense experience.[3] A naive realist view of (entirely veridical) perceptual experience is as that of a relation between the perceiver and objects of perception. Taking sensory experiences to be events, these objects of perception are to be understood as constituents of the event in question. The naive realist supposes it is an aspect of the essence of such experiential episodes that they have such experience-independent constituents.

Naive Realism is commonly taken to be falsified by the argument from illusion or hallucination. There are various formulations of the argument, few of them valid. For our purposes, we can best understand it as a form of *reductio* against Naive Realism. That is to say, one will argue that the existence of naive realist experience is inconsistent with two further claims which have broad acceptance: the first being what we might call *Experiential Naturalism*, that our sense experiences are themselves part of the natural causal order, subject to broadly physical and psychological causes; the second, the *Common Kind Assumption*, that whatever kind of mental, or more narrowly experiential, event occurs when one perceives, the very same kind of event could occur were one hallucinating.

In the context of these two assumptions, we can show that veridical perception could not be a relation of awareness to mind-independent objects, as the naive realist supposes. Either, along with sense-datum theories, one holds to the thought that sense experience is relational, and accepts that its objects must be mind-dependent; or, with representational or intentional theories of perception, one supposes that sense experience itself is not strictly a relation to the object of

McDowell (1982); see also McDowell (1994, 1995). There are significant differences in the formulation and motivation for each of these approaches. I discuss a little of this in Martin (2004).

[3] See the McDowell works cited in n. 2.

awareness at all, although typically we characterize awareness as if it were such a relation. The argument moves first through considering what the nature of hallucination must be, given Experiential Naturalism, and then generalizing from that to the case of veridical perception, using the Common Kind Assumption.

For, granting Experiential Naturalism, we need simply add the common observation that it is possible to bring about an hallucinatory experience through suitable manipulation of brain and mind. Someone who succeeds in producing an hallucination in a subject does not have to induce an appropriate correlation between the subject and any other entities beyond the subject's brain or the mind; or, if there are such necessary conditions of the occurrence of an hallucinatory experience (that other such entities should exist and be suitably related to the experience), then the causes of experience must also be sufficient to guarantee that these additional conditions obtain. From this we can derive the disjunction either that hallucinatory experiences lack any constituent elements, and hence impose no such necessary conditions on their occurrence, or that the constituent elements they have are themselves constitutively dependent on the occurrence of that kind of experience. In such a situation, the causal conditions for experience will be sufficient for it to occur, since bringing about such an experience will thereby guarantee the obtaining of what are necessary conditions for it.

Now, suppose for the moment that hallucinatory experiences do meet the second of these models: they possess constituent elements which are experience-dependent.[4] Then, by the Common Kind Assumption, whatever kind of experience does occur when one perceives, the same kind of experience can be present when one is hallucinating. So if an hallucinatory experience must be of a kind which constitutes the existence of its objects, then since the very same kind of experience is also present when perceiving, that too will constitute the existence of its objects. That is, for any aspect of the perceptual experience the naive realist hypothesizes to be a relation to a mind-independent entity, consideration of the corresponding hallucination shows the entity in that case to be mind-dependent, and hence that any experience of that kind to thereby have a mind-dependent object rather than any mind-independent one.[5] Mind-independent entities cannot then be constituents of the experience, contra the naive realist.

This gives the naive realist reason to reject this conception of hallucination, a conception familiar from sense-datum accounts, and hence one which generally people might construe as implausible anyway. The alternative is to deny that the hallucination has any constituent elements. What account of hallucination is

---

[4] This is to conceive of hallucinations along the lines discussed by sense-datum theorists from the second half of the twentieth century onwards, for example, in Jackson (1977); Robinson (1994); and Foster (1986).

[5] I assume here, in effect, that there cannot be constitutive over-determination of the veridical perceptual experience such that it is both a relation to the mind-dependent entity and the mind-independent one.

consistent with this denial? The commonest approach is to embrace a representationalist or intentionalist construal of experience. The denial that the
experience has any constituent elements must be made consistent with the
evident fact that, from the subject's perspective, it is as if there are various objects
of awareness presented as being some way or other. That is to say, whenever one
has a sense experience such as seemingly viewing a white picket fence, one's
experience has a subject matter (as we might say), there seemingly is a particular
kind of scene presented to the subject in having the experience. And it looks as if
the description of this subject matter carries with it a commitment to the
existence of what the naive realist thinks of as the constituents of experience in
the case of veridical perception. Since we deny that there are any such constituents of the experience in the hallucinatory case, our talk here must be lacking
in ontological import. We are treating the hallucinatory experience as if it is the
presentation of objects when in fact it is not. Intentional theories of experience
take the description of the subject matter of an experience to express the representational or intentional content of the experiential state. The experience has
its phenomenal character, according to this approach, by virtue of its possession
of this content. In general we take ascriptions of representational content to
psychological states to lack ontological commitment.[6]

Again, by the Common Kind Assumption, whatever kind of experience occurs
when one perceives, that same kind of event will be present when one hallucinates. So if the hallucinatory experience lacks any constituents, then the perceptual experience, being of the same kind, does not have any constituents either.
Although there may be objects which do act as appropriate values for our
quantifiers, or referents for our terms, when we describe how things are presented as being to the subject of the perceptual state, none of these should be
taken actually to be aspects of the experiential state itself, since such a kind of
experience can occur when the subject is not perceiving. On this view, even in
the case of veridical perception, when we make mention of the particular objects
which the subject is perceiving we do not describe them as parts of the experiential situation, but make mention of them to express the representational
import of the experience. Given the naive realist's commitment to thinking of
perceptual experience as genuinely relational between the subject and a mind-
independent world, this representationalist construal of hallucination is no more
amenable to Naive Realism than the sense-datum conception.[7]

---

[6] Or rather, more precisely, we may take the ascription to a psychological state of a given
representational content to lack the ontological commitment that assertion of that content (or of a
proposition corresponding to that content if the content is non-conceptual or non-propositional in
form) would involve. Some people, however, question whether one can avoid the ontological
commitment inherent in the use of some referential terms in this way, cf. McDowell (1984). I
assume that those drawn to intentional theories of perception will posit representational contents
for perceptual states which avoid these difficulties. For more on this issue see Martin (2002a).

[7] To emphasize again: this is to treat Naive Realism as committed to the idea that veridical sense
experience is, at least in part, a relation to mind-independent objects. Intentional theories of

So Experiential Naturalism and the Common Kind Assumption taken together rule out Naive Realism. The only options we would have left then would be some form of sense-datum theory or representational or intentional theory of sense experience, or a combination of the two. To defend Naive Realism, we must reject one of the other assumptions. If we do not want to deny that experience is part of the natural order, rather than some external condition on it, then we cannot abandon Experiential Naturalism.[8] Naive Realism can be preserved only at the expense of denying the Common Kind Assumption. And that is what (I) does.

There are ways of construing the Common Kind Assumption on which it comes out as trivially false. If we relax our conception of a kind of event sufficiently then any description of an event mirrors a kind of event. On that conception, it is easy to find kinds which some individual events fall under and otherwise matching individuals fail to. You paint your picket fence white on Tuesday and I do so on Wednesday: mine is a Wednesday painting, yours a Tuesday one. Given the different descriptions these seem to be different kinds of event. Since no party to the debate about perception denies that there are *some* descriptions true only of the perceptual scenario, namely, that they are perceptions rather than hallucinations, someone who wants to take the Common Kind Assumption to be a significant addition to the debate cannot be using this conception of a kind of event.

For the Common Kind Assumption to be a non-trivial falsehood, therefore, we need some conception of the privileged descriptions of experiences. For it to be a substantive matter that perceptions fail to be the same kind of mental episode as illusions or hallucinations, we need some characterizations of events which reflect their nature or what is most fundamentally true of them.[9] So one might simply reject the whole debate at this stage on the basis that there just are no interesting kinds in respect of events; and hence no way to discriminate

perception are committed to denying the relational nature of such experience, even if they are inclined to describe experience as if it were relational. The naive realist's commitment to the relational character of experience cannot be grounded solely in an appeal to the alleged 'transparency' of experience: intentional theorists typically affirm that too. Rather, the commitment to thinking of veridical perceptual experience as relational involves a further commitment—to see how that might be grounded in phenomenology see Martin (2002b; and *Uncovering Appearances* (in preparation), ch. 7).

[8] Experiential Naturalism is here conceived as a methodological or regulative assumption of both empirical work on sense experience and philosophical discussion of it. The assumption was rejected by the early sense-datum theorists (and for that reason the various forms of the argument from hallucination they employed tended to be invalid) and by some phenomenologists, for example Merleau-Ponty (1942). For a more recent discussion which rejects the principle, see Valberg (1992).

[9] Note that this is not the same thing as to assume that the events we are here interested in are themselves part of the fundamental furniture of the universe. It is quite consistent with what is claimed here that there is a more fundamental level of reality out of which the mental is somehow constructed, or out of which it emerges. All that is rejected is that we explain the salience of this level of reality merely through appeal to an inclination on our part to describe some things as similar and others as different.

among the descriptions true of both perception and matching hallucination and those descriptions true of only one. I won't address such pessimism about the state of debate directly here. Rather, I will just assume for the sake of this discussion that we can make sense of the idea that there are some privileged classifications of individuals, both concrete objects and events, and that our talk of what is essential to a given individual tracks our understanding of the kinds of thing it is. That is, I will assume the following: entities (both objects and events) can be classified by species and genus; for all such entities there is a most specific answer to the question, 'What is it?'[10] In relation to the mental, and to perception in particular, I will assume that for mental episodes or states there is a unique answer to this question which gives its most specific kind; it tells us what essentially the event or episode is. In being a member of this kind, it will thereby be a member of other, more generic, kinds as well. It is not to be assumed that for any description true of a mental event, there is a corresponding kind under which the event falls. The Common Kind Assumption is then to be taken as making a claim about the most specific kind that a perceptual experience is, that events of that specific kind can also be hallucinations.[11]

In rejecting the Common Kind Assumption, the disjunctivist might be seeking to deny that there is *anything* really in common with respect to being an experience, or being a mental state, which perceptions, illusions and hallucinations need have in common. This would be to deny even that the idea of a perceptual experience defines a proper mental kind, since all parties to the debate agree that this is a notion we can apply equally to veridical perceptions, illusions and hallucinations. Yet, given that disjunctivism seeks to defend Naive Realism, the rejection of the Common Kind Assumption only requires that one claim that the most specific kind of experience one enjoys when one perceives not occur when having an illusion or hallucination. This claim is the minimum needed to block the entailment from the claim that hallucinations cannot have mind-independent objects as constituents to the claim that the same is so of veridical perceptions. In this manner, the disjunctivist preserves Naive Realism through affirming (I) and thereby denying the Common Kind Assumption.[12]

[10] The most developed recent treatment of this kind of Aristotelianism about essence and nature is to be found in Wiggins (1980, 2001); see also Wiggins (1996). For more on the question of essence see Kit Fine's discussions of these matters in Fine (1994a, 1994b).

[11] Can one formulate the argument, and the resistance to it, by avoiding mention of kinds? The argument from hallucination is often presented in terms of the causal conditions for bringing about a given instance of perceiving. That is, it is sometimes suggested that the issue turns on whether a given perception could have occurred without being a perception, cf. Valberg (1992). But there are many reasons for denying that the very same event could have occurred in a different causal context which have nothing to do with the debate about the nature of perception. (Consider Davidson's (1969) original criterion of identity for events.) If we do not assume that an individual event of hallucinating a picket fence is identical with a given perception, some additional principle must be appealed to in order to indicate that what is true of the one must be true of the other.

[12] As should already be clear from the naive realist commitment to having entities as constituents of perceptual episodes, the disjunctivist must reject any kind of physicalism which identifies kinds

2

The commitment to Naive Realism is probably not shared by most readers, but this is not to say that the idea that some sense experiences should be relations to objects in the world around us is in itself a bizarre, or counter-intuitive, suggestion. The endless disputes about externalism and internalism in relation to psychological states should teach us that there is no clear starting point, independent of philosophical conviction, which tells us the general form that mental states must take. If one finds something puzzling in disjunctivism, then, it is not so much the commitment to Naive Realism as the consequences that such a commitment imposes on one in relation to other cases of sense experience: illusion and hallucination. But what is the disjunctivist committed to in relation to these other cases? At first sight, it may appear that all that the disjunctivist has to say is something entirely negative: that these are not cases of having the specific kind of experience one has when veridically perceiving. And hence one might think that disjunctivism avoids saying anything general about the nature of sense experience. In fact, there is something more to say here which derives from what ought to be common ground to all parties to the debate.

Michael Hinton began the debate about disjunctivism by focusing on a certain kind of locution, what he called 'perception–illusion disjunctions', for example, 'Macbeth is seeing a dagger or under the illusion of so doing'.[13] Hinton's strategy is to argue that there is no good reason to think that these disjunctive statements could not do all the work that our normal talk of appearances and experience does. That is, that there is no good reason from our ordinary ways of talking to suppose that we are committed to the existence of some special kind of experiential event which may be present equally in cases of perception and hallucination. Now, this strategy prompts a question: why pick on these disjunctions, then, rather than, say, 'Either Macbeth is seeing a dagger, or under the illusion of seeing twenty-three pink elephants'? The answer, I take it, is that the disjunction Hinton highlights has the same evidential profile as self-ascriptions of perceptual experience. Someone in a position to make a warranted judgement about their experience can also put forward one of Hinton's perception–illusion disjunctions, but not so the alternative that we suggested. One can gloss this, I suggest, by highlighting the connection between our talk of perceptual experience and the epistemic position a subject is in with respect to his or her perceptions and certain illusions or hallucinations, that they are indiscriminable from the perceptions through introspective reflection.

Suppose you start out only with the notion of veridical perception, what could introduce you to the idea of sensory experience more generally, to include

of mental episode with kinds of physical events in the subject's brain. In rejecting the Common Kind Assumption, the disjunctivist does not take a stance on whether the very same kind of local physical conditions can accompany veridical perception and hallucination.

[13] See the works cited in n. 2.

illusion and hallucination? Even if we are not engaged with Cartesian scepticism, the context of that debate offers us one route to introducing the idea. Consider your current perception of the environment around you. Perhaps you are staring out at a late spring evening; or lying in summer grass; or sitting in a dusky office reading a philosophy paper. It is quite conceivable for you that there should be a situation in which you could not tell that things were not as they are now: so it might seem to you as if you were then staring at a white picket fence, or taking in the smell of new-mown grass, even though, unknown to you in that situation, you were not doing so. Your perspective on the situation would not, in that situation, distinguish how things were from how they are now. Now we might say that how you are in that situation is a matter of having a sense experience which is not a case of perception. And, surely, it is at least cases like these which we have in mind when we think about examples of sensory experience which are not cases of veridical perception. We have a broader conception of sense experience than this, of course, for we allow that we can have illusions and hallucinations which are not veridical perceptions but which are not indiscriminable from perceptions: their character may vary wildly from what the corresponding perception would be like. But, in the context of this chapter, I want to work with the simplifying assumption that throughout we are to deal with what we might call perfect hallucinations. And, for the case of perfect hallucinations, one could get someone to track the relevant cases in just the way suggested here.[14]

It is this idea, I suggest, that disjunctivists such as Hinton use in order to explicate their preferred notion of sense experience in general, i.e., that which generalizes across veridical perception, illusion and hallucination; for, in using this Cartesian methodology, one can introduce, at least as a first approximation, the range of cases in dispute among the parties, without yet having to admit that there is something of the sort common between perception, illusion and hallucination of the kind that Hinton wishes to dispute. And hence this gives us the second commitment of disjunctivism:

(II) The notion of a visual experience of a white picket fence is that of a situation being indiscriminable through reflection from a veridical visual perception of a white picket fence as what it is.

We should immediately note three points about (II). First, the acceptability of (II) turns on how we are to understand the notion of indiscriminability here. And the relevant conception of what it is for one thing to be indiscriminable from another is that of not possibly knowing it to be distinct from the other.[15]

---

[14] For a (too brief) discussion of how we can generalize away from the case of perfect hallucination to cover illusions and hallucinations more generally, see Martin (2004).

[15] This approach to indiscriminability is developed in greatest detail in Williamson (1990). Williamson principally focuses on the case of knowledge or lack of knowledge of identities and distinctness, that $x = y$ or $x \neq y$. As I note in the text, we are concerned with the plural form of

To be somewhat more precise, since here we are concerned with knowing of individual experiences whether they are among the veridical perceptions or not, we can gloss it as:

$$\neg \Diamond K_{\text{[through reflection]}} \ \neg x \text{ is one of the } Vs$$

(That is, x is such that it is not possible to know through reflection that it is not one of the veridical perceptions of a white picket fence as what it is.)[16]

This condition is met whenever x is one of the Vs, but if there are truths which are unknowable through reflection, then the condition can be met in other ways. It should be stressed that it is no part of this discussion that we can analyse or reduce the truths concerning indiscriminability, modal facts concerning the possibility or impossibility of certain knowledge, to claims about the sorting behaviour of individuals, or the functional organization which might underpin such behaviour. As we shall see below, there are delicate questions for the disjunctivist concerning the link between a subject's failure to treat differently two situations and the claim that the two are indiscriminable for that subject.

Second, the restriction 'through reflection' is an important and central addition here. When we describe the original Cartesian thought experiment, we are considering a case in which we unknowingly find ourselves in a situation which we can't know is not one of staring at a white picket fence. But we equally have a conception of sense experiences occurring where one has been tipped off about their non-perceptual status. If I take you into the bowels of William James Hall and subject you to an expensive visual-cortical stimulator so as to induce in you the hallucination of an orange, it seems quite conceivable that I should put you in a situation which in a certain respect is just like seeing an orange. In one important respect it is not: I have told you the experiment you will be subject to. Since you have that information from my testimony, there is something you know which rules out your situation from being one in which you see the orange. Since we don't want to deny the possibility that this is a case of perfect hallucination, we need to bracket the relevance of the additional information you have acquired through testimony. This is what the appeal to 'through reflection' is

whether x is one of the Vs. This form even more obviously than the case of individual identities and distinctness raises questions about intensional versus extensional formulations.

[16] Jim Pryor and others have suggested to me that in our normal usage of 'phenomenally indiscriminable' this phrase should *not* be interpreted according to the above schema. The schema is not symmetrical: that hallucinating is not discriminable through reflection from perceiving does not entail that perceiving is indiscriminable from hallucinating; cf. Williams (1978, appendix) and Williamson (2000 ch. 6). But, the complaint goes, it is just obvious that, as we use talk of 'phenomenally indiscriminable', this relation is symmetrical.

In response, I would suggest that we should be more respectful of the etymology of the term which would support the more complex form suggested in the text. That this should lead to a symmetrical relation in the case of phenomenal states is readily explicable without supposing it analytic of the notion. For the vast majority of philosophers in this debate do make further substantive assumptions about the nature of psychological states which would allow experiential states to be indiscriminable in our sense only if they are identical in phenomenal character. And it is just these substantive assumptions that the disjunctivist challenges.

intended to do. The situation in which you are knowingly having an hallucination of an orange is like a Cartesian situation in which you don't know of the hallucination because, if we bracket that additional information, then what is available to you otherwise, i.e., what is available to you in simply reflecting on your circumstances, does not discriminate between the two situations. As we shall see in Part Two, the import of this restriction and the consequences which flow from it are central to understanding what disjunctivism is committed to, and how one should characterize one's objections to that picture of experience.

Third, we should note that condition (II) just taken by itself ought to be interpretable as at least extensionally adequate on all theories of perceptual experience. Of course, the disjunctivist's opponent will not think that this properly gives an account of the nature of sense experience, and nor, for that matter, may it really articulate the concept or conception that we all have of what sense experience is. Nonetheless, the condition cannot fail to count as a sense experience anything which genuinely is one; for, according to someone who accepts *the Common Kind Assumption*, the relevant condition for being an experience, being a P-event we might say,[17] will be exemplified by both perceptions and perfect hallucinations. In both cases, then, the x in question will be one of the Vs, namely a P-event, and so it will not be possible for one to know that it is not one.[18] The only way in which the extensions of our concept of sense experience and what is defined by (II) may fail to coincide is if (II) really is too liberal: that is, if it will include as instances of experience episodes which fail to be P-events. Now, as we will see below, the full import of this possibility is a delicate matter. But, at first sight, this is not a possibility that a theorist will wish to countenance; for, after all, if in meeting (II) we describe a situation which from the subject's own perspective is just as if one is seeing the white picket fence (as the Cartesian thought experiment suggests), then how could it fail to count as a visual experience of a white picket fence? For example, if the preferred account of experience is one in terms of sense-data, then this fact is not one entirely evident to us through initial reflection on our experience. As both intentional theorists of perception and naive realists insist, at least some objects of awareness are presented as the mind-independent objects of perception. Of course, the disjunctivist is moved to go further in this and claim that it seems to us as if we have a non-representational relation to the mind-independent objects of awareness. So, a description of how our experience is drawing solely on the need to get its introspective character correct would favour a naive realist description of it over others, and this is the same for veridical perception and for illusion or hallucination (inasmuch as these cannot be told apart from veridical perception).

[17] That is, an event of being aware of an array of sense-data with such-and-such characteristics; or being in a state of mind with such-and-such representational properties or content.

[18] Note also that, as formulated, (II) takes no stance on whether perceptions ever occur, or whether a subject need believe themselves ever to have perceived anything. All that it requires is that *we* accept that sense experiences have the character at least of seeming to be perceptions.

Therefore, there could be nothing that a non-veridical perception *P*-event would seem to possess to the subject which a non-*P*-event which was still indiscriminable from a veridical perception would thereby lack. Given this, someone who wishes to rule out such a case because it is not a *P*-event (whatever the particular account of experience is in question) seems to be offering us too restrictive an account of sense experience; for they seem to be interpreting what should at best be a sufficient condition for having a sense experience as a necessary condition. The catholicism of (II) in this case would suggest not that the account is too liberal in conditions on what is to count as experience, but rather that the theory in question (be it a sense-datum account, or some form of intentionalism) is just too restrictive in what it countenances as possible ways in which the kinds of sensory experience we have can be realized.

This suggests that the defender of the Common Kind Assumption should agree that there can be no case of one of us being in a situation indiscriminable through reflection from veridical perception which is not a case of sense experience, whatever exactly the substantive account of sense experience the theorist thereby favours. The consequence of this is to accept certain constraints on the nature of sense experience and our knowledge of it. It is common for philosophers to suppose that conscious states must be (at least to self-conscious beings) self-intimating; such states will indicate their presence and some of their properties to the subject who is in them. What is required here is much more: that there should be no circumstance in which we are awake and there be no possibility for us to detect the absence of such states. As we shall see in Part Two, this extra epistemological condition bears on the conception one has of introspective awareness of sense experience; read in the way that the Common Kind theorist requires, it is liable to introduce the need for perfect mechanisms of detection.

The disjunctivist's opponent need not reject (II) itself, or think of it as obviously implausible. They may even agree that our initial understanding of what sense experience is is as (II) dictates, but then offer a more substantive account of what it takes for something to be an experience and so meet the condition in (II). On the other hand, they may think that the condition laid down in (II) itself is too thin, or modest, as an account of our understanding of sense experience. Still, for the reasons we have rehearsed above, they are unlikely to complain that (II) gets the extension of our concept of sense experience wrong. So (II) itself is unlikely to lead to any counter-intuitive consequences and on its own can hardly be considered a particularly controversial commitment of the disjunctivist. The same is not so, though, for the combination of (I) and (II). (I) commits us to thinking that there are some sense experiences which have a distinctive nature lacked by others, while (II) insists that all of these can nonetheless be indiscriminable from each other introspectively. Together this suggests that the phenomenal characters of two experiences can be different even while one of them is indiscriminable from the other. Many have supposed that what we mean by the phenomenal character of an experience is just that aspect of it which is introspectible, and hence that any two experiences which are introspectively indiscriminable must share their phenomenal characters, even if they differ in other ways.[19]

Now, while some such complaint may have widespread support in discussions of phenomenal consciousness, it is not clear whether it should be taken as a primitive claim which is somehow obvious, and the rejection of which is incredible. After all, we can make at least some sense of the idea that distinct individuals, distinct events, and distinct scenes, can all be perceptually presented to us and yet be perceptually indiscriminable from each other. That is, suppose that the individual experiences we have of the various individuals, events and scenes we perceive thereby have as part of their phenomenal natures the presentation of those very objects; each of these individual experiences will be different from each other through featuring one object or event rather than another. Since distinct objects can be indiscriminable perceptually, it is plausible that these perceptions should be indiscriminable from each other introspectively. If so, distinct experiences will be different in ways that are not necessarily detectible through introspective reflection.[20] It may be right in the end to dismiss such theories of perceptual experience as incorrect. But if there is an incoherence here, it is a subtle one, and not so glaringly obvious a contradiction. So this throws doubt on the idea that we should view the principle that sameness of phenomenal character is guaranteed by phenomenal indiscriminability as an evident truth. If we think the conjunction of (I) and (II) generates a counterintuitive position, then there must be some further principle at work behind our thoughts which forces us to accept this strong condition.

Once one accepts that (I) and (II) are both true, then one must also deny that two experiences, one of which is indiscriminable from the other, must share phenomenal character (that is, one denies: any phenomenal character the one experience has, the other has too). But it is consistent with accepting these two principles that one hold that such experiences would nonetheless share *a* phenomenal character. One way of construing this would be to suppose that (II) fixes for one a determinable notion of phenomenal character, one which is realizable in a number of different ways. As (I) specifies, this phenomenal character is realizable in a manner specific to veridical perceptions, a manner not shared with illusion or hallucination. The sense-datum theorist and the intentionalist each offer accounts of different ways in which the same determinable can be realized. This is consistent with the rejection of the Common Kind

---

[19] In effect, this is to press what I called principle (IND), in Martin (1997): 'If two experiences are indistinguishable for the subject of them then the two experiences are of the same conscious character' (p. 81).

[20] I discuss this option for an intentional theory of perception, in Martin (2002a). There are delicate questions to be raised here about the inter-relation between the phenomenology of individual experiences and the ways in which experiences are similar or different from each other.

Assumption as long as the particular manner in which the phenomenal character is realized in the case of veridical perception could not occur in either cases of illusion or hallucination. This model also captures the thought expressed above in relation to (II), that we should not suppose that there need be a unique way in which a given phenomenal character can be realized, at least with respect to illusions or hallucinations.

Although this position would share much with disjunctivism, this does not yet capture the key thought behind disjunctivism. To employ this model as an expression of disjunctivism would be to adopt an unstable position. In addition to (I) and (II) disjunctivism requires one to take on a further commitment. Put in the most general terms, the model so far sketched leaves open both the status of the common phenomenal character among perception, illusion and hallucination, and whether this can be conceived autonomously of veridical perception, and it leaves open the conception of the ways in which that character can be realized. As we shall see, the disjunctivist needs to take a stand on both of these things, and the resulting account is more radical than anything so far sketched.

3

The easiest way to develop this is to proceed through a particular line of reasoning related to the argument from hallucination. But the main moral I want to draw is one which can be generalized away from the commitments of this argument. One formulation of the argument from hallucination focuses on questions about the causal conditions for bringing about hallucinations, and in particular works with the thought that it is possible that a hallucination can be brought about through the same proximate causal conditions as a veridical perception—what I shall call a causally matching hallucination.[21] In its standard form, this argument relies on some principle of 'Same Cause, Same Effect'. To draw a conclusion from the case of veridical perception about that of causally matching hallucination, the principle requires us to suppose a commonality among all cases in which proximate causal conditions are the same. In such a form, the principle is unsound, or so I would argue; for the principle so conceived rules out the possibility that relational states of affairs or events can form part of the causal nexus where relational states of affairs may differ purely in their distal elements.

A modified form of the argument concerns the reverse direction, from what must be true of cases of causally matching hallucinations, to what must thereby be true of the veridical perceptions they match. A weakened form of 'Same Cause, Same Effect' that requires similarity of outcomes where local causal and

---

[21] See, for example, Robinson (1985, 1994); Foster (1986, ch.II, sec. X), and, for a repudiation of his earlier acceptance, Foster (2000); for critical discussion, see Pitcher (1971) and Hinton (1973); cf. also Merleau-Ponty (1942) and Valberg (1992).

non-causal conditions are the same seems to require that similar effects are present in cases of veridical perception as in causally matching hallucination; for, since we pick out the cases of hallucination through their lack of the required conditions for veridical perception, it is unclear that any non-causal condition required for the occurrence of a specific hallucination is not thereby also present in the case of veridical perception it matches. In this case, therefore, whatever effect can be produced in the case of the causally matching hallucination, the same effect will have been produced in the case of veridical perception.

Accepting this conclusion is not in itself tantamount to affirming the Common Kind Assumption. That demands that whatever is the most specific kind of experience occurring when one has a veridical perception, the same kind of experience can occur when one has an illusion or hallucination. The most that this argument could show is that whatever is the most specific kind of effect produced when having a causally matching hallucination, that same kind of effect occurs when one has a veridical perception. But that this is the most specific kind of effect that occurs when one has an hallucination does not entail that this is the most specific kind of effect that occurs when one is veridically perceiving. Nonetheless, it does raise two pressing questions for the disjunctivist. First, what character can the hallucinatory experience possess which could also be possessed by the veridical perception without thereby being the most specific kind of mental event that the veridical perception exemplifies? Second, if there is a kind common to the veridical perception and its causally matching hallucination, what shows that what is relevant to the explanations we want to give is ever the kind of event peculiar to veridical perception rather than what is common to veridical perception and causally matching hallucination?

In answer to these two questions, one can propose the third commitment of disjunctivism:

(III) For certain visual experiences as of a white picket fence, namely, causally matching hallucinations, there is no more to the phenomenal character of such experiences than that of being indiscriminable from corresponding visual perceptions of a white picket fence as what it is.

As we can see from the logic of indiscriminability, no veridical perception can be known not to be a veridical perception. So veridical perceptions are guaranteed to meet this condition and hence exemplify the kind in question.[22] In relation to the second question, it is clear that meeting this condition cannot screen off the property of being a veridical perception from any explanatory role that the naive realist supposes that only veridical perception experiences exemplify. At the same

---

[22] This is to move too quickly. The condition of being indiscriminable from a veridical perception of a white picket fence does not necessarily specify a property or kind of event, rather than specifying a condition that individual events may meet. One might take the alleged non-transitivity of just noticeable difference to show that there cannot be kinds of experience defined in this way. For more on this, see Martin (2004).

time, we can see the answer to the first question. As those attracted to disjunctivism in the theory of perception have often been tempted to say, along-side those attracted to the idea of object-dependent thought, in cases where the relevant conditions for such a state of mind are absent, then there must be something intrinsically defective or lacking about the state. This is made explicit in the thought that while there is a positive specific nature to the veridical perception, there is nothing more to the character of the (causally matching) hallucination than that it can't, through reflection, be told apart from the veridical perception.[23]

This condition is definitely forced on one if one accepts the reasoning above involving a form of the 'Same Cause, Same Effect' principle. Although the principle there employed is sufficiently weakened to allow for the existence of (partially) externally individuated effects, some may still question whether we have any such commitment to causal principles which bridge between mental phenomena and their physical antecedents. Even in that case, I suggest the disjunctivist should be wary of holding back a commitment to (III). Once one allows that there is a more substantive characterization available across a wide range of cases of what it is for mere appearance to occur, the question arises whether such a state can also be present in the case of veridical perception. The reasons that the naive realist offers for supposing that a distinctive state is present when so perceiving do not readily translate to show that nothing else could also be occurring in such circumstances. Yet, once one is deprived of grounds for denying the presence of some such common element between perception and hallucination, then a threat of explanatory pre-emption of the common feature overcomes the claims of that which is peculiar to the case of veridical perception. The reverse causal argument demonstrates the existence of a potential explanatory competitor for the veridical perception and hence makes clear the need for a disjunctivist to specify what form of common mental kind between perception and hallucination would be consistent with disjunctivism. If one rejects the relevant weakened form of 'Same Cause, Same Effect', then there is no such direct demonstration of the existence of a common element. But that is not to say that any argument has been offered that there cannot be some such mental kind in common, that what some hallucinations exemplify can also be present in veridical perception. The concerns about explanatory exclusion or screening off do not derive solely from the 'Same Cause, Same Effect' principle, and so cannot be ignored simply by rejecting it.

It is instructive to compare and contrast the situation here with the discussion that Timothy Williamson has launched over the case of knowledge and belief. Williamson argues that it is a mistake to think that the state of knowledge is decomposable into the presence of belief with further conditions, as the

---

[23] There is a longer exposition of both this problem and how (III) offers a solution, in Martin (2004, pp. 52–70).

'traditional' approach supposes. But Williamson also argues against the idea that we should endorse a disjunctive approach to belief, taking belief to be either knowledge or purported knowledge. Instead, Williamson suggests that knowledge and belief may co-exist (accepting the common thought that knowledge entails belief) but play distinct explanatory roles.[24] Williamson's strategy in arguing his case for taking knowledge as a primitive mental state is precisely to argue for its having a distinctive explanatory role which could not be taken by belief. This is quite consistent with the idea that belief has its own explanatory role untouched by that of knowledge.

The dialectical position is different in the case of debate about perception and sensory appearance (contra Williamson); for, while there are aspects of psychological explanation where one can conceive of a division of explanatory spoils between an appeal to perceptual states, on the one hand (i.e, those not common to perception and hallucination), and an appeal to sensory experience as something common across the cases, on the other hand, there is also a central area of concern where the two notions are bound to be in competition. For consider the subject's stream of consciousness, that temporal extension of episodes and conscious processes which make up a central core of his or her biography. We can avoid the question of explanatory exclusion here if it makes sense to suppose that both perceptual episodes (peculiar only to perception) and sensory experiences (common to perception and hallucination) can occupy locations within this stream. Yet such does not seem to be the case: if we are intending to give the most determinate and specific account of how things are with a subject at a given time, thereby picking out their conscious state, either what we pick out is the perceptual episode, as the naive realist supposes, or the common sensory experience, as defenders of the Common Kind Assumption suppose. So allowing for explanatory independence of notions of perception and experience in other realms of the psychological would not settle this question where competition cannot be avoided.

The same pressure does not seem to arise for the cases of belief and knowledge. It is questionable whether either phenomenon actually belongs within the stream of consciousness (in part that turns on the relation one hypothesizes between active judgement and belief or knowledge). And, however one settles that question, we have a handle on the explanatory role of these notions within psychology independent of questions about phenomenal consciousness. While we do have a conception of how perceptual states may explain things about a subject beyond an immediate concern with phenomenal consciousness—for example, explaining how they are in a position to have some of the beliefs they have and to act as they do—the presence of such an explanatory role is already common ground before the debate about perception arises. So the focus of dispute really is over the status of the experiential episode present in conscious

[24] See Williamson (1995, pp. 558–63; 2000, pp. 41–8).

perceiving, and all parties are committed to supposing that there are competing accounts to be given of this. Extending the Williamson strategy into the debate about sensory experience is of no avail.

Hence, we can see that the way of combining (I) and (II) suggested earlier is not really available for the disjunctivist. If we suppose that (II) fixes for us a determinable notion of phenomenal character which has a variety of determinations, then we must suppose that it has some characterization as a determinable independently of any of its determinations (as we have a conception of red independent of knowledge of what it is to be scarlet or vermillion). (II) itself does not give us any such specification, since it fixes the range of cases relative to the case of veridical perception, one of the supposed determinations. Moreover, the case of causally matching hallucination gives us an example of an experience which satisfies (II) but fails to give us a determination of phenomenal character more specific than this determinable. In general, we suppose that determinables to be instantiated require that some specific determination or other is realized. On the other hand, if we seek to remove these disanalogies and posit an appropriate determination for the case of causally matching hallucination, or seek some characterization of phenomenal character in substantive terms independent of veridical perception, then we are faced with the problems of explanatory exclusion or screening off. The disjunctivist consistently can hold on to veridical perception as a special case only through denying that the notion of sensory experience, and any specification of it which can occur in the case of causally matching hallucination, have any explanatory role autonomous of that of veridical perception itself.

Another way to put this point is to highlight that there are two sides to the disjunctivist's original conception of perception and sensory appearances. On the one hand is the thought that there is something special about the 'good' case, the presence of veridical perception and the apprehension of the mind-independent world. What holds essentially of the mental state or episode present in this case is not reduplicated across illusion and hallucination, so we can hold to the intuition that such states in themselves relate us to the mind-independent world. On the other hand, though, is the thought that in the 'bad' cases, the cases of illusion and hallucination, one is in a situation which fails to be the way that good cases are, but which purports to be the way that the good case is. Were a positive characterization always possible of the bad cases independent of their relation to veridical perception, were the notion of perceptual experience construable independent of this relation, then that these cases were bad would not be something intrinsic to them. This would not be a matter of us seemingly being related to the world but failing to be so, but rather being a certain way which we might also confuse with being perceptually related. So the disjunctivist thinks that there are cases of phenomenal consciousness which are essentially failures— they purport to relate us to the world while failing to do so. Commitment (III) makes this additional element clear in a way that (I) and (II) alone cannot do.

PART TWO

4

I've argued that a disjunctivist had better endorse (III), if he or she wishes to be consistent in their position and respect the other commitments which lead one to adopt disjunctivism in the first place. But is one left with a coherent position in accepting (III)? The disjunctivist claims that sense experience in the case of causally matching hallucination is nothing more than the obtaining of certain negative epistemological conditions and what follows from them: that it is not possible to know through reflection that this is not a situation of veridical perception. But this seems to suggest that there is nothing positive to the character of the experience in itself. Could having a sense experience be nothing more than this?

Complete incredulity at this thought is voiced by A. D. Smith when he complains:

To say simply that our subject is not aware of *anything* is surely to under-describe this situation dramatically. Perhaps we can make sense of there being 'mock thoughts', but can there really be such a thing as mock sensory awareness? Perhaps there can be 'an illusion of understanding', but can there be an illusion of awareness? . . . The sensory features of the situation need to be accounted for . . . If we take as our example subjects who are fully attentive and focused, we need to do justice to the fact that such subjects in some sense take cognizance of, indeed fully attend to, sensory presentations. But if so, what else can we say other than that the subject is, as the Argument requires, aware of a non-normal object?

. . . What, however, is it for someone to *seem to confront* something? Unless more is said, we are left without any means of distinguishing the hallucinatory cases we are interested in from such quite different states as post-hypnotic suggestion, gross mental confusion, inattentiveness, jumping the gun and so on. (2002: pp. 224–5)[25]

In fact, Smith's intended target in this instance is broader than the disjunctivism we have here been discussing. Smith is concerned to reject any view according to which a particular object is sensorily presented in veridical perception, while no corresponding object is presented when one has the matching hallucination. One could hold such a doctrine and yet insist that there is something appropriately common across the two cases—that there is, for example, a common representational content which in the one context secures an object, but in the other fails to.[26] On such a view, there is something common between a case of

[25] Compare also Valberg's criticisms of Anscombe on the intentionality of sensation, in Valberg (1992).

[26] One might consider the approach developed by Tyler Burge in a number of papers, in particular, Burge (1977, 1983, 1993) as offering such accounts. I discuss such possibilities for an intentional approach to perception, in Martin (2002a). Note, in addition, that though Smith takes Evans as a target of his discussion, Evans's own view of perceptual experience is not disjunctivist.

perception and hallucination which makes both a sensory occurrence; and it is by reference to this common element that one can contrast a genuinely experiential situation with any occasion in which there is nothing sensory occurring at all, that is, that there is a common representational sensory feature. If Smith insists that that is not what is required (if he insists that what one needs is a common *object* of attention), then the complaint swiftly becomes an expression of the conviction that sense-datum theorists have, that things cannot be sensorily so unless there really is something thus and so for one to be sensing. That is hardly an intuition that many now share. Rather, those who endorse the Common Kind Assumption may well agree that there has to be *something* in common between perception and hallucination, that there must be a common way of sensing between the two which requires a unified account. What they will deny is that what is common need be thought of as any kind of object of awareness, rather than the sensory basis of attention to the environment.

Therefore, Smith's complaint seems best targeted at the disjunctivist position we have elaborated above; for affirming (III) does seem to lead to the kind of position that Smith finds incredible. Smith emphasizes the distinction between sensory and mere cognitive aspects of the mind. The specification of a situation as one in which it is not possible to know that it is not perception seems, like the condition 'seems to confront' which Smith discusses, a cognitive and not a sensory condition. In contrast to the representationalist just discussed, the disjunctivist does deny him or herself the resource of some positive element of the situation, an element which is both sensuous and common to perception and hallucination in contrast to the cases of mere intellectual disorder.

While the focus of Smith's complaint is basically an assertion of the inadequacy of the view he opposes, he does, in addition, add towards the end of the passage a briefly sketched argument through which I think we can articulate more the kind of resistance that Smith offers. Smith notes that there are cases which no one would think involve sensory experience of the relevant sort: cases of post-hypnotic suggestion or inattention. Our intuitions for such cases are that while a subject may possess some of the cognitive concomitants of sense experience, the relevant sensory state is lacking: at best the subject matches a normal subject only with respect to the cognitive consequences of sense experience, not in sense experience itself. If causally matching hallucination is assimilated to these cases, then it would seem, as Smith complains, that the possibility of hallucination is really being denied by the disjunctivist, rather than being accommodated through appeals to (II) and (III); for, surely, the complaint continues, our basic commitment is that (at least some) hallucinations are examples of genuine sense experience even if they fail to be cases of veridical perception. We suppose that there is something defective in the subject's relation

---

The brief account Evans gives in ch. 5 of his (1982) develops an account of information states on which it is possible for an information state to exist while lacking a proper object.

to the external world perceived; and not that there is merely a defect in how they relate to their own states of mind.

Smith is owed an account by the disjunctivist of how we are to distinguish cases which intuitively do not involve a visual sense experience of a white picket fence, such as when one is under the post-hypnotic suggestion that that is what one can see, from cases in which one does have such an experience but does so only through meeting the condition in (III). But, as we shall see below, there is in fact much that the disjunctivist could and would say to contrast the two kinds of case. Yet, even if an answer can be given to this, Smith may complain that it doesn't locate the difference in the right place. For Smith has in mind what the most satisfying account of the difference should amount to, and that kind of account the disjunctivist cannot offer. It is tempting to say of someone under the influence of post-hypnotic suggestion that they simply lack a mental state with the relevant phenomenal characteristics, whatever cognitive states they also possess in this situation. So the only difference that really matters between the subject of a causally matching hallucination and a post-hypnotic suggestion victim is the presence in the former case (and absence in the latter) of these phenomenal characteristics. If the disjunctivist can point to a difference between the two kinds of case which is consistent with (III), then that will relate to the kinds of condition mentioned in (II) and (III), namely, the sense in which the one situation is or is not knowably distinct from veridical perception. But such a condition seems itself to be cognitive, since it talks of what one can or cannot know. At the same time, affirming (III) seems to rule out any appeal to any further mental condition which could be present in the case of the causally matching hallucination. Hence, the disjunctivist would seem to deny the intuition that the difference here must be one of the presence or absence of the phenomenal state of mind. And it is this thought which makes Smith, or someone moved by his complaints, suppose that the disjunctivist cannot be giving an account of sense experience at all.

Now a swift riposte to this would be to point out that the disjunctivist requires that a perfect hallucination be one which is indiscriminable from a veridical perception. What more could be required of how the subject is than that this condition is met? Surely the condition of introspective indiscriminability guarantees that phenomenal consciousness is present. So the disjunctivist is not assimilating the hallucinating subject to the victim of post-hypnotic suggestion. Although I think it is right for the disjunctivist to resist Smith's characterization, as it stands this response is too swift to be adequate. Compare the concern here with the more familiar discussions of absent qualia and philosophical zombies in relation to functionalism and the conceivability argument for dualism. When a critic complains against a functionalist account of the mind that it is quite conceivable that a creature should satisfy all of the functional conditions for mentality and yet lack phenomenal consciousness, the complaint made is one external to the terms of the functionalist theory. The critic claims that we can both imagine that some creature satisfies the functionalist definition and yet lacks phenomenal consciousness as we commonly conceive it. To this the functionalist may respond that, by his or her lights, if the functionalist conditions really are met for mentality, then there is no possibility of the absence of phenomenal consciousness. What the critic puts forward either is not really possible, or has been misdescribed.

Whether the argumentative position of the initial complaint against functionalism, or the robust response to it begs the question given debate in the area is a delicate question. Matters seem more straightforward in the current case, though; for, when we turn to our more limited troubles about sensory experience, the challenge seems rather to be internal to the disjunctivist's concerns. While it is true that disjunctivism need not attempt to offer a general account of sentience as such, the disjunctivist clearly does suppose that sensory experience in certain cases amounts to more than the meeting of the negative epistemological conditions. For the disjunctivist does not suppose that veridical perception as such should simply be a matter of meeting certain epistemological conditions. Given a commitment to Naive Realism, the disjunctivist claims that veridical perception involves standing in some relation of awareness to the various objects of awareness. This additional condition is not present in the case of causally matching hallucination. So, it appears as if, by the disjunctivist's own lights, there is a positive additional characterization to be had of certain, central cases of phenomenal experience, which positive element is lacking in the case of causally matching hallucination, though unknowably so. It is this aspect of what the disjunctivist him or herself says which seems to justify the characterization of the position above, and which lies at the basis of Smith's complaint. Treating the disjunctivist's account of causally matching hallucination as a case of absent qualia, therefore, seems to be to offer an internal critique of disjunctivism.

The swift response to this challenge is simply to claim that the objection misses the fact that, since the hallucination is indiscriminable from veridical perception, phenomenal consciousness must be present. But this response misconstrues the burdens of argument. The disjunctivist who responds this way leaves untouched the worry about the coherence of his or her position: whether commitment (III) is really consistent with this alleged entailment. For, of course, it is not that Smith thinks it actually possible (or even coherent to suppose) that one should be in the same cognitive position as a subject who possesses phenomenal consciousness and yet lack such consciousness. Indeed, Smith's complaint seems rather to be that when we focus on the kind of experience we all enjoy, when we exploit our own self-awareness of that experience, we can see that it is impossible for someone to be this kind of way (the way required equally for genuine hallucination as for perception) and yet lack any positive phenomenal character. So Smith, too, would agree with the disjunctivist that if the situation really is one of being indiscriminable through reflection from a veridical perception, then matters will be phenomenologically just as in the case of veridical perception. But this is precisely because, in addition to the facts that the disjunctivist appeals to, some positive phenomenal characteristics must also be present, guaranteeing that this is a genuinely sensory occurrence. This is to contradict the claim in (III) that there is no further positive characterization to be given of the situation than that which follows from the negative epistemological properties.

The debate here is not over whether both sides should agree that the subject genuinely has sense experience in the case of causally matching hallucination in contrast to the case of post-hypnotic suggestion. Both sides should agree with that. The question is whether the disjunctivist can show that one can coherently claim this while also affirming (III). Appealing to (II) or (III) alone does not show this. Rather, if Smith's complaint mischaracterizes the situation by the disjunctivist's lights, then there must be some mistake in the reasoning which has got us to this point. There must have been something wrong in the thought that the disjunctivist is simply appealing to cognitive and not sensory features of the situation when the causally matching hallucination is taken to fulfil the condition specified in (III). But how can that condition indicate anything about the sensory character of the subject's situation? Wouldn't that be to pick out some positive feature which either will or will not be common with the case of veridical perception?

We need to identify which elements in Smith's line of thought about the situation the disjunctivist will have to reject. Now, the characterization that we extracted from Smith of the causally matching hallucination is forced upon us, I suggest, if we accept a certain picture of the relation between phenomenal consciousness on the one hand, and self-awareness of our cognitive states of response to phenomenal consciousness on the other. That is, one may conceive that the facts about phenomenal consciousness are fixed independently of whether a subject has any perspective on his or her own conscious states and is thereby self-aware of them. In general, then, it should be possible for us to settle whether someone is phenomenally conscious or not without having to make any appeal to the subject's own higher-order perspective on these conscious states. In turn, that suggests that adopting the higher-order perspective on one's phenomenal consciousness, coming to be self-aware and attentive of it, is thereby to put oneself in a position to acquire knowledge of something independent of this perspective itself. In coming to make judgements about how things phenomenally appear to one, one makes judgements about a subject matter that obtains independently of one's being in a position to make those judgements.

At the same time, we are inclined to view this higher-order perspective as one of self-awareness and self-consciousness. It is not clear that we can quite conceive of the cognitive aspect of such a state of mind as other than awareness of one's mind, and hence a form of, or ground for, knowledge. In which case, one could not be this way cognitively (i.e. with this range of judgements, formed in this way) without being self-aware and self-knowing: phenomenal consciousness would have to be present. On this picture, although the facts about phenomenal consciousness obtain independently and prior to any facts about our knowledge of it, our introspective cognition of phenomenal consciousness need not be independent of that consciousness: seeming awareness of one's conscious mind will always be genuine self-awareness.[27]

Now, in this context, it is plausible to argue that the negative epistemological properties the disjunctivist appeals to belong at the level of higher-order awareness or self-knowledge, rather than at the level of phenomenal consciousness itself. In that case, the presence or absence of the negative epistemological property will not determine the presence or absence of phenomenal consciousness, but will rather simply fix whether or not the subject is aware of these facts, and hence is self-aware or self-conscious. In the case of causally matching hallucination, the conditions specified by the disjunctivist fix only facts on the cognitive side of the divide. Where the disjunctivist claims to be characterizing sense experience without awareness of the environment, the complaint here is that they can only be describing the absence of experience with necessary ignorance of this fact. Although the claim is localized just to the case of causally matching hallucination, still the disjunctivist seems to be describing to us the case of absent qualia, or the philosophical zombie, the alleged possibility of which have plagued functionalist theories of the mind and various forms of physicalism. Since it is commonly taken to show that a theory is inadequate as an account of phenomenal consciousness if it could equally be true of a philosophical zombie, it would seem to be a failing in the disjunctivist account if it ends up claiming that in cases of hallucination we are no better off than such mythical beings.

If the disjunctivist is to resist Smith's characterization of the situation, the disjunctivist must, at the very least, reject this picture of the relation between phenomenal consciousness and our awareness of it. What alternative is there? I shall suggest that the disjunctivist needs to stress the connection between phenomenal consciousness and having a point of view or perspective on the world. The negative epistemological condition when correctly interpreted will specify not a subject's cognitive response to their circumstances—and hence their knowledge or ignorance of how things are with them—but rather their perspective on the world. This is sufficient for it to be true of a subject that there is something it is like for them to be so. In that way we can say of the subject of causally matching hallucination that they must indeed possess phenomenal consciousness precisely because, in meeting the relevant condition for the negative epistemological property, they thereby possess a point of view on the world. Though in this case, that point of view does not extend beyond how things are with them at that moment, since *ex hypothesi* perfect hallucination does not provide them with any awareness of the environment. So the subject, in this case, would possess subjectivity and thereby be conscious since there is something it is

---

[27] This is an intuition to which we will return on pp. 388–92.

like for them to be so. Appeal to further facts over and above those which provide for their subjectivity and for there to be something it is like for them to be so would thereby be redundant.

In developing the alternative account here, we need first to start with a seemingly more limited problem with the disjunctivist's appeal to (II) and (III), for these claims pick out sense experiences which are not veridical perceptions by reference to introspective reflection. So it is natural to ask: how can the disjunctivist's account be extended to account for the sense experience of creatures which lack self-consciousness, self-awareness or any introspective capacity at all? We can give a satisfactory answer to this question only after rehearsing some familiar considerations for contrasting introspective self-awareness with ordinary observation. Once we have done that, we will see that the restriction 'through introspective reflection' must work rather differently from how the model sketched above supposes. In turn, this will lay bare for us what the deeper disagreement really amounts to.

5

Suppose that dogs are sentient but lack any interesting theory of mind. In particular, let us suppose that they lack the cognitive sophistication to entertain thoughts about their own experiences and the similarities and differences among them. Note that this is not to deny them thoughts about the objects of perception and the similarities and differences among them. The disjunctive theory can make sense of the thought that a dog's visual perception of a bunch of carrots is different in character from the dog's olfactory apprehension of a bowl of meaty chunks. The first experience, after all, may have among its constituents visually manifest objects and qualities such as carrots, the orange of their flesh and the green of the leaves; while the latter experience involves the smelly presence of jelly and wet cooked meat. So far this fits with our intuitions that the world can be a relatively varied place for the dog, even if it lacks the sophistication to think about the world in as many rich ways as we can.

If we move from the case of perception alone to ask how the disjunctivist is to think of canine sensory experience including illusion and hallucination, then the answer is presumably to be supplied by (II): that the dog's experiences should be the same or different to the extent that they are discriminable or indiscriminable through introspective reflection. Yet, if we are asking of the dog's own knowledge of the sameness or difference of his or her experiences, then we already have the answer that the dog does not know of the distinctness of any of their experiences. For the dog lacks all knowledge that any given experience is of this or that kind, lacking the conceptual resources to make any such judgement. From this it seems to follow that by (II) each experience the dog has is of the same kind as any other experience that the dog has. Thought of one way, one might then suppose that the dog simply has just one kind of experience. But, given that we can make sense by the disjunctivist's lights of the various perceptions that the dog has, one may equally argue that each experience would have to exemplify every possible kind of experience that the dog could enjoy. Each experience would exemplify all, and indeed contradictory, phenomenal characteristics at once. Either way, we seem to be landed with an absurd picture.

How can the disjunctivist avoid this unfortunate conclusion? We arrive at the conclusion if we suppose that (II) is talking about the knowledge that a given individual could or could not have about the identity or difference of psychological states. Is there any other way of reading (II)?

The first move to make in response is to consider a slightly less aggravated version of the problem. (II) read in one way will generate problems for us even if we stick to self-aware human beings. Imagine the case of John who has normal sensory sensitivity but is very much in a world of his own and inattentive to things he sees or tastes. Let's suppose that John doesn't do well at telling scarlet from vermillion. Just as he is bad at telling apart samples of these shades of red, so we may suppose him inattentive at telling apart the visual experiences of these samples. In such cases it seems perfectly appropriate to say not only that John doesn't discriminate the samples or experiences, but also that he can't. But this seems to commit us to saying that the experience of scarlet and the experience of vermillion are indiscriminable for John, and hence by (II) that the experiences should be the same. Yet it was no part of our initial commitment that the experiences should have to be the same: we were making an observation about John's inclination to attend and the judgements he is liable to make; nothing need be included in this about how he will or will not experience the world to be.[28]

In response to this worry, we should note that there are different ways we can be talking about someone's inability or incapacity to do something. Often when we note not only that someone has not done something but that they could not have done it, that they lack the ability or the capacity, then we indicate that there is some particular ground present which is operative in their failure. When Nancy stumbles on the dance floor, one might say not only that she is failing to dance the tango but that she simply can't dance it. In saying on this occasion that she can't dance it, one might not mean that there are no circumstances in which she succeeds in dancing the tango, or even that normally she is able to. Perhaps Nancy is a dance instructor, and the tango is her speciality; however, this evening given how much she has had to drink, there is just no way that her limbs can coordinate successfully to produce a tango.

When we talk about particular individuals' incapacities or inabilities, therefore, we often have in mind some specific condition obtaining in them by virtue

---

[28] Note that this is not to prejudge the question how the presence of phenomenal consciousness and the possibility of attending to a phenomenon fit together—for example, I take no stance here on the proper interpretation of inattentional blindness, see Mack and Rock (1998), or change blindness, see, among others, McConkie (1979) and Dennett (1991).

of which the failure is bound to be present. That one person could not do something on a particular occasion, does not mean that they couldn't do it on some other occasion, or that others cannot, or that a different range of people could not do that thing. We can, therefore, by suitable shift of context get claims about someone's inability to come out true or false, depending on what counts as appropriately grounding a capacity or preventing them from exercising it.

However, sometimes we have ways of talking which aspire, as one might say, to greater impartiality. For example, if you take a suit to the tailor's for invisible mending, the tailor will not have lived up to his or her advertisements if they mend the clothes with thick, bright red thread but then pluck your eyes out. If clothes genuinely have had invisible mending, then the mend should not just not be visible to you, but must not be visible to anyone. Moreover, in saying that it should not be visible to *anyone*, one may well intend no restriction on this at all: it is not just not visible to the average English person who has learnt not to pay too close attention to others' attire, it is also not visible to Italians, or Americans, more used to admiring the fine textiles with which the human form can be clothed. Pushed to the limit, then, we seem to have an appeal to an impersonal talk of inability or incapacity: we are talking about what sight can discern for you, or of some aspect of the object in question, rather than some way a given individual or group of individuals is such that they can't succeed in a particular task.

Here, too, there can be different ranges of possibility we have in mind. The difference between two objects may be invisible given the normal spectrum of light that we are sensitive to. Perhaps there is a surface blemish of one which turns up only when one is sensitive to infrared or ultraviolet light. In asking about what vision can reveal to us, we can ask in terms of how vision actually is, or ways in which vision could be. In turn, the most extreme claim of incapacity to tell apart here would concern the impossibility of knowing through any way that vision could be of the obtaining of a certain fact.

Applying this to the case of introspective reflection and the case of John, we can see that in that case any appropriate claim of indiscriminability turned on incapacities specific to John—his inattention or carelessness—grounds which prevent John in particular from exercising the relevant discrimination. But when we are comparing experiences as relevantly alike or not, we are not concerned with whether John himself is particularly attentive to the subtle variations in colour appearance, or whether he has a good visual memory; rather, we are interested in whether with respect to the mode of introspective reflection the situations can be discriminated or not. So we are interested in the impersonal notion of inability or incapacity here. That is we are interested in the claim that John is in a situation for which it is impossible *simpliciter* and not just impossible for John to tell apart through introspective reflection from a veridical perception of a patch of scarlet. In this case, the experience of a swatch of vermilion will not count as indiscriminable from this perception because, although John himself might fail to notice the difference, there still is a difference between the two situations which one could through reflection come to attend to and notice. And, the disjunctivist wishes to claim, it is our understanding of this fact which grounds our recognition that John's experiences can differ from each other. Although attention typically does lead to differences in sense experience—and according to some empirical hypotheses makes for all the difference between presence of phenomenal consciousness and its absence—we do have the conception that it is possible for experience to be a certain way whether focally attended to or not. And, in this particular instance, we find quite conceivable that there was a way things were for John had he but directed his attention. In appealing to the impersonal sense of indiscriminability the disjunctivist can make sense of this conception.

Earlier we noted that Smith presented a challenge for the disjunctivist: for the account to be adequate it needs to make sense of the intuitive contrast between a victim of hypnotic suggestion, or mental confusion, and someone genuinely having an hallucination. We can now see how the disjunctivist will answer this challenge. In such cases, while there may be grounds for the particular individual why he or she will fail to know of the difference between the situation that he or she is in, and the visual perception of a white picket fence, it won't follow from this alone that his or her situation is objectively, or impersonally, indiscriminable from a veridical perception. We intuitively track the difference in contrasting how we imagine things to be presented to them, or how we conceive it as not being presented, with the individual's failure to appreciate that difference. The contrast between a case in which the subject fails to distinguish their situation from one of perceiving the picket fence and one in which their situation is such that it is impersonally indiscriminable from one of perceiving makes space for just this contrast. However, as we already remarked, to highlight the difference in these terms is not to answer the challenge in the way that Smith supposes the intuitive one. According to him, the only plausible answer is to say that the difference between the two kinds of case turns simply on the presence or absence of phenomenal consciousness, independent of any facts about what is or is not knowably different about the cases. But that is to raise again the more fundamental disagreement to which we shall return later.

In summary, while some talk of the impossibility of acting or sensing in a certain way focuses on the specific limitations that an agent or group of agents may possess, we also have ways of talking of the impossibility of doing, sensing or knowing, which are not grounded in the specific capacities or incapacities of agents. It is with reference to this notion that the disjunctivist will claim that what proponents of the Common Kind Assumption suppose are phenomenally the same are really instances of things not possibly being knowably different. Our ascription of such a psychological state to John or to the individuals involved in Smith's examples does not thereby commit us to these agents possessing any specific psychological capacities or incapacities in respect of the judgements they make over and above the experiential state so ascribed. When we ascribe such a state to someone, the focus is not on the actual psychological states that they go into in response to having an experience, or even on what states they would or might go into were conditions other than they are. To talk of the impersonal indiscriminability focuses on the mode of what is to be known about, or what is to be known about itself. It is to talk about the experiential situation.

6

But it really is not clear how establishing the possibility of impersonal claims of indiscriminability will help with our initial problem in respect of the dog. While we do use such claims without singling out any specific defects of agents, the example of invisibility still suggests that they are focused on certain aspects of agents which will not carry over to the case of the dog. For example, where we do praise the mend as being invisible, even if we need not then be speaking of any specific failing in Jones's sight, still we do seem to be talking about sight, a psychological capacity, and what can or cannot be known through its use. For example, suppose that the thread used for the mend happens to be one which reacts differently to infrared radiation from the surrounding textile. Then, while the mending is indeed invisible for us, we can conceive of possible ways that sight could have been such that the mend was visible after all. So our talk here of invisibility seems just to be talk about what it is or is not possible to know through the use of sight.

The parallel in the case of the dog is to suppose that our talk of what is or is not knowably distinct from perception by introspective reflection is to talk about the use of introspective reflection. It is to talk about the means or faculty or mechanism, or source of knowledge that introspection provides and what is or is not knowably distinct through its use. But if it is to talk about that, then it is to talk about something which is, strictly speaking, irrelevant to the case of the dog. For the dog, *ex hypothesi*, lacks the power of introspection, no less than an insentient stone does. So whatever introspection could or could not tell one about the situation the dog is in, it could not be telling the dog that, since the dog is not in a position to use it. And, one could add, it hardly helps to talk of what one could know through introspection were one in the situation of the dog. That would raise two obvious problems: what would it be about the situation which would make one's introspective judgements in that strange counterfactual situation relevant to how things actually are with the dog? And, what is it about the dog's situation that would have to be held fixed into the counterfactual situation where one introspects? Surely there is no plausible candidate other than how the dog is itself experiencing; yet we are allegedly seeking to explicate what it is for the dog to experience in terms of this counterfactual condition.

In fact, this construal of indiscriminability talk raises another problem, entirely independent of the issue of the dog. When we suppose that talk of what is or is not invisible is to talk about the power or capacity of sight with respect to certain objects or circumstances, we should also note that it is to talk of certain features of the objects of sight. This is particularly notable when we consider the invisibility of distinctness: i.e., when objects are indiscriminable through the use of sight. It is natural for us to move from talking of things being indiscriminable (where that is not tied to some specific incapacity of the judge in question) to them thereby sharing something, a look or appearance. And, if this transition from talk of indiscriminability to sameness of appearance is warranted in general, then the disjunctivist's commitment to hallucination being impersonally indiscriminable from veridical perception will lead us to talk of them sharing an appearance, in conflict with commitment (III).

For example, suppose someone presents you with a cunningly crafted bar of soap which looks just like an Amalfi lemon. Sometimes people craft soap to look lemon-like while still obviously being nothing other than soap; but we can imagine a master craftsman of soap sculpture making a soap lemon so perfectly that there is no way to tell the bar of soap from a genuine lemon, just with the naked eye. In this case the bar of soap and a real lemon may well be visually indiscriminable. And in saying this, I don't mean merely to be saying that I, with little interest in the particular ways in which the surface of lemons are textured when waxed and when not, cannot tell them apart, but rather that one just couldn't tell them apart. This impossibility of telling things apart comes with a certain objectivity attached to it. It is a fact about the two items that they are not to be told apart through sight alone. Someone would be mistaken if they thought that they could so discern them. For example, we might imagine an over-confident television chef convinced that he can spot the real lemon from the bar of soap. Moreover we may suppose that, purely by chance, what he picks as the real lemon is indeed the genuine article. In explaining his success the chef might claim that there was just a special way that the lemon looked which the soap did not, and which keyed him in to the right answer. Now, even though the chef happened on the correct item, still this claim is wrong, if the two genuinely are indiscriminable through sight. The chef is lucky in his choice, but his success is not grounded in how anything looked or how anything appeared to him, given that he was seeing things as they were.[29]

What the chef is mistaken about are not only his grounds for the judgement (or lack of them) but also something about the objects in question: in being visually indiscriminable they share something: the same appearance, or look. What is true of looks and lemons is true too of smells and tastes: if two wines just could not be told apart by use of the palate, then the two wines do share a taste; if two rags cannot be distinguished by the nose, then there will be a smell in common between them. In general, then, with respect to the senses,

---

[29] Charles Travis insisted on this point to me. Cf. also Austin (1962, ch.5).

indiscriminability of objects of sense correlates with a shared appearance, or shared object of sense.

Now this observation, no less than the last, poses a problem for the disjunctivist. For suppose that the impersonal talk of indiscriminability allows us to talk of the objects of possible knowledge, just as we can talk of the lemon and the soap. Then as when we say that two objects indiscriminable through sight must share a look or appearance, it seems as if we should say the same will hold for introspective indiscriminability. If the hallucination really is indiscriminable through introspective reflection from the perception, then the hallucination has something detectible in common with the perception, an inner appearance, or (one may feel the temptation to say) a phenomenal character. Note that this would give us *a* phenomenal sameness between the two, as proposed by the alternative response to commitment (II), but it would not yet give us what *the Common Kind Assumption* requires, that the most specific character of the veridical experience is shared with the matching hallucination. But, of course, to grant this would be to give up on commitment (III); for that claimed that all that need be in common is that the hallucination is indiscriminable from the perception. But what the above line of reasoning suggests is that the way in which objects may be so indiscriminable is really only through sharing an appearance, and hence that will be an additional feature over and beyond the merely negative epistemological property of being not knowably distinct from the perception.

We have two problems here at either end of the claim of indiscriminability. First, if we take the claim of impersonal indiscriminability about introspective reflection to be parallel to that for sight, then such ascriptions will only be significant in relation to the sense experience of creatures which possess such a mode of coming to know. So, unless the disjunctivist can offer some other interpretation, conditions (II) and (III) will be inapplicable to the case of the dog. Second, when we consider the use of such judgements in relation to the senses, such as sight, then we see that when impersonal indiscriminability holds, so too does such a sharing of a property detected through that sense: if the lemon and soap are visibly indiscriminable, then they have in common their visual appearance. Now I want to suggest that the two problems are linked. We are led to posit a common appearance in relation to sight because we think of sight as a mode of coming to be aware of a realm independent of it. But we have reasons, already partly gestured at in passing, for not thinking of introspection in this way. This gives us a reason to deny that indiscriminability requires a common appearance property in the case of introspection. But, in turn, it forces us one step further. If we are not to think of introspection as a mode or source of knowledge along the lines of claims about the visibility or invisibility of objects, how are we to construe it?

Recall that claims of indiscriminability are to be read as claims about the impossibility of knowing relative to some mode that two things are not identical, or that one thing is not a member of a given kind. So, in general there is no entailment from something's being not possibly knowably not an *F* to its being an *F*, or even some other *G*. There is no entailment from not being able to know through sight that the bar of soap is not a lemon to the claim that there is thereby something both the bar of soap and the lemon are which one *can* know through sight. What more need the two objects have in common than just that sight isn't a way of telling that the one is different from the other?

Yet, having underlined that point, we should also note that the move to the positive claim that there *is* an appearance that the bar of soap and the lemon share is one which is entirely natural for us to make. Moreover this is not just the observation that the most obvious way for something to be a fake lemon is for it to have such visible properties in common with lemons as shape and colour. Rather, it seems as if a mild form of verificationism is called for in this area, even if it is applied only within a very limited purview. In the case of visually observable phenomena, our use of sight in good viewing conditions is an appropriate way to come to know of the presence, or absence, of such phenomena. Vision, at least in optimal circumstances, is a way of coming to know things about one's environment, which things being those that vision is appropriate to tell one about. When one fails to tell apart the lemon and the soap, the failure is not a matter of the breakdown of the visual system or the conditions for viewing these objects. So, if vision is normally a way of telling whether things are thus and so within the visible world, then the fact that vision cannot tell our two objects apart suggests that there is something that it does detect in common between them.[30] And that fact, that there is something to be picked up on here, we mark with talk of the look, the visual appearance or just the appearance which the two things share.[31]

If this is the right account of why the move is legitimate in the case of vision (and, one might also suggest, in the cases of taste and smell)[32], then the move is natural to make where we suppose that we are using a source of knowledge in relation to a realm which exists independently of any one perceiver's exercise of the relevant faculty. We talk of the objects having something in common when not distinguished by one's senses because the use of one's senses is a way of

---

[30] We should note one extra complication here. It is not clear that we would talk of a distinctive look that lemons have if we lived in an environment in which there were many non-lemons which also looked just the way that lemons look. So that we talk of a distinctive look of lemons may require that the bars of soap we talk about here are something of an anomaly.

[31] Compare here Crispin Wright's (1982) discussion of observational knowledge and Christopher Peacocke's various accounts of observational concepts (Peacocke 1983, ch.4, 1986, ch.1, 1992).

[32] The case is somewhat more complex for these senses, though, for we consider smells and tastes to be the proper objects of these senses, in the way that a visual appearance of an object is not. To put the thought somewhat picturesquely, we can imagine an olfactory world inhabited solely by smells, with the smells in question linked only extrinsically to any of the common objects in the world around us; we don't conceive of the visible world as primarily occupied just by visible appearances (although perhaps some sense-datum theorists have been seduced into thinking this). Rather we suppose visible objects which possess visual appearances occupy a visual world.

determining how things are in the world independent of that exercise. We can then mark that it is not some particular limitation, or failure, on one's part, or a failure in one's senses by treating the objective indiscernibility as a positive appearance. The same story will apply to the case of introspection, therefore, only if we suppose that in self-awareness or the exercise of introspective reflection also one is detecting features of some realm of facts given independently of one's introspection, such that there can be a failure to tell apart which is not a matter simply of a subjective failing on the part of the individual enquirer.

7

This seems to raise a broader and more familiar question: to what extent is introspection like perception or observation? If we should think of introspective contact with phenomenal consciousness as relevantly similar to perceptual observation of objects, then the same move will be natural to make concerning a common appearance to introspection. It has become fairly popular to insist that introspection is not a form of inner observation, and to point out that there are key disanalogies between introspection and perception.[33] A more specific question concerns us here, though: do any such disanalogies undermine the reasoning from indiscriminability to sameness of appearance? Rather than rehearse general grounds for contrasting introspection and perception, I want to present a line of reasoning which derives from the considerations we already expressed on behalf of the disjunctivist in respect of commitment (II) above.

One familiar observation is that introspection contrasts with the sense modalities in allowing of no seems/is distinction; for, when we employ our senses to find out about the world around us, we acknowledge the possibility that things may seem a certain way to us visually or tactually without necessarily being that way. In the most favourable circumstances, proper employment of a mode of sensing can deliver knowledge of some subject matter—the use of one's eyes, or one's nose, or one's palate is a perfectly proper way to know of the size or colour of something, how it smells, whether a wine is ready to drink. But in disfavourable circumstances a subject can unwittingly go wrong in judgement through attempting to use his or her senses as they would in the best possible circumstances. In such a situation a subject may be mistaken in judgement but not at fault (epistemically) in the judgement he or she makes. When that happens the subject conforms her judgement to how things sensorily seem to her, even though how things seem is not how they are.[34] Since there are objective

---

[33] For some flavour of the varieties of discussion here, see Sydney Shoemaker (1984, originally published in *Journal of Philosophy* 1968; 1995; 1994); also compare Anscombe (1975); Burge (1996); Wright (1989, 1998); Moran (2001). For those who still favour something like an observational model, however, see Armstrong (1968); Chisholm (1969); and Macdonald (1998).

[34] The discussion here is intended to remain neutral on the question whether we should say a subject uses the same methods of enquiry across favourable and disfavourable

conditions for the correct functioning of our senses, we can conceive of the possibility of circumstances in which both things seem a certain way to the subject and the subject lacks knowledge because the conditions are not optimal for the operation of their senses.[35]

The idea that no such contrast can be drawn with respect to the inner realm is sometimes put by saying that we have direct or immediate access to our own phenomenal states.[36] But that is a somewhat misleading slogan. A naive realist about perception will insist in the case of veridical perception that one does have direct or immediate access to the environmental objects and facts which one perceives. The possibility that there can be cases in which one is subject to illusion and hence liable to error is not ruled out by the fact that in certain other cases one has direct access to the objects of awareness. So we can express the key idea in its simplest form just by ruling out the relevant parallel story for introspection that we tell for sense perception. That is to say, introspection is not like this: there are optimal circumstances for the exercise of one's introspective faculty. When such circumstances obtain, one can acquire knowledge about one's phenomenal consciousness through exercising the faculty. In less than optimal circumstances, however, attempting to employ the introspective faculty will not issue in introspective knowledge. In such circumstances a subject who does not know that the situation is disfavourable may well be reasonable in making the introspective judgements that he or she does, for such judgements will match the way that things introspectively seem. But how things seem introspectively will not be how things are phenomenally, and hence the judgement in question will not be knowledge.[37] Were this a genuine possibility, we could always significantly contrast how a subject's inner life seems to her with how it actually is: there would be the possibility (or at least conceivability) that things might merely seem to be the way she judges them to be. In denying that there is a genuine seems/is distinction we are saying that we do not conceive this as a genuine possibility, and hence that the story told is to be ruled out.

Now, in ruling this out as a coherent possibility, one denies that there are any situations in which, from the subject's perspective on her situation, her mind seems one way to her, and yet is another. It does not require one to take a stand

circumstances—whether we should say that a subject uses the same methods of enquiry when really seeing as when merely having a visual hallucination.

[35] Matters could be formulated slightly more carefully here. A subject could have knowledge in such circumstances, if on the basis of ancillary information they can know that in such circumstances, the environment can only be a certain way. For example, one can imagine an individual who knows that they are induced to have a visual hallucination of a pink elephant only in the presence of pink elephants and so comes to know that there is a pink elephant nearby when it seems to them a pink elephant is nearby. If we focus on cases of demonstrative knowledge ('That is a pink elephant') and knowledge only derivable from demonstrative knowledge, then the complication may not be required.   [36] For example, Sturgeon (1994); Chalmers (1996).

[37] This description sounds much like the scenario which Smith attributes to the disjunctivist concerning hallucination. So one might explain the intuitive force of Smith's rejection of that picture with the conviction that for the inner realm there is no seems/is distinction.

on whether one can make mistakes in one's self-ascriptive judgements. There is no reason to claim that these must be incorrigible or even infallible. Nor need one rule out the possibility that a subject may be entirely deluded about his or her own mind, just as one can be deluded about the world. Part of the point of Smith's examples discussed earlier is to highlight exactly how one can be so afflicted: through hallucinogenic medication, schizophrenic delusion, or simply hypnotic suggestion. Rather than rule these cases out, though, the insistence that there is no seems/is distinction highlights the epistemological irrelevance of these cases. A subject who is deluded into supposing that he now experiences angels talking to him need not be rationally responding to how things sensorily seem to him. That is, it need not be the case that the subject has a sensory experience as of angels, and is rationally responding to that.[38] Rather it may be that, regardless of the actual way in which the subject experiences the world, he responds in the non-rational way of judging there to be angels there. Likewise, we do not have to suppose that someone deluded about the state of her own mind, for example as to whether she is having a particular kind of experience, is misled by how her mind appears to her to be. Rather, the subject is deluded in the way that she forms her judgements in the first place, and these are not properly constrained by any grounds. When we deny that one can make sense of the seems/is distinction in this realm, all that need be denied is that we can make sense of a subject's situation being this way: describing how things seem or are from the subject's point of view characterizes her phenomenal consciousness one way; attending to how things really are, requires that we describe it another way.

There is widespread (although not universal) support for the idea that there can be no interesting distinction here between how one's phenomenal consciousness seems to one to be and how it is.[39] But agreement about why this should be so is not so widespread. I want to contrast two explanations. One holds on to an aspect of the idea that introspection is a particular kind of source, or mechanism, for knowing about an aspect of the world, just as the senses are. It may not have any visible organ, and it may not involve a particular kind of mental state which we would call introspective experience, but still it is a means by which we can come to track an aspect of reality and know things about it. That is to say, with the senses we suppose not only that there are physical

[38] Of course, it is an open question whether any psychotic or pathological delusions do involve a form of sensory illusion or hallucination. That they do so, is one active hypothesis in response to certain pathologies of belief; cf. Davies and Coltheart (2000).

[39] However, it should also be noted that the denial of a seems/is distinction is in tension with the claim that, given introspective support for Naive Realism, the only consistent sense-datum or intentional theory of perception will have to adopt an error theory of phenomenal consciousness; for that seems to require that how our sense experience seems to us to be, namely, naive realist, does not match how it really is. That this is indeed the best way to read the history of the debate about the problem of perception, I argue in my (2001). I'll mention on pp. 397 and 405 how the disjunctivist can reconcile this tension. For other theorists, I suggest it indicates not the lack of introspective support for Naive Realism, but the failure of theorists to face up to the cost of endorsing a theory of perception in conflict with appearances.

processes which underpin their operation, but that we can conceive of a privileged set of such processes whose correct operation is required for a given sense to be operating properly. Introspection will be, or rest on, a particular mechanism, if the processes which subserve it allow for the same distinction between the conditions for proper operation and their absence. The other approach takes the collapse of the seems/is distinction to indicate that there can be no such mechanism of introspection. I shall argue that the disjunctivist is implicitly committed to this latter model.

One might suggest that what is intended by those who claim that our introspective knowledge of phenomenal consciousness is direct or immediate is to rule out the possibility of certain kinds of error; perhaps on the assumption that such errors would arise only if some intermediary of some form played a role. Recall the point we stressed in relation to commitment (II): the impossibility of one's experience merely seeming a certain way without being so is not established solely by supposing that phenomenal states have the distinctive property of being self-intimating, by which I mean: being such that a subject who is in such a state is thereby in a position to know that she is in it.[40] The self-intimating nature of phenomenal states would rule out the possibility of its seeming to one as if one was presented with a pink square, when really one's experience presented solely a red triangle; for, in having an experience as of a red triangle and nothing else, one would thereby be in a position to know that one's experience was that way. But being in a position to know one's experience is that way rules out not knowing that one's experience is not a way incompatible with being that way. Hence it cannot seem to the subject as if the experience is in fact one of a pink square. The parallel reasoning will not carry over to any case in which the subject is failing to experience the world as being any particular way at all. In such circumstances, there would be no way experientially the subject would be which could intimate to the subject that he or she was that way. Rather, we simply have the absence of any experiential state. So, if it is not going to be possible for the subject to be in the error-inducing situation of its seeming as if he or she is experientially a certain way when not, then the explanation must trace to the means by which this seeming can be brought about. Hence it must trace to the means one uses in forming introspective judgements.

Given this, the claim of directness of introspective judgement adds an explanation here only if it is interpreted in one of two ways. First, it may be supposed that the means for coming to a judgement on experience is such that it is never possible for it to go wrong. If one employs it to determine whether one is having one kind of experience or another, or not having sense experience at all, then this means will have to give the right answer. Alternatively, one may claim that, even if the introspective mechanism itself can go wrong, and so potentially

[40] Williams (1978, appendix); and Alston (1989), for another attempt to tease out the competing theses about the special epistemological access we have to our own minds.

deliver the wrong answer, still the operation of this mechanism is something epistemically transparent to one: one can know when one attempts to use it whether one is succeeding in using it correctly. So, in that circumstance, there couldn't be a situation in which a subject was not in a position to know that he or she couldn't know whether things were a certain way introspectively. This alternative allows introspective mechanisms to be ordinary mechanisms within the world, prone as anything to breakdown and to improper use. But it hypothesizes for the rational agent one level up a means whose operation is, at least in principle, perfect: one just couldn't fail with due attention to determine whether one was doing things right.[41]

Now, many writers have been suspicious of the positing of any such perfect means of coming to know about the inner realm. So it has been common to suppose instead that the denial of the seems/is contrast here indicates instead that introspective access cannot be by some distinctive means or mode of coming to know one's mind. Again to stress: this thought cannot be captured simply by the claim that our access to our phenomenal states is direct or immediate: that might help explain in the good cases, when we are confronted with phenomenal reality why we are bound to get it right; but it doesn't by itself help explain why there are no bad cases, why there shouldn't be situations in which we are not properly hooked up to phenomenal consciousness as we normally suppose, but we are unable to detect why not. The requirement of super-mechanisms comes only at this stage. Rather, the alternative strategy must question how we are to understand the favourable case in which there is no question but that the subject is in a position to have introspective knowledge.

Consider again the parallel with sense perception. Suppose that the subject is in a position to make judgements because of the correct operation of some mechanism, and that the mechanism in question is an ordinary part of the world whose workings can be investigated as any other. Then there is a conceivable situation in which such investigation reveals the mechanism not to be operating correctly, but in which a subject is still liable to make judgements about his or her own state of mind. If the subject's judgement has the status of knowledge in virtue of the correct operation of the mechanism, then in such circumstances the subject would merely be making an introspective judgement and would not possess knowledge. If the subject is a rational being in this situation, then the less-than-knowledgeable judgement would conform merely to phenomenal consciousness's seeming some way to one, and not to how it really is. Since, by hypothesis, this is ruled out, there are only two possibilities: the one we have

---

[41] Strictly speaking, this is not the only alternative hypothesis. For, of course, one could hypothesize that this mechanism too is potentially faulty, but that a third mechanism is perfect and so indicates to one when the second mechanism fails. One would thereby never be in a position not to know that introspection does not reveal things the way that they are. This account, too, posits a perfect mechanism. There is an infinity of such accounts, each of which posits as its limiting mechanism a perfect one.

already canvassed, that the mechanism is such that it cannot fail or can only fail when it is knowable that it has; and the other that there is no such mechanism in the first place. In denying that there is a mechanism of introspection, one need not deny that there are certain physical conditions under which someone makes an introspective judgement. One need not deny that there are sufficient conditions for introspective knowledge. In the case of the senses, we add to this a contrast between circumstances in which the sense operates correctly and situations in which it does not. What is ruled out here is the possibility of specifying a mechanism, such that there could be a way that it goes wrong. In contrast to the sense modalities there is no particular means, or set of means, which are the introspective ones by which one derives knowledge of the inner realm. However things seem from the subject's perspective with respect to her phenomenal consciousness is how phenomenal consciousness must be, regardless of whether that seeming issues from a specific set of mechanisms that we had otherwise picked out as the introspection supporting ones.

There is a parallel here with the original moral we drew concerning commitment (II). Recall that when we fix on a circumstance as one of possibly having a visual hallucination of a white picket fence, we are concerned with things being not knowably distinct from seeing a white picket fence from the subject's point of view. Given a modest conception of sense experience, this condition does not require that one's normal means of gaining visual knowledge has actually been employed, or that it has resulted in a mental state with exactly the same characteristics as normally occur when one sees a white picket fence. All that is required is that, from the subject's perspective, things shouldn't appear any different from a situation in which one has used one's powers of sight appropriately and thereby come into visual contact with the world. Any of the various means for bringing about visual experience will, from this conception, give one sufficient conditions for having visual experience, and not any necessary condition independent of commitment (II).

In relation to phenomenal consciousness itself and introspection, the lesson is that we take 'from the subject's point of view' as, so to speak, a fixed point. If it seems to the subject as if it seems to the subject that there is a white picket fence before her, then it seems to the subject as if there is a white picket fence before her. So there can be no privileged mechanism which is required for her to be able to get right the judgement about how things seem to her. The subject's perspective on her own sense experience constitutes sense experience being that way for her.[42]

---

[42] Various authors have discussed theories of self-knowledge positing constitutive relations between the self-ascription of thoughts and the thoughts so self-ascribed. See, for example, Heal (1994); Wright (1989). A common concern with such theories is that they deprive the higher-order ascription from having a rational ground in the subject matter it concerns; cf. Peacocke (1998). The same concerns are not in play here. The constitutive connection is between the subject's perspective on his or her own mind, how it seems to be, and how his or her mind then is. This need not be

Hence, the disjunctivist has every reason to reject the idea that introspection is like perception. Introspective judgement cannot result from the correct operation of a specific mechanism of introspection without the possibility of one's phenomenal consciousness merely seeming some way to one. Since that is not possible, specifying how things seem to the subject does not introduce a perspective the subject occupies independent of the subject matter she thereby takes an interest in. Now, this conclusion bears directly both on the case of common appearances and on our understanding of how dogs can be credited sense experience in the light of the disjunctivist's commitments.

8

In the case of the lemon and the soap, we move from visual indiscriminability to a shared look via the further observation that the fact that the two objects cannot be told apart is an objective feature of them which one's use of sight tracks. But, as we have just seen, unless one wishes to posit a perfect mechanism of introspection (or tracking the use of mechanisms), we cannot suppose that one's take on how things are experientially is independent of what it is a take on, rather these two must coincide. The impersonality of one's incapacity to distinguish the two situations of veridical perception and hallucination is not matched by an objectivity tracked through introspection; for, when we say that things seem a certain way to the subject, now with respect to her own state of mind, we are not hypothesizing that she is in the best possible circumstances to tell how things seem to her, and yet still cannot find a difference between this situation and the one of veridically perceiving. The hypothesized situation is simpler than that: if she really is in a situation in which from her perspective it is as if she is having an experience as of a white picket fence, then that constitutes her being in the situation of having an experience as of a white picket fence.

And, in turn, this shows us that the impersonal ascription of introspective indiscriminability cannot be used to talk about the limitations of a given faculty or mechanism of introspection, as the parallel claims about indiscriminability through sight can be. There is no relevant mechanism of introspection to be talked about unless there can be super-mechanisms, incapable of going wrong. One cannot show the irrelevance of these claims to the case of the dog, therefore, by pointing out that the dog lacks the relevant mode of introspective access, for, if our reasoning is correct, the difference between us and the dog cannot be put down to the presence of any distinctive mechanism of introspection anyway.

What, then, do we do when we ascribe sense experience to the dog? In ascribing consciousness to a creature, we are thereby ascribing to it a point of

identified with the judgements he or she actually makes. As we have already noted, an agent may be inattentive or even deluded in their judgements even about the inner realm, so the connection drawn is consistent with supposing that self-ascriptive judgements of experience are both cognitive achievements and grounded in how things seem and are.

view or perspective on the world. This is a feature which the naive realist about perception in particular will want to stress, although its claim on us is recognized far more widely. From a subject's perspective experience is a matter (at least in part) of various objects being apparent to it; of some part of the actual world making an appearance to one. The naive realist, at least in the case of veridical perception, wishes us to understand this way of talking literally: veridical perceptual experience is constituted through one standing in a relation of awareness to the objects of perception. The same won't carry over to hallucination, though. So in general there is a question of how experience being a point of view on the world, and the non-necessity of the actual world being present to the subject, are to fit together.

The disjunctivist is moved to claim that the kind of apprehension that one has of the object of sense in the case of veridical perception is entirely absent when one has a causally matching hallucination. It is not that one fails to apprehend some aspect of the physical world and yet still latches on to something else, some inner object or sense-datum. Rather, in such cases, the subject has experience yet fails to apprehend anything at all. So, if having conscious experience involves having a point of view on the world, then having such a point of view cannot require the actual apprehension of anything. This suggests that when we grasp the idea of there being a situation which from the subject's point of view is just as if one is veridically perceiving but in which one is not, no commitment at all need be made in granting that idea to the thought that the subject *must* be aware of something, even if they are not aware of, for example, a white picket fence.

This much, I take it, even an intentionalist about perceptual experience will be inclined to accept. For the intentionalist both wants to agree that we should characterize experience when perceiving in terms of the actual objects of perception, and yet deny that any other objects fill this role when we hallucinate. So both the intentionalist and the disjunctivist will agree that in the case of hallucination it is as if the subject is being presented with objects which are not in fact there. The intentionalist wishes to add a further claim, one that the disjunctivist will deny—namely, that this fact about the situation holds by virtue of the hallucination having a certain property which the veridical perception shares, namely, having a certain representational content. The disjunctivist denies this (in committing to (III)) since the disjunctivist insists that the veridical perception is a genuinely relational state, as the naive realist claims, and not something of a kind which could equally be present in the case of hallucination. But the key point remains for both: that we cannot capture how things are from the subject's point of view without reference to what is only true in cases of veridical perception. The disjunctivist's commitment to (II) can be read, therefore, as articulating this thought: that we can only characterize how things are from the subject's perspective by reference to the veridical circumstance. In turn, the commitment to (III) indicates that in the case of hallucination we need not commit to the subject successfully picking up on anything beyond being in this circumstance of its being just as if one is in the case of veridical perception.

A consequence of the formulation of (II) and (III) is that to articulate properly what is involved in being in this situation, we must make mention of perception (a kind of mental state) and one's ability to discriminate one kind of situation in which one has a point of view on the world from other such situations (it is for the dog as if there are sausages there, not carrots). And for creatures such as ourselves, self-aware and self-conscious human beings, having such experience, with such a perspective on the world puts us in a position to articulate our plight. Any of us, suitably linguistically sophisticated, can move back from judgements about the environment surrounding us to judgements which simply concern our experiential position. As Strawson observed, experience must make room for the thought of experience itself.[43] Yet that is not to say that when we ascribe such experience to other creatures, we must thereby assume that they too are self-conscious or self-aware, even though how we conceive of their experience is such that, were a creature so to experience and be self-conscious, they would thereby be able to articulate judgements just as we in fact do.

For, as we noted above, introspection cannot be a mechanism. There is therefore nothing which has been added to phenomenal consciousness and through which we come to be aware of the character of phenomenal consciousness when we contrast our situation with that of the dog. It seeming to the subject that things seem a certain way to her can constitute things seeming that way to her. So, for a self-aware subject, phenomenal consciousness can thereby exemplify self-awareness in itself. That which in us is simply a mode of self-awareness is what we attribute to other creatures even when we do not take them to be self-aware. So the conditions in (II) and (III) attribute experience to the dog through attributing a specific take on the world, without thereby presupposing that the dog is self-aware.

In sum, although there is a temptation to suppose that when we look to what must be true of different creatures when they all enjoy a sense experience of a kind of scene, and not just a veridical perception of some particular instance, that there must positively be some phenomenal characteristics as such which they all share, the disjunctivist denies this and can do so quite consistently. For the disjunctivist what they must all have in common is just that their situations are impersonally indiscriminable through reflection from a veridical perception. What it takes for a creature so to satisfy this condition may well involve levels of similarity other than at that of experiential sameness—the same neurological organization and functioning may be nomologically required in order that creatures genuinely be indiscriminable from each other from the perspective of within. This may thereby make true broadly similar functional truths by which certain approaches to the mind have sought to define mental kinds. Where the

---

[43] Strawson (1966, p.101).

disjunctivist sticks is with supposing that these commonalities must sub-serve or define an experiential commonality where that requires more than the sharing of the negative epistemological condition.[44]

9

We have now rehearsed the various grounds for the disjunctivist to resist the characterization of his or her position that Smith sketches. The picture of causally matching hallucination as a case of unknown absent qualia is forced on the disjunctivist where we have to accept that one's introspective focus on experience is from a perspective on one's phenomenal experience, where the status of the latter is fixed independent of one's appreciation of that fact. If we think of awareness of experience in this way, conditions (II) and (III) are naturally read only as conditions on that awareness, not conditions on experience itself.

In contrast, in discussion of the contrast between introspection and observation, and the application of this to the case of the dog, we can see that conditions (II) and (III) are rather intended by the disjunctivist as the means of characterizing what a subject's perspective, either on the world, or on her own experiential situation, can amount to. Or, more exactly, the disjunctivist offers this characterization within the context of making no further assumptions about the necessary existence of objects made apparent to that subjective perspective.

The dog, the soap and the lemon together indicate why Smith's picture does not capture the situation as conceived by the disjunctivist. First, when we say of a victim of causally matching hallucination that his or her situation is one of not being knowably distinct from veridical perception of, say, a white picket fence, we need not there be talking of the specific intellectual capacities or incapacities possessed by that very individual; we need not be saying that this person is quite capable or rather incapable of exercising capacities for coming to know things about the world. Rather, our focus is on the impersonal fact that the subjective perspective, that of introspective reflection, cannot discern the difference between a situation of causally matching hallucination and that of veridical

---

[44] Likewise, the proposal here should not be read as claiming that to ascribe experience to the dog is to say that were it self-aware it would not be able to tell its situation from one in which it perceived a bunch of carrots; or to say that were an ideally reflective agent to be in the dog's situation then it would not be able to know it is not perceiving a bunch of carrots. Both of these claims may be true (though it is easy to see also how they may be falsified—perhaps dogs would be insensitive to carrots if self-aware; perhaps ideally reflective agents have very different experience from dogs). But neither can be what we mean to talk of when we ascribe experience to dogs, at best they would trade on that understanding. The counterfactuals in question might be intended as part of a reductive account of what it is to have experience, but, then, apart from the worries to which we have already gestured, the disjunctivist would also be liable to resist the account since the applicability of the counter-factual condition would be liable to seek for a common grounding in dogs across cases of perception and hallucination specified in terms other than drawn from (II), and hence would be inconsistent with (III).

perception. This fact is what is common between the dog, which lacks any powers of self-conscious judgement, and us, inasmuch as there is anything experientially in common between merely sentient creatures and self-aware agents such as mature human beings.

Second, this subjective perspective on the situation does not pick out an independent vantage point from which two possible objects of comparison are to be told apart, or treated as in some respect the same. It is common to deny that one's phenomenal consciousness could merely seem some way to one without being so—that, after all, is part of the grounds of incredulity in Smith's objection to the disjunctivist proposal. In accepting this, the disjunctivist points out that the perspective we have on our own phenomenal consciousness cannot, then, be grounded in some specific mode or source of knowing about something independent of that perspective. If it is true of someone that it seems to them as if things seem a certain way, as if they are having a certain sense experience, then they are thereby having that experience. Our reflective standpoint on our own experience cannot stand outside of it.

So, given this, the disjunctivist can point out that in characterizing the subject's circumstance in a case of causally matching hallucination as one of not knowably not being a case of veridical perception of a white picket fence, one has thereby characterized how things seem to the subject, and so characterized the course of his or her experience. If the subject is conscious, then there is something that it is like for him or her to be so. That there is something that it is like for the subject is given by the fact that we are characterizing how things seem to them, namely, that they seem in just the way they would seem to him or her were he or she veridically perceiving a white picket fence. What more could be required in order to specify a way that one can be experientially?[45]

At the same time, in spelling out how the disjunctivist seeks to rebut Smith's complaint, we are better placed to see what the deeper disagreement is between the two views. To resist Smith's characterization of the case of causally matching hallucination is not to deny that there is a significant disagreement here, and one which connects with many people's intuitions about the case of phenomenal consciousness and our knowledge of it. Rather, it is to suggest that the disagreement relates not to any denial or affirmation of the presence of phenomenal consciousness in the case of some hallucinations, but more the kind of self-awareness or introspective knowledge that one can have of phenomenal consciousness. The disjunctivist can take (III) to characterize sufficiently the subjective character of a subject's state of mind because they suppose we have no reason to claim that the only possible way in which one can come to have sense experience is through actually apprehending some object.

---

[45] In this way, too, we can see how the disjunctivist can consistently agree that there is no seems/ is distinction for sense experience, and yet that there is something essentially deceptive about the case of perfect hallucination. The essentially deceptive element relates to the subject's seemingly being in a position of awareness without in fact being aware of anything.

Return to Smith's complaint. As initially stated, it seems to affirm the kind of position familiar from early sense-datum theorists: how can things be this way if there is no object of awareness for me to sense? One can happily endorse Smith's objection here, only if one does think that what is distinctive of sense experience in any circumstance of occurrence is the presence of some actual object of sensing: that one can only be sensuously a certain way, where a genuine object of sensuous attention is provided for one's focus. That, of course, is not Smith's intention. Although he does think that there are actualized aspects of sense experience, the sensuous object of attention is not one of them.[46] So the complaint of absence here cannot literally be taken to be that of complaining that hallucination can involve the absence of an object of awareness. All theorists apart from sense-datum theorists accept that fact: they accept that there is something about the situation in the case of veridical perception which somehow is not reflected in the case of hallucination, even if otherwise we are to say that the two are experientially the same.

So, if the complaint against the disjunctivist is one of a supposed absence in the case of hallucination, one which a Common Kind Theorist can avoid, then the absence must be, so to speak, one level up, an absence purely at the level of how things are experientially with the subject, and not with the objects of such experience. Here, I suggest, is where we do find a deep disagreement which it is difficult to articulate arguments for or against.

What pushes the initial worry we started out with, I suggest, is the conviction that there must be more to causally matching hallucination. In reading this, you are not currently hallucinating. The disjunctivist agrees that there is more to your experience than just the negative epistemological property of being indiscriminable from this veridical perception; there is the positive character of the veridical perception itself. But now, one wants to say, just as I can tell that there is more in this case, so too I would be equally placed in the case of causally matching hallucination, so there must be something I am picking up on, the phenomenal character which has been left out by the disjunctivist. To adopt this position, I've suggested, is to suppose that we can fix the facts of phenomenal consciousness independently of the higher-order perspective on it, inasmuch as we think of the latter as correctly reporting or reflecting these additional facts.

And, once we acknowledge this, then we must think of the phenomenal facts that we pick up on in this way as being independent of the experience being a veridical perception, for the properties in question will have to be common to the causally matching hallucination and the veridical perception it is indiscriminable from. So it could not be that one's experience being this way in itself (as opposed to being this way in certain circumstances) constituted the kind of contact with one's environment which would explain one's ability to think about things around one and come to know how they are. Moreover, if the naive realist

----

[46] Smith (2002, ch. 9).

is right that we do conceive of our sensory experience in cases of perception as providing such a contact with the world, and we are inclined to understand our ability to think about and know of these things in terms of such experience, then recognizing our experience as only a common element to perception and hallucination comes at the cost of losing that understanding.

At best, if the disjunctivist has established that Naive Realism best characterizes how our sensory experience seems to initial reflective intuition, the position we end up in here is one of clashing intuitions. For, on the one hand, there is the thought that experience's being so, as it is now when I veridically perceive, is a matter of my standing in an appropriate relation to the world around me. On the other hand, there is the intuition that in this circumstance I am able reflectively to pick up on how my experience is and the subject of a causally matching hallucination would equally be so placed—so the phenomenal character of both experiences must be shared, and hence cannot be relational in this way.

I say that this second claim is something we find intuitive, and, apart from indicating that we find this plausible, I think it adds two further elements. The first is that, even if there is something more for us to say as to the truth of the relevant condition, we do not immediately appeal to those further considerations in order to support the claim. The appeal of the thought is more fundamental than that—one can't really conceive either of what experience, or more exactly the kind of perspective we have on experience, could be, if it is not a matter of responding to what is there. The second element is this: if this is the right place to identify the basic disagreement with disjunctivism, one which does not turn on either slips of formulation in disjunctivism, or misconception of its consequences, then, inasmuch as the objection just seems intuitive, the appropriate strategy for the disjunctivist at this stage is not so much to offer any particular argument against it (for after all it is a claim which we accept independently of the further elaborations we try to give of why we are so committed) as to explain why the principle seems so attractive to us, given that it is false. At this point what the disjunctivist needs to do is to engage in philosophical pathology.

In the closing section, I want to begin the sketch of how that might go. For, I want to suggest, one way forward is to see a connection here between the intuitions here and external world scepticism, although not quite of the form that people commonly indicate in these debates.

PART THREE

10

I've suggested that the root disagreement here relates to the epistemology of sense experience and introspective awareness of it, and that this may be connected to a response to a sceptical challenge about the external world. Now, in the introductory section, I suggested that disjunctivism is properly seen as connected to a Humean challenge of scepticism with regard to the senses, rather than the more commonly discussed Cartesian challenge raised about our empirical knowledge as a whole. I do not intend to take that contrast back here, but rather to suggest that a certain kind of natural response to the Cartesian challenge may lead us to reject disjunctivism and so have to face the Humean problem head on.

First, I want to spell out a bit more the gap between the Humean problem and the Cartesian one, before spelling out the link which may explain the counter-intuitive element in the disjunctivist's picture of experience. It is quite common when discussing empirical knowledge as a whole and its reliance on the senses, or in discussing the Cartesian sceptical challenge, to talk of sense experience as introducing a veil or barrier between one and the world. For example, towards the end of the first chapter of *The Significance of Philosophical Scepticism*, Barry Stroud reflects on the situation one finds oneself in when taking seriously the sceptical challenge to be found in Descartes's First Meditation:

What *can* we know in such a predicament? We can perhaps know what sensory experiences we are having, or how things seem to us to be . . . We are in a sense imprisoned within those representations, at least with respect to our knowledge . . . This can seem to leave us in the position of finding a barrier between ourselves and the world around us. There would then be a veil of sensory experiences or sensory objects which we could not penetrate but which would be no reliable guide to the world beyond the veil. (Stroud 1984: pp. 32–3)

Stroud suggests that when one is faced with the sceptical challenge, and has as yet no satisfactory answer to it, one cannot know, or at least take oneself to know, anything about the ordinary world around one, although one can know certain things about one's own mind. In turn, he suggests that in being in this predicament, one finds sense experience to be a kind of barrier or veil between one and the world. So a sceptical doubt which starts from a hypothesis about whether one knows oneself to be dreaming or not seems to deliver a negative verdict about the nature of sense experience itself.

Although Stroud's prose offers a smooth transition between the two thoughts, the move from external world scepticism to concerns with a barrier between the subject and the experienced world is not as obvious or straightforward as it might first appear. Suppose it is true that we have no answer to the sceptical challenge, and suppose it is also true that in those circumstances we still possess certain self-knowledge of our own states of mind, and of the character of our sense experiences in particular. Why should it follow from this alone that sense experience would act as a kind of barrier between us and the world?

Consider the following analogy: you have recently moved into an old Boston house and in the attic discovered seemingly a journal from the wars of independence. This is an intimate record, and from its close and somewhat obsessive detail, it now seems to you that you know things about the day-to-day life in late eighteenth century Massachusetts that you could not otherwise have happened on: the journal seems to give you a contact with that world. But now add that a malicious neighbour falsely, but seemingly authoritatively, informs you that the previous owner of your apartment was a fantasist and forger, given to constructing such fancies as the journal. The document you possess is not, he claims, a record of that past turbulent time, but is rather a cunning and recent fiction imagining how things must have been. Under the sway of his disturbing story, you may now feel cut off from the contact you seemingly had with the eighteenth century. It need not be that you are convinced by his story: you have some sense that he likes to deflate people in their pleasures. But, with the doubt about the provenance of the journal having been put forward so forcefully, you now need some further evidence to indicate that this is not a matter simply of fiction. And in this situation you cannot enjoy the journal as once you did. Even if the journal is genuine, you are no longer in a position, without some further evidence, to exploit the privilege it affords you of looking back into the past. You have lost the contact with that time that you found so pleasurable.

So far, the parallel with Stroud's concern with external world scepticism seems close enough, albeit on a smaller terrain. Initially, one seems to have a body of knowledge acquired through a particular source or group of sources. A sceptical doubt questions the probity of that source. One is not deprived of the knowledge of what the source claims is the case about the subject matter in question, but one is no longer in a position to trust the source, unless one can lay the sceptical doubts to rest. But in this case, I suggest, one would balk at the further move that Stroud makes in relation to the senses. There is no inclination to say that one should now see the journal as somehow a veil or barrier between one and those past events whose record one once enjoyed. For it seems, given that the journal is genuine, this indeed does provide a route back to the past, but just one which isn't now in a position to exploit. Just because one's neighbour sows the seed of doubt about the veracity of the journal, there is no reason to think that the journal thereby becomes misleading or fabrication in itself. So, likewise, we might ask of Stroud's discussion, why should the fact that in taking seriously the sceptical doubts mean that my senses now must act as a barrier between me and the world which otherwise they give me contact with, rather than simply being the facilitators of that contact, but in a way which I could not now exploit?[47]

---

[47] Tamar Szabó Gendler suggested that the story does not induce the same intuitions because it involves temporal separation from its subject matter, while the intuitions about perception concern our spatial relation to the objects in question. However, it seems to me that a variant story which preserves the spatial elements does not necessarily lead to Stroud's intuitions. While one would have the sense that a barrier is present if one accepts as true the falsification hypothesis (equivalent of the forger), there is no reason to think one's lack of knowledge of its falsity is enough to make one think of the source as a barrier. The main moral of the tale would still remain even if this worry did have some grounds: for it would not be the bare structure of the epistemological situation which led to

In contrast to this discussion, when we look to Hume, we find a more readily intelligible account of why sense experience might be thought of as a barrier between us and the world. Hume insists in section XII of the *First Enquiry* that there are different forms of sceptical challenge, some such as Descartes's, antecedent to study, science and enquiry and others consequent on it. He associates with the latter form both ancient arguments which trade on conflicting appearances and his own sceptical arguments about the senses which he claims offer a more profound challenge than other sceptical modes. The argument Hume in fact offers may not entirely convince. He hypothesizes that the vulgar suppose themselves to sense objects independent of them, but that the slightest philosophy will show this opinion to be false, and that they perceive only their own impressions or images. Hume uses the attribution of such a gross mistake in our conception of perception to undermine any argument now introduced to show that we can nonetheless reliably acquire knowledge through perception of the existence of an external world.

Whatever one thinks of the merits of Hume's argument here, he seems correct in supposing that the method of argument is very different from that employed by Descartes in the First Meditation. From elsewhere in his writings, it is clear that Descartes thinks we have only mediated perception of the objects of sense, but that assumption plays no essential role in presenting the dreaming argument or the *malin génie*. All that Descartes requires is that we can conceive of a situation in which from one's own perspective it is as if one is situated as one is now, but in which one dreams, hallucinates or is subject to some external deceptive influence. The hypothesis requires that we have a conception of the difference between normal perception and mere dreaming or hallucinating. But it does not require that we have any particular views about what normal perception must involve, beyond the thought that it would be a source of knowledge, and hence requires us to hazard no view over whether a given sense experience should fail to count as a perception of the external world, if it has not already been hypothesized to be an illusion or hallucination.[48]

---

the result. Some further assumptions have been buried in the move from sceptical quandary to imprisonment behind a veil.

[48] Although I am not sure that all parties to the debate would agree. Stroud himself, for example, writes:

[The philosopher] chooses a situation in which any one of us would unproblematically say or think, for example, that we know that there is a fire in the fireplace right before us, and that we know it is there because we see that it is there. But when we ask what this seeing really amounts to, various considerations are introduced to lead us to concede that we would see exactly what we see now even if no fire was there at all, or if we didn't know that there was one there. (Stroud 2000: p. 131)

Likewise, Wright's reconstruction of the Cartesian reasoning appeals in passing to the assumption that perception and dreaming involve the same 'manifest content' brought about through different dominant causal routes; see Wright (1991, p. 91). However, in neither case can I see that the sceptical argument requires these additional claims about the nature of sense perception.

So we seem to have at least two styles of argument here, both related to our knowledge of the external world. The one argument focuses solely on the conceivability of a situation in which one is entirely deceived in one's external world judgements, but need not take a view about the nature of sense perception itself. The other argument, in contrast, works by ascribing to us a particular conception of sense perception and then arguing that this is mistaken. Talk of the senses being a barrier or a veil between us and the world seems much more appropriate in relation to this mode of sceptical challenge. For here the implicit contrast is between how we used to believe the senses to be, giving us some kind of privileged cognitive contact with the world, and how we now believe them to be in the light of Hume's argument, or some other in its place. The mistake that Hume imputes to the vulgar has sceptical potential because it claims to falsify our beliefs about how we come to know what we take ourselves to know. While there may be no requirement that when one knows something one must also know how one comes to know it, for some cases we do have knowledge, or at least beliefs about how we have come to know something. I know that Warsaw is the capital of Poland. I am not sure how I came to know this, presumably I learnt it at school, or maybe just before, and either way through reading some authoritative text. But the specific route to that fact is not one I can retrace. When I stare at the white picket fence, though, I not only know that there is a white picket fence there, I seem to be in a position to tell how I can know that fact: it is made manifest to me in what I can see. Suppose, now, though, that I have been convinced by Hume that I am not in the kind of situation that I took myself to be in. It is not the white picket fence with which I am presented, but merely some simulacrum of the fence, an impression or image. In this case, the fact that I was mistaken about how I thought I was in a position to know that that was a white picket fence seems to undermine my confidence in knowing this fact. So my epistemic standing will now be worse than what I took it to be before I faced Hume's challenge. I may complain that given the way that Hume claims sense experience to be it lacks the virtues that I conceived sense experience to have, for it does not give me the kind of cognitive contact with the environment that I thought I had (even if it does, in fact, give me an alternative such form of contact). It is this contrast between how I conceived the cognitive advantages of my perceptual situation with how I supposedly learn them to be which warrants describing my newly discovered situation as one involving a barrier.

The simple Cartesian story does not provide the materials to warrant talk of a barrier or veil here, for the simple story in itself makes no claim about the nature of experience. The rather different Humean challenge focuses on perception and contrasts how we believe it to be with how philosophy can supposedly demonstrate it to be. This challenge does make intelligible why one could come to think of sense experience as screening off the world from our cognitive contact with it. The two challenges take different forms and draw on rather different resources. There is no obvious move from one to the other.

It should already be obvious that the arguments discussed in Part One belong in a version of the Humean sceptical challenge. The disjunctivist is motivated by the need to block the argument from hallucination offered as an attack on Naive Realism. The disjunctivist takes Naive Realism to be the best philosophical articulation of what we all pre-theoretically accept concerning the nature of our sense experience: that in veridical perception we are aware of mind-independent objects, and that the kind of experience we have of them is relational, with the objects of sense being constituents of the experiential episode. If the argument from hallucination succeeds, then no aspect of our experience can be naive realist. So, we could not be perceptually related to the physical world in the way that we pre-theoretically take ourselves to be. If our pre-theoretical conception plays any role in our understanding of what we know about the environment around us, or that of how we are able to single out and think about the objects we do, then this falsification will threaten the kinds of sceptical consequence that Hume highlights. So we can see the naive realist as a variation on Hume's vulgar, and the argument from hallucination a development of Hume's slightest philosophy. The disjunctivist seeks to block the challenge by rejecting the Common Kind Assumption.

But whether the disjunctivist can plausibly do this, we saw in Part Two, turns on one's attitude towards the awareness we have of our own sensory states. One might think that in introspective reflection we adopt a perspective outside of phenomenal experience itself, a perspective through which we track or apprehend independently holding facts about how things are with us phenomenally. Conceiving of our awareness in this way, leads to viewing the disjunctivist as claiming that causally matching hallucinations are cases in which a subject lacks any sensory experience but is deprived of the capacity to detect that lack. In rejecting this accusation, the disjunctivist affirms a different picture of how self-awareness and phenomenal consciousness interrelate. Our introspective access to our phenomenal experience contrasts with perceptual access to the world around us. In perception, we have a viewpoint on what we perceive independently of the world we perceive: and hence that we come to know that the world is as it seems reflects a substantive cognitive achievement on our part. Within the mind, on the other hand, there is no such gap to be closed by the subject's cognitive success. A subject's perspective on his or her own experience is not distinct from their perspective on the world. So the disjunctivist does not characterize our lack of awareness of the absence of experience, but rather the way in which experience itself can simply be the lack of awareness. When we consider a case of perfect hallucination, we conceive of a subject occupying a point of view on the world within which they do not succeed at all in latching on to or becoming aware of any aspect, but are rather deceived in a particular way, as if they perceived, for example, a white picket fence.

But should we simply think of our self-conscious knowledge of experience in such a situation as giving us no substantive knowledge of anything independent of our context of enquiry? I've suggested that the fundamental disagreement with the disjunctivist lies in this question. Those who find disjunctivism incredible suppose it obvious that we just recognize introspectively something which must be present in order to have experience, and so must be present for the hallucinating subject to recognize. It is this commitment that I want to suggest is connected with the Cartesian challenge, and which we might see as at work in the background of Stroud's talk of a veil of sensory experience.

How does this line of thought develop? The first thing to note is that the disjunctivist, in embracing a naive realist conception of veridical perceptual experience, claims that such mental states have as constituents the objects of perception. Second, as these are aspects of the veridical perceptual situation, the subject can attend to and form judgements about these as aspects of the experiential situation. So the subject does have knowledge of something independent of just occupying the perspective of seeming to be presented with a white picket fence, say. Moreover, that there is this aspect to veridical perception means that in the case of perfect hallucination it will seem to one as if one occupies the same sort of situation with respect to the world. That is to say, in having an hallucination one is not only deceived with respect to the environment, that it seems as if certain kinds of objects are present in one's environment, but also with respect to one's experience, that seemingly one is in a position of experiencing these objects. In both situations, therefore, it will seem to one as if there is an aspect of the experience to which one can attend and about which one can acquire knowledge independently of the perspective one takes on it. That this should merely be a matter of how things seem and not how they are in the case of hallucination is not evident within the perspective one takes on one's situation.

Turn now to the context of the Cartesian challenge. Before considering the challenge, one can see various items in the world around one, perhaps the fireplace, and the pages on which the challenge turns out to be written. One cannot only see these things, but one knows through seeing them how one knows various things about them. Faced with the sceptical challenge, and, as yet without any ready answer to it, the situation that Stroud describes in the passage cited above, one may feel deprived of knowledge both of the elements in the world around one, and also the knowledge of how one's experience can be giving one knowledge of these things. For, after all, if the knowledge one has of how one's experience provides knowledge of the world exploits one's recognition that the objects of perception are part of the experiential episode, then one cannot so recognize one's experience when gripped by the sceptical puzzle. The best that one can know of one's experience is just that it is not knowably distinct from the case of perceiving given one's perspective on matters.

While one cannot reasonably exploit one's knowledge of the objects of perception while in the grip of the Cartesian doubt, though, one need not thereby be deprived of the sense experience one has, or the ability to attend to its various elements, and hence attend to the objects of perception. It is just that, strictly speaking, one cannot take oneself to be succeeding in attending to any object or coming to know anything about it. For all that one can know from this perspective, it might merely be the case that it seems to one as if one is attending without doing so.

Yet, if one surmises that even in the face of the sceptical challenge, one does have access to the knowledge that one is attending to something, and that through so attending one can learn things about it, then one can exploit one's experiential situation to know things, at least with respect to one's experience. Note that this is not merely to surmise that one is in a position to know that it seems to one as if certain objects are present. For, as we have underlined in discussion of disjunctivism, that things are this way with one does not require one to be in a position to discover further facts about some subject matter independent of the perspective of enquiry. But to conceive of oneself as properly attending to some objects and thereby learning about them in having the experience is to suppose that there is such a subject matter which one can learn about even in the context of the sceptical challenge. Of course, so to take oneself to have access to the objects of experience is to suppose that one would have the same kind of access whether or not one is hallucinating. But the only things to which one could have such access, given how we specify the hallucinatory possibility, is if one's occupying this subjective perspective would still guarantee the existence of appropriate objects of attention. The objects in question would then have to be suitably mind-dependent. This, of course, is inconsistent with our starting thought, that reflection on one's sense experience supports a naive realist construal of the nature of experience. That is, independently of the sceptical challenge, we are inclined to suppose that our sense experience must be a presentation of a mind-independent world.

Indeed, the fact that our experience does manifestly present a mind-independent world, a feature of it immediately accessible to us when not in the grip of sceptical thoughts, may provide a motivation, albeit a self-defeating one, for conceiving of our introspective access to the subject matter of our sense experience as preserved, even in the scope of the sceptical challenge, would give one a ready and intuitive answer to the sceptical challenge. Before the sceptical challenge is raised, it seems as if there is a simple answer to the question, how do you know that there is a white picket fence there? After all, you can simply see that there is one there, and that you can see that one is there is something that you also have access to.[49] For such quotidian examples of perceptually grounded knowledge you have a ready, if shallow, understanding of how you come by the knowledge. You seem both to be deprived of the knowledge and your understanding of it when in the grip of the sceptical challenge. So a response to the sceptic which best reflected your ordinary understanding of your knowledge of

[49] Cf. here Austin (1962, p. 131).

the perceived world would be one which did appeal to your reflective knowledge of your perceptions—that this just is a case of having a white picket fence made manifest. That it seems to you that your experience has this character is not removed just by engaging with the sceptical challenge. So it is merely in the context of determining what such knowledge would have to be in order to give one an answer to the sceptical challenge that one is led to suppose that one's reflection on one's experience does give one substantive knowledge, but just knowledge of something less than the objects of experience one took it to present.

To tell the story in these terms is to invite the reader into thinking of the sceptical argument as attracting one to something like the sense-datum theory of sensory experience; for we are to suppose that reflective attention to one's experience will provide objects of awareness and knowledge, whether one is perceiving or hallucinating. Indeed, telling the story in just these terms seems to fit best both Stroud's various ways of telling the story, and Smith's original complaint (as we noted at the time). But it is also clear that disjunctivism is not the only alternative to a sense-datum theory of sense experience; one might well seek to deny that there must be objects of awareness when one hallucinates and yet insist that there is something experiential present in cases of hallucination not captured by the disjunctivist's commitment to (III).

At this point, I think, the disjunctivist can challenge back. In insisting that there must be something there in the case of hallucination which the subject can recognize to be present through introspection, and yet denying that it is any object of awareness, the theorist must suppose that the subject is, in effect, attending just to the fact that they are experiencing as such. That is, the intentionalist can differentiate his or her position from the sense-datum theorist only by exploiting the idea that we must have a distinct perspective on our inner lives from that we take in experiencing the world. This invites two comments. First, as we have noted in the discussion above on introspection, this picture is maintainable in conjunction with the widespread conviction that there is no seems/is distinction in relation to phenomenal consciousness only if the theorist commits to the existence of some perfect mechanism tracking the proper operation of introspection. Second, the insistence that there is, after all, some-thing for the subject to know, that he or she is in this distinctive kind of state, still has the element of attempting to rescue some substantial knowledge from the sceptical challenge that the story we attached to Stroud has. Even if the result is described in slightly different terms, the motivation may well be the same. And, even though the intentionalist avoids positing entities which could act as a veil, sense-data or images, still the view does not avoid the Humean problem if, as the disjunctivist argues, the conception of experience as merely representa-tional and not relational conflicts with our initial conception of it.

So, the proposal on behalf of disjunctivism is this: when initially faced with the Cartesian sceptical challenge, and as yet lacking any direct answer to it, we are tempted to re-construe the kind of self-aware knowledge we have of our sense experience such that it is preserved even in the scope of the Cartesian sceptical doubt. This would require us to view the character of such experience in terms very different from our initial pre-reflective stance on it. When we recognize that, we are then subject to the Humean challenge. The disjunctivist succeeds in blocking Hume's concerns only if they can intelligibly reject the Common Kind Assumption. Without a direct answer to Cartesian scepticism, though, the required limitations on our knowledge of our own sense experience will seem counter-intuitive.

The unacceptability of disjunctivism indicates, on this account, not its failure to take seriously phenomenal experience or the nature of subjectivity. Rather, disjunctivism takes as seriously as one could the idea that a subjective perspective on the world need impose no specific objective constraints. Instead, the unacceptability lies in the intractability of certain sceptical puzzles, and our tendency in the face of them to preserve the little knowledge that we could have through reflection on our experience.

REFERENCES

Alston, William. 1989. Varieties of Privileged Access, in *Epistemic Justification*. Ithaca, NY: Cornell University Press; original edition, *American Philosophical Quarterly*.

Anscombe, G. E. M. 1975. The First Person, in *Mind and Language*, edited by S. Guttenplan. Oxford: Clarendon Press.

Armstrong, David M. 1968. *A Materialist Theory of the Mind*. London: Routledge.

Austin, J. L. 1962. *Sense & Sensibilia*, edited by G. Warnock. Oxford: Clarendon Press.

Burge, Tyler. 1977. Belief *De Re, Journal of Philosophy* 74: 338–62.

Burge, Tyler. 1983. Russell's Problem & Intentional Identity, in *Agent, Language & the Structure of the World*, edited by J. Tomberlin. Indianapolis: Hackett Publishing Co.

Burge, Tyler. 1993. Vision and Intentional Content, in *John Searle and his Critics*, edited by R. v. Gulick and E. LePore. Oxford: Blackwell.

Burge, Tyler. 1996. Our Entitlement to Self-Knowledge, *Proceedings of the Aristotelian Society* XCVI: 108–110.

Chalmers, David J. 1996. *The Conscious Mind*. Oxford: Oxford University Press.

Chisholm, Roderick. 1969. On the Observability of the Self, *Philosophy and Phenomenological Research* 30: 7–21.

Davidson, Donald. 1969. The Individuation of Events, in *Essays on Actions and Events*. Oxford: Clarendon Press.

Davies, Martin and Max Coltheart. 2000. Introduction: Pathologies of Belief, *Mind and Language* 15 (1): 1–46.

Dennett, Daniel C. 1991. *Consciousness Explained*. New York: Little, Brown.

Evans, Gareth. 1982. *The Varieties of Reference*, edited by J. McDowell. Oxford: Clarendon Press.

Fine, Kit. 1994a. Essence and Modality, in Tomberlin, James, *Philosophical Perspectives, 8: Logic and Language, 1994*. Atascadero: Ridgeview.

Fine, Kit. 1994b. Ontological Dependence, *Proceedings of the Aristotelian Society* 95: 269–90.

Foster, John. 1986. *A. J. Ayer*. London: Routledge.

Foster, John. 2000. *The Nature of Perception*. Oxford: Clarendon Press.

Heal, Jane. 1994. Wittgenstein and Moore's Paradox, *Mind* 103: 5–24.

Hinton, Michael J. 1967. Visual Experiences, *Mind* 76: 217–27.

Hinton, Michael J. 1973. *Experiences: An Inquiry into Some Ambiguities*. Oxford: Clarendon Press.

Jackson, Frank. 1977. *Perception: A Representative Theory*. Cambridge: Cambridge University Press.

McConkie, George. 1979. On the Role of and Control of Eye Movements in Reading, in *Processing of Visible Language, I*, edited by P. Kolers, M. Wrolstad and H. Bouma. New York: Plenum Press.

Macdonald, Cynthia. 1998. Externalism & Authoritative Self-Knowledge, in *Knowing Our Own Minds*, edited by C. Wright, B. Smith and C. Macdonald. Oxford: Clarendon Press.

McDowell, John. 1982. Criteria, Defeasibility & Knowledge, *Proceedings of the British Academy*, philosophical lecture, *Proceedings of the British Academy* 68: 455–79.

McDowell, John. 1984. De Re Senses, *Philosophical Quarterly* 34: 283–94.

McDowell, John. 1994. Knowledge by Hearsay, in *Knowing from Words*, edited by B. K. Matilal and A. Chakrabarti. Amsterdam: Kluwer.

McDowell, John. 1995. Knowledge and the Internal, *Philosophy & Phenomenological Research* LV: 877–93.

Mack, Ariel and Rock, Irvin. 1998. *Inattentional Blindness*. Cambridge, Mass.: MIT Press.

Martin, M. G. F. 1997. The Reality of Appearances, in *Thought and Ontology*, edited by M. Sainsbury. Milan: FrancoAngeli.

Martin, M. G. F. 2001. Beyond Dispute, in *The History of the Mind–Body Problem*, edited by T. Crane and S. Patterson. London: Routledge.

Martin, M. G. F. 2002a. Particular Thoughts & Singular Thought, in *Logic, Thought, and Language*, edited by A. O'Hear. Cambridge: Cambridge University Press.

Martin, M. G. F. 2002b. The Transparency of Experience, *Mind & Language* 17 (4): 376–425.

Martin, M. G. F. 2004. The Limits of Self-Awareness, *Philosophical Studies* 120 (1): 37–89.

Merleau-Ponty, Maurice. 1942. *La Structure de comportement*, translated by A. Fisher. Paris: Duquesne University Press.

Moran, Richard. 2001. *Authority and Estrangement: An Essay on Self-Knowledge*. Princeton: Princeton University Press.

Peacocke, Christopher. 1983. *Sense & Content*. Oxford: Clarendon Press.

Peacocke, Christopher. 1986. *Thoughts: An Essay on Content*. Oxford: Blackwell.

Peacocke, Christopher. 1992. *A Study of Concepts*. Cambridge, Mass.: MIT Press.

Peacocke, Christopher. 1998. Conscious Attitudes, Attention and Self-Knowledge, in *Self-Knowledge*, edited by C. Macdonald, B. Smith and C. Wright. Oxford: Clarendon Press.

Pitcher, George. 1971. *A Theory of Perception*. Princeton: Princeton University Press.

Robinson, Howard. 1985. The General Form of the Argument for Berkeleian Idealism, in *Essays on Berkeley: A Tercentennial Celebration*, edited by J. Foster and H. Robinson. Oxford: Clarendon Press.

Robinson, Howard. 1994. *Perception*. London: Routledge.

Shoemaker, Sydney. 1984 (originally published *Journal of Philosophy* 1968). Self-Reference and Self-Awareness, in *Identity, Cause and Mind*. Cambridge: Cambridge University Press.

Shoemaker, Sydney. 1994. Self-Knowledge and 'Inner Sense', *Philosophy & Phenomenological Research* 64: 249–314.

Shoemaker, Sydney. 1995. Introspection and the Self (originally published 1986), in *Self-Knowledge*, edited by Q. Cassam. Oxford: Oxford University Press.

Smith, A. D. 2002. *The Problem of Perception*. Cambridge, Mass.: Harvard University Press.

Snowdon, Paul F. 1980–81. Perception, Vision and Causation, *Proceedings of the Aristotelian Society* 81: 175–92.

Snowdon, Paul F. 1990. The Objects of Perceptual Experience, *Proceedings of the Aristotelian Society, supplementary vol.* 64: 121–50.

Strawson, Peter F. 1966. *The Bounds of Sense*. London: Methuen.

Stroud, Barry. 1984. *The Significance of Philosophical Scepticism*. Oxford: Clarendon Press.

Stroud, Barry. 2000. Epistemological Reflection on Knowledge of the External World, in *Understanding Human Knowledge*. Oxford: Clarendon Press; original edition, 1996.

Sturgeon, Scott. 1994. The Epistemic View of Subjectivity, *Journal of Philosophy*: 91(5): 221–35.

Valberg, Jerry J. 1992. *The Puzzle of Experience*. Oxford: Clarendon Press.

Wiggins, David. 1980. *Sameness and Substance*. Oxford: Blackwell.

Wiggins, David. 1996. Substance, in *Philosophy: A Guide through the Subject*, edited by A. C. Grayling. Oxford: Oxford University Press.

Wiggins, David. 2001. *Sameness and Substance Renewed*. Cambridge: Cambridge University Press.

Williams, Bernard. 1978. *Descartes: The Project of Pure Enquiry*. Harmondsworth: Penguin.

Williamson, Timothy. 1990. *Identity and Discrimination*. Oxford: Blackwell.

Williamson, Timothy. 1995. Is Knowing a State of Mind?, *Mind* 104: 560–2.

Williamson, Timothy. 2000. *Knowledge and Its Limits*. New York: Oxford University Press.

Wright, Crispin. 1982. Strict Finitism, *Synthese* 51: 203–82.

Wright, Crispin. 1989. Wittgenstein's Later Philosophy of Mind: Sensation, Privacy, and Intention, *Journal of Philosophy* 86: 622–34.

Wright, Crispin. 1991. Scepticism and Dreaming: Imploding the Demon, *Mind* 100 (1): 87–116.

Wright, Crispin. 1998. Self-Knowledge: The Wittgensteinian Legacy, in A. O'Hear, *Current Issues in Philosophy of Mind*. New York: Cambridge University Press.

11

Experience without the Head

Alva Noë

Some cognitive states—e.g. states of thinking, calculating, navigating—may be partially external because, at least sometimes, these states depend on the use of symbols and artifacts that are outside the body. Maps, signs, writing implements may sometimes be as inextricably bound up with the workings of cognition as neural structures or internally realized symbols (if there are any). According to what Clark and Chalmers (1998) call active externalism, the environment can drive and so partially constitute cognitive processes. Where does the mind stop and the rest of the world begin? If active externalism is right, then the boundary cannot be drawn at the skull. The mind reaches—or at least *can* reach—beyond the limits of the body out into the world.

Can one extend active externalism to perceptual consciousness? There is a consensus that this question should be answered negatively.[1] The fact that we dream, and that neuroscientists can produce sensations by direct stimulation of the brain, shows that consciousness is a matter of what is going on in the head alone.

Or does it? The fact that some experiences can be produced by neural activity alone does not show that all experiences could be. Nor would the supposition that some not-yet-invented technology might one day enable us to produce any perceptual experience by direct neural intervention show that neural states were sufficient for experience. Just as the fact that one can manipulate a car's behavior by manipulating its engine is not enough to show that the engine is alone sufficient for the car's behavior, so the fact that one can manipulate experience by

I would like to thank Hubert Dreyfus, Benj Hellie, Susan Hurley, Sean Kelly, Mark Rowlands, Evan Thompson, and the editors of this book, Tamar Szabó Gendler and John Hawthorne, for helpful comments.

[1] Two philosophers who reject this consensus are Susan Hurley (1998) and Mark Rowlands (2002). Some philosophers (e.g. Dretske 1995 and Dennett 1987) are externalist about the content of perceptual experience, but internalist about the *vehicles* of content. On this sort of hybrid view, mental states are comparable to sunburns (Davidson 1987; Wilson 1997): The sunburn (or mental state) is literally on the skin (or in the head), but its nature depends on its world-involving causal history. In this paper I advance an externalism about the vehicles of experience.

manipulating the brain is not enough to show that the brain is sufficient for experience. We spend our lives in tight coupling with the environment (and other people). Why are we so confident that there could be a consciousness like ours independent of active exchange with the world? Why are we so certain consciousness depends only on what is going on inside us? Are we too hasty in dismissing externalism about perceptual experience?

These questions are not unmotivated. As of now, there is no account, even in roughest outline, of how the brain produces consciousness. This is widely admitted, even by leading proponents of the "consciousness is in the head" point of view, such as neurobiologists Frances Crick and Christof Koch. They write: "No one has produced any plausible explanation as to how the experience of the redness of red could arise from the action of the brain" (2003: 119). In light of this "explanatory gap," talk of neural substrates of experience can seem empty. Beyond brute correlation, we lack any intelligible connection between neural substrate and experience, and so we lack, it seems, sufficient reason to believe, of any given neural structure, that it is or could be the substrate of an experience.

Whether or not neural activity is sufficient for an experience is, or at least ought to be regarded as, an empirical question. Hurley and I have recently proposed that the explanatory gap gives us a reason for thinking that we ought to consider expanding our account of the substrate in terms of which we hope to explain perceptual experience (Hurley and Noë 2003).[2]

In this chapter I pursue related themes. My focus, however, is not on neural substrates, but rather on the phenomenology of perceptual experience. The robust "consciousness is in the head" consensus rests, I suspect, on bad phenomenology. There is a tendency to think of perceptual experiences as like snapshots, and to suppose that what is experienced, like the content of a snapshot laid out on paper, is given all at once *in the head*. But experiences are not like snapshots. Experienced detail is not given all at once the way detail in a picture is. In ways that I will try to explain, *what* we experience visually (for example) may outstrip what we actually see. From this, it does not follow that experience could not be in the head. What follows, rather, is that it might not be, or rather, that some aspects of some experiences might not always be. A modest conclusion, but one that allows that, at least sometimes, the world itself may drive and so constitute perceptual experience. The world can enter into perceptual experience the way a partner joins us in a dance, or—to change the image slightly—the way the music itself guides us.[3]

---

[2] We also argue that a range of phenomena of consciousness can be explained best not in terms of the intrinsic properties of neural activity, but in terms of the relation between those properties and the larger sensorimotor context in which the *animal* finds itself.

[3] In *Action in Perception* (2004) I extend a criticism of the snapshot conception and develop an alternative view of perceptual experience. In the final chapter of that book I take a stab at developing an externalist account of perceptual experience. This project—the elaboration and defense of this kind of externalism—is also the subject of joint work (in progress) by me and Susan Hurley.

1   A PUZZLE ABOUT PERCEPTUAL PRESENCE

It is a basic fact about perception that solid, opaque objects, when seen, have visible and invisible parts (Koenderink 1984). When you see a tomato, for example, you see its visible aspect. Euclid captured this thought when he wrote: 'Nothing that is seen is perceived at once in its entirety.'

No surprise here. What could be more evident than that you can't see the occluded portions of objects that you perceive? When you see a tomato, you can't see its back. When you see a cat behind a picket fence, you only see, strictly speaking, those parts of the cat that show through the slats.

There is a way of thinking about experience—a reasonable way—according to which these Euclidean truisms can come to seem untrue. Yes, to use Euclid's formulation, a perceived object is never perceived at once in its entirety. Nevertheless, one can hardly dispute that we take ourselves, when we see the tomato, or the cat, to have a sense of their presence—a *perceptual* sense of their presence—as wholes. In the case of the tomato, for example, you have a sense of the presence of a voluminous, ovoid, furrowed whole.

It is in defense of this reasonable way of thinking about perceptual experience that Thompson Clarke (1965) insisted that seeing is like nibbling. When you nibble a piece of cheese, you nibble it, the cheese, not merely a part of it; and so, when you see a tomato, you see precisely *it*, the tomato. It is only in special circumstances that it is correct to say, when you see a tomato, that you see only a part of it (just as, I presume Clarke would say, it is only in special circumstances that it is correct to say, when you see a tomato, that you see *the whole of it*).

P. F. Strawson (1979) aims at a related idea—also in defense of this reasonable way of thinking about experience—when he claims that one *distorts* the visual experience of a tomato, one misdescribes or mischaracterizes it, if one describes it as a visual experience as of a tomato *part* (let alone as of tomato-like sense-data). The visual experience of the tomato, when one takes it at face value, presents itself to one precisely as a *visual experience as of a whole tomato*.

There is much to be said on behalf of these defenses of familiar beliefs about perception. It would be a mistake, however, to think that they give us reason to doubt the Euclidean observation stated at the outset. For the Euclidean observation is no less well entrenched in our ordinary thought and phenomenology. Both sides in this philosophical standoff—Euclid on the one side, common sense on the other—show a tendency to lapse into dogmatism. The Euclidean insists, dogmatically, that when we take ourselves to perceive tomatoes, we "go beyond" what we really see. The "reasonable" philosopher, no less dogmatically, finds him or herself wanting to deny that our perceptual experience is confined by the limits of immediate perspective. "The plate doesn't look elliptical, it looks round!"

What I am calling the problem of perceptual presence comes clearly into focus when we acknowledge that both sides in this standoff are, in a way, right. The plate looks circular, and it looks elliptical. That is, we have a sense of the presence of the plate's circularity despite the fact that, plainly, it looks elliptical from here. And so for the tomato. When you see a tomato, you only see, strictly speaking, the visible face of the tomato; but it is also true that you are visually aware of the presence of the parts of the tomato which you don't actually see.

How can both these facts about perceptual experience be, well, just that, *facts about perceptual experience?* How can it be true, as I think it is, that we are perceptually aware, when we look at a tomato, of parts of the tomato which, strictly speaking, we do not perceive? This is the puzzle of perceptual presence: in what does our sense of the perceptual presence of a strictly unperceived feature of the world consist?

Before proceeding, two warnings. First, the puzzle of perceptual presence should not be confused with another nearby and closely related problem, namely, the epistemological problem of *the given* in perception. The problem is not with whether what is given provides sufficient rational basis for perceptual judgment, but rather with the question, *what is given?* The focus is phenomenological, on the nature of perceptual content itself. The point is that what is given is, at least apparently, rife with conflict. The plate looks round *and* it looks elliptical from here; we encounter only the visible parts of the tomato *and* we take ourselves to be aware of the presence of its strictly unperceived parts; two trees appear to be the same size *even though* the nearer tree looks larger than the farther one; a wall appears to be a uniformly colored surface, *despite* the fact that one part of the wall is visibly brighter (where it falls in direct sunlight) than a different part of the wall (which is cast in shadow).

Second, as the immediately preceding remarks indicate, the problem of perceptual presence is of surprising generality, comprising a range of perceptual phenomena not usually grouped together, including those already mentioned—occlusion shape, color constancy, apparent size—but also others as well (as we shall see).

2   FIRST STABS AT A SOLUTION

It may be tempting to bite the bullet and concede that we *don't really* see the whole tomato, or the roundness of the plate, or the whole cat, etc. We *go beyond* what is strictly given in an account of our experience when we describe what we see in this way. Our feeling that we see the whole tomato, say, is an illusion.

But this objection misses the point. The puzzle is not that it seems to us as if we see the whole tomato, when we only see part of it, or that we experience the color as uniform, when in fact it is nonuniform. This is the epistemological problem mentioned in the last section. The puzzle is that it seems to us *at once* as if we only see part of the tomato *and* as if the whole is perceptually present. It seems to us as if we see the circularity of the plate *even though* it looks elliptical. We take ourselves to sense the presence of a uniform color, even though the surface is dappled in light and thus variegated in apparent color. We take ourselves to have a perceptual sense of features we manifestly do not see and that we feel no inclination to believe we see.

Nor can it help us here to be told that although we don't *see* the hidden parts of the tomato, or the cat, we *infer* their presence. There is something to this line of thought, no doubt. After all, we know what tomatoes and cats are, we have these concepts; we make use of these concepts in fleshing out or indeed in "cognitively filling in" what is given to us. I think this must be right; however, it provides no solution to the problem of perceptual presence. It can't be the whole story. For what we want is an account not of the *thought* or *judgment* or *belief* that there is a whole tomato there, or a whole cat there, or a uniformly colored wall there. What we want is an account of our *perceptual* sense of their presence.

Crucially—and this is a phenomenological point—the cat does seem present, as a whole, *perceptually*. The voluminous tomato seems *perceptually* present. We do not merely *think* that they are present; it looks as if they are. Indeed, this sense of perceptual presence does not depend on the availability of the corresponding belief.

As an illustration of this last point, consider Figure 1, an illustration of Kanizsa's. It is natural, when looking at this picture, to say that we see a picture of a rectangle partially occluding four disks. We experience the occluded portions of the disks as visually present even though we know that they are not there (after all, this is a drawing).

In this example, then, it neither seems to us as if we see the occluded portions of the disks, nor is it the case that we think they are present but occluded. We *know* it is just a flat picture. Nevertheless, it looks as if the disks are present but

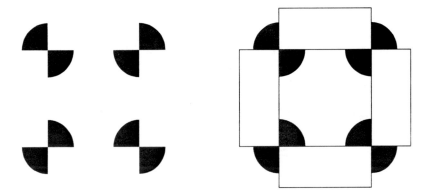

Fig. 1. Due to Kanizsa.

occluded. We experience the presence of the occluded bits even as we experience, plainly, their absence. They are present *as absent*.

Psychologists call this phenomenon *amodal* perception: perception, as it were, but not in any modality. This is not quite adequate as a characterization, however. The paradoxical quality is sharper. The phenomenon would be better characterized as amodal *visual* perception, that is, as a kind of seeing without seeing. For, crucially, even though we don't see the disks (in this case), the way in which we take them to be present perceptually is visual.

3   PRESENCE AS ABSENCE

Perceptual *presence-in-absence*—amodal perception—is, as already noticed, a widespread perceptual phenomenon. Let us consider three examples. The purpose of these examples is to illustrate the nature of the phenomenon, and to call to attention how difficult it is to give an adequate description of the relevant phenomenology.

Filling in at the Blind Spot

In his recent textbook, Steven Palmer (1999) suggests that the brain fills in to make up for the gap or discontinuity at the retinal blind spot.[4] We know this, he explains, because of the results of demonstrations such as the following. Consider Figure 2. If you shut the right eye, and fixate the cross with the left eye, you can adjust the illustration of a broken line so that the break falls in the blind spot. (This will occur when the page is about a foot from the face.) When the break falls on the blind spot, we have the experience of an unbroken line. This experience must in turn be underwritten by a neural process whereby an internal representation which has a gap in it is filled in. As Palmer writes: "The line on the retina actually has a gap in it at the blind spot, but we experience it as complete and uninterrupted when the gap falls within the blind spot. The important point is that what we experience visually conforms not to the firing of retinal receptors, but to some higher level of neural activity" (1999: 617). Neural processes of filling-in in a higher-level neural representation are what bridge the gap between low-level retinal input and experience.

Dennett (1991) has criticized this style of reasoning on the grounds that one isn't entitled to assume that the brain produces the filled-in percept by a neural process of perceptual completion. Perhaps, he suggests, the brain instead ignores the absence of information corresponding to the blind spot, thus giving rise to the gap-free percept, without requiring the actual construction of a

---

[4] See Pessoa, Thompson and Noë (1998) and Thompson, Noë and Pessoa (1999) for discussion of the blind-spot phenomenon.

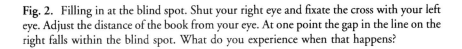

Fig. 2. Filling in at the blind spot. Shut your right eye and fixate the cross with your left eye. Adjust the distance of the book from your eye. At one point the gap in the line on the right falls within the blind spot. What do you experience when that happens?

gap-free internal representation. This line of thinking relies on the Kantian point that representations needn't have the properties they represent the world as possessing.

It is striking that Dennett, no less than Palmer, takes for granted that *it visually seems to you as if the line is filled in.* But this is a mistake, or rather, it is an equivocation. In the relevant sense of "the line looks unbroken," it isn't the case that the line looks unbroken. Perform the demonstration and pay careful attention to what you see. Notice, it does not seem to you as if you look at the break and see it is filled in there, or that the line is complete there. A better description of your experience would be: when you shut one eye and fixate the cross, you cannot see a gap in the line in your peripheral field. You do not perceive the break in the line. But not perceiving the break is different from perceiving the line filled in, or even from perceiving the absence of a break. We naturally *say* that we perceive the line as unbroken, but in saying this we are not committing ourselves to the proposition that we are in qualitatively the same state as when we actually visually examine an unbroken line.

One proposal, advanced by Durgin, Tripathy, and Levi (1995), is that the experience of the line as filled in at the blind spot is, phenomenologically speaking, like the experience of the far side of the tomato, or of the hidden portions of the disks in Kanizsa's illustration. They are visually present, but not *as seen.* As support for this point, look at Figure 2 with one eye shut, but hold up your thumb so that it blocks the gap. You now enjoy amodal visual completion of the line behind your thumb.

Phenomenologically, so Durgin, Tripathy, and Levi suggest, the experience of the line as complete when the break falls on the blind spot is just the same as the experience of the line as complete when the gap is occluded by the thumb.

This is a controversial issue and there are arguments ranging on both sides.[5] My point here is phenomenological, rather than empirical. The phenomenology of the experience of the filled-in broken line is not like that of the visual experience, in normal perceptual circumstances, of a solid line. The phenomenology is the phenomenology of presence in absence, not of simple presence.

Once we get clear about the phenomenology we can observe that even if Dennett's criticism of Palmer's argument is right, Dennett and Palmer share a commitment to a misdescription of what the experience of the line is like.

[5] See, for example, Ramachandran and Gregory (1991). For a general discussion of issues in this vicinity, see Pessoa, Thompson and Noë (1998).

Color Constancy

Color constancy is illustrated by such facts as that we do not experience a change in the color of a surface when illumination changes, and we do not experience a wall as variable in color even though it is lighter where it falls in direct sunlight than it is where it is cast in shadow. Standard thinking in visual theory would have it that the problem of color constancy is to explain the experience of sameness of color despite variation in the character of reflected light entering the eyes.

This framing of the problem of color constancy is problematic. It is true that we can perceive a wall that is illuminated unevenly as uniform in color. Nevertheless, it is also the case that when a wall is in this way illuminated unevenly, it is also visibly different in respect of color across its surface. For example, to match the color of different parts of the wall you would need different color chips. Standard ways of characterizing color constancy as a phenomenon have a tendency to explain away the fact that we experience the wall as uniform in color even when we experience the surface as visibly differentiated in respect of color across its surface. The problem of color constancy, then, is better framed as a problem about perceptual presence. We experience the presence of a uniform color which, strictly speaking, we do not see. Or rather: the actual uniform color of the wall's surface is present in perception *amodally*, it is present but absent, in the same way as the tomato's backside, or the blocked parts of the cat.

Peacocke (1983) used color constancy to illustrate the difference between the *representational content* of an experience (how the world is represented by the experience), and the *qualitative* or *sensational properties* of experience (what the experience is like apart from its representational features). The experience of the wall here and there are the same in their representational content, but they differ nonrepresentationally in their qualitative character. This seems wrong: just as our experience can present the circularity of the plate, even though the plate looks elliptical from here, so the experience can present the uniform color of the wall, even though the surface looks irregular in color. The problem of perceptual presence is a problem, precisely, about how experience can have this sort of apparently conflicting representational content.[6]

Crucially, we can experience the wall as uniform in color *and* as differently colored across its surface. Just as we can see that the plate looks circular *and* elliptical, so we can see the color is uniform *and* variable. Just as we see the circularity in the elliptical appearance, so we see the invariant color *in* the

---

[6] Kelly (2001) locates the problem in a somewhat different place than Peacocke (1983 *and* 2001). Kelly proposes that there is a qualitative difference between our experience of the two parts of the wall, and he grants that this is a difference in the representational content of our experience, a difference in how the experience presents the wall as being. But he doubts that this difference is a difference in *color* (and, in particular, that it is a difference that makes a difference to our use of color concepts).

apparent variability.[7] The color of the wall is present in absence; it is implicitly present.

Sean Kelly has urged (in personal communication) that although it is true that we can see the wall as varied in color across its surface, and that we can see it as uniform in color, we can't have these experiences at the same time. Either we attend to the uniformity of the underlying color, or to its nonuniformity, but we can't do both simultaneously. He proposes that we think of the way color appearance varies as an effect of background context. When you experience the variability of the wall's surface color, you are experiencing the different ways the single color looks as lighting varies. I am sympathetic to the idea that the way a color looks changes as lighting conditions change—and so with the idea that not every change in lighting is a change in color. I am also sympathetic to the idea that one cannot attend, simultaneously, to the constancy and the variability of color. Nevertheless, Kelly's position seems to explain away the problem of presence and constancy without explaining it. When I look at my wall now I see its uniform color *in* the variations of its apparent color across the surface. In so far as I see the constancy in the variation, I see them both at once. Experienced perceivers understand that colors, like three-dimensional objects, have aspects, and so they understand, implicitly, that changes in conditions of viewing (in position and in lighting, say, like changes in position) bring about changes in the way things look with respect to color.[8]

Change Blindness and the Experience of Detail

A fascinating phenomenon of perceptual presence is the visual experience of detail. Visual theory has tended to take as its starting point a way of thinking about seeing according to which visual experiences are like snapshots. The idea is that visual experiences represent the world the way pictures do—all at once, in sharp focus, from the center out to the periphery. This snapshot conception is captured in pictorial form by Mach's famous drawing of the visual field; it is caricatured in Gursky's well-known photograph of a Los Angeles 99 Cents Shop. The central aim of visual theory, as it has been practiced for the last century, has been to understand how the brain gives rise to this sort of snapshot-like, richly detailed experience. The problem is hard for two reasons. First, it is *ill-posed*, i.e., the two-dimensional retinal projection does not uniquely determine a three-dimensional layout. Second, the retinal image itself is defective (distorted, gappy, of uneven resolution). How, on the basis of such an impoverished stimulus, do we come to enjoy richly detailed experiential snapshots? The orthodox strategy

---

[7] Wollheim (1980: 205–26) has laid emphasis on the idea of *seeing in*. We see an object *in* a picture, for example. Just as it is the case that you see a picture, and, in seeing the picture, see what the picture depicts (and so in that sense see the depicted item in the picture), so I want to suggest that we see the uniform color of the wall *in* its variegated surface. I take up these issues in Noë (2004), ch. 4.   [8] I develop this approach to color and constancy in Noë (2004).

for answering this question is to hypothesize that the brain integrates the information available in successive fixations to form a detailed internal representation, which then serves as the substrate of the experience. *What* we experience is *what* is represented in this internal representation. Vision, according to the orthodox view, is the process whereby this internal representation is constructed.

Recent work in perceptual psychology on scene perception challenges the orthodox conception of vision precisely by challenging whether experiences are snapshot-like in the way that orthodoxy has tended to suppose. If they are not, then we are not saddled with the problem of explaining how the brain gives rise to picture-like experiences. For example, work on change blindness (and related phenomena such as inattentional blindness) weighs against the snapshot conception.[9] Our success as perceivers depends on the fact that we are very good at noticing flickers of movement and other attention-grabbing concomitants of change. We spontaneously direct our eyes to these transients and so discover change as it happens. It turns out that if we are prevented from noticing the associated flickers, or if there are no flickers—because, say, the relevant changes are too gradual—we will remain unaware of the changes going on around us, even when they are large-scale and pertinent to our interests and background concerns. In one noteworthy recent demonstration, due to Kevin O'Regan, perceivers are shown a photograph of a Paris street scene. Over the seconds that they look at the picture, the color of a car, prominently displayed in the foreground, changes from blue to red. Perceivers overwhelmingly fail to notice this change in color, even though the change is dramatic and occurs over a short period of time. When the color change is pointed out, perceivers laugh aloud and express astonishment that they could have failed to miss the change.

Change blindness does not demonstrate that ordinary perceivers tend to overestimate what they see. Given normal circumstances, we are very good at noticing changes. What change blindness illuminates is the degree to which this ability is vulnerable to disruption. Importantly, the fact of change blindness reveals that a certain theoretical account of what seeing is—the snapshot conception, and the associated idea that seeing is a process whereby a detailed representation is built up corresponding to what is seen—must be wrong. We don't seem to have easy access to such a detailed internal representation when we contemplate our environment.[10]

Scientists and philosophers have sometimes suggested that change blindness reveals that our visual consciousness is a kind of confabulation (a "grand illusion"). It seems to us—doesn't it?—as if when we open our eyes we see *everything*, the whole scene, in sharp focus, and uniform detail, right out to the edges

---

[9] For reviews of this and related phenomena, see O'Regan (in press); Simons and Levin (1997); Simons (2000); Noë, Pessoa and Thompson (2000).

[10] See Simons et al. (2002); Angelone, Levin, and Simons (2003); Levin et al. (2002); Mitroff, Simons, and Levin (2004).

of the visual field. We do not, however (as revealed by change blindness and many other experiments and demonstrations). Therefore, so this reasoning goes, the visual world is a grand illusion. Perceptual consciousness is a confabulation.

But this confabulation hypothesis is wrong.[11] Granted, we do not enjoy snapshot-like experiences, as the orthodox view had supposed and as change blindness demonstrates. But—and this is crucial—it is not the case that it *seems* to us as if we enjoy such snapshot-like experiences. We take the world to be densely detailed, yes. But we do not take ourselves to represent all that detail in consciousness at a moment in time, in the way that a picture might represent that detail at a moment in time. The snapshot conception is no part of ordinary perceptual phenomenology.

A little consideration is enough to bring this out. Consider your current visual experience of, say, the view out of your window. You no doubt have a sense of the scene outside as dense and rich in detail. If you pause to reflect, however, you will notice it is not the case that it seems to you, *now*, as if all that detail is seen by you all at once, in an instant, in sharp focus and high resolution. Some things are clearly in view, others are present only indistinctly as background elements, and some items are not really experienced at all. To bring detail into consciousness, it is necessary to probe the environment, by turning your eyes, and your head, by shifting your attention from here to there.

The suggestion that visual experience is a grand illusion rests, therefore, on a misdescription of the character of the experience of seeing. If this is so, then why do we find change blindness so surprising? Why do audiences gasp with astonishment when presented with immediate evidence of their own change blindness? Dennett (2001, 2002) has pressed this point: surprise, he has suggested, is an indicator of a foiled epistemic commitment. The question is, *what* epistemic commitment is thus shown to be foiled? It is enough to explain the surprise, I would suggest, to point out that we don't realize quite how vulnerable to disruption our ability to detect change really is. This doesn't entail that we take ourselves to see everything at once!

But there is stronger evidence that we are not committed to the snapshot conception. In daily life, we continuously move our eyes and head in order to get better looks at objects around us in the cluttered environment. Why are we *not* surprised by our need constantly to adjust and probe if in fact we take ourselves to carry around a detailed internal model with us? Moreover, if you ask me to describe my room, I don't shut my eyes and reflect on my memory of the room; rather, I look around to see what is there. Why don't we find *this* surprising? The absence of surprise at our need to move around and look is a clear indicator of the absence of epistemic commitment to the snapshot conception.

Even if we grant that the snapshot conception distorts our phenomenology, surely it remains the case that we take ourselves, at least to some degree, to be

---

[11] See the papers collected in Noë (2002b) for discussion of this issue.

perceptually aware of unattended features of the scene? After all, we do take ourselves to be aware of the environment as densely detailed, even if we do not take ourselves literally to see it all. The problem we face here is a further incarnation of the problem of perceptual presence. In what does our sense of the perceptual presence of strictly unperceived detail consist?

Each of these phenomena—filling in at the blind spot, color constancy, the perceptual experience of detail—is an instance of the perceptual phenomenon of presence in absence. We have a sense of the presence of strictly unseen or unattended visual detail; we experience the presence of a uniform color despite the apparent difference in color across the surface of the wall; we experience the line as complete even though it is not the case that we actually see the break filled in. In each of these cases, as with our examples of the tomato and the cat, what we experience visually goes beyond what we see (strictly speaking).

4   PRESENCE AS ACCESS

Do you take yourself, when you open your eyes and look, to be aware of the whole scene before you, in sharp detail, all at once? The correct answer to this, we have seen, ought to be: yes and no. Yes, in so far as you take yourself to have a sense of the presence of a richly detailed world. But *no*, in so far as it does not seem to you as if you actually see every bit of detail. There is no such thing as seeing all the detail at once, just as there is no such thing as seeing the tomato from all sides all at once.

Phenomenologically, the world is given to perception *as available.*

To solve the problem of perceptual presence—comprising as it does, a broad range of phenomena—we need to make explicit this feature of the relevant phenomenology.

We visually experience the scene before us as densely detailed without seeing all that detail, just as we visually experience the tomato as voluminous and three-dimensional even though we don't see all of it. The presence of the detailed environment—of the occluded parts of the tomato, of the uniform color of the wall's surface—consists, then, not of our feeling of immediate contact with those features, but of our feeling of *access* to those bits of detail. The detail is present *now*, though absent (unseen, out of view, partially occluded, etc.), because we *now* possess the skills needed to bring the relevant features into view.

The scene is present to me now as detailed, even though I do not now see all the detail, because I am now able—by the exercise of a repertoire of perceptual skills—to bring the detail into immediate perceptual contact. For example, I need but move my eyes, or move about, or direct my attention here or there, to bring the relevant detail to focus. The detail is present because it is, as it were, *within reach.*

The basis of our feeling of access is our possession of the skills needed actually to reach out and grasp the relevant details. We are familiar, as a general rule, with the ways our sensory experience changes as we move. Moving the eyes, blinking, turning the head, or moving the body—all this produces familiar kinds of sensory change. Familiarity with the ways sensory stimulation changes as we move is the ground of our perceptual access. Perceivers *know how* to gain access, to make contact, with the environment around them.

This is the key to the problem of perceptual presence: our sense of the perceptual presence of the detailed world does not consist of our representation of all the detail in consciousness *now*. Rather, it consists of our access *now* to all of the detail, and of our knowledge (itself practical in character) that we have this access. This knowledge takes the form of our comfortable mastery of the rules of sensorimotor dependence that mediate our relation to the world, to the surrounding detail, the cat, or the wall. My sense of the presence of the whole cat behind the fence consists precisely in my knowledge, my implicit understanding, that by a movement of the eye or the head or the body I can bring bits of the cat into view that are now hidden. And so for the tomato: my relation to the strictly unseen portions of the tomato is mediated by familiar visual laws of sensorimotor dependence. The presence of the tomato to me as a voluminous whole consists in my knowledge of the sensory effects of my movements in relation to the tomato.[12]

5 INTRAMODALITY AND INTERMODALITY

Presence is to be explained in terms of access. The *modality* of presence—whether the presence is perceptual, or merely *thought* (as it were), or whether it is visual, or tactile, say—is explained by the different *kinds of access* required, and by the different sorts of skills needed to secure access.

Contrast the felt presence of peripheral detail in the visual scene with the sense of the presence of the far side of the tomato. In both cases, the feature in question is strictly unperceived, but is sensibly felt to be present. In each case, however, the features are present, but absent, in different ways. In the one case, detail is grasped or obtained by the movement of the eye, by turning the head to the left or right. Your sense of presence at the periphery depends on your confidence that *by doing these things* you can obtain the detail. In the other case, however, you need to do very different things to obtain the detail. For example, you must move around the tomato to bring the far side into view. To the qualitative differences in the felt presence of the features, there corresponds the different

[12] Here, and in what follows, I build on the ideas presented in O'Regan and Noë (2001). See also Noë (2002a) and Noë (2004).

things we need to do to attain those features, and the different sensorimotor skills we need to deploy.

Now it is true that we have access to more than we take ourselves to experience perceptually. Not everything that is accessible is perceptually present. The room next door feels present, for example, but it doesn't feel perceptually present (as discussed in O'Regan and Noë 2001). I can't see it through the wall. The room next door is merely thought to be present. That it is not felt to be present perceptually comes out in such facts as that I know that I can jump up and down, turn around, turn the lights on and off, blink, and so on, and it makes no difference whatsoever to my sense of the presence of the room next door. My relationship to the room next door—however strongly I believe or know or assume or feel that it is present—is not a perceptual relation. My relation to hidden parts of the cat, or to the far side of the tomato, in contrast, *is* perceptual, even though I don't actually see these items. For my relation to them is mediated by patterns of sensorimotor dependence. My relation to them is affected by bodily movements.

You may wonder whether this account can be quite right. First, you might object, my visual relation to the room next door is no less mediated by patterns of sensorimotor dependence than my relation to the tomato is. *What* I need to do to produce the relevant sensory change may differ (e.g., I would need to walk out into the hall and through the door of the room next door); nevertheless, in both cases my relation is mediated by patterns of sensorimotor dependence. Second, you might question whether it is really true that I am perceptually linked to the unseen bits of the tomato or cat.

To reply to these worries: in general, sensorimotor dependencies can be characterized as having two important features. The first of these, which I have been emphasizing, is that they are *movement*-dependent. The slightest movements of the body modulate my sensory relation to the object of perception. But they are also *object*-dependent. Suppose I am looking at you and someone off to the side gets up to leave. In normal circumstances I will notice the movement and turn my eyes to it. Part of what my sense of the perceptual presence of the periphery of my visual field consists of is just this fact that movements there grab my attention. (Indeed, this in part explains our sense of the unboundedness of the visual field.)[13]

It is true, then, that there are movements of my body that will bring me into visual contact with the room next door, but it is generally not the case that movements or changes in the room next door will produce sensory changes in me. The sensorimotor contingencies mediating me and the room next door are not object-dependent (in the sense described here).

[13] This distinction between movement- and object-dependence corresponds to the distinction between bodiliness and grabbiness first presented in O'Regan and Noë (2001) (and developed in a series of unpublished papers by O'Regan, Myin, and Noë). There are differences, however, between the distinction as presented here in the text and that presented in this other work.

Now consider the tomato in front of me. True, I am unlikely to notice an ant crawling on its far side. After all, the ant is hidden by the tomato. On the other hand, the slightest movement of the tomato will grab my attention and may bring me into contact with its now occluded parts. Crucially, there is no sense in which the occluded ant feels perceptually present.

For the relation to an object to be perceptual, it must be mediated by patterns of sensorimotor dependence which are both movement-dependent and object-dependent. In this way, then, the enactive approach allows us to say that the experience of the tomato (and its backside), but not that of the room next door, is perceptual. (Or, rather, our relation to the room next door is not visual, whereas our relation to the hidden bits of the tomato is, at least to some extent.)

An objection to this proposal starts from the thought that what explains the sense of presence of the tomato as a whole, on the basis of its visible parts, is the fact that the hidden and visible parts are united by their inherence in a single object. Just as one can kick a whole table merely by kicking its leg, so one can see a whole tomato just by seeing its facing side. By the same token, so the objection goes, we ought to say that one does see the room next door by seeing the larger object (the building) of which it is a part.[14]

In reply, note that this objection is a version of the appeal to inference and knowledge considered above in section 2. I am happy to believe that the concept of objecthood shapes and constrains our appreciation of what is seen. However, I insist, as I did earlier, that this can't be the whole story. For what is needed is an account that does justice to the phenomenology itself, and phenomenologically at least some of the unseen parts of the tomato are *perceptually* present, not merely present in so far as we understand that they belong to the object we are looking at.

I grant that there is a sense in which the room next door *feels* present. And perhaps its felt presence has in part to do with our understanding that it belongs to the building of which we are perceptually aware. However, it is not present with the same liveliness, vividness, and immediacy with which some of the strictly *unseen* parts of the tomato are present. This difference corresponds precisely to the differences in the ways in which our relation to the tomato (and its unseen parts), but not our relation to the room next door, is governed by patterns of sensorimotor dependence.

This account of perceptual presence provides the basic elements of a more full-blooded account of perceptual content.[15] For the question of what does my sense of the unseen part of the tomato consist is equivalent to the question of what does my experience of the tomato's shape consist.

Consider a simple case of shape perception: A cube has six sides; there are twelve edges and eight vertices. You can never see more than three sides from a

---

[14] This objection has been raised by Edward Harcourt, Michael Martin, and the editors of this book.   [15] I offer such an account in Noë (2004).

single point of view. As you move with respect to a cube, its aspect changes dramatically. Sides come into view while others disappear. Any movement determines a set of changes in perceived aspect; any set of changes in perceived aspects determines equivalence classes of possible movements.[16]

When you see the cube from a particular vantage point, you encounter its aspect from that vantage point. When you experience an object as cubical on the basis merely of its aspect, you do so because you bring to bear, in this experience, your sensorimotor knowledge of the relation between changes in cube aspects and actual and possible movement. To experience the figure as a cube, on the basis of how it looks, is to understand *how* its look changes as you move.

Similar points, *mutatis mutandis* go for different shapes and different perceptible properties. This idea was anticipated by Merleau-Ponty (1962: 82), who wrote: "I know that objects have several facets because I could make a tour of inspection of them, and in that sense I am conscious of the world through the medium of my body."

Experiencing the ovoid character of the tomato depends on one's implicit grasp of the complicated sensory effects of movement in relation to the tomato. To experience the tomato as voluminously ovoid is to experience it as providing the possibility of a range of movement-induced sensory changes.

6   ENACTIVE EXTERNALISM AND VIRTUAL PRESENCE

With this account of perceptual presence on the table, let's return to the question of externalism and the vehicles of content. Are the vehicles of perceptual experience in the head?

It might have seemed that this question requires a positive answer. We are now in a position, however, to appreciate the possibility that perceptual experience need not supervene on neural states. The content of a perceptual experience is not given all at once the way the content of a picture is given in the picture all at once. What we experience *now* goes beyond what we represent *now* in consciousness. Detail, three-dimensionality, and color are present in experience not *as represented*, but rather *as available*. In this sense, experience has this content at a moment in time only as a potentiality. The content may be enacted; it is accessible, thanks to the perceiver's embedding in the world, and the perceiver's possession of the skills—sensorimotor, perhaps also conceptual—needed to assemble it. Perceptual experience is a temporally extended activity of skillful probing. The world makes itself available to our reach, given our skill. The experience itself comprises mind and world. It has content only thanks to the established dynamics of interaction between perceiver and world. This is the first suggestion I want to make in support of the idea that the body and the world

---

[16]   Koenderink (1984) discusses this case in detail.

may enter into the making of experience. There is a sense in which the content of the experience is not *in the head*. But nor is it *in the world*. Experience isn't something that happens in us. It is something we do.

In defense of this idea, I propose that the world is present in experience *virtually*, the way information from a remote server is present on your desktop. The world is present virtually thanks to the way we are bound to it, in bodies with the right sort of connectivities. Moving the eye, turning the head, repositioning the body, brings us the detail we need as we implicitly know that it will. The world is present in experience virtually thanks to our online, dynamic access to it.

This metaphor invites an objection. All that is present in your computer, *really*, is what is already downloaded. Information on the network is accessible, but it is not present. The *illusion* of presence (that's what it is, after all) depends only on the current state of your local machine. Isn't the same true of perception? The content of your current experience is determined by your current brain state. Crucially, this brain state includes all the needed information about the sensory effects of movement. Anyone whose brain is in a state identical to yours would have the sense of presence of the same variety of features, even if their environment were radically different!

I respond to this challenge directly in the next section. For now, two basic ideas need to be laid out. First, phenomenologically speaking, virtual presence is a kind of presence, not a kind of non-presence or illusory presence. Recall, it doesn't seem (for example) as if you can actually *see* the partially occluded bits of the cat. It only seems as if they are present in that by movements we can bring them into view. Virtual presence is all the presence we need, phenomenologically. Crucially, virtual presence can be explained given a conception of the perceiver as embodied and as situated in and coupled with an environment that affords possibilities of exploratory movement.

Second, and this may be the most important idea in this paper, experiential presence is virtual *all the way in*. This is an important disanalogy with the computer case. Consider the tomato again. You see the facing side. You can't see the far side, but you have a perceptual sense of its presence thanks to your practical grasp of sensorimotor patterns mediating your relation to it. The rear side is present virtually, but the facing side is present *simpliciter*. Notice, however, that you do not, as a matter of fact, have the *whole* of the facing side of the tomato in consciousness all at once. The facing side has extent, and shape, and color, and you can't embrace all this detail in consciousness all at once, anymore than you can embrace the whole detailed scene. This is clear to careful consideration. Take a tomato out. Look at it. Yes, you have a sense that the facing side of the tomato is all there, all at once. But if you are careful you will admit that you don't actually experience every part of its visible surface all at once. Your eyes scan across the surface and you direct your attention to this or that. Further evidence is provided by change blindness. As mentioned above, the very color of the object you are staring at can change right before your eyes without your noticing it, so long as you are not attending to the color itself!

What this shows is that you cannot factor experience into an occurrent and a merely potential part. Pick any candidate for the occurrent factor. Now consider it. It is structured too; it has hidden facets or aspects too. It is present only in potential.

The point here is not that one can only attend to a small number of features at an instant in time, although this is widely agreed to be true (Pylyshyn 1994; Sperling 1960). The point rather is this: a perceptual experience doesn't analyze or break down into experiences of atomic elements, or simple features. Experience is always a field, with structure; you can never comprehend the whole field in a single act of consciousness. Something always remains present, but out of view. All you can do is serially run through features. But the moment you stop and try to make a single feature the sole object of your consideration—*this shade of red*, for example—it exceeds your grasp. This is true even of a *Ganzfeld*. Suppose you are in a grey fog. Nothing visually distinguishes here from there. And yet, you are not given the greyness around you as a simple property. There's the color, which is spread out in space, but there's also the texture.

Qualities are available in experience as possibilities, as potentialities, but not as completed givens. Experience is a dynamic process of navigating the pathways of these possibilities. Experience depends on the skills needed to make one's way.

The upshot of this is that there is no basis, in phenomenology, for thinking that what is given now, to me, as present in my consciousness, is ever enough to account for the character of my current conscious experience. My phenomenal experience expands my immediate horizons and takes me beyond myself to the world. This sounds paradoxical, but it is not. Presence in absence, I have tried to show, is a pervasive feature of our perceptual lives.

7   DOES EXPERIENCE SUPERVENE ON INTERNAL STATES OF THE BRAIN?

The correct answer to this ought to be: "maybe."[17] I have argued that the content of perceptual experience depends on the possession and exercise of sensorimotor skill. The objector is right to push the thought that how things are with one perceptually at a given moment is controlled by one's current sensorimotor expectations, and, thus, by one's current state. However, to concede this—how could I not concede this?—is not to grant that perceptual experience supervenes on internal neural states. For it is an open question, an empirical question, whether the content and character of the sorts of perceptual experiences we

---

[17] In this section I draw on joint work with Susan Hurley. My own thinking about externalism has been shaped by engagement with her work and by our collaboration.

actually enjoy are controlled by our sensorimotor expectations *alone*. It could be, as there is now reason to suspect, that *our* experience (as opposed to some more primitive kind of experience) requires dynamic interaction with the environment. *It is an empirical question whether our brains can do the work needed to enable us to enact our virtual worlds.* It is a mistake—a prejudice really—to think this question has already been settled.

Recall the significance of the earlier discussion of the perceptual presence of detail. Change blindness shows that we do not, at a moment in time, have access to an internal representation of the visual detail. Some scientists (e.g., O'Regan 1992) have proposed that the visual system can go without such detailed internal representations since the environment can serve as a repository of information about itself. Why represent what is immediately accessible? The thought here is that an *external* representation would be just as good as an internal one. This is an important insight, one that takes the first step to demoting the significance of *internal* representations in the theory of perception. The implication is that internal representations of experienced detail are not necessary for experience.

What if they are not sufficient either? As noted at the outset, it is an uncontroversial fact about our current epistemic predicament that we don't have any understanding of what it is about the action of neural states (representational or otherwise) that gives rise to consciousness. How could internal representations of the environment be the ground of the perceiver's phenomenal experience of that environment? This explanatory cul-de-sac stands in contrast with the avenues of explanation made available on the enactive approach. For example, we have considered how the perceiver's implicit grasp of the sensory effects of movement can make the shape of an object available in perceptual experience.

We are considering the thought that detailed internal models of the environment are neither necessary nor sufficient for perceptual experience. What if, as a matter of empirical fact, they are not even possible? Change blindness raises this question. Perhaps, as a result of our phylogenetic history, we are just *bad* at storing detail, at representing. If this is how things are, then our sense of the presence of environmental detail could not consist of the fact that we have access to an internal representation, but would have to consist of our *access to the detailed environment itself*, thanks to our possession of the requisite sensorimotor knowledge and to the fact that we are *coupled* with the world. Our current experience of detail would depend on our current access to unrepresented detail.

We have already disarmed one objection to this possibility based on phenomenology: it seems to us as if the detail is represented in our consciousness all at once. This is the wrongheaded, snapshot conception of experience that I targeted earlier in this paper. It does not seem to us, when we see, that we have all the present detail in consciousness at once. The world is present—not in our minds, but as available to our inspection.

Upshot: it is an open empirical possibility that our experience depends not only on what is represented in our brains, but on dynamic interaction between brain, body and environment. The substrate of experience may include the non-brain body, and the world.

8   MODAL INTUITIONS

"Wouldn't my neural duplicate have the same experiences as me?"

Perhaps, but your neural duplicate would almost certainly be embedded in and interacting with a duplicate of your environment. What else could explain the neural identity? (This point has been discussed by Hurley 1998; see also Hurley and Noë 2003.)

"But wouldn't my neural duplicate have the same experiences as me *whatever differences there might be between its environment and mine?* This is the force of the claim that experience supervenes on the brain."

We can follow Hurley in challenging this *duplication assumption* (1998: ch. 8): who knows what would be the case in a world in which there could be neural duplicates in radically different environments? How could one decide?

It's worth recalling that arguments for *content* externalism—such as Putnam's original discussions of Twin Earth—make the assumption that physical duplicates are also phenomenal duplications, but what motivates this assumption is the supposition that they occupy qualitatively identical (if physically dissimilar) environments. In the absence of this sort of consideration, how can we even make sense of the proposal that creatures in different environments could be neural (and so phenomenal) duplicates? One strategy would be to appeal to "virtual reality". This is certainly an intelligible possibility, but not one that lends much support to the "consciousness is in the head" doctrine. First, what explains the phenomenal identity in a virtual reality scenario is not neural identity, but the environmental sameness (at some level of characterization) that drives that neural identity. What is doing the explanatory heavy lifting is the idea that the virtual environment presents the same face, as it were, to the subject. Second, in the virtual reality scenario, it is not the brain alone, but the brain as coupled to the system (perhaps including the system's designer) that suffices for experience.

I have urged that experience is a temporally extended phenomenon; it is an activity of skillful probing. If this is right, then a neural duplicate of me now, at a moment in time, won't, by dint of being my duplicate now, have *any* experience at all.[18] If the duplicate does have experience, it will be thanks to its dynamic, temporally extended interaction with the environment. But then again we must note that there is little reason to think that its experience would or could be like mine unless its environment were also like mine.

---

[18] As Mark Rowlands has emphasized in correspondence.

The internalist may be tempted to refer to dreaming as evidence that experiential states can be produced by the brain alone. But this appeal only succeeds in demonstrating (given additional assumptions) that *dream experiences* depend on neural states alone. It has been reported by the psychologist Stephen LaBerge (personal communication) that dreaming may differ from non-dream perceptual experience precisely in respect of the stability and richness of represented detail. For example, when you read a sign in a dream, and then look away and then look back, the sign almost always says something different. What explains this qualitative difference between dreaming perception and real perception may be precisely the fact that dream experiences, but not genuine perceptual experiences, do depend only on neural activity for their basis. Normal perceptual experience, in contrast, is anchored by our dynamic coupling to the world.

I have not sought to demonstrate vehicle externalism. My point has not been that the mind *must* extend beyond the limits of the head, but rather that there is no deep theoretical obstacle to thinking that (as regards experience) it might do so (at least for some range of aspects of experience).

It has always seemed that there were obstacles to thinking that consciousness could so extend beyond the limits of the skull. "Gosh—darn it, experience just feels like it's in the head." But this is bad phenomenology, I have argued, and it is probably bad science. As we have seen, detail may be present in consciousness only virtually. We thus open up the possibility of an account of (for example) the perceptual experience of detail that is consistent with its not being the case that that detail is represented at once in the head. Although of course it *could* be. The upshot is not that experience is without the head, but that it might be. The world is safe for an externalism that allows that we enact perceptual content by the exercise of sensorimotor skills over time.

REFERENCES

Angelone, Bannie L., Levin, Daniel T., and Simons, Daniel J. (2003), "The roles of representation and comparison failures in change blindness," *Perception* 32: 947–62.

Brooks, Rodney A. (1991), "Intelligence without reason," *Proceedings of the 1991 International Joint Conference on Artificial Intelligence*: 569–95.

Clark, Andy and Chalmers, David (1998), "The extended mind," *Analysis* 58: 7–19.

Clarke, Thompson (1965), "Seeing surfaces and physical objects," in Max Black (ed.), *Philosophy in America* (Ithaca, NY: Cornell University Press).

Crick, Francis and Koch, Christof (2003), "A framework for consciousness," *Nature Neuroscience* 6: 119–26.

Davidson, Donald (1987), "Knowing one's own mind," *Proceedings and Addresses of the American Philosophical Association* 60: 441–58.

Dennett, Daniel C. (1987), "Error, evolution and intentionality," in *The Intentional Stance* (Cambridge, Mass.: MIT Press): 287–322.

Dennett, Daniel C. (1991), *Consciousness Explained* (New York: Little, Brown).

Dennett, Daniel C. (2001), "Surprise, surprise (commentary on O'Regan and Noë)," *Behavioral and Brain Sciences* 24: 5.

Dennett, Daniel C. (2002), "How could I be wrong? How wrong could I be?," *Journal of Consciousness Studies* 9: 13–16.

Dretske, Fred (1995), *Naturalizing the Mind* (Cambridge, Mass.: MIT Press).

Dreyfus, Hubert L. (1999), *What Computers Still Can't Do: A Critique of Artificial Reason* (Cambridge, Mass.: MIT Press). First published in 1972.

Durgin, Frank H., Tripathy, Srimant P., and Levi, Dennis M. (1995), "On the filling in of the visual blind spot: some rules of thumb," *Perception* 24: 827–40.

Hurley, Susan (1998), *Consciousness in Action* (Cambridge, Mass.: Harvard University Press).

Hurley, Susan and Noë, Alva (2003), "Neural plasticity and consciousness," *Biology and Philosophy* 18: 131–68.

Kelly, Sean (2001), "The non-conceptual content of perceptual experience: situation-dependence and fineness of grain," *Philosophy and Phenomenological Research* 62: 601–8.

Koch, Christof (2004), *The Quest for Consciousness* (Colorado: Roberts & Company Publishers).

Koenderink, Jan J. (1984), "The internal representation of solid shape and visual exploration," in Lothar Spillmann and Bill R. Wooten (eds), *Sensory Experience, Adaptation, and Perception. Festschrift for Ivo Kohler* (Hillsdale, NJ: Lawrence Erlbaum): 123–42.

Levin, Daniel T., Simons, Daniel J., Angelone, Bonnie L., and Chabris, Christopher F. (2002), "Memory for centrally attended changing objects in an incidental real-world change detection paradigm," *British Journal of Psychology* 93: 289–302.

Merleau-Ponty, Maurice (1962), *The Phenomenology of Perception*, trans. by Colin Smith (London: Routledge); French original published in 1945.

Minsky, Marvin (1985), *The Society of Mind* (New York: Simon & Schuster).

Mitroff, Stephen R., Simons, Daniel J., and Levin, Daniel T. (2004), "Nothing compares 2 views: change blindness can result from failures to compare retained information," *Perception and Psychophysics* 66, (8): 1268–281.

Noë, Alva (2002a), "Is the visual world a grand illusion?," *Journal of Consciousness Studies* 9:5/6: 1–12.

Noë, Alva (2002b), *Is the Visual World a Grand Illusion?* (Thorverton: Imprint Academic).

Noë, Alva (2004), *Action in Perception.* (Cambridge, Mass.: MIT Press).

Noë, Alva, Pessoa, Luiz, and Thompson, Evan (2000), "Beyond the grand illusion: what change blindness really teaches us about vision," *Visual Cognition* 7: 93–106.

O'Regan, J. Kevin (1992), "Solving the real mysteries of visual perception: the world as an outside memory," *Canadian Journal of Psychology* 46: 461–88.

O'Regan, J. Kevin (in press), "Change blindness," in *Encyclopedia of Cognitive Science* (Nature Publishing Group).

O'Regan, J. Kevin and Noë, Alva (2001), "A sensorimotor approach to vision and visual consciousness," *Behavioral and Brain Sciences* 24: 883–975.

Palmer, Stephen E. (1999), *Vision Science: From Photons to Phenomenology* (Cambridge, Mass.: MIT Press).

Peacocke, Christopher (1983), *Sense and Content* (Oxford: Oxford University Press).

Pessoa, Luiz, Thompson, Evan, and Noë, Alva (1998), "Finding out about filling in: a guide to perceptual completion for visual science and the philosophy of perception," *Behavioral and Brain Sciences* 21: 723–802.

Pylyshyn, Zenon W. (1994), "Some primitive mechanisms of spatial attention," *Cognition* 50: 363–84.

Ramachanran, Vilayanur S. and Gregory, Richard L. (1991), "Perceptual filling in of artificially induced scotomas in human vision," *Nature* 350: 699–702.

Rowlands, Mark (2002), "Two dogmas of consciousness," *Journal of Consciousness Studies* 9: 158–80.

Simons, Daniel J. (2000), "Current approaches to change blindness," *Visual Cognition* 7: 1–15.

Simons, Daniel J. and Levin, Daniel T. (1997), "Change blindness," *Trends in Cognitive Science* 1: 261–7

Simons, Daniel J., Chabris, Christopher F., Schnur, Tatiana T., and Levin, Daniel T. (2002), "Evidence for preserved representations in change blindness," *Consciousness and Cognition* 11: 78–97.

Sperling, George (1960), "The information available in brief visual presentations," *Psychological Monographs* 74.

Strawson, Peter F. (1979), "Perception and its objects," in G. F. MacDonald (ed.), *Perception and Identity: Essays Presented to A. J. Ayer with His Replies* (Ithaca, NY: Cornell University Press): reprinted in A. Noë and E. Thompson (eds), *Vision and Mind: Selected Readings in the Philosophy of Perception* (Cambridge, Mass.: MIT Press).

Wilson, Robert A. (1997), *Cartesian Psychology and Physical Minds: Individualism and the Science of the Mind* (Cambridge: Cambridge University Press).

Wollheim, Richard (1980), *Art and Its Objects: With Six Supplementary Essays*, 2nd edn (Cambridge and New York: Cambridge University Press); *Art and Its Objects* first published in 1968 (New York: Harper & Row).

12

Beyond Appearances: The Content of Sensation and Perception

Jesse J. Prinz

There seems to be a large gulf between percepts and concepts. In particular, concepts seem to be capable of representing things that percepts cannot. We can conceive of things that would be impossible to perceive. (The converse may also seem true, but I will leave that to one side.) In one respect, this is trivially right. We can conceive of things that we cannot encounter, such as unicorns. We cannot literally perceive unicorns, even if we occasionally "see" them in our dreams and hallucinations. To avoid triviality, I want to focus on things that we can actually encounter. We perceive poodles, perfumes, pinpricks, and pounding drums. These are concrete things; they are closely wedded to appearances. But we also encounter things that are abstract. We encounter uncles and instances of injustice. These things have no characteristic looks. Percepts, it is said, cannot represent abstract things. Call this claim the Imperceptibility Thesis. I think the Imperceptibility Thesis is false. Perception is not restricted to the concrete. We can perceive abstract entities.

This may sound like an obvious claim. We often use perceptual terms widely to say things such as: "I perceive a lack of agreement" or "I see where you are going with that argument." But, by most accounts, these uses of perceptual terms are either metaphorical or, at any rate, different from the use of perceptual terms in cases that more directly involve the sense modalities: "I perceive distant rumbling"; "I see a red light over there." The abstract cases are interpreted as involving the sense modalities, if only indirectly. The presumption is that we must first pick up something with our senses and then judge that there is, say, a lack of agreement. Moreover, the abstract cases are presumed to require a level of mental representation that is not perceptual in format. I want to deny all of this. Perceiving abstracta can be just like perceiving concreta.

Those willing to abandon the Imperceptibility Thesis might dig in their heels elsewhere. If there is no semantic gulf between percepts and concepts, there

I am deeply indebted to two anonymous referees and, especially, Tamar Gendler. This paper benefited tremendously from their detailed comments and excellent advice.

might be a gulf between *sensations* and concepts. As I will use the term, a sensation is a state in a perceptual stream that is phenomenally conscious. On the face of it, sensations are even more restricted than percepts. We can perceive concrete entities, because they are closely wedded to appearances, but, intuitively, we can sense only appearances themselves. We can sense poodly appearances, but sensing a poodle, where that means having a phenomenal experience of the property of being a poodle, seems impossible. There are no poodle qualia. Sense-data theorists traditionally made claims like this, and, as we will see below, an alluring argument can be marshaled in support. If we cannot sense concrete entities, sensing abstract entities is entirely out of the question. Sensations, it is said, cannot represent anything abstract. Call this claim the Insensibility Thesis. I think the thesis is false.

Most people agree that we can conceive of abstract things, but many deny that we can perceive and sense abstract things. Or, more accurately, they assume that percepts and sensations cannot have abstract contents. If we can be said to perceive and sense abstract things, it is only indirectly by combining percepts or sensations with concepts. On this approach, percepts and concepts do not represent abstract things, but perceivings and sensings can represent abstract things when combined with concepts, which are presumed to be something other than percepts and sensations. In other words, some authors allow that we can perceive something or sense something *as* falling under an abstract concept, where that means we produce a complex mental state that has both a percept or a sensation and a concept. Importantly, the semantic heavy lifting is done by the concept. Percepts and sensations do not themselves represent abstracta in these cases. Those who think that we can sense and perceive abstracta indirectly still hold the Imperceptability and Insensibility Thesis. The point might be made by saying that such authors think we cannot perceive or sense abstracta directly. Percepts and sensations cannot represent abstracta themselves.

In this chapter, I will present evidence against the Imperceptibility Thesis and the Insensibility Thesis. That evidence is partially empirical. We are led astray by pretheoretical intuitions about the semantic properties of the representations available to our senses. Research on the nature of concepts and their interactions with sensory processes reveals a different picture. We can, in principle—if not always in practice—sense and perceive just about anything that we can conceive.

1   WHAT CAN WE PERCEIVE?

1.1   Seeing Things

To navigate through these issues, we need to clarify some terminology. First of all, we need a working definition of perception. I will treat "perceiving" as a success term. Uses in the case of hallucinations and dreams are parasitic on successful seeing. On the success interpretation, an organism O *perceives* something X only if:

(i) X impinges on O's sensory transducers;
(ii) O forms a corresponding perceptual representation as a result;
(iii) that representation is matched against stored representations that represent X.

This requires a few more definitions. A *sensory transducer* is a psychophysical mechanism that converts physical magnitudes into mental states or mental representations. Something *impinges* on a sensory transducer on an occasion if its instantiation causes transduction in that transducer on that occasion (where causation can be cashed out in counterfactual terms). A *perceptual representation* is a representation in a dedicated input system. A *dedicated input system* is an information-processing system that takes inputs from sensory transducers (and possibly elsewhere), and forms representations that have the function of representing inputs from those transducers. Dedicated input systems typically use proprietary codes; they use representations that have some syntactic and semantic properties not found in other input systems. As should be clear this definition applies only to uses of the word "perception" that involve these senses. Intellectual uses ("Descartes was very perceptive") don't count. The third condition in my definition refers to matching. Here, some caveats are necessary. Matching does not necessarily involve comparing two token representations. As I am using the term, matching can also occur when an input *triggers* a stored representation. The key idea is that perceiving involves recognition.

Some might take issue with the recognition requirement. Dretske (1969) argues that we can perceive something without recognizing it. He calls this non-epistemic perceiving. We can say, "I must have seen you at the market, but I didn't recognize you." On my definition, this is not a case of perceiving, though I would allow that it is a case of seeing. I have the conceptual intuition that seeing can be non-epistemic, but perceiving can't. Nothing will ride on this. Dretske's notion of non-epistemic perceiving can be captured by dropping condition (iii).

That does not mean that my definition is equivalent to what Dretske calls epistemic perceiving. I aim for something that is stronger than Dretske's non-epistemic perception, but weaker than his notion of epistemic perception. I think we need something in between. There are two reasons for this diagnosis.

First, Dretske may blur an important distinction that can be found in the pages of Wittgenstein (1953). Wittgenstein contrasts ordinary cases of seeing with "seeing-as." The latter phrase is colloquially reserved for cases where we need to apply a special skill or interpretive act. We can see a cloud as a warthog, but it sounds odd to say I see this fork *as* a fork. When I see the fork, I just recognize it. One might call this recognitional seeing. Recognitional seeing is not non-epistemic. A tarantula can see forks in a non-epistemic sense, but a tarantula cannot see a fork in the way we can, because tarantulas cannot (I presume) recognize forks. Recognitional seeing requires the capacity to represent forks as such. But recognitional seeing differs from seeing-as in at least three respects. First, seeing-as involves two stages. Initially an object is recognized, and then it is interpreted in a new way. A duck is re-construed as a rabbit. Second, recognition need not involve the application of a concept. Concepts are representations that can be actively tokened by an organism (Prinz, 2002). In recognition, we often use representations that can only be tokened passively. I can recognize certain things that I cannot bring readily to mind in imagination or reflection. Recognition outstrips conceptualization. Seeing-as usually doesn't. To re-construe a perceived object, we typically deploy concepts (though perhaps not always—swapping figure and ground, for example, can be done without concepts). Third, recognitional seeing is always factive, and seeing-as is often not. When we see a cloud as a warthog, there is no avian swine. Dretske does not use "epistemic seeing" to subsume non-factive cases, but neither does he distinguish epistemic seeing from seeing as. I want to make it explicit that perceiving, in the sense outlined above, is not equivalent to seeing-as.

There is a second contrast that I want to draw between recognitional seeing and epistemic seeing in Dretske's sense. Dretske (1981) argues that epistemic seeing involves a process of digitalization. Information that is nested at one stage of sensory processing becomes un-nested. In the fork example, this might work out as follows: at some stage in visual processing, representations carry the information that a fork is present, by carrying information about other features, which are natural signs for the property of being a fork. In particular, we represent forkhood via forky appearances. At this stage of processing, one cannot perceive a fork as such. One cannot have forkhood as the object of perception. To perceive forks epistemically, we need to digitalize. We need to extract forkhood from forky appearances through a further stage of processing that abstracts away from the appearances and represents forkhood. A digitalized representation of forkhood does not represent forkhood in a way that depends on carrying information about forky appearances. For example, it might be a representation that is triggered by an open-ended range of forky appearances. If a representation is triggered by an open-ended range, it cannot represent any one of those appearances because it will not carry the information that any one of those appearances has been instantiated. Such a representation represents forkhood as such.

I reject this account of epistemic seeing. It entails that we can epistemically see forks only if we have representations that abstract away from forky appearances. This strikes me as terribly implausible. I think we can visually recognize forks, and hence epistemically see them, by means of fork images: representations that encode features of forky appearances. Dretske does not offer a good way of accommodating this possibility. I will suggest a way below. My proposal is compatible with Dretske's approach to intentionality, but it differs from the digitalization theory of epistemic seeing. That is why I prefer to talk about recognitional seeing (which is, in my terminology, just visually perceiving).

The first condition in my definition of perception makes it clear why we can perceive only those things that we encounter. In order for something to impinge on the senses, it needs to be present to do the impinging. But what exactly does presence require? As a first pass, we can say something is present if it is here now. This needs to be qualified. Consider very distant objects, such as stars. What could "here and now" mean such that stars count as being here now? It is tempting to say that something counts as "being here now" just in case it is accessible to our senses here now. This, of course, is circular if we are hoping to define accessibility in terms of presence. We can do a little better, however, if we go back to the idea of impingement. If impingement is a causal notion, then we can say that "being here" means being instantiated within sufficient spatio-temporal proximity to have causal impact on sensory transducers. I will eventually argue that this allows for the perception of abstract things.

To make sense of this claim, we will need a characterization of abstractness. Abstract is the opposite of concrete, or at least the opposing pole on a spectrum. These terms are tricky, however, because they are used differently by philosophers and psychologists. In saying that we can perceive anything that we can conceive, I must argue that we can perceive abstracta in both the psychological and philosophical sense, assuming such things (a) exist and (b) are conceivable. I will sometimes use the shorthand "philosophically abstract" and "psychologically abstract" to capture the contrast. In much of the discussion, I won't bother with modifiers because context can disambiguate or because both kinds of abstractness are relevant.

In psychology, the concrete/abstract contrast is sometimes defined with reference to perceptibility; concrete things are perceivable and abstract things are not. Such definitions clearly won't do for this inquiry, because I think abstract things are perceivable. But I think we can capture the basic idea behind the psychologists' definition. Abstract and concrete can be *indirectly* defined in terms of perceptibility.

It all begins with appearances. Appearances must be defined relative to the senses. They are powers that external things have to cause representations in our dedicated input systems. Two things have the same appearance (from some vantage point) if they cause perceptual representations that are intrinsically type-identical (from that vantage point). Two things have similar appearances if the intrinsic properties of the perceptual representations they cause are similar. By "intrinsic properties," I am thinking of the kinds of properties that we would mention in describing perceptual representations at a psychological- or personal-level of description—properties such as shapes or colors. By analogy, think of the visual information captured on the celluloid of a film (perhaps a 3D film). When we watch a film, we assign meaning to the images that pass before our eyes, but the film itself just captures shapes, colors, and movements. Appearances are like that. For simplicity, I will be assuming here that perceptual representations are like mental pictures. Abstractness and concreteness can be defined relative to appearances. A thing is concrete to the extent that it would appear alike across different encounters when it impinges on the same sensory transducers under the same viewing conditions. A thing is abstract to the extent that it appears different across encounters. This characterization works for objects, events, and properties (though I will not talk about events). An object is concrete to the extent that it appears alike across encounters with it. A property is concrete to the extent that it appears alike across encounters with its instantiations. Properties have their appearances via their instantiations. The property of being a flounder is relatively concrete; the property of being a fish is less so; and the property of being a sea creature is even less concrete than that.

Here I must step back from the main thread of discussion to pursue a metaphysical aside. I want to clarify how the psychological abstract/concrete distinction relates to the homophonic metaphysical distinction, and I want to show that the Imperceptability Thesis seems plausible whether or not one believes in universals. To philosophically trained ears, talk of concrete properties sounds odd. Philosophers agree that concrete entities can exist in space and time, but they are divided as to whether properties can exist in space and time. Trope theorists say they can, and universalists typically say they cannot. Talk of "concrete properties" is fine for trope theorists (though they often use the term "abstract particulars"). For trope theorists, all properties are concrete in the philosophical sense. Notice, however, that this does not make all properties concrete in the psychological sense. For there is no guarantee, on trope theory, that two tokens of the "same" property will appear alike. Talking about two tokens of the same property is shorthand for talking about two tropes that bear a certain equivalence relation. Trope theorists talk about "exactly resembling tropes," but "resemblance" here must not be understood in terms of appearance. Trope resemblance is usually taken to be a primitive relation, not analyzable in perceptual terms.

Trope theorists are often skeptical about the existence of philosophical abstracta. For them, there is no special puzzle about perceiving properties, because all properties are instantiated instances. But that does not mean trope theorists deny the Imperceptibility Thesis. Trope theory does not entail that we can perceive things that are abstract in the psychological sense. On trope theory, ordinary property terms refer to equivalence classes of tropes, rather than individual tropes. Our concepts can represent these equivalence classes, but what about our perceptions? There is nothing in trope theory to guarantee that we can perceive equivalence classes of tropes. Equivalence classes of tropes are often psychologically abstract (their members have different appearances). It is far from obvious whether such entities are perceivable. Thus, trope theorists may be strongly inclined to accept the Imperceptability Thesis.

Now consider universalists. Unlike trope theorists, they deny the existence of metaphysically concrete properties, because they think properties are abstracta in the philosophical sense. But they can accept concrete properties in a psychological sense. When I use the phrase "concrete properties" this can be translated into metaphysically benign talk by interpreting it as "properties whose *instantiations* are psychologically concrete." Universalism seems to entail that we can perceive instantiations of properties, not the properties themselves. If properties are philosophically abstract, then they do not exist in space and time. If that is the case, they don't seem to be in a position to impinge on our senses. Thus, like trope theorists, universalists may be strongly inclined to accept the Imperceptibility Thesis. The Imperceptibility Thesis does not hinge on a particular theory of properties.

That ends my metaphysical aside. And now back to our main question: what is perceivable? The most intuitive answer is that we can perceive appearances and we can perceive objects that are philosophically concrete, and when we do so, we do it by recognizing psychologically concrete properties. As properties get less concrete, they become less perceivable. Psychologically abstract properties, which are poorly correlated with appearances, cannot be perceived. Philosophical abstracta cannot be perceived either, because they do not come into physical contact with the senses. This, I think, captures folk intuitions about perceptibility. If questions about what we perceive were best answered by folk intuitions, the Imperceptibility Thesis would be confirmed. We can undoubtedly *conceive* of properties that are very abstract in both philosophical and psychological senses, but such properties cannot be perceived. If we encounter an event that instantiates injustice or a sentence that has the property of being true, we cannot perceive these properties. Injustice and truth can be encountered, but, intuition proclaims, they are imperceptible. This is the intuition I want to reject.

First, one qualification is required. Folk psychology allows us to say, "He could see the injustice of her actions," or "I can see that you are right." This might be taken as evidence for widespread folk acceptance of the thesis that I will be defending. I don't think that is the right interpretation. In the introduction, I suggested that such locutions exploit a metaphorical or extended use of perceptual vocabulary. Notice that it sounds a little weird to say, "I *literally* saw the injustice in her actions," or "I could see the injustice, despite the fleck of dirt in my eye." Blind people can see abstract things, in this extended sense. Tiresias could see that Oedipus was doomed. There is no entailment from "I see P" to "I see." In the cases such as "seeing injustice," the folk will resist the inference emphatically. After all, injustice doesn't look like anything. I will part company with the folk. I think we can see abstract things in a literal way— i.e., via the senses.

1.2   Abstract Images

The Imperceptibility Thesis says that we cannot see any of the abstract properties that we encounter. Its denial is the thesis that we can perceive some abstract things. I want to go even farther and argue that virtually no abstract property is, in principle, imperceptible. In making this case, I will focus on visual perception, although it will be easy to extrapolate from my examples how abstract perception could arise in other modalities.

To make the case for seeing abstracta, I will begin with a general theory of how perceptual representations represent. By default, we should assume that perceptual representations represent in the same way that other kinds of mental representations represent. If we have a good theory of representation, then the question about perceptual content becomes an empirical question. We need not worry about mongering intuitions or relying on introspection.

This is not the place to *defend* a theory of mental representation, but fortunately many defenses can be found in the literature. The kind of theory that I favor derives from Dretske's (1986) teleological/informational intentionality. I have defended a version of Dretske's approach against standard objections elsewhere, and I have applied it to concepts and to emotions (Prinz, 2000b; 2002; 2004). Roughly, the idea is that mental representations represent that which they have the function of detecting. Put a bit differently, a mental representation represents that which it is set up to be set off by. Two conditions are implied here. First, there is an informational condition: the representational content of a representation must be something that is capable of setting off that representation. If a mental representation M represents a content C, then instances of C have the power to cause tokens of M when they are encountered. This causal link must be reliable. In his initial formulations, Dretske (1981) captured the idea of reliability by supposing that, within certain boundary conditions, the probability of C given a tokening of M is equal to 1. This is too strong a requirement, and it saddles Dretske with the extra burden of specifying what those boundary conditions are. One can get by with the simpler claim that Cs have the power to cause Ms.

The second condition in Dretske's psychosemantics is teleological: a representation must be *set up* for the purpose of being set off by that which represents. Talk about purposes can be cashed out historically. Roughly, the idea is that a representation type M came to exist by virtue of being set off by an instance or instances of its content. Ms would not exist were it not for prior encounters with Cs. Those encounters can occur in the learning history of a particular representing organism or (with innate representations) in that organism's ancestral past. Dretske's first condition ensures that my *water* concept will refer to a substance that is typically clear and tasteless, for those are the substances that set off *water* tokens. Dretske's second condition selects out the specific clear, tasteless, liquids, that played a role in the acquisition of my *water* concept, namely H_2O.

I think Dretske's theory of intentionality must be supplemented with one more condition. Content is further constrained by what I have called semantic markers, following Putnam (Putnam, 1975; Prinz, 2002). As I use the term, a semantic marker is not a kind of representation, as the term may imply, but a way of using a representation. Different patterns of use determine what general ontological category a representation represents. For example, semantic markers determine whether a representation represents an individual or a natural kind. If there were no semantic markers, it might be indeterminate whether my water concept referred to H_2O in general or to the specific sample of H_2O that was ostended when I first learned the concept. Semantic markers are also used to determine whether a representation represents distal or proximal stimuli, and they may play a role in coping with certain forms of Quinean indeterminacy. Patterns of use may include inferential roles that distinguish between interpretations that would be equally viable if content were determined entirely by stimulus detection and causal history. I mention this add-on to Dretske's theory for completeness. It will not play much of a role in the discussion below.

The Dretskean approach to intentionality is controversial, but it is widely regarded as one of the best theories under contention. Other approaches to intentionality are compatible with the conclusions that I will draw about perception, but I will assume that Dretske's theory is essentially correct. Given that assumption, we can return to the question of perceptual representation. The question about what perceptual representations represent can now be traded in for the question of what those representations are set up to be set off by. This is an empirical question. It requires investigating, for any given perceptual representation, what sets it off and how it came into being. As an example, take a population of cells in a particular region of primary visual cortex. We can measure what sets these off by determining what kinds of stimuli are present when they fire. Perhaps they are responsive to lines at a particular angle of orientation. To determine how these cells came to be responsive to lines of that kind, we must engage in some historical guesswork. We can surmise that they came to have their current response profile in virtue of events in the organism's lifespan or in virtue of events in the organisms evolutionary past (or, most plausibly, some combination of these). If we conclude that these cells came to detect angles by virtue of having been set off by angles by the past, then we conclude that they are angle representations. Other cells in the visual system are responsive to colors, directions of motion, depth, and so on.

Now consider a more complex case. There are cells in higher visual areas that seem to be responsive to specific kinds of objects, rather than colors or shapes. For example, it is known that monkeys have cells in the fusiform gyrus that are especially responsive to faces (e.g., Desimone, 1991; for humans, see Kanwisher et al., 1997). It is not unreasonable to think that they are set up for this purpose, given the importance of faces for social creatures. It is also known that the visual stream is highly plastic. An encounter with a novel object can cause cells in the visual system to become responsive to that object in the future. For example, if you show a monkey a piece of wire bent in a peculiar pattern, cells in the inferotemporal portion of its visual stream will become detectors for that very pattern (Gauthier and Logothetis, 2000). It has been surmised that small populations of inferotemporal cells become detectors for individual objects, such as particular faces (Gross and Sargent, 1992). Kreiman et al. (2000) have found individual cells in human medial temporal cortex that respond to multiple images of the same person. They found, for example, a cell in one subject that was responsive to pictures of Bill Clinton. It is safe to assume that this cell was set up for the purpose of Clinton detection. It came to play that role through encounters with Clinton (or images of Clinton). (Things may be more complicated for cells that respond to Saddam Hussein, because he allegedly had a group of look-alikes standing in for him in public appearances.)

A cell that is responsive to Clinton's face may be interpreted as representing Clinton's face. Clinton's face is not merely an appearance. It varies across angles, expressions, and viewing conditions. Clinton's face is a concrete object, though; it is closely correlated with appearances. Note, moreover, that Clinton's face is highly correlated with Clinton, the person. A cell that reliably detects Clinton's face is, thereby, a Clinton detector. Cells that are involved in detecting *particular* faces may attain this function in virtue of the fact that they are good tools for detecting particular persons. The idea of being a good tool might be captured by downstream effects. Millikan (1989) explains the teleological contribution to content by appeal to "consumers," the systems that make use of representations. If used to coordinate responses towards a person, and not just a face, the cell that responds to Clinton's face may have the function of detecting Clinton. Such downstream effects may be one way of cashing out the idea of semantic markers. The Clinton face cell may, in virtue of its use, be marked as a person-representation. If so, this cell is a Clinton representation, and not just a Clinton-face representation.

Clinton, of course, is a relatively concrete object, so the existence of Clinton representations in the visual stream would not establish the possibility of seeing things that are abstract. But the Clinton example will help provide a strategy. Let's shift to a more abstract domain. Consider numerosity. When we perceive groups of objects we can perceptually determine whether there are, say, three objects or four. We share this ability with infants, nonhuman mammals, and birds (Dehaene, 1997). Groups of three vary significantly in their appearances, but the visual system is capable of tabulating quantity across a wide range of variation. Let us suppose, plausibly, that there are cells in the visual system that have the function of firing when we encounter groups of three. I think such cells represent the property of threeness or, at least, the property of being a three-item group. They are invariant across a wide range of concrete inputs, none of which are correlated well with their firing. Threeness has the highest degree of correlation. Moreover, these cells are used to keep track of quantity. They contribute to simple arithmetic, and, when we see a group of three strawberries, say, we know to reach and grasp three times.

Of course, this won't help with larger numbers. To represent exact quantities much larger than three, Deheane makes the obvious suggestion: we count. More specifically, Deheane says we use representations of number-words in our language systems. These representations are perceptual. They are representations of the sounds or symbols used in linguistic communication. To determine that there are, say, fifty-seven toothpicks on the table, we just shift attention from pick to pick, assigning each a label: one, two, three . . . By the time we get to the fifty-seventh toothpick, we form a visual image of it along with an auditory image of the word "fifty-seven." This is a perceptual state, and it is one that is set up to be set off by sets of fifty-seven items. We can thereby perceive sets with arbitrarily high cardinalities (though performance limitations will prevent us from going too far). By this method, we can perceive the difference between a chiliagon and a 999-sided figure. We need only count the sides!

The Dretskean approach to semantics can explain how we represent things that are abstract in the psychologists' sense. A representation can refer to things that do not appear alike if it is reliably caused by those things, despite the differences in their appearance. Specific populations of numerosity neurons represent threeness, because those neurons are best correlated with threeness, and not any particular group of three things.

This story about how we refer to psychologically abstract properties only delays the question about philosophical abstracta. That question is even more pressing. The philosopher will object that, though threeness may be correlated with cells firing, it cannot be causally responsible for their firing, because threeness doesn't exist in space and time. Only concrete instantiations of threeness can have causal efficacy. Thus, our cells can represent instantiations of threeness, but not threeness itself. One might reply by stipulating that representation does not require causation, but only correlation and function. But this won't help. If threeness exists always, then it is correlated with every mental representation that ever gets tokened. And, even if representation doesn't require causation, perception, as I have defined it, does. Fortunately, there is a solution.

Notice, first, that the problem of referring to properties has an analogue in the case of referring to concrete individuals. Strictly speaking, our mental representations of individuals (such as Clinton) are not correlated with the *existence* of Clinton. Clinton always exists (or at least he exists until he dies), so his existence is correlated with all my representation tokens. To get around this problem, we define reference in terms of *encounters*. My Clinton representation is tokened when I encounter him (or representations of him, in which case reference is one step removed). Above, I said that we encounter something if it becomes causally accessible to us. Now, it would be crazy to deny that properties are causally efficacious. For many philosophers, causal efficacy is a necessary condition for realism. If properties exist, they must pull their weight. One way to explain the causal efficacy of properties is by appeal to counterfactuals. *Very* roughly, we can say that a property P is causally efficacious in item O's bringing about effect E, if E would not have occurred if O had not instantiated P. Properties need instantiations to have an impact, but, once instantiated, they deserve causal credit. If we buy into this picture, there is no problem saying that we encounter properties. We come into causal contact with them (via their instantiations). So reference to properties can be characterized in the same way as reference to concrete individuals. (Fodor (1990) even argues that we only refer to properties, because he thinks that reference depends on laws, and laws are defined in terms of properties.) I conclude that perceptual representations can refer to abstract properties. We need to be able to say that properties are causally efficacious, and once we do that (by whatever theory of causation turns out to be correct), then we have the resources to attribute abstract contents to perceptual states.

The preceding story explains how a universalist can allow reference to abstract properties. The problem of abstract reference facing trope theory is different. I have been talking about abstractness in the philosophical sense. Trope theorists deny that such properties exist, so they need not worry about how something that isn't in space and time can have a causal impact on the world. Properties are tropes and tropes are present. But trope theorists face a related problem. They must explain how a concept could refer to an equivalence class of exactly resembling tropes. The members of an equivalence class are rarely compresent. If representation depends on detection relations, how can a representation refer to an equivalence class?

The question can be addressed by dissecting the notion of reliable causation. A representation that is caused by a particular trope will also be caused by exactly resembling tropes. Thus, there is a distributive sense in which such a representation is caused by the equivalence class of tropes, i.e., it is caused by the members of that class. Compare: pinpricks cause pain. Furthermore, a representation that is caused by all (or most) tropes in a class, is also better correlated with the class than with any individual member of the class. The class itself has no causal efficacy above and beyond the efficacy of its members, but, semantically, it is the class, and not the members that have the kind of causal correlation. When we talk about reliable causal relations between two things, we mean a relation that is causal and highly correlated. The relation between equivalence classes of tropes and tokenings of a mental representation satisfies both of these conditions. The class is causally related to the tokenings via its parts, and it is correlated with tokenings, when taken as a whole. The causation is distributive and the correlation is collective. If we interpret the Dretskean account so as to allow this, reference to trope classes will be secured.

I conclude that mental representations in our perceptual systems can refer to both philosophical and psychological abstracta. They can refer to properties whose instances don't look alike, and they can refer to those properties (and not just their instances) even if they are universals or equivalence classes of tropes. If defensible, this is a useful result. But, for my thesis, something stronger is required. I want to show that we can perceive *any* conceivable abstract thing that we can encounter. To defend this claim, it will help to consider another example of abstract perception.

Suppose you are teaching a class and you want to find out how many of your students are philosophy majors. Being a philosophy major is an abstract property. Philosophy majors do not look alike. So you tell your students to raise their hands if they are philosophy majors. I would contend that a visual representation of raised hand under these circumstances quite literally represents being a philosophy major. When we ask people to signal something through hand-raising, we effectively assign the perception of those hands a particular informational function. For a brief interval, the perception caused by raised hands reliably detects the property of being a philosophy major, and those perceptions are selected to serve that purpose. We can think of the perceptions as having a "passing function" assigned temporarily for a particular purpose.

This is a surprising result. I am not claiming merely that we can infer that there are philosophy majors by looking at raised hands. I am claiming that the perceptual state caused by raised hands represents the property of being a philosophy major. It represents that property, since that's what it is set up to be set off by. Folk intuitions allow only that we can perceive properties like this in an indirect way. It is hardly controversial to say that we can "perceive" abstract properties by first perceiving something else that indicates that the abstract property has been instantiated, and then representing the abstract property in a subsequent mental episode. On this model, seeing the property of being a philosophy major is very different than seeing red. I want to claim that there is no difference. Seeing red is a matter of having a visual state that represents red. Seeing the property of being a philosophy major is a matter of having a visual state that represents that property. By assigning transient meaning to our visual states, we can literally and directly see the property of being a philosophy major.

This case underscores the fact that percepts can come to represent abstract properties in at least two ways. The first way is illustrated by the numerosity example discussed above. In cases like that, perceptual systems *store* representations that detect abstract properties. We see threeness by matching a visual experience against a representation of threeness that is built into the visual system. Here, the "matching" that takes place between occurrent percept and stored percept does not require calling up a representation from somewhere outside of the visual system. A visual encounter with three objects triggers a representation of threeness by directly activating it in the visual stream. The hand-raising case works differently. There, we assign a meaning to perceptual states by matching it to an image that is called up from elsewhere. We call up an image of raised arms, and that image is *transiently* linked to our beliefs about what raised arms indicate in this context. Both kinds of examples present a challenge to the Imperceptibility Thesis. They show that we can represent abstract properties in perception. A fan of the Imperceptibility Thesis might concede the point, but deny its generality. The case of numerosity perception may be very unusual, and the hand-raising case is a bit contrived. We still need a more general argument for the perceptibility of abstract things.

I think such an argument is available and, indeed, it falls out of the semantic theory that I just endorsed. If Dretskean semantic theories are right, then everything that we can represent is represented using Dretskean detectors or combinations thereof. Let's consider abstract concepts, such as *injustice* or *truth*. If these things are to represent in a Dretskean manner then they must be either reliable detectors for those abstract properties, or combinations of reliable detectors. Detection is a relationship between mind and world. In order for an item in the mind to become a detector for something out there, the thing out there must cause that item to occur. That causal relation must be mediated by the senses. The senses are the only avenue by which things out there can cause states in here. So, if Dretske is right about reference, then referring concepts must be, at the very least, built up from representations that get correlated with the world through perceptual representations. Those representations may be extremely complex. They may be highly variable. They may include representations of words, sentences, or other public symbols. But, no matter what, they must be perceptual. Every referring concept, no matter how abstract, must be linked to a collection of perceptual representations that play an indispensable role in establishing reference. This is going to be the key point in debunking the Imperceptibility Thesis.

Consider some examples. Suppose you want to know whether a particular statement is true. Someone says, "It is snowing outside." You want to see if she is being honest with you, so you have a look at the window, and you see snow. When you see that snow, it confirms that it is snowing outside, and it also confirms that the sentence "It is snowing outside" is true. You can be said to *perceive* the truth of that sentence insofar as you used your concept of truth to establish a way of recognizing truth through perception.

Here's another example: it is possible to perceive an uncle, but, intuitively, it is not possible to perceive the property of being an uncle. That property seems too abstract. But this intuition is a bit hasty. If you go to a family gathering and want to determine whether there are any uncles present, you can simply search for people you know to be uncles. If you recognize your own uncle nestled on the sofa while searching for uncles, your perception of him qualifies as a perception of unclehood. It is not just a perception of an instance of unclehood, but, arguably, a perception of unclehood itself since you have assigned perceptions of uncles the transient meaning of unclehood. The perceptual representation caused by seeing your uncle has the function of detecting that abstract property on this occasion.

Now consider moral concepts. I think we often apply concepts such as *good* and *bad* by paying attention to our emotions. If you experience guilt after doing something, your perception of the guilt represents that you have done something bad. It represents that moral fact, because guilt is set up to be set off by bad behavior (Prinz, forthcoming). This kind of account does reasonably well for thin moral concepts, in Williams's (1985) sense, but it is less plausible for more sophisticated moral concepts, such as *injustice*. It is less plausible that any particular emotion reliably indicates the presence of injustice. Indignation may be designed to register injustice, but to know that you are indignant and not merely angry, you need to know something about the factors that triggered that emotional response. Let's consider how one might recognize injustice without relying on telltale emotions. Instances of injustice are events of various kinds. Suppose you read in the paper that a federal court has upheld a decision to allow a corporation to maintain discriminatory hiring practices. These are just words on a page, but as you read them you engage in a series of inferences, mediated in large part by language. "That's unjust!" you conclude. The concept you are expressing manages to refer to the property of injustice, whatever that is, precisely because it is causally responsive to situations of this kind. There are events in the world, such as bad court decision, that are unjust. These events are often encountered indirectly through linguistic symbols. Through linguistic inference, we can derive the conclusion that these events each involve an authority-sanctioned unequal distribution of costs or benefits to equally deserving individuals or groups. But a token instance of the concept of injustice need not be comprised of that complex description, and the recognition of injustice need not involve a complex linguistic inference. Recognition requires only that we have some mental representation, *of any kind*, that has been set up to be set off by inequitable distributions. Suppose that we infer, through linguistic inference, that a particular event would be unjust if it were ever to occur. When that event subsequently does occur, we can represent it as unjust without going through all of the inferential steps. Imagine that you have been following the court battle between a corporation and those against whom the corporation has discriminated, and you have come to the conclusion that the jury would be acting unjustly if they were to favor the corporation. Imagine, further, that you are in the courtroom when the judge reports the jury's decision. When you hear the words "not guilty," your representation of those words in this context carries the information that an injustice has occurred. Here, I would contend, you are literally perceiving injustice. You are perceiving injustice because you have assigned a passing function to the words "not guilty." Those words are, at this moment, a tool for detecting injustice. Just as we can perceive a philosophy major by seeing a hand, we can perceive injustice by hearing a couple of words.

These examples can be used to illustrate the problem with Dretske's (1981) theory of digitalization. In that earlier work, Dretske argued that you can epistemically represent a property in perception only by forming a representation that carries information about that property without carrying information about other properties in which that property is nested. In other words, if A carries information about B (but not conversely), a representation of A is not thereby a representation of B. To represent B, one needs a representation that abstracts away from A. One can represent forkhood only by abstracting away from forky appearances. The examples that I have been offering do not depend on an abstraction process of this kind. Consider uncles again. When you use a mental image of your uncle to determine whether there are any uncles in the room, you do not abstract away from his appearance. Your uncle image continues to carry information about your uncle's appearance. However, for that moment, it serves as a representation of the property of being an uncle by virtue of the function it has been assigned. Dretske's (1986) teleological theory of content can be played against his earlier proposal by showing how we can bypass the need for digitalization.

The present proposal bypasses the need for digitalization in a second way. Dretske (1981) implies that digitalization is a *stage* in information processing: we first represent appearances using one representation, and then go beyond appearances using another. There is one representation of uncle-like appearances, and then an abstract representation registering the presence of uncles. I think these two stages can be collapsed. The representation of unclehood is token identical to the representation of uncle appearances. We perceive the abstract property *by means of* a perceptual representation of a concrete particular.

This alternative to the digitalization story has an important implication. There is a sense in which everyone might agree that we can perceive abstract entities. Everyone might agree that we can use appearances and concrete objects as evidence to confirm that an abstract property has been instantiated. I can see that Barbara is a philosophy major because she raised her hand. This kind of talk is commonplace, and, if interpreted in a certain way, it is uncontroversial. I see that Barbara is a philosophy major by virtue of the fact that she raised her hand. I see abstractions by virtue of their concrete signs. The use of the phrase "by virtue of" renders the "seeing" indirect. I don't literally see that Barbara is a philosophy major, if that means I directly experience that through vision. Rather, I see something else (her hand) which allows me to conclude that she is a philosophy major. This modest suggestion is not the one that I am defending. I am not suggesting that we *indirectly* perceive abstract things *by virtue of* directly perceiving concrete things. Rather, I am suggesting that we *directly* perceive abstract things *by means of* directly perceiving concrete things. The perception of abstract things is direct, because it does not require that we perceive something else in advance. And it is perception "by means of" the concrete things, because our images of concrete things *constitute* our perceptions of abstract things; they are not merely instrumental causes of those perceptions. Thus, we literally perceive unclehood and the property of being a philosophy major. This is a controversial claim, but I think it is true.

The controversial claim also generalizes. Every concept that refers by reliable detection can be triggered by a perceptually mediated encounter with the world. The perceptual representations that cause a concept to be tokened on such an encounter *could* be set up as passing representations of the property designated by that concept. I would actually take this one step further. I believe that concepts *just are* stored records of perceptual states. Once we adopt the view that concepts refer by reliable detection and recognize that detection is perceptually mediated, we must conclude that every concept for which this story is true is associated with a collection of perceptual representations that play this mediating role. Those representations can be said to constitute a mental file. Elsewhere, I have argued that we should define concepts in terms of mental files of this kind (Prinz, 2002). On any given occasion when a concept is tokened, it will be mentally represented using a representation drawn up from a particular file, i.e., the file that establishes a reliable relation with the property represented by that concept. Those representations will vary from occasion to occasion as context demands. Since these files comprise nothing but stored perceptual representations, every token of a concept will itself be a stored perceptual representation. Concepts that do not refer by reliable detection are built up from those that do. If this theory is right, then all concepts are stored records of percepts or combinations of stored percepts (where "percept" is shorthand for perceptual representation). This is not an original proposal. It is a redressing of the theory of concepts defended by Locke and Hume.

This is not the place for a defense of concept empiricism. I want only to trace out an important implication. If empiricism is true, then all our referring concepts, no matter how abstract, are built up from stored percepts. For any concept built up from stored percepts, there should be some condition under which those percepts could be matched with percepts caused by an encounter with objects or events in the world. When such a match takes place, we can be said to perceive the property represented by the percepts used to achieve the match. Thus, if empiricism is true, we should be able, in principle, to perceive the properties represented by any referring concept, no matter how abstract, provided those properties can be encountered. This means that the Imperceptibility Theory is deeply mistaken. Seeing is not restricted to the concrete.

One doesn't need to be an empiricist to accept this conclusion. The crucial premise is that abstract concepts can be associated with perceptual representations, and, indeed, that they must be in order to secure reference to properties in the world. Concepts themselves do not need to be identified with percepts; they need only be associated with percepts. If the non-empiricist accepts this, then there is only one more premise needed to secure abstract perceiving. If a percept that is associated with an abstract concept is applied in perceptual recognition, it imparts the meaning of the concept with which it is associated. In other words, when we recognize things by using stored percepts that we have previously associated with a concept (permanently or in passing), those percepts represent whatever the associated concept represents. If representation is determined by detection and function, this assumption is very plausible. Percepts that are associated with concepts have the function of detecting whatever the associated concept detects. Anyone tempted by this approach to psychosemantics should be comfortable with the idea of abstract perception.

This story is not just Humean; it is Kantian. Kant tells us that concepts without percepts are empty. He also tells us that concepts are rules for constructing perceptual representations, and that, in imagination, we bring concepts to bear on perceptual episodes (a theory of imagination that he shared with Descartes). Any theory that allows abstract concepts to bear on perception via the deployment of perceptual representations has the resources to debunk the Imperceptibility Thesis. Empiricist theories make this possibility especially obvious, but empiricists are not alone.

2 WHAT CAN WE SENSE?

2.1 The Realm of the Senses

The claim that we can *perceive* abstract properties does not entail that we can *sense* abstract properties. Perceiving and sensing are not the same thing. Sensing occurs when something that impinges on our sense organs causes a sensation. I will define a "sensation" as a representation in a dedicated input system that is consciously experienced. By "conscious," I mean phenomenally conscious or having qualitative character.

It is sometimes presumed that sensations are not representational. Traditional sense-data theories, for example, propose a level of perceptual processing that is qualitative, but uninterpreted. Perception is the process of assigning meaning to sense-data. I think this picture is implausible. If representation amounts to functional detection, then representation goes all the way down. The earliest stages in sensory processing are involved in detecting information. Sensations carry information, and they have the function of doing so. But what sort of information do they carry? What do our sensations represent?

Intuitively, sensations are representationally impoverished in comparison with perceptions. It seems perfectly natural to say that we represent concrete objects in perception. It is not very controversial to say that we perceive tigers, tables, and typewriters—as such. It seems less plausible to say that we sense these things. If we restrict sensation to those aspects of perception that have phenomenal character, then it is natural to conclude that we cannot represent anything that makes no phenomenal difference. Sensing a real tiger and a Hollywood prop tiger can be qualitatively alike. The content of those sensations must, therefore, be alike as well. And, conversely, if two sensations are phenomenally different, they must have different content. A sitting tiger looks different from a prancing tiger, and that difference in looks is a difference in our sensations. Such sensations must differ in content. Using the terminology from above, it seems that sensations represent appearances. They represent colors, shapes, textures, and sounds from particular vantage points.

This is an argument for the Insensibility Thesis. If sensations represent appearances, then they cannot represent anything abstract. Indeed, they cannot represent some things that are not maximally concrete. Things are concrete to the extent that they appear alike. Tigers appear alike, but not maximally so. Only appearances themselves have this guarantee. The appearance of something from a particular vantage point is the power it has to cause perceptual representations in a viewer from that vantage point. Two appearances are type-identical if they are powers that could cause identical perceptual representations. The argument that we can perceive only appearances goes as follows:

P1. Sensations represent only things that make a phenomenal difference.
P2. Appearances are the only things that make a phenomenal difference.
 C. Thus, sensations represent only appearances.

One might try to challenge this argument by rejecting the second premise. One might argue that something other than appearances contributes to phenomenology (see Siegel, this volume, ch. 14). I don't find this plausible. I suspect that most of our perceptual representations are picture-like (or like sound recordings or textures, etc.). In vision, that means perceptual representations capture things like shapes and colors. To say that phenomenology goes beyond appearances is like saying that phenomenology includes features that could not be captured by a camera or a tape recorder. Is there any reason to think that this is the case?

Philosophers who believe that phenomenology outstrips appearances typically appeal to introspection. They point to examples in which we are invited to recognize that the same appearances can be phenomenally different. Block (1995) gives the example of hearing words. If a monolingual English speaker hears the German word *Hund* it is just a sound. If a German speaker hears it, the experience is phenomenally different. Does this show that phenomenology goes beyond appearances? I think not. The problem is, if we grant the two listeners have different phenomenal experiences, we can explain those differences in terms of further appearances. The German speaker may form a visual image of a dog, or an auditory image of an associated word; she may have an emotional feeling of familiarity or recognition; she may form spontaneous motor images of dog-related behaviors. Hearing familiar words triggers a cascade of responses, documented through a thousand lexical priming studies, which may impact phenomenal experience.

This response reveals a serious danger of appealing to introspection when arguing for differences in phenomenology. Introspection may do a reasonably good job of telling us when two phenomenal experiences differ (especially if one can experience them consecutively, which is difficult in Block's example), but introspection is less accurate when it comes to telling us what such differences consist of. This fact is precisely what undermined introspectionism as a methodology in psychology. Wilhem Wundt and his followers insisted that all experiences were constituted by images. Dissenters, such as Oswald Külpe and Robert Woodworth, claimed that we could have imageless thoughts. Roughly, the debate was about whether phenomenal experiences included features that were not specific to any sensory modality. Both sides used the same experimental methods: they asked subjects (often serving as subjects themselves) to do some mental task and then report on whether any imagery had been used. For example, they asked subjects to form the intention to move, and report what it felt like. Unfortunately, the different camps got correlatively different results (see Woodworth, 1906). Defenders of imageless thought got subjects to claim that they were not experiencing any images when they formed the intention to move, and opponents of imageless thought got subjects to explain every aspect of their experience imagistically. The intention to move might be reported as a tensing of the muscles or as a kinesthetic image of a movement. With no way to adjudicate between these sides, the methodology had to be abandoned. The moral is that intuitions about what kinds of representations are used in phenomenal experiences are unreliable. Those who use introspective evidence to support the claim that phenomenology outstrips appearances are offering too little.

In the debate about imageless thought, I think we have independent reason to favor Wundt. In particular, I think we have reason to think that all the mental representations used in thought are modality specific. There are no amodal symbols, no common code, and no language of thought (Prinz, 2002; Barsalou, 1999). If this is right, then no thought, conscious or unconscious, is imageless. Some of the evidence for this claim comes from the fact that we find modality-specific representations throughout the brain. There is no center of thinking or cognitive engine that hovers above the input systems. So-called higher cognitive structures often contain modality-specific subregions, and any regions that have claim to being polymodal typically play an auxiliary role in thinking; they reactivate modality-specific regions of the brain or coordinate transfer of information between the senses. In addition, when we look at brain activity during cognitive tasks, we see modality-specific activation. For example, when we ask people to form the intention to move, areas of motor cortex (unsurprisingly!) are especially active. If thought were imageless, we might expect to see loci of activation in a modality-neutral region, which could be regarded as the central executive that makes decisions about behavior before issuing motor commands.

These remarks about modality specificity also bear on the question of whether phenomenology outstrips appearances. They offer a way of explaining the intuition that favors that hypothesis. When you look at a table, it doesn't seem that you are merely experiencing colors and shapes. You seem to be experiencing tablehood. Phenomenologically, it seems like a table experience. I have been trying to suggest that such intuitions are unreliable, but I also think they can be explained. If empiricism is right, then our concept of tables comprises stored images of tables. So, if we were to represent the property of tablehood in thought, we would use an image. The images available to us in sensation may seem to represent objects (rather than mere appearances) by virtue of being very much like the representations used to represent objects. When we form *judgments* about our phenomenal states, we assume that they represent objects, but the phenomenal states themselves may represent nothing but appearances. This undercuts any attempt to refute P2 in the argument for the Insensibility Thesis. Empiricism can help explain away the persistent belief that phenomenology outstrips appearances.

Does this mean that the Insensibility Thesis is right? I am inclined towards a negative answer. The culprit is P1, not P2.

2.2 Deep Sensations and the Duality of Content

I argued against the Imperceptibility Thesis by arguing that perception involves matching incoming percepts to stored percepts. Under certain conditions, the incoming percepts can take on the semantic content of the stored percepts. The stored percepts can represent abstract properties and, therefore, so can the incoming percepts. This argument hinges on the claim that perceiving involves recognizing. The matching process is a recognition process. Sensation does not require recognition. Indeed, I think that sensation takes place at a level of processing within our input systems that typically precedes the level at which recognition is achieved (Prinz, 2000a). So there is no trivial way to adapt the argument against the Imperceptibility Thesis to the Insensibility Thesis. Another strategy is needed.

My skepticism about the Insensibility Thesis stems from empirical work on perceptual systems in the brain. A little background will help. Perceptual systems are hierarchically organized. Low-level perceptual subsystems capture information about local features of a stimulus. In vision, for example, low-level subsystems encode information about small edges derived from discontinuities in light. Intermediate-level subsystems integrate local features together into more coherent representations. In vision, intermediate-level representations encode information about contours and surfaces. They achieve some degree of color constancy, superimpose illusory contours, and encode information about depth derived from binocular disparity. No level of processing in the visual stream corresponds more faithfully to what we report in conscious experience (Jackendoff, 1987; Prinz, 2000a). High-level perceptual subsystems use representations that are invariant across a range of perceiving conditions. In vision, high-level representations are often relatively invariant across orientations, scale changes, and even changes in handedness (whether a feature of a stimulus is on the right or the left). These invariant representations are ideally suited for object recognition. If perception were to be located within the visual stream, high-level areas (in inferotemporal cortex) would be the best bet. Sensation, on the other hand, is better identified with intermediate-level representations.

So far, this offers little hope for the opponent of Insensibility. If sensation precedes recognition, then it precedes the stage at which representations of abstract properties are recruited for matching. There may, however, be a role for abstract representations in sensation. It is well known that pathways in our input systems travel both forwards, from our sensory receptors, and backwards, from higher perceptual areas. In the visual system, for example, there are massive back projections from inferior temporal cortex, associated with high-level vision, back into prestriate areas, associated with intermediate-level vision. The exact function of these back projections is unclear, but there are some reasonable hypotheses. One of the most plausible suggestions is that back-projections are used to form mental images (Kosslyn, 1994). In imagery, we reactivate perceptual systems using representations stored in memory. High-level representations, which can be relatively schematic, are used as instructions for reforming rich sensory arrays. The images that result inherit their meaning from the concepts or words that guide their formation. If you form an image of George Washington, it will represent Washington by virtue of having been drawn up from a mental file that has the function representing Washington. Mental images almost certainly re-engage intermediate-level perceptual areas, because images are often conscious and consciousness arises at the intermediate level.

Back-projections are clearly used during mental imagery tasks, but there is also physiological evidence that back-projections are active during conscious visual perception (e.g., Lamme and Roelfsema, 2000). One explanation is that imagery is used during perception to improve performance (Kosslyn, 1994). Information coming through our sensory receptors is often degraded. In vision, the objects around us are often occluded, poorly illuminated, insufficiently foveated, or moving too quickly to be adequately perceived. We take in enough information to make good guesses about object identity, but doing so often requires that we fill in information that has been lost. To do this, we use available information to call up less degraded perceptual representations from memory, which can be back-projected into earlier visual areas to enhance the signal. As Plato notes in *The Republic*, our input systems allow us to make guesses as to what we are perceiving, and those guesses then help us perceive. A good guess can also tell us where to saccade or focus attention, increasing the chances of picking up the details relevant for recognition. In sum, Kosslyn speculates that perception and imagery work in concert. Something like this may happen all the time. Even when an input is clear, high-level perceptual centers may send back efferent signals for other purposes. Back-projections result in a "re-entrant" processing loop, which may have computational advantages, just as back-projecting connectionist nets can outperform feed-forward nets (Edelman, 1993). Projecting images backwards can also facilitate binding. Treisman's (1998) influential theory of attention postulates high-level feature maps, which help us associate shapes with colors in vision. When a visual stimulus is presented too quickly, we sometimes bind the colors to the wrong shapes. Longer exposure allows us to produce more stable high-level representation and project them back into earlier processing subsystems.

Bringing this together, perception may work in the following way. After transduction, a signal is propagated through a hierarchically organized sequence of subsystems, which begin by producing representations of local features and move on to representations that are more global and invariant. Sensations occur at the intermediate stage, between these two extremes. When a high-level representation is formed, it is matched against representations stored in memory. This process sometimes occurs before the perceptual system can fully discern a stimulus—a kind of perceptual guessing. The resulting high-level representation, whether a mere guess or not, is back-projected into earlier perceptual subsystems. This improves the signal, facilitates binding, and allows for selective, strategic processing.

After back-projection, sensations are no longer purely bottom-up. They are blends of incoming signals and mental images produced by centers further down the processing stream. The representations used downstream, which have been matched with representations stored in memory, can inherit semantic properties from those stored representations. This was one of the points that I tried to defend in the discussion of perception. Now I want to suggest that the semantic properties of high-level perceptual representations that have been matched against stored perceptual representations can be exported to earlier processing levels. Sensations can take on new meaning once they intermingle with representations coming down from on high.

Suppose you see a dog. Initially, your sensations will represent nothing but the appearance of that dog—an ephemeral array of colors and shapes. But, in a few dozen milliseconds, recognition is achieved, and the resulting high-level representations are projected backwards. The sensation may remain unchanged, phenomenologically, but it is now a blend of incoming signals and top-down signals. Just as a mental image of a dog would represent a dog, this blended conscious percept may represent a dog. It incorporates a representation, drawn from memory, that was set up to be set off by dogs.

This account can be extended to allow for the sensation of abstract properties. If the arguments of section 1 go through, then we can perceive just about any abstract property that we encounter. In perceiving abstract properties we relate incoming percepts to stored percepts that have been set up to detect abstract properties. Those very same stored percepts can be back-projected. I can form a mental image of injustice by projecting back an image of a scene stored in the mental file by which I track injustice perceptually. The image would presumably be a depiction of an event in which something unjust had occurred. It represents injustice insofar as it is drawn up from the injustice file. I can also back-project such an image in real time, while perceiving unjust events. The result will be sensations of injustice. In this way, we can perceive properties that are extremely abstract. There may be performance constraints on what can be back-projected, but I doubt that there are any limitations in principle. The contents of sensation are no more limited, in principle, than the contents of perception. The Insensibility Thesis is false.

At this point, one might be tempted to enter an objection. When I form an image of an unjust event, say a judge upholding an unjust verdict, it does not seem to be an image of injustice. Indeed, the whole idea of an image of injustice seems bizarre. Some people have the intuition that we can consciously experience concrete objects, in addition to appearances (e.g., one can have an image of a dog), but having an image of injustice is beyond the pale. Injustice just can't be depicted. Isn't this a *reductio* of the hypothesis that I have been defending?

I think this intuition can be partially accommodated without accepting premise 1 in the core argument for the Insensibility Thesis. According to that premise, sensations represent all and only things that make a phenomenal difference. The intuition that we cannot represent injustice in an image derives from the fact that an image of injustice would be indistinguishable from an image of a certain class of appearances. An image of injustice might be indistinguishable from an image of the sound of the phrase "not guilty" as it falls from a judge's lips. Since these images look alike, there is a strong inclination to say that they represent the same thing, namely, a mere appearance. We might *infer* that the appearance is *evidence* for injustice later on in processing, but that has no bearing on the content of the sensation itself.

I think this contention is wrong, but not entirely off-base. One wants a way of capturing what images have in common, qua images. Suppose I form an image of my dog, Fido. It might be indistinguishable from an image caused by seeing my neighbor's dog, Rover. I submit that these two images differ in content. But there is clearly a sense in which they are alike. That similarity might be captured by simply saying that they feel alike, but this leaves us with the thorny problem of how to individuate and compare conscious feelings. It seems we can characterize the similarity in the two images as a similarity in content. They seem to represent the same appearances.

This invites a proposal. Perhaps sensations have two different kinds of content. On the one hand, they represent superficial appearances. On the other, they represent the deeper properties that those appearances are used to detect. I recognize Fido by his appearance. An imagistic representation of Fido represents Fido *and his appearance*. A painting of Fido also represents Fido and his appearance. It is designed to represent both. I suspect that nothing represents Fido without also representing some perceivable attribute of Fido, including the name "Fido," which represents the word "Fido" (I would argue) as well as the dog.

Now go back to injustice. An image of injustice will represent whatever appearance we are using to detect injustice on a particular occasion. But that does not prevent it from representing injustice itself. Representations have dual content. This suggestion can actually be found in the pages of Locke's *Essay* (1690). He says that ideas (which are, arguably, conscious images, for Locke) represent both nominal and real contents. The real content of an idea is, often, some deep property or essence that can be very loosely correlated with appearances. Nominal contents are appearances; they are the superficial features that we use to identify and classify things. The nominal content of our idea of gold comprises properties such as yellowness and hardness. The real content is gold, the substance, which has an essence that was (in Locke's time) unknown. I have argued elsewhere that Locke's dual-content thesis is right for concepts (Prinz, 2000b). I have also argued that it is true for emotions. An emotion represents an appearance of bodily perturbation, and it represents an organism-environment relation that bears on well-being (Prinz, 2004). Now I am suggesting that sensations can have dual contents as well.

The first premise in the argument for the Insensibility Thesis is partially right. Sensations do represent those things that make a phenomenal difference, and those things are appearances. But the premise is partially wrong. Sensations do not only represent appearances, they can also represent deeper properties, including properties that are highly abstract. The intuition that sensations cannot represent abstract properties is mistaken. How do we know it's mistaken? The leading theory of how mental representations represent entails that sensations represent abstract properties under certain circumstances. We have independent and solid reasons for believing that sensations go beyond appearance. Thus, the intuition that they don't is mistaken. This entails that we shouldn't trust our intuitions about sensory content. And, if we cannot trust our intuitions about sensory content, then the main support for the first premise falls away. The claim that sensations represent only appearances is based on the assumption that our intuitions about what mental representations represent are completely reliable. They arc not. A good psychosemantic theory must accommodate intuitions about paradigm cases, but we should expect to give up other intuitions once a good theory is selected.

If I am right, then sensations can have content that makes no phenomenal difference. When we sense an abstract property that content does not alter the character of experience. We can experience something without it affecting our experience. This is not at all paradoxical when we consider that semantic content can, in general, be determined by factors external to the representations that have that content.

3   CONCLUSION

I have been arguing that we can sense and perceive abstract properties. So far, however, I have been a little bit vague about the limitations on abstract sensation and perception. If I am right, then every referring concept can be represented using perceptual representations, and these can, in principle, be used in perceptual matching or sensory back-projection. Thus, the range of things we can conceive does not significantly exceed the range of things that we could perceive. Perhaps we rarely deploy abstract concepts during perception. Perhaps limits on memory or the size of the mental-imagery buffer or other performance factors place limits on the perceivable. Perhaps concepts that get their meaning through combination, rather than reliable detection, are too cumbersome to use in our input systems. I am agnostic about these questions. My point is that the alleged representational gulf between perception and conception may be much smaller than we usually realize.

REFERENCES

Barsalou, Lawrence W. (1999). Perceptual Symbol Systems. *Behavioral and Brain Sciences*, 22, 577–609.

Block, Ned. (1995). On a Confusion about a Function of Consciousness. *Behavioral and Brain Sciences*, 18, 227–47.

Dehaene, Stanislas. (1997). *The Number Sense: How the Mind Creates Mathematics*. Oxford: Oxford University Press.

Desimone, Robert. (1991). Face-Selective Cells in the Temporal Cortex of Monkeys. *Journal of Cognitive Neuroscience*, 3, 1–8.

Dretske, Fred. (1969). *Seeing and Knowing*. Chicago: University of Chicago Press.

Dretske, Fred. (1981). *Knowledge and the Flow of Information*. Cambridge, Mass.: MIT Press.

Dretske, Fred. (1986). Misrepresentation. In R. Bogdan (ed.), *Belief: Form, Content, and Function*. Oxford: Oxford University Press.

Edelman, Gerald M. (1993). Neural Darwinism: Selection and Reentrant Signaling in Higher Brain Function. *Neuron*, 10, 115–25.

Fodor, Jerry A. (1990). A Theory of Content II. In *A Theory of Content and Other Essays*. Cambridge, Mass.: MIT Press.

Gauthier, Isabel and Logothetis, Nikos (2000). Is Face Recognition Not So Unique After All? *Cognitive Neuropsychology*, 17, 125–42.

Gross, Charles G. and Sargent, Justine (1992). Face Recognition. *Current Opinion in Neurobiology*, 2, 156–61.

Jackendoff, Ray. (1987). *Consciousness and the Computational Mind*. Cambridge, Mass.: MIT Press.

Kanwisher, Nancy, McDermott, Josh, and Chun, Marvin. (1997). The Fusiform Face Area: A Module in Human Extrastriate Cortex Specialized for the Perception of Faces. *Journal of Neuroscience*, 17, 4302–11.

Kosslyn, Stephen M. (1994). *Image and Brain: The Resolution of the Imagery Debate*. Cambridge, Mass.: MIT Press.

Kreiman Gabriel, Koch Christof, and Fried Itzhak. (2000). Category-Specific Visual Responses of Single Neurons in the Human Medial Temporal Lobe. *Nature Neuroscience*, 3, 946–53.

Lamme, Victor A. F. and Roelfsema, Pieter R. (2000). The Distinct Modes of Vision Offered by Feedforward and Recurrent Processing. *Trends in Neurosciences*, 23, 571–9.

Locke, John. (1690/1975). *An Essay Concerning Human Understanding*; P. Nidditch (ed.). Oxford: Clarendon Press.

Millikan, Ruth. G. (1989). Biosemantics. *The Journal of Philosophy*, 86, 281–97.

Prinz, Jesse J. (2000a). A Neurofunctional Theory of Visual Consciousness. *Consciousness and Cognition*, 9, 243–59.

Prinz, Jesse J. (2000b). The Duality of Content. *Philosophical Studies*, 100, 1–34.

Prinz, Jesse J. (2002). *Furnishing the Mind: Concepts and Their Perceptual Basis.* Cambridge, Mass.: MIT Press.

Prinz, Jesse J. (2004). *Gut Reactions: A Perceptual Theory of Emotion.* New York: Oxford University Press.

Prinz, Jesse J. (forthcoming). *The Emotional Construction of Morals.* Oxford: Oxford University Press.

Putnam, Hilary. (1975). The Meaning of "Meaning." In K. Gunderson (ed.), *Language, Mind, and Knowledge* (pp. 131–93). Minneapolis: University of Minnesota Press.

Treisman, Anne. (1998). Feature Binding, Attention and Object Perception. *Philosophical Transactions of the Royal Society of London B: Biological Sciences*, 353, 1295–1306.

Williams, Bernard. (1985). *Ethics and the Limits of Philosophy.* Cambridge, Mass.: Harvard University Press.

Wittgenstein, Ludwig. (1953). *Philosophical Investigations*; G. E. M. Anscombe (trans.). Oxford: Blackwell.

Woodworth, Robert S. (1906). Imageless Thought. *The Journal of Philosophy, Psychology, and Scientific Methods*, 3, 701–8.

13

On the Ways Things Appear

Sydney Shoemaker

I

When we see, things look various ways to us. When we perceive in other ways, things feel certain ways, sound certain ways, smell certain ways, and taste certain ways. In addition to the ways objects of touch feel to us, there are also ways parts of our bodies feel to us, as when we are nauseous or in pain.

What are these "ways"? A natural thought is that the ways are simply properties things appear to us to have. Appearing a certain way is (it is natural to suppose) appearing *to be* a certain way, and *being* a certain way is having a certain property. It is also a natural thought that the properties are what traditionally have been regarded as "sensible qualities"—in the case of vision, these would include colors and shapes. The way something looks is how it looks, and one can certainly respond to the question of how something looks to one by saying that it looks a reddish-brown, or that it looks elliptical in shape.

But sometimes we speak of the way something looks as the same or similar to, or as different from, the way something else looks, where we do not mean that the thing looks to be the same, similar or different with respect to color, shape, or the like. If the surface of a table is partly in shadow, one may say that the way the shadowed part of it looks is different from the way the unshadowed part of it looks, without implying that the two parts look to have different colors. And, supposing that the table is brown, the way the shadowed part looks may be the same as the way an unshadowed surface in another part of the room looks, where the latter is of a darker shade of brown than the table surface; and this can be so

Thanks to David Chalmers and Brad Thompson for comments on an earlier version of this chapter. Thanks also to Thompson, and to other members of the 2002 NEH Summer Institute on Consciousness and Intentionality, for discussions that loosened my earlier adherence to the *Ways = Properties principle*. Versions of the paper were presented at Duke University, Union College, The City University of New York Graduate Center, and at the "Content and Concepts" conference at UC Santa Barbara in February 2004 (where Sean Kelly was my commentator). My thanks to the audiences on all of these occasions for good comments. Finally, I am grateful to the editors of this volume, Tamar Gendler and John Hawthorne, for their very helpful comments.

even though the two surfaces do not look to have the same shade of color.[1] Here it is differences in illumination that account for differences in the ways things of the same color look. It is also well known that the way a thing of a certain color looks to a subject may be influenced by the colors of adjacent objects, or by what the subject saw immediately before seeing the thing in question—these are cases of simultaneous or successive contrast. Where the ways things of a certain color look are different in different circumstances, or where things of the different colors look the same in certain circumstances, it may in some cases be right to say that in some of the circumstances an object looks to have a color it doesn't have; and this would allow the way it looks to be a color it is represented (correctly or incorrectly) as having. But this will not normally be true in the case of shadowed and unshadowed objects, and it will not always be true in cases involving simultaneous or successive contrast.

Where looking the same, similar or different ways is not a matter of looking to have the same, similar or different colors, shapes or sizes, let us speak of the ways as "phenomenal" ways things look. It is phenomenal ways things look, and more generally phenomenal ways things appear, that I shall be concerned with here, and usually I shall omit the qualifier "phenomenal." If ways things look are properties they look to have, then some of the ways involved in color perception, namely the phenomenal ones, have to be properties other than colors—and properties for which we have no names.

The situation may seem different in the case of taste, smell, and hearing. If the way X tastes is the same as the way Y tastes, and X tastes sweet, then Y tastes sweet, whereas the shadow case shows that it is not true that if the way X looks is the same as the way Y looks, and X looks dark brown, then Y looks dark brown. Terms like "sweet," "bitter," "sour," and "salty" seem more closely tied to ways things taste than color terms and shape terms are to ways things look. Likewise for terms like "acrid" used to describe smells, and terms like "shrill" used to describe sounds. But we often speak of similarities and differences in the way things taste or smell or sound when we have no names for the properties—if there are such—which our experience represents things as having when they taste or smell certain ways. I might say in certain circumstances that the way a flute sounds is the same as the way a violin sounds, without having any name for a property shared in such circumstances by flutes and violins, or by the sounds produced by these instruments.

---

[1] Two different cases can be distinguished here. In one case there are sufficient cues about the illumination for it to appear to one that, as is in fact the case in the envisaged situation, the two surfaces differ in color. I think that there is a good sense in which it can be true even in such a case that the "phenomenal" ways the two surfaces look can be the same, even though one looks to be in shadow and the other doesn't. Another possible case is that in which there are not sufficient cues about illumination to enable one to see that the surfaces differ in color—and also there are not misleading cues that make it look as if they have the same color. Here it can certainly be the case that the ways the two surfaces look can be the same while the surfaces do not look to have the same color; and this will not be the case that one is misperceiving the color of either surface.

Describing one's symptoms to a doctor, one might say that the way one's abdomen feels is the way it feels when one is hungry, but that it often feels that way when one has recently eaten. There may or may not turn out to be a single physiological condition responsible for both one's hunger feelings and those one is reporting to the doctor. But such a condition is unlikely to be a property that one's experience attributes to one's abdomen; and if there is such a property, it is one for which one lacks a name.

Turning to temperature perception, consider a variation on the example, discussed by Locke and Berkeley, in which a basin of water feels warm to one hand and cold to another. Let our case be one in which the subject has just been out of doors on a cold day, with her right hand gloved and her left hand ungloved, and now places the two hands (the glove having been removed) in two different basins of water of different temperatures, and in which the way the colder water in basin A feels to her left hand is exactly the same as the way the warmer water in basin B feels to her right hand. There may be some inclination here to say that the experience involving her left hand is illusory—a matter of water of feeling warmer than it is. But it is not plausible to suppose that there is a particular way the water must feel in order for the perceiver not to misperceive its temperature. Let's suppose that the perception of the temperature of the water in basin A with her right hand counts as veridical. Suppose that the temperature difference between the two basins of water is slight, although noticeable, and consider someone who, owing to a physiological difference from our subject (thicker skin perhaps), is such that when he is in the same circumstances as our subject, water that is of the temperature of that in basin A feels to him the way water with the temperature of the water in basin B would feel to our subject in those circumstances. He makes pretty much the same temperature discriminations as our subject, but each way the water can feel is paired in his case with a slightly higher temperature than it is in the case of our subject. It is not plausible that such a subject would be misperceiving—that his experience would be representing things as having higher temperatures than they in fact have. If the ways are properties, they are different properties than the temperatures, and they are properties for which we lack names.

This last case should remind one of the inverted spectrum scenario, which takes us back to the case of color. If spectrum inversion is a possibility, as I have argued elsewhere that it is, this gives us an additional reason for thinking that if something's appearing a certain way is a matter of one's experience ascribing a property to it, our color perception involves the perception of properties that are not colors (1982, 1996, 2003). A case of spectrum inversion, of the sort that we are interested in, must be one in which the invertees do not differ in their beliefs about the objective colors of things; if one of them thinks the tomato before her is red, the other, in the same circumstances, will think the same. If Jack and Jill are spectrum inverted relative to each other, this will involve, for example, the way red things look to Jack being the same as the way green things look to Jill, and vice versa, and likewise for other pairs of colors. This cannot be a matter of Jack's experience ascribing to red things a different color than Jill's experience ascribes to them, for if it were they would have different beliefs about the colors of these things.[2] So, if the ways the things look are properties represented by the experiences, the different properties ascribed to red things by Jack's and Jill's experiences cannot be colors.

The view that there are nameless properties other than the colors that we perceive in color vision, and that spectrum inversion would consist in the invertees having experiences that represent different properties of this sort when they are perceiving things having the same color, and also sometimes perceiving the same property of this sort when they are perceiving things different in color, is one that I have defended in several places (1994, 2000). It is also a view that Michael Thau (2002) has defended. As will be seen, Thau and I hold different versions of it. But both of us have claimed that this view enables one to combine the view that spectrum inversion is possible with the view that the phenomenal character of perceptual experience consists in its representational content; the phenomenal character of color experiences will consist in that aspect of their representational content that has to do with the representation, not of colors per se, but of nameless properties that are correlated with colors in the experience of a particular sort of subject but could in principle be associated with different colors in the experience of different sorts of subjects. And both of us have held that this permits one to do justice to the Moorean "transparency" intuition— that when we attend to our perceptual experience, what we attend to is what that experience represents. It differs from other accounts of transparency by saying that our introspective access is not in the first instance to colors represented by our experiences but is rather to the nameless properties correlated in our experience with those colors.

Lying behind this view is the assumption that something's appearing a certain way is always a matter of its appearing to have some property. I will call this the "Ways = Properties Principle."[3] I have mentioned two routes from this principle to the view that our perceptual experience represents objects as having nameless properties that are different from the sensible qualities as usually conceived, i.e., colors, shapes, etc.. One, advanced both by Thau and by me, is the argument from the possibility of spectrum inversion just sketched. The other, not mentioned by Thau, is from the fact that in actual cases the ways things appear can be different when there is no difference in "objective" sensible properties like colors, or the same when the objective sensible qualities differ, and that in some of these

---

[2] This is not undisputed. Some, including Fred Dretske (personal communication), think that it is coherent to suppose that the contents of someone's color experiences might be systematically mistaken while the contents of his perceptually based color beliefs are normally true.

[3] If one equates *looking a certain way* with *looking to be a certain way*, the Ways = Properties principle will seem obviously true. My doubts about the principle began when Brad Thompson pressed me on whether these should be equated.

cases there is no misperception, and so no representing things as having properties they do not have. Thau has a further argument, based on a variation of Frank Jackson's Mary argument, that I shall not discuss. My concern in the next section will be with whether the nameless properties view can be correct. I shall first consider my own version of it, including Thau's criticism of it, and then Thau's version.

II

I have taken the nameless properties to be what I initially called "phenomenal properties" (1994) and more recently have called "appearance properties" (2000). These I have held to be relational properties of things—properties the having of which by a thing consists either in that thing's actually causing experiences of a certain sort in a perceiver (in which case it is an "occurrent appearance property") or in the thing's being disposed to produce experiences of a certain sort in perceivers of one or more sorts (in which case it is a "dispositional appearance property"). I have held that the phenomenal character of an experience consists in that aspect of its representational content that is the representation of appearance properties, and that it is to this that we have introspective access. I have also held that while appearance properties are relational, they are not represented in our experience *as* relational. Nor are they represented as intrinsic; about such matters the content of our experience is noncommittal.

This last feature of my view is the basis of Michael Thau's main criticism of it. He agrees that if I hold that the appearance properties are relational, I must deny that they are represented as such. But he argues that if I make this denial then I must invoke modes of presentation in order to explain the subjective difference between different appearance properties—e.g., between the one I perceive red things as having (and someone inverted relative to me perceives green things as having) and the one I perceive green things as having (and someone inverted relative to me perceives red things as having). If I were aware of these *as* properties consisting in the causing (or disposition to cause) different sorts of experiences, that would explain the subjective difference; but since I am not, the difference must reside not in *what* I perceive but in *how* I perceive it, and so in different modes of presentation. But, according to Thau, once I allow modes of presentation to enter into the determination of perceptual content, I lose the motivation for introducing the appearance properties. Instead of saying that spectrum inversion would involve the different subjects perceiving the same color by perceiving different appearance properties, and perceiving different colors by perceiving the same appearance property, I might as well say that the different subjects differ in the following way: what for one of them is the mode of presentation for the color red is for the other the mode of presentation for the color green, and vice versa. There is then no need to hold that appearance properties enter into the content of perceptual experience. Notice that holding this view would amount to abandoning the Ways = Properties principle. Sameness or difference of ways of appearing would amount to sameness or difference of modes of presentation, not sameness or difference of properties represented.

I will argue later that if this argument works against me, basically the same argument works against Thau. But, before I argue that, I want to present a different objection to the view that ways of appearing are appearance properties.

I should make clear that nothing I am about to say is intended to call into question that there *are* appearance properties as I have characterized them. I think there clearly are. The question is whether these properties are represented in our perceptual experience, are properties things appear to us to have, and so can serve as ways things appear to us.

The difficulty is that each appearance property can be characterized as the property of appearing a certain way. I characterized appearance properties above as properties things have in virtue of causing or being disposed to cause experiences of certain sorts. But the intent was that they be properties things have in virtue of appearing certain ways—either appearing certain ways to certain perceivers (producing experiences of appropriate sorts in them) or being disposed to appear certain ways to certain sorts of perceivers (being disposed to produce experiences of appropriate kinds in perceivers of those sorts). In the case of color vision, the appearing will be looking. So we have to ask: do things we see look to have properties of looking certain ways? If a given way, call it W, is the property of looking a certain way, that way had better be way W; it can hardly be the case that the way something looks is the property of looking some *other* way! But if way W is the property of looking way W, then the property will be the property of looking to have a certain property, namely itself! And, what might seem worse, the property W will be identical with the property *looks W*, which will be identical with the property *looks to look W*, which will be identical with the property *looks to look to look W*, and so on ad infinitum.[4]

Is this regress vicious? It might seem that it is, because it might seem that it makes it impossible to complete an answer to the question of what way W is. But it is not clear that this is so. Particular ways of looking can be picked out demonstratively—"looking way W is looking *that* way"—or by descriptions like "the way chartreuse things look to observers with thus and such perceptual systems in thus and such conditions." If the demonstrative "that," or a description of the sort just mentioned, can succeed in picking out an appearance property, the identification of ways with appearance properties is no bar to our being able to specify what a particular way is; and I am not able to see that the

---

[4] An objection along these lines was presented to me by Zoltan Szabò; it took a while for me to feel its force.

regress presents any bar to ways, regarded as properties, being picked out demonstratively or by description.

While holding that way W is identical with the property of looking way W may seem incoherent, I do not think that it is. Doesn't this amount to saying that way W is a property something has just in case it looks way W? Many perceivable properties are such that things that one sees can have them without looking to one to have them; here we are saying that there is a class of properties, namely ways of appearing, each of which is such that something one sees has it just in case it appears to one to have it. This doesn't mean that an experience representing such a property cannot be illusory—it is not ruled out that someone could hallucinate a state of affairs in which something has such a property. The claim is about the things that have these properties; for each property of this sort, if something has it then it appears to have it (either in the occurrent or the dispositional sense), and if something appears to have it (either appears to some particular subject to have it, or appears to have it in the sense that it is disposed to appear to have it to appropriately placed subjects) then it has it. I do not see that there is any incoherence involved in this.

There does seem to be an incoherence involved in supposing that when such a property is perceived, the content of the perception is that the thing has the property of appearing to have that very property. It will not do to say that the content is: this thing has the property of appearing to have a certain property, namely that very property. The "namely" clause does not tell us what the "certain property" is. But from the fact that the property is in fact a property that is identical with the property of appearing to have it, we cannot conclude that it is perceptually represented as such. Perhaps in the perceptual representation it is picked out, as it were, demonstratively.

Still, the consequence of the view that the ways are appearance properties— namely that each of them is a property that is identical with the property of appearing to have it—is prima facie counterintuitive. And many people also find counterintuitive the view that we perceive colors by perceiving properties distinct from them, and that each color experience ascribes two different properties. It may seem that this view is sufficiently counterintuitive that we should instead accept Michael Thau's alternative view that the ways—the nameless properties that are not colors, shapes, etc., but nevertheless tell us about the colors, shapes, etc. of things—are intrinsic properties of things, and that our color experiences ascribe these instead of, rather than in addition to, the colors.

Let me begin by addressing Thau's claim that to explain the subjective difference between different appearance properties I must invoke modes of presentation. Now, I think that I have an explanation of the subjective difference between appearance properties. I have maintained that the relations of qualit- ative similarity and difference amongst experiences are functional relations, and that it is central to the functional role of qualitative difference that when experiences are qualitatively different this results in a corresponding difference in how the environment is represented and an awareness that there is such a difference (2000). Given that different appearance properties constitutively involve qualitatively different experiences, this seems to me to explain the subjective difference between such properties in a way that does not depend on the subject perceiving the appearance properties *as* relational properties involving experiences. Does this explanation invoke modes of presentation? It does if speaking of experiences as qualitatively similar or different, and so as having features ("qualia") in virtue of which these relations hold, itself counts as invoking modes of presentation. But if so, what becomes of Thau's claim that the modes of presentation can serve as modes of presentation of the colors, thus removing the need to introduce appearance properties into the story? The introduction of appearance properties is motivated by the desire to respect the Moorean intuition that the qualitative character we are aware of in introspection is that which our experience attributes to the perceived object, and to do this without holding that the attribution of qualitative character to the perceived object is a projectivist illusion. Merely holding that experiences have modes of presentation in the thin sense just sketched, i.e., qualitative features that determine how things appear, does not achieve this, since it is compatible with a projectivist view.

But suppose for the moment that Thau is right, and that my account does need modes of presentation in a way that undermines its motivation? Why isn't the same true of his account? What is his explanation of the subjective difference between two of his nameless intrinsic properties—e.g., those correlated in his experience with red and green? The explanation can't be just that the properties are different, and are both perceived. After all, on my account the appearance properties are different and are both perceived, yet Thau doesn't think this is sufficient to explain the subjective difference. And why should it make a difference that his properties are intrinsic and mine are relational? One would think that to explain the subjective difference between two perceivable intrinsic properties one would need to appeal to a difference in their causal powers, presumably grounded in a difference in how they are physically realized, that explains not only why they are different properties but why they impact differently on creatures with certain sorts of perceptual systems. Presumably, Thau does not think that we perceive his nameless intrinsic properties *as* having certain causal powers, or *as* having certain sorts of physical realizations. So, it would seem, it is as much true on his view as it is on mine that what grounds the subjective difference is not something we are immediately aware of in perceiving the properties. So if I need modes of presentation, why doesn't he?

There are two reasons why a commitment to modes of presentation would be unacceptable to Thau. First, a point he makes against me would apply to him as well; once modes of presentation are introduced, we might as well take them to be modes of presentation of the colors themselves, and say that spectrum inversion consists not in the invertees perceiving red things to have different properties but in their perceiving the color red by means of different modes of presentation. So allowing modes of presentation would undermine his motivation for introducing his nameless intrinsic properties. Second, Thau is in fact a committed Millian, and thinks that modes of presentation can play no role in mental representation, whether it be that involved in belief or that involved in perception.

Given his argument against me, it would seem that Thau can escape commitment to modes of presentation only by holding about his nameless intrinsic properties a very strong version of what Mark Johnston (1992) has called "Revelation," namely, that their nature, and so everything relevant to what makes them similar or different, is revealed to us in our perception of them. And there are indications that he does hold this. He claims that there cannot be names of these properties, and that the only way to refer to them is demonstratively. This would seem to rule out their being physically realized; for if they were physically realized, presumably they could in principle be picked out by their sets of physical realizers, which would provide a way of fixing the reference of public language names of them. So one sort of hidden nature is ruled out. And it also seems to be ruled out that these properties can be individuated by, and that the subjective differences amongst them can be explained in terms of, causal features of them that are not revealed to us in our perception of them. He suggests that his view allows colors to be regarded as dispositional properties: "each color C can be defined as a disposition to cause a representation involving the property perceptually correlated with C" (2002: 236), where the property perceptually correlated with a color is one of his (necessarily) nameless intrinsic properties. But this suggests that colors preempt whatever causal role in affecting our experience we might want to assign to the nameless intrinsic properties. And it is hard to see what other causal role they could have that would not be preempted by the colors and their physical realizers. Given his argument against me, I think he *needs* these properties to be without physical realizers and without causal powers in order to escape commitment to modes of presentation. But if indeed these are properties that can only be designated demonstratively, are not physically realized, and are without causal powers, I think we should conclude that there are no such properties. No real property that we perceive could be like that.

In a footnote to his paper "A Mind–Body Problem at the Surface of Objects," Mark Johnston attributes to Thau, whose dissertation he was then supervising, the view that perception attributes to objects a set of "colorlike qualities which surfaces could not have or be perceived to have" (1996: 219). This would be a version of what I have called "figurative projectivism." If, as I argued above, his nameless intrinsic properties could not be among the perceived properties of objects, adopting figurative projectivism is the only way he could save the view that these properties are represented in perception. And since he holds that these are the *only* properties that are perceptually represented, this would commit him to a radical error theory, one according to which every property attributed to objects in our experience is one that the objects do not and could not have. This is an unbelievable view. And I think it is clearly not his current view.

Elsewhere Thau offers a slightly different reason for holding that my view is committed to modes of presentation.[5] I need modes of presentation, he thinks, to explain how it is that the appearance property I see when I see red things seems incompatible with the appearance property I see when I see green things, when in fact, on my view, these are not incompatible. They are not incompatible because I might be seeing the tomato to have one of them while someone spectrum inverted relative to me is seeing it to have the other of them, when neither of us is misperceiving. He thinks that I can only explain this by saying that in my experience these properties are presented by different and incompatible modes of presentation. Now I think that this is explained by something I said earlier, namely that qualitative similarity and difference relations amongst experiences are functional relations. Part of what constitutes a qualitative difference between two experience types is that things perceived by subjects having experiences of those two types are perceived as different, and it is impossible for one and the same subject to perceive something by means of an experience of one of these types and at the same time perceive it—in the case of vision, in the very same portion of the field of vision—by means of an experience of the other type. This makes certain pairs of appearance properties, e.g., the one I see red things as having and the one I see green things as having, incompatible relative to every sort of perceptual system—no matter what the nature of one's perceptual system, and so no matter what objects one sees as instantiating these properties, one cannot simultaneously perceive something as having, on the same portion of its surface, both of these appearance properties. This can be so even though members of these pairs are not incompatible *simpliciter*, and can be perceived as belonging to the same object at the same time, as long as they are perceived by subjects with different sorts of perceptual systems. I do not see that this commits me to modes of presentation.

The advantage Thau thinks his view has over mine is that whereas the appearance property I see red things as having and the appearance property I see green things as having are not in themselves incompatible (creating, he thinks, the need for modes of presentation to explain why they seem incompatible), the nameless intrinsic property his theory says I see red things as having is incompatible with the nameless intrinsic property his theory says I see green things as having—so these properties seeming to be incompatible is explained by their actually being so. For reasons indicated above, I question whether the fact that properties are incompatible will by itself explain their seeming to be so. But what

---

[5] This is in an unpublished paper entitled "What to do When your Relationships Fail," which is a later version of his contribution to an APA book symposium (Central Division, 1999) on my *The First Person Perspective and Other Essays*.

I want to point out now is that what he says here reveals a difference between the way in which he thinks that spectrum inversion is possible and the way in which I think it is. We both think that two people could differ systematically in the ways things of the various colors appear to them, while not differing at all in what colors they believe objects to have. I have taken it that this does not involve misperception on the part of either party. Thau agrees that it does not involve either party misperceiving the *colors* of things, because he thinks that strictly speaking we don't perceive the colors at all; what we perceive are nameless intrinsic properties that are correlated with the colors. If the role of the nameless intrinsic properties in his theory were the same as the role of the appearance properties in mine, his view would be that in a case of spectrum inversion one of the invertees might be veridically perceiving red things to have the nameless intrinsic property that the other is veridically perceiving green things to have, and vice versa. Were that true, these different nameless intrinsic properties would not be incompatible. Apparently he holds instead that one or the other of them would be misperceiving—would be systematically misperceiving things as having nameless intrinsic properties that they don't have. But this misperception would not result in that subject having any mistaken beliefs about the colors of things, or being in any way disadvantaged in coping with the world. And, as best I can see, there would be no way in which it could be determined which of them was misperceiving and which was perceiving correctly. Worse than that, given that the view allows the possibility of this sort of systematic misperception, there would be no way in which we could establish whether *we* are veridically perceiving the nameless intrinsic properties we represent things as having or are systematically misperceiving them. This view seems to me just as bad as the figurative projectivist view that all perceivers are systematically misperceiving objects as having intrinsic properties that no object ever has.

Suppose that Thau were to hold instead that in a case of spectrum inversion the invertees could both be veridically perceiving the objects to have the nameless intrinsic properties their experiences represent them as having. Then he would lose his basis for saying that my view requires modes of presentation in a way his doesn't. And there would be an additional problem. Let F be the nameless intrinsic property Jack sees red things as having and Jill sees green things as having, and let G be the nameless intrinsic property Jack sees green things as having and Jill sees red things as having. Assuming that, in the same circumstances, Jack's experiences are veridical just in case Jill's are veridical, then it would seem that F and G are necessarily coextensive. What would distinguish them? Apparently they would not be distinguished by their causal powers, since Thau's view seems to leave no room for assigning them causal powers. Could they be distinguished by the fact that the experiences of them are phenomenally different? No, for on Thau's account differences in phenomenal character of experiences would have to consist in differences in the properties represented by the experiences.

III

Where does this leave us? If phenomenal ways things appear are properties of the things that appear, it would seem that they must be either relational properties such as my appearance properties or nameless intrinsic properties of the sort Michael Thau thinks they are. I think that they certainly cannot be the latter, for the reasons I have given, and we have seen that the supposition that they are the former has some counterintuitive consequences. Should we then abandon the Ways = Properties principle? And, if we do, what alternative account can we offer?

One alternative has already been mentioned, at least by implication. Michael Thau holds that my view is committed to there being modes of presentation governing the representation of appearance properties, and that once modes of presentation have been introduced I might as well drop the appearance properties from the account and say that in a case of spectrum inversion the difference between the invertees' experiences of the tomato is a difference in modes of presentation—a difference in *how* the one perceived property, red, is represented, rather than a difference in *what* properties are represented. So one alternative would be to hold that ways are modes of presentation. This would give us a Fregean version of representationalism (or intentionalism) about the phenomenal character of perceptual experience. Such a view has recently been defended by David Chalmers (2004) and by Brad Thompson (forthcoming).

As I have mentioned, while I think that Thau needs modes of presentation for his nameless intrinsic properties if I need them for my appearance properties, he is in fact a Millian who rejects altogether the appeal to modes of presentation in explaining mental representation. If his arguments against modes of presentation are successful, the alternative just mentioned is ruled out. I will not here take a stand on this. What I want to do now is present a suggestion that may count as a version of the view that phenomenal ways are modes of presentation, but which in any case seems to me promising.

I take as my point of departure the claim made by John Campbell that "the qualitative character of a color-experience is inherited from the qualitative character of the color" (1993; see also Campbell 2002). Campbell (2002) holds a "relational" view of experience, according to which the perceived object and the perceived properties are literally parts of the experience, so on his version of the inheritance view the experience inherits the qualitative character by including an instantiation of the color that has it. But it is in the spirit of one version of the representational view of the phenomenal character of experience to say that the experience inherits the qualitative character of the color because its phenomenal character simply consists in its representing that qualitative character.

Such views are usually taken to rule out the possibility of spectrum inversion. And so they do if they take it that each color has *just one* qualitative character, so that if an experience represents that color it must, in the relevant sense, "inherit" just that qualitative character.[6] But we needn't invoke the possibility of spectrum inversion in order to see that it is wrong to suppose that for each color there is a *single* phenomenal character that an experience must have if it is to be an experience of that color. The falsity of that supposition follows from the fact, pointed out at the beginning of this chapter, that the (phenomenal) way something looks can be different from the (phenomenal) way something else looks without those things being represented as having different colors (or differing in any of their other objective sensible qualities), and that the way something looks can be the same as the way something else looks without the things being represented as being of the same color—and that these things can happen without there being any misperception. The way a veridically perceived color looks, and so the phenomenal character of the experience of it, depends on lighting conditions and a variety of other conditions. This is a fact of everyday experience. What the possibility of spectrum inversion amounts to is that the way a veridically perceived color looks also depends on the nature of the perceptual system of the subject; among other things, on the structure of the perceiver's color "quality space," and on what similarity and difference relations the subject perceives among the physical properties that are realizers of the colors. As I have recently argued elsewhere (Shoemaker 2003), I think that it is beyond question that perceivers with differently constituted visual systems can, in the same viewing conditions, perceive the same colors while having experiences of them that are phenomenally different, and perceive different colors while having experiences of them that are phenomenally the same. This can also be put by saying that even if we hold viewing conditions constant, the way something of a given color looks to someone with one sort of perceptual system can be different from the way something of the same color looks to someone with a different sort of perceptual system, and that the way something of a given color looks to someone can be the same as the way something of a different color looks to someone with a different sort of perceptual system.

Elsewhere I have defended a version of the view that in virtue of having a certain color quality space, a visual system "selects" certain objective properties in the world to be colors and certain relations between these to be relations of color similarity and difference (Shoemaker 2003). On my version of this view, the same property can be selected as a color by different visual systems that give it different similarity relations to other colors, and so different positions in the subjects' color quality spaces. We can now add to this that different visual systems select different aspects of those properties to be the qualitative characters these properties present, to creatures with those visual systems, under certain viewing conditions.

---

[6] In my terminology, experiences have phenomenal character while properties of objects in the world have qualitative character. This leaves open what the relation between these characters is.

Given this, in whatever sense colors have qualitative characters that can be inherited by perceptual experiences, thereby determining the phenomenal character of those experiences, they must have *multiple* qualitative characters. A color will have different qualitative characters corresponding to the different ways it can look (without being misperceived) in different viewing conditions, and also different qualitative characters corresponding to the different ways it can look to different observers owing to differences in their perceptual systems. The sets of qualitative characters possessed by different colors will overlap; this is what makes possible spectrum inversion, and it is also what makes it possible for the way a light-brown object in shadow looks to be the same as the way a dark-brown object not in shadow looks. Let us say that when someone veridically perceives something as having a certain color, one of its qualitative characters presents itself to that person. It goes with this that when someone's experience represents, whether veridically or not, the instantiation of a certain color, it represents there being an object having a color that is presenting a certain qualitative character to that person.[7]

Qualitative characters, as conceived here, are aspects of properties in the world. A property's having the qualitative characters it does is part of its essential nature; and if the property is an intrinsic property of a thing, then having a property with that qualitative character is intrinsic to the thing. And these are aspects of the property that are represented in perceptual experience. Why shouldn't these be the (phenomenal) ways things look or otherwise appear? Perhaps this counts as a version of the suggestion that the ways are modes of presentation; for one could say that that the qualitative character a color presents, or is perceived as presenting, determines *how* the color is represented, and in that way determines the phenomenal character of the experience. But since the qualitative character is an aspect of the color, one can also say that *what* is perceived, or is represented as being perceived, determines the phenomenal character of the experience.

If one tries to dispense with qualitative characters of perceived properties, represented in perceptual experience, and to make do only with phenomenal characters of experiences serving as modes of presentation (as on the views on Chalmers and Thompson—see n. 9), one will still need to deal with the fact that the phenomenal character of veridical experiences of a given color can be different in different circumstances (e.g., different lighting conditions), and for

---

[7] In his insightful comments on this paper at the Santa Barbara conference (see n. 10) Sean Kelly questioned whether this claim is true. He claims that when one is perceiving in what he calls the "engaged attitude," where one is attending to what colors things have and not to the ways things look, the qualitative characters are not represented in one's experience. He also claims that when one is in what he calls the "detached attitude" (or "painterly attitude"), and is attending to the looks of things, the colors are not represented. I am not persuaded that he is right. But his claim is compatible with most of what I say, including my claim that colors have multiple qualitative characters whose representation gives experiences of them their phenomenal character—at least when the perceiver's attention is on the ways things look.

creatures with different sorts of perceptual systems. So the same color will have to have a number of different modes of presentation associated with it. To say that this variation is only a variation in the *how* of perceptual representation, and in no way a variation in *what* is represented, seems to me at odds with the phenomenology. When the light-brown object in shadow and the dark-brown object not in shadow look the same to me, the sameness is experienced as being *out there*—and in such a case the perception can be perfectly veridical. Similarity in the presenting manifests itself in represented similarity in what is represented, and in the absence of perceptual illusion requires that there be similarity in what is represented. More generally, the best gloss on the Moorean transparency intuition is that the qualitative character that figures in the perception of the color of an object is experienced as in or on the perceived object. A modes-of-presentation view that dispenses with qualitative characters in objects could account for this aspect of the phenomenology only by adopting a projectivist view according to which our experiences project onto perceived objects qualitative features that they do not possess. Such an error theory is to be avoided.

Nothing that I have said addresses the question of what determines what color one's experience represents when in having it one is presented with a particular qualitative character. Presumably for each color there will be a "canonical" way it appears to observers of a certain sort in normal viewing conditions, and normally experiences in which an object presents one with the qualitative character associated with this canonical way will represent the object as having that color. But partly as the result of learning, and partly through the operation of a wired-in color constancy mechanism, phenomenally different experiences in which different qualitative characters are presented will also represent that color in circumstances that are in one respect or another abnormal.

Qualitative characters are closely related to what I have called appearance properties. If something with a certain color presents one of its qualitative characters, the thing will have the occurrent appearance property associated with that qualitative character. And if in certain circumstances an object is disposed to present one of the qualitative characters of its color to observers of certain sorts, the object will have the dispositional appearance property associated with that qualitative character. Since different colors can in different circumstances, or when viewed by different sorts of perceivers, present the same qualitative characters, things having different colors can have the same appearance property. And since the same color can in different circumstances, or when viewed by different sorts of observers, present different qualitative characters, things of the same color can have different appearance properties. But if we allow that the perception of a color involves its presenting to the perceiver one of its qualitative characters, we can dispense with the view that perceiving an object to have a color involves perceiving it to have an appearance property distinct from that color.

I began the current discussion with the idea that our color experiences "inherit" their phenomenal character from the qualitative character of the colors themselves, and then claimed that to be tenable this view must allow that the same color will have many different qualitative characters, different ones of which it presents to observers depending on the circumstances (lighting conditions, etc.) and the nature of the observers. But this talk of "inheriting" phenomenal or qualitative character is a ladder I now want to throw down behind me. All I want to retain is the idea that there is a necessary correspondence between phenomenal characters of color experiences and qualitative characters of colors, this because each of the phenomenal characters can be thought of as a representational feature of the experience, which it has in virtue of representing the instantiation of a color presenting that qualitative character. Like my former view, which equated the phenomenal character of color experiences with that aspect of their representational content that has to do with the representation of appearance properties, this view is a version of representationalism about phenomenal character. And like my former view I believe that it does justice to the Moorean transparency intuition; asked to attend to one's perceptual experience of color, all one can do is attend to the way something appears with respect to color (or, if one is hallucinating, how one is appeared to with respect to color), and this is to attend to what qualitative character a colored object is perceived as presenting (or, in the case of hallucination, what qualitative character it appears to one that some object is presenting).[8]

---

[8] The claim that there is a necessary correspondence between phenomenal characters of color experience and qualitative characters of colors needs to be qualified, for reasons given in my 2003. Consider a case of spectrum inversion in which Jack's experiences of a certain color are phenomenally different from Jill's experiences of the same color. As I am now conceiving this, that color presents one qualitative character to Jack and a different one to Jill. One possibility is that the causal features of the color that are involved in the production of Jack's experiences of the color are different from those involved in Jill's experiences of that color, and one might in that case identify the different qualitative characters of the color with these different sets of causal features of it. But it needn't be like this. It might be instead that when the color is viewed by both Jack and Jill, its proximate effect on Jack's perceptual system is the same as its proximate effect on Jill's perceptual system (e.g., in both, the cells on the retina are affected in exactly the same way), and that the difference in their perceptual experiences is due to differences in the way this proximate effect is processed in the two systems in later stages of the perceptual process. In that case, there would be a good sense in which the very same sets of causal features of the color contribute to causing the phenomenally different experiences. If we identify qualitative characters with sets of causal features, this give us a case in which the presentation of the *same* qualitative character produces, in different perceivers, experiences *different* in phenomenal character. If we want to preserve the correspondence between phenomenal characters of experiences and qualitative characters of colors, we will have to give up identifying the latter with sets of causal features of color properties. Now in the present example, the color has both the power to produce one sort of experience in the likes of Jack and the power to produce another sort of experience in the likes of Jill, and while these powers are grounded in the same causal features of the color there is a sense in which they are different—one is a power to produce one effect, and the other is a power to produce a different effect. So we might preserve the necessary correspondence by taking these different powers to be the different qualitative characters that are presented by the color to the different observers. But given that the causal features that ground one of these powers are the same as those that ground the other, and that the powers are different because of the different phenomenal characters that experiences have when they are exercised, it would only be in a very Pickwickean sense that the phenomenal characters of the experiences could be said to be "inherited from" qualitative characters of the colors.

IV

Earlier I suggested that while the way a thing of a certain color looks can be the same as the way a thing of a different color looks without there being any misperception, it seems necessarily the case that if the way something tastes is the same as the way a sweet thing tastes, and there is no misperception, then both things taste, and are, sweet. What goes for sweet seems to go for bitter, sour, and so on. This suggests that while colors are not (phenomenal) ways things appear, properties such as sweetness, bitterness, and the like are (phenomenal) ways things appear, namely, ways things taste.

I have said that if we speak of colors as having qualitative characters, we should allow that each color has a set of different qualitative characters. We can take it that any sensible quality has a set of qualitative characters. But this should not rule out the possibility that there are some sensible qualities that differ from colors in having only one member in their sets of qualitative characters. Perhaps this is true of the properties expressed by the terms "sweet," "bitter," and so on. When this is so, the property will be necessarily coextensive with the appearance property associated with its one qualitative character, and arguably identical with that appearance property. Perhaps sweetness, bitterness, and so on just are appearance properties. So my abandonment of the view that our color experiences represent appearance properties associated with the qualitative characters of the colors does not commit me to denying that it is ever the case that what a perceptual experience represents is an appearance property.

Elsewhere I have held that when a person feels a pain in his foot, he is perceiving a certain sort of appearance property (what I used to call a phenomenal property) in his foot (Shoemaker 2000). There can be disagreement as to whether it can be strictly correct to say that what is in the foot *is* pain; for there are considerations that point towards saying that the pain is a perceptual experience that represents one's foot as being some way, and that experience is presumably not in the foot. Be that as it may, it is certainly the case that when one feels pain in one's foot, there is a way one's foot feels—a qualitative character is presented to one, as located in one's foot. Perhaps in some sense one is also perceiving damage in one's foot. But it would seem forced to say that there is some property one perceives as being instantiated in one's foot which is such that under different circumstances, or to different sorts of perceivers, that same property appears different ways (presents different qualitative characters). I find it more natural to say that the property perceived to be instantiated in one's foot has only one qualitative character in its quiver of qualitative characters, and is an appearance property. The same applies to itches, feelings of nausea, and to the mostly nameless feelings one experiences in various parts of one's body.

What are we to say of felt warmth and coldness? Temperatures are properties of objects at least as objective as colors, and the temperatures responsible for feelings of warmth and coldness can feel different depending on the circumstances, and perhaps depending on the nature of the perceiver. But it is questionable whether terms like "hot," "warm," "cool", and "cold" are always used to ascribe the same ranges of temperatures. Sometimes, I think, saying that something feels warm is just saying that it feels a certain (phenomenal) way; it is saying that it has a certain appearance property.

I said above that it might be that terms like "sweet" stand for appearance properties. But couldn't there be something analogous to spectrum inversion in the case of tastes—a difference between two subjects, such that the things both call "sweet" taste different to them, and perhaps such that there is a way things can taste such that to one of them the things they call sweet taste that way while to the other the things they call sour taste that way? This raises a variety of issues that I cannot pursue here. If someone were such that the things that both he and we call sweet made him pucker up his lips, and if in general he responds to the taste of such things as we do to the taste of a lemon, I think we would be reluctant to hold that he means by "sweet" what we do, even if he applies it to the very things we do. I would be inclined to describe the case by saying that he uses the word "sweet" to report the appearance property we use the word "sour" to report.

On my former view the phenomenal character of experiences can be said to consist in the representation of appearance properties. On my present view the situation is more complicated: sometimes the phenomenal character consists in the representation of appearance properties; sometimes it consists in the representation of one or another of the aspects of perceivable properties that I have called qualitative characters. Both the former view and the present view can look circular—for, while phenomenal character is characterized in terms of the representation of appearance properties or qualitative characters, appearance properties and qualitative characters are characterized in terms of how they affect or are disposed to affect the phenomenal character of experiences. My way of avoiding circularity is laid out elsewhere (Shoemaker 2000), and I will not repeat it here. I will only mention that it consists in a "package deal" account that simultaneously defines "phenomenal character" and "qualitative character," and involves an appeal to something I have long insisted on—functionally definable relations of qualitative similarity and difference between experiences, and qualia as features of experiences that ground these relations.

IV

I began this chapter by observing that we speak of things as appearing various ways to us, and asking what these "ways" are. It seemed at least a natural suggestion that the ways things appear are properties they appear to have—this I called the *Ways = Properties Principle*. But in the case of what I have called "phenomenal" ways of appearing—where we speak of similarities and differences in ways things appear without intending to speak of similarities and differences in the "objective" properties things are perceived as having—this suggestion ran into difficulties. One candidate for being the set of properties that are the ways is the set of what I have called appearance properties. If we take these to be perceived, and perceptually represented, they seem the ideal candidate; for then the ways things appear will be the same or different just to the extent that the appearance properties they are perceived as having are the same or different. But the idea that these are perceived seems problematic, because of the oddity of saying that a given way something appears is the property of appearing that way, and so the property of appearing to have the property of appearing that way, and so the property of appearing to have the property of appearing to appear to have the property of being that way, and so on *ad infinitum*. Many people also find it odd, at best, to hold that our color experiences necessarily represent properties other than the colors, and represent the colors only by representing these other properties. I do not think that these oddities constitute a knockdown refutation of the view that appearance properties are the ways; but perhaps they are a reason for looking for a less paradoxical-sounding account of what the ways are. The other version of the Ways = Properties Principle I considered was Michael Thau's view that the ways are nameless intrinsic properties. That view I found unacceptable because it seems to me unbelievable that there are properties of the sort his account requires these to be.

It may be that the question of what the ways things appear are is as misplaced as the question of what "sakes" are—what kind of entity is the sake for which something is done. It may be that we can understand what is said when we speak of the ways things appear as similar or different without assigning any ontological status to ways. But I have suggested that we might think of the ways as the "qualitative characters" of perceived properties that determine the "phenomenal characters" of the experiences of them.[9] It is compatible with this suggestion that sometimes a perceived property has just one qualitative character, and can be identified with the property of presenting that qualitative character or being such as to present it—in other words, can be identified with an appearance property.

---

[9] There may be cases in which something looks, phenomenally, a certain way but does not present a qualitative character of its color (or, in the terms of my former view, does not have the corresponding appearance property). Suppose I have an after-image with eyes open, and its position in my visual field coincides with that of some object. The object might appear to have the color of the after-image, thereby looking a certain way, without its color presenting the qualitative character that normally goes with looking that way. My experience would in this case represent the object as having a color that presents that qualitative character, and would be to that extent illusory; but the object would be seen, and the way it looks could be the same as the way some other object looks, where the color of the latter is presenting that qualitative character. If this is possible, we cannot say in general that the ways are qualitative characters—although we can say that when something looks (phenomenally) a certain way, it is represented as having a property that presents a qualitative character. Here I am indebted to discussion with Doug Meehan.

In such cases the Ways = Properties principle holds. But in the case of color, where the same color can present different qualitative characters under different viewing conditions, or to different sorts of perceivers, it seems better to say that the ways are not properties of external things but aspects of such properties. This provides the same benefits as the view that the ways are appearance properties in all cases. It does justice to the Moorean transparency claim about introspection of perceptual experiences; in introspecting the experience we see through it to the property it represents, and here this means seeing through it to the qualitative character which the property is represented as presenting. And it permits one to hold that the phenomenal character of perceptual experiences is an aspect of their representational content, and to hold this compatibly with holding that spectrum inversion is possible—this because sensible qualities can have multiple qualitative characters, and can overlap in their qualitative characters, thereby making it possible for the same property to present different qualitative characters to different sorts of perceivers, and for different properties to present the same qualitative character to different sorts of perceivers.

REFERENCES

Campbell, John (1993), "A Simple View of Color," in John Haldane and Crispin Wright (eds), *Reality, Representation, and Projection* (Oxford: Oxford University Press).

Campbell, John (2002), *Reference and Consciousness* (Oxford: Clarendon Press).

Chalmers, David (2004), "The Representational Character of Experience," in B. Leiter (ed.), *The Future of Philosophy* (Oxford: Oxford University Press).

Hilbert, David and Kalderon, Mark E. (2000), "Color and the Inverted Spectrum," in Steven Davis (ed.), *Color Perception: Philosophical, Artistic and Computational Perspectives* (Oxford: Oxford University Press): 187–214.

Johnston, Mark (1992), "How to Speak of the Colors," *Philosophical Studies* 68: 221–63.

Johnston, Mark (1996), "A Mind–Body Problem at the Surface of Objects," *Philosophical Issues* 7: 219–29.

Shoemaker, Sydney (1982), "The Inverted Spectrum," *The Journal of Philosophy* 79: 357–81.

Shoemaker, Sydney (1994), "Phenomenal Character," *Nous* 28: 21–39.

Shoemaker, Sydney (1996), "Intrasubjective/Intersubjective," in Shoemaker, *The First-Person Perspective and Other Essays* (Cambridge: Cambridge University Press).

Shoemaker, Sydney (2000), "Introspection and Phenomenal Character," *Philosophical Topics* 28: 247–73.

Shoemaker, Sydney (2003), "Content, Character, and Color," *Philosophical Issues* 13: 253–78.

Thau, Michael (2002), *Consciousness and Cognition* (New York: Oxford University Press).

Thompson, Brad (forthcoming), "Senses for Senses."

14

Which Properties are Represented in Perception?

Susanna Siegel

In discussions of perception and its relation to knowledge, it is common to distinguish what one comes to believe on the basis of perception from the distinctively perceptual basis of one's belief. The distinction can be drawn in terms of propositional contents: there are the contents that a perceiver comes to believe on the basis of her perception, on the one hand; and there are the contents properly attributed to perception itself, on the other. Consider the content:

(#) that Ms Elfenbein went to Ankara.

Suppose that you believed that Ms Elfenbein is out of town only if she went to Ankara. And suppose you went to her house, and found that her curtains were drawn, that her mailbox was overstuffed, and that repeated ringings of her doorbell went unanswered. Then you would reasonably come to believe (#) on the basis of your visual experience. But (#) does not seem to be properly attributable to your visual experience itself (in this case). We seem to be able to distinguish what is presented perceptually from what we go on to believe. We can draw this distinction, no matter how much or how little overlap there may be between them.

The same point can be put in terms of the properties that are represented in visual experience. Consider the property of being round. This is a property that something can be seen to have. And if one can perceive that a surface is round,

Versions of this paper were presented at Vassar, Utah, the 2002 NEH Summer Institute on Consciousness and Intentionality, Syracuse, Arizona, Michigan, ANU, Taipei, UNC-Chapel Hill, and NYU. I am grateful to the audiences on these occasions for much helpful discussion. For criticism and discussion along the way, many thanks to Ned Block, Alex Byrne, David Chalmers, Fred Dretske, Rich Feldman, Hartry Field, Justin Fisher, Michael Glanzberg, Güven Güzeldere, Terry Horgan, Amy Kind, Jeff King, Bill Lycan, John Morrison, Ram Neta, Christopher Peacocke, Richard Price, Jim Pryor, Stephen Schiffer, Charles Siewert, Maja Spener, Jason Stanley, Daniel Stoljar, Scott Sturgeon, Jonathan Vogel, and the editors of this volume.

roundness, the property, can be represented in visual experience. Contents and properties, then, are related in the following straightforward way: if a subject S's visual experience has the content that a thing x is F, then S's visual experience represents the property of being F.

It is relatively uncontroversial that color and shape properties of some sort are represented in visual experience.[1] Being orange and being spherical, for example, are properties that we can sensorily perceive a basketball to have. (I'm assuming that if shape properties are represented in experience, then so are some depth properties.) I'll also be assuming, somewhat more controversially, that in experience we also represent ordinary objects. The class of ordinary objects is notoriously difficult to define, but it is clear enough to support theorizing by psychologists—for instance, theorizing about what *concept* of object infants have. And plenty of examples of ordinary objects can be given—cats, keys, tables, and the like.

The main question addressed in this chapter is whether any properties are represented in visual experience, besides the ones standardly taken to be so represented. Do any sensory experiences represent any properties other than color, shape, illumination, motion, their co-instantiation in objects and successions thereof? I will focus on visual experiences, and argue that some visual experiences do represent properties other than these. Although the properties other than these do not form a natural class, it will be useful to have a label for them. Because they include, though are not limited to, natural kind properties, and because one of my examples will involve such a property, and finally because "kind" begins with "k", I'm going to call the rest of the properties *K-properties.*[2] The thesis I will defend is:

Thesis K: In some visual experiences, some K-properties are represented.

Defining K-properties in the way I have brings into focus some alternatives to Thesis K. Consider the following extreme view about the properties represented in visual experience: visual experience is akin to what David Marr called the *2 1/2-D sketch.* Roughly, the 2 1/2-D sketch represents color, shape, and illumination properties of facing surfaces, but does not represent which surfaces belong to the same object, or how those surfaces continue out of view. (That's what the "1/2" is for: some facing surfaces are represented as farther away than others; but the sketch does not represent full volumetric information.)

---

[1] There has been much discussion recently about which properties in the natural world (if any) are the colors, and about whether any of those properties are the same as the properties represented in color experiences (see essays in Byrne and Hilbert (1997)). Though hardly anyone denies that colors are represented in color experience (though see Thau (2002)), some have proposed that visual experience represents properties easily mistaken for the colors. (Defenders of this last view include Shoemaker (1994, and this volume, ch. 13.) Neither of these positions departs very far from the intuition that properties very much like colors are paradigms of what is presented in visual experience.

[2] K-properties also exclude some properties that one might think of as kinds, such as the property of being red.

A slightly more permissive view is that visual experience represents that some surfaces and edges—for example, those making up a cup's handle and the rest of the cup—are grouped together into fully volumetric (3D) units. More permissive still is the view that visual experience represents colors, shapes, volumetric groupings, and objects. Thesis K is even more extreme: it allows that in addition to all these things, visual experience represents properties such as being a house, and being a tree.[3]

The views I've just mentioned differ on what the veridicality conditions of visual experience are. The less committal the contents of visual experience, the less misperception there is. For instance, suppose you and your brother come across a bowl full of expertly designed wax fruits. Your brother is fooled into thinking that there are ripe juicy peaches and pears in the bowl: he *believes* that there are peaches and pears in the bowl, and this belief of his is false. The scene doesn't fool you, let's suppose, but only because you already believed on some non-perceptual basis—for instance, from reading your daily horoscope's predictions—that you would see some fake fruits today. Because you have this background belief, you suspect trickery, and, unlike your brother, you don't end up *believing* that there are peaches and pears in the bowl. Might there be in such a case some sort of error in your visual experience, even if not in your belief? A *perceptual* error would be one from which not even your suspicion protects you. If you misperceive, then your visual experience's content is false: your visual experience tells you that there are peaches and pears on the table, and that is incorrect, so the experience is falsidical. In contrast, if no perceptual error is involved in this case, then the contents of your visual experience are less committal, but correct: they tell you, for instance, that the contents of the bowl have certain colors and shapes. So if you misperceived, then, in suspecting that things were not as they looked, you corrected for an error at the level of visual experience. Whereas if your visual experience told you something less committal about what you each saw in the bowl (as it would, for instance, if Thesis K were false), then your suspicion saved you from making an error at the level of belief in the first place. These two descriptions of the situation assume different accounts of what contents visual experience has.

My defense of Thesis K goes as follows. First, I will discuss some cases in which a perceiver is disposed to recognize a K-property on the basis of visual experience. I'll argue in each sort of case that such sensitivity makes a difference to the phenomenology of visual experience. Furthermore, I'll suggest, its making

---

[3] Though I have assumed here that experiences have contents, in the sense introduced in the text, the main question of the chapter can be posed without assuming that they do. Experience may represent properties, even if it consists in a relation to a perceived particular object and its property instances, as some disjunctivists about visual perception hold. (see Martin (1997)). An analogous question would then arise: namely, which properties are such that their property instances can (partially) constitute experiences? Similarly, if experience is the having of sense-data, where these are sensory afflictions that are not assessable for accuracy, the analogous question is what properties sense-data can have.

a difference to visual phenomenology is a reason to think that visual experiences represent the K-property to which the subject is sensitive. The discussion will proceed with preliminary clarifications in section 1, a discussion of why it matters whether Thesis K is true in section 2, and the case involving recognitional dispositions in section 3. I conclude in section 4 by considering some implications of Thesis K.

1   PRELIMINARIES

Before proceeding any further, some terminology needs to be clarified: *visual experience*, its *phenomenology* and *contents*, and what it is for visual experience to *represent a property*.

Visual experiences are mental events of the sort that typically occur when a subject is seeing. These events determine the way things look to the subject. Substantive questions arise in determining what the relevant meaning of "look" is. We cannot discern which aspects of experience are the visual ones simply by determining which English sentences of the form *It looks to S as if . . .* are true. You could speak truly when you say "It looks to me as if Ms Elfenbein went to Ankara," yet not be reporting the contents of your visual experience.[4]

Visual experiences have phenomenal character, or more simply a phenomenology. The phenomenal character of a visual experience is what it is like to have that visual experience. In general, I will say that events of sensing, such as seeing, have a sensory phenomenology. Using terminology in this way, blindsight is not a form of sensing.[5]

What it is like to have a visual experience is easy to confuse with what it is like to have the overall experience—including kinesthetic, emotional, and perhaps

---

[4] One might question whether there is any use of "looks" that is appropriate for this stipulation. As J. L. Austin (1962: 43) pointed out, gasoline looks like water. This seems to be a fact about gasoline that obtains independently of anyone's mental states. (We seem to be able to make sense of the idea that gasoline would look just the same, even if there were no perceivers.) Inspired by Austin, one might conclude that there is no mental property we have while seeing, in virtue of which things look the way they do; and, therefore, the working definition offered is a non-starter, since it says that visual experience is just such a mental property.

The Austin-inspired point brings out that there are multiple uses of "looks." Even if its use in "gasoline looks like water" does not tell us about any particular perceiver's mental state, there are other uses of "looks" that do tell us about this, as when we say "it looks to S as if there is something red and white over there." It could look this way to S even if there is nothing red and white over there, whereas (worries about fiction aside) "gasoline looks like water" could not be true if there were no such thing as gasoline. This is relevant use of "looks." Since "looks" has such a use, our working definition of visual experience is not doomed from the start: the Austinian use of "looks" is not the only use available.

[5] In blindsight, although there does not seem to the subject to be anything in her visual field, if forced to guess between certain parameters (e.g., which way a line is oriented), subjects guess correctly more than half the time. For further discussion of perception without awareness see Dretske (this volume, ch. 4).

imaginative components—of which the sensory experience is a part. Suppose you see a golden pentagon while sitting cross-legged in a garden, feeling cheerful. "What it is like to see the golden pentagon" could reasonably be taken to pick out either the phenomenal character of the overall experience, or the phenomenal character of the visual experience of which it is a part. What it is like to see a golden pentagon differs from what it is like to see a rocky hillside. More generally, a visual experience V counts as phenomenally the same as a visual experience V′ just in case V and V′ have the same phenomenal character. V and V′ could be phenomenally the same, even though the subject of V feels cheerful while the subject of V′ feels gloomy.

What needs clarification next is the notion that visual experiences have contents. The contents of visual experience are the sort of things that have accuracy conditions. If a visual experience has the content that there is a golden pentagon in front of one, then this content is accurate just in case there is a golden pentagon in front of one.

Some philosophers have denied that visual experiences have contents, even in this minimal sense. If a visual experience is nothing but a "raw feel," for instance, then it has no contents. In assuming that visual experiences have contents, I am assuming that they are not merely raw feels.[6]

When experiences have content, they represent—perhaps inaccurately—that such-and-such is the case. They represent that certain things have certain properties. For example, when you see a ripe tomato under normal circumstances, your experience represents the tomato surface as being red. In general (as I suggested at the start), when experiences represent that a thing x has property F, it is representing the property F. So visual experiences represent properties.

Thesis K says that some K-properties are sometimes represented *in visual experience*. Being represented in visual experience is one way in which properties can be represented. Some visual processes represent properties, where such representation has no associated phenomenology. In contrast, when a property is represented in experience, its being so represented has an associated phenomenology.

Now, it is a theoretical question, with many competing candidate answers, exactly what relation being represented in experience has to sensory phenomenology. The notion of being represented in experience that figures in Thesis K leaves open whether there is any explanatory relation between property-representation and sensory phenomenology, and whether either of these constitutes the other. Given what's built in to the notion of being represented in experience, Thesis K amounts to this: in whatever sense the representation of color and shape properties can have an associated sensory phenomenology, the representation of K-properties can too.

---

[6] This leaves open that visual experiences can also have intrinsic, non-representational features of some sort, where these are not themselves truth-apt, and are also not parts of contents. So I am not assuming anything about the existence of such non-representational features, one way or the other.

Finally, for all I've said about being represented in experience, a property can be represented in experience, even if the subject of the experience possesses no concept of that property. According to some philosophers, subjects can sensorily represent a determinate hue, even when they are not disposed to recognize that hue on subsequent occasions.[7] Experiences of colors are supposed to be the paradigm case of non-conceptual sensory representation. I don't know of any discussion of the topic that presents a K-property as an example of a property that can figure in what have come to be called "non-conceptual contents" of experience. The arguments for Thesis K in this chapter won't challenge the implicit assumption that K-properties, perhaps unlike some color properties, can be represented in experience only if the subject has *some* sort of disposition to recognize their instances (assuming that they have multiple instances). But this assumption will not be built into the very notion of property representation in experience. That notion is neutral on what it takes for a property to be represented in experience.

2   WHY IT MATTERS WHETHER THESIS K IS TRUE

I said earlier that asking what shall count as a misperception is a way of making vivid the issue surrounding Thesis K. Why does it matter whether Thesis K is true, and what counts as a misperception? It matters for at least four reasons.

First, the problem of intentionality is sometimes posed as the problem of how it is possible for a subject to be in a contentful state. A verdict on what counts as a misperception would constrain the explanandum for the case of visual experience. That is, a verdict on what may count as a misperception places a constraint on accounts of how it is possible for there to be contentful visual experiences in the first place. If visual experience cannot represent that there are peaches on the table, then whatever makes it the case that a visual experience has the content it does had better not allow that visual experiences represent the property of being a peach.

Second, there may be general skeptical worries that get going only if the contents of visual experience turn out to be informationally impoverished. Suppose, for example, that veridical experiences could only provide information about the colors and facing surfaces of objects, and not about which facing surfaces belong to the same object, or whether or not they continue out of view. Could such visual experiences play the justificatory role claimed for them by a correct theory of justification? Someone might reasonably doubt that they could. Settling what contents visual experiences have will determine whether such a challenge is worth attempting to formulate.[8]

---

[7] For discussion, see the articles in Gunther (2003).

[8] Even if Thesis K is true, that would not necessarily be the end of the skeptical challenge mentioned. In principle, merely entertaining the skeptical could change the contents and phenomenology of an experience in such a way that even if the experience started out representing

A third reason why the truth of Thesis K matters has to do with recent research on pathological conditions known as delusions of belief, such as those found in Capgras Syndrome, which is a condition in which patients seem to believe that people close to them have been replaced by impostors. An important empirical question for psychiatry is what the nature of the delusion is: roughly, whether it is a normal response to an unusual experience, or whether instead it is an unusual response to a normal experience.[9] In forming empirically testable hypotheses about delusions of belief, it is useful to have independent support from the philosophy of perception about what sorts of contents experiences can have.

The fourth reason why it matters whether Thesis K is true relates to the role of experiences in justification. Let a w-world be a world with the actual laws of nature, in which subjects have the same perceptual equipment as we do. Consider the following claim:

(+) If two visual experiences in a w-world differ in which properties they represent and all other factors relevant to justification are the same, then they differ in which propositions they provide justification for believing.

Suppose that visual experiences provide immediate justification for believing a proposition p, where this means that the justification provided by visual experience does not depend on any other factors. Assuming that experience provides immediate justification in virtue of the properties it represents, claim (+) will be true if any difference in properties represented makes a difference to justification provided.

Even theories that deny that there is such a thing as immediate justification can accept (+). Suppose that visual experiences provide evidential support for propositions only with the addition of certain special background beliefs on the part of the subject. According to claim (+), if two subjects in a w-world have exactly the same background beliefs (which themselves have the same epistemic status) and their visual experiences differ in what properties they represent, then different propositions will be evidentially supported by the visual experience combined with the background beliefs.

Let us take another example. Suppose that which propositions visual experiences provide justification for believing depends on the environmental conditions in which the visual experiences are had. For example, suppose that which

K properties, as a result of entertaining the skeptical hypothesis it ceased to represent them. It is an open question whether entertaining the skeptical hypothesis would change experiences in just this way.

[9] For discussion, see Coltheart and Davies (2000). More generally, Davies, Coltheart, and colleagues agree with Maher (1974, 1999) that several delusions in addition to Capgras are beliefs, and that part of what makes them pathologies is an experiential component in response to which the subject forms the delusional belief. Given these assumptions, one task for future research is to develop and test hypotheses about the nature of the experience.

propositions the subject is justified in believing depends on whether the belief-forming process, of which the experience is a part, is reliable. According to claim (+), if such mechanisms in two subjects in a w-world are equally reliable and their visual experiences differ in what properties they represent, then different propositions will be such that the visual experience combined with the environmental conditions justify the subject in believing them.

If claim (+) is true, then what propositions one's visual experience contributes to providing justification for will depend on which properties visual experience represents. But is claim (+) true?

Claim (+) is very strong. It says that in any w-world, every difference in properties represented by experience matters for what an experience, combined with other factors relevant for justification, provides justification for believing. A claim at the opposite extreme says that in any w-world, no difference in properties represented by experience makes a difference for what an experience, combined with other factors relevant for justification, provides justification for believing.

This latter claim seems false. It would be odd if, in a w-world, what contents visual experiences had was totally irrelevant to what propositions the experience (together with any other epistemically relevant factors) provided justification for believing. For example, holding environmental conditions constant, compare two visual experiences, one of an undifferentiated blue expanse, the other of a dairy farm. Now consider the claim that the propositions that the experience together with these conditions provide justification for believing are exactly the same. This claim seems not to respect the basic point that what one sees makes a difference to what one is justified in believing. The falsity of this claim is enough to make the general issue of what shall count as a misperception matter. But this is compatible with the denial of (+). I'm not sure whether a claim as strong as (+) is true.[10] But I think something is true that's stronger than the basic point that what one sees makes a difference to what one is justified in believing.

Consider two entirely veridical w-world experiences had by Boring and Rich. Boring and Rich are facing a fruit bowl. Boring's experience represents only colored shapes, whereas Rich's represents that there is a bowl of fruit on the table.

Now, Boring's experience supports invariances that Rich's experience doesn't. Both experiences represent properties that some rubber balls can look to have, as well as representing properties that peaches can look to have. But consider the result of combining each experience with the belief that rubber balls look to have certain shape and surface-shape (texture) properties—properties that both experiences represent. Arguably, combining this belief with Boring's experience

---

[10] One might propose to accept (+) on the basis of the claim that one is justified in ascribing to oneself an experience that represents properties F and G if one has an experience that represents F and G and not otherwise. I'm dubious about the latter claim, however.

yields some sort of evidence that there are rubber balls in the bowl: visual experience represents that there are certain colored volumes; the background belief is that some rubber balls look to have the property of being spherical and (let's say) orangey-pink.

In contrast, combining Rich's experience with the belief that rubber balls look to have certain color and shape properties does not seem to yield the same evidence. Rich's experience represents that there is fruit in the bowl (along with representing the color and shape properties that Boring's experience represents). Now, nothing is both a rubber ball and a piece of fruit. So the fact that Rich's experience represents the property of being fruit weakens the evidence for there being rubber balls in the bowl.

I think this sort of case shows that the justificatory role of experiences is not indifferent to whether it represents K-properties or not. I haven't tried to defend the claim that Boring and Rich—the subjects—are justified in believing different propositions. But I have given a reason to think that, as factors in justification, the experiences of Boring and Rich are not interchangeable.[11]

I now turn to the case for Thesis K from recognitional dispositions.

3   RECOGNITIONAL SENSITIVITY TO K-PROPERTIES

My case for Thesis K involves experiences in which the subject's beliefs about what she is seeing seem to affect visual phenomenology. Changes in beliefs about what one is seeing don't always bring about changes in one's visual phenomenology. A case in point is the Müller-Lyer lines, which continue to look as if they differ in length, even after one learns that they don't. But there seem to be other cases in which changes elsewhere in the cognitive system do bring about phenomenal changes. The argument for Thesis K depends crucially on *intuitions* about these examples, or others like it. Before turning to examples of such changes, some remarks about methodology are in order.

It is often best to avoid arguments that rest ultimately on intuition, since there can be at most a stand-off between a proponent of the argument and someone who does not share the intuition. In this case, however, appeals to intuition of some sort are unavoidable. Perhaps this is why other defenders of Thesis K have not tried to offer arguments for it at all, but have opted instead simply to give convincing *descriptions* of the phenomenology.[12] The discussion here is an attempt to split the difference between description and argument,

---

[11] I've been considering only one type of factor besides experience that is relevant to justification—namely, background beliefs. But I suspect you could make a similar argument using different non-experiential factors, such as external ones.

[12] A contemporary example of such a writer is Charles Siewert, who offers excellent descriptions of the phenomenon (1998: ch. 7).

by starting with a minimal intuition, and then mapping out exactly what an opponent of Thesis K would have to deny if she accepts the initial intuition.

What about the initial minimal intuition? What happens if someone doesn't share it? It seems reasonable to expect there to be some intuitions that elicit broad agreement, since visual experience is something to which one has first-person access. The exact nature and limits of such access is a topic unto itself. But the intuitions on which the case for Thesis K rests are simple and modest: they are intuitions about whether there is a change in phenomenology between two sorts of situation. It would be quite a radical view that denied that there were *any* such cases in which first-person access could detect a change in phenomenology. The case for Thesis K counts on there being first-person access to the fact that there is this sort of change, but does not assume that with such access alone one can discern the exact contents of visual experience.

Let me turn to two examples of changes in the cognitive system that seem to bring about phenomenal changes. Both involve the gradual development of properly grounded recognitional dispositions.

The first example involves the disposition to recognize semantic properties of a bit of text, grounded in knowledge of how to read it. Although Thesis K concerns only visual experience, it is useful to begin with an auditory example. Almost everyone has experienced hearing others speak in a foreign language that one doesn't understand, and that one can't parse into words and sentences. The phenomenology of hearing the same speech when one does understand is markedly different.

This contrast has a visual analog. Consider a page of Cyrillic text. The way it looks to someone before and after she learns to read Russian seems to bring about a phenomenological difference in how the text looks. (Christopher Peacocke makes a similar phenomenological claim in ch. 3 of *A Study of Concepts*.)[13] When you are first learning to read the script of a language that is new to you, you have to attend to each word, and perhaps to each letter, separately. In contrast, once you can easily read it, it takes a special effort to attend to the shapes of the script separately from its semantic properties. You become disposed to attend to the

---

[13] Peacocke writes:

Once a thinker has acquired a perceptually individuated concept, his possession of that concept can causally influence what contents his experiences possess. If this were not so, we would be unable to account for differences which manifestly exist. One such difference, for example, is that between the experience of a perceiver completely unfamiliar with Cyrillic script seeing a sentence in that script and the experience of one who understands a language written in that script. These two perceivers see the same shapes at the same positions. . . . The experiences differ in that the second perceiver recognizes the symbols as of particular orthographic kinds, and sequences of the symbols as of particular semantic kinds. (1992: 89)

In this passage, in addition to claiming that two experiences of reading Cyrillic text would differ phenomenally, Peacocke also seems to be making an argument, with the phenomenal claim as a premise, that which concepts one possesses can causally influence which contents one's experiences have. I'm endorsing the phenomenal premise, without endorsing the argument.

semantic properties of the words in the text, and less disposed to attend visually to the orthographic ones.

The second example involves a different recognitional disposition. Suppose you have never seen a pine tree before, and are hired to cut down all the pine trees in a grove containing trees of many different sorts. Someone points out to you which trees are pine trees. Some weeks pass, and your disposition to distinguish the pine trees from the others improves. Eventually, you can spot the pine trees immediately. They become visually salient to you. Like the recognitional disposition you gain, the salience of the trees emerges gradually. Gaining this recognitional disposition is reflected in a phenomenological difference between the visual experiences you had before and after the recognitional disposition was fully developed.

The argument for Thesis K from these cases has three substantial premises, plus a premise that is unproblematic if the cases are convincing. Let E1 be the sensory experience had by a subject S who is seeing the pine trees before learning to recognize them, and let E2 be the sensory experience had by S when S sees the pine trees after learning to recognize them. E1 and E2 are sensory parts of S's overall experiences at each of these times. I'm going to call the premise that is unproblematic if the cases are convincing premise (0):

(0) The overall experience of which E1 is a part differs from the overall phenomenology of which E2 is a part.

Claim (0) is supposed to be an intuition. It is the minimal intuition one has to have, for the argument to get off the ground.

(1) If the overall experience of which E1 is a part differs from the overall phenomenology of which E2 is a part, then there is a phenomenological difference between the sensory experiences E1 and E2.

(2) If there is a phenomenological difference between the sensory experiences E1 and E2, then E1 and E2 differ in content.

(3) If there is a difference in content between E1 and E2, it is a difference with respect to K-properties represented in E1 and E2.

If no experiences represent K-properties, then there will be no difference between E1 and E2 with respect to K-properties represented in them. So if (3) and its antecedent are true, then Thesis K is too. An analogous argument could be made for the case of the Cyrillic text.

Premises (0) and (1) entail that there is a phenomenological difference between the *overall* experiences of which E1 and E2 are parts. It specifies that it is a difference in *sensory* phenomenology (the phenomenology of sensing). Premise (0), in contrast, allows that the phenomenological difference is not a difference in sensory phenomenology, but in phenomenology of some other sort.

Given premise (0), there are three ways to block the inference from these cases of recognitional dispositions to Thesis K. First, one could deny that the phenomenological changes are sensory. This would be to deny (1). Second, one could grant that they are sensory, but deny that there is any accompanying representational difference (i.e., any difference in contents of E1 and E2). This would be to deny (2). Finally, one could grant that the phenomenological changes are accompanied by a representational change, but deny that the change involves any representation of K-properties. This would be to deny (3). I will consider each of these moves in turn.

Premise (1): Non-Sensory Phenomenology?

Let me start with the first way of attempting to block the inference to Thesis K. There are various kinds of phenomenology besides sensory phenomenology. There is the phenomenology associated with imagination, with emotions, with bodily sensation, with background phenomenology, and perhaps with some non-sensory cognitive functions. If the phenomenological change described in the two cases is non-sensory, the two most plausible suggestions seem to be that it is a change in some sort of cognitive phenomenology, or in background phenomenology. Someone might be tempted to re-describe the text and tree cases so that as far as sensory phenomenology is concerned, the experiences had with and without recognitional dispositions are the same; but that the difference in phenomenology of overall experiences is due to a non-sensory factor. If these descriptions were correct, then the examples would not bear on what properties *sensory* experience represents at all, hence would not bear at all on Thesis K.

The strategy of the opponent I'm considering, then, is to re-describe the tree and text cases by invoking non-sensory phenomenology, and thereby avoid making a commitment to Thesis K. Let's consider cognitive phenomenology first.

What structure would such re-descriptions have to have? Well, first, there would have to be an *event* in the stream of consciousness, other than the event of sensing (seeing, hearing, etc.), that allegedly has the phenomenology. Just as events of sensing have an associated phenomenology, and just as events of imagining and having (some) emotions have an associated phenomenology, so too if there is cognitive phenomenology, there must, it seems, be some events in the stream of consciousness that the phenomenology attaches to.[14] Second,

---

[14] To say that an event of sensing has an associated phenomenology leaves open whether there is any phenomenological commonality to all such events. This seems implausible for sensing as such, though perhaps more plausible within each of the modalities. But the demand on the denier of (1) is merely to show that there is an event that is not sensory and has an associated phenomenology, not to show that there is a phenomenological common element to all events, or to all events involving the same attitude, that are both cognitive and have an associated phenomenology.

assuming that the mental event involves a propositional attitude of some sort, a plausible account would have to be given of the *attitude* involved in the event, and of the *content* of that attitude.[15] Finally, some reason would have to be given to think that the phenomenology involved really isn't sensory. So, for the strategy to succeed, plausible accounts are needed of four things: the *event* in the stream of consciousness that has the (alleged) non-sensory phenomenology; the mental *attitude* it involves; the *content* of that attitude; and the factors that make the phenomenology non-sensory.

The general idea behind the strategy is that the *familiarity* that one gains in gaining a recognitional disposition is reflected in cognitive phenomenology. I now want to list some of the options for the event types, attitudes, and contents that an opponent of Thesis K who followed this strategy might invoke, in accounting for this feeling of familiarity. Though the list of options is not put forward as exhaustive, they are natural ones to consider (and the only ones that come to mind after much consideration). Once they are on the table, it will be easier to assess the case against Thesis K.

It is natural to list the events and attitudes together. They include:

(i)   forming a judgment;
(ii) dwelling on a belief;
(iii) entertaining a hunch or intuition;
(iv) entertaining a proposition by having it pass through your mind, without committing to its truth.

These are four sorts of events that can occur in the stream of consciousness. Entries (i)-(iii) are *commitment-involving*: the attitudes are all related to belief, and its accompanying commitment to the truth of the thing believed. Hunches and intuitions are like beliefs in that the subject accepts their content for certain purposes. For instance, in testing a hypothesis, one may reason as if a hunch or intuition were true. Entry (iv), in contrast, does not involve any such commitment. This distinction will be useful shortly.

What about the content of the attitudes involved in the event? Since the events are supposed to be brought about in part by gaining a recognitional disposition, the contents should reflect this gain in some way. Some reasonable options include these (I'll stick to the case of the trees):

(a) *That* is a pine tree (mentally demonstrating a tree).
(b) I've seen trees with *that look* before.
(c) I recognize *that kind of tree*.
(d) *That kind of tree* is familiar.

---

[15] When I discuss the strategy of denying (2), I will consider a version of this strategy that allows cognitive phenomenology to be had by an event that does not involve any propositional attitudes, or contents thereof.

These are supposed to be contents of mental states, rather than contents expressed by actual uses of sentences. As such, the proposal that there are attitudes that have (a)–(d) as contents involves a notion of a demonstrative thought, independent of the notion of what is expressed by an actual use of a demonstrative. The contents are analogs for thought of contents expressed by uses of sentences.

Suppose we combine any of these contents into any of the attitudes and events in the first list. Then we will have a candidate for an event with phenomenology. The denier of (1) will still owe some account, however, of what makes the event that has the phenomenology *non-sensory*. (I'm assuming that if the event is non-sensory, then so is its associated phenomenology.)

Let me now examine one instance of the strategy I've outlined for denying (1). In the tree case, the suggestion comes to this. How the tree looks before and after you become disposed to recognize pine trees is exactly the same: it looks to have certain color and shape properties. But at the moments when you recognize the tree, you experience a feeling of familiarity, and this feeling accounts for the phenomenological change before and after you gain the disposition. So, on this suggestion, the way the tree looks stays the same, before and after you become disposed to recognize it; but the phenomenology of "taking" the tree to be familiar contributes to the phenomenal change accompanying E2. For the purpose of discussion, I'll select the event and attitude of dwelling on a belief, and content that *that kind of tree* is familiar (so, (ii) and (d)).

I'm going to raise two objections to the view that the phenomenological change in the tree case consists exclusively in a change in cognitive phenomenology, where the cognitive phenomenology is had by event and attitude (ii) with content (d). The first objection would also apply, if the event and attitude were (i) or (iii), and if it had any of the four contents listed. My second objection is more general: it would apply to any combination of the events, attitudes, and contents listed.

The first objection focuses on the events with commitment-involving attitudes. Suppose that you're an expert pine-spotter looking at some pine trees in the forest. Then someone tells you that the forest has been replaced by an elaborate hologram, causing you to cease to dwell on the belief that you're looking at a familiar tree. If an event such as (ii)(d) were what contributed to the phenomenological change before and after acquiring the disposition to recognize pine trees, then we would expect your acceptance of the hologram story to make the hologram look as the forest looked to you before you knew how to recognize pine trees. But intuitively, the hologram could look exactly the same as the forest looked to you after you became an expert. So the familiarity with pine trees does not seem to have its phenomenological effects at the level of belief.

The case against the proposal that the feeling of familiarity is conferred by a belief holds equally well against the proposal that substitutes any of the commitment-involving events/attitudes for the one I chose for purposes of discussion.

Hunches and intuitions, like beliefs, seem to be attitudes that one could lose by accepting the testimony described above. If anything, hunches and intuitions are *less* resistant than beliefs are to counter-evidence—if the belief wouldn't survive accepting hologram testimony, then neither would hunches or intuitions.

The objection I've just made would not threaten a version of the strategy that invoked a non-commitment-involving attitude, such as entertaining a proposition without committing to its truth. So let us focus on a version of the proposal that appeals to an event of this sort. On this version of the proposal, in the tree case, when you look at the tree after having gained the recognitional disposition, you undergo a mental event, distinct from sensing, that has a phenomenology of its own. This is an event (we're supposing) of entertaining the proposition that *That kind of tree* is familiar, where this proposition passes through your mind, without your committing to its truth.

Here it is important to keep in view the aspect of the proposal that posits an event (supposedly a "cognitive" event) occurring in the stream of consciousness. This proposal predicts that there will be a phenomenological difference between your experiences of seeing the pine tree before and after you learn to recognize trees, only to the extent that such an event is occurring. If no such event is occurring, then, this proposal predicts, there will be no phenomenological change of the sort invoked in the original example.

The second objection targets this aspect of the proposal. An event's occurring in the stream of consciousness is not akin to having a tacit recognition (or misrecognition) of something as a tree. It is something explicit, rather than tacit. But the phenomenological change in the original tree example seems to be the sort that does not always involve an explicit entertaining of a proposition such as (d). Consider a comparable thought from Charles Siewert:

[t]hink of how individual people look different to you after you have gotten to know them than they did when you first met. Notice how different your neighborhood looks to you now that you have lived there for a while, than it did on the day you first arrived. (1998: 257–8)

What can happen with a neighborhood, it seems, can happen with trees as well. The phenomenological change is the sort that we can infer by remembering how different things looked before we became familiar with them. Becoming aware of the phenomenon involves thinking of something—a person, a neighborhood, or a kind of object, such as a tree—as familiar. But simply undergoing the phenomenon does not have to involve this. There need not be, it seems, an extra event, beyond sensing, for the phenomenological change to take effect.

I've raised this objection against the proposal that invokes a non-commitment-involving attitude. But it works equally well, if it works at all, against the proposal invoking a commitment-involving attitude.

At this point, the denier of premise (1) might reply to the objection by claiming that the event in question could have a content such as (d) explicitly, without the event being the sort I've described. After all, the denier might point out, sensory experience has its content explicitly, without involving something analogous to *saying* to oneself something like (d) (e.g., "well how about that, that's a tree," etc.).

If the putatively non-sensory event does not involve something analogous to saying to oneself something like (d), and if it is supposed to be something other than an event of visually appearing, then it becomes less clear that it is accompanying an event in the stream of consciousness at all.

Let me now consider the proposal that the phenomenal change is a change in background phenomenology, rather than a change in cognitive phenomenology attached to an occurrent event. Someone who denied premise (1) might claim that although the phenomenological difference between E1 and E2 is not sensory, neither does it belong to a specific cognitive event in the stream of consciousness.

Drunkenness and depression may be two examples of standing, background states that affect overall phenomenology. As against premise (1), someone might claim that recognitional dispositions are like drunkenness and depression in the crucial respect: they too are standing states of a subject that can affect overall phenomenology—and, indeed, the objector will claim, that is just what happens in the text and the tree cases.

To defeat premise (1) in this way, what the objector would need is a reason to think that changes in standing states can affect overall phenomenology in some way other than by causing changes in sensory phenomenology. Depression and drunkenness may involve at least some such changes: depression can cause things to look grey; drunkenness can cause them to look blurry. The relevant analogy has to be between changes in overall phenomenology that are not the result of changes in sensory phenomenology. The changes must be akin to changes in mood.

Having a recognitional disposition, however, is not phenomenologically like being in a mood at all. Moods have relatively non-local effects on phenomenology: almost *nothing* seems exciting during depression; nearly *everything* seems exciting during drunkenness. In contrast, being disposed to recognize pine trees does not have such overall phenomenological effects. So, whatever phenomenal change results from gaining recognitional dispositions, it does not seem to be a change in background phenomenology.

Let me now consider how the text example fares, if (1) is false and the phenomenological difference in how text looks before and after one learns to read it is a difference in cognitive, as opposed to sensory phenomenology.

A fan of premise (1) can grant that there are some cases in which reading a text does involve undergoing events that have a phenomenology, and that are arguably non-sensory. Lingering on a sentence while deliberating about whether it is true has a phenomenology, and arguably such an event is non-sensory. It could happen, for instance, if you weren't perceiving anything at all, but simply entertaining the proposition expressed by the sentence.

Contrast this phenomenology with that of being bombarded by pictures and captions on billboards along the highway. This seems a visual analog of the blare of a loud television, or a fellow passenger's inane cell-phone conversation. Understanding the text on the billboard as you drive by isn't a deliberate affair; rather (if the billboards have been positioned correctly), it just happens. It would please the advertisers if you lingered over every billboard's message, but no such event need occur in order for you to have "taken in" the semantic properties of the text as you whizz by. This suggests that the "taking in" can be merely sensory.

So far, I've considered two ways to deny (1). One way is to propose that the phenomenal change is a change in cognitive phenomenology that is attached to a specific event in the stream of consciousness. The other way is to propose that the phenomenal change is a change in background phenomenology. I've given reasons to think neither of these ways of denying premise (1) in the argument in for K will succeed. I now turn to the strategy of denying premise (2).

Premise (2): A Non-Representational Phenomenological Change?

The denier of (2) tries to block the inference from the examples of phenomenological change to Thesis K, by claiming that phenomenological changes are unaccompanied by any representational change at all.

Premise (2) is a consequence of a more general claim, one that is controversial in the philosophy of mind. This is the claim that with *any* change in the sensory phenomenology, there is a change in the content of sensory experience. But premise (2) itself is much more limited. It just makes a claim about phenomenology of the sort at issue in the two cases.

If (2) is false, then there is such a thing as a non-representational feeling of familiarity. This could be part of sensory experience, or part of some sort of cognitive event. Either way, it would be a feeling of familiarity that could be had even in the absence of perceiving, or seeming to perceive, anything as being familiar.[16] It would not represent anything as being familiar, but rather would be akin to a sensory affliction. It would be a raw feel. The proposal is not that there

---

[16] One might think that recent findings about the structure of face-recognition provides evidence for the existence of an non-representational feeling of familiarity. According to some neuropsychologists, the face-recognition system has at least two components: an affective component that registers when a face is familiar, and a semantic component devoted to recognizing faces (see Young (1998)). These elements seem to come apart in prosopagnosics's, who have the same differential affective reactions as normal perceivers do to pictures of familiar famous people, on the one hand, and to pictures of complete strangers, on the other (as measured by skin conductance tests), but who claim not to know who any of the people pictured are. Even if there is a mechanism devoted to affect of familiarity, however, that does not show that there is non-representational *phenomenology* of familiarity. The structure of underlying mechanisms of face recognition may not be mirrored by phenomenology. For us to have the phenomenology of seeing a familiar face, it may be that more than positive skin-conductance reaction is needed. (Indeed, it seems that more is needed, since otherwise we would expect the prosopagnosics's reports to be more equivocal than they are, to the effect that the person pictured seems familiar, yet cannot be named).

is merely a non-representational *aspect* to a representation of familiarity. Rather, the proposal is that the feeling of familiarity is entirely non-representational.[17]

Against this idea, my defense of (2) is that familiarity is not the sort of thing that could be felt without any representation of something as familiar. The best attempt to make the case for the contrary ends up positing a representation of familiarity after all.

One would expect a raw feeling of familiarity, if there was such a thing, to leave one with a sense of confusion, since if it was clear to the subject what was being felt to be familiar, then this would seem to make the feeling representational after all. Suppose, for example, you see someone who acts toward you as a stranger would, and this seems inappropriate to you, but you can't at first figure out why. In response to this feeling of strangeness, you might think to ask the person whether you have met before. But the feeling you have that leads you to ask it, someone might suggest, is a raw feeling of familiarity. It is a variety of "déjà-vu."

In the case above, the sense of confusion comes from the fact that though you take the person to be familiar, you don't recognize who they are. There are two aspects to this experience: you represent something as familiar without recognizing it, and you represent something as familiar, without at first realizing that it is so represented. The first aspect is definitive of déjà-vu: a place, or a sound, or a situation strikes you as familiar, without your being able to discern what is familiar about it. This is simply a less specific representation of familiarity—it is not a case of a feeling that does not represent anything as familiar. So the putative case of a raw feeling of familiarity does not illustrate this after all. And if that case doesn't illustrate it, it is hard to see what kind of case would.

Premise (3): Exclusively Non-K Representation?

I now consider the third response to the argument for Thesis K, which is to reject premise (3) while granting (0)–(2). Premise (3) says that the difference in content between E1 and E2 is a difference with respect to K-properties represented in E1 and E2.

Both the tree and the text examples involve a gain in recognitional dispositions, and it will be useful to keep in mind what sort of structure recognition has. A perceiver who can recognize trees by sight seems to have some sort of memory representation, and some sort of perceptual input, such that the input "matches" the memory representation, and the cognitive system of the perceiver registers that this is so. Empirical theories of object recognition are supposed to explain the nature of each of these components (the memory, the input, and the

---

[17] Contrast the case of color, where some philosophers argue that there are both non-representational and representational features of color experience: color properties are represented in experience, but color experiences also have non-representational features (e.g., Block (1996)).

matching), and the mechanisms that underlie them. Part of what's at issue in the debate about Thesis K is whether visual experience is an input to such processes of recognition, or an output of such processes. Whichever empirical and philosophical theories turn out to be correct, some structure such as this seems built in to the very notion of recognition.

One sort of proposal about the contents of E2 that a denier of premise (3) might invoke would involve the notion of a pine-tree shape-gestalt. Suppose that when you learn to recognize pine trees by sight, your experience comes to represent a complex of shapes—leaf shapes, trunk shapes, branch shapes, and overall pine tree shapes. This complex is an overall pine-tree gestalt. The pine-tree-shape gestalt is general enough that it can be shared by differently looking pine trees. But it is specific enough to capture the look shared by exemplary pine trees. The pine-tree-shape gestalt is invariant across differences in shape of particular pine trees.

For an experience of seeing a tree to represent a pine-tree-shape gestalt, it need not be part of the content of experience that the tree seen is similar to other trees with respect to such-and-such shapes. It is enough simply to represent the respects in which various pine trees are in fact similar. A pine-tree-shape gestalt, then, is not by definition something that can be represented in experience, only if the subject is disposed to believe that the different things instantiating it are the same shape. But all things that have it have a complex shape property in common.

It seems plausible to suppose that pine trees share a pine-tree-shape gestalt, to the extent that pine trees, varied though they may be in size and other features, have some quite general shape properties in common. If there were such a thing as a tree-shape gestalt, then the denier of (3) could invoke this as the non-K property that E2 represents and E1 doesn't. I'm going to call this proposal for denying (3) Anti-K.

Anti-K: E1 and E2 differ with respect to the pine-tree-shape-gestalt properties they represent, and neither represents any K-properties.

In the tree case, as Anti-K would describe it, the perceiver's experiences come to represent the tree-shape-gestalt as part of the same process by which the perceiver comes to have a memory representation "matching" that shape gestalt.

I don't know of a knock-down argument against Anti-K. But the strategy of invoking the representation invariant color-shape complexes to underpin phenomenological changes does not seem generally available. Consider, for example, the property someone's face can have of expressing doubt. One could learn to recognize when the face of someone, call him X, was expressing doubt. X might even belong to a group of people whose faces all express the doubt in the same way. Initially, one might not know that X and his kin are expressing doubt when they look that way. But this is something one could learn to recognize by observing them. In this sort of case, it seems implausible to suppose that there must be a change in which color and shape properties are represented before and after one learns that it is doubt that the face so contorted expresses. One could initially wonder what the contortion of the face meant, and come to believe that it is an expression of doubt only after repeated sightings of it and interaction with the person. This change in interpretation seems to be one that could be accompanied by a phenomenological change as well.

Once they are adjusted to be about the face case, the other two premises of the argument still seem to go through. Exactly the same considerations apply in the case of premise (2). In premise (1), the argument for ruling out non-sensory phenomenology also seems to go through as before, but in the face case another alternative to sensory phenomenology seems relevant—namely, emotional phenomenology. Here, it seems possible in principle that X could learn to detect a look of doubt on Y's face without X's having any emotional response—Y might not be anyone significant for X, such as a talking head on television.

As for premise (3), an opponent who granted the initial intuition that there is some phenomenal change accompanying the gain of a recognitional disposition might say that the phenomenal change is sensory, but that the novel phenomenology is associated merely with coming to represent the property of being a familiar expression. This option seems to be ruled out by considering a variant of the face case involving two subjects. Consider a counterfactual situation in which X contorts his face in exactly the same way, but in which that contortion expresses bemusement rather than doubt. One could come to learn that it expresses bemusement in the same way as in the first case, by extended observation and interaction. But it seems plausible to suppose that the phenomenal change in each case would be different: one sort of phenomenology for recognizing the doubtful expression, and another sort for recognizing bemusement.

Finally, return to the text example to see how it fares with respect to premise (3). The original intuition was that before and after you learn to read Russian, the same page of Cyrillic text will look differently to you. You might love the look of Cyrillic script, keep a page nearby at all times, and study its shapes carefully. Then, after learning to read Russian, you see by reading it that it is a page of insults. Even if you attended to colors and shapes of the Cyrillic script as thoroughly as possible before learning to read it, you would still experience the page differently once it became intelligible to you.

I've argued that gaining a disposition to recognize K-properties can make a difference to visual phenomenology, and that this difference is accompanied by a representation of K-properties in visual experience. In the next section, I consider why it matters whether Thesis K is true.

4   SOME IMPLICATIONS OF THESIS K

I will conclude by discussing some implications of Thesis K, and of the considerations I've appealed to in support of it.

First, if Thesis K is true for reasons of the sort given here, then visual perception as a whole is at most partly informationally encapsulated: which contents visual experiences have can be influenced by other cognitive processing. Even if visual experiential representations of some properties cannot be influenced by what happens in other parts of the cognitive system, visual experiential representations of other properties can be. If the argument here is sound, our perceptual systems may include modular "input systems" of the sort described by Fodor (1983), but these systems will not be ones with which visual *phenomenology* is exclusively associated.

Second, my case for Thesis K has proceeded without appealing to any specific theory of intentionality for experiences. The pine-tree example might be taken to suggest that one of the K-properties that visual experiences can represent is the natural kind property of being a pine tree. Since it is widely held that any mental state that represents natural kind properties has contents that are externally determined, it is natural to ask what relation Thesis K bears to the thesis that some experiential contents are externally determined.

Externalism about experience content is the view that physical duplicates can differ in which contents their experiences have. Since Thesis K is silent on what makes it the case that experiences represent what they do, it is clearly compatible with externalism about experience content.

Suppose that Thesis K is made true by visual experience representing natural kind properties, such as the property of being a pine tree. And suppose one accepts externalism. It is open to someone who accepts both of these claims to hold that physical duplicates whose environments differ (where only one includes pine trees) have the same visual phenomenology. This would entail that the property of having that visual phenomenology is not *identical* with the property of representing the property of being a pine tree in experience.[18] But it is compatible with the view that that visual phenomenology *supervenes* on the contents of visual experience.

Thesis K is also compatible with the denial of externalism. Even if one accepts that natural kind properties can be represented in visual experience only if externalism about experience content holds, one need not accept such externalism in order to accept Thesis K, because Thesis K can be true even if natural kind properties are not represented in experience.

Consider the case discussed earlier involving dispositions to recognize pine trees. If one rejects externalism but accepts that E2 in the example is an experience that represents some K-property, one has two options. First, one can hold (contrary to the received view) that the property of being a pine tree can be represented even by someone who was never in contact with pine trees. Second, one can hold that the K-property that comes to be represented in E2 is not the property of being a pine tree, but a more general K-property (possibly a kind

---

[18] For a defense of this position, see Tye (1995, 2000).

property that is not a natural kind property) that both pine trees and superficially similar trees share.

In sum, although Thesis K is compatible with externalism about the contents of experience, it does not require it. The argument for Thesis K does not appeal to any theses about content-determination. Depending on which such theses one accepts, however, and depending on views about the exact relation between content and phenomenology, one may reach different verdicts on exactly what K-property would come to be represented in the pine-tree example (assuming that the rest of the argument for Thesis K is accepted).

Finally, if Thesis K is true, then it seems reasonable to expect that K-properties other than the property of being a pine tree (or some more general K-property) and semantic properties of texts are represented in visual experience. There are two routes to generalizing the conclusion beyond the two specific properties used as examples in the argument. One route is to run exactly analogous arguments for other cases in which becoming sensitive to property instances has an effect on overall phenomenology. The argument structure leaves open, however, whether analogous considerations will always be available—and to that extent, the first route to generalizing the conclusion may turn out to be somewhat limited.

There is, however, a second route to generalizing the conclusion. Thesis K has some prima facie plausibility. One role of the argument given here is to provide positive reason to think that at least some K-properties are represented in visual experience. And if some such properties are, then it is plausible to think that others are as well.

REFERENCES

Austin, John L. (1962), *Sense and Sensibilia* (Oxford: Clarendon Press).

Block, Ned (1996), "Mental Paint and Mental Latex," in Enrique Villanueva (ed.), *Philosophical Issues 7: Perception* (Atascadero: Ridgeview Publishing Company): 19–49.

Byrne, Alex and Hilbert, David (eds) (1997), *Readings on Color*, vol. 1 (Cambridge, Mass.: MIT Press).

Coltheart, Max and Davies, Martin (eds) (2000), *Pathologies of Belief* (Oxford: Blackwell).

Fodor, Jerry (1983), *The Modularity of Mind* (Cambridge, Mass.: MIT Press).

Gunther, York H. (ed.) (2003), *Essays in Non-Conceptual Content* (Cambridge, Mass.: MIT Press).

Maher, Brendan A. (1974), "Delusional Thinking and Perceptual Disorder," *Journal of Individual Psychology* 30: 98–113.

Maher, Brendan A. (1999), "Anomalous Experience in Everyday Life: Its Significance for Psychopathology," *The Monist* 82: 547–70.

Martin, Michael (1997), "The Reality of Appearances," in Mark Sainsbury (ed.), *Thought and Ontology* (Milan: Franco Angeli): 81–106.

Peacocke, Christopher (1992), *A Study of Concepts* (Cambridge, Mass.: MIT Press).

Shoemaker, Sydney (1994), "Phenomenal Character," *Nous* 28: 21–39; reprinted in Byrne and Hilbert (1997): 227–46.

Siewert, Charles P. (1998), *The Significance of Consciousness* (Princeton: Princeton University Press).

Thau, Michael (2002), *Consciousness and Cognition* (New York: Oxford University Press).

Tye, Michael (1995), *Ten Problems of Consciousness* (Cambridge, Mass.: MIT Press).

Tye, Michael (2000), *Color, Consciousness and Content* (Cambridge, Mass.: MIT Press).

Young, Andrew W. (1998), "Covert Face Recognition in Prosopagnosia," in Andrew W. Young, *Face and Mind* (Oxford: Oxford University Press): 282–312.

15

Nonconceptual Content, Richness, and Fineness of Grain

Michael Tye

As I view the scene before my eyes, there is a way the world looks to me. If the world is that way, my visual experience is accurate; if not, my experience is inaccurate. My visual experience, then, has correctness conditions: it is correct or accurate in certain circumstances; incorrect or inaccurate in others. Visual experiences, like beliefs, are *representations* of how things are. Accordingly, visual experiences have representational content.

It is often said that the representational content of visual experience is *rich*. Another common claim is that there is a *fineness of grain* to visual experience. A third view, also quite widely accepted, is that the representational content of visual experience is *nonconceptual*. Notwithstanding the popularity of these views, it is still not fully clear what is being claimed nor how exactly the three views are connected.

The purpose of this essay is threefold. First, I want to present a clarification and partial defense of the thesis that visual experiences have nonconceptual contents.[1] Second, I want to explain and defend the view that visual experience is representationally rich. This necessitates a discussion of several psychological experiments, the results of which bear upon the view. Finally, I want to discuss how the thesis of richness relates to the thesis of fineness of grain (held most often in connection with our experiences of shades of color); and I want to spell out carefully how both theses relate to the thesis of nonconceptual content.

I would like to thank Tamar Gendler and John Hawthorne for extensive and very helpful written comments. I am indebted to Mark Sainsbury for general discussion on the topic of nonconceptual content and to Alex Byrne, Peter Carruthers, David Hilbert, and Terry Horgan for a discussion over cocktails of dot patterns after an APA symposium in Chicago on nonconceptual content. I also owe thanks to Ned Block and Chris Peacocke for their comments on this text delivered at the first NYU philosophy conference at the Villa La Pietra in Florence (as well as to members of the audience). Thanks, finally, to two anonymous referees for their observations.

[1] For a fuller defense that brings in considerations lying beyond the scope of this essay and having nothing to do with visual experience in particular, see Tye (forthcoming).

The chapter is divided into six sections. In Section I, I address some preliminary terminological matters and I take up the question of what it is for an experience to have a nonconceptual content. Here I suggest that the standard way of understanding nonconceptual content is unsatisfactory and I make a proposal of my own. In Section II, I turn to a discussion of Sperling's classic experiment (1960) on *sensory memory*. This is used to motivate on empirical grounds the thesis that visual experience has a rich content. Section III considers whether recent change blindness experiments in psychology show that richness is an illusion. In Section IV, I elucidate the familiar claim that there is a fineness of grain to the content of visual experience (notably color shade experience) and I relate it both to the thesis of nonconceptual content and to the thesis of richness. Section V addresses various responses that are available to the content conceptualist in connection with the issue of fineness of grain in visual experience. Section VI discusses an example that may seem to create serious difficulty for my proposal about nonconceptual content.

I   NONCONCEPTUAL CONTENT, THOUGHT CONTENT, AND CONCEPT POSSESSION

Before we can take up the question of what it is for an experience to have a nonconceptual content, some preliminary remarks are necessary on how I shall be using the terms "concept" and "thought content" in this essay. The content of a thought, as I shall understand it, is what is thought and intuitively what is thought individuates in a fine-grained way. Consider the case of the thought that coriander is a spice. Intuitively, what I think when I have this thought is not what I think, when I think that cilantro is a spice. The two thoughts play different roles in rationalizing explanations. This is why it is possible for me to *discover* that coriander is cilantro. The concepts *coriander* and *cilantro* have the same referent, but the way in which the referent is presented in the two cases is different. One who thinks of coriander (cilantro) as coriander thinks of it under a different guise or in a different way from one who thinks of it as cilantro. So, the content of the one thought is different from the content of the other.

In general, I take thought contents to be indicated by the "that"-clauses used to attribute thoughts. Moreover, in the first-person case, I take the content attributed via the "that"-clause to be the content of the thought, assuming that the thought ascription is true.[2] In the third-person case, the situation is more complicated. Here the thought ascription is sometimes counted as true even if the content of the thought is not the same as the content attributed, so long as

---

[2] This is to oversimplify a little. A further assumption is that the thought ascribed is a present thought. (We have privileged access to the contents of our present thoughts, not to the contents of our past ones. See here McLaughlin and Tye (1998)).

there is sufficient similarity between the two. Accordingly, I take the "that"-clause in such a case to indicate that the thought has a content that, in the given context, is sufficiently similar to the content of the sentence embedded in the "that"-clause.

As I use the term "concept," concepts are not linguistic terms in a public language. They are mental representations of a sort that can occur in thought.[3] Thoughts are composed of concepts and the contents of concepts individuate in a fine-grained way. As illustrated in the case above of the concepts *cilantro* and *coriander*, concepts that refer to the same entities can differ in their content. Indeed, concepts can differ in their content even if they refer to the same entity in all possible worlds. For example, the concept *Hesperus* has a different content from the concept *Phosphorus*, even though they both refer to the planet Venus in all possible worlds. This is why the thought that Hesperus is a planet is a different thought from the thought that Phosphorus is a planet. Similar comments apply to the concept *four* and the concept *two times two*. A small child who can count to four has the former concept; but she may not yet have learned how to multiply and thus may lack the latter concept. Such a child can think the thought that four is greater than three without being able to think the thought that two times two is greater than three. Likewise, in my view, the concept *fortnight* has a different content from the concept *fourteen days*. One might be misinformed and believe that a fortnight is ten days without thereby believing that fourteen days is ten days. Concepts of which one has a partial understanding are still concepts one may exercise in belief and thought.

So far I have not said anything directly about concept possession. This too merits some brief preliminary discussion. What is it for a given concept to be a concept of *mine*? What is it for me to *possess* a concept? A straightforward answer is just this: I possess a given concept *C* if and only if I am able to exercise *C* in my thoughts. This answer is not very informative, however; for under what conditions can I exercise a concept in my thoughts? Given the phenomenon of partial understanding, the ability to exercise a concept in thought does not require full mastery of the concept. But this ability surely does require at least partial understanding of the concept. And once one has at least a partial understanding, one can employ the concept in thought. So, another answer to the above question is: I possess the concept *C* if and only if I have at least a partial understanding of *C*. On this intuitively attractive view, one cannot possess the concept *fortnight*, for example, unless one grasps that a fortnight is a period of time. Similarly, one cannot possess the ordinary concept *red* unless one grasps that red is a color.

A stronger requirement on concept possession is given by Gareth Evans's Generality Constraint (1982). A simple way to state the constraint, idealizing

---

[3] For other uses of the term "concept," and a helpful discussion of nonconceptual content, see Byrne (2005).

away from limitations imposed by short-term memory and attention, is as follows: for any concepts a thinker possesses, the thinker can think any thought that can be formed from those concepts. This constraint places a necessary condition on concept possession and it is compatible with the above proposals, so long as I am capable of exercising a concept C in my thoughts only if I am capable of thinking any thoughts that can be formed from combining C with other concepts I possess. Those who hold that thought is systematic and productive will happily grant this; but not everyone will accede to such a requirement.

It might be objected that I can possess concepts that are available *only* for use in experience (on a conceptualist view of experience), so that not all my concepts need be ones that I am capable of exercising in thought. But if experience is conceptual, it must be capable of standing as a reason for belief and the subject of each experience must be capable of appreciating its justificatory role, of inferring the content of the belief from the content of the experience. So, the subject must be capable of exercising concepts in thought that are deployed in experience after all.

With these largely terminological matters out of the way, we are now ready to take up the thesis of nonconceptual content for experiences. On the usual understanding of this thesis, a visual experience E has a *nonconceptual* content if and only if (i) E has correctness conditions; (ii) the subject of E need not possess the concepts used in a canonical specification of E's correctness conditions.

The first point to note here is that the thesis, as just stated, does not preclude the nonconceptual content of a visual experience from being the content of a thought of another subject. For what makes the content nonconceptual for subject S is simply the fact that S need not herself have the relevant concepts and thus need not herself be in a position to form the relevant thought. Moreover, the nonconceptual content of an experience E of a subject S can even be the content of a thought of S, given the above thesis. All that is required in such a case is that S *need* not possess the pertinent concepts to undergo the experience: thus, were S to lose the concepts and with them the capacity to have such a thought, that would not preclude her from having the experience, if the content of the experience is nonconceptual.

It appears, then, that, given the usual understanding of the thesis of nonconceptual content, *as far as the nature of content itself goes*, there need be no distinction between conceptual and nonconceptual content. All the thesis, as usually stated, requires is that visual experiences be contentful *nonconceptual states*, where a contentful nonconceptual state is a contentful state, the tokening of which does not involve the exercise of concepts.

We see therefore that the original thesis of nonconceptual content for visual experiences leaves open three possibilities: 1) such experiences are nonconceptual states having conceptual contents (and thus are the same as thoughts along the content dimension only); 2) such experiences are nonconceptual states having fine-grained nonconceptual contents (and thus are similar to thoughts along the content dimension); 3) such experiences are nonconceptual states having coarse-grained contents (*robustly* nonconceptual contents, as I shall call them).

Since conceptual contents have fine-grained individuation conditions, those philosophers who embrace nonconceptualism for visual experience and who opt for alternative (1) above face the following very awkward question: how can an experience *E* of a subject *S* have a fine-grained content without being built from concepts? Those philosophers who embrace nonconceptualism and who opt for alternative (2) face the same awkward question and a further one, namely: how can an experience *E* of a subject *S* have a fine-grained content without that content being conceptual?[4] Perhaps these questions can be answered adequately, but I am skeptical. Accordingly, in my view, the advocate of nonconceptual content should embrace alternative (3) (or, better, a slightly more cautious formulation of alternative (3), namely, that visual experiences have contents that are robustly nonconceptual and, *insofar as* they have such contents, they are nonconceptual states). For the remainder of the chapter, this is the alternative I shall endorse.

But what is the robustly nonconceptual content of an experience? One answer is that such a content is a set of possible worlds. Another answer is that each robustly nonconceptual content is a possible state of affairs built out of worldly entities. Of these two answers, I accept the second, since it fits best with my views on the transparency of experience (Tye 1995, 2000, 2003). But for the purposes of the rest of this chapter it will not matter whether the former unstructured account of content is preferred to the latter structured one.

On the structured account, it is plausible to break down the relevant possible states of affairs into two basic types: 1) structured complexes of specific particular items, properties, and relations; and 2) structured existential states of affairs involving properties and relations (and plausibly the subject of the experience). Suppose, for example, I see the facing surface *S* of an object *O* and it looks red to me. My visual experience intuitively represents *S* as having the property of being red. At this level, my experience is accurate if and only if *S* is red. But my experience also has something important in common with certain other visual experiences not directed at *S*. Suppose, for example, that *O* is replaced with another object *O'* that looks just like *O* or that I am hallucinating a red surface so that phenomenally it is for me just as it is in seeing *S*. Intuitively, in all three cases, it seems to me that *there is* a red surface before me. At this phenomenal level, my experience is accurate if and only if there is a red surface before me.[5] This content is existential, not involving *S*, though it does also include the subject of the experience.

The structured account delivers *coarse-grained* contents in that representations with such contents (unlike representations having conceptual contents) cannot

---

[4] Relatedly, why *couldn't* such a fine-grained content be the content of some thought?

[5] In reality, of course, things will be much more complex than is indicated in this statement of correctness conditions. The existential content for the case in which I see surface *S* will involve not just red but a determinate shade of red, a surface orientation, distance away of the apparent surface, 2-D location relative to the viewer, etc.

represent the same particulars, properties, and relations arranged in the same possible object-involving states of affairs or the same properties and relations involved in the same possible existential states of affairs and yet differ in content. On the unstructured account, coarseness of grain follows from the fact that sameness of content is guaranteed by sameness of correctness conditions in all possible worlds. The two accounts do not yield the same degree of coarseness of grain in robustly nonconceptual contents. For one thing, some may wish to deny that necessarily co-instantiated properties (and relations) are identical. For another, on the structured view, some necessarily co-obtaining states of affairs can differ even if necessarily co-instantiated properties (and relations) are identical. Consider, for example, the object-involving state of affairs of X's being red and the necessarily co-obtaining state of affairs of there being exactly one actual F that is red, where "actual" is understood as a rigidifier and X is the actual F. These states of affairs differ in their structure and thus are different states of affairs, on the structured account, but there is no difference in content on the unstructured alternative. The upshot is that the unstructured account is more coarse-grained than the structured one.

The issue of whether the thesis that visual experiences have coarse-grained contents conflicts with the claim accepted by nonconceptualists that our experiences of shades of color are *fine-grained* is one I shall take up in Section IV. In the next section, I want to turn to another related topic, that of the richness of visual experience.

II SPERLING'S EXPERIMENT AND THE THESIS OF RICHNESS

There is empirical evidence that supports the view that visual experience has a *rich* content. One important piece of evidence is provided by Sperling's well-known experiment on sensory memory. The relevance of this experiment to the thesis of richness will be brought out in due course. I begin with a general discussion of the experiment and other related effects.

Subjects were shown an array of letters, composed of three rows with four letters in each (see Figure 1). The array was presented for 50 mseconds in the center of the subjects' field of view, followed by a blank field.

The subjects were asked to report what they saw, under two different sets of conditions. In condition 1, subjects were asked to identify as many letters as possible. In condition 2, subjects were asked to identify letters in a single row. The chosen row was identified by a tone (high for the top row, medium for the middle row, and low for the bottom row), the use of which had been explained to the subjects in advance. The tone was not played until *immediately after* the display was extinguished.

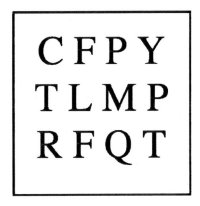

Fig. 1. The set of letters shown in Sperling's experiments.

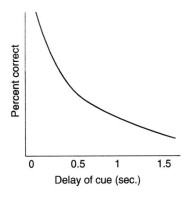

Fig. 2. Partial report accuracy when the cue is delayed by various intervals.

Sperling found that in condition 1, subjects were only able to identify at most one-third of the twelve letters. In condition 2, however, subjects were typically able to report correctly at least three out of the four. The accuracy of the subjects' reports about the contents of the row in the latter condition diminished if the time of presentation of the tone from the disappearance of the array was delayed. As the time delay increased, the accuracy decreased, as shown in the graph above, (Figure 2).

How are these facts best explained? Sperling hypothesized that there is a visual *sensory memory* that fades away very quickly. In the case of the subjects in condition 1, the act of reporting all the letters takes too long: the sensory memory fades by the time that the subjects have reported one-quarter or one-third of the letters, with the result that they cannot report the remainder. In the case of the subjects in condition 2, when the tone sounds, the sensory memory is still available and it persists long enough for the subjects to report three or four of the letters in the relevant row of four. Since in condition 2 the subjects do not know until the tone sounds which row to report on and the tone does not occur until after the array display is turned off, the fact that the subjects successfully report at least three of the four letters in the appropriate row shows that the sensory memory preserves information about the letter shapes in *all* the rows.

In saying that the sensory memory fades very quickly, Sperling is best understood as making a remark about visual information. Initially, all twelve letter shapes are represented; less information is available through time and very quickly no information remains. Of course, the time at which the sensory memory is formed need not be the same as the time at which the array is displayed or the time at which it disappears. In general, represented time need not be the same as time represented, and this case is no different.[6]

What Sperling and other psychologists call in the above case the "visual sensory memory" is what we would call in ordinary life the look or the appearance of the array. According to Sperling, after the array has been extinguished, it *appears* still to be displayed.

It may be wondered why we should accept that the sensory memory itself operates at the phenomenal level. Why should we agree that the memory trace is a visual appearance? Sperling tested for this by varying the brightness of the field in which the array was displayed immediately after the array disappeared. He found that with a bright post-target field, the success rates at identifying letters were significantly worse, just as they would be were we asked to read what is projected on a screen in a room that gets more and more brightly illuminated. The interference effect in the latter case is at the level of experience: the screen appears more blurry (and thus less easy to read) as the lighting condition changes. So too in the former.

Other experiments support Sperling's position. For example, when subjects are shown two brief random dot presentations, one after the other, such that when superimposed they form single letters, the subjects accurately report the letters, provided that the time gap between the presentations is 300 mseconds or less (Eriksen and Collins 1967). Evidently, the initial display appears to last longer than it really does by some 300 mseconds; the result is that the letters appear to "pop out" of the dot patterns, according to the subjects.

That the visual sensory memory system operates at the level of visual appearance is also shown by the experience of lightning during a storm. Suppose you see a single flash of lightning in the sky, lasting about $\frac{1}{2}$ second. In reality, the flash is made up of three or four very brief flashes, each lasting only 2 mseconds. You experience a persisting flash for $\frac{1}{2}$ second, however, rather than three or four very brief separate flashes, because of visual sensory memory: before the first very brief flash fades in your experience, the second one occurs, and likewise for the third and fourth, with the result that it looks to you as if there is single, continuing flash.

---

[6] For more on this topic, see Tye (2003).

Fig. 3. The saccades produced while viewing a picture.

Further facts about human vision support the view that visual sensory memories are representations whose contents are directly involved in the contents of everyday visual experiences. Consider the phenomenon of eye saccades. As we view a picture or read a book, our eyes move around in a quick, jerky way. These movements or saccades last from 25 to 200 mseconds. Above is an illustration of the saccades produced while viewing a picture (Figure 3).

It is well known that sensitivity to visual input is shut down during saccades. Visual information is processed only during eye fixations (the pauses when the eye is not moving), which each last 100–200 mseconds.[7] Our *experience* of the picture in figure 3 does not have black-out periods or blank intervals, however. Why is this? If our eyes are moving around with no information getting in during the periods of movement, why isn't our experience like that we would get were we to view the results of filming a scene through a moving video camera that had been turned on and off during filming?

One plausible answer is that the visual sensory memories generated during fixations carry information about the parts of the picture fixated on, even after the fixations have ceased, and do so moreover until the next fixation. Given this

---

[7] Rayner et al. (1981) showed that only the first 50 mseconds of each fixation are used to extract information when reading.

hypothesis, if the memories operate at the level of appearances, there will be no black-outs in viewing the picture.

The proposal I am making, then, is that at any given time visual experiences represent whatever the visual sensory memories represent at that time, whether the experiences occur in situations in which stimuli are only briefly visually presented or in situations in which the stimuli are continuing. This is not to say that the experiences represent *only* what the visual sensory memories represent. For example, there are facts about change, continuity, and succession that are represented in visual experiences and that are not captured in sensory memories.[8] My point is that at each moment, the visual experiences humans undergo are at least as rich representationally as the sensory memories. And what Sperling's results strongly suggest is that the sensory memories are rich not only in that they represent more than their subjects actually judge to be present, but also in that (typically) they represent more than their subjects are *capable* of judging to be present.

Normal humans are unable to *identify* many of the letters in the Sperling experiment. They do not *notice* which letter shapes are apparently present in the rows not corresponding to the tone that is played and thus they form no beliefs as to which letters those rows contain. Even so, the letters to which the subjects are not attending appear in ways that *would* have enabled the subjects to identify them, *had* their attention been directed differently. This claim, it is worth noting, is also in keeping with the beliefs of the subjects about their experiences. Presented with a briefly displayed Sperling array, subjects believe that there are twelve *letters* in the array and indeed that they see all twelve. They also believe that the letters are all equally well-defined. Their inability to identify many of the letter shapes, even though the information needed for such identifications is present in their visual experiences, derives from how rapidly the sensory memories fade: there is simply not enough time for the subjects to process cognitively the information about more than three or four letter shapes.

I should emphasize that the points above do not assume that information about the identities of the unattended letters is itself coded in the subjects' visual experiences. Indeed, I am making no strong claim about the level of information contained in the experiences about unattended regions of the Sperling array. I find it plausible to suppose that non-local information about shapes is encoded[9] (even though this is not the standard view in psychology on the matter); but this does not matter for present purposes. So long as information is present about the contents of the unattended rows on the basis of which shape and letter identifications could have been made, had attention been directed differently, the relevant visual experiences are representationally rich.

---

[8] For a detailed discussion of the experience of change, continuity, and succession, see Tye (2003).   [9] This too is the view of Ned Block (1995: 244).

III   THE ILLUSION OF RICHNESS

Some psychologists and philosophers have claimed recently that we are under an *illusion* that we experience more than we consciously notice (O'Regan and Noë 2001). Our visual awareness, they say, is really sparse, instead of being detailed and rich. We are subject to the illusion of richness because as soon as we ask ourselves whether we are experiencing something in the field of view, our eyes go to it and it is then available for cognitive processing.

Kevin O'Regan (2000) calls this "the refrigerator light illusion." Every time we open the fridge door, the light is on. This might lead someone to believe that the light is on all the time. Analogously, every time we turn our attention to something, we are conscious of it. This fosters the illusion that visual consciousness of things is present even when we are not attending to them. In reality, things in the field of view to which we are not attending do not *look* any way to us. We do not experience those things. They are only *potentially* within our phenomenal experience.

Recent work in psychology on change blindness has been held to support this view (O'Regan 2000). Where two complicated images are shown to subjects in short succession, and the images are the same except for one change, the change is extremely difficult to discern, provided it is not part of the subjects' conception of what the picture is about. For example, when subjects are shown a picture of a man eating lunch with a woman, followed quickly by the same picture with a shift in the location of the railing right behind where the couple are seated, subjects typically do not notice any difference. And this effect often persists even if the two pictures are shown to subjects one after the other, several times in a row (Figure 4).

Why should this be? If visual experience is itself sparse in its representational content—if its content extends no further than what is consciously noticed—then the answer is obvious.

Another equally good explanation, however, is that the subjects do not notice any difference because they do not *attend* to the position of the railing. Studies of eye movements in subjects who fail to notice a difference in the two pictures show that their search for a change is largely focused on the man, the woman, and the contents of the table. Had the subjects been given the additional instruction to focus on the railing, they would have noticed the change easily enough. But without that instruction, the alteration in the position of the railing is missed.[10] This is perfectly compatible with supposing that the subjects do see the railing and that it appears in different positions in the two pictures.

---

[10] The same is true in the case of the woman wearing a gorilla suit who dances a jig on a basketball court while two teams are passing a ball around. Since the subjects viewing a tape of the game are given the task of counting carefully how many times the ball changes hands, their eyes are glued to the ball and they fail to notice the "gorilla".

Fig. 4. Example of change blindness.

Moreover, the claim that the subjects do not see any difference in the position of the railing is consistent with the railing's appearing to the subject in different positions; for, as ordinarily understood, this claim would be counted as true only if the subjects do not see *that* there is any difference in the position of the railing and the railing can appear in different positions without that difference being noticed.

Perhaps it will be replied that the temptation to think that we *see* unattended regions in the field of view and thus that they *appear* to us in certain ways derives from the mistaken thought that if there are regions in the field of view that are not seen, then our experience will be unacceptably "gappy." Consider, for

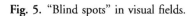

Fig. 5. "Blind spots" in visual fields.

example, the so-called "blind spots" in our visual fields corresponding to the places on our retinas where the optic nerve leaves the eyeball. Close your left eye and look at the cross in Figure 5 above.

As you move the book away from your eyes, at about 6 inches away, you will cease to notice the disk on the right. This is your blind spot for the open eye. With the book in this position, you do not see the disk on the right. But there is no "gap" in your experience. For phenomenologically what happens is that initially you have an experience of a black disk in the relevant region of your field of view, and then later you cease to get information from that region about any surface and your brain then "fills in" the region so that the right half of figure 5 appears to you to be a continuous white surface. Thus, for example, were the color of the page as a whole changed from white to yellow, while your right eye remained close, the right half of figure 5 would change in its appearance from one of a uniform white surface to one of a uniform yellow one. The experience you undergo in such a case is in error: it *mis*informs you that the surface to the right of the cross is white throughout initially, and then a continuous yellow, when in reality it contains a black disk surrounded by a uniform white or yellow. So, although you do not see the black disk, you have an experience as of a filled region where the disk is in fact located.

The phenomenon of "filling in" occurs also in the case, discussed by Dennett (1991: 354), of the Marilyn Monroe wallpaper. You walk into a room and immediately have a visual experience as of a wall full of identical photographic portraits of Marilyn Monroe. For you to identify a picture as being of Marilyn Monroe, it has to fall within the scope of the high resolution foveal part of the retina. Parafoveal vision is much weaker. For example, if five differently colored pencils are held at arm's length on the right side of the visual field but nowhere near the periphery, as you look straight ahead, you won't be able to identify their colors correctly. So, how is it that you *immediately* have an experience that represents hundreds of Marilyn Monroe pictures? You certainly do not foveate on each of them in the time it takes for you to have the experience. Your eyes saccade only four or five times each second, so foveation on each picture is impossible.

The explanation is that you foveate on several Marilyn Monroe pictures and your brain then generalizes to the others, since it receives no contrary shape information. So, you have a visual experience as of hundreds of Marilyn Monroes.

Imagine now that, as you walk into the room, things are as above, except that many of the photographic pictures of Marilyn Monroe, lying in your parafoveal vision, are replaced by ones of Madonna (during her Marilyn Monroe period). Your brain "fills in" as before, so again you have a visual experience as of hundreds of Marilyn Monroes. This time, your experience is in error.

The situation just envisaged would be difficult to realize physically, given that your eyes saccade often and the regions of your field of view that fall under parafoveal vision change correspondingly. But it would not be impossible. Indeed, there are actual cases of "filling in" of this sort. Consider, for example, the results of an experiment in which subjects were asked to read a story on a screen. Using a computer program, words lying in the parafoveal regions of vision were changed to sequences of nonsense characters, so that as each subject's eyes moved across the screen in the process of reading, different words were altered. The subjects noticed nothing awry. It did not seem to the subjects that the screen contained a mixture of words and nonsense sequences. It seemed to the subjects that the screen was filled with words. Indeed the effect was so complete and surprising to the psychologist who designed the experiment (Grimes 1996) that, when he tried the experiment on himself, he thought that the equipment was malfunctioning!

Filling in, then, is a common phenomenon. And it may well be that in at least some cases of change blindness, objects on which the subjects are not foveating are *not* seen, any more than is the cross in the blindspot of the visual field. But at least where things lie *within* the scope of foveal vision, as in the case of the railing in the picture of the man and the woman eating lunch, there is reason to think that the relevant regions of the visual field are seen and that our visual experiences contain information about them whether or not we notice that information. This follows from the results of the Sperling experiment.[11] In that experiment, the tone has the effect of focusing the subjects' attention on one particular part of the array that apparently is still before them. Since the sensory memory carries information about the contents of the various cells of the top, middle, and bottom rows of the array (all of which lie within foveal vision)—even though there is room for dispute about just how high-level this information is—and the sensory memory is a phenomenal representation, the results of the change-blindness experiments do not undermine the thesis of richness for visual experience. Indeed, the opposite seems to be the case. The Sperling experiment provides reason to believe that at least in some contexts we experience *more* than we notice; thus, the view, supposedly supported by the change-blindness data, that consciousness is *restricted* to what we notice is in trouble.[12]

---

[11] A referee notes that this also follows from other psychological work on change blindness in which there are shown to be implicit effects of the objects to which the subjects are supposedly blind. See here Henderson (1997); Hayhoe et al. (1998); Fernandez-Duque and Thornton (2000); Williams and Simons (2000); Hollingworth et al. (2001).

[12] See Cohen (2002) for further discussion of change blindness in a similar spirit (brought to my attention by a referee).

IV   FINENESS OF GRAIN

One reply that might be made to Sperling's experiment is that, even though sensory memories are involved in everyday visual experience, still the results, properly generalized, show only that visual experiences *often* or *typically* contain more information than their subjects are able to extract cognitively. But what of the case in which the content of the visual experience remains unchanged through time? Suppose, for example, that the array is *not* extinguished in Sperling's experiment. Then, by suitable shifts in their acts of attention, the subjects *can* identify all the letters. Even so, it might well be insisted, there is a determinacy of detail in the letter shapes (and also for that matter in the background color shade of the array) that goes beyond the subjects' conceptual repertoires. This needs further elucidation.

The claim that there is a fineness of grain in visual experience that cannot be captured by the concepts possessed by the subject of the experience (or at least any ordinary subject) dates back to Gareth Evans in *The Varieties of Reference* (1982: 229). John McDowell (1994: 56) puts Evans's underlying thought this way: think of ordinary color concepts such as those expressed in "red," "green," "blue" as concepts of bands on the spectrum. Evans's point is then that color experiences present properties that correspond to something like lines on the spectrum, namely, minimal shades of red, blue, green, etc. (where a minimal shade is one for which there is no other shade that is a shade of it).

Here are some further representative quotations from those on Evans's side of the fence. First, Chris Peacocke:

If you are looking at a range of mountains, it may be correct to say that you see some of them as rounded, some as jagged. But the content of your visual experience in respect of the shape of the mountains is far more specific than that description indicates. The description involving the concepts round and jagged would cover many different fine-grained contents which your experience could have, contents which are discriminably different from one another. (1992: 111)

More recently, Richard Heck has commented:

Before me now, for example, are arranged various objects with various shapes and colors, of which, it might seem, I have no concept. My desk exhibits a whole host of shades of brown, for which I have no names. The speakers to the sides of my computer are not quite flat, but have curved faces; I could not begin to describe their shape in anything like adequate terms. The leaves on the tree outside my window are fluttering back and forth, randomly, as it seems to me, as the wind passes over them—Yet my experience of these things represents them far more precisely than that, far more distinctively, it would seem, than any characterization I could hope to formulate, for myself or for others, in terms of the concepts I presently possess. The problem is not lack of time, but lack of descriptive resources, that is, lack of the appropriate concepts. (2000: 489–90)

Let us, then, distinguish three different claims about visual experience. First, in typical cases, visual experiences are rich. This is to be understood as the thesis that typically visual experiences contain more information than their subjects are able to extract cognitively (in belief or judgment). Second, visual experiences are fine-grained. This is usually formulated as the thesis that visual experiences represent the world with a determinacy of detail that goes beyond the concepts possessed by the subjects of those experiences. However, there is a problem with this formulation. For the fineness-of-grain thesis is surely not supposed to conflict with the view that we can use demonstrative concepts in *judgments or beliefs* based on experience to pick out experienced details. What the thesis of fineness of grain demands is that visual experiences represent the world with a determinacy of detail that is not capturable conceptually *in the experiences themselves*. From here on, this is how I shall understand fineness of grain. Finally, visual experiences have robustly nonconceptual contents.

How are these three claims related? Sperling's experiment supports richness, but visual experiences could be rich, as revealed in that experiment, without having a nonconceptual content. For the thesis of richness alone does not rule out the possibility that visual experiences are conceptual states whose conceptual contents contain more information than the belief-forming processes can handle under certain constrained circumstances (such as those in the Sperling experiment). Nor does richness entail fineness of grain. Consistent with the thesis of richness, it could be that to the extent that details are represented in experiences, they are represented conceptually. Fineness of grain, moreover, does not entail richness, since, if visual experience is detailed in a way that is not capturable by concepts employed in the experiences, it does not follow that the subject will not be able to bring the experienced details under concepts (including demonstrative ones) that the subject is capable of exercising in *judgments or beliefs* based on those experiences (as noted above). Finally, fineness of grain does entail that visual experiences have nonconceptual contents, as the latter thesis is usually understood. So, if, as I suggested in Section I, the most plausible version of the thesis that visual experiences have such contents is that they have robustly nonconceptual contents, then fineness of grain certainly supports the robustly nonconceptual thesis.

To suppose otherwise, indeed to suppose more strongly that there is actually a conflict between the proposal I am making about the content of visual experience and the above claim of fineness of grain on the grounds that robustly nonconceptual content is coarse-grained, is to confuse different notions of grain. To say that the content of an experience of a shade of color is coarse-grained (in the sense relevant to the thesis of robustly nonconceptual content) is to say something about how its individuation conditions are fixed by sets of possible worlds or by arrangements of properties and relations in possible states of affairs. It is not to say anything about the kinds of properties (or relations) represented. Patently, experiences having contents with such coarse-grained individuation conditions can nonetheless differ by virtue of representing different, minimal shades of color.

So, richness is not something that the advocate of nonconceptual content can appeal to on behalf of her view (at least in any direct way); but fineness of grain is—provided that it really is the case that our visual experiences represent the world with a determinacy of detail that is not capturable conceptually in the experiences. This is the focus of the next section.

V   REPLIES BY THE CONCEPTUALIST

Some philosophers claim that the determinacy of detail in visual experience *can* be captured by concepts at play in the experiences. They thus reject the thesis of fineness of grain, as presented above. The onus is upon such philosophers to spell out how the determinacy of detail in visual experience is represented conceptually.

What is needed, according to the first view I shall consider, is simply the acknowledgment, in the case of color experience, that some of our color concepts pick out minimal shades of color. This is one view adopted by McDowell in *Mind and World*.[13] He comments: "What is in play here is a recognitional capacity, possibly quite short-lived" (1998: 57). McDowell's thought, elucidated more clearly in a subsequent symposium on *Mind and World*,[14] is that there is a recognitional capacity that persists for a little while *after* an experience of the shade recognized and thus a recognitional concept is exercised. More specifically, according to McDowell, the conceptual content

This is colored (with) *S*

is in the content of the experience, where *S* is a general recognitional concept of a fine-sliced shade.

This is not convincing. Human memory is limited. We abstract away from details to avoid information overload. We have recognitional concepts such as *red, green, blue*, and more specific ones such as *scarlet*, and *bright scarlet*. But we do not have recognitional concepts for minimal shades. The recognitional capacities to which McDowell adverts simply do not exist. The ordinary person cannot recognize red_{27}, even after having just seen it. People who are shown a patch of color and then very shortly afterwards are asked whether a second patch has the same shade of color or a minimally different one do not do well at the task.[15] Of course, if the original patch is re-presented *before* the original

---

[13] I say one view here, since there seem to be two different views on offer in *Mind and World*, the second of which will occupy us shortly.

[14] In *Philosophy and Phenomenological Research* (1998).

[15] See here Hurvich (1981); Halsey and Chapanis (1951); and Raffman (1996).

experience is over—and that will not be until roughly one-third of a second or so after the original patches are removed, given Sperling's data—then the match will be made successfully. But this does not show a recognitional capacity. For that requires the capacity to recognize the given hue when it comes again *after* the initial experience ends.[16]

A second reply the conceptualist might make to the alleged fineness of grain in visual experience is to allow that the subject of an experience of a minimal shade lacks a general recognitional concept of that shade, but to insist that it does not follow that the experience has a nonconceptual content, since the subject can conceptualize the given shade in the experience via a general, fine-grained perceptual concept that the subject is hard-wired to exercise in the given situation.

Such a "concept" is one that never enters memory. The subject possesses the concept, on one natural way of understanding the above proposal, by having a hard-wired disposition to exercise the concept in certain circumstances. This, however, seems very implausible. In general, the disposition to exercise a concept in certain circumstances does not confer the ability to exercise the concept in one's thoughts. For example, Frank Jackson's Mary, while in her black-and-white room, does not possess *phenomenal* concepts of a sort the rest of us exercise in our introspective awareness of experiences of the various hues, since she does not know what it is like to experience the hues. And, not knowing this, she does not have any understanding of the relevant phenomenal concepts. So, she is not capable of thinking thoughts into which such phenomenal concepts enter. But Mary in her room *does* have the disposition to exercise those concepts in classifications she makes of how objects appear to her if and when she sees objects with the various hues.

One way to try to handle this difficulty is to insist that the relevant, general, fine-grained concepts are possessed only at the times of their exercise. They are automatically manufactured on the spot, as the subject undergoes the experiences; the concepts are then lost as soon as the experiences are over. The obvious trouble with this view is that if such concepts occur in the subject's experiences then they must be concepts the subject possesses and hence concepts that the subject is capable of exercising in thought. But if these concepts can occur in the subject's thoughts as well as in her experiences, and they really are general concepts, then the subject should be able to think thoughts that use the concepts even when the experiences are not present; and this conflicts with the hypothesis that the relevant concepts are lost once the experiences end.

Here is another problem. Suppose that I am viewing a colored patch and that my visual experience conceptually represents this patch as red_{25}. Suppose further that my experience is not fleeting: I am staring at the patch for a considerable

---

[16] Another objection is that there cannot be recognition for a *first-time* experience of a property; but that experience still has a specific representational content: the world still appears a certain way to the subject of the experience (Peacocke 2001).

length of time. While my experience lasts, can I think to myself a thought which exercises this concept, for example, the thought that I am seeing something with shade red$_{25}$? It seems to me that the only thoughts I can form at such a time about red$_{25}$ have a demonstrative content. I can mentally "point" at the shade I am experiencing. I can think of it as that shade or that shade of red or perhaps just that. But, if my thoughts here *seem* to me to have a demonstrative content, then, given that I have privileged access to the contents of my thoughts (that I can know via introspection alone what I am thinking),[17] they do have such content. It seems, then, that I cannot think the thought that I am seeing red$_{25}$, from which it follows that I do not possess the general concept red$_{25}$. And, if I do not possess this concept, then I cannot exercise it in *my* visual experience.

This brings me to the third reply that the conceptualist might make, namely, to suggest that the concept for a shade employed by visual experience is indeed demonstrative. The obvious immediate question for this reply is: what form does the demonstrative concept in the experience take? McDowell (1994) appeals to the demonstrative *that shade*. To experience a particular shade, red$_{27}$, say, is to have an experience of something as being of that shade, where the latter is to be understood as involving the application of the concept *that shade* to red$_{27}$. On this view, seeing a shade is the same as or at least to be modeled on seeing something *as* having that shade.

The difference, then, between seeing red$_{27}$ and red$_{28}$ is the difference between applying the concept *that shade* to red$_{27}$ and applying it to red$_{28}$. The concept *that shade*, in the context of the one experience, refers to red$_{27}$; the concept *that shade*, in the context of the other experience, refers to red$_{28}$. The two experiences thereby have different correctness conditions and thus different contents.

This is problematic, as has been noted by several philosophers (but most forcefully by Peacocke 1998, 2001). First, which concept exactly is exercised in the experience of a particular shade of red? The concept McDowell appeals to is the concept *that shade*. But why not *that shade of red*? Or *that color*? Or *that red*? There seems no non-arbitrary way of deciding between these candidates— they all seem equally eligible—and thus no fact of the matter as to which one is applied in the experience. It appears, then, that the problem of differences of grain between conceptual resources and experience of shades is genuine but opposite to that envisaged by Evans. For now we have too many available concepts for each shade rather than too many shade experiences for each available concept.

Second, McDowell's proposal appeals to a demonstrative concept that uses a general sortal, *shade*. The latter is a recognitional concept. The idea that in order to undergo an experience of a particular shade of red, something a very small child can do, from a very early age, one must possess the concept *shade*, is absurd.

---

[17] Assuming my faculty of introspection is working properly. For more on privileged access, see McLaughlin and Tye (1998).

To possess the concept *shade*, one must possess a cognitive grasp of the difference between a shade and a color that is not a shade, classifying red$_{27}$ as a shade, for example, and red as not. It seems to me quite likely that some high schoolers do not grasp the concept *shade*!

One way to handle these problems is to appeal to a pure demonstrative *that*. In connection with this possibility, Peacocke comments:

Someone could be introduced to the general concept timbre, applicable to sounds, by his first having an experience leading him to judge, "That's beautiful", referring specifically to the timbre of, say, a clarinet. It may be that our listener only later applies the concept timbre to the instance he had already perceived and thought about. ("That sound" could be too unspecific to capture what he experienced as beautiful.) (2001: 246)

But what is the referent of the demonstrative in the color case? The obvious answer is: the particular shade. *Which* shade? Suppose I am viewing a color patch with the shade red$_{18}$. Pointing at the patch and the shade, on the basis of my experience, I say, "That has that shade." Should we suppose that the concept *that*, exercised in the experience with respect to a shade, refers via a sample of the shade, namely, the shade of the patch the subject is viewing? Then, on the sample view, both my remark and my experience are accurate. However, if I am *mis*-perceiving the patch and experiencing it as having a shade different from the one it actually has, then my experience will not represent the patch as having *that*, understood as the actual shade of the patch, at all. So, the content of my experience cannot be demonstrative.

The conceptualist might respond that, whatever may be the case for the demonstrative *expression*, "that shade," the demonstrative concept exercised in the *experience* is a concept of the shade the given surface *appears* to have. But, now, in the case of misperception, there is no sample of the color in the world. So, how is the referent of the concept fixed? The obvious reply is that it is fixed by the content of the subject's experience: the concept refers to the shade the given experience represents the surface as having. However, this reply is not available to the conceptualist about the content of visual experience; for the content of the demonstrative concept is supposed to be *part* of the content of the experience and so the concept cannot have its referent fixed by that content (Heck 2000: 496).[18]

There is a further problem. Consider the case of shape. Suppose you and I are both viewing the same shape. The concept *that*, in this case, refers to the shape. But suppose you experience it as a square and I experience it as a regular diamond, so that there is a difference in how things appear, in the contents of our experiences. That difference hasn't been captured by appeal to the demonstrative

---

[18] One nonconceptualist, Chris Peacocke, does not notice this problem. As a result, in a recent essay he comments, "Since these unsupplemented perceptual-demonstratives exist, and can pick out fine-grained properties, the anti-conceptualist should not try to rest his case on fineness of grain" (1998: 610). This concession seems to me too hasty.

here. Peacocke says:

We will not do justice to the . . . phenomenology of experience if we restrict ourselves to those contents which can be built up by referring to the properties and relations which the perceived objects are represented by the experiences as possessing. We must, in describing the fine-grained phenomenology, make use of the notion of the *way* in which some property or relation is given in the experience. (2001: 240)

He continues:

The same shape can be perceived in two different ways, and the same holds for shape properties, if we regard them as within the representational content of experience. Mach's example of one and the same shape that can be perceived either as a square or as a regular diamond is a familiar example . . . an object can be perceived either as a square, or as a diamond, in either of the standard orientations relative to the perceiver. (2001: 241)

Now Peacocke himself is a nonconceptualist about the content of experience. But his comments above suggest another possible reply the *conceptualist* might make to the problem of accounting for the determinacy of detail in our visual experiences, namely, that each such detail is represented via the exercise of a demonstrative concept *that way*, which refers to a way a property is presented—in the case of shape experience, to the way a shape is presented.

However, suppose the case is one of misperception so that the presented shape isn't actually the given way. Then the concept *that way* exercised in the experience picks out the way the shape appears in the experience—that is, the way the shape is represented in the experience. So, the referent of the concept *that way* is fixed by (part of) the content of the subject's experience. But the content of the demonstrative concept is supposed to be *part* of the content of the experience, and thus again the concept cannot have its referent fixed by that content.

Furthermore, does it really make clear sense to talk of the way a shape is presented in experience or the way a color is presented (as Peacocke does)? If it does not, then the claim that the demonstrative concept *that way* picks out such a way is not properly intelligible. We may happily allow, of course, that if something looks red, say, it looks a certain way, namely, red. But the way here is the way the *thing* looks. Redness, the property, is not experienced as being given in a certain way (other than as belonging to the thing).[19] Similarly, I would say,

---

[19] It might be held that where there is an inverted spectrum, red is given in experience something other than the normal way. However, I deny this. To one who has an inverted spectrum, red things do not appear red. They appear green. So, red itself is not given in experience to the invert in any way. Red things are so given. They are given as green. Of course, this commits me to holding that color inversions are a form of misperception, but this seems to me the correct view (both for the standard inverted spectrum case and for the more recherche versions). For more here, see my 2000: chs 4 and 5. There is another possible account of color inversions worth mentioning, namely, that red things are experienced as red by the invert, but they are also experienced as having another surface quality which makes the redness of those things manifest, and this quality is different from the one that makes redness manifest for normals. On this view, there is no misperception with

for the case of shape. The shape, squareness, viewed as a universal, is not pre-sented in experience in any particular way. Individual squares are so presented.[20]

Of course, each such square—each particular—is, in one sense, a colored shape. But it is only relative to this use of "shape" that it is uncontroversial that shapes can be presented in different ways in experience. Thus, viewing a figure, I can experience its shape as a regular diamond, say, as Peacocke asserts, and not as a square only insofar as *the figure* is presented to me in experience as regular diamond-shaped (and not as square). The figure, in looking regular diamond-shaped, to me looks a certain way. This way is not a way a shape property looks.

Peacocke's own position, as noted above, is nonconceptualist. He thus must face the awkward questions I raised earlier for any nonconceptualist who takes the content of experience to individuate in a fine-grained way, namely: if experiences are nonconceptual states, then how can they have fine-grained individuation conditions? Further, how can the contents of such experiences be fine-grained and yet fail to be conceptual? Peacocke, of course, believes that the fine-grained view of nonconceptual content is necessitated by a proper account of examples like the one from Mach of squares and diamonds. Peacocke is mistaken, however, as I shall try to show in the final section.[21]

VI   SQUARES AND DIAMONDS

According to Peacocke, the property of being a square is the same as the property of being a regular diamond.[22] Thus, the robustly nonconceptual content that X is square is the same as the robustly nonconceptual content that X is a regular diamond. However, there is a difference between how X looks, when X looks square, and how X looks, when X looks regular diamond-shaped (or vice versa). This phenomenological difference, Peacocke believes, is one that cannot be accounted for by appeal to robustly nonconceptual content.

---

respect to the color of red things. But, equally, there is no need to countenance ways, considered as entities distinct from properties and relations; for the qualities now grounding color inversions are qualities of things.

[20] In general, in my view, it is a mistake to model our awareness of qualities on our awareness of particulars. When we see particulars, they look various ways to us but the qualities of which we are conscious in seeing these particulars do not look any way. Our awareness of the relevant qualities is direct. It involves no mode of presentation. To suppose otherwise is to take the first step down the slippery path that leads to the thesis of revelation. And the thesis of revelation is a philosophical thesis (not a thesis of common sense) and one that (by my lights) generates a world view that is clearly unacceptable.

[21] Again, I want to stress that the above discussion of demonstratives does *not* undercut the view that the fineness of grain in visual experience can be represented conceptually in *demonstrative judgments or thoughts* made on the basis of experience. What I have argued is that the *visual experiences themselves* do not represent details *via* demonstrative concepts.

[22] This claim is very plausible and I shall not challenge it in what follows. (I have contested it elsewhere (Tye 2003: 173–4), but I now prefer the response below.)

To see what is wrong with this argument, consider the following parallel argument. The way something looks, when it looks square, is different from the way it looks, when it feels square by touch. The same property—squareness—is represented in both cases. So, the robustly nonconceptual content of the experience of *X*'s looking square is the same as the robustly nonconceptual content of the experience of *X*'s feeling square by touch. So, the phenomenological difference between the way *X* looks and the way *X* feels by touch cannot be captured solely via appeal to robustly nonconceptual content.

The standard way of responding to the second argument is to note that when something looks square, many other properties are represented in addition to squareness—properties not represented when something feels square by touch. For example, the color of the object is represented, its distance away, its two-dimensional location relative to the eyes. In the haptic case, the shape is represented as belonging to a surface with which one is in bodily contact; the temperature of the surface is represented; there is a more detailed representation of the degree of solidity.

In similar fashion, I maintain that when something looks square, certain properties are represented that are not represented when the same thing looks regular diamond-shaped (or vice versa). This can be brought out as follows. Consider first the case in Figure 6 of two different figures, one of which looks square and the other of which looks regular diamond-shaped: Here, it is obvious that there is a difference in the (viewer-relative) properties represented in the two cases. For example, *X* looks to be resting on a side; *Y* does not. *Y* looks to be standing or balanced on a point; *X* does not. *X* looks to have two vertical sides; *Y* does not. *X* looks to have two horizontal sides; *Y* does not. *Y* looks to have inclined sides; *X* does not.

Now consider Figure 7. In this example, the square, *X*, inside the rectangle on the left, can look square. When it does so, it looks different from the figure, *Y*, on the right. Here, again, there is a difference in (viewer-relative) properties represented. When *X* looks square, *X* looks to have an inclined base; *Y* does not. In such circumstances, *X* looks tilted; *Y* does not. *Y* looks upright; *X* does not.

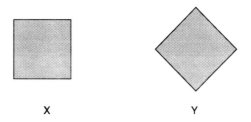

X   Y

Fig. 6. Example 1: difference in (viewer-relative) properties represented.

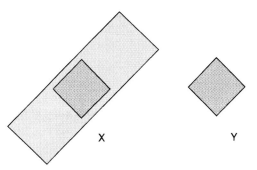

Fig. 7. Example 2: difference in (viewer-relative) properties represented.

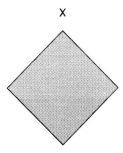

Fig. 8. Example 3: difference in (viewer-relative) properties represented.

In the third example, shown in Figure 8, we have a single figure, *X*, that can look either square or regular diamond-shaped. If *X* looks square, *X* looks to have an inclined base. *X* then looks tilted. If *X* looks diamond-shaped, *X* looks upright. So, when *X* looks square, *X* is represented as having the property of being tilted; this property is not represented as belonging to *X* when *X* looks diamond-shaped.

Note that when something looks tilted, it can look tilted at a variety of orientations (see Figure 9); but in each such case, the figure is represented as having the property of being tilted.

Chris Peacocke (1998) has objected to this proposal on two grounds. First, figures such as *X* in example 3 (Figure 8) can sometimes look square without looking tilted, as when one sees an appropriate pattern of floor tiles. Second, the appeal to tilt as a ground of the phenomenal difference between looking square and looking regular diamond-shaped ignores the role symmetry is agreed to play by psychologists in such experiences.

Consider the second point first. For a symmetrical figure such as a square, tilt goes with a certain sort of symmetry, namely symmetry about an axis bisecting two opposite sides. If the figure, *X*, looks tilted to the right (left), it looks

Fig. 9. A tilted figure: various orientations.

symmetrical about an axis inclined 45 degrees to the right (left). It is precisely because there is such an inclined axis of symmetry that *X* looks tilted in the relevant direction. If *X* looks upright, as it does if it looks regular diamond-shaped, it looks symmetrical about a vertical axis of symmetry, one that bisects two opposite angles. In looking tilted, *X* does not thereby look upright, since the visual experience tracks the first symmetry and not the second. Of course, *X* actually has both symmetries, but the property of being symmetrical about an axis bisecting opposite sides is not necessarily co-instantiated with the property of being symmetrical about an axis bisecting opposite angles. In the case of a vase figure, for example, the figure is symmetrical about an axis that bisects the top and bottom sides of the vase but it is not symmetrical about an axis that bisects two opposite angles.

In the case of the pattern of floor tiles, it seems to me that their looking square, say, at least requires that they look to have a certain symmetry, as Peacocke himself would grant, and the relevant symmetry is about an axis the direction of which (relative to the perceiver) intuitively is represented in the experience. But, if this is so, then (on the nonconceptualist view), contra Peacocke, the square will automatically look tilted in a certain direction relative to the perceiver.[23] The conclusion I draw is that the familiar example of squares and diamonds provides no good reason to move away from the view that the nonconceptual content of visual experience is robust.[24]

---

[23] It is also worth stressing that the coarse-grained account I am proposing of the nonconceptual content of experience can account for the rational transition from something's looking square to the judgment that it is square (given the right circumstances), since the thing in question will then look to have certain properties it will not look to have in the case it looks regular diamond-shaped. The nonconceptual representation of these properties in the former experience justifies the transition (via a reliable process) to the judgment that a square is present rather than to the judgment concerning a diamond shape.

[24] Alex Byrne has suggested to me that although the case of squares and diamonds can be handled in the way I propose, there is another similar case which creates difficulty, namely, that in which I experience nine dots first as making up three rows of three and second as making up three columns of three. Here there is a clear phenomenal difference in how the dots look but not one, according to Byrne, that can be handled in terms of a difference in robust nonconceptual content, since the property of making up three rows of three dots is necessarily co-instantiated with the property of making up three columns of three dots. (Of course, this presents a problem for the view that experiences have structured, robustly nonconceptual contents only on the assumption that necessarily co-instantiated properties are identical.)

My reply unsurprisingly is that there are other represented properties in terms of which the difference in content can be drawn. For example, when the dot pattern looks made up of three rows

REFERENCES

Block, Ned (1995), "On a Confusion about a Function of Consciousness," *Behavioral and Brain Sciences* 18: 227–47.

Byrne, Alex (2005), "Perception and Conceptual Content," in Ernest Sosa and Matthias Steup (eds), *Contemporary Debates in Epistemology* (Oxford: Blackwell).

Cohen, Jonathan (2002), "The Grand Grand Illusion Illusion," *Journal of Consciousness Studies* 9, 141–57.

Dennett, Daniel (1991), *Consciousness Explained* (Boston: Little, Brown).

Eriksen, C. W. and Collins, J. F. (1967), "Some Temporal Characteristics of Temporal Pattern Recognition," *Journal of Experimental Psychology* 74: 476–84.

Evans, Gareth (1982), *The Varieties of Reference* (Oxford: Oxford University Press).

Fernandez-Duque, Diego and Thornton, Ian M. (2000), "Change Detection without Awareness: Do Explicit Reports Underestimate the Representation of Change in the Visual System?," *Visual Cognition* 7: 324–44.

Grimes, John (1996), "On the Failure to Detect Changes in Scenes across Saccades," in Kathleen Akins (ed.), *Perception* (New York: Oxford University Press): 89–109.

Halsey, R. M. and Chapanis, A. (1951), "Number of Absolutely Identifiable Hues," *Journal of the Optical Society of America*, 41: 1057–8.

Hayhoe, Mary M., Bensinger, David G., and Ballard, Dana H. (1998), "Task Constraints in Visual Working Memory," *Vision Research* 38: 125–37.

of three dots, it looks divided into three rows. It does not look this way when it looks made up of three columns of three dots. Then it looks divided into three columns. Patently, the property of dividing into three rows is not identical with the property of dividing into three columns (some dot patterns with three rows divide into four columns). Further, in the dot pattern of three rows of three, the bottom three dots appear to compose a row (as do the three dots immediately above them and the three dots immediately above those dots). They do not appear this way when the dot pattern looks made up of columns. Since the property of composing a row is possessed by dots elsewhere that are laid out in a row without there being any columns, it is not the case that the property of composing a row can be redescribed in column terms such that the property, so described, is represented when the dot pattern of nine is experienced as dividing into three columns.

There is a further case mentioned by David Chalmers in this volume which also deserves a quick response. Chalmers asks us to imagine an "El Greco" world in which everything is stretched ten times in one direction but in which structure and dynamics are otherwise the same. In this world, Chalmers says, long, thin rectangles look phenomenally square even though the visual experiences they generate, being normally caused by long, thin rectangles, represent them as having a certain sort of rectangularity. This supposedly creates difficulty for any coarse-grained view of the content of experience. There is no real difficulty, however.

Ask someone in the El Greco world to trace out in space the shape of something that looks square to her. What will this person draw? A long, thin rectangle? I don't think so: kinesthetic feedback will tell her that cannot be right. A square? Again, I don't think so: that won't *look* right. Ask this person to feel out the shape of an object that looks square to her. How will it feel? Will all the sides feel to be the same length? Surely not. In general, touch corrects vision. The stick that looks bent in water no longer looks bent once its shape is felt by hand. So, it is unlikely that the thin rectangle will continue to look square. Why? Obvious answer: because the case is one of shape illusion (or normal misperception and in this respect like the Müller Lyer). Accordingly, long, thin rectangles are *not* represented in visual experience in the El Greco world as thin rectangles. They are represented as square.

Heck, Richard (2000), "Nonconceptual Content and the 'Space of Reasons,'" *Philosophical Review* 109: 483–523.

Henderson, John M. (1997), "Transsaccadic Memory and Integration During Real-World Object Perception," *Psychological Science* 8: 51–5.

Hollingworth, Andrew, Williams, Carrick C., and Henderson, John M. (2001), "To See and Remember: Visually Specific Information is Retained in Memory from Previously Attended Scenes," *Psychonomic Bulletin and Review* 8: 761–8.

Hurvich, Leo M. (1981), *Color Vision* (Sunderland, Mass.: Sinauer Associates).

McDowell, John (1994), *Mind and World* (Cambridge, Mass.: Harvard University Press).

McDowell, John (1998), "Response to Peacocke," *Philosophy and Phenomenological Research* 58: 414–19.

McLaughlin, Brian and Tye, Michael (1998), "Is Content-Externalism Compatible with Privileged Access?," *Philosophical Review* 107: 349–80.

O'Regan, J. Kevin (2000), "Experience is not Something We Feel but Something We Do," talk at ASSC 2000.

O'Regan, J. Kevin and Noë, Alva (2001), "A Sensorimotor Account of Vision and Visual Consciousness," *Behavioral and Brain Sciences* 24: 939–1011.

Peacocke, Christopher (1992), "Scenarios, Concepts, and Perception," in Tim Crane (ed.), *The Contents of Experience: Essays on Perception* (Cambridge: Cambridge University Press): 105–35.

Peacocke, Christopher (1998), "Nonconceptual Content Defended," *Philosophy and Phenomenological Research* 58: 381–8.

Peacocke, Christopher (2001), "Does Perception Have a Nonconceptual Content?," *Journal of Philosophy* 98: 239–64.

Raffman, Diana (1996), "On the Persistence of Phenomenology," in Thomas Metzinger (ed.), *Conscious Experience* (Thorverton: Imprint Academic; Paderborn: Mentis): 293–308.

Rayner, K., Inhoff, A. W., Morrison, R. E., Slowiaczek, M. L., and Bertera, J. H. (1981), "Masking of Foveal and Parafoveal Vision during Eye Fixations in Reading," *Journal of Experimental Psychology: Human Perception and Performance* 7: 167–79.

Sperling, George (1960), "The Information Available in Brief Visual Presentations," *Psychological Monographs* 74: 1–29.

Tye, Michael (1995), *Ten Problems of Consciousness* (Cambridge, Mass.: MIT Press, Bradford Books).

Tye, Michael (2000), *Consciousness, Color, and Content* (Cambridge, Mass.: MIT Press, Bradford Books).

Tye, Michael (2003), *Consciousness and Persons: Unity and Identity* (Cambridge, Mass.: MIT Press, Bradford Books).

Tye, Michael (forthcoming), "The Nature of Nonconceptual Content."

Williams, Pepper and Simons, Daniel J. (2000), "Detecting Changes in Novel, Complex Three-Dimensional Objects," *Visual Cognition* 7: 297–322.

Index